DISHONORABLE
PASSIONS

Also by William N. Eskridge Jr.

Gay Marriage: For Better or for Worse?

Equality Practice: Civil Unions and the Future of Gay Rights

Gaylaw: Challenging the Apartheid of the Closet

Constitutional Stupidities, Constitutional Tragedies

The Case for Same-Sex Marriage

William N. Eskridge Jr.

DISHONORABLE PASSIONS

Sodomy Laws in America

1861–2003

VIKING

VIKING
Published by the Penguin Group
Penguin Group (USA) Inc., 375 Hudson Street,
New York, New York 10014, U.S.A.
Penguin Group (Canada), 90 Eglinton Avenue East, Suite 700,
Toronto, Ontario, Canada M4P 2Y3 (a division of Pearson Penguin Canada Inc.)
Penguin Books Ltd, 80 Strand, London WC2R 0RL, England
Penguin Ireland, 25 St Stephen's Green, Dublin 2, Ireland (a division of Penguin Books Ltd)
Penguin Books Australia Ltd, 250 Camberwell Road, Camberwell,
Victoria 3124, Australia (a division of Pearson Australia Group Pty Ltd)
Penguin Books India Pvt Ltd, 11 Community Centre,
Panchsheel Park, New Delhi–110 017, India
Penguin Group (NZ), 67 Apollo Drive, Rosedale, North Shore 0632,
New Zealand (a division of Pearson New Zealand Ltd)
Penguin Books (South Africa) (Pty) Ltd, 24 Sturdee Avenue,
Rosebank, Johannesburg 2196, South Africa

Penguin Books Ltd, Registered Offices: 80 Strand, London WC2R 0RL, England

First published in 2008 by Viking Penguin, a member of Penguin Group (USA) Inc.

1 3 5 7 9 10 8 6 4 2

Photograph credits
Chapter 1: From *Leaves of Grass* by Walt Whitman (1855); 3: Library of Congress;
4: William Dellenback. By permission of The Kinsey Institute for Research in Sex, Gender, and
Reproduction; 5: Rainbow History Project; 6: Copyright © by Fred W. McDarrah; 7: Courtesy
of the California History Room, California State Library, Sacramento, California; 8 and 12:
Susan Browning Chriss; 9: William Eskridge; 10: Mitchell Katine; 11: © Tomas Gaspar.
All rights reserved.

Maps and graphs by Virginia Norey

LIBRARY OF CONGRESS CATALOGING-IN-PUBLICATION DATA
Eskridge, William N.
Dishonorable passions : sodomy laws in America, 1861–2003 / William N. Eskridge Jr.
p. cm.
Includes bibliographical references and index.
ISBN 978-0-670-01862-8
1. Sodomy—United States—History. 2. Sodomy—United States—Cases. 3. Sex crimes—
United States—History. 4. Sex and law—United States—History. I. Title.
KF9328.S6E84 2008
345.73'02536—dc22   2008002733

Printed in the United States of America
Set in Minion   Designed by Francesca Belanger

For Kathleen "Kitty" Blalock Hardwick and her children:
Patrick, Alice, Susan, and Michael

Acknowledgments

This book originated with the Reading Group that Jeanne Goldberg, Mark Agrast, Paul Wolfson, Marcia Kuntz, Robert Raben, Sarah Goodfriend, Jeff Blutinger, and I founded fifteen years ago under the auspices of the Gay and Lesbian Attorneys of Washington, D.C., or GAYLAW. This ongoing group of legal intellectuals has sustained me through my career, and has been the source of all the fine literature I have read in recent decades. In 2002–03, most members of the Reading Group worked on briefs in *Lawrence v. Texas*, where the Supreme Court considered whether consensual sodomy laws violate the U.S. Constitution. I authored the brief submitted by the Cato Institute in that case, and the Supreme Court opinions drawing from my work encouraged me to write this book.

I am greatly indebted to Dean Harold Hongju Koh of the Yale Law School. Dean Koh provided me with extensive financial and other support services without which I should not have easily been able to complete this project. Invaluable research assistance was provided by the following Yale Law students: Alex Berlin (Class of 2008), Daniel Bird (2005), Sarah Bishop (2008), Daniel Freeman (2007), Michael Gottlieb (2006), Jamal Greene (2005), Sara Jeruss (2008), Frederick Liu (2008), Curtis J. Mahoney (2006), Christopher Mandernach (2008), Natalie Ram (2008), Darsana Srinivasan (2007), Elisa Weygul (2007), Bree Grossi Wilde (2006), and Rob Yablon (2006).

Certain colleagues and associates have provided invaluable assistance for specific chapters. I am indebted to Alexander Glage (NYU Law, Class of 2007) for conversations, historical research, and fundamental insights about Walt Whitman, one focus of chapter 1, and Sigmund Freud, discussed in chapter 2. Beth Hillman suggested parallels to the seventeenth-century Puritans, as classically understood by Perry Miller, that proved most insightful to me. Historians Jonathan Ned Katz, Allan Bérubé, George Chauncey, Lisa Duggan, John D'Emilio, Lillian Faderman, and Elizabeth Lapovsky Kennedy made chapters 2 and 3 easier to write, because they have provided essential factual materials and important analysis of the creation of "homosexuality" as a significant social and legal category. David Johnson has done pioneering work to recapture what he calls the "Lavender Scare" (I have adapted that terminology as

"Lavender Terror"). Diane Rossell (Washburn University School of Law, Class of 2005) helped me with the Kansas materials discussed in chapter 6. Michael Gottlieb interviewed several relevant actors for chapters 6 and 7. Conversations with Fathers Timothy Healy and Leo O'Donovan, presidents of Georgetown University during my happy tenure at America's leading Roman Catholic law school, very much assisted me in writing about the politics of preservation in chapter 7; also helpful is my ongoing relationship with Lynn Wardle, a leading Mormon family law scholar and my counterpoint in roughly a dozen public debates on same-sex marriage and other topics. Rick Thompson and his associates with the section on gay interest issues of the Texas Bar Association helped me in many ways to understand Texas political culture, discussed in chapter 10.

No one has contributed to this book more than Patricia Page, my administrative assistant and crack researcher at the Yale Law School; Gene Coakley, the backbone of the Yale Law Library for almost half a century (and counting); and Scott Matheson, cherished teaching colleague and my expert on state legislative histories. Dozens of archivists all over the United States have been very helpful, often way above the call of duty. I owe particular gratitude to the librarians at the Manuscript Reading Room of the Madison Building of the Library of Congress (Washington, D.C.), as well as those at the National Archives (Suitland, Maryland), the Kenan Research Center of the Atlanta Research Center, the California State Archives (Sacramento), the Florida State Archives (Tallahassee), the Special Collections of the Columbia University School of Law Library (New York City), the Mudd Library at Princeton University (Princeton, N.J.), the Rare Books and Special Collections of the Harvard Law School Library (Cambridge, Mass.), the Rare Books and Special Collections of the Tarlton Law Library at the University of Texas (Austin), the Powell Papers at the Washington & Lee School of Law (Lexington, Va.), the Boston Public Library, the Nashville Public Library, the New York Public Library, the Philadelphia Free Library, the St. Louis Public Library, the San Francisco Public Library, the Chicago Police Department Archives, and the Los Angeles Police Department Archives (Pasadena).

I have presented selected chapters of the book to law school workshops at New York University, the University of Texas, the University of Minnesota, Emory University, Yale University, the University of Florida, and the University of Kentucky; I learned from each experience, and appreciate the sympathetic feedback from those law professors. NYU's Legal History Colloquium not only generated the most useful comments I have ever received on a book manuscript, but provided essential encouragement and methodological advice. I am particularly indebted to William Nelson (the convenor and grand pooh-bah), Felice Batlan, Richard Bernstein, Dan Hulsebosch, Bernard Freamon, Harold Forsythe, Serena Mayeri, John Reid, and Jed Shugerman for their detailed comments at and after the colloquium. At the other workshops,

I received particularly valuable comments from Vicki Schultz, Adrienne Davis, Karen Engel, Willie Forbath, Robert Gordon, Nan Hunter, Harold Koh, Miranda Oshige McGowan, David McGowan, Diane Mazur, Larry Sager, Alan Schwartz, Ed Stein, and Kenji Yoshino.

For general encouragement, special mention must be made for Elizabeth Eskridge, Lois Van Beers, Len Becker, Mark Agrast, Judith Sandalow, and Hans Johnson.

I dedicate this book to Kathleen "Kitty" Blalock Hardwick and her four children: Patrick Hardwick, Alice Hardwick Ahrer, Susan Hardwick Browning Chriss, and Michael Hardwick.

Contents

DISHONORABLE
PASSIONS

Introduction

What was the "crime against nature"? Why did the American colonies make it a capital offense in the eighteenth century, and the states regulate it as a serious felony after independence? How did our understanding of the crime against nature (also traveling under the name *sodomy*) change after the Civil War? Why is it no longer a crime when consenting adults engage in it? In the process of answering these questions, I shall tell a story about sexuality, gender, and law in American history.

American statute books and judicial opinions ritualistically described the crime against nature as "detestable and abominable." For most of American history, this was fundamentally a Christian, religious judgment. The crime against nature was the sin of Sodom, whose citizens sexually assaulted an angel of God and were punished with "brimstone and fire" (Genesis 19:24).* Sodomy, or something like it, was an "abomination" to the Israelites (Leviticus 20:13–15). Although Christ Himself said nothing on this subject, the early Christian church taught that the "dishonorable passions" of those who "exchanged natural relations for unnatural" were displeasing to God (Romans 1:26). Many Christians and some Jews still consider sodomy the gravest sin, even though they accept other practices that the Old Testament condemns as "abomination" (*to'eva*)—cross-dressing (Deuteronomy 5:22), wearing cloth with mixed fabrics (Leviticus 19:19), and sowing "discord among the brethren" (Proverbs 6:16).[1]

As chapters 1 and 2 of this book will demonstrate, secular authorities have also condemned the crime against nature, on grounds that echo the religious objections. Like the author of Genesis, who reported God's judgment on Sodom, which extended beyond the rapists to the entire rape-tolerant community (Genesis 19:12–29), Puritans like John Winthrop and neo-Puritans like Anthony Comstock and Robert Bork condemned the crime against nature as a disgusting threat to the community and claimed that a society that tolerated unnatural sexuality was one that "slouches toward Gomorrah," Sodom's twin city on the

*All Bible quotations are from the Revised Standard Version (RSV) unless otherwise noted.

plain. Like Saint Paul, who observed that "men committing shameless acts with men" would receive "in their own persons the due penalty for their error" (Romans 1:27), early-twentieth-century doctors thought sodomy reflected a "degeneration" that could be diagnosed through examination of the deformed body. More recently, Bible-based objections to sodomy have resurfaced in their own religious rather than secular terms, as religious fundamentalists reentered American politics (chapter 7).[2]

Yet the crime against nature has lost most of its sting, for the religious as well as the secular among us. Indeed, consensual private sodomy is no longer an enforceable crime in the United States. This book traces the rise, evolution, decline, and fall of the crime against nature, from a capital offense with great symbolic importance to an object of judicial nullification. A history of the crime against nature is, in some ways, a history of American sexuality and its social and legal regulation. That is, sodomy's tale reflects the evolution of a culture that has remained ambivalent about the morality of pleasure. This book also, perhaps surprisingly, touches on our rich history of identity-based social movements—not just the gay and lesbian rights movement, but also the civil rights and women's movements and the traditional family values (TFV) countermovement. Finally, the history of sodomy illuminates some central themes of American politics, including the role of constitutional law in the continual reshaping of American law.

What Was the Crime Against Nature? Why Was It Abominable?

Although he termed the crime against nature "infamous," Sir William Blackstone also considered it "unmentionable," and for centuries no English-language statute defined precisely what conduct constituted the crime against nature. Case law specified sodomy to include anal intercourse by a man with a woman or girl, another man or boy, or a beast; women could only commit sodomy by lying with a beast (chapter 1). However ill-defined, the crime against nature was a cornerstone of the Anglo-American legal regime regulating sexuality. From the sixteenth to the twentieth century, the norm reflected in that regime was procreative marriage. Adultery and fornication laws insisted that sexual activities occur only within marriage; sodomy and seduction laws insisted that the sex be procreative.[3]

The vagueness of the crime against nature, and its central role in this normative regime, rendered it elastic and mobile, so that it might include other nonprocreative sexual activities. Once they became aware that many Americans, in our booming cities, were engaging in oral sex, some judges and many legislators between 1879 and 1921 extended sodomy laws to include fellatio, oral sex performed upon a man (chapter 2). Although the crime against nature had traditionally involved a penis, cunnilingus—oral sex performed upon a woman—came within the scope of some sodomy laws in the course of the twentieth century (chapter 3). The purview of sodomy laws did not end with oral sex, however. Most of the Americans actually charged with committing the crime against nature did so with minors, and the records in these cases reveal a broad range of sexually stimulating or abusive activities, including touching and fondling erogenous zones. Even as jurisdictions adopted new child molestation statutes to regulate these activities, the crime against nature remained a fallback charge, and in some jurisdictions even included masturbation.[4]

Although the crime against nature's regulatory ambit has been quite dynamic, it has in our culture drawn its force from a relatively stable collection of human impulses: *disgust* Americans feel toward sensual activities that remind us of our animal natures; fears of *pollution*, especially when sexuality, gender role, and racial identities are combined, and of *predation*, especially as regards our children; and *self-definition* that depends on creating symbolic others who are our degraded opposites. All these themes can be understood through an exegesis of the warning Saint Paul gave the church at Corinth: "[N]either fornicators, nor idolaters, nor adulterers, nor the effeminate, nor abusers of themselves with mankind [sodomites], nor thieves, nor covetous, nor drunkards, nor revilers, nor extortioners, shall inherit the kingdom of God" (1 Corinthians 6:9–10 [King James Version]).

Disgust. All the activities condemned by Saint Paul are self-indulgent: the fornicator and the like engage in actions that serve no rational function characteristic of godly society and instead represent purely selfish indulgence in transient pleasure seeking. The objection here is something more than a utilitarian disdain for activities that do not contribute to self- or community improvement, however. The fundamental objection is that when man indulges his sexual or other primitive appetites, he is forfeiting the capacity for reason and morality that separates us from the beasts. It is "unnatural" for human beings *(imago Dei)* to behave like animals, and nowhere is this more evident than in matters of sexuality. "The body is not meant for immorality, but for the Lord" (1 Corinthians 6:13). While the body ideally should not be polluted by sexual activities of any sort (7:8, 25–27), it is no sin to marry, according to Saint Paul, "[f]or it is better to marry than to be aflame with passion" (7:9). The goal of a Christian marriage is to join as sexual partners two believers who beget and rear clean children (7:12–14). Influential church fathers such as Saint Augustine read Saint Paul to focus on the "dishonorable passions" (Romans 1:26) in his list to the church at Corinth.

America's Puritans followed this thinking closely, such that Richard Mather and William Thompson could in 1650 summarize 1 Corinthians 6:9–10 as simply admonishing that "neither whoremongers nor adulterers, nor drunkards, nor any that walk in such waies and works of the flesh, shall have any inheritance in the kingdome of God." Nothing is more unworthy of human beings than sex for pleasure alone, because then nothing separates us from beasts. Marriage can justify pleasurable sex engaged in by a man and a woman seeking to procreate—an option unavailable to the sodomite. English and colonial laws followed Leviticus 20:13–16 in associating bestiality with sodomy in the same prohibitory statutes (chapter 1).[5]

These moral connections did not die with the seventeenth-century Puritans; indeed, neo-Puritan moralists of the nineteenth and twentieth centuries deepened the relationship between sex for pleasure and beastliness. Now the emphasis was on different-race sexuality, especially between persons of English and African descent. While miscegenation laws were primarily enacted out of fears that different-race procreative sex would create a "mongrel race" of citizens, American racists also associated "inferior races" with importing nonprocreative sexual practices that might corrupt the "white" race. Scientists published serious papers claiming that sodomy and cross-dressing originated in Africa and were foreign imports into the United States.[6]

Paul Rozin, a modern social scientist, maintains that our expressions of moral disgust arise out of emotional efforts to distance ourselves from physical functions that are "reminders of our animal vulnerability." As our most deeply animal function, sex is the subject of the greatest disgust, so much so that almost anything related to it remains appalling to some people. In America, sex is still often guilty unless proven innocent—as by God—or (nowadays) state-sanctioned marriages.[7]

Pollution. One group condemned by Saint Paul are predatory, selfish pleasure seekers inflicting harm on others. Like the adulterer, thief, and extortionist, the sodomite preys on victims, usually children. In both Puritan times and today, sodomy laws have overwhelmingly been enforced against mature men assaulting boys, girls, and less-powerful adults. The other focus of Saint Paul's list are those who pollute the public culture. Like the idolator, the covetous, the drunkard, and the reviler, the "effeminate" disrupts society with his impious *public* display. Many sodomy prosecutions, then and now, have involved sexual activities that disturbed the peace because they shocked "innocent" observers.[8]

Again, the moral judgments embodied in these Pauline concepts have retained their power in the modern era. The anthropologist Mary Douglas understands moral taboos as a matter of *pollution*. Human beings derive emotional and intellectual security from familiar patterns, and institutions and practices, as well as the labels they deploy and the lines they draw, achieve much of their power by their ability to organize our thinking about an untidy world. Moral revulsion, therefore, is a reaction to phenomena and practices that do not fit labels or that cross lines. Certain physical phenomena (such as sodomy) are disgusting to many of us because they threaten the boundaries between human being and animal; others (effeminacy) threaten social boundaries and even stable identities. Interracial sex has traditionally been the most prominent example of this phenomenon in American culture, but homosexuality may have outpaced it in the late twentieth century.[9]

Today, the (homosexual) sodomite is often constructed as predatory because he is public. Although few Americans today believe that gay men and the occasional lesbian actually assault children and unsuspecting heterosexuals, they are bothered by the fact that the public celebration of homosexuality—sex for pleasure alone—is predatory in its supposed effect—namely, to lure naive and innocent children into hedonistic lifestyles and away from traditional marriage. Society itself will then fall into irreparable decay, for once traditional moral lines are blurred, the argument goes, all lines will disappear, and people will do whatever they want. In *The Republic*, Plato criticizes such an anything-goes society, where "each lives along, day by day, gratifying the desire that occurs to him." Such a formless society inevitably degenerates, according to Plato, because citizens end up "paying no attention to the laws, written or unwritten, so that they may avoid having any master at all." Just as immorality and sexual license reportedly caused the decline and fall of the Roman Empire, so they will be fatal to the survival of any society.[10]

Destabilization. Saint Paul's First Letter to the Corinthians addresses identities, not practices: rather than saying that fornication disqualifies one from joining the kingdom of God, for example, he warns that fornicators cannot join. Following Christ, Paul suggests that believers may have committed various sins, such as fornication or sodomy, but God will forgive those sins if the sinners sincerely repent. Hence one's identity as a Christian depends on renunciation of such conduct and a vow to try and live a holy life. Unlike Christ, Saint Paul constructed a religious identity in large part by distinguishing the Christian from what he is *not*—idolator, fornicator, and so on. Thus, the cement that holds together the community, as well as gives the Christian person his distinctive identity, is disapproval of sexual nonconformists.

Within the Pauline Christian community, the existence of an unrepentant fornicator or sodomite would have been destabilizing. The same idea is characteristic of neo-Puritan thinking throughout American history and continues to have purchase today, as illustrated by William Ian Miller's synthesis of the work of Rozin and Douglas. "Our durable self is defined as much by disgust as by any other passion. . . . It installs large chunks of the moral world right at the core of our identity, seamlessly uniting body and soul and thereby giving an irreducible continuity to our characters." Disgust is "especially useful and necessary as a builder of moral and social community. It performs this function obviously by helping define and locate the boundary separating our group from their group, purity from pollution, the violable from the inviolable."[11]

The seventeenth-century "effeminate" (which many scholars today translate as "male prostitute") suggests a deeper point here. The man who assumes female gender roles in some ways occupies a unique place on Saint Paul's list. Unlike the other sinners, the effeminate has neither harmed anyone (the thieves, revilers, etc.) nor committed forbid[den] [...] fornicators, sodomites, etc.). His offense, rather, is that [...] on of the most fundamental boundary in human exist[ence] [...] demarcation of man from woman. Because the male [...] partner, he has violated the gender role of males as ins[...] cross-dresser, which Deuteronomy 22:5 condemns as a [...]

The Homosexualization [of the] Crime Against Nature

Reflecting twentieth-century terminology, the Revised Standard Version's translation of 1 Corinthians combines the effeminate and the sodomite under one classification, the "homosexual." Although this was not an identity category that Americans would have understood until the 1890s, in the course of the twentieth century, homosexuality became synonymous with sodomy (chapters 2–6). This phenomenon flows, in part, from the logic of the crime against nature and its underlying anxieties. When heterosexual intercourse involves oral sex, anal intercourse, sexual fondling, and other play, it can often be linked to human projects beyond animalistic pleasure, perhaps as foreplay preceding procreative sex or as a reinforcement to the moral ties of marriage. Oral sex between two men or two women, in contrast, satisfies neither of these conditions. Hence, the open homosexual, unlike the heterosexual, by his or her very presence flouts the sex-not-for-pleasure norm, as well as the norm of strict gender distinction.[13]

This logic played out in interesting and often dramatic ways because of social changes that placed pressure on the ever-malleable crime against nature. The overriding phenomenon between the Civil War and World War II was diversifying urbanization: the United States steadily evolved from a rural and small-town Anglo-American society to a predominantly urban one, with the cities increasingly diversified by race and ethnicity (chapters 2–3). The accepted standard of marriage and procreation gave way to a more liberal one, with more choices for middle-class women in particular. The new norm, which achieved wide public acceptance by the 1920s, was marital rather than procreative marital sex (chapter 2). Our culture still pressured everyone to marry, but wives successfully claimed the right to limit the size of their families, without giving up the pleasures of sex with their husbands. In addition to contraceptive devices, which were openly embraced, twentieth-century wives and husbands engaged in unprecedented amounts of oral sex and other nonprocreative activities. Although oral sex was added to law and society's elastic understanding of the crime against nature, many Americans found it a tolerable variation. Homosexual sodomy, on the other hand, remained an intolerable variation, because it violated still-fixed gender roles and lacked any possible connection to procreation or marriage. Men and women who engaged in oral sex in the context of marriage or dating could contrast their healthy and natural sexual activities with the depraved and unnatural activities of "homosexuals and other sex perverts" (the boilerplate language of the era), even though they were often practicing exactly the same activities.[14]

Diversified urbanization also meant that more Americans were exposed to a wide variety of sexual couplings, which alarmed them and motivated them to establish strong boundaries separating moral from immoral activities. Particularly disturbing were different-race, same-sex, and intergenerational couplings, all of which crossed hallowed cultural lines. Between 1890 and 1950 alarmed citizens petitioned their state and local governments to create a detailed regulatory system of sexual line drawing. Although the code they demanded was novel in most respects, the petitioners presented it as a return to old-fashioned moral values. Municipal and state governments responded with increasingly detailed laws regulating sexual activities, including miscegenation, cohabitation, sodomy, and indecency with minors, and created a police apparatus to enforce those laws. Even the national government evolved from a night watchman, primarily responsible for the nation's defense and international trade and relations, to a pervasively regulatory authority (chapter 3).

The half-generation after World War II (1945–61) was both the golden age and the dark age of sodomy law in America. From Pauline and other traditionalist perspectives, it was the golden age, for American society and law unequivocally and prominently stigmatized and discouraged the crime against nature, now broadly defined. Those persons whose characteristic sexual conduct was sodomy, the "homosexuals," were not only legal criminals, but also political outlaws theoretically excluded from the franchise, jury and military service, government jobs, professional licenses, and if foreign even entry into the United States.

Local, state, and federal government officials and employees devoted millions of hours to carrying out these policies. The nation has never committed more resources to sexual purification than it did during the McCarthy era. From the perspective of homosexuals themselves, of course, this was a dark period of terror.[15]

Sodomy Laws, the Constitution, and Culture War

Most of this book tells the story of sodomy laws after 1961, and the story is one of heated debate, identity politics, and constitutional challenge (chapters 4–11). As the reader will already know, this is not a story that ends well for consensual sodomy laws. Yet the process by which such laws ultimately found themselves at their social, political, and constitutional Alamo is one that no one could have predicted in 1961. Even in historical retrospective, the process was filled with unexpected twists and turns. Consider some reasons for this surprise-filled history.

Law and Sociopolitical Identities

The rule of unintended consequences dominates the history of sodomy law in America. The most direct effect of sodomy laws in the twentieth century was not to enforce traditional morality (the aim of such laws), but instead to empower law enforcement officers, hospital personnel, military commanders, and others who encountered homosexuals and other violators. Many exercised their power to invoke the law against these criminals, but others bargained for leniency in return for money, humiliation, or even sexual favors. That consensual sodomy laws contributed to private blackmail and public corruption (especially with police forces) was a powerful pragmatic argument against such laws (chapter 4).[16]

In contrast, sodomy prohibitions had no discernible effect on the incidence of the forbidden activities; this contributed to liberal arguments against such laws (also chapter 4). At its pinnacle during the golden/dark age, the crime against nature was apparently practiced more widely than ever before, notwithstanding greater police resources devoted to its detection. Even homosexual intercourse, both illegal and socially penalized, reached new levels after World War II. For some "homosexuals" of the period, the illegality of the "love that dare not speak its name" was part of its lure. While society found it important to draw lines separating acceptable from prohibited sexual behaviors, those engaged in sexual misbehavior found those lines erotic and alluring. Not infrequently, the line drawers and the line violators were the same people (chapters 2–3).[17]

Moreover, the terrorizing regulatory regime actually fueled the development of a coherent homosexual subculture (chapters 4–5). During World War II, for example, many soldiers did not realize they had "homosexual" feelings until they were interrogated by military personnel. After the war, government witch hunts drove thousands of homosexuals out of their closets and provided common experiences and enemies to tens of thousands more. Although the homosexuals who pushed back against state persecution numbered in the dozens during the 1950s, those numbers swelled in the 1960s. After the Stonewall riots of 1969, lesbians, gay men, and bisexuals came out of their closets in unprecedented numbers, aggressively demanding not only the repeal of sodomy laws but also full recognition of homosexual citizens as no less worthy and moral than heterosexuals (chapter 6). Just as state persecution failed to cleanse public culture of homosexuality, so efforts by gay people to change the law did not necessarily establish equal citizenship for homosexuals. Instead, gay people's politics of recognition had the opposite effect, helping stimulate the creation of a "traditional family values" countermovement that asserted a powerful politics of preservation (chapter 7). [18]

Like the politics of sodomy enforcement, the politics of sodomy reform had had unexpected consequences, in large part arising out of its effect on people's understanding of their own identities. Before 1961, religious fundamentalists were often divided among themselves, with Catholics and Protestants in bitter contests for people's souls. After 1961, Baptist as well as Catholic and Jewish fundamentalists have found common ground in opposing moral hedonism associated with abortion, nonmarital cohabitation, and homosexuality; in the 1980s, the AIDS epidemic, also associated with homosexuality, deepened the sense of crisis. So long as their religious identities were invested in preventing the state from "promoting homosexuality," the stakes of the sodomy debate got higher (chapters 7–8). The 1990s saw further turns in both homosexual and religious identity, and these changes affected the sodomy debate profoundly (chapters 9–10).

Institutional Diversity and Multiple Forums for Challenge

In theory, one protection that minority groups in the United States have against vicious, unjustified state invasions of their liberties is the multiple layers of government. For a state government to create an outlaw class of productive citizens, the state legislature must adopt stigmatizing laws acceptable to the governor who must sign them and the judges who will interpret them. Even then, individual group members might be protected by the discretion vested in local enforcement or the mercy of juries. And the national government can trump state exclusions and penalties with preemptive legislation (Congress) or rights protection (Supreme Court). This constitutional regime of separation of powers and federalism protected sexual and gender minorities against the harsh operation of the antihomosexual terror regime of the 1950s.[19]

Although there were collateral consequences at the national level, laws criminalizing consensual and other forms of sodomy were *state* statutes. Whether inspired by pragmatic or humanistic reasons, reformers had a variety of institutional forums for challenging consensual sodomy laws within each state: law reform commissions created by state governors or bar associations; legislative committees acting on their recommendations; state judges applying such laws; and municipal police departments and prosecutor's offices. The precise politics of sodomy reform varied from state to state, depending on the strength of traditionalist attitudes toward sexuality and gender roles; the ability of the state's gay subculture to attract allies without alarming mainstream citizens; and the willingness of straight officials to stick their political necks out for the despised minority (chapters 4–6).

The state-by-state politics of sodomy reform also evolved in response to the changing gay and traditionalist identities mentioned above. Once identity politics hardened around the issue of consensual sodomy, the institutional focus also shifted. With traditionalists mobilized, state legislative repeal became more difficult, but the equally mobilized minority of open lesbians, gay men, bisexuals, and transgendered people turned to the courts, just as racial minorities and women had done before them. Indeed, gay people relied on and sought to expand the constitutional equality rights won by people of color and women from state as well as federal judges (chapters 5–9). Like the legislative battles, the judicial battles changed over time: the early focus was the U.S. Supreme Court (chapters 7–8), but after 1986 the focus shifted to state higher courts (chapter 9) before ultimately returning to the Supreme Court (chapter 10). At the nation's highest court, the fate of consensual sodomy laws was more decisively influenced by the personal views of the justices and the views of their perceived audience than by the precise constitutional arguments made by the parties.

Constitutionalism and Culture Conflict

For most of American history, the limited public discourse about the crime against nature was dominated by moral and religious tropes (chapter 1). After 1890, supporters of sodomy laws "modernized" their discourse by translating its essential points (disgust, pollution, boundary maintenance) into scientific and medical terminology. The immoral "sodomite" condemned by scripture morphed into the "degenerate" who threatened the health of the body politic (chapter 2).

After 1945, sodomy discourse was further modernized by translating the religious and medical images into social utilitarian ones (greatest good for the greatest number). The "predatory homosexual" was a threat to the public good and the family because he assaulted or otherwise corrupted defenseless children and was a constant source of temptation to youth (chapter 3). Even after many lesbian and gay Americans came out and challenged these stereotypes, traditionalists argued to receptive mainstream audiences that sodomy reform would "promote homosexuality" (chapters 5–7).[20]

Combined with the difficulty of legislative reform, the ability of sodomy law proponents to adapt their defense to new social consensuses drove the men and women subject to consensual sodomy laws toward constitutional arguments made available by the civil rights, women's rights, and pro-choice movements that came before. In theory, constitutional rights are trumps negating the force of moral or utilitarian agruments and, hence, valuable for minorities marginalized in the democratic process. In practice, constitutional rights did not work that way at all. Rather than trumps, constitutional "rights" were themselves a product of the social and political clash pitting fundamentalists and other religious persons against gay people and their allies. Thus, rights recognition was not a predictable function of precedent and other sources of law; personal political variables invariably figured in the mix. Judges outraged by ill treatment of gay people by the state construed the constitutional materials to invalidate consensual sodomy laws, while those unsympathetic to homosexuals or fearful of public backlash construed the materials to uphold such laws (chapters 6, 8–10).

Not only were constitutional rights part of the political process by which sodomy laws were evaluated, but they affected the political process and thereby introduced a new dimension of variability and unpredictability. Contrary to the assumptions lawyers had in the civil rights era (roughly 1954–1981), winning a constitutional right did not necessarily ensure triumph for the prevailing group. For example, the Supreme Court's dismissive attitude toward gay people's privacy claims galvanized the progay social movement (chapters 8–9), while more sympathetic Supreme Court treatment did not necessarily advance gay people's interests much and perhaps not at all (chapters 9–11).

Most surprising was the effect of same-sex marriage litigation on the constitutional politics of sodomy reform. The conventional wisdom among academics and journalists is that the mere possibility of a same-sex marriage ruling from the Hawaii Supreme Court triggered a backlash that galvanized traditional family values groups and set back equality for gay people, maybe for a long time. Contrary to this conventional wisdom, the same-sex marriage issue created positive as well as negative political reactions (chapters 10–12). Even as national and state legislatures precluded recognition of gay marriages, middle-of-the-road

Americans were struck by the fact that gay marriage was neither a joke nor a political stunt. Gay and lesbian couples, including couples raising children, undermined all the old stereotypes about homosexuals: not only were they not predatory, but many of them shared the core values of commitment and family that their traditionalist opponents cherished.

Chapter 12, which revisits some of the people who figure prominently in the sodomy reform debate, contemplates some lessons of this history for constitutionalism itself. Not only are judge-articulated constitutional rights little more than another institutional variable in the larger identity politics involved in sodomy reform, but rights articulated by legislators and governors can be just as important to constitutionalism as those articulated by judges. What does this mean for the future of gay rights in the United States? For same-sex marriage recognition?

American Body Politics and the Crime
Against Nature, 1860–81

*L*eaves of Grass is not only America's first
great collection of poetry, but an important document in our cultural and even political history. The first (1855) edition of *Leaves*
did not carry the name of its thirty-six-year-
old author, but offered only a portrait. The
poet stares directly at the reader, his felt hat
tipped at a jaunty angle. A fellow Brooklynite
described Walt Whitman (1819–1892) as a
man "[o]f pure American breed, of reckless
health, his body perfect, free from taint from
top to toe, free forever from headache and
dyspepsia, full-blooded, six feet high, a good
feeder, never once using medicine, drinking
water only." He was "always dressed freely
and clean in strong clothes, neck open, shift

Walt Whitman

collar flat and broad, countenance of swarthy transparent red, beard short and
well mottled with white, hair like hay that has been mowed in the field and lies
tossed and streaked—face not refined or intellectual, but calm and wholesome—
a face of an unaffected animal—a face that absorbs the sunshine and meets savage or gentleman on equal terms."[1]

In *Leaves of Grass*'s opening poem, later entitled "Song of Myself," Whitman
announced himself as the authentic poetic voice of America. "I am the poet of
the body, / And I am the poet of the soul." He brashly suggested that the two were
intertwined, and equally dignified.

Through me forbidden voices,
Voices of sexes and lusts . . . voices veiled, and I remove the veil,
Voices indecent by me clarified and transfigured . . .
I believe in the flesh and the appetites,

Seeing, hearing and feeling are miracles, and each part and tag of me is a
    miracle.

Addressed to women as well as men, manual laborers and sex workers, farmers
and longshoremen, people from all walks of life, "Song of Myself" was less about
Whitman than about America itself. It trumpeted the individuality, physicality,
and diversity of the poet's fellow citizens in a free, nonrhyming style befitting the
provocative subject matter.[2]

In *Leaves*' third (1860) edition, Whitman added the "Children of Adam" and
"Calamus" poems. Even more explicitly than "Song of Myself," the "Children of
Adam" sequence celebrates the sacredness of the body and the joy of sex. "Without shame the man I like knows and avows the deliciousness of his sex, / Without
shame the woman I like knows and avows hers." The poet extols the sexual "in-
terpenetration" of man and woman: "Through you I drain the pent-up rivers of
myself, / The drops I distil upon you shall grow fierce and athletic girls, new artists, musicians, and singers."[3]

The "Calamus" series glorifies what Whitman called "adhesiveness" between
men. The first poem, "In Paths Untrodden," sets the tone. The poet has "[e]scaped"
from the "standards hitherto publish'd." "No longer abash'd," he "[r]esolv'd to
sing no songs to-day but those of manly attachment." In a draft version, Whitman closed the poem:

I proceed for all who are or have been young men,
To tell the secret of my nights and days,
I celebrate the need [of the love] of comrades.

These words extol the individual, idiosyncratically "escaping" convention and
living a "concealed but substantial life," tied to his fellow citizens by "the love of
comrades." (The published version dropped the bracketed language.) The natural adhesion one independent man feels for another quite unlike him is the personal bond that assures the future of democracy.[4]

At the same time that Whitman was celebrating a democracy of comrades,
Elizabeth Cady Stanton (1815–1902) and Susan B. Anthony (1820–1906) were
demanding that democracy include women. Stanton and Anthony met in 1851
at a lecture sponsored by the American Anti-Slavery Society, and theirs became
a friendship that would change American history. "[W]e demand the full recognition of all our rights as citizens," they proclaimed, including rights to vote,
serve on juries, enter into contracts, enjoy joint control over the lives of their
children, and be free of domestic violence. In response to a decade of their activism, New York in 1860 enacted a law enabling married women to contract in

their own names; the state had allowed married women to own property since 1848. Like Whitman, Anthony and Stanton supported President Lincoln's emancipation of slaves in 1863 and the abolition of slavery in the Thirteenth Amendment (1866).[5]

The mother of seven children, Stanton was a matronly and substantial woman, fiercely intelligent (a student of law as well as philosophy) and unconventional, vocal on the subject of women's and her own sexuality. She read Whitman's "Children of Adam" poems with interest and amusement, agreeing with the poet that female sexuality had been too long ignored and suppressed, and that women's legal equality was linked with sexual freedom, starting with the right to divorce.[6]

As if recalling her early years as a temperance reformer, Anthony had a stern, piercing stare that was anything but sensual. But she, like Whitman, was emotionally and intellectually sustained by same-sex relationships. The "Calamus" poems were a product of Whitman's self-reflection after his beloved Fred Vaughn had left him in 1857. The poet then focused his special affections on Peter Doyle, a former Confederate soldier he had met in Washington, D.C., after the Civil War and consorted with until 1874, and later on Harry Stafford, an uneducated eighteen-year-old who was Whitman's constant companion till Stafford married, in 1884. Like Whitman, Anthony never married and formed her only important attachments to persons of the same sex—Stanton in the 1850s, Anna Dickinson in the 1860s, and Emily Gross in the 1890s until Anthony's death.[7]

Oscar Wilde hailed Whitman as "the herald of a new era," the "precursor of a fresh type." Today, some scholars argue that the "fresh type" represented by Whitman as well as Anthony was the "homosexual." Citing the fact that Anthony shared her bed with women like Stanton and Dickinson and addressed her letters to them with such endearments as "My Dear Chicky Dicky Darlint," they read her as a pioneer of female sexual relationships. Whitman, for his part, apparently engaged in petting, erotic touching, and oral sex with other men.[8]

Such speculations, however, inevitably fall into the trap of becoming anachronistic: there was no such concept as "homosexual" in 1860; the term did not enter the English language until 1892. It is also quite likely that neither Whitman nor Anthony was a "sodomite," as that term would have been legally understood in the 1860s. Viewed in the context of their own era, however, Whitman, Stanton, and Anthony could all be considered sex-and-gender rebels, and as such might have been regarded as Apostles of Sodom by their puritan contemporaries. Because they challenged the normative regime that American sodomy laws enforced, they *were* a fresh type of American—bold men and free women who did not marry and whose closest emotional relationships were with persons of their own sex. Their *body politics* were a rejection of the biblical ideal, whereby individuals could find sexual satisfaction only within religious procreative marriage. They called on women and men to reclaim and deploy their bodies for their own projects and enjoyment, not those dictated by traditional religion.

Their liberatory body politics did not go unchallenged. Indeed, traditionalists responded to the new liberalism in sexual politics represented by figures like Whitman, Stanton, and Anthony with their own moralizing body politics, reminiscent of the Puritans' defense of their Bible-based regime. Like the Puritans in the 1690s, the neo-Puritans of the 1860s attempted to defend a legal and moral status quo threatened by changing social conditions. To do so they referred to similar tropes of the body: the sexual freedom entailed in the new ideas was denounced as fundamentally disgusting, a force that would pollute the body politic, which needed to purify itself through ritual purges and suppressions. Both positions are also relevant to the great constitutional codifications of the abolitionist project, the Reconstruction Amendments, which have been a key battleground in the dialectical struggle between the inclusionary individualism of Whitman, Stanton, and Anthony, versus the community-based traditionalism of their critics. It is the evolution of that struggle that has driven the history of American sodomy laws.[9]

American Sodomy Laws, 1533–1871

From colonial days up until the nineteenth century, American law decreed sodomy, buggery, or "the crime against nature" a capital crime. Exactly what constituted sodomy and its various synonyms remained, however, vague and largely unspoken—and therefore rendered it an elastic and dynamic concept. At the behest of King Henry VIII, the Reformation Parliament of 1533 had made "the detestable and abominable vice of buggery committed with mankind or beast punishable by death." That statute in effect secularized offenses that had traditionally been regulated by the Roman Catholic Church, which Henry was renouncing. The buggery law had its roots in scriptural admonitions. Leviticus 20:13 says, "If a man lies with a male as with a woman, both of them shall have committed an abomination [to the Lord]; they shall be put to death, their blood is upon them." If either a man (20:15) or a woman (20:16) lies with a beast, not only must the human be executed, but so too the beast, for "their blood is upon them." In Romans 1:24, Saint Paul charged that the Romans were "dishonoring their bodies among themselves," which is the worst of sins against God. Unfortunately, none of these scriptural sources specifies precisely which sexual acts are considered to be abominable.[10]

Although Englishmen engaged in a wide array of sexual practices in the early modern era, relatively few were prosecuted under buggery laws. When they were, norms of legalization produced more determinate definitions. English courts ultimately interpreted the buggery law to forbid anal intercourse between two men or between a man and a woman (sodomy) and any sexual congress between a man or woman and an animal (bestiality). The Act of 1533 did not apply to oral sex between humans or to any intercourse between women. There were likewise no authoritative cases involving masturbation.[11]

The seventeenth-century American colonies adopted a variety of approaches to sexual transgression, all harsh in theory but less so in practice.[12] The southern and middle colonies followed English law. For example, Virginia's 1610 code made rape, adultery, and sodomy capital offenses. Men outnumbered women on the colony by a ratio of three to one; the Virginia Company periodically disciplined the randy young men for behavior that upset the public order. In 1624–25 Captain Richard Cornish was tried and executed for assaulting and sodomizing William Cowse (or Couse), an indentured servant and steward on the ship *Ambrose*. This is the only recorded sentence of death for sodomy or buggery in Virginia; after the mid-seventeenth century, sex crimes were less strongly enforced generally. Other southern and middle colonies (Georgia, the Carolinas, Maryland, Delaware, New York) followed the Virginia model, where sodomy— which again was not clearly defined—was a capital offense, but almost never enforced.[13]

Founded by the Quaker William Penn, Pennsylvania was a relatively lenient jurisdiction. Penn's "Great Law" of 1682 abolished the death penalty for all crimes but murder. The code punished "the unnatural sin of Sodomy or joining with beasts" with property forfeiture, public whipping, and six months at hard labor for the first offense and life in prison for the second. In 1700 Pennsylvania raised the sodomy penalty to life imprisonment for the first offense, adding, "And if he be a married man, he shall also suffer castration, and the injured wife shall have a divorce if required." Under a companion statute, "negroes" suffered the death penalty if they committed buggery. After 1718 Pennsylvania reinstated the death penalty universally for "sodomy or buggery." County court records, comprehensively examined by the historian William Nelson, reveal no convictions for sodomy in colonial Pennsylvania.[14]

Promulgated by the Massachusetts Bay Colony in 1641, *The Capitall Laws of New England* followed the Levitical language in decreeing death for men "lying" with "mankinde" and for women or men having "carnall copulation" with "any beast, or bruit creature." Prominent ministers throughout New England had a broad understanding of what might be included as natural law crimes enforceable in Massachusetts Bay and its satellites (Plymouth; New Haven, Connecticut; New Hampshire; and Rhode Island). Most ministers of the seventeenth century considered almost any kind of sexual assault on a girl to be a "sodomitical act," and some included masturbation by a man in the company of another person as well as "unclean practices" between women. In 1656 the New Haven Colony prohibited under pain of death men lying with men, women lying with women, masturbation, and any other "carnall knowledge." This was the broadest sodomy statute in the colonial era, but Plymouth and Massachusetts also prosecuted female sexual intimacy as noncapital crimes ("lewd behavior" or "unseemly practices"). When New Haven merged with the Connecticut Colony in 1665, the crimes of masturbation and women lying with women disappeared from the statute books. There is no indication of any reported colonial prosecution of women for intimacy with other women after 1649.[15]

Altogether records indicate fewer than ten sodomy executions in the seventeenth-century colonies. Almost all of them were matters of either forcible sodomy (as in the Cornish case) or sex with animals. An unusual incident involved William Plaine (or Plane), one of the founding fathers of Guilford, Connecticut. In 1646, before there was a statutory prohibition, he was prosecuted for "unclean practices." Massachusetts governor John Winthrop described his case:

> [B]eing a married man, he had committed sodomy with two persons in England, and . . . he had corrupted a great part of the youth of Guilford by masturbations, which he had committed, and provoked others to the like above a hundred times; and to some who questioned the lawfulness of such filthy practice, he did insinuate seeds of atheism, questioning whether there was a God, etc. The magistrates and elders (as many as were at hand) did all agree, and gave divers reasons from the word of God. And indeed it was *horrendum facinus* [a dreadful crime], and he a monster in human shape, exceeding all human rules and examples that ever had been heard of, and it tended to the frustrating of the ordinance of marriage and the hindering of the generation of mankind.[16]

Plaine's case, a vivid example of the Puritans' broad understanding of criminal law and the relatively elastic categories they deployed, also illustrates three kinds of goals that colonial sodomy laws served. One was to protect vulnerable persons—minors, but also women and male subordinates such as Cornish's victim—from sexual assault or even exposure of sex organs, as well as from the seeds of "atheism." Second, the prosecution was meant to protect the institution of procreative marriage generally—and that of Plaine and his wife, Anna, in particular. The couple had no children, perhaps because William was uninterested in his wife sexually. After William's execution, Anna wed John Parmelee, a marriage that also had no issue before Anna died, in 1651.[17]

A third purpose was the maintenance of community purity and order. The Massachusetts Puritans drew the same lesson from the story of Sodom (Genesis 19:1–29) that Saint Paul did when he warned the congregation in Rome that the whole community was at risk if it did not purge itself of the "inventors of evil" (Romans 1:30). "Though they know God's decree that those who do such things deserve to die, they not only do them but approve those who practice them" (1:32). In the other colonies, public order was a more important consideration. "Pennsylvania's Quakers worried about sexual misconduct that led to public scandal but did not want to publicize private sins, because publicity only had a 'tendency . . . to raise up strife and discord.'"[18]

The seventeenth century was the high point for the expansive interpretation and aggressive enforcement of sodomy and other sexual morality laws in America. The Puritans' theocracy eventually splintered in response to social change and its ministers' own blunders, such as the witch trials of the 1690s. In the next century, there were less-aggressive monitoring of people's private activities by church and state and virtually no executions for sodomy. The only notable capital case was the summary conviction of "Mingo, alias Cocke Negro, for forcible Buggery" in Massachusetts on January 30, 1712. It is not clear that even Mingo was executed, as he was the slave of the state's chief justice and was recorded as a mourner at the justice's funeral in 1717. Ironically, the falloff of sodomy enforcement in the colonies coincided with major increases in such policing in London, Paris, and Amsterdam—European cities where noticeable subcultures of sexual minorities were beginning to alarm middle-class communities.[19]

The colonies' struggle for independence, and the Constitution of 1787, reinforced a spirit of individualism that was characteristic of the new United States of America. Even New England lawmakers abandoned the broad Puritan understanding that the state ought to be an intrusive "enforcer and guardian of Christian society," and accepted a new regime where the state respected and preserved individual liberty. Between 1786 and 1826, all the original thirteen states (except the Carolinas, where enforcement was nonexistent) revoked the death penalty for sodomy.[20]

After independence, all the original thirteen states, and almost all subsequent ones, adopted laws criminalizing sodomy and attempted sodomy. Instead of labeling the offending conduct as buggery (as in the Act of 1533) or "lying" with men (*Capitall Lawes*), most states termed the offense "sodomy" or "carnal knowledge" or "the infamous crime against nature," the terminology favored by the English jurist William Blackstone. None of these new statutes defined precisely what conduct constituted this crime, but American courts and commentators uniformly followed the English buggery precedents in regarding it as the penetration of a man's penis inside the rectum of an animal, of a woman or girl, or of another man or boy. Nineteenth-century judges were usually unwilling to read sodomy laws expansively or to interpolate biblical admonitions into state criminal codes.[21]

Given this background, even if Whitman and Anthony had engaged in erotic activities with persons of the same sex in the 1850s, it is doubtful that either would have violated New York's law criminalizing the "detestable and abominable crime against nature." Nothing Anthony could have done with another woman—neither cunnilingus (oral sex) nor mutual masturbation—would have been covered, because a male penis had to be involved to constitute illegal sodomy. Kissing, masturbation, and even oral sex between two men also fell outside the legal definition of sodomy, and New York had no catchall crime like "lewdness" that would forbid such public nonprocreative sex. Accordingly, Whitman would have violated the state sodomy law only if he had engaged in penetrative anal sex with another man.[22]

Even if Whitman engaged in anal intercourse (for which there is no evidence), it is most unlikely that he would have been arrested for violating the state sodomy law, for its operational purpose was to regulate sexual assaults. New York's criminal code in 1850 listed sodomy as one of the "crimes against the person"— associating it with rape, carnal knowledge of a girl, and mayhem. This suggests that sodomy laws filled a regulatory gap as regards what we would today consider nonconsensual sex. Because rape or seduction required vaginal penetration by the penis, an adult male who forced himself anally upon a woman, girl, boy, or weaker man could be prosecuted only under sodomy laws in the 1860s. Indeed, the "grave sin" that precipitated God's destruction of Sodom was the mob's threat to rape the male angels who were Lot's guests (Genesis 19:1–14); in the same spirit, New Haven's 1656 statute announced that "Sodomiticall filthinesse . . . is committed by a kind of Rape, nature being forced, though the will were enticed."[23]

A widely accepted legal rule of evidence reinforces the notion that sodomy laws were understood, in the nineteenth century, primarily as instruments to regulate sexual assault. As was true of the rule followed in rape cases, a man could not be convicted of sodomy based on testimony of a sexual partner who was his "accomplice," a willing adult partner. The partner's testimony was admissible if she or he was an unwilling participant or was a minor incapable of granting consent. So even if Whitman had engaged in anal sex with Vaughn, neither could have been successfully prosecuted if each was the accomplice of the other and there were no corroborating witnesses.[24]

Consistent with the regulatory emphasis on nonconsensual sex, the earliest reported sodomy case in the United States was the Maryland Court of Appeals's decision in *Davis v. Maryland* (1810). Baltimore County prosecutors accused William Davis of "assaulting, and attempting to commit *Sodomy*" on William Carpenter, a "youth" of nineteen. "[W]ickedly and devilishly," Davis with "force and arms" did "beat, wound, and illtreat" the victim. This was the standard formula for a sodomy charge, so we do not know exactly what transpired in this case, but the accusation sounds like a typical instance of rape. The historian Jonathan Ned Katz has identified 105 reported nineteenth-century cases involving sodomy, buggery, or the crime against nature. Excluding the decisions that did not reveal the sex or even the species of the parties involved, the reported cases fall into three roughly equal groups: bestiality with barnyard animals and the occasional ferret, sex between an adult man and a boy or "youth," and assaults by adult men upon women and weaker men. It is not clear whether any of these involved conduct we would now consider "consensual."[25]

Another factor that was key in sodomy cases was whether the sexual activity in question was flagrant and notorious. Both as written and as applied, nineteenth-century sodomy laws helped maintain public order and decency. Unlike New York, most states included sodomy in the category of "crimes against public morals and decency," among which were open adultery; distributing obscene literature; public indecent exposure; lewd cohabitation; and blasphemy in public places. Even when there was a public dimension to sexual activity, sodomy prosecutions were hard for the state to prove, as illustrated in *Medis v. State* (1889). A Galveston, Texas, jury convicted Charles Medis and Ed Hill of committing sodomy upon Milton Werner; each was sentenced to ten years in the penitentiary. The matter had come to the law's attention when two outsiders entered a room and observed Medis "in flagrante delicto" with Werner, and Hill lying six feet away, reading a newspaper. The Texas Court of Criminal Appeals overturned the conviction, on the ground that Werner was a consenting participant, and therefore the jury should have been instructed that his inculpatory testimony required corroboration. Texas was, in fact, the site of a quarter of the 105 cases Katz found—far more than any other state, and four times the number arising out of New York. Most of the Texas incidents involved sex with animals—usually cows, mares, or mules. In the South, most sodomy prosecutions involved bestiality; an entire jurisprudence developed as to what kinds of animals could be the objects of the crime. In some jurisdictions, sex with small birds was exempt.[26]

A final reason for Whitman's immunity from crime-against-nature laws lies in their pattern of (non)enforcement. In practice, police rarely enforced sodomy laws against anyone before 1880, even when such illegal activities were notorious in the community. In 1842 the *New York Sporting Whip* reported the names of men "who follow that unhallowed practice of Sodomy," including three "old and lechrous villains" who had seduced younger men. The "king of the Sodomites" was one Captain Collins, "who has been the instrumental cause of the death of a young man, who was employed by the monster as barkeeper; who was forced nightly to lie with beasts in the shape of men, by the order of his employer." Another named sodomite was Sally Binns, a curly-haired young man who characteristically wore "a snuff-colored frock, and fashionable pantaloons," and openly solicited men for unnatural intercourse on lower Broadway. While the *Whip* primarily identified men who assertedly engaged in sexual assaults and disrupted public spaces, and its exposé called for these "monsters" to be prosecuted, there is no record that any of these individuals was even arrested, nor were the dozens of "male prostitutes" who plied their trade in lower Manhattan. In the eight decades between 1786 and 1873, only twenty sodomy cases were prosecuted in the "City of Eros," which had a population of 1,912,000 by 1880.[27]

San Francisco followed the same pattern. Same-sex intimacy of all sorts was common in this rough-and-tumble Gold Rush town, which was ninety percent male and already known as "Sodom by the Sea." San Francisco's Barbary Coast (today's North Beach) offered unattached men more saloons and brothels per capita than anywhere else in the world, and the carousing was not limited to the heterosexual variety. Male prostitutes frequented the brothels and one Turkish bath. "Vice and depravity rules this limbo between the Paris Montmartre and the New York Bowery—but life, laughter and gayety too." Although San Francisco was by 1880 a Sodom-soaked city of 234,000 people, its police force arrested a total of just twenty-six men for the crime against nature between 1860 and 1880. During this same period, the police arrested almost a thousand women for prostitution, 162 men for rape, and forty-five men and women for cross-dressing.[28]

In 1871 a sexual advice manual reported that "every unnatural lust . . . is practised, not in rare or exceptional cases, but deliberately and habitually in the great cities of our country." The author described "restaurants frequented by men in women's attire, yielding themselves to indescribable lewdness," as well as "literature so inconceivably devilish as to advocate and extol this utter depravity." Little of this "depravity" was pursued by the law. Between 1865 and 1880 the police arrested a total of nine men for sodomy in Boston, eight in Chicago, one in Cincinnati, eight in Philadelphia, five in St. Louis, and none at all in Cleveland, Nashville, Atlanta, and Richmond (even though a category for sodomy was included in the local police reports).[29]

The 1880 Census reported that only sixty-three prisoners were then incarcerated for crimes against nature in the entire country. Thirty-eight of them were in the South; only five were New Yorkers like Whitman. Thirty-two of the prisoners were males of color, and eleven of the white prisoners were foreign (European) born.[30] Charges were almost never pressed against native-born educated white males; the men named by the *Whip* in 1842 as sodomites were all immigrants. Indeed, these "horrible offenses" were typically regarded as "foreign to our shores—to our nature they certainly are." The crime against nature was thus seen as a foreign infection threatening to native purity. Another assumption was racist and links the *Whip*'s stories with the pattern of arrests in the South. Because the crime against nature was "monstrous," only men of inferior "races" would commit it. (In the nineteenth century, the concept of "race" included what we would consider ethnicity, and so Jews and Frenchmen as well as Africans were considered to be of different races than Englishmen.) A third assumption was that the law needed to control and discipline these foreign activities engaged in by inferior races, lest the pollution infect Anglo-American youth. As the *Whip* put it, the "diabolical enticements" of sodomites (the promise of sinful pleasure) exerted an "allure," and the city needed to stop the contagion "lest their children should know that such crimes can be committed."[31]

The *Whip*'s commentary thus identifies three key symbolic purposes of sodomy laws. First, these statutes represented moral disapproval of *immoral acts,* not just of sexual assault (which was their main legal purpose), but also of "unhallowed practices." Second, sodomy laws helped define a particular category of people as *social outcasts.* The "beastly crew" of sodomites were considered "monsters" (also "brutes" and "miscreants") and were linked to other inferior groups, such as immigrants and freed slaves. In New York, sodomites were "mostly of the Hebrew race," proclaimed the *Whip*; several of the men outed by the paper, such as Sally Binns, were also derided as effeminate and unmanly. Third, sexual offense statutes were expressions of *community purity.* Again, going beyond their ostensible legal purpose (public decency), the symbolic goal of sodomy laws was to reinforce the notion that the only "pure" form of sexual expression was procreative sex within marriage. The sodomites identified by the purple press were also threatening because sodomy was an "allure" that could tempt and corrupt the boy as well as the young man.

American Body Politics: Themes of Disgust, Contagion, Community

There is a broader way of understanding the body of American sodomy law that connects the Puritan regime to the one in place after the Civil War. While criminal law is primarily prohibitory, when the state prohibits, it also implicitly allows, and that allowance may be viewed as a form of encouragement. By outlawing many sexual activities, the Puritans' seventeenth-century code of crimes at the same time endorsed and normalized a Bible-based code of conduct.

Although not articulated in religious terms, the normalizing standards suggested by American criminal law in the 1860s were little different, in substance,
from those of Puritan New Haven and Massachusetts. Both made it a crime for a
man and woman to have procreative sex outside of marriage (fornication or
adultery), especially if the sex involved force (rape) or a minor (seduction). Even
within marriage, it was a crime for husband and wife to engage in nonprocreative activities (sodomy). Anal sex, or sodomy, outside of marriage was triply
immoral because it was nonmarital, nonprocreative, and probably nonconsensual. Because American criminal law did not attempt to legislate female intimacy
or oral sex, it did not perfectly fence out all nonmarital or nonprocreative
sex. (Because the age of consent was low, usually ten years, the regime also did
not criminalize sexual activities between adults and adolescents.) Even if it was
not comprehensive, the body of law was clear in its intentions, and that clarity
extended to gender roles, particularly the notion that a woman's place was to be
a mother and a wife. (In the same vein, a number of ordinances made cross-
dressing a crime, in reference to the prohibition cited in Deuteronomy 22:5, that
"[a] woman shall not wear anything that pertains to a man.")[32]

Walt Whitman, Elizabeth Cady Stanton, and Susan B. Anthony all challenged
the norms underlying American law regarding sex crimes. They did so by proposing a new politics of the body, one that appealed to an American public
that was urban as well as rural, female as well as male, working-class as well
as middle-class, and increasingly not Anglo-Saxon. These writers spoke to an
America of the future, urging rejection of the moral status quo.[33]

Consciously reflecting urban working-class values, Whitman's poetics rejected the idea that physical purity demanded that sexual pleasure be enjoyed
only in the romanticized context of marital procreation. "Song of Myself" revels
in the appetites of the body. Contrast Saint Paul's idealism, only grudgingly allowing sexual pleasure within marriage, with Whitman's "Native Moments":

Give me now libidinous joys only,
Give me the drench of my passions, give me life coarse and rank,
To-day I go consort with Nature's darlings, to-night too,
I am for those who believe in loose delights, I share the midnight orgies of
    young men[.]

His "dearest friend" will be one who "shall be lawless, rude, illiterate, he shall be
one condemn'd by others for deeds done." Other *Leaves* suggest that those deeds
might include masturbation, prostitution, oral sex, even sodomy. "O you shunn'd
persons, . . . I will be your poet[.]"[34]

Although he depicted the male body more vividly, Whitman's celebration of the physical corpus also extended to women of all stations. Many of his passages are traditional in their extolling of women's role as universal mothers, but others present women as public citizens equal to men. "The idea of the women in America (extricated from this daze, this fossil and unhealthy air which hangs about the word *lady*) develop'd, raised to become the robust equals, workers, and, it may be, even practical and political deciders with the men[—]or, rather, capable of being so, soon as they realize it." It was Stanton and Anthony who pioneered that project when, in 1869, they formed the National Woman Suffrage Association (NWSA). Despite its title, NWSA had a broader agenda, seeking equal rights for women in the workplace, marriage, and the home—a project that entailed a rejection of accepted religious ideas. Stanton, for example, drafted a feminist response to the patriarchal passages (many from Saint Paul) in the Bible.[35]

Stanton and Anthony's feminist agenda also maintained that women should have the right to control their own bodies and the circumstances of reproduction. Thus, they supported mutuality within marriage and the freedom to exit unhappy, nonmutual marriages. "There is no other human slavery that knows such depths of degradations as a wife chained to a man whom she neither loves nor respects," said Stanton. One solution was to make it easier for women to divorce abusive husbands; an alternative was to avoid marriage altogether. In "Homes of Single Women" (1877), Anthony argued, "If women will not accept marriage *with subjection* [to the husband], nor men proffer it *without,* there is, there can be, *no alternative.* The women who *will not be ruled* must live without marriage" [Italics in original]. Although Anthony addressed her proposal to single women, the homes she described were ones where unmarried women lived with their sisters or friends in "co-partnership." She praised such women as the front line of women's equality, and as "balanced, well-rounded characters." Stanton and Anthony also rejected compulsory motherhood within marriage and urged women to avail themselves of contraceptives and other mechanisms to prevent unwanted pregnancies.[36]

Whitman's "Children of Adam" poems also focused on women's bodies as the foundation for a new politics, a proposal that did not go unanswered. While the critical response to the first edition of *Leaves* was negative—Rufus Griswold castigated it as "stupid filth" composed by someone "with the soul of a sentimental donkey that had died of disappointed love"—the critical abuse intensified after the "Children of Adam" sequence was added in the 1860 edition (see below). In 1865, Whitman lost his job at the Indian Bureau, as part of Interior Secretary James Harlan's campaign to establish "rules of decorum & propriety prescribed by a Christian civilization," a regime inconsistent with the unruly *Leaves.*[37]

The official response to the early feminists was even more ferocious. Politi-

cians and judges emphatically rejected women's suffrage, on the ground that it
would draw women away from the home and thereby undermine the family.
Anthony was arrested and convicted of a federal crime for voting in 1872. Having condemned abortion in 1857, after the Civil War the American Medical Association successfully lobbied for state legislation banning abortions and the sale
or use of contraceptives. Also responding to women's claims, husbands retaliated
with physical violence. Wife beating, though no longer authorized by the law,
became a national epidemic—from which judges averted their eyes, concluding
that marital privacy interests precluded relief.[38]

Stanton's views on women's ownership of their bodies were often linked to
(and sometimes confused with) those of the "free love" writers such as the feminist Victoria Woodhull, and moralists were prone to condemn both feminism
and free love as obscene.[39] The leader in these efforts was Anthony Comstock, the
secretary and chief special agent of the New York Society for the Suppression of
Vice from 1872 to 1915. Comstock was combative in all senses of the term—
morally, emotionally, even physically. After an 1874 scuffle with a pornographer
left his face scarred, he grew the muttonchop whiskers that became his trademark. Inspired by religious faith and concern for children, he brought a single-
minded obsession to eradicating obscene materials. The Comstock Act of 1873
made it a federal crime to send such literature, as well as contraceptive or abortion materials or devices, through the federal mail. Although most of Comstock's
prosecutions involved indecent pictures and literature, his most publicized sting
operations involved sexual advice manuals, birth control materials, offers to perform abortions, and feminist tracts. Indeed, Comstock's first recorded arrest
(March 2, 1872) was Patrick Bannon, an Irish Catholic who was charged with
possession of "Women's Rights Convention" publications and sent to jail for one
year for violating pre-Comstock federal law.[40]

Comstock particularly targeted individuals he regarded as leaders of the vice
movement. In 1872 he prosecuted Woodhull herself, who had (rightly) accused
the moralist Henry Ward Beecher of adultery. While Beecher managed to survive
the scandal, Woodhull was forced to flee the country to escape the society's harassment. Comstock arrested Ezra Heywood when he published the free-love
sensation *Cupid's Yokes* (1877), which mocked marriage as an oppressive institution; although convicted, Heywood was pardoned in 1878. Whitman himself lost
his Boston publisher in 1881 when the Boston branch of the society persuaded
the district attorney that *Leaves* was obscene. In 1883 Comstock arrested Heywood again, this time for reprinting Whitman's "To a Common Prostitute" and
"A Woman Waits for Me" (the poet's two most objectionable works, according to
the Boston censors in 1881), but the prosecutor refused to press charges. On his

third try, in 1890, Comstock finally succeeded in sending Heywood to prison, which ultimately killed the man.[41]

This revival of the Puritan ethos was both inflamed by and eventually superseded by new social developments, including urbanization, immigration, the end of slavery, and new opportunities for women. The same changes in society that gave rise to feminism and the free-love movement created alarm among classes whose status was threatened. Most men not only resisted women's equality demands but were emotionally unsettled by them. Native-born Americans were shocked by the wave of "pauperism, ignorance and degradation" (Stanton's words, ironically) that swept ashore from Ireland and Germany, and Irish immigrants were described as "simian," "savage," and "sensual." The slaves freed by the Emancipation Proclamation worried the North almost as much as they did the South. The term *miscegenation* originated in an 1864 anti-Lincoln tract, which warned that the first of this new wave of arrivals to mingle sexually would be Irish women and African men.[42]

No period in American history saw more social change than that between *Dred Scott* (1856) and the Fifteenth Amendment (1870). Faced with less-dramatic circumstances, the original Puritans had fought back with their own moralizing politics of the body, culminating in the witch trials. Neo-Puritan Comstockery developed a similar response after the Civil War. Its efforts were particularly powerful because they spoke to the psychological needs of Americans in times of unsettling demographic and social upheaval.[43]

Morality and Disgust

The most common response by traditionalists to the new body politics was that it was *disgusting*. Griswold dismissed the 1855 *Leaves* as the reflection of a "degrading, beastly sensuality." Appalled that the "Children of Adam" poems in the 1860 edition reduced "the congress of the sexes [to] a purely animal affair," Juliette (a.k.a. Calvin) Beach could not finish reading the collection: "I write simply to express my unqualified disgust with the portions I have read." William Dean Howells sarcastically summarized the reaction: "The Misses Nancy of criticism hastened to scramble over the fence, and on the other side, stood shaking their fans and parasols at the wretch [Whitman], and shrieking, 'Beast! Beast!'" But even Howells, a fan of Whitman's, admitted that the "utter lawlessness" of *Leaves* gave pleasure only to "those who believe liberty to mean the destruction of government," while "disgusting many persons of fine feelings."[44]

Traditionalist reactions to propositions defended by early feminists were similar. In the classic statement of his agenda, *Traps for the Young* (1883), Comstock's standard denunciation of feminist or free-love materials was that they were "vile" or "disgusting." Supporters wrote the society of their "feelings of disgust on these damnable creatures in human shape who vend or deal in obscene literature." Even birth control, not an item on Comstock's primary agenda, called forth harsh rhetoric: "Let men and women live a life above the level of beasts." Allowing contraception "would debase sacred things, break down the health of women and disseminate a greater curse than the plagues and diseases of Europe."[45]

Griswold's and Comstock's attitudes help link the moral politics of the neo-Puritans of the 1690s with those of later periods. "Traditionalist" moral systems do not simply wither away when social circumstances change and thus arguably render them obsolete. Like seventeenth-century Puritan culture in decline, latter-day Puritans retaliated, reasserting their moral code and demonizing its new critics. The rhetoric of disgust they so often resorted to reflected and appealed to emotions that supported traditional morality. As modern social scientists put it, "moral judgment is caused by intuitive moral impulses and is followed (when needed) by slow, ex post facto moral reasoning."[46]

According to the philosopher Elisabeth Young-Bruehl, sexual disgust, especially when expressed in an extreme manner, is often a coping mechanism for hysterical personalities such as Comstock and many of the seventeenth-century Puritans. Such individuals are often deeply disturbed by their libidinal or aggressive emotions and seek to manage them by projecting such emotions onto demonized objects of their disgust. "The prejudiced acts of hysterical characters really or symbolically attack the power they feel their victims have for getting too great a share of life's satisfactions—that is, life's erotic satisfactions." Hysterical feelings manifest themselves as acts of humiliation and denigration, putting the objects "in their place." If large numbers of people join in such emotions in a collective hysteria, they tend to create a demonized class, which they view as primitive, sexualized, effeminized, dark, and animalistic. Under extreme cultural conditions, such as those accompanying slavery, that class can even be deemed as subhuman.[47]

Purity, Pollution, and Boundary Maintenance

If viewed in a positive light, attitudes like disgust and boundary maintenance are useful in that they help constitute both individual and community identity. Young-Bruehl suggests that certain personality types are particularly obsessive about boundary maintenance, and are dependent on routines and established categories as a way to manage their lives. Like hysterical personalities, obsessive ones develop emotional prejudgments that help them control their anxieties, especially sexual ones. "[O]bsessionals purge themselves of polluting thoughts and desires by displacing them onto others, who then are experienced as dirtying and assertedly polluting." Obsessional feelings need a scapegoat group, to which is attributed individual or social ills. While hysteria creates an underclass that is animalistic and disgusting, obsession understands its objects as contagious or predatory, but often hidden, which means they must be hunted out. In some historical circumstances, such as those giving rise to the Salem witch hunts, group obsession becomes paranoia, hatred becomes a duty, and revenge a virtue. The enemy must be exposed and then annihilated.[48]

Traditionalist responses to free love and feminism reveal the power of cleansing rituals. Writing in 1855, Griswold condemned Whitman as worse than the filthiest pauper. Both "leave a foul odor, contaminate the pure, healthful air," but at least the "slave of poverty" has a "sense of shame." Griswold regretted that he had not the temerity to quote more of Whitman's obscenities, much like a critic of the 1860 edition of *Leaves*: "His indecency is protected against the critics as a skunk is protected against the hunters. It is safe because it is too filthy to handle, and to noisome even to approach."[49]

While the Comstock Society's first annual report acknowledged that "[n]o language can describe the disgust and loathing with which pure minds must regard the traffic" in feminist and free-love tracts, it also worried that these "shrewd and wily" purveyors are "so stealthy and persistent" that they "have succeeded in injecting a virus more destructive to the innocency and purity of youth, if not counteracted, than can be the most deadly disease of the body." Comstock is one of the great obsessives in American history. In 1897, he reported that he had protected youth by arresting 1,220 malefactors; seizing 872,507 corrupting pictures, 64,723 pounds of obscene books, and 97,132 articles for immoral use; and halting the illegal mailing of 121,913 indecent items.[50]

"Hunt these men as you hunt rats, without mercy." Like William Plaine, these miscreants did not just assault vulnerable youth, they changed them. "Every new generation of youth is sent out into the world as sheep in the midst of wolves," said the society's vice president. "The danger, however, is not that they will be devoured by them, but that they will be transformed into wolves." So when a student at a boarding school receives a package of smut, "the boy breaks the seal and lets the monster loose. . . . Passions that had slumbered or lain dormant are awakened, and the boy is forced over a precipice, and death and destruction are sure, except the grace of God saves him." By corrupting youth, the feminist and the pornographer "strik[e] at the heart of the Republic," sapping "the foundation of society and implant[ing] the principles of decay and certain death in the body politic."[51]

Reflecting the rising social and intellectual influence of doctors, Comstockerite metaphors were often heavily medical in nature—lewd and feminist ideas were characterized as contagious diseases, viruses, cancers, poisons. Comstock himself was viewed as a doctor who went forth with tentative remedies: "[T]here is no way whatever to cut out this cancer which is eating away the heart of society, but to put in the knife and tear out the venomous part. . . . Gentlemen! Let us purify this city if it be by fire and sword."⁵²

Traditional Gender Roles and Family as the Basis for Civic Community

Young-Bruehl's third kind of emotional coping mechanism completes my account of morality-based politics of preservation. For Freudians like Young-Bruehl, sexism is ultimately based on narcissism: "[T]he child . . . assumes all beings are like himself and disparages the woman when he discovers she is other." The male child can recover the familiar image of the mother by constructing his own family and sexuality through the lens of patriarchy, in which the husband presides over the wife and children. "When, under the weight of familial organization, [woman's] difference does not disappear, it is controlled legally, exploited and then, when even that repression does not silence the difference, the male is made . . . the universal category."⁵³

Whitman's "Song of Myself" seeks to turn narcissism into a strategy for inclusion. He befriends and identifies with long lists of Americans—the carpenter, duck shooter, spinning girl, farmer, lunatic, journal printer, "quadroon girl," gentleman dancers, "newly-come immigrants," the "squaw wrapt in her yellow-hemm'd cloth," steamboat deckhands, the Yankee girl working in the mill, drovers and peddlers, the opium eater, a prostitute, the train-fare collector, and so forth. Hundreds of different individuals populate "Song," and Whitman merges them all into a vision of American democracy, which (in the person of Whitman) embraces them all. What makes the poem so dazzling is its panoramic inclusiveness, a contemporary equivalent to the exclamation of the Roman playwright Terence, "Nihil humanum *mihi* alienum est" [Italics added]. (Nothing human is alien *to me.*) Whitman's inclusiveness is resolutely narcissist, however. "I say it is as great to be a woman as to be a *man,* And I say there is nothing greater than the mother of *men.*" The universal referent is, finally, man.⁵⁴

Stanton and Anthony's project was a more direct challenge to male narcissism. They attacked the radical merger of wife with husband, which the law guaranteed when it denied wives property and contract rights and made divorce impossible. Women, they insisted, must be understood on their own terms, not just as wives and mothers of men, however romanticized. Stanton and Anthony rejected the era's separate-spheres philosophy. Education, work, the franchise, and jury service should all be domains available to women, not just the home and hearth. Most radical was Anthony's notion that women could live rewarding and productive lives in all-female households. True to the narcissism of the time, men responded to this proposal with denial for the most part, and incredulity for the rest.[55]

During the trial of the liberal marriage critic George Train, Comstock was appalled by the "most disgusting set of Free-lovers." He described the women as "thin-faced, cross, sour-looking, each wearing a look of 'Well I am the boss' and 'Oh, for a man.'" While these feminists had abandoned their natural roles as mother and helpmate, they still *really* yearned for a real man, if any would have them. But the men in the courtroom, "unworthy the name of men," were "licentious looking, sneakish, contemptible, making a true man blush to be seen near them."[56]

Reconstruction: Recognition and Preservation

As Whitman was adding "Calamus" and "Children of Adam" to *Leaves* in 1860, America was marching toward civil war. Lincoln, "gentle, plain, just and resolute . . . saved the Union of these States," and although "My Captain" fell, "cold and dead," at war's end, his abolitionist Republicans presided over the constitutional Reconstruction of America in 1865–77. The Reconstruction Amendments—the Thirteenth, Fourteenth, and Fifteenth, but especially the Fourteenth—revolutionized the U.S. Constitution and provided a framework for examining the social conditions in which America's sodomy laws of the time were situated.[57]

The Principles of the Fourteenth Amendment

The first sentence of Section 1 of the Fourteenth Amendment grants national citizenship to "[a]ll persons born or naturalized in the United States," thereby overruling *Dred Scott*. The following sentence ensures national rights against the states:

> No State shall make or enforce any law which shall abridge the privileges or immunities of citizens of the United States; nor shall any State deprive any person of life, liberty, or property, without due process of law; nor deny to any person within its jurisdiction the equal protection of the laws.

As legal scholars have established, the Fourteenth Amendment not only altered the relationship between Americans and state governments, but also transformed the very meanings of citizenship and rights. As originally understood by the abolitionist coalition that sponsored and ratified the amendment, Section 1 articulates three principles that limit the authority of state governments, especially with regard to their criminal codes. As they were enforced in 1868, state sodomy and crime-against-nature laws did not, as a general matter, violate Section 1.[58]

The Legality Principle. The Fourteenth Amendment's Due Process Clause was copied from the Fifth Amendment, which in turn was inspired by the Magna Carta's concept of *per legem terrem*. For the government to act "according to the law of the land," state officials were required to follow the rule of law and not their own biases. A criminal sanction, for example, should not be levied unless the populace had sufficient notice that this particular conduct had been determined to be criminal. Nor should criminal sanctions depend on the whim and caprice of individual law enforcement officers; there must be guidance, preferably from the legislature.

In 1868, when the Fourteenth Amendment was added to the Constitution, twenty state codes made the "crime against nature" a felony, often mentioning "sodomy" as well; ten other states labeled the crime "sodomy" or "buggery" or "carnal knowledge" (or some combination). No state defined those terms, but due process did not require exact statutory definition if a term had an accepted legal meaning, such as could be supplied by the common law. Between independence and 1890, American state courts faithfully followed the common law's limitation of the crime against nature to an act of anal sex committed by an adult man against a woman, boy, girl, another man, or animal (or by an animal against a woman). So while there was no due process problem applying those thirty crime-against-nature or sodomy laws to such conduct, any innovative application of them—such as in a case of sex between women—should have been unconstitutional, because it would have been well beyond the customary meaning of the statutory language.[59]

Six state criminal codes (Indiana, Iowa, Nebraska, New Hampshire, Ohio, Vermont) did not include crime-against-nature laws. Informed by Fifth Amendment due process notions, the Supreme Court had ruled that the federal government could not prosecute common-law crimes. Accordingly, the Fourteenth Amendment would presumptively have been read to preclude judges from expanding the ambit of state statutory crimes. Vermont's Supreme Court did later recognize "buggery" as a common-law crime in 1899; that decision was probably wrong under the Fourteenth Amendment (an argument the Vermont court did not consider). New Hampshire presented a variation. Its criminal code, adopted in 1867, did not report the crime against nature, nor did the 1843 and 1851 codes. But the legislature had enacted a statute in 1812 making it a crime if a "man lye with mankind." It is not clear how the framers would have evaluated this unusual situation.[60]

The Liberty Principle. The Declaration of Independence asserts that it is "self-evident" that men "are endowed by their Creator with certain unalienable Rights," those rights being "Life, Liberty, and the Pursuit of Happiness." The Constitution is a thoroughly libertarian document. Following Blackstone, the framers would have understood liberty to include common-law rights of personal security, or "a person's legal and uninterrupted enjoyment of his life, his limbs, his body, his health and his reputation," subject to regulation "for the general advantage of the public"; of personal freedom to move about; and of personal property, namely, "[t]he free use, enjoyment, and disposal of all his acquisitions, without any control or diminution save only by the laws of the land." Article IV of the Constitution prohibited states from denying "privileges and immunities" such as these to out-of-staters. Justice Bushrod Washington authoritatively read the Privileges and Immunities Clause to protect people's substantive rights "to pursue and obtain happiness and safety; subject nonetheless to such restraints as the government may *justly* prescribe for the general good of the whole." Copying this language from the Constitution of 1787, the Fourteenth Amendment's Privileges or Immunities Clause probably meant that the states had to respect these same kinds of liberties for their own citizens as well.[61]

As they were enforced in the nineteenth century, crime-against-nature statutes would not have offended the Privileges or Immunities Clause. Under the liberty principle recognized in 1868, an individual could enjoy "the use of his life, his limbs, his body," for pleasurable sensations, so long as this enjoyment did not constitute an assault against an unconsenting person *and* did not create a public nuisance, as through third-party witnesses. Moreover, Americans were free to enjoy the use of their "acquisitions," including the privacy of their homes, "without any control or diminution save only by the laws of the land," namely, laws targeting the home.

The Principle Against Class Legislation. The Declaration of Independence also announces that "all men are created equal." Applying this principle to the states, the Reconstruction framers emphasized that "the American system rests on the assertion of the equal right of every man to life, liberty, and the pursuit of happiness." Introducing the proposed Fourteenth Amendment, Senator Jacob M. Howard said it would "abolis[h] all class legislation in the States and [do] away with the injustice of subjecting one caste of persons to a code not applicable to another." This rule against class legislation was widely accepted by the state conventions ratifying the amendment. Although the immediate beneficiaries of the anti–class legislation principle were the freed slaves, the framers understood the principle to apply more generally, for "there is no more effective practical guaranty against arbitrary and unreasonable government than to require the principles of law which officials would impose upon a minority must be imposed generally."[62]

The framers would not have recognized "sodomites" as a protected "class," any more than they would have recognized a class of rapists or child molesters. (In the nineteenth century, these categories overlapped substantially.) The only plausible complaint supported by this principle would have been against the South's enforcement of sodomy laws almost exclusively against men of color. But the number of arrests was so small and their connection with a larger scheme of exclusion so remote in the 1870s that the claim would have undoubtedly failed. A more pertinent question was whether the principle against class legislation could be extended to the body of state laws discriminating against women. Not only were women universally excluded from the franchise and jury service, but many states also blocked them from certain occupations, professional licenses, and business endeavors, and some still even denied married women ordinary property and contract rights. States were also starting to regulate women's freedom to obtain early-term abortions. Whether such laws violate the Fourteenth Amendment depends on how broadly one interprets its language.[63]

An Inclusionary Vision of the Fourteenth Amendment

Due process, privileges and immunities, and equal protection were, like the crime against nature, elastic terms. Most criminal laws contain fuzzy edges, restrict liberties, and draw lines creating inequalities. When are such features inconsistent with the Fourteenth Amendment? For example, did the Fourteenth Amendment guarantee women the right to vote? On its face, apparently not. Although the Reconstruction Congress that drafted the Fourteenth Amendment did consider Stanton and Anthony's arguments, it declined to bar sex-based discriminations. Indeed, Section 2 of the amendment provides a remedy if the right to vote in federal elections "is denied to any of the *male* inhabitants of each State." Stanton and Anthony accordingly opposed the ratification of the Fourteenth Amendment, as well as the Fifteenth Amendment, which ensured men of color (but not women) the right to vote. The "special legislation" limiting women's opportunities was, they believed, indefensible. "Christ's golden rule is better than all the special legislation that the ingenuity of man can devise: 'Do unto others as you would have others do unto you.' . . . We ask no better laws than those which you have made for yourselves."[64]

In 1869, before the Fifteenth Amendment was ratified, Virginia Minor opened the Women Suffrage Convention with an argument that the Fourteenth Amendment *did* ensure women the right to vote: (1) Section 1 guarantees *citizens* national "privileges or immunities." (2) The ultimate "privilege" of national citizenship is the right to vote. (3) Women are "citizens" under Section 1. There-fore, Section 1 guarantees women the privilege of voting. The NWSA embraced this "New Departure" argument and urged it on voters and Congress in 1870–71. Arguing for a bill to extend the vote to women in the District of Columbia, over which Congress has plenary jurisdiction, Stanton supplemented Minor's text-based argument. A broad reading of the Privileges or Immunities Clause is con-stitutionally preferable because it is more consistent with the Guarantee Clause of Article IV, ensuring states a "republican form of government," and the Bill of Attainder Clause of Article I, which protects against the singling out of disfa-vored groups for criminal treatment. Victoria Woodhull presented an even more expansive version of this argument later in 1870: the freshly ratified Fifteenth Amendment reflected the Constitution's steady expansion of the franchise, and the universal recognition of women's legal autonomy suggested that this amend-ment should be read expansively as well. In 1872 Stanton deployed such an evo-lutive analysis to the Fourteenth Amendment argument and uttered a famous objection to originalism: "If we are to be governed in all things by the men of the eighteenth century, and the twentieth by the nineteenth, and so on, the world will always be governed by dead men."[65]

At the same time feminists were struggling with the Reconstruction Amend-ments, Whitman was working out his vision of constitutionalism in *Democratic Vistas* (1870). Like Stanton and Anthony, he endorsed "woman's entrance amid the arenas of practical life, politics, the suffrage, &c." Whitman anticipated Stan-ton's "dead men" argument in his vision for new forms in poetry. "It must bend its vision toward the future, more than the past. *Like America*, it must extricate itself from even the greatest models of the past, and, while courteous to them, must have entire faith in itself, and the products of its own democratic spirit only." His most distinctive contribution was a positive understanding of govern-ment, "not merely to rule, to repress disorder, &c., but to develop, to open up to cultivation, to encourage the possibilities of all beneficent and manly outcrop-page, and of that aspiration to independence, and the pride and self-respect la-tent in all characters." The role of law, "higher than the highest arbitrary rule, [is] to train communities through all their grades, beginning with individuals and ending there again, to rule themselves." The goal of democracy is that "men, the nation, as a common aggregate of living identities, affording in each a separate and complete subject for freedom, worldly thrift and happiness, and for a fair chance for growth, and for protection in citizenship, &c.," must "be placed, in each and in the whole, on one broad, primary, universal, common platform."[66]

A great challenge for any society is to find the proper balance between dis-tinctive individualism and the needs of the community. *Democratic Vistas* opens with a reference to John Stuart Mill's *On Liberty* (1859), which Whitman invokes for its notion that America must give "full play for human nature to expand itself in numberless and even conflicting directions." The dignified, sensual individual Whitman depicted in *Leaves* becomes the connected citizen in *Vistas*. "The purpose of democracy" is the idea "that man, properly train'd in sanest, highest freedom, may and must become a law, and series of laws, unto himself, surrounding and providing for, not only his own personal control, but all his relations to other individuals, and to the State." A nation seeking both perfect individuality and perfect solidarity faces a paradox.[67]

Whitman appreciated Lincoln's insistence that a Re-United States must be a government serving and responsive to the former slaveholders as well as to the former slaves. "Of all dangers to a nation . . . there can be no greater one than having certain portions of the people set off from the rest by a line drawn—they not privileged as others, but degraded, humiliated, made of no account." Even people considered to have a higher social standing have a role to play in the body politic. As "Nature's stomach is fully strong enough not only to digest the morbific matter always presented, not to be turn'd aside, and perhaps, indeed, intuitively gravitating thither—but even to change such contributions into nutriment for highest use and life—so American democracy's."[68]

A Puritan Vision of the Fourteenth Amendment

Between 1870 and 1874, Congress and the Supreme Court rejected feminist readings of the Reconstruction Amendments, with an argument that was largely phrased in the argot of original intent, with a narcissistic edge: *we* (males) participated in these amendments, and we did *not* intend them to enfranchise women. Their focus, rather, was race discrimination, and the targeted beneficiaries were the freed slaves. There is more to this story, however. Many of the same congressmen and justices who invoked original intent (race discrimination) to reject feminist arguments soon enough turned their backs on the freed slaves and signaled the constitutional acceptability of race-based segregation and anti-miscegenation laws. Legislators and judges came to understand the Fourteenth Amendment pragmatically, in light of public opinion: the American people did not, as a whole, favor equal rights for women, free lovers, or (ultimately) the former slaves.[69]

Competing with the inclusionary interpretation of the free lovers and feminists was a puritan reading of natural-law moralists, who articulated their standard concerns within the rhetoric of constitutional structure and rights. As before, Comstock and his society best exemplified the goals of this puritan constitutionalism. Its first principle is *purposive* and dynamic: it is the responsibility of the government to advance the public welfare, especially the moral integrity and even purity of the body politic. The public good entails the flourishing of key institutions—the family, the church, schools—that the state should affirmatively support. These institutions and the state should work together to create a culture where youth will be able to develop without pollution. The Comstock Society argued that obscene books and feminist tracts "strik[e] at the foundations of [our] civil, social, and religious life" because they "*attack specially and fatally the youth*. What shall be the society of twenty years hence if the boys and girls of to-day are smitten by this leprosy?"[70]

The second principle of puritan constitutionalism is *antiliberal:* individual liberties must give way to the public good. As Comstock explained it, "[F]reedom sought by our forefathers to worship God did not mean to serve the devil. . . . Freedom to speak or print does not imply the right to say or print that which shocks decency, corrupts the morals of the young, or destroys all faith in God. Neither [freedom nor liberty] drags mankind downward, sanctions wrong-doing, or links man to the lowest elements of his nature." He was aware of and rejected Mill's arguments: "Liberty to them [the liberals] is not the liberty of the patriot that rejoices in the freedom from crime, and the terrors of the criminal class; but rather freedom to them means a right to ignore the rights of others." This was a perceptive analysis, and one that Comstock applied especially to abortion. In the name of a woman's liberty, quacks were murdering "ante-natal human beings," a violation of both natural law and third-party liberties.[71]

The third principle of puritan constitutionalism is *traditionalist:* the state should follow and embrace the natural order of things; naturalized distinctions are not even "discriminations," properly speaking. In *Bradwell v. Illinois* (1872), the Supreme Court unanimously rejected Myra Bradwell's challenge to her exclusion from the practice of law. The majority opinion ruled that practicing a trade was not a national right ensured by the Privileges or Immunities Clause. While Justice Joseph Bradley and two others felt economic interests were protected by the clause, they still denied relief, on the ground that judges ought not interpret the Constitution as inconsistent with the merger one expects when a woman marries:

The constitution of the family organization, which is founded in the divine ordinance, as well as the nature of things, indicates the domestic sphere as that which properly belongs to the domain and functions of womanhood. The harmony, not to say identity, of interests and views which belong, or should belong, to the family institution is repugnant to the idea of a woman adopting a distinct and independent career from that of her husband. . . . The paramount destiny and mission of woman are to fulfil the noble and benign offices of wife and mother. This is the law of the Creator.

Comstock surely agreed with this articulation, for he saw mothers as the primary glue holding the family together and protecting youth against corruption.[72]

Neither the framers of the Fourteenth Amendment, nor free lovers like Whitman and Stanton, nor neo-Puritans like Comstock would have considered crime-against-nature laws unconstitutional in the 1870s. A lot changed in the next century, however, as social and political developments affected the language and operation of sodomy laws, objections to them, and even the politics of preservation that supported them, until the turn of a new millennium.

CHAPTER TWO

From the Sodomite to the Homosexual, 1881–1935

Illustrations of Freda Ward and Alice Mitchell
from an 1892 Memphis newspaper

Married with three children, John Addington Symonds nevertheless nurtured feelings for other men, which were clarified when he read *Leaves of Grass* at Trinity College, Cambridge. In 1872 he reported to Whitman his own researches on "passionate friendship" in ancient Greece and Renaissance Italy. Suggesting that Whitman's "Comradeship" was "on a par with the Sexual feeling for depth & strength & purity," Symonds begged the poet to "tell me more about the Love of Friends!" Whitman responded evasively to this and subsequent inquiries. In 1890 Symonds put the matter unambiguously: "In your conception of Comradeship, do you contemplate the possible intrusion of those semi-sexual emotions and actions which no doubt do occur between men?" And, as a moral and legal matter, was Whitman "prepared to leave them to the inclinations and the conscience of the individuals involved?" Symonds endorsed the European approach, which forbade coercion and guarded against "outrages of public decency," but did not interfere in private intimacies between consenting adults. Whitman rejected the "entirely undream'd & unreck'd possibility of morbid inferences—wh' are disavow'd by me & seem damnable." After a short ramble, he concluded with a remarkable lie: "I have had six children," and one southern grandchild.[1]

By 1890 Whitman was much more cautious than he had been thirty years earlier. Near the end of his life, he was anxious to preserve his legacy, *Leaves of Grass*, and with the tide of Comstockery waxing, he was increasingly alert to the fine line between his naturalistic endorsement of sensual pleasures, and what might be perceived as pornographic smut (in "Children of Adam") and sexual abomination ("Calamus"). In 1882 Whitman lost his Boston publisher because the local Comstock society and prosecutors deemed *Leaves* obscene and lascivious. In fact, his main critic, Thomas Higginson, was obsessed with younger men and projected his own "polluted" sexual feelings onto *Leaves*.[2]

The year of Whitman's death, 1892, saw a new neo-Puritan interest in unnatural sex between women, epitomized by Alice Mitchell (1873–1898) and Freda Ward (1875–1892). These classmates at Miss Higbee's School in Memphis, Tennessee, wore their hair in short curls. The brunette Alice is depicted with a strong jaw and a determined look, in contrast to the fair-haired and soft-featured Freda. The two women exchanged passionate letters and were apparently lovers. In 1891 the sixteen-year-old Freda agreed to become eighteen-year-old Alice's wife. They planned to elope and marry, with Alice passing as a man, "Alvin J. Ward." Their families discovered this scheme and separated the girls. When Freda later agreed to marry Ashley Roselle, Alice was inconsolable. On January 25, 1892, she approached Freda near a levee. Wielding her father's shaving razor, Alice reached from behind and slashed her friend's throat, and Freda bled to death before she could receive medical attention. The newspapers feasted on this "Very Unnatural Crime" and the ensuing trial. Acquitted on grounds of insanity, the defendant spent the rest of her life in an asylum.[3]

Alice Mitchell exemplified a new kind of miscreant. Some called her an *invert*, an individual who had taken on the gender role of the "opposite" sex. Others deemed her a *degenerate*, an evolutionary backward step. In the new century, the most popular term would be *homosexual*. Whatever the terminology, this new devil was increasingly visible and correspondingly threatening to respectable urbanites. At the same time that Americans were growing obsessively concerned about protecting children from sexual abuse, they constructed the image of the (male) homosexual as a predator victimizing their sons and daughters. Likewise, as Americans were becoming increasingly concerned about protecting white women against sexual assault by black men, they constructed the image of the lesbian as a vampire preying on their daughters. The country was in the throes of a sex panic: the sexuality represented by the homosexual child molester, the black rapist, and the vampire lesbian was out of control, contagious, and ruinous for America's youth, its families, and the very core of society.[4]

Those new myths and identities led to a revisionism that now viewed Walt Whitman, who had been criticized in the 1860s for sexualizing the female body, as more dangerous for his suggestion of erotic relations between men. In "Walt Whitman's Anomaly" (1913), Dr. W. C. Rivers read the "Calamus" poems as evidence of inversion. "If ever one had the woman's soul in a man's body, it was he." Likewise feminists like Susan B. Anthony were labeled "man-haters" and charged with seducing young women away from their intended husbands. The psychiatrist William Lee Howard said that "the female possessed of masculine ideas about independence" and the "female sexual pervert, are simply different degrees of the same class—degenerates." These reinterpretations fueled a revolution in American sodomy law, a revolution that expanded regulatory attention and reconstructed the crime so that women as well as men could now commit it.[5]

Novel Urban Identities: New Women, Prostitutes, and Fairies

This emerging national anxiety found its greatest expression in big cities. Fueled by immigration from Europe, New York's population soared to 2,507,414 in 1890; with the migration of southern blacks northward, its population doubled in the next thirty years to 5,620,048, according to the 1920 Census. Other cities followed a similar pattern. By 1920, Philadelphia had grown to 1,823,779 inhabitants; Baltimore to 733,826; Washington to 437,571; Chicago to 2,701,705; St. Louis to 772,897; San Francisco to 506,676. Los Angeles exploded, from 50,395 (1890) to 576,673 (1920). The United States was transforming from a relatively homogeneous, rural, farm-based society to an ethnically diverse, urban industrial one. These demographic changes produced new patterns of sociability and sexual behavior, with sexual variety openly flourishing. The confluence of so much social novelty—a shift in racial balance, expanded roles for women, and sexual couplings unimaginable in 1860—created an anxiety that moral, social, and class lines were collapsing. To shore up those lines, moral reformers identified classes of miscreants who most openly challenged traditional mores: the New Woman, the prostitute, and—a synthesis of the first two— the predatory degenerate, a catchall category that included black rapists, child-molesting inverts, and vampire lesbians.[6]

The New Woman

A major effect of post–Civil War urbanization was to present more opportunities for middle-class white women, more of whom were now able to earn higher educations, enter the workforce, and postpone or avoid marriage and children.

Although she represented only a small percentage of the population—and a percentage that included few women of color—the "New Woman" became a critical part of American society and intellectual life. Among the many accomplished women were the authors Willa Cather and Gertrude Stein; the educators Mary Woolley (Mount Holyoke) and M. Carey Thomas (Bryn Mawr); and the social reformers Frances Kellor and Florence Kelley.[7]

Perhaps the most remarkable of all was Jane Addams (1860–1935), who in 1889 founded Hull House in Chicago's Ward 19, a diverse neighborhood that included 50,000 indigent eastern European immigrants. Hull House was a residence for women working in this community, and hosted a range of social and political events generated by neighbors. Addams believed that relief for the poor should be a cooperative effort between the community and those seeking to help. Her paper on "The Subjective Necessity for Social Settlements" (1892) argued that Hull House epitomized the "social function to democracy." Addams went beyond Whitman's notion that democracy was built on adhesive ties among comrades and Anthony's insistence that women should be part of civic life. "To make the entire social organism democratic," she maintained, required social intercourse and mutual learning across lines of class, race, religion, and sex.[8]

Many of the New Women who came of age between 1880 and 1920 found their most important relationships with other women, a choice Anthony had praised in "Homes of Single Women." Jane Addams's life partner was the universally beloved Mary Rozet Smith, a full-time volunteer at Hull House, Addams's alter ego, and her financial angel, who helped fund Addams's plans to expand the house into a vast complex that spanned several city blocks. Relationships such as this were called "Boston marriages," after Henry James's depiction in *The Bostonians* (1886), which itself was based on the long-term union between his sister, Alice, and Katharine Peabody Loring. No one openly marked Boston marriages as sexual relationships, and many surely were not. The most famously sexual of these partnerships was between Gertrude Stein and Alice B. Toklas, who met in San Francisco and began living in Paris in 1903. We cannot know whether Addams's relationship with Smith had a sexual component, in part because Addams destroyed their correspondence, believing it to be "too intimate" to be shared.[9]

A more widespread practice than Boston marriages was "smashing," which was popular at women's colleges. "When a girl takes a shine to another, she straightaway enters upon a regular course of bouquet sendings, interspersed with tinted notes [etc.], until at last the object of her attentions is captured, the two become inseparable." The ever-serious Addams was one of the few college-educated young women of her era (and the next) *not* to have formed crushes on her fellow students and teachers; everyone else smashed, or so it seems from contemporary accounts of student life at women's schools. The mutual attachment of Mitchell and Ward at Miss Higbee's School began as a smash.[10]

One reason Mitchell's case received so much national publicity was that she came to represent the New Woman Run Amuck. Many middle-class men were nostalgic for the Jacksonian ideal of True Womanhood, which was nurturing, nonsexual, and confined to the domestic sphere. They lamented that New Women were invading the civic sphere and were no longer supporting the important project of perpetuating the Anglo-American race by bearing and raising lots of children. Manifestations of this restorationist goal were Civil War–era laws criminalizing abortion and the distribution of contraceptives, moves that limited (married) women's ability to plan childbearing. Feminists were tagged as enemies of the family, and women like Addams were potentially suspect in that they established lives sustained only by female affection.[11]

Mitchell was particularly threatening in her appropriation of the male "crime of passion" and, worse, in her plan to marry Ward. The press breathlessly reported earlier examples of women who passed as men and married other women. Even more objectionable was Mitchell's persuading the impressionable Ward to go along with the travesty. If this well-educated young woman could be convinced to renounce men and nature, why not anyone's daughter? Or wife? By 1900, even ordinary passionate friendships between women became "laced with ambivalence and danger; they might become too intensely romantic or substitute for marriage."[12]

Prostitutes in the City of Eros

Whitman associated the "populous city" with sensuality. "Yet now of all that city I remember only a woman I casually met there who detain'd me for love of me, Day by day and night by night we were together." Had such a woman requested a fee, Whitman would not have been fazed. "You prostitutes, . . . who am I that I should call you more obscene than myself?" As he tramped down Broadway in the 1850s, Whitman would have passed dozens of brothels and hundreds of streetwalkers, with working-class immigrant or slave roots and little formal education. Sex workers could make ten times as much money on the street, at a saloon, or in a bawdy house as they could in a sweatshop. As many as ten percent of the young women in the "City of Eros" engaged in prostitution for some period in their lives during the nineteenth century. Although the New York market for sex and erotic entertainment was the largest, most American cities saw a thriving sex business after the Civil War.[13]

The commercialization of sex had a potentially revolutionary impact on Americans' attitudes and practices. Prostitutes, for example, helped popularize nonprocreative sex. Fellatio (oral stimulation of the penis) was a favored activity among sex workers, because it posed no risk of pregnancy and in most markets brought a higher price, as it was a service most wives wouldn't provide. Some bordellos that offered this amenity advertised themselves as "French houses." Female sex workers also engaged in cunnilingus (oral stimulation of the clitoris), either as part of a sex show for male clients or for their own satisfaction. In 1878, Comstock reported women putting their heads "between the legs of one another and their mouths upon the sexual organs or the vagina.... Others feigned intercourse with each other and sucked each other's breasts." Many brothels and saloons were also places where male prostitutes, often mere boys, hung out and engaged in oral or anal sex for pay.[14]

The female prostitute was the antithesis of True Womanhood: she was not only engaging in nonprocreative sex outside of marriage, but she was offering men a pleasurable alternative to marriage, and doing so in public—from the soliciting streetwalkers to the sex shows in bawdy houses to cruising in saloons. By midcentury the alarmed middle class of St. Louis, San Francisco, and other cities adopted the European philosophy of regulating prostitution and zoning it into "red light" districts, an example Whitman urged New York to follow: "There are certain propensities and passions inherent in our nature which will have vent in one shape or another, despite all the legislative wisdom of communities." Permitting but regulating these practices would provide a "safety valve for the . . . excesses" associated with sex work, especially sexually transmitted diseases. In 1867, a bill was drawn up to that effect but was never introduced in the New York legislature because of opposition from Anthony, who argued that women's lives were being destroyed by traffic in their bodies. St. Louis soon thereafter ended its experiment in regulation rather than prohibition.[15]

From 1870 through 1920 American cities of all sizes and in all regions witnessed purity movements, which brought together wealthy men, feminists, and religious leaders dedicated to the eradication or, more realistically, curtailment of the oldest profession. New York's periodic antivice campaigns between 1892 and 1920 generated thousands of pages of private reports and legislative hearings that serve as the best sources for the sociology of prostitution even today. Antiprostitution laws were constantly updated by the New York legislature between 1881 and 1921, with corresponding increases in arrests. Although such societies were not as prominent in southern cities, their police forces were also active. St. Louis was probably the biggest enforcer per capita in the nation, arresting between one thousand and fifty-two hundred women (and sometimes men) for various prostitution-related offenses every year between 1877 and 1921. In St. Louis and other southern cities, most of those arrested were women of color. In New York and other northern cities, daughters of immigrants predominated.[16]

Fairies and Cross-Dressers

Not only did America's population explosion produce larger communities of nonconforming women, but it also fostered a subculture of Sodom. Much of this subculture consisted of male prostitutes—soldiers, workers, and unemployed men who earned money for sex, usually for receiving oral sex. By 1900 New York's Broadway and San Francisco's Presidio were focal points for male sex workers. Whitman associated with these comrades; his "Populous City," purporting to recall a one-night stand with a woman, was originally written with a male lover in mind. By 1890, however, this subculture was dominated by self-consciously feminized men who called themselves "fairies." Many cross-dressed and posed as "female impersonators," and they had their own vernacular, friendship networks, and social centers. New York's chief hangout was Paresis Hall, a saloon in the Bowery, so named by the police based on the medical term for a psychopathic interest in sex. As one shocked observer recounted, "most of [the patrons] are painted and powdered; they are called Princess this and Lady So and So and the Duchess of Marlboro, and get up and sing as women, and dance; ape the female character; call each other sisters and take people out for immoral purposes." Paresis Hall was the meeting place for the "Cercle Hermaphroditos."[17]

There was also public interest in women passing as men—the ploy that Alice Mitchell planned for her elopement. New York's Murray Hall, a biological female and Tammany politician, was twice married to women who divorced him for carrying on with other women. San Francisco's famous cross-dresser Jeanne Bonnet was described as a "man-hater," with "short cropped hair, an unwomanly voice, and a masculine face which harmonized excellently with her customary suit of boys' clothes." Renouncing men in 1875, she organized a gang of prostitutes who supported themselves by petty theft. While lying in bed waiting for her lover, Blanche Buneau, Bonnet was murdered in 1876, probably by a vengeful pimp. Like New York, San Francisco had its share of saloons frequented by female impersonators, the best known being the Dash on Pacific Street. Fairies and other men cruised for partners in the Barbary Coast saloon district and near the Presidio. For such quick encounters, fellatio was the preferred method of intercourse.[18]

In 1889 Dr. Frank Lydston reported a "colony of male sexual perverts" in Chicago and in "every community of any size." These people "operate in accordance with some definite and concerted plan in quest of subjects wherewith to gratify their abnormal sexual impulses. Often they are characterized by effeminacy of voice, dress, and manner." In contrast to men, "women usually fall into perverted sexual habits," mainly oral sex, "for the purpose of pandering to the depraved tastes of their patrons rather than from instinctive impulses." Lydston was referring to sex workers, but also mentioned a "woman of perfect physique, who is not a professional prostitute [but] who has a fondness for women." Chicago's Anti-Vice Commission later confirmed his account through its own private army of investigators. "It appears that in this community there is a large number of men who are thoroughly gregarious in habit; who mostly affect the carriage, mannerisms, and speech of women; . . . who lean to the fantastic in dress and other modes of expression, and who have a definite cult with regard to sexual life."[19]

A subsequent survey claimed that sexual inversion was widespread in the United States, with New York, Boston, Philadelphia, Washington, Chicago, St. Louis, Milwaukee, New Orleans, and San Francisco as the "homosexual capitals." To that list should be added Baltimore, Los Angeles, Long Beach, Portland (Oregon), and Seattle.[20] Although their numbers were modest, these visible communities of fairies, cross-dressing men and women, and male prostitutes were highly alarming to the respectable citizens who served on antivice commissions. Typically, Comstock's reaction to them went beyond shock: "These inverts are not fit to live with the rest of mankind. They ought to have branded in their foreheads the word 'Unclean,' and as the lepers of old, they ought to cry 'Unclean! Unclean!' as they go about, and instead of the [crime-against-nature] law making twenty years imprisonment the penalty for their crime, it ought to be imprisonment for life." Like prostitutes, "these inverts" did more than commit immoral acts; like lepers, they were a status group defined by their perceived disease as much as by their actions. Comstock's society assisted the New York police in apprehending fairies and male prostitutes. Antivice study commissions, especially those in Chicago and New York, documented the increasing public presence of fairy culture and cross-dressing. These societies and commissions also became vehicles for the spread of a new vocabulary for discussing sexual and gender minorities.[21]

State Mechanisms for Controlling Sexual Inverts and Degenerates

Rather than criticizing prostitutes, sodomites, and fairies for conduct that violated a natural law or religious ideal, as Comstock did, a new breed of scientists—the sexologists—assigned them a status that represented an *inversion* of their biological sex and a physical or mental *degeneration* (downward evolution). While this represented a key shift in thinking about same-sex intimacy, it reflected the same underlying tropes found in Saint Paul and Anthony Comstock: namely, a disgust with sex for pleasure alone; a yearning for pure lines of gender role and identity; and an obsession with the possibility that sexualized human beasts would pollute the entire culture and send it into decline. What the American sexologists added to this framework was not so much their quasi-scientific terminology, but a focus on race.[22]

The most influential early sexologist was Richard von Krafft-Ebing, author of the widely read *Psychopathia Sexualis* (1886; English translation 1892). Krafft-Ebing's theories rested on biologically based assumptions about men's and women's different sexual instincts. Man "has beyond doubt the stronger sexual appetite" and is "aggressive and impetuous," while nurturing woman "remains passive" as the man woos her. Such gender differences were profound, and "[t]he higher the anthropological development of the race, the stronger these contrasts between man and woman, and vice versa." Krafft-Ebing took it as a given that normal, healthy sex consisted of vaginal intercourse between a masculine male and a feminine female; he then systematically categorized an array of deviations from this norm, most of them rooted in a congenital defect in the deviant's brain or constitution. "Inversion" by women or men, in which they revealed physical or psychological characteristics of the opposite sex, was for Krafft-Ebing a leading sexual pathology, one that reflected a broader mental or physical "degeneration," or reversion to a prior evolutionary status. Fairies were obvious examples of his thesis. Starting in the 1899 edition, Krafft-Ebing told Alice Mitchell's story as an inversion tragedy.[23]

Anticipating some of Krafft-Ebing's ideas, American doctors reported in the early 1880s that when individuals' "sex is perverted, they hate the opposite sex and love their own; men become women and women men, in their tastes, conduct, character, feelings and behavior." Dr. James Kiernan, another Chicago medic, viewed Alice Mitchell as a classic invert, with a man's brain in a woman's body. Dr. Charles Hughes of Barnes Medical College in St. Louis agreed with Kiernan's diagnosis but objected to the Mitchell insanity verdict. Although she committed "sexual perversity" with another woman, such people "are moral perverts, not lunatics." Reflecting greater overall social anxiety, most Americans were less sympathetic to the female invert than Krafft-Ebing had been. Kiernan closed his Mitchell article with a warning that, as a result of the press coverage of her case, "sex pervert crimes of all types are likely to increase."[24]

Anglo-American sexologists also linked female inverts like Mitchell to feminists and their agenda. Dr. James Weir argued in 1895 that the New Women, like prostitutes, were just as much victims of "psychic atavism as was Alice Mitchell." Like Mitchell, "every woman who has been at all prominent in advancing the cause of equal rights [has] either given evidences of masculo-feminity (viraginity), or has shown, conclusively, that she was the victim of psycho-sexual aberrancy." In *The Intermediate Sex* (1908), Edward Carpenter noted, approvingly, that "the movement among women towards their own liberation and emancipation . . . has been accompanied by a marked development of the homogenic passion among the female sex." The British sexologist Havelock Ellis explained why: "[H]aving been taught independence of men and disdain for the old theory which placed women in the moated grange of the home to sigh for a man who never comes, a tendency develops for women to carry this independence still farther and to find love where they find work. These unquestionable influences of modern [feminism] cannot directly cause sexual inversion, but they develop the germs of it, and they probably cause a spurious imitation."[25]

Although Ellis ridiculed it, American doctors embraced Krafft-Ebing's idea that any departure from strict binary gender roles (man = masculine, woman = feminine) represented a degeneration to more primitive forms. Theodore Kellogg, for example, maintained that degeneracy could be recognized by certain telltale characteristics—including "[p]recocity, or retarded evolution of intellect"; "exaggerated conscientiousness or absence of moral sense"; and "one-sided talents, display of fantastic genius." Dr. Lydston maintained that all vice and crime could be traced to "the degenerate classes," those "persons of low grade of development, physically and mentally, with a defective understanding of their true relations to the social system in which they live. . . . In them, vice, crime, and disease go hand in hand." Prostitutes (with inordinate sexual desire) and sexual inverts (with inappropriate sex and gender roles) were two of the chief degenerate classes, and they contributed to a dramatic surge in perverted sexual practices in urban areas. Lydston believed in evolutionary reversion, whereby the prostitute and invert abandon the inhibitions of civilization and revert to subhuman, animalistic desires. Degeneracy was a social disease that could be passed on to the next generation, through both inheritable characteristics and the bad example set by degenerates for the young.[26]

The Americans' extension of Krafft-Ebing's philosophy was also a function of this country's hysterical anxiety about racial mixing.[27] Dr. Irving Rosse of Georgetown associated sexual perversions with prehistoric "troglodytes," barnyard animals, prostitutes, and people of color. His main touchstone for perversion involved a "band of negro men" of "androgynous character" whose rites of phallic worship were raided by the Washington police; he also cited arrests, mainly of blacks, in Lafayette Park, a notorious site for male-on-male solicitation in the shadow of the White House. Dr. Hughes reported on the "drag dance" in Washington and St. Louis, "which is an orgie of lascivious debauchery beyond open power of description." The St. Louis event featured black men dressed in women's garb, dancing with white men—which led a horrified Hughes to call it a "miscegenation dance." "Social reverse complexion homosexual affinities are rarer than non reverse color affinities, yet even white women sometimes prefer colored men to white men and vice versa."[28]

Lydston's 1904 book on social disease devoted an entire chapter to the "degenerated" practices of racial minorities and primitive cultures. "Physical and moral degeneracy—the latter involving chiefly the higher and more recently acquired attributes—with a distinct tendency to reversion of type is evident in the Southern negro. This physical and moral degeneracy and atavism is especially manifest in the direction of sexual proclivities," Lydston wrote. "The removal by his liberation of certain inhibitions placed upon the negro by slavery itself . . . has been especially effective as a causal factor of sexual crimes among the blacks of the South." One probable source for Lydston's generalization was Dr. Hunter McGuire of Richmond, Virginia. During his tenure as president of the American Medical Association, McGuire published a letter to Lydston remarking on the "sexual perversion in the negro," evidenced by the alarming incidence of rapes against white women and girls. In that single, chilling letter, McGuire linked perversion, disease, racial degeneracy, and genocide (through lynching and natural selection). As the historian Lisa Duggan has observed, the American press was instrumental in popularizing the lynching narrative, in which a sexually crazed black man assaults a white woman, at the same time it was popularizing the sapphic slasher narrative, in which a sexually crazed lesbian assaults a white woman.[29]

New Elaborations of the Crime Against Nature

In *A Problem in Modern Ethics* (1896), Symonds laid out a detailed case against consensual sodomy laws: they imposed great harm on congenital "inverts," without offering any corresponding social benefit. In 1915 Havelock Ellis joined his collaborator in supporting this reform. For the cultural reasons suggested above, there was no constituency for such a proposal in the United States. Even when Symonds pressed him, in private correspondence, to support the European approach (where only forcible sodomy would be considered a crime), Whitman demurred.[30]

Between 1881 and 1923 no state seriously considered narrowing its sodomy prohibitions to include only sex with minors or coerced adults. The three states without sodomy laws in 1881 adopted them in short order—Ohio in 1885, Iowa in 1892, Washington in 1893. Except for Wyoming, every territory admitted to the Union after the Civil War (Alaska, Arizona, Hawaii, Idaho, Montana, New Mexico, Nevada, North Dakota, Oklahoma, South Dakota, and Utah) had a territorial sodomy law that carried over upon statehood. Existing sodomy laws were expanded, updated, and enforced more energetically. Whereas the 1880 Census identified sixty-three prisoners convicted of this crime, the 1890 Census identi-fied 224, an increase greatly exceeding growth in the general population. Much higher numbers were recorded in the new century, when states further expanded the reach and penalties of their sodomy laws. In short, there was a revolutionary expansion of American sodomy law and its enforcement between 1881 and 1921.[31]

Expanding the Crime Against Nature to Include Fellatio. As Americans flocked to booming cities, they found not only bordellos and sexual freedom, but improved personal hygiene and public parks and (soon) restrooms, which fueled an explosion of fellatio in the generations after the Civil War. (The inven-tion of the zipper for men's pants, around 1893, made the "quickie" oral en-counter even easier.) Fairies did it, female as well as male prostitutes did it, wives did it occasionally, and a criminal jury found that Oscar Wilde did it.[32]

But as a legal matter oral sex was not classified as a crime against nature—until June 11, 1879, when Pennsylvania enacted the first detailed statutory speci-fication of what conduct constituted sodomy:

> [T]he terms sodomy and buggery . . . shall be understood to be a carnal copula-tion by human beings with each other against nature, *res veneria in ano,* or with a beast, and shall be taken to cover and include the act or acts where any person shall wilfully and wickedly have carnal knowledge, in a manner against nature, of any other person, by penetrating the mouth of such person; and any person who shall wickedly and indecently suffer or permit any other person to wickedly pene-trate, in a manner against nature, his or her mouth, by carnal intercourse, he, she and every such person committing any of the acts aforesaid, or suffering the same to be committed as aforesaid, shall be guilty of the crime of sodomy or buggery.

The Pennsylvania statute was not only the first English-language law to include oral sex as sodomy, but also the first to include females as intended defendants in human sodomy cases. (Women could be guilty of bestiality under the older stat-utes.) Following the Pennsylvania approach of specifying fellatio as a crime against nature more precisely within state sodomy laws were New York (1886), Ohio (1889), Wyoming (1890), Louisiana (1896), Wisconsin (1897), Iowa (1902), Indiana (1905), Washington (1909), Missouri (1911), Oregon (1913), Nebraska (1913), North Dakota (1913), Virginia (1916, 1923), and Minnesota (1921).[33]

Six years after the Pennsylvania law, the British Parliament enacted the Labouchere Amendment, appended to a prostitution-regulatory bill. The 1885 law made it a misdemeanor, punishable by up to two years in prison, for "[a]ny male person" to commit "any act of gross indecency with another male person." The law was aimed at oral sex between men. True to its Puritan heritage, Massachusetts became the second American state to criminalize oral sex, when its legislature in 1887 made it a crime for any person to commit "unnatural and lascivious acts" with another. It was the Labouchere Amendment, and not the Act of 1533, that ensnared Oscar Wilde in 1895, and the publicity from Wilde's case motivated Michigan to copy Labouchere with its own gross indecency law in 1903. Eight other states adopted new laws aimed at oral sex and other, unspecified, "lascivious acts."[34]

Most of the individual state statutes were introduced following local scandals in which the public learned that men were engaging in unnatural practices not covered by the traditional crime-against-nature laws. In the most famous example, the police in Long Beach, California, arrested thirty-one men for oral sex in 1914 after two undercover officers infiltrated two sex clubs. Befriending men attracted to them, the officers lured them into compromising positions in public restrooms, bathhouses, or private apartments, where spying colleagues arrested the "degenerates." The newspapers raised an alarm against these "devils" committing "a horrible enormity besides which ordinary prostitution is chastity itself." Legally, however, these men had committed no felony; some were charged with vagrancy, just a misdemeanor, and the florist Herbert Lowe was acquitted of all charges by a jury.[35] Responding immediately to the general public outrage, the California legislature in 1915 added to the penal code's list of serious felonies "fellatio" and "cunnilingus" (changed, in 1921, to "oral copulation").[36]

In other states the specification of sodomy to include fellatio came through dynamic police and judicial interpretation of existing laws. The police often arrested undesirables for offensive acts first and then sought legal justification after the fact, so existing sodomy laws were sometimes applied to instances of oral sex. (Recall Comstock's report of the female sex workers in 1878.) Interpreting elastic terms such as "crime against nature," judges sometimes achieved the same result through reasoning by analogy: oral sex is like anal sex (sodomy) in its inability to contribute to the procreative project. As the Illinois Supreme Court said in the leading case, *Honselman v. People* (1897), fellatio "is as much against nature . . . as sodomy or any bestial or unnatural copulation as can be conceived." *Honselman* was followed by the highest courts of Georgia (1904), South Dakota (1910), North Carolina (1914), Alabama (1914), Nevada (1914), Delaware (1915), Kansas (1915), Montana (1915), Idaho (1916), Oklahoma (1917), Hawaii (1922), Arkansas (1925), Maine (1938), and three other states after World War II.[37]

Most state courts, however, did not follow *Honselman*. Because the state law used the common-law term "crime against nature," the Texas Court of Criminal

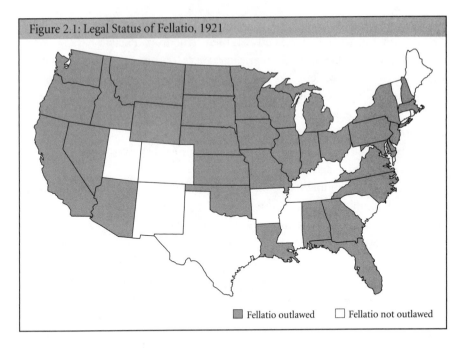

Figure 2.1: Legal Status of Fellatio, 1921

Fellatio outlawed   Fellatio not outlawed

Appeals in *Prindle v. State* (1893) followed common-law precedent and limited the crime to anal sex. As they had done in *Medis* four years earlier, the judges expressed disgust that the law failed to reach this equally abominable conduct, but hoped that the legislature would fix the problem. This was an invitation the Texas Legislature did not take up until 1943, when it updated its sodomy law to include oral sex. The highest state courts in California (1897), Kentucky (1909), Nebraska (1910), Arizona (1912), Utah (1913), Virginia (1923), Colorado (1927), New Mexico (1953), and New Jersey (1953) followed *Prindle* and specifically rejected the expansive approach of *Honselman*. In all these states, the narrow judicial interpretation was overridden by legislation broadening the definition of sodomy or creating a new crime. As figure 2.1 reveals, fellatio—a crime nowhere in 1878—was a crime in almost all states outside the South by 1921.[38]

Expanding the Crime Against Nature to Include Cunnilingus. While legislators generally were quick to address the practice of fellatio, there was less urgency when the issue was intercourse that did not involve a penis. Because Pennsylvania's 1879 statute defined the crime against nature to include "carnal knowledge" by "penetrating the mouth" of another person, it targeted fellatio but not necessarily cunnilingus. The Illinois Supreme Court, which had decided that fellatio was a crime against nature in *Honselman*, ruled that cunnilingus was not in

People v. Smith (1913). It is not entirely clear which state first made cunnilingus a crime. In 1886 the New York legislature expanded the crime against nature to reach anyone who "carnally knows any male or female person by the anus or by the mouth." At common law, "carnal knowledge" required penetration by a male penis; also, New York required proof of "penetration" *by* the sexual organ, presumably the penis. Thus, the statute's plain meaning excluded cunnilingus. On the other hand, a knowledgeable authority suggested in 1917 that "penetration" of a woman's sexual organ by a tongue could satisfy the statute. In 1895, North Dakota redefined the crime against nature to include carnal knowledge by or with the mouth, but without a penetration requirement.[39]

Louisiana amended its sodomy law in 1896 to include the "crime against nature . . . with the sexual organs, or with the mouth." In 1914 the Louisiana Supreme Court stated that the amendment expanded common-law sodomy to include fellatio, "and perhaps that other perversion called 'cunnilingus,' committed with the mouth and the female sexual organ." More clearly covering cunnilingus was Oregon's 1913 law, which made it a crime to engage in "any act or practice of sexual perversity," or to "sustain osculatory relations with the private parts of any man, woman, or child." California's 1915 law, noted above, was the first to identify specifically "cunnilingus" and "fellatio" as felonies.[40]

By 1921 seventeen other states deployed the old "crime against nature" or "carnal knowledge" terminology to include fellatio (where the penetration requirement was clearly met). It was possible—but remained unclear—that such language would also apply to cunnilingus. Six states (Arizona, Florida, Maryland, Massachusetts, New Hampshire, and New Jersey) with new terminology intended to cover fellatio might also have included cunnilingus. Fourteen states and the District of Columbia did not in 1921 consider oral sex of any sort a crime. At least six states (Illinois, Michigan, Missouri, Nevada, Pennsylvania, and Wisconsin) made fellatio a crime but apparently not cunnilingus.[41] In Georgia, cunnilingus was a crime, but only when a man did it to a woman, and not when two women engaged in the activity. In Virginia, it may have been a crime in 1921, but only if two women engaged in it (a gap the legislature filled in 1924).[42]

As this survey of the states suggests, state criminal law did not yield a consensus as to the legality of oral sex between two women. Figure 2.2 displays this complexity.

Special Laws Protecting Children and Preventing Procreation. Like many of the other nineteenth-century sodomy cases, *Honselman* involved sex between an adult and a youth. The year after he translated *Psychopathia Sexualis* into English, Dr. Charles Chaddock published an article documenting that "rape of

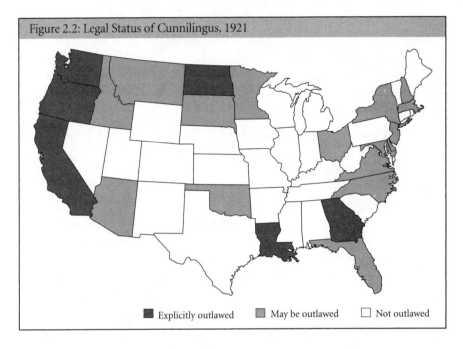

Figure 2.2: Legal Status of Cunnilingus, 1921

■ Explicitly outlawed   ■ May be outlawed   □ Not outlawed

children is the most frequent form of sexual crime," involving as many as eighty percent of reported cases. These rapes were not limited to penile-vaginal intercourse, but more often involved masturbation, genital manipulation, and oral and anal sex. Reflecting degeneracy theory, Chaddock opined that "sexual perversion (erotic fetishism) might lead to an unnatural preference for children." In the same text, Travis Gibb drew on his experience with New York's Society for the Prevention of Cruelty to Children to catalog the many ways that children could be sexually abused by adults, with emphasis on cunnilingus and fellatio.[43]

Children's protection groups as well as doctors clamored for targeted legal intervention. In 1881 Indiana amended its sodomy law to include enticement of minors "to commit masturbation," and in 1897 Michigan created a separate and more serious crime for sodomy with boys. After 1900 most states adopted criminal laws protecting the sexual purity of male as well as female children. In 1897 Wisconsin established a new crime of taking "improper liberties" with minors of either sex, with seven states adopting similar laws before World War I. In 1907 Illinois criminalized "any immoral, improper or indecent liberties with any child of either sex, under the age of fifteen years," and the commission of "lewd and lascivious act" on a child. Illinois in 1915 expanded the law to criminalize lewd and lascivious conduct committed in the presence of a child. Most popular were statutes making it a crime to "contribute to the delinquency of a minor," a concept inaugurated by Massachusetts in 1906. Nineteen states, mostly with urban centers, had such statutes by the end of World War I.[44]

A different kind of intervention married law and medicine. In 1893 Dr. F. E. Daniel argued that "rape, sodomy, bestiality and habitual masturbation" were serious crimes that should be punished with the loss of civil rights, including the right to vote and to procreate. In 1907 Indiana enacted a law allowing the sterilization of "confirmed criminals, idiots, rapists and imbeciles." A more typical statute was the one adopted by Iowa in 1911; it required sterilization of inmates judged to be "moral or sexual perverts." Thirty other states adopted similar measures, many of them specifically targeting sodomites and degenerates.[45]

The most comprehensive regulatory regime in place by 1921 was California's. In addition to its seduction, sodomy, and oral copulation laws, the California legislature made it a crime to commit a lewd act with a child under age fourteen (1901), to send a minor to an "immoral" place (1905), to commit "degrading, lewd, immoral" practices in front of a child (1907), or to contribute to the delinquency of minors (1915).[46] New York adopted similar laws in the 1920s. In contrast to established seduction statutes, these new laws not only protected boys as well as girls, but defined the arena of sexual violation more broadly, to include oral and anal sex, sexual touching, fondling, and even just observing sexual activities. To give added force to these new proscriptions, California in 1909 enacted a law providing for the sterilization of any person convicted of two or more sexual offenses if he or she also showed evidence of being a "moral or sexual pervert." By 1930 almost seven thousand Californians were sterilized, many of them prostitutes and homosexuals. In 1937 the state expanded the law to apply also to anyone committed to a state hospital if he or she was "afflicted with, or suffers from . . . perversion," and the number of sterilizations rose accordingly (peaking at 848 in 1939).[47]

Aggressive Enforcement of Sodomy Laws

The broadening of crime-against-nature laws had immediate relevance for local enforcement, as the number of sodomy arrests skyrocketed. The main factor linked with a dramatic surge in a city's sodomy law enforcement was the state's explicit authorization to apply the law to oral sex. For example, Philadelphia's sodomy arrests jumped from one a year to double digits soon after Pennsylvania's 1879 law went into effect; a similar trend can be observed in New York City, Baltimore, St. Louis, Richmond, and Los Angeles. The most direct evidence exists for Boston, whose police separately reported "unnatural acts" (oral sex) arrests after the creation of this new crime by the Massachusetts legislature in 1887.

Between 1880 and 1886 the police arrested a total of thirteen men for sodomy, about two per year. Between 1887 and 1900 the police arrested fifteen men for sodomy (one per year), but ninety-eight men and seven women for what they called "unnatural lascivious activities" (seven per year). Controlling for population increases in the cities for which we have arrest data, a comparison of arrests before oral sex was illegal, with arrests after illegality, yields a statistically significant difference.[48]

The largest increases in sodomy arrests and prosecutions came after 1900. Sodomy arrests in twelve big cities, based on detailed police reports, soared from a yearly average of 30 in the period 1881–85 to 141 in the period 1901–5, then to 247 in the period 1911–15—an almost tenfold increase in a generation. The bigger numbers were driven by the largest cities, which were also the sites for private antivice campaigns—New York, Philadelphia, Chicago, and St. Louis. (See figure 2.3 for the dramatic New York numbers.) The expansion of the definition of sodomy to include oral sex also contributed to the increase. A third factor was the focus on children. Forty-four percent of the reported sodomy cases for 1896–1925 involved sex with children, compared with twenty-seven percent for 1880–95 and less than a quarter for the nineteenth century as a whole. Because municipal police forces started reporting crimes against children in special categories in this period, the statistics for "sodomy" or "crime against nature" probably underreport the incidence of arrests.

Even augmented to offset underreporting, however, the number of arrests for the crime against nature remained relatively modest. New York City, for example, arrested 630 men for sexually assaulting minor women in 1921, more than six times the number arrested for the crime against nature, which was primarily enforced when minor males were the victims. Boston's arrests for fornication and adultery were more than one hundred times those for the crime against nature between 1870 and 1921. St. Louis arrested 290 men and women for the crime against nature between 1874 and 1921, about one-tenth of the number arrested for rape and about 0.3 percent of the nearly 90,000 women and men arrested for prostitution during the same period. In short, urban enforcement resources before World War I remained overwhelmingly focused on nonmarital heterosexual intercourse.

The 1880 Census reported only one woman incarcerated for sodomy or the crime against nature, but that changed in the next generation. New York City's annual police reports regularly reveal female perpetrators of sodomy after 1890. Thirty-one of the 601 persons arrested between 1901 and 1910 were women. Boston arrested nine women for oral sex between 1889 and 1899, almost ten percent of the arrests for such crimes; in the twentieth century, women were regularly arrested for oral sex, almost always for providing fellatio to men. Al-

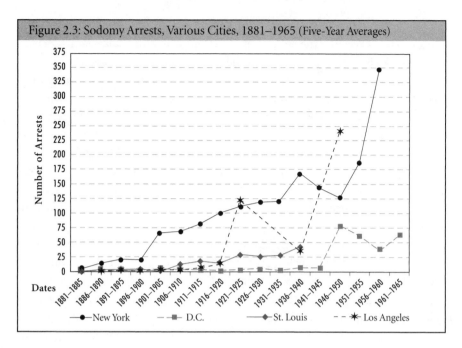

Figure 2.3: Sodomy Arrests, Various Cities, 1881–1965 (Five-Year Averages)

though these numbers remain minuscule compared with those for men, they reflect a remarkable turning point in the history of sodomy: women as well as men were now responsible actors in the theater of perverted sexuality.[49]

During this period the enforcement of sodomy laws was often racially slanted, as it had been in the nineteenth century. In Washington, D.C., an overwhelmingly white city, eighty percent of the people arrested for sodomy between 1881 and 1921 were African American, a pattern followed by many other southern cities. On the other hand, data available for Baltimore suggest that this was not inevitable. Until Maryland adopted its "perverted practices" law in 1916, almost no one was arrested for sodomy (anal sex); afterward the police did a brisk business, even arresting a few women in 1917, once the law included oral sex. In contrast with Washington, just under one-quarter of Baltimore's sodomy arrests between 1906 and 1921 were people of color, a relatively modest figure for a segregated society.[50]

New Sodomy-Solicitation and Degeneracy Laws

Most oral sex was hard to detect. Drawing from their experience with prostitution laws, antivice societies realized that more fairies could be brought to justice for soliciting (rather than engaging in) sodomy. In New York, the purity campaigns of the 1890s resulted in a major state legislative investigation by the

Mazet Committee. Citizens complained that "degenerates," "male harlots," and fairies were "thronging the streets" of the city; many of the complaints focused on Paresis Hall. George Hammond of the City Vigilance League assured the committee in November 1899 that the "unmentionable crime" had "increased wonderfully within the last six months," because of the proliferation of "resorts for male prostitutes" and "degenerates." In January 1900, the Mazet Committee's report documented the rise of degeneracy and the crime against nature. Less than three months later, the legislature expanded the definition of illegal vagrant to include "[e]very male person who lives wholly or in part on the earnings of prostitution, or who in any public place solicits for immoral purposes." The language was broad enough to include male inverts as well as pimps for female prostitutes.[51]

In 1915 New York's antivice "Committee of Fourteen" (1904–32) lobbied the legislature to adopt Senator Robert Wagner's bill to expand the definition of vagrant even further, to include any person "who loiters in any thoroughfare or public or private place for the purpose of inducing, enticing or procuring another to commit lewdness, fornication, unlawful sexual intercourse or any other indecent act," or who "procures a person who is in or near any thoroughfare or public or private place, to commit any such acts." A 1919 statute, also sponsored by the Committee of Fourteen, amended the vagrancy law to cover anyone who "offer[s] to secure another" person for prostitution or lewd acts. As amended, the vagrancy law was regularly applied to harass or arrest fairies.[52] Codifying an 1845 statute responding to riots in which people had dressed up as Indians, yet another subsection of the vagrancy law made it a crime if "[a] person who, having his face painted, discolored, covered or concealed, or being otherwise disguised, in a manner calculated to prevent his being identified, appears in a road or public highway." The police enforced this law against cross-dressers.[53]

Even more than the sodomy and vagrancy laws, the New York City police relied on the state disorderly conduct law to monitor and harass people they were calling "Degenerates" (under the larger category, "Prostitutes"). Proclaiming that male degeneracy was even worse than female prostitution because "the pervert . . . is constantly seeking converts to his practice," the Committee of Fourteen and the New York Society for the Suppression of Vice not only pressed the police to enforce the law vigorously, but assisted them. Arrests for "degeneracy" increased from 92 in 1916 to 605 in 1921. Most of the defendants were arrested for fondling other men in public toilets and movie theaters; almost all were convicted. After a Nassau County judge questioned the legality of the broad application of the open-ended law, a coalition of prosecutors and citizen groups persuaded the legislature to specify the definition of the crime in 1923. The new law made it illegal for "[a]ny person who with intent to provoke a breach of the peace, or whereby a breach of the peace may be occasioned . . . [f]requents or loiters about any public place soliciting men for the purpose of committing a crime against nature or other lewdness."[54]

California followed a pattern similar to New York. California's vagrancy law targeted female prostitutes, but was simplified and broadened in 1903 to include anyone who was either a "common prostitute" or an "idle, or lewd, or dissolute person, or associate of known thieves." Another 1903 statute made it a misdemeanor to "outrag[e] public decency" and to "personif[y] any person other than himself" with "intent of accomplishing any lewd or licentious purpose." These two laws were applied in the same broad way New York's vagrancy statute was—to permit police to harass and sometimes arrest fairies, inverts, and cross-dressers. Most of the charges in the 1914 Long Beach sting were under these statutes.[55]

Because of public concern about prostitution, most states at the turn of the century had broad vagrancy statutes, and almost all had public lewdness, disorderly conduct, or indecent exposure laws that were mainly enforced against men behaving lasciviously. While male pimps, drunks, and rowdies were the primary objects of these laws, they were increasingly enforced against male inverts in big cities where fairies were becoming a public presence—not just New York and San Francisco, but also Chicago, St. Louis, Los Angeles, Cleveland, Detroit, Boston, Philadelphia, Baltimore, and Washington, D.C. The inverted populations of most southern cities were much smaller and less visible, and for that reason there was little enforcement in Richmond, Atlanta, Miami, Birmingham, New Orleans, Houston, Dallas, Nashville, and Memphis before 1921.[56]

The Homosexual, 1921–35

Samuel Neal Kent (1873–1943) was an Episcopalian priest who was appointed chaplain for the Young Men's Christian Association in Newport, Rhode Island, the home of the Newport Naval Training Station. A quietly handsome, bookish-looking man with a strong jaw and piercing blue eyes, Kent was a tireless servant of the Lord. Soon after he arrived in Newport in September 1918, the worst influenza epidemic of the century broke out. With chaplains as well as sailors becoming deathly ill, Kent spent almost a month indefatigably attending to men at the naval hospital. The grateful boys applauded "Pop Kent" as a "good soldier," and his dedicated service made him an epitome of Christian brotherhood.[57]

But to Chief Machinists' Mate Ervin Arnold, Kent was just another pervert. A former undercover state detective, Arnold was assigned to Newport in February 1919. He learned that the naval station housed a "gang of perverts"—David

"Beckie" Goldstein, Frederick "Theda Bara" Hoage, Billy "Salome" Hughes, and more than a dozen others—who cross-dressed and sought out sex with other men. Arnold began spying on them and reported his suspicions to naval superiors. In March Dr. Erastus Hudson authorized him to deploy undercover operatives to "allow the pervert[s] to solicit them." After a court of inquiry assembled evidence against a few dozen sailors, Assistant Secretary of the Navy Franklin Roosevelt authorized Arnold and Hudson to expand the investigation to the surrounding community. Arnold's undercover agents befriended Kent, accepting car rides from him and sleepovers at his apartment. Several reported that Kent masturbated and performed oral sex on them. At the end of July state police arrested Kent for "lewd and scandalous behavior" with Arnold's operatives.[58]

Because the operatives had been willing participants, they were considered accomplices whose testimony needed corroboration to obtain a conviction. Judge Hugh Baker acquitted Kent, who checked into a sanitarium. Federal agents later tracked him down and arrested him a second time, for violating a federal statute that made it a crime for civilians to solicit military personnel "for the purpose of lewdness." The federal trial, in January 1920, was an elaborate replay of the first. Kent denied the allegations and introduced a string of public figures who attested to his respectability; the implicit argument was that a man of Kent's rectitude, vouched for by other rectitudinous men, could not be a degenerate. On humiliating cross-examination, the operatives admitted they had repeatedly ejaculated in the defendant's mouth or hand. The jury took only a few hours to acquit.[59]

After Kent's acquittals, the Episcopal bishop James DeWolf Perry persuaded the Navy Department to convene a second court of inquiry. "[Y]oung men, many of them boys, in the naval service have been compelled under the specific orders of officers attached to the office of naval intelligence to commit vile and nameless crimes on the persons of others in the navy service or have suggested these acts be practiced." These charges, denied by Hudson and Arnold, were swept under the rug by the court of inquiry. Under pressure from press and clergy, and sniffing partisan blood, the Senate Naval Affairs Committee continued the investigation, and in 1921 a subcommittee condemned the undercover activities as "deplorable, disgraceful, and unnatural."[60]

The Newport prosecutions transcended old-fashioned understandings about sodomy and sexual inversion. As a technical matter, Kent and the other defendants had not committed the crime against nature, for like the common law, military regulations in 1918–19 stated that oral sex was not sodomy (a loophole that was addressed after the Newport scandal).[61] More important was that the federal agents had engaged in the same conduct as those accused—and reported that this form of physical pleasure came "naturally" to them. One operative,

Charles Zipf, described his encounter with Kent: "Put his arms around me, kissed me, began rubbing my penis. . . . Nature took a hand and I discharged." Many of the defendants had none of the characteristics associated with degeneracy. Kent was resolutely all-American, which may have helped him earn his acquittals, even as the less-educated fairies were being sent to prison for exactly the same conduct. Among those court-martialed, however, was macho sailor Thomas Brunelle, Salome Hughes's "husband," a man who derived physical pleasure from having his penis fellated in the same way the investigators had.[62]

Sigmund Freud's *Three Essays on the Theory of Sexuality* (1905, revised 1920) provided a superior framework for understanding and evaluating the new sexualized world revealed by the Newport scandals. Freud's most helpful concept was to distinguish between a person's sexual object and his sexual aim. Like the Newport investigators, Brunelle enjoyed receiving fellatio as a sexual aim. Unlike the investigators, he was a homosexual whose sexual object was other men. For a person with a "normal" sexual orientation, the sexual object is an adult human of the opposite sex, with the sexual aim being penile-vaginal intercourse. According to Freud, "perversion" of sexual aim involves erotically pleasurable activities not focused on penile-vaginal intercourse; perversions are "pathological" when the nonprocreative activity takes the place of the normal aim. Thus, oral sex and anal sex are both perversions deviating from and, in the case of homosexuals, entirely supplanting the normal sexual aim. Also, the Senate subcommittee was right to be concerned that young sailors were being encouraged to engage in perverted acts. Rejecting Krafft-Ebing's view that homosexuality is congenital, Freud's theory of mobile and evolving sexuality suggested the possibility that oral sex with homosexuals might derail the young operatives' own paths to mature procreative heterosexuality.[63]

Freud also questioned moralists' extreme distinction between acceptable procreative intercourse and perversions/sodomy. "It is only in the rarest instances that the psychical valuation that is set on the sexual object . . . stops short at its genitals. The appreciation extends to the whole body of the sexual object and tends to involve every sensation derived from it." Thus, "activities connected with other parts of the body," including oral and anal sex, become legitimate "sexual aims," often connected with penile-vaginal intercourse. In this way, Freud suggested not just a continuum of sexual aims—from "normal" procreative intercourse to "fetishistic" variations like oral sex—but an interconnected continuum where normal intercourse is connected with fetishes. One consequence of Freud's theory is that a moral system insisting only on procreative intercourse, without any erotic attention to other body parts, is itself fetishistic and unnatural.[64]

The foregoing analysis provided grist for American traditionalists to both broaden and narrow their understanding of "perverted," and presumptively criminal, practices. Even when his or her sexual aim was nonprocreative oral sex, the sexual object of the heterosexual remained someone of the opposite sex, and so the possibility of productive procreation could always be imagined. This was not the case for the homosexual, whose sexual aim was inherently sterile; it could never be associated with procreation, given that the homosexual's choice of a sexual object was someone of the same sex. Just as officials were expanding the range of sodomy laws' reach to include oral sex, Freud's theory provided a justification for narrowing their enforcement to the unproductive, pleasure-loving, sterile homosexual. Additionally, Freud's understanding of childhood sexuality and its fragile evolution toward maturity fueled Americans' concerns about adult sexual stimulation of minors. Parents and the state should do everything possible to prevent the child's evolution toward good (productive) heterosexuality from being derailed in the direction of bad (sterile) homosexuality.

Unlike the traditionalists, however, Freud approached sexual deviations in a comparatively nonjudgmental way. He viewed sex mainly as a source of pleasure—implicitly including pleasure between persons of the same sex and (for heterosexual relations) pleasure for women as well as men. While Freud considered nonprocreative aims to be perversions and homosexual desires to be inverted, he was basically unfazed by these departures from the norm and vigorously criticized thinkers who associated sexual deviation with degeneracy, asserting, "Inversion is found in people who exhibit no other serious deviations from the normal." Traditionalists, however, rejected this feature of Freud's thought. Their attitude, which still has deep moral resonance for most Americans, was that engaging in sex purely for pleasure is morally inadmissible. Like Saint Paul, Americans believe sex guilty unless connected to something productive, such as procreative marriage or, perhaps, committed relationships.[65]

Although Freud's understanding of women's sexuality seems unsophisticated today, it was an advanced view in 1920 and was eagerly embraced by feminists. Margaret Sanger, for example, maintained that women deserved sexual pleasure within marriage, but should not have to run the risk of pregnancy; hence, married women ought to have access to birth control information and devices. After World War I many Americans accepted the Freud-Sanger idea that pleasurable sex (including oral sex) was good and that women deserved sexual satisfaction within companionate marriages. Mainstream authors invoked Freud to draw a new line consistent with the American ideal of individual fulfillment: no longer was sex for procreation the compulsory rule; it was replaced by compulsory heterosexual marriage.[66]

Indeed, the Americans who embraced Freud's ideas were in the process of changing their sexual repertoires. "Beginning in the 1920s, the sexual script for opposite-gender sex became more elaborated to include more kissing, more caressing of the body, more manual genital contact, and, more recently, more oral sex." Such attitudes helped usher in more than a decade of relative tolerance for nonprocreative sex, albeit mainly as a prelude to the "main event." Although urban police continued to arrest men for sodomy, the arrests did not keep pace with the explosion in oral sex, which probably appeared in the first third of the twentieth century. Consistent with Freud, homosexual sodomy remained a focus of moral disapproval, because it could never be legitimized as a prelude to procreative sex. Nonetheless, homosexual subcultures thrived and became important landmarks in public culture—especially the jazz clubs and saloons in Harlem, the drag balls in Chicago, and San Francisco's drag clubs. Thousands of Americans came to the conclusion that they were homosexual, and that their preferred sexual activities were felonious in every state of the Union. As a result, these men and women started leading the double life—bowing to social convention at work and even marrying persons of the opposite sex, while socially and romantically consorting with other homosexuals on the side.[67]

The Legacy of Walt Whitman: The Love of Comrades Among White Male Homosexuals

Historians have provided rich accounts of gay life in America's biggest cities in the 1920s and early 1930s, especially Boston, Chicago, Los Angeles, New York, San Francisco, Seattle, and Washington, D.C.[68] The government records for the Newport scandal reveal that homosexual subcultures existed in smaller cities as well. As best illustrated by the published interviews with homosexual men that were conducted in the 1930s by the Committee for the Study of Sex Variants, the arm-around-the-shoulder camaraderie among men celebrated by Walt Whitman had come a long way by the 1930s.[69]

Three kinds of men populated these subcultures of Sodom. First were those who had sex with other men but did not self-identify as homosexuals. The Newport investigators fell into this category, as did many married men, male sex workers, and working-class men who enjoyed receiving oral sex. Such men played the traditional male role of penis inserter and were not aware of, or did not care about, homosexuality. Some were even homophobic. Gene S. had been having sex with men since the age of five, but told the Sex Variants Committee that "pansies" should be "stamped out," as Hitler was doing. Many places were available for such men to find others willing to have anonymous sex, including such well-known cruising spots as San Francisco's Barbary Coast and Presidio, New York's Bowery and Central Park, North Michigan Avenue in Chicago, Washington's Lafayette

Park, and Los Angeles's Pershing Square. A man could obtain a lunchtime blow job at public restrooms throughout the country; public parks and other secluded areas served the same purpose.[70]

The other two categories were men who self-identified as homosexuals. Most were middle-class individuals who had sexual feelings for which society now provided terminology and organizing concepts. Jeb Alexander (1899–1965), a proofreader at the Government Printing Office for four decades, was a student at Washington and Lee College when he fell in love with C. C. Dasham from Mississippi. "He has the palest green eyes I ever saw," Alexander wrote in his diary for January 2, 1919. "I feel my life has changed forever." In the 1920s, as he cruised for sex at Lafayette Park, pursued and ultimately bedded "Dash," and fell in with a coterie of gay friends and former lovers, his identity took shape as a "Calamite," after his favorite author, Whitman, "a Government clerk, like myself. Often, I yearn toward Walt as toward a father, look up at his picture, then close my eyes and feel him beside me, rugged and strong with his gentle hands caressing and comforting me." Alexander's clique of friends also read Ellis and Freud, and flocked to gender-bending movies such as *Chained*, a life of Rodin that was originally entitled *The Inverts*.[71]

Randall Hare, Alexander's first love, whom he picked up in Lafayette Park, lived the double life after he married a woman. Most of the men interviewed by the Sex Variants Committee dissembled, and several were married. Angeleno Harry Hay (born 1912) had openly declared his homosexuality while a student at Stanford University. By the 1930s he had become a left-wing activist and aspiring actor, and because both the Communist Party and Hollywood officially condemned homosexuality, Hay retreated back into the double life. Like most of his lovers (including Will Geer, later to be famous as Grandpa Walton), Hay married, in 1938.[72]

Given the social stigma associated with homosexuality, almost all homosexuals would have preferred the double life, but many were unable to pull it off. Like other Newport fairies, Beckie Goldstein was too effeminate to pass persuasively as a heterosexual and so made the best of his situation, even starring as a drag queen in official Navy productions. Although Jeb Alexander despised effeminacy, he was a walking catalog of stereotypes—fussy, opera-loving, snidely condescending toward women, campy. At the 1928 office Christmas party, Alexander received a box of chocolate cigarettes, with handwritten doggerel from a coworker: "If as a smoker you enjoy a 'good drag,' You'll find these a very particular 'fag.'" They knew what Alexander was, and he now knew that they knew. "I lost all pleasure in the gathering."[73]

In big cities, homosexuals had a rich array of institutions that constituted a gay subculture. By George Chauncey's account, New York in the 1920s was home to dozens of speakeasies where gay and straight commingled in illegal boozing; "pansy clubs," featuring entertainment by female impersonators; jazz spots in Harlem, where white and black people of all orientations socialized against a background of great music; Greenwich Village bookstores and Broadway theaters, where homosexuals could read or view avant-garde gender-bending stories; and several gay baths and brothels. No other city featured such a wide array of choices, but most cities of any size outside the South offered at least some of them.[74]

World War I and its aftermath yielded an explosive increase in the amount of sexual interaction between men. The detailed record developed by the Newport investigations reveals that even outside the big "homosexual capitals," not only were men having a lot of sex with men, but the sex was quite diversified. All the Newport fairies seemed to enjoy oral sex, and some were "French specialists." Others, the "pogues," enjoyed anal sex. Many, including Kent, enjoyed Whitman-esque activities such as kissing, erotic touching, and sleeping curled in another man's arms. About a third of the men interviewed by the Sex Variants Committee in the 1930s enjoyed anal sex, and more than half oral sex; most mentioned that they liked "soul-kissing" and mutual touching. Almost none limited himself to just one kind of sex. Some liked intercrural intercourse (penis between another man's thighs), others demanded imagination and role-playing, and still others were turned on by cross-dressing. Not a few wanted passionate romance above all. The New York sex variants were more versatile than the Newport fairies had been. The fairies (1910s) generally followed the so-called woman's role, giving oral sex and receiving anal sex. A quarter of the sex variants (1930s) said they liked simultaneous mutual fellation, the "sixty-nine" position. More than half of them reported sexual preferences that did not map consistently onto the male (always a penis inserter) or female (always a penis receiver) roles.[75]

We have no reliable statistics for sexual activities among men before and after World War I, but it is likely that there was a good deal more man-with-man sex after the war than there had been before. And more of it was deemed illegal. Not only was oral sex newly criminalized, but so were sex or lewd behavior with minors and solicitation in a public place to commit oral or anal sex. Kissing, masturbation, and intercrural sex remained legal if done with adults, but not with minors, as they were "indecent liberties." By 1935 thirty of the forty-eight states had at least one statute generally protecting minors against sexual molestation, including fondling and masturbation. And sodomy law enforcement focused on anal and oral sex with minors.[76]

In 1923 Harry Hay worked for a summer on tramp steamers. One night he walked the Santa Barbara beach with a handsome twenty-five-year-old colleague, Matt. Harry clasped Matt's hand, and Matt pulled him close and kissed him.

Retreating to a grove of trees, the two men made love. Afterward, Harry admitted this was his sexual initiation; he was only fourteen. (At six feet three inches tall, he had convinced the steamer company that he was twenty-one.) Matt was panic-stricken: he had not only violated California's sodomy law (a possible ten years in prison), and its new oral copulation law (fifteen years), but he feared that he had also violated the state law against committing a lewd act with a minor (twenty-three years). He was justifiably concerned. Los Angeles was devoting more resources to enforcing sodomy laws (123 men were arrested in 1923), focusing particularly on sex with boys. Almost ninety percent of the reported California sodomy cases between 1920 and 1946 involved either rape of an adult or sex with a minor. In the country as a whole, eighty percent of the reported sodomy cases for 1926–40 involved forcible oral or anal sex with adult men (four percent) or women (seventeen percent) or sex with boys (forty-eight percent) or girls (ten percent).[77]

According to accounts from Washington, Chicago, Los Angeles, and New York, however, sodomy and sodomy-solicitation laws had a modest *direct* effect on the lives of white gay men in those cities. Although the District of Columbia did not have an explicit sodomy law until 1948, its police arrested a few people each year for common-law sodomy, and the majority of those apprehended between 1921 and 1940 were men of color. As whites, Alexander and his friends were exempt from the law. This pattern was replicated throughout the South, where men of color remained the primary targets of morality-based laws.[78]

Although Illinois had a sodomy law, which judges construed broadly, the legendarily corrupt Chicago police only episodically enforced it. Their reports list an average of forty-three people arrested for sodomy each year in the 1920s, a tiny number for a city teeming with fairies and homosexuals among its four million people. New York City arrested an average of 124 men and women each year, not a much more impressive number for a city of almost seven million in 1930, and the arrests involved mainly immigrants and people of color. (Of the Sex Variant respondents, only one said he had been arrested for sodomy, with a "colored boy in Baltimore.") The large majority of those arrested were having sex with minors. Native-born white men having sex with one another would not have gone to jail for sodomy but might well have been picked up for soliciting the crime against nature (the degeneracy category). An average of 560 men each year were arrested for this crime; more than three-quarters of them received either suspended or short (under two-month) jail sentences.[79]

But sodomy and, especially, antisolicitation laws did have an important indirect effect on the lives of white men in most large cities, because they empowered police officers. Police forces were predominantly staffed with underpaid working-class ethnic minorities, many of whom harbored prejudices or resentment against middle-class homosexuals—and the law allowed them to monitor, harass, and sometimes abuse these presumptive criminals. Jeb Alexander bitterly resented the surveillance of an undercover cop he dubbed "the Sneak": "Am I to be one of the ones picked out, made a scapegoat, watched and harassed? . . . Why in God's name would human society want its morals to be watched over by a creature with a soiled hat and a cheap coat?"[80] Peter R., one of the Sex Variants respondents, said that New York City police would demand sex from him and on one occasion arrested him for vagrancy when he refused to comply. Sex crime laws were so vaguely worded that they could be interpreted to cover almost any offensive conduct, which gave the police tremendous discretionary power. Most settled for monetary payoffs—the typical pattern in Chicago, San Francisco, and other cities.[81]

The most important effect of sodomy laws, however, was the extent to which they situated homosexuals outside the normal protections of the law. When Rudolph von H. (one of the Sex Variants respondents) was stabbed at a Hollywood gay party, the police were less interested in finding the culprit than in inculpating the victim as a homosexual. Many individuals felt they could victimize homosexuals with legal impunity, and they were usually right. Thus, Sidney H. was accosted by two "detectives" in a hotel restroom and threatened with arrest unless he paid them $25, which he did. Norman T. paid blackmail money until he was broke. Although blackmail was itself illegal, its victims were afraid to go to the police, who would (at best) have ignored the violations of law. As Eric D. put it to the Sex Variants Committee, "Homosexuals are preyed upon because they are timid and don't wish to bring in the aid of the law." Max D.'s young butler stole his car, and he did report the crime. When they apprehended the culprit, he claimed that Max had engaged in "perverted" sex with him, a charge that created a public scandal and ended Max's marriage.[82]

The Legacy of Jane Addams: Romantic Relationships Among White Lesbians

The New Women of Jane Addams's generation often lived their lives with female partners—and, like proper ladies, said not a word about sex. Antivice moralists, Mitchell-crazed journalists, and the American Freudians did away with that reticence by speaking openly and in detail about women's sexual feelings, including those for other women. When Ruth Fulton (1887–1948) enrolled at Vassar in 1905, the culture of smashing was at its height but was drawing cautions from moralists and doctors. Smashing, they argued, must not detract from a woman's central mission, which was to marry and have children. The intense Fulton bowed to this conventional wisdom and married Stanley Benedict in 1913. Ruth Benedict found married life unexciting, but pursued her professional interests and was admitted to study for a Ph.D. in anthropology under Franz Boas at Columbia University.[83]

In fall 1922 Benedict became Boas's teaching assistant. One of their students was a petite Barnard College dynamo by the name of Margaret Mead (1901–1978). There was an immediate electricity between the two women—a teacher-student smash—with a mutually acknowledged sexual tension. Benedict wrote in her diary that Mead was the female "companion in harness" she needed to complement Stanley. Also married, Mead embraced a philosophy of free love and reciprocated Benedict's feelings. Both women had read Ellis and Freud, yet neither was prepared to label her sexuality. By the end of 1924 they were committed partners. According to their friends, they consummated their sexual relationship in the summer of 1925 beneath a rock formation at the rim of the Grand Canyon, just before Mead left to do her initial fieldwork in Samoa.[84]

Unlike Jane Addams and Mary Rozet Smith, Ruth Benedict and Margaret Mead were not life partners. Although their personal and professional lives were intertwined until Benedict's death, they each remained married to men (in Mead's case, a series of husbands). Katharine Bement Davis's celebrated 1928 survey of the sex lives of twenty-two hundred middle-class white women suggests that, in some respects, theirs was a common pattern. Although ninety percent of American women married, they were more interested in sexual fulfillment than their mothers had been. Following Sanger's advice that marital pleasure need not be encumbered by procreation, three-quarters of the thousand married women surveyed by Davis used contraceptives; almost ten percent had had sex before marriage and had had abortions. Thirty-one percent experienced "intense emotional relations with other women," with fourteen percent recognizing the relationship as sexual *and* admitting that it was accompanied by "overt homosexual practices," namely, mutual masturbation and "contact of genital organs" (presumably including oral sex). In contrast to Benedict and Mead, only two percent of the married women admitted that they had such relations with other women after their marriages. Almost all those respondents said that the female relationships had no significant ill effect on their marriages.[85]

Davis's survey also found that sixty percent of the twelve hundred unmarried women had intense emotional relations with other women; thirty-one percent of those recognized the relationship as sexual *and* admitted that it was accompanied by "overt homosexual practices." Such answers—indeed, such questions—would have been unthinkable when Addams was a young woman. Following the doctors, the Freud-saturated media began to examine women's sexual relationships. A series of controversial Broadway plays, such as *The Children's Hour* (1935), as well as popular novels, most notably *The Well of Loneliness* (1929), focused on lesbian characters. Attempts to censor them only raised their visibility. Thoughtful women all over America considered their own sexuality. By 1935 Mead concluded that she was a "mixed type"—what we would call a bisexual today—while Benedict understood herself to be a lesbian.[86]

Benedict's lesbian self-identification bothered Mead, who associated it with mannishness and degeneracy. Mead was also concerned about sodomy laws, but only in an abstract way. The intimacies these women shared in 1925 fell outside the sodomy laws of most states at the time. The first American appellate court to report a woman-with-woman sodomy decision, in 1939, ruled that Ella Thompson and her female partner could not commit the crime against nature without more-specific statutory language. On the other hand, females were arrested in modest numbers for sodomy, unnatural acts, and oral copulation with men, though the charges almost always involved fellatio. Seventy-four of the 3,502 persons (two percent) arrested for sodomy in New York between 1911 and 1940 were women. Between 1921 and 1935, Boston police arrested thirty-two women for unnatural acts, eight percent of total arrests for that crime. In Baltimore, an average of one to two women were arrested each year between 1917 and 1945.[87]

The women arrested for oral sex after World War I were, as before, primarily sex workers. Some of them may have been working-class lesbians, who were starting to achieve some public visibility. By the 1920s and 1930s working-class lesbians had begun meeting other women in saloons in New York, Buffalo, Chicago, San Francisco, and other cities. It was there that "butch-femme" roles were worked out, butches dressing like men and acting tough, competing for and protecting their femme charges. As one sociologist described lesbian parties in Chicago, "some of [the women] would put on men's evening clothes, make love to the others, and eventually carry them off in their arms into the bedrooms."[88]

The most famous post-Prohibition bar dedicated to a largely lesbian clientele was opened in San Francisco by Mona Sargent in 1934. The bar was a meeting place for butch-femme couples. Featuring singing waitresses and, later, cross-dressed women offering popular tunes, Mona's also attracted sexual tourists. In 1938 the police were shocked when they discovered women dressing as men and dancing with women. Although they arrested Mona for running a "disorderly house," the club reopened and continued its bohemian ways for two more decades. Less-famous lesbian bars included Tony Pastor's and Ernie's in New York, the Barn in Cleveland, Oakland's White Horse, the Roselle Club and the Twelve-Thirty Club in Chicago, and Tess's Café and the Café Gala in Los Angeles.[89]

Creating Their Own Legacy: The Gay Harlem Renaissance

Between 1890 and 1930 southern whites created apartheid, a violent reign of terror against African Americans, whose supposed inferiority was accompanied by
a mythic sexualization. At the same time that the press was featuring sapphic-
slasher scenarios, it was popularizing a lynching narrative, in which oversexed
black men raped white women and were punished by an energized (white) community through a public hanging. As Lisa Duggan has argued, each myth involved a vulnerable white woman tempted away from marriage to a white man
by an unnatural liaison.[90]

At the symbolic level, the record of sodomy charges against black people only
deepens Duggan's account. A large majority of those arrested in the South for
sodomy or unnatural solicitation before World War II were African American.
The association of blacks with sodomy, prostitution, and rape not only helped
construct a public consensus that people of color were a degraded, sex-crazed
race, but also helped exclude black men from public citizenship. In the same
period that southern states were adopting antimiscegenation and other apartheid laws, they were adopting statutes that stripped citizens of their right to vote
if they committed "crimes of moral turpitude"—including rape and sodomy.
Just as northern states had adopted similar laws between 1840 and 1861 in order
to marginalize working-class immigrants, southern states between 1865 and
1890 adopted disenfranchisement laws in order to ensure political marginaliza-
tion of African Americans.[91]

To escape these conditions, 1.5 million southern blacks moved north between
1915 and 1921, many of them to New York. By 1920, Harlem, in the northern
part of Manhattan, had become a black enclave, and one consequence was the
famous "Harlem Renaissance" of 1920–1935. The promoters of the Renaissance
emphasized literature that revealed the humanity of African Americans, but the
humanity suggested by its younger participants was often sexual and gay as well
as black.[92]

Harlem in the 1920s became what Lewis Mumford calls a *sexual interzone*—a
mixed-race area where gender-bending men and women socialized. Nowhere
was the synergy of race, sexuality, and gender diversity more apparent than in
music. Gertrude "Ma" Rainey, a bisexual, was the mother of the blues. Displacing
gospel music as the central musical genre of people of color in New York, the
blues were pervasively sexual and nonconformist. The lyrics of Ma Rainey, Bessie
Smith, and Billie Holiday were ambivalent about marriage and celebrated wom-
en's sexual and economic independence. In "Young Woman's Blues," Smith
gushed, "No time to marry, no time to settle down / I'm a young woman and ain't
done runnin' 'round." Black women could not enjoy the luxury of domesticity,

because they typically had to work outside the home. The blues were also notable for depicting female protagonists as free from both husbands and children.[93]

And sometimes free from men altogether. Rainey's "Prove It On Me Blues" flaunted her own feelings toward other women and teased the state for its censure:

> Went out last night with a crowd of my friends,
> They must've been women, 'cause I don't like no men. . . .
> They say I do it, ain't nobody caught me,
> They sure got to prove it on me. . . .

The Chicago advertisement for the record depicted "a plump black woman, looking much like Ma Rainey, in a man's tie, hat, and jacket, talking to two entranced feminine flappers. In the distance, observing them, there is a policeman." The cops kept an eye on Ma Rainey, and in 1925 she was arrested for hosting a lesbian orgy. Her former lover Bessie Smith bailed her out of jail.[94]

Many of the male prose writers of the Harlem Renaissance were sexual as well as racial minorities. The novelist Claude McKay and short-story writer Richard Bruce Nugent were openly homosexual. Nugent, a sensual and unconventional man who had been run out of Washington, D.C., by respectable black families, created nonstereotypical images of men who loved other men. Not only did he reject the notion that gay men were effeminate, but in stories like "Smoke, Lilies and Jade" (1926) he dismissed the idea of sexual orientation as a defining category. In "Geisha Man" (1925), he asked, "Is it wrong to love bodies?" without any reference to their sex. Others, like Langston Hughes, had intimate relations with men and did understand themselves as homosexual. The elegant Countee Cullen was a closeted homosexual whose Whitmanesque poetry contained many coded gay references.[95]

Many blacks felt sympathy with marginal white fairies and dykes, and a large number were personally tolerant of sexual and gender variation among people of color, especially if it was confined behind closed doors. But Harlem blacks resented white people's sexual colonization of their neighborhoods, and most Baptist churchgoers disapproved of sodomy and inversion. Integrationists like W. E. B. DuBois feared that the (homo)sexualization of the Renaissance would discredit its achievements and reinforce stereotypes of African Americans as sexually rapacious and deviant. Many saw homosexuality as a disease that corrupt white culture imposed on blacks. Although fairies encountered almost none of the mean-spiritedness in Harlem that they faced in lower Manhattan, African-American clergy and press regularly inveighed against contamination of Harlem by the homosexual "disease." In 1929 the Reverend Adam Clayton Powell led an antivice campaign that exposed homosexual hangouts and netted a number of arrests, mostly of black fairies soliciting sex in public lavatories.[96]

Notwithstanding its ambivalence, Harlem was the site that best carried forth the romantic political ideals of Whitman and Addams into the new century. Countee Cullen's poem "Tableau" (1925) is one notable update of Whitman's notion of inclusion across artificial social barriers. Dedicated to Cullen's white lover, Donald Duff, the poem opens: "Locked arm in arm they cross the way, / The black boy and the white." Invoking Whitman's "We Two Boys Together Clinging" (1867), Cullen adds a racial dimenson to male camaraderie and underscores its radicalism in an era of Sigmund Freud and Jim Crow. The "dark folk" stare at the boys "[f]rom lowered blinds," while "the fair folk talk" openly, presumably scandalized that the boys "should dare / In unison to walk." "Oblivious to look and word," the boys "see no wonder / That lightning brilliant as a sword / Should blaze the path of thunder." Just as Addams argued that democratic community requires commingling of social classes, Cullen suggested that democratic community (impossible in the South) requires commingling of the races. Not just love but democracy was at stake in the boys' crossing the homo-miscegenation line.

CHAPTER THREE

The Antihomosexual
Kulturkampf, 1935–61

Raised by his Quaker grandparents in West Chester, Pennsylvania, Bayard Rustin (1912–87) knew he was a homosexual by age fourteen. He told his grandmother, the civil rights activist Julia Rustin, that he preferred men. "And she said, 'Is that what you really enjoy?' I said, 'Yes, I think I do.' Her reply was, 'Then I suppose that's what you need to do.'" Her response reflected a cautious tolerance. While Julia believed that Bayard's sexual orientation was nothing to become alarmed about—he was still the same bright-eyed boy with the sweet smile she had loved since his infancy—neither was it cause for celebration. Julia worried that homosexuality would cause her boy a great deal of trouble in the world. It gave white people

Bayard Rustin

another reason to hate and assault him, and created anxiety among respectable black folk, who felt it was a discredit to the race.[1]

Bayard Rustin found much satisfaction in his sexual romps with other men, but his life's mission lay in grand political causes. His inspirations were the Social Gospel of his Quaker upbringing; the Harlem Renaissance, where he met Alain Locke and other barely closeted black gay men; and Mahatma Gandhi's philosophy of nonviolent protest, which he embraced in 1941 when he joined the pacifistic Fellowship of Reconciliation (FOR). Rustin's refusal to serve in the armed forces landed him in the Ashland (Kentucky) Federal Correctional Institute in 1944. Ever the activist, Rustin urged the warden to commence a gradual desegregation and helped the inmates to engage in organized, nonviolent resistance. Prison also gave Rustin plenty of time for reading, including Henry Canby's 1943 biography of Walt Whitman. Critics in the 1930s trained their attention on the relationship between Whitman's nonconforming sexuality and the greatness of his poetry, including the "Calamus" poems. While Canby could not admire Whitman as a homosexual, he did connect the poet's "passionate, physical love" for men with "strong creative intellects, whose imaginative sympathies penetrate beyond sexual differences." This, too, was Rustin's aspiration: like Whitman, he did not see himself as a homosexual, but derived energy and imagination from his nonconforming passions.[2]

Emerging from prison in 1946, Rustin began his career as a leader in the civil rights movement, initially under the auspices of FOR and its offshoot, the Congress for Racial Equality (CORE). He combined this work with intense cruising of other men wherever he was located. Both activities resulted in frequent arrests, including at least three for homosexual solicitation (in New York and North Carolina). On January 21, 1953, Rustin gave a speech on world peace to the American Society of University Women in Pasadena, California. Afterward, he walked the streets, searching for sexual partners. Sometime after two o'clock in the morning, Rustin approached two twenty-three-year-old white men, Marvin Long and Louie Buono, who had been driving around looking, also unsuccessfully, for female companionship. "[Rustin] asked us if we wanted to have a good time," one of the pair said later. When they didn't understand the offer, Rustin was more specific: "[H]e could blow us." Long and Buono accepted, and soon afterward, police rousted the three from the backseat of the automobile and arrested them for "sex perversion," or felonious oral sex. Newspapers reported that a "nationally known Negro lecturer" was in jail on a morals charge. As they usually did in such cases, prosecutors only charged Rustin with "lewd vagrancy," a misdemeanor, in return for a guilty plea. The judge sentenced all three men to sixty days in jail.[3]

The Pasadena arrest was a turning point in his career. Like Whitman, Rustin had always seen himself as a universal figure, a mediator among the races, religions, and classes. After the arrest, he lost control of that identity, for he would henceforth be the Negro homosexual, "Brother Outsider." If Pasadena marked the end of Rustin's future as a visible leader of the civil rights movement, it was a new beginning for him as an influential behind-the-scenes strategist. Two years after Pasadena, he was sent to support the Montgomery, Alabama, bus boycott. Rustin arrived just after a grand jury had indicted the boycotters, and he made a Gandhian suggestion: don't wait for the sheriff to arrest you; turn the event into a public display of pride. The next morning, dozens of Negroes, dressed in their finest clothes, marched to the courthouse and turned themselves in, to the applause of hundreds of supporters, and to the shock of white bystanders. Thus commenced a beautiful (if rocky) friendship with Dr. Martin Luther King Jr., who embraced the Gandhian philosophy. "Rustin was as responsible as anyone else for the insinuation of nonviolence into the very heart of what became the most powerful social movement in twentieth-century America."[4]

The half-generation after World War II was a period of enormous social and demographic turmoil, as the Great Depression gave way to the Second World War, in turn followed by the Cold War. As they had in the 1870s, Americans coped with new anxieties through a body politics that involved familiar themes of disgust, purity and pollution, and the moralization of difference. The objects of the earlier morality politics had been wide-ranging and diffuse— pornographers, feminists, free lovers, abortionists and family planners, degenerates, sex inverts, Catholics, Mormons, immigrants. The new panic was more focused, its targets ostensibly domestic Communism and child molesters, but increasingly the focus was "homosexuals and other sex perverts." The paranoid domestic politics of the 1950s ultimately expended more resources in its antihomosexual witch hunts than in its anti-Communist ones (though most Americans saw them as the same campaign). As a homosexual who had once been a Communist, and remained a "colored" civil rights "agitator," Rustin was triple poison.

What most distinguished the purity politics of the 1950s from that of the 1870s was the role of the government. Turn-of-the-century Comstockery was essentially private entrepreneurship, which cooperated with state police to carry out purity campaigns favored by local elites. By 1935 the pervasive regulatory state was itself poised to lead the purity crusade. Rustin's life dramatically illustrates this shift. The state mostly left him alone before World War II, but dominated his life afterward. During his term in federal prison for war resistance, his every move was monitored by state agents. After prison, his career focused on the goal of ending state-sanctioned apartheid, and his nonviolent protest activities led to a series of new arrests for disorderly conduct and other offenses. By the 1950s J. Edgar Hoover's Federal Bureau of Investigation was monitoring his activities. Rustin believed that the FBI set him up for the Pasadena arrest and then used it to discredit him. FBI wiretaps of Dr. King's private conversations yielded further sexual gossip about Rustin, which Hoover's men dutifully publicized.[5]

The social meaning of sodomy crystalized during this period, and by 1961 it was a thoroughly homosexualized term. Even though most adult Americans had engaged in oral sex, they did not consider themselves felons, because only "homosexuals and other sex perverts" engaged in the *crime* against nature. Moreover, states began enforcing criminal sodomy laws at levels never before imagined, and created entire regulatory regimes built up on the assumption that (suspected) homosexuals were felons, literal outlaws. State-sponsored witch hunts and monitoring not only ruined the lives of countless homosexuals but undermined the homosexual's ability to successfully lead a double life. In the 1930s Rustin assumed he could date men on the "down low," while carrying on with his career as an activist. The Pasadena arrest shattered that assumption, as similar incidents did for thousands of other lesbians and gay men. By ripping the masks off so many of them, and by interrogating millions of Americans about their sexual orientation and campaigning against homosexuality, the state created a cadre of homophile activists with nothing to lose, and only intensified public interest in the subject.

High Anxiety and America's Sex Panics, 1935–61

The historian Estelle Freedman argues that after World War I, American regulation of sexuality shifted from a focus on female corruption to a focus on male sexual aggression, a theme that reached an apex after 1935, when child molestation became a national obsession. The legal record, however, suggests that the transition started earlier, focusing on aggression against children starting in the 1890s (chapters 1–2). Outside the South, arrests for male-aggressive sex crimes against women and children steadily increased after 1900. In New York, for which we have the most complete data, arrests for both sodomy (sexual assaults on male minors) and rape (sexual assaults on female minors) steadily increased after 1900, peaking at more than a hundred (sodomy) and almost a thousand (rape) per year in the late 1920s. Each major city exhibited somewhat different patterns, but in cities as disparate as Atlanta, Baltimore, Boston, Chicago, Los Angeles, St. Louis, and Washington, D.C., arrests for rape, child molestation, and sodomy spiked in the 1910s and continued to increase dramatically after World War I ended. In some cities arrests fell off in the early 1930s, before strongly rebounding later in the decade, which Freedman cites as the beginning of heightened regulatory attention on the child-molesting "sexual pervert." The period after World War II saw multifarious and ambitious new regulatory programs to control male sexual aggression, as well as huge rises in arrests for sodomy, rape, and child molestation.[6]

Consistent with Freedman's idea that 1935 was a turning point, New York City's annual average number of arrests for impairing the morals of a minor was 258 for the period 1930–34, but rose to 344 for the period 1935–39. Sodomy arrests showed a similar surge, from an annual average of 115 for 1930–34 to an annual average of 164 for 1935–39, the biggest increase in sodomy arrests that New York saw in the early twentieth century (figure 3.1). Almost ninety percent

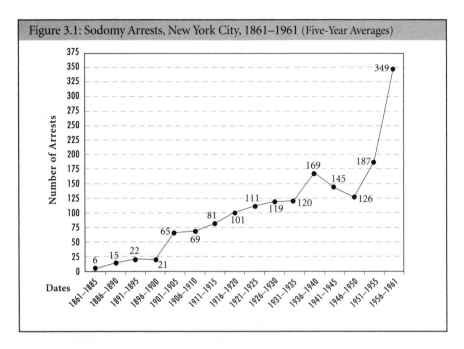

Figure 3.1: Sodomy Arrests, New York City, 1861–1961 (Five-Year Averages)

of the sodomy arrests involved minors. A similar trend can be observed in some of the other large cities.[7]

The growing number of sodomy and other sex crimes was accompanied by a major regulatory focus on homosexuality. Demonized as sexual psychopaths, sex perverts, and child molesters, homosexuals became the new enemy of the people. Their greater visibility made them the perfect repository for Americans' obsession with and guilt about sexual pleasure, gender-bending, and even racial segregation. Like the Comstock Society's earlier efforts, the antihomosexual politics of the mid-twentieth century deployed a moralizing body politics of disgust, contagion, and forced assimilation. But the goal of the new politics was different—to reaffirm a new norm of companionate marriage—as was the forum in which it played out, as participants now arrayed their efforts around the government.

Changing Demography and New Social Anxieties

The conventional explanation for the sodomy arrest boom is that Americans became frantically concerned about sex crimes against children. But why? There is no reliable evidence that there was an uptick in *actual* assaults against minors, just more discussion and enforcement. Also, given that most assaults were by men against girls, why was there so strong a focus on homosexuals? We cannot understand the regulatory interest in sodomy without understanding why homosexuality became a national obsession during this period. Social anxiety about homosexuality was fueled by such factors as guilt over a secret boom in oral sex among married couples, nostalgia for old-fashioned marriage, and concerns about racial mixing. As Americans became fearful of sexual chain reactions that would destroy the nation's moral fiber and expose them to external as well as internal enemies, the resulting philosophy of containment made homosexuals the universal scapegoat.

Projection of Sexual Guilt. Dr. Alfred Kinsey started taking personal sex histories in 1938, and within a decade he had collected about 12,500 of them. Although not a random sample of Americans (Hoosiers and homosexuals were overrepresented), his survey provides a rough profile of the sexual practices of whites born between 1890 and 1930. According to Kinsey's data, eighty-five percent of white males had engaged in fornication, between thirty and forty-five percent had committed adultery, fifty-nine percent had engaged in oral sex, seventy percent had patronized prostitutes, and seventeen percent had had sex with animals. Most of this activity was still technically illegal; Kinsey concluded that sex felons "constitute more than 95 percent of the total male population." By age forty, fifty percent of the women in Kinsey's sample had violated fornication laws, twenty-six percent had committed adultery, nineteen percent had had homosexual contact with other women, around one-fifth had received oral stimulation (cunnilingus), and another one-fifth had given it to a man (fellatio). The generation that came of age after World War I routinely engaged in "petting" (kissing, oral sex, stimulation of the breasts) before marriage.[8]

Such behavior continued unabated after the wedding. As sex manuals had been insisting since the 1920s, petting before coitus could spice up or save a marriage. Only 0.2 percent of Kinsey's sample of married women had *not* engaged in petting with their husbands. Fifty-four percent of the married women reported receiving cunnilingus, and forty-nine percent gave fellatio to their husbands. Most of these respondents understood that oral sex was considered a sin and were, to some extent, ashamed of their secret perversion. Deeper was the guilt felt by an indeterminate number of husbands and male relatives engaging in or fantasizing about sex and masturbation with children in their own families. One way human beings deal with deep-seated guilt about their sexual feelings and activities is to project them onto an outgroup. America had an outgroup tailor-made for such purposes—homosexuals.[9]

The Roaring Twenties had seen homosexual subcultures become publicly visible in large urban areas outside the South. Once a critical mass of homosexuals had congregated in a city, gay ghettos and venues for male cruising became apparent to the surrounding population. After Prohibition ended, in 1933, bars and clubs catering to a lesbian and gay clientele also became evident, and for the first time in American history lesbians claimed public space through this culture. After World War II, lesbian and gay bars grew like weeds in a vacant lot.[10]

Many alarmed Americans projected their own real or imagined crimes onto this sexualized and increasingly visible minority. There is no better example than J. Edgar Hoover (1895–1972), the bulldog who was his era's Comstock. The unmarried FBI director's closest relationship was with Clyde Tolson, his second-in-command at the agency. While there is no consensus as to his sexual and gender preferences, serious scholars agree that Hoover was fascinated by sexual deviation and cross-gender attire and obsessed with people who crossed sexual and racial lines, such as the adulterous Martin Luther King Jr. and the promiscuous Bayard Rustin. He considered these men to be as much "sex perverts" as the men who preyed on children. Producing a stream of popular articles like "How *Safe* Is Your Youngster?" Hoover was both hysterical exemplar and public cheerleader for the sex crime panics of this period.[11]

A Culture of Containment and Nostalgia for Old-Fashioned Marriage with Children. The audience for Hoover's propaganda included Americans who yearned in unsettled times for the reassurance of what they considered "traditional" marriage. During the Great Depression, men who could not find work postponed marriage, and divorces continued their century-long climb. World War II disrupted marriage in a different way, breaking up relationships: most men went to combat, and many women entered the labor force to sustain the war effort. Spurred by economic necessity, women assumed more public duties— working outside the home, serving in the armed forces, and even running for public office. Married women came into the workplace and public life in unprecedented numbers. Wives often enjoyed these new responsibilities, but felt some guilt about neglecting their families. Husbands appreciated the extra income, but many feared that their manhood had been diminished.[12]

As World War II ended the pent-up nostalgia for old-fashioned marriage was released dramatically. Between 1946 and 1955 more Americans wed than at any other point in modern history; they had children immediately, and even the divorce rate dipped (temporarily). These trends cut across racial, economic, and social lines. The comeback of marriage reassured men and women that traditional boundaries were intact after the great traumas of war and depression. The post-1945 thirst for normalcy fed into what Elaine Tyler May calls a "culture of containment" that helped calm anxieties about security in the wake of external threats from the Nazis and Communists. Containment required that accepted lines be reaffirmed—albeit in the process redefined. Thus, young Americans having oral as well as procreative sex within marriage came to understand their own conduct as consistent with a new "traditional" norm, companionate marriage. This new conformism also involved a deep suspicion of the *un*married. The homosexual not only epitomized the unmarriageable American, but he or she was a threat to the marriageability of the next generation—the children.[13]

Because they invested a great deal of effort and emotion into successful child-rearing, diligent parents' worst nightmare was having a homosexual child. Such offspring would not fulfill their destiny of replicating themselves and were headed for a life of trouble. Parents assumed, or hoped, that children's homosexuality could not have come from them, but must have been inflicted by someone else—the "predatory homosexual" or the "vampire lesbian." Recall Comstockery's metaphor, that sexual wolves will not just devour your little lambs, but transform them into wolves (chapter 1). Because these particular wolves were usually in sheep's clothing, many parents felt that homosexuals should be exposed as well as despised.[14]

An early example of the operation of this paradigm came in spring 1944. A concerned mother wrote the Women's Army Corps, complaining that the WAC training camp at Fort Oglethorpe, Georgia, "is full of homosexuals and sex maniacs," one of whom had molested her "little [twenty-year-old] girl" and who "will continue to use her spell over other innocent girls who join up with the WAC." The Army assigned Lieutenant Colonel Birge Holt and Captain Ruby Herman to the case. The investigators recommended separation or treatment only for women who were having sex with other women (sodomites) *and* were not interested in relationships with men (homosexuals) *and* displayed other cross-gender habits, such as dressing in men's attire. The Fort Oglethorpe investigation was a particularly revealing experience in that it underscored the growing concerns with excessive sexuality, the insistence on sharply defined gender roles, and the fear of predation, all of which were already converging to create an image of the homosexual as public enemy number one.[15]

Concerns with Racial (etc.) Contagion. Immigration from Europe and Asia had fueled much of the late nineteenth century's sociosexual anxiety. Although this influx abated after Congress set rigid quotas on immigration in 1924, an internal migration soon took its place. Between 1915 and 1950 more than three million African Americans moved from the rural South to New York, Chicago, Detroit, Washington, Los Angeles, Atlanta, and other growing cities; a million more joined them in the 1950s. Northerners who had disparaged southern whites for their racism now found themselves alarmed by new economic competition and social networking by such great numbers of "colored people." As a star high school student and athlete, Bayard Rustin learned that whites accepted token integration, but as an adult he discovered that white tolerance fell as black numbers rose. To make matters more tense, people of color began demanding higher legal and social status, as well as better jobs. Julia Rustin's National Association for the Advancement of Colored People (NAACP) was becoming a household word in the 1930s and 1940s.[16]

One sign of the backlash against this demand for recognition was white people's discipline of hypersexualized black bodies. Lynchings of innocent black men for allegedly raping or accosting white women had always been a centerpiece of apartheid's reign of terror, and in segregation's final decades, legalized lynchings continued this tradition, as hundreds of innocent black defendants were hustled to death sentences or long prison terms for such putative rapes. A variation on that theme was the episodic prosecution of black men for assaulting white children. Like lynchings of old, these incidents could mobilize a community. In 1959 Houston police found the body of twelve-year-old Merrill Bodenheimer stuffed in an icebox. They arrested seven African-American youths (aged thirteen to seventeen) and extracted confessions that they had raped and murdered the white boy. These confessions were probably bogus, but the boys were saved from a legal lynching only by an open letter from Merrill's mother, denouncing the racist response of the authorities.[17]

While there are no national data breaking down sodomy arrests by race, survey evidence for particular cities suggests that police attention to sodomy continued to focus disproportionately on black men. In the 1930s, when only six percent of its adult male population was nonwhite, twenty percent of New York City's sex offenders were black, as were twenty-one percent of those arrested for sodomy. In the 1940s, San Francisco, with a smaller black population, reported that fifteen percent of its convicted sex offenders were African American. For California as a whole (with a four percent black population) ten percent of the sex offenders were black. In Washington, D.C., in the 1950s sixty percent of those arrested for sodomy and seventy-two percent of those arrested for indecent acts with minors were black men, in a city that was two-thirds white. In contrast, Baltimore continued to arrest black men for sodomy and perverted practices at relatively low levels in most years.[18]

This period also saw a modest migration of Latinos from Puerto Rico and Mexico into some American cities, and these new residents accounted for an even more disproportionate number of sex crime arrests. In New York, Puerto Ricans accounted for five percent of sex crime arrests, a far higher proportion than their tiny representation in the population. California's Mexican population was officially estimated at two percent in the 1940s, but Mexicans accounted for ten percent of all those convicted of sex crimes, twenty-eight percent of all convicted rapists, and twenty-one percent of convicted "sodomists."[19]

Police, prosecutors, and judges who often showed some mercy to white defendants typically dealt more harshly with defendants of color. A Broward County, Florida, judge faced two defendants who admitted "unnatural sex acts." The white defendant was sentenced to jail for thirty days; the black defendant, described by the prosecutor as an "animal," went to prison for fifteen years. In California, where ten percent of convicted sex offenders were black, twenty percent of those who went to prison for sex crimes were African American and thirteen percent were Mexican American. The focus on minorities' supposed animalistic sexual conduct and the widespread concern with maintaining boundaries or purity connected racism to homophobia in a complicated way. Society was more likely to be harsh on the black or brown man or woman who dared to have sex with whites of the same sex (as Rustin regularly did).[20]

The New State-Supported Norms: Companionate Racially Pure Marriage and Compulsory Heterosexuality

The rhetoric of this period involved a moralizing body politics similar to that of the 1870s and 1880s, the era of the United States' first major purity campaigns, and once again themes of disgust, pollution, and traditional gender roles were central. What was different now was the norm. In the 1870s the norm was procreative (white) marriage and compulsory (white) motherhood. By the 1930s and 1940s, it had become companionate racially pure marriage and compulsory heterosexuality.[21]

Another difference between the old and new campaigns was the role of government. The state had served as Comstock's junior partner, but after 1933 governmental institutions played a much more active role in defining body politics. Public officials came to consider themselves the guarantors of the institution of companionate marriage, a duty that obliged them to maintain a vigilant alertness for pollution by homosexuality and other alien influences. Consider the following examples. It was during World War II that the armed forces first established procedures and standards for screening homosexuals and gender minorities, so that they could be barred from service; the military also formulated detailed standards for expelling practicing homosexuals who managed to slip through the porous screening mechanism. After World War II the federal government excluded homosexuals from the civil service as well as the military, and likewise adopted more-effective monitoring practices. Between 1956 and 1964, the "Johns Committee" of the Florida legislature engaged in a wide-ranging search to identify homosexuals employed in the state civil service and in schools. These important campaigns reinvigorated the old Comstock-era rhetoric and applied it, powerfully, to enforce a norm of compulsory hetero-sexuality.[22]

Just as traditionalist Americans in the 1870s did not necessarily agree with Comstock's extremism, so many in the 1940s did not support the views of such neo-Puritans as J. Edgar Hoover. Still, it was the most extreme who were the most outspoken, and Hoover and his allies continually vilified homosexual conduct. After the war, Hoover terrified a generation of parents with the warning that "[t]he most rapidly increasing type of crime is that perpetrated by degenerate sex offenders," who wanted to do unspeakable things to children. Like Comstock, he was loath to specify the nature of the disgusting acts, but he painted their perpetrators as "depraved human beings, more savage than beasts." Going even further than Hoover, California judge Paul Vallée ruled in 1951 that only "lewd and dissolute" people committed the crimes of sodomy or sex perversion, and regularly denounced "homosexual activity" between con-senting adults from the bench, deeming it "illegal, immoral, disgusting, and indecent."[23]

In 1964 Florida's Johns Committee published *Homosexuality and Citizenship in Florida*. Its purple cover portrayed two young naked men in a lascivious em-brace, and inside was a depiction of a blond boy in bondage. Unlike Hoover, the Florida legislators did not shrink from describing the acts they were condemn-ing. ("Homosexuality is, and for too long, has been, a skeleton in the closet of society.") The end of this government publication included a glossary of termi-nology, which was the most sexually explicit description of homosexual activities available in the period, ranging from mutual masturbation to "golden showers." Few homosexuals were familiar with all the terms included in the glossary, such as "dinge queen" (a "negro homosexual") or "sea food" ("Homosexuals in the Navy"). Its association of homosexuals exclusively with unusual or predatory sexual activities led to the committee's decisive conclusion: you cannot be a gen-uine citizen, or even a decent human being, in America if you are not hetero-sexual.[24]

The rhetoric of pollution was even more specific than the discourse of dis-gust, and is best exemplified by North Carolina senator Clyde Hoey's Committee Report (1950), which recommended that "homosexuals and other sex perverts" be excluded from federal government employment. Drawing from conclusions of the medical establishment, the report asserted that "those who engage in overt acts of perversion lack the emotional stability of other persons." And "indulgence in acts of perversion weakens the moral fiber of an individual to a degree that he is not suitable for a position of responsibility." These weak people are by nature predatory. "[P]erverts will frequently attempt to entice normal individuals to engage in perverted practices. This is particularly true of young and impressionable people who might come under the influence of a pervert." Such homosexual predation can be institutional as well as personal. "One homosexual can pollute an entire office. Another point to be considered . . . is his tendency to gather other perverts around him."[25]

The Johns Committee warned that "a great many homosexuals have an insatiable appetite for sexual activities and find special gratification in the recruitment to their ranks of youth." Its report cited examples of teachers frequenting glory holes, coaches assaulting players, and adults luring teenage boys into prostitution rings. Echoing Comstock, the committee argued that the homosexual is *worse* than the (heterosexual) child molester. "The homosexual prefers to reach out for the child at the time of normal sexual awakening and to conduct a psychological preliminary to the physical contact. The homosexual's goal and part of the satisfaction is to 'bring over' the young person, to hook him for homosexuality. Whether it be with youth or with older individuals, homosexuality is unique among the sexual assaults considered by our laws in that the person affected by the practicing homosexual is first a victim, then an accomplice, and finally himself a perpetrator of homosexual acts."[26]

While this rhetoric seems overwrought today, many people accepted it because homosexuals were visible enough to be alarming but not accessible enough to become humanized. This helped reinforce such notions as the idea that homosexuals blurred sharp gender lines. The Army's screening procedures during World War II, for example, taught that homosexuals could be recognized by "feminine body characteristics" or "effeminacy in dress and manner," as well as by such symptoms as a "patulous [expanded] rectum." The Army paid less attention to lesbians, but the Fort Oglethorpe investigation did set its sights on women known to wear men's clothing. After the war the Navy gave scripted lectures to WAVES, emphasizing the evils of homosexuality: "By [homosexual] conduct, a Navy woman may ruin her chances for a happy marriage," and poison relationships with "normal women" and her own family. This was an unusually clear statement of the postwar philosophy that was the basis for a New Eden of marriage, a ranch house, and 2.2 children.[27]

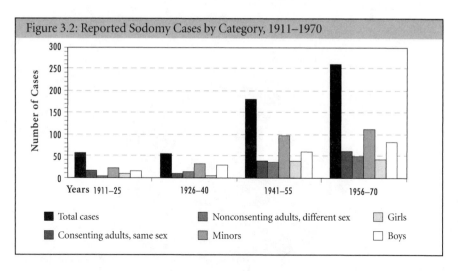

Figure 3.2: Reported Sodomy Cases by Category, 1911–1970

The Politics of Sodomy Enforcement: Panics and Manias

After a lull in enforcement during World War II, sodomy arrests rose dramatically between 1946 and 1970. It appears that yearly sodomy arrests went up threefold or more in New York City, San Francisco, and Los Angeles, cities with the most vigorous enforcement efforts before the war; that Baltimore, Miami, Philadelphia, Seattle, Washington, D.C., and other large cities had equally impressive increases, while Chicago, Cleveland, and St. Louis probably did not; and that southern cities such as Atlanta, Charleston, Dallas, Houston, Memphis, Nashville, and Richmond for the first time in their histories saw sodomy arrests in the double digits. Even small towns such as Boise, Idaho, initiated serious sodomy law enforcement. Although there are no national sodomy arrest data for this period, the general trend can be quantified in another way: for the years 1940–70, sodomy laws generated four times the number of reported appellate decisions as in the previous thirty years (1910–40).[28]

Figure 3.2 also suggests a general stability in the pattern of enforcement during the first two-thirds of the twentieth century. Sixty percent (261 out of 440) of the sodomy cases reported between 1940 and 1970 involved homosexual activities. Even though most of the oral sex in America was conducted in marital bedrooms, often by unwilling wives, there was only one reported case involving marital sodomy. Those arrested for the crime were usually men having sex with men; the portion of such arrests rose in the 1950s and 1960s. Consistent with the centurywide focus on protecting children, fifty percent of the reported cases (221 of 440) involved sex between adults and minors, two-thirds of whom were boys.

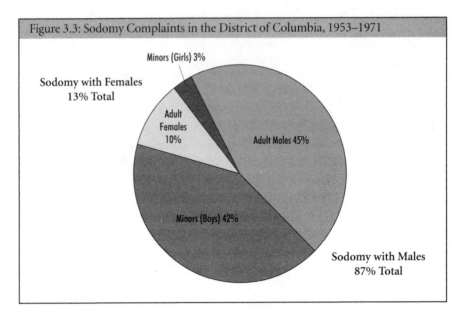

Figure 3.3: Sodomy Complaints in the District of Columbia, 1953–1971

Minors (Girls) 3%

Sodomy with Females
13% Total

Adult
Females
10%

Adult Males 45%

Minors (Boys) 42%

Sodomy with Males
87% Total

Just under forty percent of the cases involved sexual assault on adult women (81 of 440) or girls (76 of 440).

There is a bias in these statistics, because they cite only reported cases, including appeals from sodomy convictions. The trends they depict might be adjusted by comparing them with the data for sodomy *complaints* in the District of Columbia from 1953 to 1971 (figure 3.3). As with the reported cases, fifty percent of the D.C. complaints were made on behalf of minors. But more than eighty percent of the D.C. complaints (much higher than the sixty percent of the reported cases) involved homosexual sodomy. Contemporary accounts indicate that homosexuals were less likely to appeal sodomy convictions, and so the actual incidence of homosexual sodomy arrests is likely to be closer to eighty percent, consistent with the D.C. data.[29]

Both the reported cases and the D.C. complaints suggest that the large majority of sodomy arrests involved nonconsensual conduct, either sexual assault on an adult man or woman, or sex with a minor who could not legally consent. But the number of arrests involving consensual activities was also rising. The best evidence comes from New York City, where during the 1930s as many as ninety percent of the sodomy arrests were for nonconsenting activities. Twenty-three percent of the sodomy defendants arraigned in New York City's Magistrates' Courts between 1951 and 1959 were charged with consensual activities, a number that spiked to fifty-three percent between 1960 and 1962. While most of the consensual sodomy cases involved sex in a quasi-public place such as an automobile, park, restroom, or subway, the biggest innovation of postwar sodomy law enforcement was an unprecedented focus on homosexual activities in private bedrooms between consenting adults. Reported cases from states in all parts of the country illustrated such police invasions to nab male and sometimes even female homosexuals.[30]

One way to understand the politics of sodomy law enforcement in the 1940s and 1950s is to revise Estelle Freedman's thesis. After 1870, American criminal law grew increasingly concerned with the sexual abuse of children, boys as well as girls. After 1935, and especially after 1945, that primary focus was joined with a strong secondary one of demonizing homosexuality anytime it came to the public's attention—even if that was the result of police sting operations, bar raids, or invasions of the home. Even the discreet homosexual was terrorized by being labeled an enemy of the people and threatened with public exposure and ruin if a nosy neighbor or an entrepreneurial policeman chose to persecute him or her.[31]

Antisodomy campaigns often followed a panic scenario, where one incident triggered a wave of media and political attention, resulting in a frenzy of homosexual arrests, detentions, and harassment by police. Publicity surrounding the murder of William Simpson, a homosexual man, triggered a Miami panic in 1952, with a bigger "Miami Hurricane" following two lurid sex crimes against children in 1954; the murders of three Chicago boys led to police roundups of homosexual men all over the Midwest in 1955; Stephen Nash's 1956 confession that he had killed several homosexuals triggered an antihomosexual cleanup operation in Santa Monica. Other panics were politically motivated. In 1937–38, Mayor Fiorello LaGuardia ordered a purification of homosexual cruising areas to make New York City a presentable host to the World's Fair. Responding to parental complaints, Atlanta police chief Herbert Jenkins devoted hundreds of officers to antihomosexual sting and cleanup operations between 1954 and 1958.[32]

Most famous was the "Boys of Boise" panic. On October 31, 1955, three blue-collar men were arrested for having "unnatural relations" with teenage boys in Boise, Idaho. The minors were reportedly part of a larger "homosexual ring" of youth who agreed to receive oral sex for pay. The local newspaper expressed surprise that such a "cancerous growth could have taken roots" in this city of 34,000 and demanded an "immediate and systematic cauterization." In the ensuing weeks, the police arrested fourteen more men, including a lawyer, a banker, and a haberdasher. Responding to mounting public concerns, the city council urged not only that all these defendants be "convicted and sentenced, but also that all those who live outside the law are vigilantly watched and rigidly prosecuted." In 1956 police interviewed hundreds of suspected homosexuals and widened the dragnet to include married men committing the crime against nature with adults. By 1957 all but one defendant had pleaded guilty to sodomy or lewd behavior charges, and a jury convicted Gordon Larsen, a married man who committed sodomy with another adult man. Eight defendants received sentences of five years to life in prison.[33]

The Boys of Boise episode reflected the same kind of paranoia that spooked audiences watching the movie *Invasion of the Body Snatchers* (1956). Just as alien spores infected Americans and turned them into pod people in the movie, Idahoans believed that boys "infected" by homosexuals would themselves become homosexual and would, in turn, "infect other boys." Like pod people, homosexuals were Trojan horses, fifth columns undermining society from within. Just as humans triumphed in the movie when Dr. Miles Bennell exposed the pod people and purged them of their spores, so Boise hoped by exposure and expulsion of homosexuality to purify itself and its bored teen population. Considering the fate of a banker who pleaded guilty to oral sex with young men he picked up at the YMCA, Judge Oliver Koelsch realized that neither the defendant nor his paid companions would benefit from a stiff penalty but sent him to prison for seven years nevertheless in order to preserve community purity. Leniency when the crime against nature had been exposed could, he said, lead to "mass conscience deterioration" and "social disorder." This same *Body Snatcher* philosophy applied to homosexual sodomy between consenting adults. As prosecutor Blaine Evans said, "You've *got to get these guys,* because they strike at the core of society, I mean the family." Police accordingly took no interest in oral sex between husbands and wives, even though the Idaho law considered such conduct a crime against nature.[34]

In effect, the Boise cleanup was an antihomosexual Kulturkampf. A Kulturkampf is a state campaign to domesticate or erase a minority. In the half-generation after the war, American political leaders engaged in an ambitious campaign of demonizing and purging homosexuals from public life. These leaders included not only hysterical zealots like Hoover, but also Americans like Governor Earl Warren of California (1943–53), Nebraska senator Kenneth Wherry (1943–53), Florida governor Charley Johns (1953–55), and Los Angeles police chief William Parker (1950–66).[35]

Expansion of Sodomy Laws, 1935–61

Linda Joyce Glucoft, the six-year-old daughter of Jules and Lillian Glucoft of the Crescent Heights section of Los Angeles, wandered into the home of her friend

Rochelle Hausman on November 14, 1949. Wearing a blue plaid dress, bright red shoes, and yellow socks, Linda encountered Rochelle's grandfather, Fred Stroble, an Austrian immigrant, who tried to molest the little girl. Linda screamed and turned to run, but Stroble grabbed her and strangled her with his necktie. He wrapped the child in a blanket and carried her outside, where he made sure she was dead by stabbing her with a knife and striking her with an axe. Police discovered Linda's body the next day and arrested Stroble, who had previously assaulted at least six other girls in the area. Linda's murder was front-page news in the state's newspapers for two weeks, during which time police reports of assaults on children skyrocketed. FBI director Hoover called for "total war against sex fiends," and California parents wrote the state attorney general, legislators, and the governor, demanding legal reforms to head off further atrocities of this sort. The state government responded with new laws and enforcement vigilance. Although Stroble and most other child molesters had assaulted girls, the primary targets of the legal reaction were male homosexuals. The person who spearheaded the greatest antihomosexual Kulturkampf in American history was California's governor, Earl Warren (1891–1974).[36]

Warren is best known as the chief justice who authored *Brown v. Board of Education* (1954) and led the Supreme Court to constitutionalize a wide range of rights for minorities and criminal defendants. While this affable Swede became the smiling face of American liberalism, as attorney general (1939–43) and governor (1943–53) of California, he championed one of the most illiberal state acts of the century—the detention and internment of Japanese-American citizens during World War II. As this episode suggests, Warren's political philosophy was more closely tied to early-twentieth-century Progressivism than to late-twentieth-century liberalism. Progressives advocated an activist government dedicated to the public interest, including the preservation of a pure American culture. That meant scrupulous attention to "foreign threats," as Warren understood Japanese Americans, and to ideological contamination, as Warren understood Communism. Homosexuality contained elements of both, and Warren fought it too.[37]

Central to Warren's Progressive philosophy was "the right of the government to maintain a decent society." Anything that discouraged men from leading wholesome family lives was indecent to Warren, whose own greatest treasures were his supportive wife, the former Nina Meyers, and their six children. Sexual expression outside a companionate marriage such as his own was suspect. Warren would never have acknowledged knowing any homosexuals, though his legislative assistant Beach Vasey was apparently gay. "[L]ess the masculine type than the people that Warren usually had around him," the diligent, methodical

Vasey was the object of emotional outbursts from the typically unflappable governor, irritated that the man was "a little bit on the gentle side." Warren tolerated his secretary because he was as closeted as possible, and therefore not the social pollution someone like Rustin would have seemed. A prosecutor for more than twenty years, Warren believed in a moral police power to protect *families* against predators and polluters. Like other fathers, he had an emotional, violent streak when exposed to aggressive, child-threatening deviant sexuality. He reportedly said, after reviewing a smutty book in an obscenity case, "If anyone showed that book to my daughters, I'd have strangled him with my own hands."[38]

No state better exemplified the social trends contributing to public homophobia than California. Every decade of the twentieth century saw significant changes in its social demography, as its population swelled through migration from the East and Mexico. Sexual minorities had been visible in San Francisco since its origins, and the 1920s saw expanded visibility of gay men on the beaches and in the public restrooms, bars, and parks of Los Angeles, San Diego, and other booming southern California cities. The same factors that fueled a popular obsession with the Communist threat to national security (sending Bill Knowland and Richard Nixon to the Senate in 1946 and 1950) also motivated middle-class concern about domestic security against child molesters and homosexuals. Legislators such as H. Allen Smith, a former FBI agent representing Los Angeles, reflected an aggressive form of this concern, as they pressed for highly regulatory sex crime legislation.[39]

On November 22, 1949, a week after Linda Glucoft's murder, Governor Warren joined the FBI's call for an all-out war against sex criminals. In early December he summoned a special session of the legislature and convened a Law Enforcement Agencies' Conference. Between 1949 and 1953, California transformed its sex crime laws, and what began as a panic became a decade-long mania in which state and local governments cooperated to identify, expose, and imprison "sex perverts" of all sorts, but particularly homosexuals. Advocates were working in the nation's capital and many other states to promote similar measures, though they were more often in the Hoover than the Warren mold.[40]

Specifying, Monitoring, and Expanding the Crime Against Nature

With homosexuals emerging as public enemy number one, America's legislators updated their criminal codes. The last jurisdiction within the continental United States to make sodomy a statutory crime was, ironically, the District of Columbia, under Congress's authority. In order to "strengthen the laws as they deal with sodomy and perverted practices," the Miller Act was passed in 1948. As California had done in 1921, Congress made sure that the District's new statutory crime went beyond the common law, to include "taking into the mouth or anus the sexual organ of any other person or animal." (Although it did not do so as clearly as California, Congress probably meant to criminalize cunnilingus as well as fellatio.) At a point when most married couples were engaging in oral sex, Congress and most state legislatures had made it a felony.[41]

The Miller Act provided that a single act of sodomy could lead to ten years in prison, twenty years if an adult committed the crime with a minor (under age sixteen). This was a formidable punishment, but Warren's California outdid even Congress in this respect. In 1945 the California legislature amended its habitual offender law, adding sodomy to the list of crimes for which a second offense meant an automatic sentence of life in prison. In the wake of the Glucoft murder, Governor Warren procured legislation doubling the penalty for sodomy (a new maximum of twenty years in prison), and adding oral copulation and loitering around a public toilet to the crimes triggering recidivism enhancements. Later that year, the legislature added oral copulation and sodomy to the list of crimes where a third conviction required mandatory life imprisonment. A year before he became chief justice, Warren signed a law eliminating the maximum sentence for consensual sodomy, thereby making it a potential life sentence for the first offense; the maximum penalty for consensual oral sex remained fifteen years in prison, with a mandatory minimum sentence of three years if the partner was under the age of fourteen or the oral copulation was forcible.[42]

California's one "liberalization" was a 1950 amendment to the oral copulation law, giving judges a choice between sending violators to prison for up to fifteen years or to county jail for up to one year—in effect creating a misdemeanor alternative within the felony copulation law. Assemblyman Smith, a dedicated homophobe, justified the liberalization because many homosexuals were escaping punishment under the harsher law. As prosecutors told his committee, "[i]f two men of lawful age are living together, that when they attempt to prosecute them under [the oral copulation felony law] they find that the juries, in many instances, are not interested in returning a guilty verdict. Further, that to sentence the subject and, in some instances, the victim, to the penitentiary only acts as a 'quarantine' of the individual for a period of time, and does not help in the over-all solution of the sex-crime problem."[43]

California's new regime illustrates three innovative approaches to sodomy regulation that set a pattern for the future. First, there was explicit statutory recognition that forcible sodomy and sodomy with minors were more blame-worthy than sodomy between consenting adults. Earlier in 1950 New York had recast its sodomy law as three separate crimes: (1) consensual sodomy, re-duced to a misdemeanor, with felony punishment for (2) forcible sodomy and (3) sodomy with minors. The idea of *consensual sodomy* as a distinct legal classification originates in this period. Michigan and other states considered joining New York in differentiating between the three crimes, but only Cali-fornia did, in the 1950 oral copulation amendment. (There was no analo-gous leniency for consensual sodomy, perhaps because most of those arrests were for unconsented activities.) Although the decency-promoting state could not ignore homosexuality, it could distinguish among different levels of abomination.[44]

Second, there was both explicit articulation of what constituted the crime against nature, and open-ended authorization for police to target related activities. Following California's 1921 law, new statutes explicitly described sodomy to include both anal and oral sex, or made oral sex a separate crime. Following the trend described in chapter 2, most jurisdictions with discernible lesbian subcultures made sex between two women a felony—California, the District of Columbia, Florida, Massachusetts, New York, and Texas.[45] And stat-utes protected minors against not just sodomy and oral copulation, but also "indecent liberties" of any sort, which could include sexual touching, fond-ling, masturbation, and so forth.[46] Some of the new laws were also prophylactic, empowering police to arrest "sex perverts" before they actually did anything. In 1927 California made it a crime to loiter close to public schools and other places where schoolchildren congregated. At Warren's special session, the legisla-ture expanded the law to make it a crime to loiter in or about public toilets in parks.[47]

Third, the new criminal law regime was highly punitive, as figure 3.4 re-veals. The crime against nature carried a potential life sentence in Georgia, Idaho, Nevada, and California (for recidivists) and sixty years in North Carolina. Only nine states had maximum penalties of five years or less for sodomy between consenting adults. The large majority of states had maximum penalties between five and fifteen years in prison. Also, the law occasionally imposed minimum sentences. Although these could be avoided if prosecutors agreed to accept a guilty plea to a lesser charge, the mandatory minimum increased the power of the prosecutor to insist on guilty pleas.[48]

Another innovation was to extend the punishment visited on sex offenders beyond their time in jail. In 1947 the California legislature unanimously passed a law to require convicted sex offenders to register with the police in their home

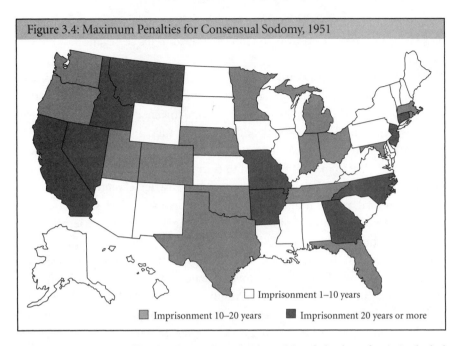

Figure 3.4: Maximum Penalties for Consensual Sodomy, 1951

☐ Imprisonment 1–10 years

▨ Imprisonment 10–20 years   ■ Imprisonment 20 years or more

jurisdictions. State officials objected to the breadth of the law, for it included consensual sodomy and oral copulation defendants. "Congenital homosexuals may often be convicted" under these provisions, which posed no problem, "but very often one party to the act is not abnormal, but merely of low moral character and sometimes the person so involved is only partially responsible because of intoxication." At Warren's suggestion the legislature later extended the registration law to include the thousands of persons (almost all of them homosexual men) convicted of lewd vagrancy, a crime with an infinitely elastic definition. In 1951 and 1952 Congress considered but failed to enact a law imposing national registration on sex offenders.[49]

The main purpose of registration was to create a statewide data bank with information about convicted homosexuals and other sex offenders. In 1950, during Warren's special session, the legislature required local sheriffs to send fingerprints of people arrested for sodomy, oral copulation, lewd vagrancy, and various crimes against minors to the state Bureau of Criminal Investigation. The state bureau shared this and other information with the FBI, which in 1950 was assembling a national data bank of sex offenders and known homosexuals, information that Director Hoover used to pressure officials to cooperate with him and to punish perceived enemies. For example, on August 13, 1963, Senator Strom Thurmond of South Carolina would insert into the *Congressional Record* the Los Angeles County Jail's booking slip for Bayard Rustin's 1953 arrest, a sheet the L.A. police provided the Bureau of Criminal Investigation, which passed it on to the FBI, and which Hoover slipped to his segregationist allies in Congress.[50]

Well before Warren became governor, California had joined New York in making it a crime for a homosexual to ask another man to engage in anal or oral sex in private places such as the home. This misdemeanor was called "disorderly conduct, degeneracy" in New York and "lewd vagrancy" in California. This idea went national after World War II. In 1953 Congress amended the District's indecent exposure law to make it unlawful to commit any "obscene or indecent" exposure, sexual proposal, or act anywhere in the District. Congress intended to ensure criminal prosecution of private homosexual acts or solicitation, by removing the common-law public-place requirement for indecency, lewdness, or lewd solicitation. Other jurisdictions followed Congress's lead, and by 1960 twenty-one states (including Florida, Massachusetts, Michigan, New Jersey, North Carolina, and Ohio) had removed public-place requirements from their lewdness and indecency statutes. As a result, in most of the United States it became a crime not only for same-sex couples to engage in private consensual sodomy but even to propose such conduct at any time or place. [51]

Medicalization of the Crime Against Nature

For decades California led the nation in sterilizing "sex perverts" (chapter 2). In 1941 the state established procedures for *asexualization,* or castration, of "moral or sexual degenerate or pervert" prisoners who were repeat offenders.[52] In light of *Skinner v. Oklahoma* (1942), which invalidated Oklahoma's similar sterilization policy, it is not clear that California could have constitutionally castrated or sterilized anyone, but Earl Warren helped create a more Kafkaesque mechanism: hospitalize and "treat" them. During the Depression police and doctors often worked together in plausibly humane ways. Pauline (Pauli) Murray (1911–1976), a North Carolina civil rights activist, was picked up by police while hitchhiking on a road outside Providence, Rhode Island, on March 1, 1940. Wearing men's clothing and disoriented, Murray told the probation officer she was a homosexual but wanted to change her sex from female to male. The officer took her back to New York City, where the police referred her to Bellevue Hospital. Murray's friend Adelene MacBean arranged for her to be released to a private sanitarium. At no point was Murray arrested—nor had she committed a crime—but the police facilitated medical treatment for gender and sexual deviation that Murray acquiesced in and may have welcomed.[53]

These informal social arrangements were now becoming legally formalized. Before Murray's episode, state legislatures in Michigan (1935), Illinois (1938),

California (1939), and Minnesota (1939) had enacted *sexual psychopath* laws. The pioneering Michigan law established special procedures for identifying people convicted of sex offenses who "appear to be psychopathic, or a sex degenerate" or a "sex pervert," precisely how most doctors would have described Murray (or Rustin). Once identified, such persons could be committed for an indeterminate time in state mental hospitals, until cured. California's law was more moderate, aimed only at defendants predisposed "to the commission of sexual offenses against children." In 1945, however, the legislature removed this requirement, which freed the state to send men convicted of adult homosexual activities to hospitals for indefinite periods of time, based on doctors' testimony that those men were "inverts."[54]

Between 1946 and 1957 twenty-nine states, including all the urbanized jurisdictions outside the South, enacted new sexual psychopath laws or expanded existing ones. The Miller Act created a psychopath statute for the District, which permitted civil commitment without even a criminal charge (the Murray scenario). Although publicly justified by concerns about child molestation, only Florida, Oregon, and South Dakota limited their statutes to sex crimes involving minors. The most common jurisdictional basis was conviction for sodomy, including consensual activities. In California, the District of Columbia, Florida, Illinois, Indiana, Iowa, Michigan, Minnesota, Missouri, Nebraska, New Hampshire, and Washington—almost half the jurisdictions with sexual psychopath laws—simply a *charge* of consensual sodomy or another sex crime could trigger the statutory procedures (the Rustin scenario). In 1949 California's legislature created procedures allowing indefinite detention of "sexual psychopaths." The director of mental hygiene objected that this rule was "the result of hysteria" and was "vicious because under it a person who would ordinarily be sent to prison for a short term can be compelled to remain in prison for the rest of his life." Governor Warren signed the bill into law without hesitation.[55]

In states such as New York and California, most people committed as sexual psychopaths were men having sexual contacts with minors, but this was not true elsewhere. Half of the first hundred sexual psychopaths adjudicated in New Jersey were convicted of adult sodomy, fellatio, and "lewdness," New Jersey's code word for homosexual overtures; one psychopath was a black man committed for following a white woman. Almost a quarter of Indiana's committed psychopaths were men in jail for sodomy or "unnatural" sex with consenting adults. In other states, significant minorities of sexual psychopaths were confirmed homosexuals convicted of the crime against nature.[56]

Few jurisdictions had the facilities required to treat people committed as sexual psychopaths, and the treatment at the existing facilities could be inhuman.

The most infamous of the treatment institutions was California's Atascadero State Hospital, a thousand-bed facility authorized by Governor Warren three weeks after Linda Glucoft's murder and opened in 1954. About sixty percent of its population was sex offenders, including some convicted of consensual adult sodomy or oral copulation. Inmates of all sorts were subjected to experimental therapies, including lobotomies, electrical and pharmacological shock therapy, and castration. The lobotomies, explained an Atascadero doctor, helped the patients lose "their fear and hate and become noticeably friendly." According to homosexual alumni, one treatment at Atascadero was aversion therapy: a muscle relaxant rendered the patient temporarily unable to breathe, which made him feel as if he were suffocating, a terrifying experience. In Ohio's Lima State Hospital, homosexual "psychopaths" were dosed with trancypromine, a potentially lethal antidepressant.[57]

Mass Implementation of Sodomy and Homosexual Solicitation Laws

Where same-sex intimacy did not involve force or a minor, the state was usually the complainant and had to flush out the homosexual from the shadows. The mechanisms for such aggressive enforcement had been developed in New York and California during the Comstock era: (1) police stakeouts of homosexual hangouts, which was the best way to obtain evidence of oral sex and indecent exposure; (2) decoy or sting operations, whereby an undercover officer would loiter in a homosexual cruising area, attracting sexual solicitations from other men; and (3) police raids, which netted large numbers of socializing homosexuals and charged them with disorderly conduct, cross-dressing, and other minor offenses. The period after 1935 did much to regularize, popularize, and modernize such tactics.[58]

Regularization came in most cities through the creation of police department vice or morals squads. Vice squads consisted of officers exclusively devoted to ferreting out sex and drug crimes, and (judging from annual police reports) their productivity was measured by the number of prostitutes, sexual perverts, and drug dealers they arrested. After 1946 their attention increasingly focused on homosexuals. In an extreme example, sodomy or solicitation of sodomy generated almost sixty percent of the arrests by Philadelphia's morals squad in 1949, its first year of operation, and in 1950 the squad was hauling two hundred homosexuals into court each month. Given public anxiety about sex crimes, Philadelphia's and other vice squads were able to increase their jurisdiction and their budgets. Higher budgets alone could create a "boom" in sex crimes, because they could finance more decoys and tearoom spies.[59]

These new vice squads developed tactics more invasive than police had used before the war. Decoy cops reportedly made advances on shy homosexuals, sometimes forcing themselves on their prey until they uttered the magic words that could constitute solicitation. Spying on homosexuals often meant spending hours perched above public toilets, peeking into parked cars, and trailing suspects. In one case, San Diego vice agents observed Eldridge Rhodes, a black man reputed to proposition sailors, walking with Thomas Earl, a white man. The police followed the pair to a hotel room. One officer allegedly saw the two naked men embrace by peeking through a door crack and then observed them engage in oral sex by peering through the glass transom over the door. The intrepid agents broke through the door and arrested the startled sex felons. Unlike other (same-race) defendants, they did not get the benefit of a reduced charge (lewd vagrancy) and, as sexual psychopaths, they were sent to Atascadero for an indefinite time.[60]

Most remarkably, raids carried out by police departments in many cities resulted in wholesale arrests of gender and sexual deviants, including unprecedented numbers of women. The homophile press of the period reported a 1955 raid on the Pepper Hill Club in Baltimore, which led to 162 arrests for disorderly conduct, based on observations of same-sex hugging and kissing; a 1956 raid on Hazel's Bar near Redwood City, California, that yielded ninety arrests (including ten women) on lewd vagrancy charges; a 1957 raid on Jimmie's Tavern in Tampa, Florida, where twelve women were arrested for their "mannish" dress; a series of raids by Philadelphia police in 1959 seizing dozens of men and women from the Hummoresque Coffeehouse and other cafés; a 1960 raid on the Tay-Bush Café in San Francisco, which resulted in 103 arrests (fourteen women) for same-sex dancing, under the charge of disorderly conduct; and a 1962 raid of the Yuga drag ball in Jefferson County, Louisiana, which netted ninety-six.[61]

Antivice campaigns yielded an unprecedented number of arrests of homosexuals between 1946 and 1961. In New York sodomy arrests had averaged 130 in the 1930s, but increased to an average of more than 200 per year after the war. Arraignments for degeneracy (homosexual solicitation), which averaged 570 per year in the 1930s, averaged 2,850 in the last five years of the 1940s and fell back to an annual average of 1,560 in the 1950s. Los Angeles saw arrests for sex perversion and sodomy increase from forty persons in 1940 to 483 in 1948 (the only data available for the 1940s). Lewd vagrancy (homosexual solicitation) arrests went up from 166 to 1,555 in the same period. Other cities saw much lower overall numbers but similar trends: sodomy and solicitation arrest figures exponentially higher than before World War II.[62]

For the country as a whole, there were some two to three thousand arrests per year for sodomy between 1946 and 1961. Exact data is available for eight cities (including New York and Los Angeles, the biggest enforcers), which cumulatively generated an average of almost a thousand arrests each year. With one thousand arrests as the baseline, there were at least as many and perhaps twice that number in other parts of the United States, including (1) big centers of antihomosexual police campaigns, which did not include specific sodomy numbers in their police reports (namely, Atlanta, Chicago, Cincinnati, Detroit, Miami, New Orleans, Pittsburgh, Portland, San Diego, St. Louis, and Seattle); (2) dozens of medium-size or small cities with known antihomosexual campaigns (such as Boise and Tampa); and (3) hundreds of jurisdictions that arrested only a handful of sodomites each year. There were more jurisdictions like this than anyone would have imagined. For example, none of the South Carolina cities had visible gay communities or mounted antihomosexual campaigns, but the state attorney general reported an average of ten arrests per year for the crime against nature in the state for the period 1946–1961.[63]

Most of the two to three thousand arrests were for sex between an adult male and a minor; some were for forcible male-female sex. Based on direct evidence from New York City and the District of Columbia, a reasonable estimate is that thirty to forty-five percent of the arrests were for consensual same-sex adult intimacy. Hence, between 600 (thirty percent of 2,000) and 1,350 (forty-five percent of 3,000) Americans, on average, were arrested each year for oral or anal sex with a consenting adult. While some sodomy defendants went to jail or a mental hospital for several years, most were able to plea-bargain to a lesser offense, and white first-time offenders usually suffered no jail time.[64]

Many more male homosexuals were apprehended for committing misdemeanors, such as homosexual solicitation, indecent exposure, and loitering at a public restroom. Lesbians were arrested in much smaller numbers for cross-dressing, indecent exposure, and disorderly conduct. In New York and Los Angeles, the ratio of arrests for lesser (homosexual) crimes to arrests for sodomy was quite large, more than twenty to one.[65] But most cities did not devote as many resources to this area as New York and Los Angeles, nor was toilet loitering considered a crime elsewhere. A conservative estimate is that, for the country as a whole, misdemeanor arrests were ten to fifteen times the number of sodomy arrests in this period. Given a multiplier of ten to fifteen, an educated guess is that between 6,600 (600 times ten, plus 600) and 21,600 (1,350 times fifteen, plus 1,350) people, mostly men, were arrested each year (1946–61) for nonconforming gender or sexual behavior that inflicted no tangible harm on other persons.

Given that these assumptions are conservative, the actual arrest figures were probably higher.

Additionally the police accosted or detained tens of thousands more homosexuals without arresting them. Narrative accounts of gay and, especially, lesbian lives during this period suggest that police harassment, detention, and brutality were more common than arrests for sodomy or solicitation. Because they were empowered to arrest lesbians, police officers felt completely free to bully them, and not a few used that power to coerce them into having sex with them in return for not arresting them or their dates. Leslie Feinberg's *Stone Butch Blues* recounts the particular cruelty law enforcement personnel visited on bulldyke (butch) lesbians, who usurped the male sexual role as well as gender attitude and attire. Although the large majority of lesbian and gay encounters with the police were not this harsh, tens of thousands of gay people had some manner of frightening encounter with the police each year during the half-generation after World War II.[66]

Exposing and Erasing the Homosexual, 1946–61

Rose Levinson (born 1933) grew up in New York City, where forty percent of Jewish Americans lived during World War II. After the war, thousands of Jewish families migrated each year to southern Florida. Levinson did so in 1950 to enter the University of Miami, where she met her second serious girlfriend, Laura. They were a classic "butch-femme" couple: when they went to lesbian bars, Rose combed her short brown hair back into a "duck's ass" and wore trousers, while Laura wore blouses and skirts. Early in 1951 the two women visited the Pan American, a downtown Miami club, entering it shortly after the Miami police had occupied it. Although they had done nothing but walk into a homosexual hangout, the young women were arrested for vagrancy, but they were released after several hours at the jailhouse.[67]

This experience taught Levinson that the modern regulatory state had trained its eyes on homosexuals, who therefore had to be careful about how they conducted their lives. As Levinson would learn when she went to law school, also at the University of Miami, police harassment and arrests were just the most visible feature of the official campaign against homosexuality. The Truman and Eisenhower administrations were the stepchildren of the New Deal, and both presidents supported a campaign to purge the federal government and the armed forces of known homosexuals, to keep homosexuals and sex perverts out of the country, and to censor any written or visual material portraying homosexuality in a positive or humane light. Every level of American government dedicated some regulatory resources to the antihomosexual Kulturkampf, a loosely coordinated effort to cleanse America's public culture of homosexuality and to contain confirmed homosexuals to the margins or closets.

The Federal Kulturkampf: Preserving the Purity of the Civil Service, the Military, the U.S. Mail, and the Nation's Borders

When Rose Levinson graduated from law school, in 1954, her employment options were much more limited than those of other graduates. Few law firms in southern Florida would hire Jewish attorneys; fewer still would hire females. Many talented women worked for the federal government, but Levinson knew that for her this was a risky option, given her sexual orientation. The postwar period saw the federal government not only create a heterosexuality requirement for civil service and military employment, but enforce that requirement through intrusive investigative techniques.

In testimony before a Senate subcommittee in 1947, Secretary of State George Marshall was admonished for "the extensive employment in highly classified positions, of admitted homosexuals, who are historically known to be security risks." Republican senator Kenneth Wherry of Nebraska accused the Truman administration of running a government crawling with subversives and sex perverts. President Truman adopted a loyalty security program to weed out Communists and also started looking for homosexuals in earnest. Between January 1947 and April 1950, the administration investigated 192 cases of "sex perversion" in civil government, and most of the targets were discharged or resigned. During the same period, 3,245 personnel were separated from the military— triple the discharge rate during World War II. In 1949 the Defense Department announced a firmer policy of excluding all "known homosexuals" from the military.[68]

When the D.C. vice squad told the Senate in 1950 that there were five thousand homosexuals still working for the government, Senator Wherry called for a full-fledged investigation, asking "Can [you] think of a person who could be more dangerous to the United States of America than a pervert?" There followed a steady stream of bipartisan rhetoric associating homosexuality with Communism: both were secretive, worldwide coalitions of aliens scheming to destroy America and undermine family values. "It is a known fact," proclaimed Representative Miller, "that homosexuality goes back to the Orientals [i.e., Communist China]; that the Russians are strong believers in homosexuality." Coming from the opposite direction, two journalists argued, "Communism actively promotes and supports sex deviation to sap the strength of the new generation and make the birth of another problematical."[69]

Over the next seven months, the Truman administration stepped up its efforts, investigating 382 civil servants (most of whom resigned), and the Senate authorized the Hoey Committee investigation described above. Consistent with the Hoey Committee's approach, the Civil Service Commission had secretly interpreted its regulation barring from federal employment people who engage in "immoral conduct" to include "homosexuality and other types of sex perversion" as "sufficient grounds for denying appointment to a Government position or for the removal of a person from the Federal service." To enforce this policy, the commission began checking the fingerprints of job applicants against FBI files of arrests across the country. Between 1947 and 1950 the agency denied government employment to 1,700 applicants because they had "a record of homosexuality or other sex perversion." In 1951 the State Department fired 119 employees for homosexuality, and only 35 as other security risks (Communists); the figures were 134 and 70, respectively, in 1952.[70]

A similar cleansing occurred within the armed forces. Implementing the 1949 directive, the Army instructed enlisted men to report anything concerning "overt acts of homosexuality," and officers were to investigate such reports "thoroughly and comprehensively." The armed forces engaged in periodic witch hunts, the most effective way to uncover lesbianism. The Office of Special Investigation identified and expelled eleven lesbians at Kessler Air Force Base in Biloxi, Mississippi, by pressuring women to name other lesbians in order to avoid incarceration themselves. Investigators exposed twenty suspected lesbians at Lackland Air Force Base and several more at Wright-Patterson. Hundreds, perhaps thousands, of female soldiers were asked, "Have you ever thought of making love to a woman?" Between 1950 and 1965, the armed forces separated between two thousand and five thousand persons as suspected homosexuals; the rate of discharge was much higher for women than for men.[71]

At the same time that Senator Hoey's committee was studying ways to purge homosexuals within the government, Senator Patrick McCarran's Judiciary Committee was drafting a law to keep them from entering the country. McCarran's comprehensive redraft of the immigration law focused on excluding Communists, anarchists, and other subversives. Reflecting fears that homosexuals were subversive, the bill also excluded all "persons afflicted with psychopathic personality, or who are homosexuals or sex perverts." (As a Nevada judge, McCarran had authored one of the earliest judicial opinions including oral sex in the crime against nature.) Upon the assurance of the Public Health Service that the term "psychopathic personality" was broad enough to "specify such types of pathologic behavior as homosexuality or sexual perversion," the Senate as well as the House judiciary committees settled for an exclusion simply of "persons afflicted with psychopathic personality," which was the exclusion finally enacted as section 212(a)(4) of the McCarran-Walter Act of 1952.[72]

The Eisenhower administration was even more antihomosexual than its predecessor. In April 1953 Eisenhower issued Executive Order 10,450, which officially added "sexual perversion" as a grounds for investigation and dismissal under the federal loyalty-security program. In the next two years more than eight hundred federal employees resigned or were terminated because they had files indicating "sex perversion," which typically meant charges—but not convictions—of loitering, solicitation, or disorderly conduct. Although the rate of such expulsions abated in the late 1950s, the Eisenhower administration continued its industrial security program, which denied security clearances to private as well as public employees who engaged in "immoral" conduct or "sex perversion." The historian David Johnson estimates that five thousand suspected homosexuals lost their civil service jobs in the first decade of the Cold War—thousands more than were released because of Communist affiliations. The McCarthy era's official enemy was Communism, but its everyday fodder was the homosexual.[73]

Moreover, the Eisenhower administration initiated an episodic campaign to disrupt any kind of homosexual politics or press. Although the earliest homophile organizations were completely law-abiding, the FBI infiltrated them, recorded their internal discussions and activities, and occasionally harassed them. Prodded by Senator Alexander Wiley, Joseph McCarthy's Wisconsin colleague, the Post Office reviewed each issue of *One, Inc.* (the earliest mass-mailed homophile publication) and refused to carry the October 1954 issue because an advertisement, a lesbian-friendly short story, and a poem about homosexual cruising were deemed lewd and obscene under the Comstock Act. The November 1955 issue intimated that the FBI was filled with "Tory" homosexuals. Hoover and Tolson personally directed FBI agents to confront the journal, to identify and expose homosexuals associated with it, and to coordinate their activities with postal authorities and prosecutors.[74]

The California Kulturkampf: Protecting the Purity of Schools and Licenses

The federal purge of this period also stimulated analogous state witch hunts. Under Governor Warren and his successor, California's policy was to cleanse public education and the professions of homosexuality, and to close down the most visible site of homosexual community, the lesbian or gay bar. Following the Warren approach, Rose Levinson's Florida showed how witch-hunting state governments could inflict more terror on the average homosexual than the federal government.

Public Education. In an attempt to guard children's fragile sexuality, public education was monitored more carefully. Under California law, a person who engaged in "immoral conduct" (including sodomy and oral copulation) could not be a public school teacher. To give this rule greater enforcement bite, the legislature in 1951 adopted Warren's proposal to require law enforcement officers to notify the state and local education departments of the arrest of any public school teacher for a sex crime. The following year, the legislature directed the state board of education to deny or withdraw teaching certificates for any person convicted of sodomy, oral copulation, lewd vagrancy, or various crimes against children. School districts were prohibited from employing anyone guilty of those offenses. Hundreds of gay men resigned or were fired after minor scrapes with law enforcement.[75]

Florida saw an even more vigorous campaign to purify public education. In 1957, Hillsborough County (Tampa) commenced an investigation of homosexuality in the public schools. After staking out lesbian bars, pressuring informants to identify suspected homosexuals, and conducting a trip to Anna Maria Island to spy on lesbian activities, the sheriff by the end of the year had discovered almost sixty admitted or confirmed homosexual teachers, most of whom resigned their posts. Inspired by this and other local investigations, the Johns Committee engaged in a six-year campaign to remove homosexuals from state schools (1958–64). The campaign identified suspected homosexuals who were high school teachers, college students, and university professors. Most of the suspected homosexuals resigned or were dismissed. The committee also pressured the state board of education to revoke teachers' certificates, which the legislature seconded with a 1959 statute authorizing certificate revocation for "moral misconduct" and a 1961 statute setting forth expedited procedures for revocation. Near the end of its tenure, the Johns Committee announced that the board had revoked seventy-one teachers' certificates (with sixty-three more cases pending); fourteen professors had been removed from the state universities (nineteen pending); and thirty-seven federal employees had lost their jobs, while fourteen state employees faced removal in pending cases.[76]

In 1958 the Johns Committee investigated reports that both the president and the dean of students at the University of Florida were practicing homosexuals. The two officials resigned, and the committee's investigator turned up extensive evidence of homosexuality among students as well as faculty. Suspects were placed under oath and pressed to identify other homosexuals; almost all of them cooperated. Sixteen students were suspended or withdrew from the university, and twenty-five were placed on probation because of the committee's revelations. Smaller-scale investigations occurred at Florida State, Florida A&M, and the University of South Florida. Hundreds of students dropped out or transferred because of pressure from school administrators. After the Depression, institutions of higher education became the front line of the national campaign to suppress homosexuality. Bayard Rustin had been compelled to leave college because of his affair with another man. Pauli Murray feared expulsion from the Howard Law School in 1943 when her affair with a female undergraduate was exposed.[77]

Professional Licenses. Like teachers, other professionals could not ply their trades without state licenses, and most states had prohibitions authorizing regulators to deny or revoke licenses of people exposed as homosexual sodomites. In California, as in other states, "gross immorality" was a statutory basis for professional disciplinary action against doctors, dentists, pharmacists, embalmers, and guardians. The most common basis for revoking a professional license in most states, conviction of a "crime involving moral turpitude," reached dozens of occupations in California. Because these crimes were a matter of public record, which the state police supplied to relevant agencies, homosexual professionals sometimes saw their licenses challenged or withdrawn.[78]

Florida had a regulatory regime similar to California's, and the Johns Committee supplied licensing agencies with information about the sexual orientation and activities of professionals within the state. A number of doctors and not a few lawyers lost their licenses. In 1956 Rose Levinson was arrested on vagrancy charges in Miami Beach with a (straight) girlfriend. Although the charges were dismissed, the FBI brought her in for questioning when she applied for membership in the Florida Bar Association. "After they got over their initial embarrassment, they had the nerve to ask the big L question, 'Are you a lesbian?' Of course, I was 'shocked' that they had asked such a thing." Levinson became a member of the bar association but curtailed her social life, avoiding lesbian or even mixed (gay and straight) bars and social scenes.[79]

Liquor Licenses. The end of Prohibition meant a new beginning for state regulation of liquor sales. California's alcoholic beverage control (ABC) law allowed regulators to revoke a premise's liquor license if it was "contrary to public welfare and morals." Following the practices developed in New York and New Jersey before the war, the Warren-era ABC Department invested significant resources in campaigns to identify and discipline bars serving lesbians, gay men, and female prostitutes. The most celebrated investigations involved Sol Stoumen's Black Cat Bar, a gay mecca near North Beach in San Francisco. Its first license revocation case grew out of an investigation in 1949, in which undercover agents witnessed same-sex dancing, hand holding, and affection on the premises. After the courts overturned the revocation for its tenuous relationship to public morality, the California legislature in 1955 amended the law to require license revocation for any premises permitted to become a "resort for illegal possessors or users of narcotics, prostitutes, pimps, panderers, or sexual perverts"; the law directed the liquor authorities to consider as evidence "the general reputation" of the premises. On the basis of the new law and evidence of homosexual kisses and caresses, as well as lewd propositions made by patrons to undercover investigators, the ABC Department revoked the Black Cat's license again in 1957 (but once again the courts intervened to thwart it). At the same time, the department was seeking to close dozens of other bars, including Pearl Kershaw's Oakland bar, which lost its license because investigators spotted women dancing with women, two men displaying wedding rings, and same-sex fondling.[80]

Michigan, New Jersey, New York, Texas, and Virginia adopted similarly explicit policies denying liquor licenses to clubs and bars catering to homosexuals or prostitutes, and New York's State Liquor Agency (SLA) implemented its policy with aggressive undercover work similar to that in California.[81] Most respectable people supported these policies as a way to prevent the coalescing of social networks before they could seduce young people and contaminate local neighborhoods. Middle America also approved of the notion that the state should disrupt and terrorize such social spaces. Unlike the revocation of professional licenses, which was episodic even in the most aggressive states, major resources were invested in campaigns to shut down homosexual bars. In 1960 the SLA closed thirty gay bars in New York City, and the ABC Department did the same to twenty-four bars in San Francisco the following year. The Black Cat lost its final appeal in 1963. But, like the hydra, every bar that closed spawned two more to take its place.[82]

The Miami Kulturkampf: Protecting the Purity of Public Spaces

Although the twentieth century witnessed steady expansions of national jurisdiction, most Americans' interactions with government still came at the local level. Federal and state Kulturkampfs remained for many people abstractions, with no direct effect on their lives. Unfortunately for Rose Levinson, however, when she showed up in Miami in 1950, the city was on the verge of conducting its own Kulturkampf.

The conditions for antihomosexual backlash mirrored those of the country as a whole: young veterans and their families were seeking reassurance of the purity of public spaces in the wake of a large demographic shift, as sleepy WASP Dade County began to make room for Jews, African Americans, and Cubans. In 1950 Florida voters rejected cosmopolitan senator Claude Pepper (1939–51) in favor of George Smathers (1951–69), who stood for strict containment of Communism, racial mixing, and sexual freedom. Like California under Earl Warren, Miami introduced a steady stream of antihomosexual laws and stepped-up but highly politicized enforcement.[83]

In 1952 Councilmember Bernard Frank, inveighing against "degenerate bars and hangouts," called on Police Chief Walter Headley to remove all "sex degenerates and female impersonators" from the city. Although his Miami Beach counterpart had already conducted an antihomosexual campaign, Headley was hesitant. "If I ran all the homosexuals out of town," he observed, "members of some of the best families would lead the parade." Miami newspapers, meanwhile, went on the attack. "Is Greater Miami in Danger of Becoming a Favorite Spot for Homosexuals and Sexual Psychopaths?" asked the *Herald*. Mayor Abe Aronovitz declared war on public homosexuality. Over the next two years Aronovitz procured ordinances making it a municipal crime for homosexuals to congregate or be served alcohol in a licensed business, to cross-dress, or to commit "any indecent or lewd act" that could be seen by another person (such as an undercover policeman).[84]

The antihomosexual "Miami Hurricane" reached full force in August 1954. In the course of one night the Miami Beach police swept the beach, arresting men, essentially for feminine dress and behavior, while Dade County sheriff Tom Kelly raided eleven Miami and Miami Beach bars, arresting nineteen patrons, including one "fighting barmaid" charged with striking a deputy. The following month, Acting Governor Charley Johns (before he became the chair of the famous Johns Committee) appointed a state boxing commissioner to "coordinate the Miami campaign against perverts." By the end of the year, every Miami gay bar was out of business. The Hurricane then turned on Kelly, who in the 1956 sheriff's race was accused of racial mixing and homosexual activities. Observed one wag, "It does go to show how hard it is to tell the witches from the witch hunters."[85]

In 1960 police stumbled upon evidence of a network of call boys, pornographers, and wealthy Dade County patrons. Working with the state police, the ABC agency, and the Johns Committee, Sheriff Kelly gathered the names of 150 young men involved in these "homosexual rings," several of the adult ringleaders, local consumers as well as manufacturers of child pornography, and 13,000 names on a worldwide mailing list. Rather than breaking the back of what appeared to be a genuine menace, Headley and Kelly continued to focus enforcement resources on bar raids and entrapping lonely men into soliciting police undercovers. As those investigations petered out, Rose Levinson found her niche in the law—representing those lonely hunters. For most of her clients, judges eagerly accepted assurances that they would seek psychiatric counseling and dismissed charges. Clients who got caught repeatedly, or who had sex with minors, often went to jail, though usually not for long.[86]

The Miami Hurricane was unusually dramatic, but most of the nation's major cities (New York, San Francisco, Philadelphia, Washington, Los Angeles, Atlanta, Seattle, Boston) and many minor ones (like Boise and Tampa) engaged in some version of such antihomosexual policies. (A possible exception was Chicago, where the police often left gay institutions alone, in return for regular bribes.) Combined with the federal and state campaigns, these local efforts aimed at complete erasure of homosexuals and their institutions from public culture. The goal of such disparate figures as Earl Warren, J. Edgar Hoover, Kenneth Wherry, and Charley Johns was to reassure American families that they were secure from danger, and their children safe from sexual pollution. Gay individuals like Bayard Rustin and Rose Levinson were prohibited from engaging in sexual activities with persons of the same sex, from publicly soliciting other homosexuals, from hanging out with them in identifiably lesbian and gay bars, from teaching in public schools or universities, from serving in the armed forces or the civil service, and from publishing homosexual propaganda.

On paper this regime of antihomosexual laws, regulations, and police practices eerily recalled the virtually identical antihomosexual rules of Nazi Germany under Chancellor Adolf Hitler. There were even American analogs to concentration camps: California's Atascadero was popularly known as the "Dachau for Queers," notorious today for its human medical experimentation. In practice, however, America's antihomosexual Kulturkampf was aimed at exposure, not extinction, of homosexuals. Ironically, though the witch hunts sought to erase homosexuality from public life, the campaign's legal mechanisms ultimately created greater visibility.[87]

In 1955 the Delaware Port Authority proposed to name a new Delaware River bridge connecting Philadelphia and Camden, New Jersey, the Walt Whitman Bridge. In December the Camden diocese of the Roman Catholic Church publicly opposed this plan: Whitman's "life and works are personally objectionable to us," it declared, because he was a "homo-erotic" sodomite. For the next year the authority was inundated with letters opposing (and some supporting) the naming. While most of the opposition was conveyed in code, referring to the "Godless and selfish" features of Whitman's "destructive egotism," much of it was openly homophobic: "Whitman's major works exhibit a revolting homosexual imagery that is not confined to a few isolated passages but permeates the fetid whole."[88] The naming went ahead despite the campaign. To this day, Philadelphia, the City of Brotherly Love, and Camden, Whitman's final home, are connected by the Walt Whitman Bridge.

CHAPTER FOUR

The Case(s) Against
Sodomy Laws, 1935–61

Constructed of beige limestone mined from nearby quarries, the buildings of the University of Indiana at Bloomington form a physical campus that is handsome, solid, and uniform in style, a campus where generations of midwesterners have received a serious, practical education. On April Fools' Day 1935, the world's leading authority on the gall wasp, Professor Alfred C. Kinsey (1894–1956), presented a discussion paper on "Biological Aspects of Some Social Problems" to the Indiana University faculty. Most of the paper was as bland as its title, a summary of recent primate studies and other scholarship bearing on the biology of human sexuality. But it closed with a dramatic challenge.

Alfred Kinsey

Social prejudices and religious taboos about human sexuality, Kinsey maintained, had had devastating effects on millions of people. "The currently accepted list of sex perversions are, almost without exception, rooted in primate behavior and, in that sense, natural; if divorced from their present-day social reactions, most of them would have little effect on the security of the home or the propagation of the race." The laws of a modern society ought not be based on such superstitions, the entomologist argued. Ignorance about sexual realities and frustration of natural sexual instincts caused "most of the social problems and the sexual conflicts of youth." Tackling these real social problems and contributing to genuine social utility required jettisoning religion as a source of guidance and turning instead to science.[1]

Although he was born in Hoboken, New Jersey, and educated at Bowdoin and Harvard, Alfred Kinsey's lifelong Indiana University appointment made him a citizen of the Midwest. He certainly looked the part. A fine aquiline nose connected his thin, tightly pursed lips to a broad forehead, topped by bushy hair, parted in the middle. Careless about clothes, Kinsey favored bow ties and un-pressed tweed jackets. Intense gray-green eyes seethed with barely suppressed impatience—an impatience that now had him ready to abandon his landmark entomological work and tackle the great topic of the century, sexuality. Kinsey aimed to persuade America that the prescriptions of the "Social Problems" paper were valid and should serve as the basis for law reform.

His campaign started in Bloomington, where, in the summer of 1938, Kinsey offered an elective course on marriage. His opening lecture analyzed human sexuality from a social and propagation-of-the-species point of view. The biggest problem, he told the students, was shame-based ignorance and religion-based taboos about natural sexual activities. This was the course's normative point, but most of the lectures were descriptive—detailed scientific analyses of the biology of reproduction, the mechanics of coition and birth control, and "individual variation," the subject of Kinsey's last lecture. "[N]o two individuals are alike" in their sexual tastes and preferred practices, he argued. Although people were ashamed of engaging in acts they had been told were "abnormal," Kinsey urged students to consider that most such practices were more common than moralists were willing to admit and that everyone enjoyed some activities that most others did not. The criterion ought not be "normal," but "functional": Does an activity undermine the purposes of sexual activities—namely, reproduction, pleasure, and sociability? Given those goals, "there are only three kinds of sexual abnor-malities: abstinence, celibacy, and delayed marriage. Think about this," Kinsey told the students.[2]

What probably shocked some of them, and most of the townspeople in Bloomington, was Professor Kinsey's assumption that sexual variation is benign and that there is nothing wrong with pursuing sex for pleasure. Although Walt Whitman and Sigmund Freud had introduced Americans to these ideas, they had done so through metaphor and poetic generalization, while Kinsey issued blunt declarations and then backed them up with massive support from human case studies and comparative zoology. The entire country eventually learned about the idea of benign sexual variation when Kinsey published his ground-breaking reports, *Sexual Behavior in the Human Male* (1948) and *Sexual Behavior in the Human Female* (1953). In them he challenged all the cultural foundations for the crime against nature: disgust at nonprocreative or nonmarital sex; the idea of nonconforming sexuality as impure and socially polluting; and identity grounded on rigid lines and roles. The professor was certain that Americans would abandon these superstitions once they considered the scientific evidence he had assembled to show that enormous human sexual variation is natural, that sexual expression is necessary and liberating for the individual and healthy for society, and that categorization of sexual behaviors or identities is arbitrary and socially wasteful.

Kinsey adamantly opposed consensual sodomy laws, the first public figure in American history to take an unequivocal position against them. His main criticism reflected his liberal morality: sexual conformity imposed by social or legal coercion is highly destructive and ought to be resisted. The philosophical basis for this liberal objection had deep roots in English jurisprudence and had a receptive audience among the American legal academics who proposed the Model Penal Code, the great criminal-law-reform document of the century. These academics were even more impressed with pragmatic objections to consensual sodomy laws that Kinsey also documented. When it adopted the Model Penal Code in 1961, Illinois became the first state in American history to repeal its consensual sodomy law.

The scientists and lawyers who were involved in sodomy reform in the 1940s and 1950s were all married with children. But some were homosexual or bisexual—including the good Dr. Kinsey, who befriended and bedded dozens of men in the course of his career as a sex researcher. His firsthand knowledge of the frustrations and terror that the law visited on homosexuals fueled his lifelong crusade against sodomy laws. Other Americans, cast out of their closets by the sexuality police of the McCarthy era, spoke as open homosexuals. Going beyond Kinsey's libertarian and practical arguments, early homophile activists argued that homosexuals were a minority group that had been deprived of its civil rights by the prejudiced majority. They accepted Kinsey's liberal and pragmatic arguments but added a third point: consensual sodomy is actually joyful and good; it ought to be celebrated and not just decriminalized.

The Benthamite (Liberal and Practical) Case Against Sodomy Laws

Many theorists maintain that the criminal law should be expressive, condemning activities that are "immoral." Rejecting expressive theories, especially natural-law ones, the British philosopher Jeremy Bentham (1748–1832) maintained that the goal of law is to establish regulations that improve overall social utility, the "greatest good for the greatest number." In "On Paederasty," an unpublished essay written in 1785, Bentham criticized consensual sodomy laws for undermining social utility. Although British intellectuals made Benthamite arguments against consensual sodomy laws throughout the twentieth century, Alfred Kinsey was the first to advance them in the United States.[3]

"On Paederasty"

William Blackstone's *Commentaries on the Laws of England* (1765) reflected the expressive approach. For Blackstone, judges were the main agents of the law, discovering it from precedent, or from previous articulations reflecting the fundamental values and practices of England. One of the fundamental laws of England was the buggery statute, which applied the death sentence to a "crime not fit to be named." Contrary to Blackstone, Jeremy Bentham's *Theory of Legislation* (1821) argued that law ought to be regulatory, not expressive. Hence, offenses against taste were presumptively not within the state's authority.[4]

Bentham applied this utilitarian philosophy to crime-against-nature laws in his essay "On Paederasty."[5] He argued that England's buggery statute did not contribute to overall social utility and therefore should be repealed. He offered two primary reasons, one liberal and one practical. However distasteful sodomy might be to the majorty of Englishmen, some did derive great pleasure from this activity, so the social cost of sodomy laws was substantial. Was there a corresponding social benefit? Bentham thought not. Historical experience was inconsistent with prior claims that sodomy debilitated persons who committed it, undermined marriage and led to depopulation, or harmed women. As a matter of fact, the reason for sodomy laws was "antipathy," the disgust and prejudice many people had for those practicing the crime against nature. Invoking the Spanish Inquisition's persecution of Jews and Moors, Bentham argued that laws based on antipathy epitomized tyranny. John Stuart Mill's *On Liberty* (1859) applied Bentham's premises to support the modern libertarian argument that the state should leave people alone unless they are harming others. The libertarian presumption suggests that sodomy between consenting adults in private places should not be a crime, but sodomy without consent (including with minors) or in public places should be regulated.[6]

"On Paederasty" offered a second set of reasons why crime-against-nature laws were in derogation of overall social utility. While Bentham's liberal reasons examined the direct effect of such laws, his practical ones examined their indirect effect. The ease of charging an enemy with sodomy and the high stakes of such charges created terrible risks of "false and malicious prosecutions," as well as extortion by sexual partners, bystanders, or the police. Moreover, such laws reinforced social prejudices against persons who should, at worst, be pitied. In subsequent notes not incorporated into the essay, Bentham also suggested that crime-against-nature laws disrupted genuine "bonds of attachment" between men that were often a positive social good.[7]

These were remarkable arguments in 1785, when the crime against nature was still officially unmentionable—and a capital offense. In his notes Bentham sadly concluded that this was not a topic susceptible to public reason. Anyone who would apply a dispassionate analysis to the subject would stand accused: "Miscreant! You are one of them then." Accordingly, he did not publish "On Paederasty" and it was unknown for almost two hundred years, until Louis Crompton published it in 1978.[8]

It took another century for Bentham-like arguments against sodomy laws to find other advocates in English-speaking countries. The British sexologist Havelock Ellis and the classicist John Addington Symonds concluded from their study of sexual inversion that many people found great pleasure in consensual sodomy, that the main effect of crime-against-nature laws was to encourage blackmail by private parties or policemen, and that such laws had no effect on the incidence of homosexuality. (The last point was an innovation, as Bentham had no conception of homosexuality as a sexual orientation.) In the 1915 edition of *Sexual Inversion*, Ellis proposed that "if two persons of either or both sexes, having reached years of discretion, privately consent to practise some perverted mode of sexual relationship, the law cannot be called upon to interfere. It should be the function of the law in this matter to prevent violence, to protect the young, and to preserve public order and decency"—and nothing else. Consensual sodomy laws should be repealed.[9] In European presses, homosexuals such as Edward Stevenson (writing under a pseudonym) and Magnus Hirschfeld made the same liberal and practical arguments for sodomy deregulation.[10]

American Intellectuals (Indirectly) Supporting Bentham's Arguments, 1935–39

Before World War II no American public intellectual or political leader endorsed these Benthamite arguments against consensual sodomy laws. Anthropologists raised some doubts, however, that classifying nonprocreative sex as a "crime against nature" reflected a universal human moral "truth." Ruth Benedict demonstrated in *Patterns of Culture* (1934) that sexual behaviors or gender roles that were considered deviant in one society, such as homosexuality or cross-dressing in America, might be accepted or even valued in others, as with the *berdache* (an intermediate sex) tradition in Native American tribal cultures. Margaret Mead's *Sex and Temperament in Three Primitive Societies* (1935) suggested that our obsession with the distinction between masculine and feminine traits and roles was idiosyncratic to Western culture and that "homosexuality" was not an organizing category that had universal applicability. Activities (like sodomy) that were harshly penalized in the United States were either tolerated or just mildly discouraged elsewhere in the world.[11]

Benedict and Mead were outspoken critics of rigid gender roles and privately agreed with Ellis's brief against New York's consensual sodomy law—a law that both women had repeatedly violated, with each other and with other women as well as with men (including their husbands). Yet neither spoke out directly against such laws. Like Bentham 150 years before, they were afraid of being stigmatized as homosexuals themselves, especially as the backlash was gathering power in the 1930s. Even tony Columbia University was not immune. One of their mutual friends (involved in a messy divorce) threatened to expose Benedict as a lesbian, and by implication Mead as well, in the summer of 1939. Although the situation was resolved, both women drew from the episode a lesson about the fragility of their professional standing, and they subsequently took a less provocative stand in their published work.[12]

As women in a male-dominated profession who were breaching social norms and violating the law, Benedict and Mead were unusually vulnerable. Male scientists were no more outspoken, however. In a 1937 symposium Dr. Karl Bowman of Bellevue Hospital in New York invoked sexologists like Ellis and anthropologists like Mead to conclude that "there is no general agreement as to what constitutes normal sex behavior" and to question the repressive attitude of our culture. "Homosexuality" itself was not a stable category. Given "great individual variations" in sexual preference and behavior, Bowman blandly concluded that there was no "simple, easy formula" for regulating human sexuality and that "more study and research are needed." The most direct public criticism of consensual sodomy laws before World War II was by Dr. Joseph Wortis of Johns Hopkins Medical School. Crimes against nature involved conduct that is natural for many people, he observed. Although New York's sodomy law was so infrequently enforced against consenting adults as to have little deterrent value, it could be defended as expressing a social taboo (against nonprocreative sexuality) that was essential to the perpetuation of the race. He concluded, however, that legislatures should consider "whether or not the law is entitled to interfere with sex practices engaged in discreetly by otherwise normal and responsible adults."[13]

Bentham in Full Bloom: The Kinsey Reports (1948 and 1953)

The timidity of East Coast intellectuals to assail consensual sodomy laws in the late 1930s makes Alfred Kinsey's lectures in the Indiana University marriage course (1938–40) all the more remarkable. The classes were a sensation—

popular among the students but controversial among the faculty, townspeople, and alumni. Kinsey's critics assailed him for the graphic nature of his lectures, replete with slides showing aroused reproductive organs, and for his soliciting students to provide him with their sexual histories. In 1938 Kinsey developed a written questionnaire probing a person's sexual repertoire and preferences, and the following year he started gathering the information through private oral interviews that were, for the large majority of respondents, an experience somewhere between confession and communion. In 1940 the university gave Kinsey a choice between continuing the marriage course and receiving university support to broaden his collection of sex histories. It was an easy choice for the ambitious researcher, and for the next sixteen years Kinsey and a few hand-picked colleagues gathered detailed sexual biographies of more than twelve thousand Americans. His research was financed by Indiana University, the National Research Council (after 1941), and the Rockefeller Foundation (after 1946). The Rockefeller money also enabled Kinsey to establish the Institute for Sex Research in 1947.[14]

Like Benedict and Mead, Kinsey understood that the best strategy to undermine crime-against-nature laws was through description, strictly following the objective methodology of science. In 1947 he pulled together his research to write *Sexual Behavior of the Human Male*, a massive description of the sexual practices of more than fifty-three hundred American men. Like his gall wasp books, *Human Male* was densely packed with methodological essays, 162 tables and 173 graphs reporting the data and lengthy analysis. While the stated goal of the book was to report "an objectively determined body of fact about sex which strictly avoids social or moral"—that is, subjective—"interpretations of the fact," its unstated goal was to overthrow the traditionalist philosophy of proper sexual activity and its regulation.[15]

Almost every American man engaged in a variety of sexual practices, and they made him very happy, Kinsey reported. Sexual variation was both ubiquitous and usually benign, and that ubiquity mocked state criminal codes: more than ninety-five percent of the adult population violated America's sex laws, and most were serial offenders. Obviously, America's sex laws were not being enforced, nor should they be, the book argued. The people committing these acts, over and over again, were the bedrock of America. The book found that the early-maturing respondents, typically the most sexually active, were the "more alert, energetic, vivacious, spontaneous, physically active, socially extrovert, and/ or aggressive individuals in the population."[16]

The shocking force of Kinsey's data was most evident in the long chapter on "Homosexual Outlet." Homosexuality/heterosexuality, Kinsey attempted to show, was a continuum rather than a binary divide. "Males do not represent two discrete populations, heterosexual and homosexual. The world is not to be divided into sheep and goats," Kinsey famously declared. "Only the human mind invents categories and tries to force facts into separated pigeonholes." Thus, it was arbitrary to label someone a "homosexual" (just as Benedict and Mead had demonstrated the arbitrariness of the masculine and feminine labels). Contrariwise, if a man was to be considered a homosexual based upon a single erotic act with another man, as the federal government was maintaining during the lavender terror, the country was full of homosexuals. Thirty-seven percent of the male population had had at least one overt homosexual experience to orgasm after age sixteen, while an additional thirteen percent had reacted erotically to other males without orgasm; half the male population had experienced significant homosexual erotic attraction during adulthood. Eighteen percent of the male population had had at least as much homosexual as heterosexual experience over at least a three-year period; ten percent had been predominantly homosexual for at least a three-year period, with eight percent being completely homosexual for at least that period. Four percent of the white male population was exclusively homosexual (a Kinsey rating of six) for their entire adult lives. However those numbers are interpreted—and Kinsey did present the numbers to make them more dramatic—they indicated the existence of a great deal of homosexuality and sodomy in America.[17]

Kinsey carefully controlled press access to the page proofs of *Human Male*, so that when it was shipped by the publisher in January 1948, dozens of articles appeared simultaneously everywhere in the country. The book was an overnight sensation. *Human Male* was both praised and assailed for its fact-based approach to a controversial topic. Everyone read or perused the book, and many Americans assigned themselves Kinsey numbers. (On the zero-to-six scale, exclusive heterosexuals rated a lowly zero, and homosexuals a six, a sly bit of Kinsey humor.) After the initial rush of publicity, serious critics weighed in. There was much to criticize in the report: its lack of a random sample, its emphasis on the mechanical (was there an orgasm?) over the emotional and the cultural, and its dismissive tone toward psychology and psychiatry and other softer sciences. Reviewers recognized that, beneath its mountains of fact, *Human Male* was a normative book. Most appreciated the central norm: human sexual variation is tolerable, and the majority of it is completely benign from society's point of view.[18]

Kinsey and his coauthors continued this theme in *Sexual Behavior in the Human Female*, published in 1953. *Human Female* opened with a scathing analysis of the newer sexual psychopath laws and repeated the prior book's Benthamite critique of consensual sodomy laws. But the new volume was an even broader perspective on sodomy (broadly defined). The Kinsey team found that twenty-eight percent of the women sampled had experienced significant erotic attraction to other women (compared with fifty percent of the male sample to men), and thirteen percent had had homosexual experiences to orgasm (compared with thirty-seven percent of the male sample). For some Americans, the fact that a woman could even achieve orgasm with another woman was a surprise. The most important fact in the volume also came as a surprise to most men and many women: female orgasms originated in the clitoris, not the vagina. Hence penile-vaginal (procreative) sex did not guarantee a female orgasm, while cunnilingus (considered sodomy in many states) generally did. This finding exposed not only the pointlessness of the law, but also its sexist premises. The only *legal* sexual conduct ensured the man, but not the woman, an orgasm.[19]

Human Female triggered a more polarized reaction than the previous volume. Although many Americans, especially women, felt the report was refreshingly honest, others were repelled by its open embrace of sexual variety and critique of traditional gender roles. Traditionalists now realized that Kinsey's work represented a serious challenge to their natural-law perspective, and they responded vigorously. The respected theologian Reinhold Niebuhr criticized Kinsey's underlying liberal assumption that sexual pleasure should be a primary human end as "absurd hedonism." Obliterating traditional ethical distinctions, Niebuhr warned, would lead to "moral anarchism." Niebuhr's friend Jackson Tolby lamented that Kinsey "does not seem to have any comprehension of the conditions for the coexistence of people as opposed to the conditions for the realization of the desires of the individual. He does not grasp the sociological fact—tragic though it is—that community is purchased at the price of individual self-restraint." The evangelist Billy Graham said, "It is impossible to estimate the damage this book will do to the already deteriorating morals of America."[20]

Responding to such objections, J. Edgar Hoover's FBI initiated an investigation, and an ongoing harassment, of the Institute for Sex Research, for importing and handling lewd materials. In 1954, House Republicans launched a congressional investigation into private foundations supporting subversive research projects (i.e., Kinsey), whereupon Dean Rusk announced that the Rockefeller Foundation would no longer support the institute. Desperate to fund his continuing research, Kinsey died of heart failure in 1956.[21]

The Model Penal Code's Case Against Sodomy Laws

In 1935, American criminal law was essentially a hodgepodge of moral prohibitions. Each state had its own criminal code, and those codes had a sedimen-
tary quality: conduct considered objectionable in 1850 remained a crime long
after public opinion had shifted, and new crimes were added on top of old
ones, to reflect new moral concerns. Offenses like fornication, adultery, and
sodomy reflected a nineteenth-century viewpoint, in which procreative marriage was the exclusive domain of sexuality. In a layer above those prohibitions
were twentieth-century rules restricting public conduct—sexual solicitation,
loitering in public places, cross-dressing, displays of morally squalid movies or
plays, and so forth.[22]

A new generation of Benthamite lawyers, judges, and academics was critical
of this state of affairs. Columbia Law School professors Jerome Michael and Herbert Wechsler (1909–2000) proposed a new paradigm in their pathbreaking
casebook, *Criminal Law and Its Administration* (1940). Instead of expressing society's moral code—or, practically speaking, the moral code of bygone years—
Michael and Wechsler argued that "the criminal law, like the rest of the law,
should serve the end of promoting the common good," precisely along Benthamite lines. A morals-based theory of criminal law was unjust, because it "requires
[the state] to inflict pain upon others, regardless of its effect upon social welfare."
Thus, "no legal provision can be justified merely because it calls for the punishment of the morally guilty." Although the Michael and Wechsler casebook said
nothing about the crime against nature, its philosophy provided an analytical
framework hostile to making consensual sodomy such a crime, especially in light
of the data Dr. Kinsey provided after the war.[23]

Critical Approaches to Sexual Psychopath Laws:
Why Criminalize Consensual Sodomy?

Although most states adopted sexual psychopath laws between 1935 and 1961
(chapter 3), New York was perhaps the only one that soberly studied the problem before enacting such statutes. In 1947 the legislature passed a law to commit defendants to indefinite hospitalization if they were convicted of certain
sex crimes (including consensual sodomy and solicitation, but not rape) *and* the
court found the defendant could not control his sexual impulses. Even though
the bill was supported by prosecutors and both political parties, Governor
Thomas Dewey (1943–55) vetoed it. The Republican nominee for president in

1944 and again in 1948 was a no-nonsense Benthamite. As New York County district attorney, Dewey had broken up a massive homosexual-blackmail ring by encouraging homosexuals to press charges. A focus on public harm was his mantra. "[T]he bill does not distinguish between the different degrees of social harm that may result from the acts of sexual psychopaths. There are some who commit their acts privately, and they are their own greatest victims. Incarceration for life of such persons . . . seems unnecessarily inhuman and least calculated to provide a cure." He insisted that the legislature study the matter further.[24]

Dewey's reasons for the veto were drawn from a letter from the original drafter of the bill, Magistrate Morris Ploscowe (1904–1975). A judge in many homosexual solicitation cases, Ploscowe objected that his original proposal had been amended in the legislature to drop rape and to add solicitation for the crime against nature as a basis for commitment. The latter crime, "used primarily to deal with persons guilty of homosexual behavior in subway and theatre toilets," was not, Ploscowe maintained, "sufficiently dangerous or antisocial" to merit such extreme treatment. Ploscowe's concern was widely shared. Reflecting the same Benthamite attitude as the Michael and Wechsler casebook, judges and magistrates throughout New York registered objections to sleazy police tactics and overenforcement of the state's loitering and sodomy-solicitation laws; some had even started to throw out convictions. Why should any kind of consensual activities be subject to such a grave deprivation of liberty?[25]

In 1948 the governor appointed a blue-ribbon Committee on the Sex Offender. Filled with pragmatists, the group engaged in a study of 102 sex offenders incarcerated at Sing Sing and consulted Kinsey and other experts. In 1950 the committee presented to the legislature a moderate proposal for the treatment of violent or child-molesting sex offenders. At Kinsey's urging, the committee's bill amended the penal code to reduce consensual sodomy to a misdemeanor; forcible sodomy and sodomy with a minor (under age eighteen) remained felonies. The new consensual sodomy law was politically feasible because it was featured as a minor provision in a bill that was accepted by police and prosecutors as tough on sex crimes. Because all the press attention focused on the new protections against sexual psychopaths, few New Yorkers even realized their sodomy law was being liberalized. The Roman Catholic Church's lobbyist, Charles Tobin, expressed "concern[s] with certain substantive features of the bill," but ultimately acquiesced in the governor's pragmatic coup.[26]

Between 1946 and 1961 no other state reduced the penalty for consensual sodomy, and most increased it. Still, state legislatures were willing to establish blue-ribbon commissions to review existing sexual psychopath laws, and commissions published reports in New Hampshire (1949), Michigan (1951), Pennsylvania (1951), Virginia (1951), Illinois (1953), New Jersey (1953), California (1954), Oregon (1956), and Minnesota (1959). Like Dewey's committee, state sex-crime study commissions were billed as data-collecting organs: How serious is the problem of sex crimes? What can the legislature do to reduce them? The men running the most ambitious study commissions—Karl Bowman in California, Frank Allen in Illinois, Paul Tappan in New Jersey—accepted the Benthamite philosophy and as allies of Kinsey drew normative conclusions from their factual quests.[27]

The Illinois Commission on Sex Offenders, established in 1951, interviewed dozens of relevant officials and experts and sifted through a considerable amount of data. Its members spent a whole day reviewing data with Kinsey. The professor was a big hit with the commission, especially its chair, Professor Frank Allen of Northwestern University Law School. The two men were a study in contrasts. With his drill-sergeant haircut and intense energy, Kinsey was feisty, and combative if crossed. Tall and WASPy, with thinning brown hair, Allen was placid, judicious, and unflappable. Kinsey was a zealous crusader with a sharp tongue; Allen a detached observer with a dry wit. Kinsey's Olympian and highly unconventional sex life would have been incomprehensible to Allen. Yet Allen appreciated Kinsey's fact-based presentation and agreed with Kinsey's skepticism about using the criminal law to punish immorality rather than third-party harms. And the facts reported by Kinsey were spot-on, including Kinsey's charge that consensual sodomy laws generate police corruption. Some members of the commission had direct evidence of such corruption in Chicago, where police were "harassing homosexuals outrageously. There were tales of outright blackmail, threats that were effective" because of the "devastating" effect of exposure.[28]

Allen's report for the commission was openly Benthamite and demonstrated that Kinsey's findings, which "permeate all present thinking on the subject," suggested the futility of regulating private activities between consenting adults and the desirability of focusing enforcement resources on conduct that causes the most harm. The commission's report recommended that criminal regulation should focus on (1) "repetitive compulsive acts" that invaded other people's privacy, such as spying by Peeping Toms; (2) "forced relations," such as rape; and (3) relations involving minors. Consistent with that overall philosophy, the commission recommended that greater penalties for "homosexuality" should be reserved "for violent and aggressive acts," with acts committed in public places or with minors being reclassified as misdemeanors. "Homosexual acts" between consenting adults in private should not be criminal.[29]

Model Penal Code and Sodomy Reform

Located in downtown Philadelphia, the American Law Institute (ALI) is the grand assembly of law reform, a collection of America's most eminent lawyers, judges, and academics. Since its founding in 1922–23, the ALI has developed systematic and comprehensive "model" codes for subject areas ranging from commercial law to trust and estate law. In 1951, after study and discussion over several decades, the institute committed itself to drafting a systematic Model Penal Code (MPC) to replace the chaotic body of crimes unsystematically collected in the codes of most states. It asked Professor Wechsler to be the reporter, the academic coordinator for the project. Not surprisingly, Wechsler's philosophy was based on the harm principle: the criminal law should only regulate conduct which causes harm and should leave morals regulation to religious authorities. As his associates on the project, Wechsler chose Benthamites who agreed with that premise—Paul Tappan, Morris Ploscowe, Frank Allen, and other men who were involved in legislative study commissions recommending repeal of consensual sodomy laws.[30]

The associate reporter who handled sexual offenses was Professor Louis Schwartz (1913–2003) of the University of Pennsylvania School of Law. A tall, elegant man with thick, graying hair, Schwartz had served in the Justice Department between 1936 and 1946, during which he absorbed the New Deal's liberal philosophy. As Allen had done in Illinois, Schwartz and his associates in 1952–53 gathered reams of materials, including the Kinsey reports, and shared their recommendations and materials with the ALI's Council in 1953–54.[31]

Schwartz circulated his final draft of the sex offense provisions to the ALI's Advisory Committee in early January 1955. Section 207.5 ("Homosexual Imposition, Public Solicitation") made it a serious felony for a person to force "deviate sexual intercourse" on someone else of the same sex or to have such intercourse with a minor (under age eighteen). Such intercourse between consenting adults was not to be considered a crime, but "[a] person who in any public place solicits deviate sexual intercourse with individuals with whom he had no previous acquaintance commits a misdemeanor." Section 207.5 was, on the whole, a liberalization, for it proposed what no state had been willing to do—decriminalize consensual sodomy entirely. The solicitation provision took back some of that liberalization, for it would have filled a regulatory gap in some states. And the definition of "deviate sexual intercourse"—"contact for purposes of sexual gratification between the sex organ of one person and any part of the body of another except the sex organ of a person of the other sex"— was an expansion of American criminal law. In 1955 oral sex was not a crime against nature in some states, and cunnilingus was clearly targeted in only a handful. If public or unconsented, this conduct would have been made illegal by the MPC.[32]

Accompanying section 207.5, Schwartz submitted a scholarly comment on "Deviate Sexual Gratification." Starting with the Kinsey data showing extensive homosexual activities in the country, the comment was skeptical that the criminal law should do much about it. Schwartz made the standard liberal arguments: consensual sodomy creates "[n]o harm to the secular interests of the community" and is a moral matter better left to "spiritual authorities"; existing laws are "substantially unenforced" and only create opportunities for police harassment and blackmail; scarce enforcement resources are better deployed against activities that cause serious harm. He added a few more pragmatic arguments to the list: the criminal sanction "probably deters some people from seeking psychiatric or other assistance for their emotional problems"; enforcement of consensual sodomy laws requires the police, like the Newport investigators in 1918, to engage in demoralizing behavior.[33]

Schwartz provided little justification for the public-solicitation prohibition, beyond an analogy to public heterosexual activities (like open cohabitation) that were "an open flouting of widely held standards of morality." He later explained that the target of this provision "is not private immorality but a kind of public 'nuisance' caused by congregation of homosexuals offensively flaunting their deviance from general norms of behavior." But he conceded that there was some tension between the public-solicitation provision and the decriminalization of private conduct. "People may be deeply offended upon learning of private debauchery." Should criminality then turn on "the level of gossip to which the moral transgression gave rise"? Schwartz thought not. "As I search for the principle of discrimination between the morals offenses made punishable only when committed openly and those punishable even when committed in secrecy, I find nothing but differences in the intensity of the aversion with which the different kinds of behavior are regarded."[34]

Wechsler called this kind of reasoning "principled pragmatism," and his support for Schwartz's compromise ensured its approval by the advisory committee. But if this was to be the basis for judgment, the whole compromise was vulnerable to the objection that *any* kind of homosexual conduct was deeply offensive to the community. Although Kinsey had found widespread homosexual conduct, the fact remained that most Americans found it disgusting and its very existence polluting, for it was a naked embrace of sex *only* for pleasure. This argument was indeed put forward during debate on the March 1955 draft by the ALI's Council. Unlike the advisory committee, dominated by academics, the council consisted of barons of the legal profession, about half of whom were from traditionalist states of the South, Midwest, and West. They were more interested in the "pragmatism" than the "principle" of sex crime reform. The two senior figures were Judges John Parker (1885–1958) of the Fourth Circuit and Learned Hand (1872–1961) of the Second Circuit.[35]

Although rejected by the Senate as too conservative on race and labor matters when President Hoover nominated him for the Supreme Court in 1930, Parker was the most respected judge in the South and reflected its courtly traditions. In council, he argued that "deviate sexual practices were either symptom or cause of moral decay and should be repressed by law." Learned Hand, perhaps the greatest federal judge not to have served on the Supreme Court, was an old Bull Moose, with bushy gray eyebrows dominating a face furrowed by eighty-three years. Strongly agreeing with Schwartz that "discreet" sexual behavior between consenting adults ought not be criminal, he nonetheless supported the proposal to retain consensual deviate sexual intercourse. Hand feared that "failure to make a concession to violent emotional hostility among legislators and the public at large might jeopardize acceptance of the Model Penal Code as a whole."[36]

At the direction of a large majority of the council—the Parker traditionalists and the Hand pragmatists—Schwartz prepared a new draft of section 207.5 that made deviate sexual intercourse between consenting adults a misdemeanor, as New York had done in 1950. But he appended a comment, tracking his earlier essay, explaining why he disagreed with the council's recommendation. Schwartz also expanded the definition of deviate sexual intercourse to include "penetration of the male sex organ into any opening of the body of a human being or animal [other than coition] and any sexual penetration of the vulva or anus of a female by another female or by an animal."[37]

On May 19, 1955, Schwartz presented the council's sex crimes provisions to the body of the institute in its annual proceedings at the stately Mayflower Hotel in Washington. He outlined the Benthamite philosophy underlying those provisions, and accordingly sexual assault was the main conduct criminalized; conversely, fornication and adultery were omitted as crimes, with little discussion. In the afternoon session, Schwartz urged the institute to follow this example and delete the consensual sodomy misdemeanor that had been inserted by the council. Judge Parker opposed the motion, leading with the Hand argument: "[T]he attitude of the Institute would be largely misunderstood" if it decriminalized conduct considered a felony everywhere in America, and "its work would be discredited in the minds of many people whose good opinion we should desire to retain." Parker dismissed Schwartz's concern that such laws were not much enforced: "There are many things that are denounced by the Criminal Code that cannot be prosecuted with success. But it is important that they be denounced by the Criminal Code in order that society may know that the state disapproves." Judge Hand immediately disagreed; unenforced crimes reflecting moral disapproval were not appropriate for a criminal code. Although he had opposed decriminalization in council, "I have finally come to the conclusion that the chance of prejudicing the Code is not sufficient to warrant opposition to making the law as we who think it is not a subject of criminal prosecution, think it should be."[38] Within minutes of Hand's comment, a young lawyer remarked, "[I]f we are going to be criticized as we are, I prefer to be criticized by people who I think represent an outmoded and unsound viewpoint, rather than be criticized by the more modern and up to date."[39]

By a vote of thirty-five to twenty-four, the institute supported the motion to drop consensual sodomy as a misdemeanor. In light of the reporter's emphatic (and Wechsler's tacit) support, this was a slender margin of victory. It was probably Hand who tipped the scale, for most of the membership were lawyers in the Northeast, and would have been impressed by the conversion of the man they viewed as the greatest judge in America. Schwartz enthusiastically implemented the institute's decision and also revised the sodomy section to reflect other developments in the code's complicated drafting history. The final version defined "deviate sexual intercourse" more conservatively, as "sexual intercourse per os or per anum between human beings who are not husband and wife, and any form of sexual intercourse with an animal." As earlier versions had done, the final MPC made this a crime only if it was forcible (or its equivalent) or with a minor. A separate section made public solicitation of same-sex intercourse a misdemeanor. The new draft went through the same elaborate process as the 1955 draft had done, but with no controversy over the sodomy provisions. The ALI adopted the final draft in May 1962.[40]

Illinois Decriminalizes Consensual Sodomy, 1961

A test of Judge Parker's Mayflower arguments soon presented itself. Between 1955 and 1970, most states established bar-sponsored criminal code revision commissions. Wisconsin recodified its criminal law in 1955, before the MPC could have any influence, but the bar association in neighboring Illinois established a blue-ribbon Joint Committee to Revise the Illinois Criminal Code in 1954. The joint committee consisted of sixteen (later twenty-one) eminent lawyers, but the bulk of the work was accomplished by the drafting subcommittee, chaired by Professor Allen, who had moved from Northwestern to the University of Chicago Law School. Allen's subcommittee included Professor Charles Bowman of the University of Illinois School of Law and the prosecutor (later governor) James Thompson.[41]

The joint committee was receptive to the Benthamite approach to sex crimes and to sodomy repeal in particular. As Allen recalled it, "[M]uch of our work was an expression of ideas in the air at the time. Kinsey was important." Allen's work with the earlier sex crime committee had framed his thoughts for the code revision. He had witnessed the Parker-Hand debate at the Mayflower in 1955 and had cast one of the votes to remove consensual sodomy from the MPC. Although only Allen read all of it, the joint committee was strongly impressed by the 1957 Wolfenden Report, which recommended that England decriminalize consensual sodomy. The report's Benthamite argumentation and the publicity it generated reinforced the Kinseyesque ideas that Allen was supporting.[42]

"Some of what we did was a direct result of our observation of police practices." Allen was "convinced that the police in Chicago were harassing homosexuals outrageously," an impression supported by first-person accounts. Before 1935, Chicago police left homosexuals pretty much alone, in return for payoffs. In the 1950s, they continued to take the money, while still arresting and harassing drag queens, fairies, and butch lesbians.[43]

The joint committee's proposed criminal code, completed in November 1960, reserved the criminal sanction for sexual conduct that was forcible, imposed on minors, or "openly flouts accepted standards of morality in the community." Although it followed the ALI in having no provision criminalizing consensual sodomy in private places, the joint committee's proposal departed from the MPC in several respects. Based upon Kinsey's finding that sex with animals is almost always in the context of "youthful 'experiments' rather than part of a pattern of conduct" contributing to the youth's deterioration, the joint committee omitted it from its definition of deviate sexual intercourse. It also narrowed the MPC's public indecency provision and declined to criminalize solicitation of deviate sexual conduct: "This is essentially a private rather than a public irritation. Since it is an act not likely to be noted by parties other than those admittedly involved, it is a secretive situation extremely difficult of proof or disproof—and thus, lends itself again to dangers of extortion and blackmail." The proposed code did, however, criminalize the "lewd fondling or caress of the body of another person of the same sex" in a public place.[44]

The Illinois and Chicago bar associations approved the proposed code in December, and it was introduced in the legislature in January 1961 with some concern that the entire project might be undermined by the sodomy decriminalization. The bill was referred to subcommittees chaired by Senator Robert Canfield, a conservative downstate Republican, and Representative Abner Mikva, a liberal Democrat from the south side of Chicago. Canfield and Mikva held seven joint hearings, including two in Chicago, to canvass public opinion on the legislation. This was the first time in Illinois history that subcommittees from different chambers had jointly coordinated their public hearings, and the legislators heard opposition to various provisions from the defense bar, the National Rifle Association (which managed to alienate every subcommittee member by what Mikva characterizes as "fanatic" statements), and the Roman Catholic Church.[45]

The Council of Catholic Churches objected to the proposed MPC-based defenses to criminal abortion for cases where the pregnancy posed a threat to the health of the mother, resulted from rape or incest, or involved an irremediably deformed fetus. Representing the Joint Committee, Charlie Bowman worked out a deal agreeing to strike out the new abortion defenses, leaving only the existing one (when the abortion was necessary to save the life of the mother) but in return "asked that [the church] not object to any other provisions of the code. While they had some reservations about some of the sex offense provisions, and especially the repeal of the offense of 'Crime Against Nature,' they did not object in the legislature after we amended out the abortion defenses." Bowman later recalled that the coalition never expected the abortion defenses would be accepted, "but having them in there gave me a good 'bargaining' tool on the rest of the provisions."[46]

After that hurdle was negotiated, the proposed Illinois Criminal Code met little opposition. The ACLU, state prosecutors, and both political parties signed off on the bill. Legislators ultimately deferred completely, without any idea of what they were supporting. This lazy politics may have made sex crime reform possible; as Allen put it, "Illinois was the best state in the nation to accomplish law reform, because no one in the legislature read the bill."[47]

The conditions for enacting the legislation were fragile, however. Dawn Clark Netsch, the governor's legal counsel and a former student of the revered Professor Allen, recalls: "We all knew the code was eliminating sodomy as a crime. It was just understood that you didn't say anything about this. It was there; everybody knew it was there—but it might go away if it was discussed openly." Occasionally, someone came close to doing so. During the House debate, one frustrated downstate representative exclaimed, "You know what this means! This means that the only way [sex is] illegal in Illinois is if you're doing it on the front porch and blowing a bugle! And you can do it with either sex!" He sat down, an embarrassed silence ensued, and the bill advanced without further comment. On

May 25, the House passed the criminal code reform bill 148 to 1. The Senate followed, 57 to 0, on June 28. Governor Otto Kerner signed it with fanfare on July 28, 1961.[48]

The Civil Rights Case Against Consensual Sodomy Laws

When they cast their lot against consensual sodomy laws, people as different as Alfred Kinsey, Frank Allen, Charlie Bowman, and Dawn Clark Netsch—all midwesterners—were appealing to the common good. Their reasons were liberal and pragmatic: however morally objectionable sodomy might be, the state could not legitimately or effectively regulate it when consenting adults engaged in such activities within the home. Largely excluded from this debate were the Americans most clearly affected by the public debate—homosexuals themselves. They listened fearfully from their closets, but a few started to make their own arguments against sodomy laws. Between 1950 and 1961, homosexuals began to view themselves as an unfairly persecuted minority whose civil rights were violated by consensual sodomy laws.

Homosexuals as a Persecuted Minority with Civil Rights

Although sexually active with men since age fourteen, the minor Hollywood actor Harry Hay (born 1912) married fellow Communist Party member Anita Platky in 1938. The physically striking pair was a model couple, adopting two daughters. But Hay continued sleeping with men and ultimately left both Platky and the party because he considered himself unalterably homosexual. After he read the Kinsey report in 1948, it occurred to him that homosexuals met the neo-Marxist definition of an oppressed minority, just as blacks did: they had a common language (gay slang) and territory (gay ghettos), as well as a common psychology and (sub)culture. If the Kinsey one-in-ten number was anything close to correct, the homosexual minority was potentially quite substantial, but still vulnerable. As Hay later put it, "I knew the government was going to look for a new enemy, a new scapegoat. It was predictable. But Blacks were beginning to organize, and the horror of the holocaust was too recent to put the Jews in this position. The natural scapegoat would be us, the Queers. They were the one group of disenfranchised people who did not even know they were a group because they had never formed as a group. They—we—had to get started."[49]

In August 1948, Hay became a founder of "Bachelors for Wallace," single men supporting the Progressive Henry Wallace for president. Encouraged by this experience and by his lover, Rudi Gernreich (later to become a prominent fashion designer), Hay believed the time had come to organize homosexuals as a social movement, and in 1950 he drafted a prospectus to establish a permanent homophile group. Its premise was that homosexuals, like people of color, were a minority unfairly subjected to social prejudice and state persecution and discrimination. Like blacks, homosexuals were entitled to civil and political rights against state discrimination. It was this sensibility that Hay and Gernreich brought to the Mattachine Society of Los Angeles, which they and a few other white male homosexuals founded in 1950–51.[50]

Writing as Donald Webster Cory, Edward Sagarin made similar arguments in *The Homosexual in America* (1951), a book that popularized the message to a small but growing national audience. Some readers independently drew Hay's conclusion from Sagarin's book: persecution should stimulate resistance. The playwright James Barr had this experience after he was drummed out of the Navy as a homosexual. "For the first time in my life it was not a completely personal issue with me. . . . [I]n defending myself I was forced to defend the rights and concepts of a group numbering hundreds of thousands."[51]

Mattachine cofounder Dale Jennings had a similar awakening, with more far-reaching consequences. In 1952 he was accused of soliciting sex from an undercover policeman. The officer followed him home and all but forced his way into his apartment; frightened that he was going to be beaten and robbed, Jennings claimed that he made no advances before the officer arrested him. All the Mattachine founders had been similarly mistreated by the notorious L.A. police, and at the March meeting the still-secret society decided to fight the charges. Its members formed a Citizens' Committee to Outlaw Entrapment, which made Jennings's case a public issue. LAPD tactics reflected an "unconstitutional police conspiracy which, under cloak of protecting public morals, threatens not only all Minorities but civil rights and privileges generally." The lawyer they retained won Jennings a hung jury (eleven to one for acquittal) and dismissal of the charges. Jennings's own account emphasized how important it was for homosexuals to work together against oppression. "It is unification for self-protection." If every homosexual rolled over when kicked by the police, they would keep kicking; only by kicking back could homosexuals hope to be left alone. "Were all homosexuals and bisexuals to unite militantly, unjust laws and corruption would crumble in short order," Jennings concluded.[52]

Word-of-mouth news of the verdict generated great enthusiasm for Mattachine, whose membership exploded from a handful to several thousand in southern California and San Francisco. Parallel Mattachine organizations were established in New York (1955), Chicago (1955), Denver (1956), Boston (1957),

Washington (1957), Detroit (1958), and Philadelphia (1961), to name only the major cities. At this point, Mattachine could have taken off as a grassroots organization, militantly asserting that it was illegitimate for the majority to deprive the gay minority of its civil rights, including the freedom to engage in consensual sexual activities without state interference.[53]

A civil rights claim differs from a utilitarian policy claim. It does not entail a cost-benefit analysis, as it does not ask what's good for the majority. A right is a minority's trump against the majority's supposed public benefit. The NAACP asserted that people of color had the right to be afforded procedural protections when the state prosecuted them and to have access to segregated institutions. Mattachine could have followed the NAACP's example and initiated a litigation campaign to build up a constitutional case against police tactics or against sodomy laws themselves, or, like the Southern Christian Leadership Conference (SCLC), it could have mobilized protests against these denials of gay civil rights. Notwithstanding its early success, however, Mattachine did neither.

The Daughters of Bilitis/Mattachine Jurisprudence of Privacy

The failure of Mattachine to become an activist civil rights organization was partly a failure of leadership. Although visionary, Hay was not a gifted strategist, as Bayard Rustin was for the SCLC. Hampered by the secretive cell system he had learned from the Communists (most of Mattachine's early membership knew one another only by pseudonyms) and distracted by personal matters (such as divorcing his wife, in 1951), Hay was unable to build Mattachine, and his associates proved even less capable. Hay also failed to reach out beyond middle-class white men, which gave a hollow ring to Mattachine's analogy of homophobia to racism. (Indeed, no civil rights leader, including the homosexual Rustin, publicly agreed with the comparison.) But Mattachine's failure was also one of followership. You cannot lead a mass social movement when the mass is still cowering in its closet. As Sagarin/Cory ruefully put it in 1951, "[t]he homosexual is, unfortunately, in a position before the law where he cannot effectively fight back.... Laws whose unconstitutionality is considered by many to be patent remain unchallenged because no one dares come forward."[54]

In 1953 Harold Call, a businessman, ousted the disorganized founders from control of Mattachine. For the remainder of its history, the society followed the safe course of education and persuasion, rather than the avant-garde strategy of constitutional litigation and street activism. That same year, its members started publishing *One, Inc.,* the first widely circulated homophile journal; the *Mattachine Review* was first published in 1955. San Franciscans Del Martin and Phyllis Lyon formed the Daughters of Bilitis (DOB), and it published *The Ladder* from

1956 to 1970. DOB was formed for the benefit of lesbians but shared one major goal with the Mattachine groups: "Investigation of the penal code as it pertains to the homosexual, proposal of changes to provide an equitable handling of cases involving this minority group, and promotion of these changes through due process of law in the state legislatures."[55]

Although gay activists and some historians have criticized Mattachine and DOB for their apologetic and assimilative politics, the groups had some striking accomplishments within an extremely hostile culture. They also developed a coherent philosophy and a civil rights vision that has proved more enduring than the Marxist philosophy of its more radical members. The philosophy featured three ideas.[56]

First was the *rule of law*. As the Jennings case suggested, "law enforcement" personnel regularly broke the rules, and their abuses were exposed and criticized in DOB and Mattachine publications. This not only positioned homosexuals as law-abiding citizens, but also educated them about the many protections afforded by the rule of law in the United States. In the 1950s the California and federal supreme courts were enforcing old and recognizing new constitutional rights for people questioned or arrested by the police. The homosexual's first line of defense was to know his protections, and thousands of men carried with them copies of Mattachine's list of "Your Rights in Case of Arrest."[57]

The second theme of the DOB/Mattachine philosophy was *tolerance* and *inclusion*. Whatever anyone thought of their activities, homosexuals did not harm others and posed none of the public threats the antihomosexual terror attributed to them. Hence, as a substantive matter, the state was unjustified in making their consensual private activities a crime. Bowing to some conventions while altering others, DOB and Mattachine "[did] not advocate sexual license" but "believed that sexual activities between two willing and consenting adults should not be a legal matter governed by public law but rather a matter of individual personal morals." Published just months after the ALI's vote to decriminalize consensual sodomy, this statement could have been written by Louis Schwartz, who in January 1955 had considered "fundamental" the "protection to which every individual is entitled against state interference in his personal affairs when he is not hurting others." This homophile jurisprudence of privacy had a singular advantage in the 1950s: it did not require straight Americans to endorse or value homosexuality—then an unachievable goal—but only asked them to give the homosexual the same private (sexual) space that heterosexuals enjoyed as a matter of course. This jurisprudence also offered America an attractive exchange: leave us in peace, and we'll be discreet.[58]

The third idea central to the homophile philosophy was *procedural correct-*

ness: "Change can only be accomplished in the proper way and manner and by the proper people." Accordingly, Mattachine and DOB urged their members and friends to write legislators urging criminal law reform and dreamed of forming alliances with elite organizations like the ACLU and the ALI. The fourth issue of *Mattachine Review* saluted Learned Hand for his decisive intervention in the May 1955 ALI debate, and both the *Review* and the *Ladder* devoted considerable attention to the Wolfenden Report. Although their support was not relevant, DOB and Mattachine felt their approach was vindicated when the California legislature repealed its "lewd or dissolute person" (vagrancy) law, which police used to harass and arrest homosexuals almost at will. The new law left sexual solicitation (and public loitering for that purpose) a misdemeanor, but the homophile groups considered the reform an important step toward recognizing gay people's privacy rights.[59]

Unlike the ACLU and the NAACP, the homophile movement did not press minority rights in norm-establishing constitutional litigation. None of its leaders was a lawyer, and funds were short. A further reason was the overwhelming whiteness and the predominant maleness of the homophile groups; until Ernestine Eckstein, an African American, became president of DOB New York in 1969, there were no people of color leading these organizations. The black civil rights movement generated the judicial precedents that inspired the homophiles and protected many of them from the police—a debt Mattachine and DOB did not sufficiently appreciate. They did not even imagine coalitions with other civil rights or even feminist groups. Just as the homophiles were starting to think about sodomy deregulation as a civil right, Planned Parenthood was engaged in litigation pursuing a *constitutional* right of privacy that would have suited the homophile agenda, had its leaders been better connected with East Coast civil liberties and feminist groups.[60]

The Jurisprudence of the Bar Culture: Gay Is Good and Homo Equality

In 1961, the Mattachine Society's nationwide membership was 230; DOB's was 115. Fewer than a thousand people (including several dozen FBI agents) read their magazines. In contrast, tens of thousands of lesbians, gay men, bisexuals, transgendered people, and straight tourists flocked to lesbian and gay bars that year. Notwithstanding police raids and liquor license revocations, those bars proliferated after World War II. Most major American cities had a variety of bars that served as the foundation for local lesbian and gay communities and subcultures.[61]

The best account of such a bar-based subculture is that assembled by the

Buffalo Women's Oral History Project, headed by Madeline Davis and Elizabeth Lapovsky Kennedy. As they demonstrate, these bars were the terrain where a modern lesbian identity was shaped, at the height of the Kulturkampf. Buffalo's bars drew women from all over northern New York and even Canada. While most of their patrons were working class, others were teachers or owned their own businesses. What they found in the lesbian-friendly bars were places where they could make friends, meet potential sexual partners, and claim public space that had traditionally been denied to women in America. The prevailing lesbian social script in the 1940s and 1950s was the *butch-femme* one, as noted in chapter 3. The butch partner was sexually and usually personally assertive, physically as well as metaphorically wearing the pants in the relationship. The butch was expected to protect her femme partner, and many couples readily displayed affection in public. In the bar or on the street, a butch-femme pair was therefore recognizable as a homosexual couple—unlike the Boston marriages of discreet women such as Susan B. Anthony or Jane Addams in previous eras.[62]

Lesbian identity, including the butch-femme dynamic, was also shaped by state persecution, as astounded police harassed and sometimes brutalized these women. Although female couples were violating New York's sodomy law, butch lesbians were usually arrested for cross-dressing, public indecency, or disorderly conduct. At the height of this harassment emerged the *street dyke,* a full-time bar queer who appeared in public in jeans or overalls, often with a pretty girl on her arm and always prepared to fight off fag-bashing bullies and police. While polite society—including the Daughters of Bilitis—disdained the street dyke and the stone butch, they were heroes in the bars.[63]

Not as committed to community-building as their sisters, gay men created a culture of Whitmanesque camaraderie in their own bars. It was this friendliness tinged with sexual tension that attracted Alfred Kinsey to Chicago's gay scene. He first visited its bars in 1939, as part of his project to collect Americans' sexual histories, and the boys embraced him, had sex with him, and introduced him to hundreds of men happy to submit to the interview. Kinsey's visits to gay bars deepened his outrage at Illinois's sodomy law and gave him vivid stories of police brutality and injustice—some of which he later shared with Professor Allen's law reform commissions.[64]

Nowhere was this culture more vital than in San Francisco, home to dozens of lesbian and gay bars, including the world-renowned Mona's and Finocchio's. The greatest bar of all was the Black Cat, on the corner of Montgomery and Washington streets. It was a "bohemian bar where women smoked in public, where people believed in free love, and where there were artists wanting to talk about their artwork." The Black Cat did not come into its greatness, however, until cross-dressing José Sarria became a waiter there. Although his Colombian-born mother encouraged his ambition to be a teacher, that vocational possibility became moot when Sarria was arrested for lewd vagrancy (homosexual solicitation) at the public restroom of the St. Francis, a tony Nob Hill hotel. The resourceful Sarria landed on his feet when he got a job at the Black Cat.[65]

With his impish sense of humor and theatrical flair, the handsome Latino encouraged homosexual customers to enjoy being with comrades who accepted them as they were, and at the same time teased straight couples ("So who's your boyfriend?") and asked them to accept for the moment that *they* were the variants tolerated in the good-humored gay bar. During the 1950s Sarria became increasingly flamboyant—adding red pumps to his partial drag attire, regaling the crowd with campy readings from news items, and (on Sunday afternoons) delivering in a fluid tenor gay comic operas that left the customers, gay and straight, in tears of laughter. At the end of these performances, he would lead everyone in a rendition of "God Save Us Nellie Queens" (to the tune of "God Save the Queen"). "I sang the song as a kind of anthem, to get them realizing that we had to work together, that we were responsible for our lives. We could change the laws if we weren't always hiding."[66]

As Nan Alamilla Boyd observes, Sarria and his colleagues created an atmosphere in which "it was no longer shameful to be gay. . . . By enforcing a culture that assumed everyone in the bar was gay—and gayness was not simply the norm but a preferred way of being—the bar sacrificed quiet anonymity for a surge of cultural pride—a pride in being different." Unlike the white, male, middle-class members of the Mattachine Society, habitués of the Black Cat included people of color, gender-benders, lesbians, and working-class or unemployed queers. Almost all of them had had unpleasant or traumatic interactions with the sexuality gendarmerie, and many suffered from frequent police harassment. After 1959, some of these marginal homosexuals were intensely politicized by the intersection of Sarria's affirmation of their dignity and renewed harassment by the city.[67]

In his first term, San Francisco mayor George Christopher (1956–64) aggressively harassed lesbian and gay bars and their denizens. In the 1959 election, however, City Assessor Russell Wolden attempted to smear the mayor with the charge that he was the favorite of the Mattachine Society, until the media revealed that Mattachine support for the mayor had been engineered by an operative of Wolden's campaign. For the first time, homosexuality was the major issue in a big-city election campaign. Most voters were repelled by Wolden's phony injection of "perversion" into politics, and Mattachine sued him for defamation. Del Martin saw this issue as a rallying point for lesbians and gay men to register and vote—and many of them answered her call to become more politically active. After Wolden's loss at the polls, gay people were permanently mobilized as a voting bloc. It was a small group—but one that was beginning to persuade nongay residents that homosexuals should not be treated like garbage.[68]

In early 1960 the famous "gayola" scandal erupted in San Francisco, when the press revealed that police officers had been demanding bribes and kickbacks from the city's gay bars (which they still mercilessly harassed). The smug self-righteousness of the accused cops attracted sympathy for gay people from journalists and some of their readers. One reporter asked the attorneys involved in one of the gayola prosecutions whether "gay bars" were acceptable. City prosecutors as well as defense attorneys said yes. "These people have to drink someplace, and like any minority group they're entitled to equal accommodations" and even, in the words of one prosecutor, "equal protection" of the law.[69]

By now the infuriated bar gays were no longer willing to accept second-class treatment. Their spokesman—and later their empress—was Sarria, who in 1961 sought a seat on the eleven-member San Francisco Board of Supervisors, the city's governing body. With a campaign fund of less than $500 and public appearances mainly at the Black Cat, Sarria ran as an openly gay Latino on the platform "Gay is Good." He won 5,613 votes. "While the press waffled on the 'problem' of homosexuality, activists like Sarria proposed a counter-discourse, claiming that gay is good and that homosexuals constituted a potentially powerful political constituency."[70]

Sarria's Gay is Good motto had an ambiguous relationship to the politics of sodomy reform. On the one hand, Gay is Good supported the Bentham-Kinsey case against consensual sodomy laws by insisting that they disrupted human flourishing. Indeed, Sarria's claim offered a potential response to the powerful Niebuhr-Tolby objection to the Bentham-Kinsey case: homosexual sodomy was not just base pleasure seeking, but a basis for social flourishing and community-building. On the other hand, Sarria's claim was not even comprehensible, much less credible, to the large majority of straight Americans. For them, the testimony of a bar queen that homosexuality was "good" carried no more authority than the testimony of an addict that drug use was "good." From this perspective, Sarria's campaign posed a threat to the liberal and pragmatic case for repeal of the crime against nature, because it potentially reinforced Americans' understanding of homosexuals as selfish and predatory, insisting on "their" deluded sense of morality regardless of the consequences for society and the family.

By presenting homosexuals as an aggressive social group *demanding* equal treatment, and not as a collection of individuals for whom the state should accord sympathy, Gay is Good was political poison in the context of American culture in the early 1960s. Although Kinsey was, secretly, in tune with the gay-affirming bar culture exemplified by the Black Cat, most reformers were not. Shortly before his death, in 2007, Allen recalled that he and other tolerant midwesterners were unable to understand the Gay is Good argument for sodomy reform. Indeed, Allen was certain that if open homosexuals like Sarria had serenaded the Illinois legislature with claims that gay people were just as worthy as straight people, and *not* tolerable misfits, their pride would have given sodomy reform the kiss of death. Thus the political conditions under which Illinois pioneered sodomy reform (tolerant pragmatism and substantial ignorance about the burgeoning homosexual subculture) were at risk if gay people became too liberated and emerged from their closets. Yet that is precisely what happened after 1961.[71]

CHAPTER FIVE

Homo Equality and Sodomy Reform, 1961–69

Franklin Edward Kameny (born 1925) epitomized the straight-arrow ideal of the Eisenhower era. Interrupting his higher education at Queens College in New York, he proudly served his country as a soldier in World War II. Of average height and with thinning hair, Kameny had a strong jaw, a linebacker's shoulders, an infectious smile, and a husky laugh that ensured his popularity with other men. He was also highly intelligent, earning an astronomy Ph.D. from Harvard in 1956. But Kameny was anything but a straight arrow. In May 1954, on his twenty-ninth birthday, he had come to the realization that he was a homosexual. After years of repressed desire, he took to sex with other men

Frank Kameny campaign poster

"like a duck to water," as he typically put it. In August 1956 Kameny journeyed to San Francisco to attend the annual meeting of the American Astronomical Society. He came into the city by bus, which deposited him at the old Key Terminal. He retired to the men's restroom, where a man standing at the neighboring pissoir reached over and fondled his genitals. Kameny responded in kind. Two police officers were observing the men from behind a one-way mirror, and after a few minutes they emerged and arrested the men.[1]

Just one of thousands of homosexuals ensnared in Mayor George Christopher's police dragnets, Dr. Kameny was "a naive young man, easy pickings for those undercover cops." This arrest could have effectively ended his life then and there. If the district attorney had charged him with attempted oral copulation, a state trial judge could have ordered him incarcerated indefinitely as a statutory "sexual psychopath," and he would have been sent to Atascadero State Hospital. Fortunately, prosecutors charged Kameny with only the municipal offense of lewd conduct. After successfully petitioning the court to expunge the charges, Kameny believed he could move on.

In July 1957 he took a job with the Army Map Service, where he helped perfect techniques for precise measurement of distances between points in the United States and points across the ocean. While he was on an extended trip gathering data for the measurement project, the Civil Service Commission (CSC) learned of the San Francisco restroom incident. When Kameny returned to Washington, D.C., in November, investigators confronted him: "We have information that leads us to believe you are a homosexual. Do you care to comment?" He did not care to comment and was discharged. Shocked that he would be considered an enemy of the state because of his sexual feelings, the astronomer went into a deep depression. Impoverished after a year of living off his meager savings, he subsisted on twenty cents per day. He grew so thin that it was painful for him to sleep on his side.

But unlike thousands of other sexual outlaws, Kameny fought back, appealing his dismissal all the way to the U.S. Supreme Court. Filed on January 27, 1961, his pro se petition for Supreme Court review started with the liberal *discourse of privacy* that undergirded the Model Penal Code and the Wolfenden Report, but which Kameny articulated in constitutional terms. Thus, he argued that the rule barring federal employment of people who commit "immoral conduct" was inherently arbitrary, because the government had no business gathering or relying on information about people's personal affairs. The vague "immoral conduct" bar imposed an "odious conformity" on federal employees. Kameny maintained that the state could not, as a constitutional matter, impose moral conformity on its citizens, except where a person's conduct was harming other citizens. He linked this limitation to the Free Speech Clause of the First Amendment, for denying a class of dissident citizens state employment was one method the state could use to "attempt to tell the citizen what to think and how to believe."[2]

Having made this libertarian case against his discharge, Kameny shifted constitutional gears. The federal government's broad exclusion from employment, he argued, "makes of the homosexual a second-rate citizen, by discriminating against him without reasonable cause." As the Kinsey reports had shown, such exclusion affected as many as a third of the American people. There was, moreover, no scientific basis for the belief that people in this group were psychopathic. "The average homosexual is as well-adjusted in personality as the average heterosexual," as the research of Dr. Evelyn Hooker had recently established. Because such persons were capable of excellent government service, excluding them was presumptively irrational. That irrationality stood in contrast to the purpose of the American government, "to protect and assist *all* of its citizens, not, as in the case of homosexuals, to harm, to victimize, and to destroy them." The CSC's discriminations, Kameny argued, "constitute a discrimination no less illegal and no less odious than discrimination based upon religious or racial grounds, a personal discrimination which is . . . 'so unjustifiable as to be violative of [the Fifth Amendment].'"[3]

On March 22, 1961, the justices unanimously voted to deny Kameny's petition. That marked the end of the litigation, but the beginning of Kameny's lifelong campaign for equal gay citizenship, a campaign that included a race for the District's nonvoting delegate to Congress in March 1971. His argument went beyond the liberal politics of privacy, which begged the government to tolerate pitiable but harmless homosexuals, and asserted a Progressive *politics of recognition*. Accepting the state's assertion that homosexuals are presumptive sodomites, Kameny denied that assertion any normative force: there was no connection between sodomy and any kind of civil harm; homosexuals were honorable people entitled to full equality. Echoing José Sarria's Gay is Good philosophy, Kameny's politics of recognition asserted that the state was *constitutionally* obliged to repeal not only sodomy laws, but all discrimination against gay people.[4]

If Kameny's brief was a turning point, it was a point with more than one turn. By revealing how widely practiced and harmless sodomy was, Kinsey had supplied a basis for practical arguments to support the libertarian idea that the state should not regulate people's private sex lives. These enabled lawyers and doctors to find common ground with mainstream politicians and religious leaders. In Illinois, the result was the deregulation of consensual sodomy in 1961. Decriminalization would have been impossible if legislators had thought that they were advancing civil rights for homosexuals—precisely Kameny's claim—by deregulating sodomy. Although the new civil rights case against sodomy laws electrified hundreds of homosexuals in the 1960s, it also alarmed many heterosexuals, stiffening resistance to sodomy law reform throughout the United States. Even legislators who favored the repeal of miscegenation, fornication, and adultery laws feared the charges of "promoting homosexuality" that were entailed by sodomy repeal efforts.

More important, the increasing prominence of homosexual subcultures and their insistence on civil rights completed the century-long transformation of the idea of sodomy itself—from rapelike conduct by predatory monsters against women, men, or animals, to any kind of sexual activity between two people of the same sex. While sodomy had long been a metonym for homosexuality, it was substantially subsumed within homosexuality by 1969. Confirming the exclusive association of sodomy with homosexuality, Kansas and Texas redefined "deviate sexual conduct" (the Model Penal Code's term for sodomy) to include *only* homosexual activities—a move so consistent with social norms that it passed without public comment anywhere.

Gay People's Politics of Recognition and Sodomy Reform, 1961–65

By 1961 America's biggest cities all had discernible gay and lesbian subcultures.[5] Homosexuals who came of age after World War II were more likely to become sexually active and less likely to be ashamed of their orientation and their activities than the previous age cohort had been. Many of those homosexuals were angry at the state's discriminatory treatment of them. They were fed up with "this degrading of our personalities by the state. Merely to live, we must assert ourselves as homosexuals," and "accept it or not, we will force our way into open society; you will have to acknowledge us." This demand for acknowledgment and homo equality called for what political scientists term a *politics of recognition.*[6]

To pursue this new politics, gay people—predominantly middle-class white men—formed new organizations in the cities where they were most abused by the government and harassed by the police. The main groups were the Mattachine Societies of New York (1957) and Washington (1957, 1961); the Daughters of Bilitis in San Francisco (1955), New York (1957), and Philadelphia (1968); Philadelphia's Janus Society (1964); Mattachine Midwest (1965); the Circle of Friends in Dallas (1965); Mattachine Florida (1966); Houston's Promethean Society (1967); and San Francisco's Society for Individual Rights (1962) and Committee for Religion and the Homosexual (1964). While helping foster robust subcultures and stimulate some political involvement, these modest efforts had little effect on America's regulation of homosexual sodomy during the 1960s.

New Mattachine Societies in Washington and Philadelphia: The Limits of White Male Activism

Kameny learned that the Supreme Court had denied his petition for review by reading the March 26, 1961, edition of the *Washington Star*. He decided to fight this discrimination politically. In August 1961, Kameny and fifteen other men met at the Hay-Adams Hotel to reestablish the Mattachine Society of Washington, D.C. (MSW). After he introduced the gentlemen to his agenda, Kameny announced, "I understand that there is a member of the Metropolitan Police Department here. Could he please identify himself and tell us why he's here." He had been tipped off by one of the participants, who recognized Louis Fochett, a notorious vice officer responsible for arrests of hundreds of gay or bisexual men. Fochett mumbled an explanation and left the room. Apparently, the D.C. police had been informed of the meeting, perhaps by the FBI, which had been spying on Mattachine New York.[7]

In an earlier era homosexuals would have run for cover. But Kameny and his colleagues were determined to proceed with their plans and adopted a constitution for MSW, which announced their goals unequivocally and without apology:

To secure for homosexuals the basic rights and liberties established by the word and spirit of the Constitution of the United States,

To equalize the status and position of the homosexual with those of the heterosexual by achieving equality under law, equality of opportunity, equality in the society of his fellow men, and by eliminating adverse prejudice, both private and official,

To secure for the homosexual the right, as a human being, to develop and achieve his full potential and dignity, and the right, as a citizen, to make his maximum contribution to the society in which he lives.

A month later Kameny learned that Illinois had repealed its consensual sodomy law. In August 1962, MSW publicly insisted that equal citizenship for gay Americans was not possible so long as consensual sodomy was a crime. Government for, by, and through the people had an obligation to repeal those laws.[8]

Kameny's call for reform had a mixed reception. After 1962, MSW made sure that District homosexuals knew their constitutional rights and were willing to secure legal representation; police dragnets and undercover cops now met with community-based objections. Sodomy arrests peaked in 1962 and then fell to relatively low levels for the remainder of the decade, as illustrated in figure 5.1. Although MSW had some success in discouraging sodomy law enforcement, it had none in securing sodomy law repeal. Under the authority of Congress, the District of Columbia was governed by special House and Senate committees. Southern senators and representatives took particular interest in serving on these committees, and they ran the District like a plantation. This was not conducive to gay rights reform, for southerners were particularly unsympathetic to open homosexuality. When Justice Hugo Black (a New Deal liberal) was a judge in Alabama, he encountered a case in which a man charged with assault claimed

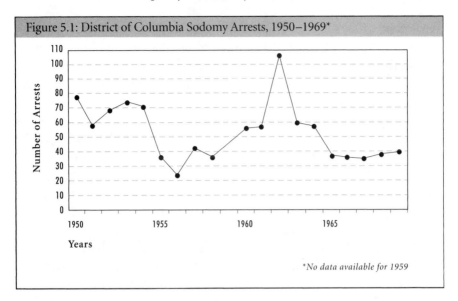

Figure 5.1: District of Columbia Sodomy Arrests, 1950–1969*

*No data available for 1959

that the male victim had "made advances." Black dismissed the charges, "found the pervert guilty of disorderly conduct and gave him the maximum sentence. 'That kind of thing will destroy a society,'" he reportedly told his son. Most southerners, and many northerners, in Congress were a lot less liberal than Black. "With the exception of one or two members of Congress," recalls Kameny, "our pleas for equal treatment were greeted with hostility or, in most cases, silence."[9]

Indeed, MSW's only business before Congress arose out of southern revulsion. In 1963 MSW registered as an educational organization under District of Columbia law, which would enable it to solicit funds. Representative John Dowdy in turn introduced a bill to revoke Mattachine's license. A yellow-dog Texas Democrat, Dowdy had no truck with uppity minorities. At August hearings he was adamant that Congress do something about "queers" and "fairies" who were polluting the public culture. Kameny begged to differ: gay people were more numerous than Dowdy suggested—existing in large numbers even in Texas—and Congress should promptly repeal the law making homosexual activities between consenting adults a crime. Although the House of Representatives passed Dowdy's bill by a 301–81 vote, it died in the Senate. The brouhaha did bring MSW valuable publicity, but it also provided clear evidence that Congress would be unwilling to reconsider the District's consensual sodomy law. Dowdy was later convicted of bribery, conspiracy, and perjury. He charged that his prosecution reflected the desire of "homosexuals and urban renewal interests" to discredit him.[10]

Another reason for MSW's political marginality during the most liberal decade of American history was its inability to form coalitions with other progressive civil rights groups. Kameny repeatedly made a point of equating gay people's struggle against homophobia with black people's struggle against racism, and visited black gay bars to pass out MSW flyers entitled "You Are Welcome," but the outreach had almost no success. Kameny can remember only a few African Americans ever participating in MSW—even though black men had historically been the main target of the District's sporadic sodomy enforcement, which had reached a peak of 106 arrests in 1962. Almost all gay and lesbian blacks lived discreet double lives. The District's African-American middle class and its vibrant Baptist churches tolerated gays in their midst, and even in their pulpits, but only so long as they did not "flaunt" their homosexuality. Moreover, politically engaged people of color had more pressing priorities. Gay black men, like Bayard Rustin, focused their energies on the civil rights movement, which was on the verge of political breakthroughs. Some black lesbians, like Pauli Murray, became involved with the emerging "second wave" of women's rights.[11]

Ironically, MSW's best opportunity came immediately after the Dowdy hearing. In 1963 all the leading civil rights movements joined in a planned March on Washington, which had been proposed and directed by Rustin. The goal was to show mass support for the proposed Civil Rights Act, which southern senators were stalling with a marathon filibuster. On August 2, 1963, the segregationist senator Strom Thurmond of South Carolina charged that the march was being planned by Communists and subversives. When the media ignored his claims, Thurmond published in the August 13, 1963, *Congressional Record* a copy the FBI had supplied him of Rustin's 1953 arrest sheet for "sex perversion" in Pasadena, and tried to smear the entire movement with "Mr. Rustin's ludicrous record." Although most disapproved of Rustin's trysts with other men, the civil rights leaders publicly defended him. On August 28 the march drew 250,000 women and men (including nine MSW members) to the Washington Mall. Their assembly and Dr. King's "I Have a Dream" speech changed American history.[12]

Thurmond's August 13 speech was a classic mixture of race-baiting, gay-bashing, and anti-Communist paranoia—a reactionary strategy that was ripe for attack. Yet neither Kameny nor MSW issued a press release, showed solidarity with their civil rights colleagues, or made an effort to contact Rustin or the other organizers. Kameny recalls only one interaction between the homophile and civil rights leadership: when he asked that homophile literature be distributed at a SCLC event, the organizers declined to do so.[13]

At the same time that the civil rights movement was gaining national stature, the second wave of feminism was taking off, following the publication of Betty Friedan's *The Feminine Mystique* (1963). Although Friedan presented herself as a bored Jewish housewife dissatisfied with the bad deal women faced in marriage, the ideas in her book were adapted from the European leftist intellectuals Gunnar Myrdal and Simone de Beauvoir. Myrdal and Beauvoir had analogized women's experience to that of people of color: both groups were oppressed by systematic discriminations that had no natural or rational basis, and individuals in each group lived their lives within the stigmatizing ideology of patriarchal racism. The race analogy was a powerful idea, and Pauli Murray worked to give it constitutional bite through her work for the President's Commission for Women in 1963 and, later, in connection with the ACLU. Like Rustin, Murray, who was a black lesbian working in Washington in 1963, had no connection with MSW. MSW had several female members, most prominently Lilli Vincenz, a lesbian who had been dishonorably discharged from the Army, but it was almost as disconnected from the emerging women's rights movement as it was from the civil rights one.[14]

Activism in Philadelphia offered a partial contrast. Established in 1961, Philadelphia's Janus Society enjoyed significant support from lesbians. Its first chair was Mae Polakoff, a "stereotypic Jewish suburban lady," and its secretary was Joan Fleischmann, a schoolteacher. Like Kameny, they embraced the radical idea that lesbians and gay men were a persecuted minority seeking their civil rights. In January 1963 Janus joined with MSW, Mattachine New York, and DOB New York to form an Eastern Conference of Homophile Organizations (ECHO). On Labor Day weekend, ECHO held its first conference, at Philadelphia's Drake Hotel. The primary topic of the gathering was the legal persecution of homosexuals through sodomy and solicitation laws and civil service exclusions. The younger participants not only accepted the conference's homo equality theme, but demanded that the movement be more militant. One twenty-six-year-old firebrand, Janus's Clark Polak, physically threatened the manager of the hotel, who tried to cancel the conference because of its sexual content.[15]

After the ECHO conference, Polak won the presidency of the Janus Society. Under his hardworking leadership Janus attracted many more members, almost all of them young white males. It raised money, staged bigger events, and converted its newsletter into *Drum*, a magazine mixing male homoerotica, news, and pro-gay propaganda. Like Kameny, Polak believed that homosexual intimacy was morally good and that the state had no business prying into gay people's private lives or discriminating against them in any way. In its January 1964 newsletter, Janus called for Pennsylvania to adopt the Model Penal Code, including its deregulation of consensual sodomy and fornication: "[P]rivate sexual acts of consenting adults are matters of individual preference and are not rightfully the concern of the law." Polak was unsuccessful in attracting mainstream attention to his proposal, however, and was unaware that the Pennsylvania Bar Association (advised by Professor Louis Schwartz) was drafting a revised penal code. More-over, Polak's leadership style and agenda alienated the increasingly outspoken lesbian community.[16]

In 1964, Marge McCann and Joan Fleischmann re-created Mattachine Phila-delphia as a better sex-integrated alternative to Janus. It also had a different agenda, one focusing on employment discrimination by the government. (On July 4, 1965, Kameny, Barbara Gittings, and other Mattachine activists protested state job discrimination by picketing Independence Hall, an event repeated an-nually until 1970.) The sodomy law, lesbians also argued, was rarely deployed by the police to arrest women, whereas gay men were regularly hauled off to jail. Some took a different point of view after the police raided Rusty's, a lesbian bar, and apprehended twelve women. Just as the police arrived, Byrna Aronson kissed her partner on the cheek, and an officer arrested her. "And I said, 'What for?' He said, 'Sodomy.' I just started to laugh." The raid on Rusty's radicalized Aronson and other lesbians. When Philadelphia's DOB reorganized itself as the Homo-phile Action League (HAL) in 1968, it asserted as its main purpose "to strive to change society's legal, social, and scientific attitudes toward the homosexual in order to achieve justified recognition of the homosexual as a first class citizen and a first class human being." Like Janus, HAL made sodomy repeal a top prior-ity, but neither group established any connection to the legal and political figures who were already working on the matter. In fact, the bar association's committee had already completed its draft penal code, reducing consensual sodomy to a misdemeanor.[17]

Legislative Resistance at the State Level: Florida and New York

As in Pennsylvania, legislatures and bar associations all over the country con-cluded that their state criminal codes were outdated, incoherent, and ineffective, and lawyers resolved to revise, update, and recodify them. By 1969 nine states had adopted new criminal codes, and more than twenty others had code revision commissions working on comprehensive penal law reform.[18] Advised by Ben-thamite academics who accepted the idea that criminal law should attack only social harms, commissions relied on the Model Penal Code as their template. Because the code decriminalized consensual sodomy, this topic invariably emerged, but states did not rush to follow Illinois's lead to decriminalize entirely. In 1967, Minnesota's legislature revised the sex crimes portion of its code and reduced consensual sodomy to a gross misdemeanor, but did not decriminalize it. In states with discernible lesbian and gay communities, there was particularly strong political pressure to preserve consensual sodomy as a crime, lest the state be seen as "promoting homosexuality."[19]

The most elaborate reported discussion occurred in June 1964 within Florida's criminal law reform Advisory Committee. Reflecting on Kinsey and his philosophy, the committee's four medical experts urged that Florida decriminalize sodomy for the same liberal and practical reasons Illinois had. "[T]he homosexual who engages in homosexual activities exclusively with other homosexuals in private presents no harm or danger to society, and . . . ordinarily it is not their compulsion to cruise and try to involve children; . . . the child molester is in another group." One expert opined that "ours is supposed to be a free society, and he felt it to be immoral to invade the privacy of human beings if they are in no way encroaching on the rights of another human being."[20]

The judges and law enforcement officers on the committee disagreed, arguing that consensual sodomy could not be separated from homosexuality, which was a public menace. By their account, homosexuals preyed on children, were security risks and untrustworthy employees, and carried disease and contagion. Accordingly, the law enforcement officials recommended not only that the "crime against nature" be retained as a felony in Florida, but also that the felony be expanded beyond anal and oral sex, to include "[a]ny act providing or tending to provide sexual gratification between two persons of the same sex." For the Florida lawyers, there was no separation of the public and the private for the homosexual: "[T]o ignore consenting [homosexual] adults in private would certainly be to condone their actions and before long the problem would be out of control." Even sodomy performed in the home corrupted children and perpetuated a criminal class that had just been exposed by the Johns Committee's "purple report." The Florida legislature declined to adopt the proposals and, in 1967, created a new Law Reform Commission to approach criminal law reform more systematically.[21]

If any state were to follow the example of Illinois, one might have guessed it would be New York—where Republicans like Governor Nelson Rockefeller and Democrats like Senator Robert Kennedy competed for liberal and even gay voters. The state had reduced consensual sodomy to a misdemeanor in 1950 without public backlash. It would be only a small step to decriminalize consensual sodomy altogether, which is precisely what New York's Temporary Commission on Revision of the Penal Law recommended in 1964. Chaired by Assemblyman Richard Bartlett and advised by Professor Wechsler, the commission followed the Model Penal Code to decriminalize consensual sodomy.[22]

Bartlett and Wechsler were only vaguely aware of the growing lesbian and gay community in the state. They did not know about Mattachine or DOB New York, or that its new generation of leaders—Dick Leitsch, Craig Rodwell, Randy Wicker (Mattachine) and Barbara Gittings and Kay Tobin (DOB)—shared Kameny's vision of homo equality. These leaders, in turn, did not know sodomy reform was on the legislative agenda until the commission issued its report. For Mattachine, the main priority in 1964 was police entrapment of gay men, as part of Mayor Robert Wagner's effort to clean up the city during the World's Fair.[23]

While DOB and Mattachine played no role in the decriminalization campaign, they did figure in the opposition. Religious leaders were nervous about the decline of sexual morals and the advance of homosexuality in public culture. Two commission members dissented from the decriminalization of adultery and consensual sodomy—Assemblyman Julius Volker from Buffalo and Senator John Hughes from Syracuse, both Catholic Republicans. At public hearings the Catholic Welfare Committee joined in the opposition. If adultery and sodomy were decriminalized, the church argued, the state would be understood as accepting immoral conduct, and this would only encourage people to engage in more of it. (The church did not insist that fornication remain a crime.) Bartlett, a devout Catholic, did not waver in his position: criminal sodomy laws were neither humane nor socially productive. The commission backed him, but Volker and Hughes served notice that they would take their case to the legislature.[24]

Bartlett and Volker agreed to allow the reform bill to proceed to a vote as written, but to accompany the reform bill with two bills amending the new code: one criminalizing adultery, and the other consensual sodomy. In the Assembly, Volker justified the amendments as "inspired by the entreaties of churchmen who fear we would be appearing to give passive approval to deviant [sic] sexual practices." The sodomy amendment passed 115–16. Many different constituencies voted for it—Jews and Protestants as well as Catholics, liberals as well as conservatives. The adultery amendment achieved only a 73–49 majority, which was not sufficient for passage; on a second vote, it squeaked through. When a discouraged Bartlett called Wechsler to report the votes, the latter drily replied, "Well, that figures. There are a lot more of us than there are of them."[25]

Although everybody knew the controversy over the sodomy bill only concerned homosexuals, DOB and Mattachine did no lobbying in Albany. In contrast, Charlie Tobin, the longtime lobbyist for the Catholic Church, was welcomed in every office as he drummed up support for the Volker amendments. In the upper chamber of the legislature, Senator Hughes made the public space argument: if freed from legal restraints, homosexuals "would become more public in their displays." Opposing the sodomy amendment, Senator Joseph Zaretsky said, "I oppose making criminals out of sick people because they are sick." The appeal of pity for sick homosexuals may have narrowed the vote. The Senate adopted the sodomy amendment 39–16, and the adultery one by 38–17.[26]

The new penal code and the sodomy and adultery amendments all went to Governor Rockefeller. Adhering to the deal that had ensured passage of the code, Bartlett recommended that the governor sign all three bills. Volker and Hughes insisted that the governor sign the amendments, lest the state be accused of lending "tacit approval of immoral conduct." Opposed to the amendments were the Bar Association of the City of New York, the ACLU, and the Mattachine Society of New York. Coming late to the debate, Mattachine argued that the sodomy amendment reflected legislative "intolerance and ignorance." Although the consensual sodomy law was almost never enforced, "its very existence encourages a sense of estrangement from and disrespect for the law and for those who enforce it." In June 1965, the governor signed all three bills.[27]

The experience of sodomy reform in New York and Florida was, in the end, quite similar. While enough homosexuals lived in each state to arouse anxiety among traditionalists—especially Baptists in Florida and Catholics in New York—and thereby to harden opposition, there were not enough open homosexuals to constitute a political reason for legislators to think twice about voting for criminalization. Gay activists' claims that homosexuals are decent people not afflicted with mental illness may also have undermined sodomy reform, for most opponents of criminalization believed homosexuals to be sick. Under these circumstances, sodomy law supporters latched onto the various no promo homo rationales: sodomy reform would "promote" homosexuality from a criminal status to just a sickness, and perhaps even to normalcy if gay activists had their way, as well as fueling increased homosexual activism. They would, of course, be proved right about that.

San Francisco's Society for Individual Rights and Los Angeles's Mattachine Society

Equal citizenship also became the rallying cry for gay activists in San Francisco. With William Beardemphl and other activists, José Sarria, the Black Cat's singing waiter, organized the Society for Individual Rights (SIR) in early 1964. Like MSW, SIR maintained that gay people were a persecuted minority denied their constitutional freedoms by prejudiced state officers. SIR informed its members of their legal rights through its glossy monthly, Vector, and assembled a network of lawyers to represent gay and lesbian defendants. As Beardemphl put it, the case for gay rights rested on "present[ing] the homosexual as he is—by far and large a responsible and moral member of his community and one seeking only the equal protection of the laws." Within three years, SIR saw its membership grow from 250 to more than 1,000, making it the largest homophile organization in the country. Like Mattachine New York and Janus in Philadelphia, however, SIR was out of touch with statewide sodomy reform. Between 1964 and 1967, the legislature's Penal Code Revision Project drafted new sex crime provisions—with no input from SIR. Following the Model Penal Code, Project Director Arthur

Sherry proposed to deregulate consensual sodomy. The election of conservative Republican Ronald Reagan as governor in 1966, however, buried sodomy reform for the next eight years.[28]

SIR did, however, cooperate with other local homophile groups. One product of these alliances was the Council of Religion and the Homosexual, a forum that included mainstream clergy. The council's first public event was a costume ball at California Hall, on Polk Street, for New Year's Day 1965. Although the council secured permission from the police, more than a dozen officers nonetheless showed up to harass the costumed crowd. They arrested Herb Donaldson and Evander Smith, the lawyers advising the council, and Nancy May, a straight woman working with it. The Protestant ministers and their wives who had organized the event could not believe what they had witnessed, and the next day seven ministers held a press conference to denounce police "intimidation, broken promises, and obvious hostility" to law-abiding clergy and minorities. DOB leaders Del Martin and Phyllis Lyon worked with other leaders to establish a Citizens Alert to report police abuse. Just as Kameny's MSW had been able to discourage police enforcement of sodomy and antisolicitation laws in the nation's capital after 1962, DOB and Citizens Alert apparently stifled excessive enforcement in San Francisco.[29]

Los Angeles presented a contrast. Unlike San Francisco, where the homophile professionals worked with the class- and race-mixed gay bar clientele to form a community by the mid-1960s, Los Angeles's gay population remained relatively isolated even from one another. L.A. gays responded tepidly to the abuses accompanying police enforcement of California's antihomosexual laws. Between 1962 and 1964, the LAPD arrested an average of 770 men (and a few women) each year for committing the felonies of sodomy or oral copulation. Between May 1964 and April 1965, the police arrested 2,994 Angelenos for committing the misdemeanors of lewd vagrancy and public indecency, laws enforced only against soliciting homosexuals. In San Francisco, New York, Washington, or Philadelphia, such a pattern would have triggered organized protests and press coverage. It was not until 1967 that gay Angelenos staged public demonstrations against LAPD abuses.[30]

Homophile leaders ranging from Lilli Vincenz and Frank Kameny in Washington to José Sarria and Bill Beardemphl in San Francisco to Barbara Gittings and Clark Polak in Philadelphia to Dick Leitsch in New York had, by the latter half of the 1960s, formed a consensus that gay men and lesbians deserved equal treatment by the state as well as toleration of their private conduct. Allowing ECHO to lapse, these and other activists formed the North American Conference of Homophile Organizations (NACHO). In April 1966, the initial NACHO planning conference adopted this central resolution: "Homosexual American citizens should have precise equality with all other citizens before the law and are entitled to social and economic equality of opportunity." NACHO later endorsed "Gay is Good" as the slogan of the homophile movement. Explicit in this agenda was the proposition that gay people were *citizens,* not *outlaws.* Implicit was the notion that consensual sodomy laws must be repealed.[31]

The Constitutional Right to Privacy and Sodomy Reform, 1965–69

The libertarian and pragmatic arguments that persuaded Illinois legislators to repeal their consensual sodomy law were, by 1965, often counterbalanced by community and religious concerns that repeal would promote homosexuality. Just as the political process was becoming less friendly to sodomy repeal in states with visible homosexual communities, the Warren Court offered a new possibility for reform through judicial invalidation. As Clark Polak put it, "Law reform will not be effectuated through State Legislatures. . . . We see the solution within the Federal Court system, with the Supreme Court as the final voice. The Connecticut birth control decision points the way—invasion of privacy." Polak was referring to *Griswold v. Connecticut* (1965). Although the Court would not advance gay rights in the 1960s, *Griswold* fueled a national conversation about the balance between individual sexual freedom and community mores that called consensual sodomy laws into constitutional question.[32]

Griswold v. Connecticut *and the Constitutional Privacy Right*

Planned Parenthood engaged in decades of activism to persuade state governments to make contraceptives available in order to give women greater control over the timing of their pregnancies. In *Poe v. Ullman* (1961), Yale law professor Fowler Harper (formerly a colleague of Professor Kinsey) argued for the group that sexual pleasure is a key feature of individual flourishing, and that state laws restricting personal sexual choices made by consenting adults are presumptively invalid invasions of liberty interests protected by the Constitution's Due Process Clause. Five justices dodged these arguments by voting to dismiss the appeal on procedural grounds.[33]

Two of the four dissenting justices offered theories for invalidating the Connecticut law, which banned the use of contraceptives. William O. Douglas was a maverick liberal who treasured human independence. He read the Due Process Clause to protect individual liberties implicit in the concept of a "free society." The principle was antitotalitarian: "[F]reedom bootlegged around the law is freedom crippled." Douglas objected to Connecticut's requirement of sexual conformity. The Constitution does not allow the state to commandeer family and medical relationships to its own agenda, for that is the essence of totalitarianism. Although he did not adopt Harper's Kinsey-based assertions about the centrality of sexual expression to individual flourishing, Douglas's dissent was consistent with such an approach.[34]

A patrician of the law, John Marshall Harlan was neither liberal nor traditionalist. He read the liberty protection of the Due Process Clause not as a simple expression of abstract individualism, but as a "balance which our Nation, built upon postulates of respect for the liberty of the individual, has struck between that liberty and the demands of organized society." The balance is one informed by history, "the traditions from which it developed as well as the traditions from which it broke. That tradition is a living thing." The living tradition of our common law has rendered marriage a central institution, and indeed a primary mechanism whereby individual desire and community norms are balanced. "The laws regarding marriage which provide both when the sexual powers may be used and the legal and societal context in which children are born and brought up, as well as laws forbidding adultery, fornication and homosexual practices which express the negative of the proposition, confining sexuality to lawful marriage, form a pattern so deeply pressed into the substance of our social life that any Constitutional doctrine in this area must build upon that basis." Because Connecticut's law meddled with the core marital decisions that must be left to husband and wife—the form of sexual intimacy and the planning of childbearing—it upset that historical balance and was therefore unconstitutional. Harlan's dissent was an effort to provide a constitutional middle ground between Kinsey's hedonism and the Catholic Church's meddling traditionalism, a ground using history to help set the complicated relationship between individuals and society.[35]

Given such powerful, if clashing, dissenting opinions, Planned Parenthood and its allies at Yale Law School continued their campaign against Connecticut's law. Estelle Griswold, the director of Connecticut's chapter of Planned Parenthood, and a New Haven married couple brought another lawsuit, and the Court granted review in 1964. Harper was on his deathbed and unable to participate in *Griswold*, but his libertarian approach was followed by the briefs for Estelle Griswold (written by Yale law professor Thomas Emerson and Catherine Roraback), Planned Parenthood (Morris Ernst and Harriet Pilpel), and the ACLU (Melvin Wulf). All stressed the same "basic freedom, namely, the right of married people to have sex relations *and* (not *or*) to decide whether to bring new life into the world." The state's interference with this right "in light of the facts of human sexuality, the traditional place of marriage in our society and the obvious need, medical and otherwise, for many couples to plan or limit their families, cannot

rationally be defended." Like Harper's brief in *Poe*, the briefs in *Griswold* emphasized that the state ought not be able to require married couples to choose between the health or life of the wife and the sexual abstinence of the couple: given
the realities of the human sex drive, abstinence is not possible for most couples
or is destructive of their relationship.[36]

At the justices' *Griswold* conference, Chief Justice Earl Warren was inclined to
overturn the law, because it intruded too broadly into the "most confidential
relationship in our society"—namely, marriage. Other justices propounded various doctrinal theories to support the chief's conclusion—a right of association
"on the periphery" of the First Amendment's protection (Douglas); the Due Process Clause's protection of liberty (Harlan); and a nontextual "right to marry,
maintain a home, have a family," perhaps related to the Fourth Amendment's
"right to be let alone" (Tom Clark). A clear majority voted to invalidate the anticontraception law, and Warren assigned the opinion to Douglas. Most of Douglas's opinion consisted in an effort to find zones of privacy within the "penumbras"
of the Bill of Rights, a departure from his own *Poe* dissent. Although his analysis
of the *source* of the privacy right moved further away from Harlan's position,
Douglas's articulation of the *scope* of that right moved toward Harlan's relational
position, for it stressed the fact that this was a right of a *married* couple to choose
the terms of their sexual relations and family planning. Such a right was "older
than the Bill of Rights."[37]

In dissent, Justices Hugo Black and Potter Stewart objected that there was no
textual basis for a *constitutional* right of privacy. Agreeing with Black on this
point, Justice Byron White nevertheless agreed with the Court's result because he
found no rational basis for the state's outdated law. Concurring, Justice Arthur
Goldberg (joined by Warren and Brennan) responded that the Ninth Amendment provided a sufficient textual hook for such a right: "The enumeration in
the Constitution, of certain rights, shall not be construed to deny or disparage
others retained by the people." Echoing Harlan (who concurred in the Court's
judgment based on his *Poe* dissent), the concurring justices argued that the rights
"retained by the people" are those recognized by our legal traditions—including
the sanctity of marriage. Like both Douglas and Harlan, therefore, they emphasized Connecticut's intrusion into the marital relationship. The concurring
opinion concluded with an admonition that the right of privacy does not prevent the state from regulating sexual misconduct. "'Adultery, homosexuality and
the like are sexual intimacies which the State forbids . . . but the intimacy of husband and wife is necessarily an essential and accepted feature of the institution
of marriage, an institution which the State not only must allow, but which always
and in every age it has fostered and protected.'"[38]

By this account, not a single justice suggested that consensual sodomy enjoyed any constitutional protection. The six justices who voted to strike down the law emphasized its intrusion into (heterosexual) *marital* relations, and four of those six (Warren, Harlan, Brennan, and Goldberg) explicitly stated that a tradition-based approach gave the state room to regulate "homosexuality and adultery," the same pair of sins the New York legislature was targeting for community concern. Three justices (Black, Stewart, and White) declined to recognize a *constitutional* right of sexual privacy. Nonetheless, the Court's recognition of such a constitutional right opened the courts as a forum for gay people and their allies to attack sodomy laws in states whose legislatures would not budge. *Griswold* set in motion an intimate but controversial involvement of federal and state judges with gay rights advocates that endures to the present day.

The American Civil Liberties Union and Sodomy Law Reform

The ACLU has a well-earned reputation for defending the liberties of the most unpopular minorities, but for much of its history that stance did not extend to sexual minorities. On January 7, 1957, at the height of the antihomosexual Kulturkampf, the ACLU declared: "It is not within the province of the Union to evaluate the social validity of the laws aimed at the suppression or elimination of homosexuals. We recognize that overt acts of homosexuality constitute a common law felony and that there is no constitutional prohibition against such state and local laws on this subject as are deemed by such states or communities to be socially necessary or beneficial."[39]

On the other hand, the ACLU never denied that homosexuals should be afforded full protections of legal procedures and rules. Union-affiliated attorneys were virtually the only ones who would represent homosexuals dismissed from the armed forces or the civil service in the 1950s and early 1960s. San Francisco ACLU attorneys Mitchell and Juliet Lowenthal tirelessly represented gay men in criminal proceedings and lesbian or gay bars whose licenses were revoked. ACLU-affiliated Professor Monroe Freedman represented the Mattachine Society of Washington, D.C., (MSW) at the 1963 Dowdy hearings. The Florida ACLU provided lawyers and other assistance to Richard Inman's battles against the many antigay discriminations in that state.[40]

An ACLU member since 1950, Frank Kameny turned to Union attorneys for advice and counsel after he was dismissed from the Army Map Service. In November 1961, at the same time that he was creating MSW, Kameny was one of the founding members of the National Capital Area ACLU (ACLU-NCA). Its affiliated attorneys represented—often with great success—gay or bisexual men discharged from the civil service throughout the 1960s. In 1964 David Carliner, the president of ACLU-NCA, challenged the national Union's assumption that "homosexuality is 'not now a pressing problem in civil liberties terms.'" To the contrary, "homosexual conduct continues to provide the ground for a substantial number of discharges from government service and the police activity to ferret them out has been the source of continuing civil liberties violations." The national ACLU's Due Process Committee took up the issue of homosexual conduct and concluded, in a memorandum of November 24, 1965, that the ACLU should adopt the ALI's position that private sexual behavior between consenting adults was no concern of the law. Before the ACLU's governing board, Pilpel and Carliner argued that the principle they were fighting for in the birth control cases was "the right to do with one's body what he wishes." This was "a very fundamental civil liberty," and the ACLU's position should be that the right of privacy that the Union helped win in *Griswold* protected sodomy as well as other sexual behavior between consenting adults. In December the board agreed.[41]

The Union issued a new "ACLU Statement on Homosexuality" on August 13, 1967. Invoking the Model Penal Code (MPC), the Union declared that *Griswold*'s "right of privacy should extend to all private sexual conduct, heterosexual or homosexual, of consenting adults. The judgment of such conduct, including its morality, is the province of conscience and religion, but is not a matter for invoking the penal statutes of the secular state." Creating a constitutional principle from Louis Schwartz's MPC commentary, the Union also condemned the arbitrary enforcement of sodomy statutes as deeply inconsistent with the "equal protection of the law." The Union, however, also followed the MPC in affirming the state's authority to criminalize public solicitation. "The public has the right to be free from solicitation, molestation, and annoyance in public facilities and places."[42]

While this document represented an important statement of the constitutional rights Frank Kameny advocated in his 1961 Supreme Court brief, it was (characteristically) Kameny himself who was the first to criticize the new ACLU statement. "The overwhelming majority of arrests of homosexuals, the country over, are not sexual acts in any private (or even public) context, but for solicitations of one sort or another," he observed, recalling his own arrest ten years earlier. "Basically, what you are doing by legalizing private homosexual acts, but leaving anti-solicitation laws of *all* kinds indiscriminately on the books, is to say, by analogy, that it is legal for two people to have dinner together, but illegal for one to invite the other to that perfectly legal dinner." Kameny also reminded the Union that many antisolicitation statutes focused only on sodomy solicitation and therefore discriminated against lesbians and gay men. Even the proudly liberal ACLU was sensitive to the distinction between *private* homosexual intimacy and *public* homosexual solicitation. Like the ALI a decade earlier, the ACLU was not willing to support constitutional protections for the latter, for it mobilized all the traditionalist concerns about "promoting" homosexuality and endorsing sex for pleasure as a moral good.[43]

The Cases of Alvin Buchanan and Clive Michael Boutilier

While the ACLU was honing its new gay-friendly understanding of the Constitution, others were invoking *Griswold* to challenge state sodomy laws. Gay residents of Seattle, Washington, were shocked by the arrest of the Reverend Keith Rhinehart for sodomy in 1965. The police may have framed the married Rhinehart, as the testimony of his alleged sexual partner (a male hustler) changed repeatedly. After the court sentenced the minister to ten years in prison, a coalition of gays and straights formed the Dorian Society in 1966, in part to support Rhinehart's appeal. The reverend's main argument was that he was innocent and the evidence against him fabricated; his backup argument was that Seattle enforced its sodomy law in a discriminatory manner. The twelve to twenty-five arrests made each year focused exclusively on homosexual activities, even though Kinsey had shown that most straight couples also engaged in sodomy. His final contention was that the sodomy law was "unconstitutional in that it purports to make criminal, private consensual acts which are not affected with sufficient public interest to be the subject matter of the exercise of the police power of the state." The Washington Supreme Court summarily rejected all these arguments, and Rhinehart languished in prison until 1972, when a federal judge vacated his sentence because it rested on perjured testimony.[44]

The first full-fledged privacy challenge to a consensual sodomy law was brought by Dallas attorney Henry McCluskey Jr. on behalf of Alvin Buchanan. Homosexual subcultures became visible in Texas's largest cities in the 1960s, and the predictable result was police surveillance and arrests. Between 1963 and 1969, Dallas police apprehended an average of sixty-nine men a year, most of them in the shadow of the revolving Pegasus atop the Magnolia Petroleum Building in downtown Dallas. (Within blocks of the Pegasus were the YMCA, several gay bars, and cruising areas.) During the winter of 1969 Buchanan, "a stocky man with dark piercing eyes," was arrested twice for having oral sex in public restrooms, once in a municipal park and then at Sears Roebuck. The Texas trial judge sentenced him to two concurrent five-year prison terms for these violations.[45]

Police harassment had inspired Dallas gays to form a "Circle of Friends." A member of the Circle, McCluskey appealed these convictions within the state court system but, at the same time, brought a lawsuit in federal court seeking an injunction against further enforcement of Texas's consensual sodomy law. In addition to Buchanan, plaintiffs included Travis Strickland, a Dallas gay activist who said he feared arrest, and a married couple, Michael and Janet Gibson, whose marital intimacies were also subject to the Texas sodomy law. McCluskey argued that the Texas sodomy law violated the privacy rights of all four plaintiffs. Following *Griswold*'s reasoning, the three-judge court ruled that the married couple, but not the gay men, had a privacy right to engage in consensual sodomy. But Judge Sarah Hughes also struck down the entire Texas sodomy law because it was unconstitutionally overbroad; hence the gay plaintiffs benefited from the married couple's successful claim. Hughes's is the first judicial decision invalidating a state sodomy law because of its invasion of privacy rights.[46]

A determined traditionalist, Dallas district attorney Henry Wade appealed this judgment directly to the U.S. Supreme Court. McCluskey filed a cross-appeal, challenging Judge Hughes's distinction between sodomy between spouses (constitutionally protected) and between unmarried persons (unprotected). Like the ACLU, he read *Griswold* as a starting rather than a stopping point. In addition to the privacy problem, Texas's criminal code was fiercely discriminatory. For consensual oral sex in a public restroom, the gay defendant could receive a fifteen-year prison term, while penile-vaginal sex in the same restroom carried with it no jail time and a $100 fine. In support of Buchanan and representing twenty homophile groups, NACHO filed an amicus brief pressing the equality issue and arguing that sodomy laws remain on the books in states like Texas "primarily to punish, harass and otherwise denigrate the male homosexual, to make him feel inferior, unworthy, and an outlaw of society."[47]

The Supreme Court did not rule on these arguments. Instead, the Court vacated the judgment and remanded the case to the lower court to consider whether it was proper to enjoin future prosecutions of the statute when the state courts stood ready to adjudicate actual convictions, such as Buchanan's. A Texas state appellate tribunal overturned one of the sodomy convictions against Buchanan on the ground that the police violated the Fourth Amendment when they spied inside a closed toilet stall, but reaffirmed the second sodomy conviction. Making the same arguments he had made in 1970, McCluskey petitioned the Supreme Court to review the remaining conviction. In February 1972, the justices unanimously declined to hear the case, and Buchanan went to Texas's Ramsey Prison. He died in 1999, at age sixty-one. Attorney McCluskey passed away even earlier, murdered in 1973 by William Hovila, who claimed to be his lover.[48]

In 1969, the ACLU for the first time applied its 1967 statement in a constitutional context. NYU professor Norman Dorsen, a former clerk to Justice Harlan, became the Union's general counsel in 1968. A cosmopolitan New Yorker, he and his wife, Harriette (also a lawyer), knew many homosexuals and considered state persecution of them a core offense to a legitimate constitutionalism. Dorsen's vision was to ensure that the ACLU take firmer positions in favor of the free speech and personal privacy of the most unpopular Americans, while at the same time insisting on equal citizenship for women and gay people. At his insistence the Union agreed to represent two gay men (Richard Schlegel and Robert Larry Adams) who had been dismissed from federal employment and denied security clearances. Dorsen's briefs to the Supreme Court relied on the same arguments that Kameny had raised in 1961: gay people are good citizens, homosexuality is an acceptable variation from the norm, and antigay discrimination is "odious," unjust, and contrary to the equal protection component of the Fifth Amendment. While "irrational fears and prejudices abound . . . the government may not add its approval or sanction to these prejudices. Otherwise, Negroes, communists, and bastards would not have been entitled to the constitutional protections that the Court has consistently provided" these minorities.[49] Solicitor general and former Harvard Law School dean Erwin Griswold defended the employment discrimination. "[H]omosexuals are still looked on with much disfavor, and their sexual conduct is frequently made criminal. . . . The willingness of a person to engage in behavior which flouts social and legal norms . . . justifies a reluctance to trust him with national secrets." The Supreme Court allowed the antigay judgments to stand without comment.[50]

In the Kameny, Buchanan, Adams, and Schlegel cases, the Supreme Court, without recorded dissent, ducked serious constitutional issues posed by gay people's demands for recognition. The homophile leaders and the ACLU were optimistic in thinking that the Warren Court would extend to homosexuals the same privacy rights that *Griswold* had recognized for married couples or the same antidiscrimination principle that *Brown* had established for people of color. The Court's reluctance was illustrated by the fate of Clive Michael Boutilier (1934–2003). The oldest son in a large Nova Scotian family, Boutilier had dropped out of school to work full-time and emigrated to New York for better job opportunities. In 1965, when he applied for citizenship, he admitted that he had been arrested on a charge of sodomy and had engaged in oral and anal sex with other men as well as women. On the basis of these admissions, the Public Health Service certified that Boutilier was a person "afflicted with psychopathic personality." Under the McCarran-Walter Immigration and Nationality Act of 1952, that was grounds for deporting Boutilier back to Canada.[51]

Boutilier desperately wanted to stay in the United States—not just because of his job, but also to be with his life partner, Eugene O'Rourke. Supported by the ACLU and Polak's Homosexual Law Reform Society (HLRS), immigration rights attorney Blanch Freedman represented him. Freedman introduced expert evidence that Boutilier was not "psychopathic," as scientists used that term. Nor was he exclusively homosexual, as he had periodic intercourse with women. The INS rejected this evidence as irrelevant, on the ground that Congress in 1952 intended to exclude all "homosexuals and sex perverts" as per se psychopaths. The INS, however, was actually not quite so certain about that contention. During its deliberation in Boutilier's case, the agency proposed that Congress clarify its authority by amending the statute to exclude immigrants afflicted with "sexual deviation" as well as "psychopathic personality." Without significant debate Congress enacted that amendment in October 1965, two months after the INS ordered Boutilier deported.[52]

Engaged in her own life-and-death struggle with scleroderma, Blanch Freedman took the case all the way to the Supreme Court. Her brief presented Boutilier as a respectable person who could not reasonably be classified as a psychopath. HLRS filed an amicus brief arguing that medical evidence provided no support for the INS's supposition that homosexual activities or homosexuality was *any* evidence of a "psychopathic personality," and the INS's per se rule was unconstitutional because it was unconnected with the expert consensus. Freedman died on April 16, 1967. The Court affirmed the INS several weeks later. Justice Clark's opinion for the Court reasoned from Boutilier's admitted sodomy that he was a "homosexual" and from his homosexuality that he was afflicted with "psychopathic personality." Clark ignored the possibility that Boutilier might be bisexual and dismissed the medical experts' suggestion (supported by the statute's legislative history) that not all homosexuals were psychopaths.[53]

Tom Clark was a social conservative from Texas, but the eminent liberals of the decade were of like mind on this issue. Thurgood Marshall, the great NAACP lawyer, was the solicitor general who authorized the federal government's brief that Clark followed. Chief Justice Warren, the Progressive who as governor had sponsored California's antihomosexual Kulturkampf (chapter 4), conceded at conference in Boutilier's case that "a homo immigrant might not be psychotic," but ultimately joined Clark's opinion. Justice Black, the mastermind of the Warren Court's liberal activism in the 1950s, suggested that the statute could be interpreted either way, but that he leaned toward the view that "psychopathic personality means sexual deviate," the term used in the 1965 statute. Decided two years after *Griswold*, the majority opinion in *Boutilier* was an aggressively antihomosexual reading of vague statutory language.[54]

Boutilier illustrates the social limits of the privacy right. Not only would cautious judges like Harlan be unwilling to extend privacy-based protections to long-regulated homosexual intimacies, but more-liberal judges like Warren were uncertain about using the Court's political capital to protect homosexuals against state discrimination. Indeed, all six justices joining Clark's *Boutilier* opinion apparently accepted stereotypes about gay people that were widely believed by men of their age group—not only the notion that homosexuals were afflicted with mental illness, but also that they were a threat to the social order. Even the dissenting justices treated the homosexual as a pitiable "freak," who "is the product of arrested development."[55]

The Supreme Court's disposition had a devastating effect on Boutilier. Brokenhearted, he tried to commit suicide, and then was shipped back to Canada, where he remained, a quasi invalid for the rest of his life. Because of the deportation, he never saw O'Rourke again and never enjoyed another long-term relationship. Clive Michael Boutilier died, practically alone, on April 12, 2003.

The Sexual Revolution and the Official Homosexualization of Sodomy Law, 1965–69

At the same time that the Supreme Court was reaffirming traditional assumptions about sexual "deviance" in *Boutilier*, American sexual mores and behaviors were changing. Old taboos were falling, including those against interracial sexuality, sex outside of marriage, and oral sex. The baby boom generation was coming of age, and it proved to be a generation of sexual rebels. Boomers had sex outside of marriage, had sex in public, engaged in sodomy—and were open and unashamed about it. Suddenly, it appeared that millions of Americans accepted the liberal view of sexual morality, that sex for pleasure alone is acceptable. Changing public opinion supported sex crime liberalization along Model Penal Code lines. Indeed, young people's insistence that the state not interfere in their lives threatened social turmoil if criminal law did *not* liberalize. But at the same time, traditionalists continued to argue that the state has responsibility for setting good examples for the community (especially its young people) and maintaining a "decent" public sphere. In the 1960s, America clearly had to construct a new line between sexual freedom and community values. That line was provisionally drawn across the backsides of homosexuals, still the universal scapegoats.

The Sexual Revolution

The engine of the sexual revolution was young heterosexual women. Helen Gurley Brown's *Sex and the Single Girl* (1962) celebrated women's sexual liberation once the Pill and other forms of contraception allowed them to enjoy sexual pleasure without the risks of pregnancy. As they entered adolescence and young adulthood, female baby boomers still aspired to be married, but an increasing number of them combined that goal with earning college degrees, pursuing careers, and enjoying sexual pleasure. Young men felt the same way about sexual emancipation. Between 1963 and 1975 a sex-positive attitude swept the country.

Demographers have documented the primary effects of this revolution, which included a widespread willingness to engage in sexual intercourse before marriage; the rise of sexual cohabitation and childbearing outside of marriage; the postponement of marriage and childbearing; the decline in the number of children per family; and steady increases in divorce rates.[56]

Some of the most interesting features of the sexual revolution have not been well documented. Although we know that the baby boomers engaged in penile-vaginal sex earlier and outside of marriage, we do not know about the incidence of other sexual activities. Anecdotal evidence suggests that fellatio and, especially, cunnilingus were increasingly popular. As researchers William Masters and Virginia Johnson publicized in *Human Sexual Response* (1966), the female orgasm originated in the clitoris, not the vagina. Because the clitoris retracted during penile-vaginal sex, "normal intercourse" celebrated by traditionalists was unlikely to produce an orgasm for the female partner, unless it was accompanied by oral or manual stimulation. This may have encouraged more homosexual experimentation among women. If cunnilingus stimulated the primary source of pleasure for women, men were sexually expendable.[57]

The baby boomers were hardly the first generation to find joy in nonmarital and nonprocreative sex, but they were the first to proclaim it openly and without shame. This attitude was part of a larger antiauthoritarianism. Boomers not only defied their parents, but denounced their values as morally obsolescent. Feminists as well as people of color embraced Simone de Beauvoir's suggestion in *The Second Sex* that, because the racism and patriarchy of American society pervasively affected the lived experiences of women and blacks, the progressive project entailed reclamation of "genuine" identities from the "false consciousness" created by oppressive stereotype-based ideologies. For women, this insight spawned consciousness-raising groups, where participants shared their experiences and feelings so that they could confront the many areas of their subordination and seek firmer grounding as women.[58]

Although of the same generation as boomer parents, José Sarria, Barbara Gittings, and Frank Kameny were precursors of this new morality. Their pro-gay politics of recognition involved a similar rejection of (religious) authority, a similar celebration of sexual fulfillment as an end in itself and not as an instrument of procreation, and a similar insistence that the objects of oppression reclaim their humanity. Did the baby boomers appreciate these coincidences? Many did not. Even in the late 1960s, few lesbians, gay men, or bisexuals were willing to "drop the mask" of compulsory heterosexuality, for those who did often encountered hostility—from progressives as well as from traditionalists. When Del Martin and Phyllis Lyon joined the National Organization for Women (NOW) in 1968, they applied as a couple. The national treasurer accepted the application enthusiastically, but when NOW president Betty Friedan found out, she was furious, and abolished the couple's membership. Friedan feared her movement would be tagged with the scarlet letter of homosexuality.[59]

Communities of color were even less accepting. Gay Latinos such as cross-dressing Sylvia Rivera (a New York City gay activist) were tormented by other young Hispanic men, who considered effeminacy degrading to their sense of manhood. Rivera's own grandmother despaired that his gender and sexual variation would lead to tragedy for him. Leading black nationalists such as Malcolm X and Huey Newton were openly homophobic; some black leaders blamed homosexuality for destroying the black family. Eldridge Cleaver condemned "Black homosexuality" as the "extreme embodiment" of a "racial death-wish." Homo-miscegenation—sex between black and white men—was the worst offense: "The white man has deprived him of his masculinity, castrated him in the center of his burning skull, and when he submits to the change and takes the white man for his lover as well as Big Daddy, he focuses on 'whiteness' all the love in his pent-up soul and turns the razor edge of hatred against 'blackness'—upon himself. He may even hate the darkness of the night."[60]

On the other hand there is evidence that the generation of Americans born between 1946 and 1961 was more accepting of homosexuality than their parents' generation. In 1973 the National Opinion Research Center asked respondents whether homosexuality was wrong. One-third of the boomer generation responded that homosexuality was just sometimes wrong or not wrong at all, in contrast to one-sixth of their parents' generation. Although more than eighty percent of the parents' generation and almost two-thirds of the children's generation believed homosexuality to be immoral, these percentages are probably much lower than those one would have found in the 1950s, when virtual unanimity of opinion made such a question not worth asking.[61]

Anecdotal evidence supports the claim that attitudes about homosexuality were moving away from unmitigated disgust or anxiety, and toward ambivalence or even tolerance. Mainstream books like David Reuben's best-selling *Everything You Always Wanted to Know About Sex** (**But Were Afraid to Ask)* began to discuss homosexual activities in a fairly neutral manner, and informed readers that oral sex between women was the height of female pleasure. "Dear Abby," the nation's most popular personal advice column, followed Sigmund Freud in advising parents that homosexuality was acceptable. Even antigay authors conceded that "[h]omosexuality used to be 'the abominable crime not to be mentioned.' In the sexy '60s, it is not only mentioned; it is freely discussed and widely analyzed."[62]

Sodomy Repeal in Connecticut, 1969

Almost everything the baby boomers did in their water beds was against the law. Unlike earlier generations, who told no one but Alfred Kinsey about their sexual nonconformities, the boomers publicly flaunted their violations. Because increasing numbers of America's youth openly cohabited in nonmarital sexual unions, the Model Penal Code's deregulation of sex outside of marriage attracted increasing support from law enforcement officials as well as civil libertarians. Although Illinois had decriminalized consensual sodomy and adultery in 1961, its new criminal code had retained open and notorious sexual cohabitation as a misdemeanor. In contrast, New York's 1965 code deregulated fornication and cohabitation because those laws were so widely flouted that lawmakers feared disrespect for the rule of law in general if extramarital but heterosexual intercourse remained criminal.

By the end of the decade legislators could no longer deny that the younger generation's defiance of sexual convention extended to oral sex as well as fornication and cohabitation. Ironically the first state to act on this development was the same one that had been the last to repeal its anticontraception law: Connecticut. This state was in most respects the ideal forum for sodomy reform: the citizens were well-educated, local politics was liberal, and there was no discernible homosexual community that would generate the anxieties that killed sodomy reform in New York. The only roadblock, and a considerable one, was potential opposition from the Roman Catholic Church.

Chaired by House Speaker Robert Testo and populated with law enforcement experts and scholars, Connecticut's Commission to Revise the Criminal Statutes proposed in 1967 that consensual sodomy, fornication, and adultery be decriminalized. Two years later, it submitted to the legislature a suggested code incorporating those changes. Emphasizing pragmatic reasons for decriminalizing consensual sexual activities in the home, the commission cautioned that "its position should in no way be regarded as moral condonation or approval of certain sexual activity which is now criminally prohibited; rather, its position is that for sound reasons of public policy these questions are better dealt with by authorities—spiritual, medical, judicial, etc.—other than those involved in criminal-law enforcement."[63]

As the Illinois legislature had done, the judiciary committees of the Connecticut Assembly and Senate held joint hearings on the proposed code on March 29, 1969. The commission's director, David Borden (later chief justice of the Connecticut Supreme Court), explained and defended the code's deregulation of consensual private activities, and he was joined by the ACLU and the Caucus of Connecticut Democrats. The state should not be regulating people's private activities, they argued, and the archaic laws then in place were inevitably applied in arbitrary ways. The caucus complained that the sex crime laws were still disproportionately deployed against different-race couples. Testifying on behalf of police officers, Sergeant Roach of the Guilford Police Department endorsed the sex crime downsizing. "We are finding problems enforcing these laws because the courts take a lenient view of them for the most part, [and] people themselves feel it's not wrong to be so involved."[64]

Surprisingly, the Roman Catholic Church raised no public objections to the new code. While the church's neutrality might have been the result of internal diocesan politics, it is likely that it reflected larger concerns. As in Illinois eight years earlier, the church's primary focus in 1969 was the issue of abortion, which from its perspective was literally a matter of life and death. In a tacit trade-off, the commission left abortion a crime. Also, in a state like Connecticut, where there was no visible homosexual subculture, sodomy reform would not be read as "promoting homosexuality." Under these circumstances even most Catholic legislators were more concerned with other sex crimes. Indeed, by acclamation, the House amended the commission's bill by reinserting adultery as a crime (in language drafted by Borden). House sponsor John Carrozzella, a devout Catholic, supported the amendment, because he wanted to signal that "this legislature recognizes the sanctity of the family unit."[65]

There was no proposal to criminalize either fornication or sodomy—until the bill reached the Senate. Senator Raymond Lyddy, a Republican from wealthy Fairfield County, proposed an amendment to retain all the existing sex crimes. A Catholic graduate of Holy Cross and Georgetown, Lyddy acknowledged that these crimes were seldom enforced but urged his colleagues to retain them for larger reasons:

> [According to the commission's bill], an individual can act as he pleases, as he chooses, without any regard for any kind of law or [traditional] precept. . . . This is a complete disregard for any moral aspect in our laws. Good or bad. Every one is a God unto himself. Do what your conscience says. Do what you want to do. . . . Look what happened under our so-called new morality. We've had increases in crime and juvenile delinquency. We've had drug addiction. . . . The destruction of private property. Riots.

Lyddy's speech was an eloquent statement of traditionalist morality: sex for pleasure is not morally acceptable; decriminalizing sodomy is the obliteration of all moral lines in matters of sexuality; the result would be the formless and ultimately lawless society lamented in Plato's *Republic*. Although many senators supported Lyddy, the Senate narrowly passed the commission's bill, with the adultery amendment.[66]

On July 8, 1969, Governor John Dempsey, another Catholic, signed the criminal law reform package that made Connecticut the second state to decriminalize consensual sodomy.[67] Connecticut's willingness to take this step owed much to the willingness of law enforcement as well as religious figures to recognize that oral sex was so widely practiced that the law's legitimacy would suffer if it were left a crime. On the other hand, this decision left many religious people dissatisfied, for they felt decriminalization sent a message inconsistent with their sense of a moral community and its obligations to youth. Although it did not prevail in Connecticut, this viewpoint remained dominant elsewhere.

Sodomy Reform in Texas and Kansas, 1968–69

In 1965, the Texas Bar Association created a Committee on Revision of the Penal Code. Chaired by Page Keeton, the longtime dean (1949–74) of the University of Texas School of Law, the committee consisted of more than two dozen state legislators, judges, prosecutors, and defense attorneys. The pragmatic and politically savvy Keeton sought the right blend of reform and reaffirmation in the law revision. Like other criminal-law reform groups, the Texas committee took the Model Penal Code as its template. A variety of law professors worked on the sex crime provisions of the draft—Fred Cohen, Joel Finer, and finally Dean Keeton himself. The academics strongly believed that private activities between consenting adults were no business of the law.[68]

On June 7, 1968, Keeton circulated a preliminary draft of proposed sex crime provisions: the draft left fornication, adultery, bestiality, and consensual sodomy *un*regulated. As Keeton put it, "penal sanctions are in opposition to the basic right of men to be free in society, and the right to privacy. In fact, there may be serious constitutional questions about such a law, including not only an invasion of privacy [*Griswold*], but also its operation as cruel and unusual punishment." Because such laws were difficult to enforce and criminalized widely practiced behaviors, they gave the police broad discretion and contributed to abusive practices as well as blackmail. Keeton acknowledged the main objection that "to legalize such activities is to condone them," leading to a "general breakdown of the moral fibre of the community. However, there is not one shred of evidence to support this position."[69]

On June 28 the committee met at the Etter Alumni Center of the University of Texas to discuss this draft. The draft's failure to criminalize fornication, adultery, and cohabitation passed without dispute, but traditionalists pounced on the proposed deregulation of consensual sodomy. Bexar County (San Antonio) district attorney James Barlow objected because "he was opposed to legalizing homosexuality.... [Y]ou would have every deviate in the United States coming to Texas and he didn't want to open Texas to homosexuals by legalizing it." Harris County (Houston) district attorney Carol Vance had heard that there were "colonies of homosexuals in hotels" after Illinois's sodomy repeal. Representing the law enforcement community, Glenn Conner reported that Texas police overwhelmingly favored retaining "homosexuality" as an offense because "the act itself is so destructive of moral fiber and so insidious—especially regarding the young."[70]

San Antonio judge Archie Brown, a relative liberal, offered a reason for reconsideration. "On the other hand, sending a homosexual to prison is more like a reward than a punishment." In his preliminary memorandum, Keeton had suggested that, for the homosexual, "imprisonment itself is very much like throwing Br'er Rabbit in the briar patch." The outspoken Vance found this bizarre argument compelling, and he too urged that the punishment for "homosexuality" be reduced.[71]

A staff member "inquired whether the committee also wanted to cover heterosexual deviate sexual intercourse. Mr. Conner, Judge Brown, and the rest of the committee agreed that they did not want to deal with consensual heterosexual deviate sexual intercourse." Vance suggested that homosexual intercourse be a gross misdemeanor, with a maximum one-year jail sentence. "[A]ppreciat[ing] a legislature's embarrassment when confronted with the assertion that it is approving homosexual conduct by taking it out of the criminal law," Seth Searcy III, the director of the law revision project, wondered whether homosexual sodomy might be condemned in the penal code, but without penalty. The suggestion met with silence from the committee. One member moved the addition of a new section "making homosexuality between adults in private a gross misdemeanor," a motion the committee approved by a vote of five to four. The critical fifth vote was Judge Brown, who believed that gay people enjoyed a constitutional right of privacy to engage in consensual sodomy, but feared that complete deregulation would sink the entire code project. "How [could] the representative from Polk County go back home and explain why he endorsed homosexuality?"[72]

While it would take the Texas legislature another five years to enact the compromise agreed to by Keeton's committee (chapter 10), the Kansas legislature enacted the same idea in 1969. Between 1963 and 1968, the Kansas Criminal Law Recodification Committee worked through these same issues, ultimately deciding to decriminalize fornication, open cohabitation, and adultery for the liberal and pragmatic reasons adduced in the MPC commentary: "Obviously, the committee and its members do not by this omission intend to express approval of unconventional sexual conduct. However, the committee feels that irregular sex relations between consenting adults involve moral considerations that are largely personal, and that the social injury or affront resulting from such acts is not sufficiently grave to bring them within the purview of the criminal law. Moreover, experience has demonstrated the difficulty of enforcement of such restraints." Although the same privacy and difficulty-of-enforcement reasons were applicable, the committee retained criminal penalties for consensual sodomy, a misdemeanor carrying a prison term of up to three years.[73]

When the Kansas Senate Judiciary Committee marked up the penal code reform bill, it redrafted the consensual sodomy provision to criminalize "oral or anal copulation" *only* "between persons who are not husband and wife or consenting adult members of the opposite sex." The redraft provoked no controversy and sailed through the legislature, which battled instead over the liberalized abortion allowances the Judiciary Committee added at the behest of physicians. One member of the Judiciary Committee later questioned the new sodomy provision: "[W]hy opposite sex—if consenting adults ok—why go half way?" But the council let it pass without public comment. Governor Robert Docking, a moderate Democrat, signed the bill in April 1969. With no public discussion, Kansas had become the first state to officially criminalize same-sex but not different-sex sodomy.[74]

Two months later, the homosexuals spoke back.

CHAPTER SIX

The Crime Against Nature
After Stonewall, 1969–75

In the early morning of Saturday, June 28, 1969, New York police raided a seedy Greenwich Village gay bar, the Stonewall Inn. Located at 53 Christopher Street, right off Sheridan Square in the heart of the gay ghetto, the Stonewall had been reopened as a gay bar by an assortment of neighborhood oddballs who were in partnership with a henchman of the Genovese family. "Fat Tony" ran the club, "Blond Frankie" manned the door, and "The Skull" operated a blackmail operation on the second floor. Although patrons complained that the Stonewall was dirty and overpriced, they flocked to it because it was a large two-floor space where they could socialize and dance. Like San Francisco's Black Cat, it was a place where queer was normal, and so-

Stonewall celebration

ciety's prejudice could be forgotten. Despite receiving regular mafia payoffs, cops raided the Stonewall once a month, and the bar's drag queens, butch lesbians, and assorted fairies knew the drill: line up against the wall and suffer degrading verbal and some physical abuse from the men in blue. A few might go to jail, and the bar would close for the night.[1]

The June 28 raid, which began around 1:20 a.m., did not follow the usual pattern. Some customers refused to show their IDs and sassed the officers. As arrested patrons were led from the bar, a cheering crowd of street youths, hustlers, and passersby formed on the street. One officer slugged a drag queen. Accounts differ as to what happened next, around 2:00 a.m. Some say that a transvestite hurled a rock at the police, others say a Puerto Rican youth tossed a beer can. The historian David Carter thinks it was a bulldyke who threw the first punch. "Whoever acted first," what transpired was "an avalanche of bottles, stones, an uprooted parking meter, and the setting of several bonfires. The police scurried for cover and barricaded themselves inside the bar." The mob broke down the door, and someone tossed lighter fluid and a match into the building, which burst into flames.[2]

The trapped police escaped the burning bar when reinforcements from the city's Tactical Patrol Force arrived, shortly after 3:00 a.m. This riot squad spent two hours clearing the West Village streets of hundreds of flame queens, dykes, and angry homosexuals. "They would chase us down the street and we'd just go around the block and come back and chant things and throw bottles," recalls Craig Rodwell, a young activist. Gay youth taunted the police, calling them "faggot cops," "girls in blue," and "Lily Law," as well as forming Rockettes-style kick lines and chanting ditties such as, "We are the Village girls, we wear our hair in curls, we wear our dungarees above our nelly knees." In response, the police savagely deployed their nightsticks to beat and bloody any faggot or queen they could run down, including many bystanders. At dawn the community surveyed the scene and covered it with graffiti. "They invaded our rights." "Support Gay Power." "Drag Power." Even more intense rioting and police-queer confrontations occurred the next night.[3]

The Stonewall riots were not only an opportunity for thousands of gay New Yorkers to vent their anger, but also an opportunity to share a new pride. Surveying the Stonewall shortly after the riots, the poet Allen Ginsberg remarked, "You know the guys there were so beautiful—they've lost that wounded look that fags all had ten years ago." Among those energized by the Stonewall riots was Martha Shelley, a diminutive (five-foot-four-inch) lesbian who became a firebrand for a new cause. A month later, Shelley and Marty Robinson organized a rally of more than five hundred lesbian and gay activists under the triumphal arch in Washington Square Park, three blocks east of the Stonewall Inn. They fired up the crowd with a new defiant tone of "Gay Power." On July 31, they formed the Gay Liberation Front (GLF). Shelley insisted on using the term "Gay," rather than the old euphemisms (such as Mattachine), and others added "Liberation Front," after the liberation army seeking to expel Americans from Vietnam.[4]

GLF and the dozens of similar organizations that sprang up in cities all over America after Stonewall created a new gay rights spirit. "If you are homosexual, and you get tired of waiting around for the liberals to repeal the sodomy laws, and begin to dig yourself—and get angry—you are on your way to being a radical." Unlike the fifties politics of privacy or the sixties politics of recognition, gay radicals set forth a politics of transformation. "[T]he function of a homosexual is to make you uneasy," Shelley warned. "We didn't want to be accepted into America the way it was," she recalled. "We wanted America to change." This kind of politics was angry, confrontational, and destabilizing. Its leaders often disrespected older, more cautious lesbian and gay pioneers and sought alliances with other liberationist organizations—the New Left and the antiwar movement; women's liberation groups; and the Black Panthers.[5]

Gay liberationist thought owed much to existing radical theories popular among the college-age baby boomers. Such theories taught that existing social attitudes and institutions were structural impediments to equality and freedom; victims of the false consciousness needed to reclaim themselves through critique or consciousness-raising and to create new institutions. Activists like Shelley contributed some important ideas to radical thought, such as a critique of sex negativity. Americans' sodomy disgust, it held, is just a local example of their general revulsion against natural sexual functions. Sex in America is presumed guilty until proven innocent, such as through production of a marriage license. Going beyond Kinsey's critique that this kind of attitude is itself unnatural, gay liberationists argued that it was a form of exploitation. To satisfy their own neuroses, traditionalists colonized the bodies of citizens by imposing on them a regime of sexual repression. An implication of radical thought was that traditional morality's focus on boundary maintenance and social pollution reflected the same kind of politics as traditional racism. The racist (like the homophobe) insisted on respecting traditional race (sex and gender) lines and believed that crossing those lines, especially through transgressive sexual behaviors, would pollute society and cause its decay.[6]

In the most original contribution, radical feminists maintained that the pillar of patriarchy was the rigid gender roles inherent in compulsory heterosexuality. The mainstay of oppressive stereotypes holding women down was the notion that the natural role of a woman is to marry a man, administer the marital household, and bear and raise "his" children. Shelley pressed these critiques in particularly radical directions. By her account, both gender role and sexual orientation are false and confining categories. Not only must women and gay people escape them, but so must men and straight people. "We want to reach the homosexuals entombed in you, to liberate our brothers and sisters, locked in the prisons of your skulls."[7]

Ideas like this were deeply threatening to most Americans, including other radicals with whom gay liberationists were trying to form alliances. The Black Panthers were a case in point. Founded by Huey Newton and Bobby Seale in 1967, the Panthers were run by black men who held relatively conventional views about women and gays. (One common Panther putdown for the police was that they were "faggots and cocksuckers.") In August 1970, on the eve of the Revolutionary People's Constitutional Convention to bring together all radical groups, Newton released a letter supporting the women's and gay liberation movements. That "sometimes our first instinct is to want to hit a homosexual in the mouth and to want a woman to be quiet," Newton explained, were irrational responses to the possibility that straight men might themselves be homosexual or sexually dominated by women. Agreeing with the liberationist analysis of sexuality and gender, Newton proclaimed women and gays "oppressed people" with whom blacks should express solidarity. Although her colleagues applauded the statement, Shelley believed it was "patronizing." Many feminists found the convention unresponsive to their concerns for control of their bodies and respect as political equals, while people of color found the radical lesbians racially insensitive in their complaints that they were "fucked over" by black men.[8]

Other baby boomers found the ideas of gay liberation exciting. Lesbians and gay men flooded out of their closets in unprecedented numbers (thousands, rather than the dozens before 1969) and into organizations like GLF and the Gay Activists Alliance (GAA), which focused on political reform. It also caught the imagination of many straight Americans, some of whom were feminists, such as Marilyn Geisler Haft. A graduate of the NYU Law School, she readily understood Shelley's notions that sexuality and gender-bending were liberating for everyone. From her point of view, people's distaste for homosexuals was no different than anti-Semitism, racism, and misogyny. As a young ACLU lawyer, Haft met and befriended gay men such as E. Carrington (Cary) Boggan, a West Virginia native who took his Wake Forest law degree to New York City, where he became active in GAA. Just as GAA superseded the more radical GLF, lawyers like Boggan replaced street activists like Shelley as speakers for the gay community. Gay *liberation* was overshadowed by gay *rights*.[9]

The key to obtaining gay rights was the repeal of consensual sodomy laws. Although such laws had never been strictly enforced against adults having sex in private places, they were increasingly invoked as a rationale to discriminate against the post-Stonewall horde of openly lesbian and gay citizens. For the first time, gay people became seriously involved in the legislative lobbying effort against sodomy laws. Sodomy reform itself came out of the closet. The ACLU and the Lambda Legal Defense and Education Fund (founded by Boggan and Bill Thom) challenged consensual sodomy laws on constitutional grounds, and lobbying groups such as the National Gay Task Force challenged them on political grounds. While sodomy reform continued to emphasize privacy rights applicable to all Americans, reformers also openly maintained that sodomy laws had legal effects on lesbians and gay men that were inconsistent with the equal citizenship the Constitution ensured for them.

But gay activism carried a hefty political price. With the homosexual subculture and its advocates, like Shelley, becoming more visible and militant, it became more and more difficult for sodomy repeal to sneak in through the back door of the Model Penal Code (MPC). Few Americans believed that "Gay is Good," and most felt threatened when they read that the "homosexual agenda" demanded an end to age-of-consent laws and "patriarchal" marriage as well as sodomy laws. As a result, the gay rights movement increasingly turned to constitutional lawyers like Haft and Boggan.

The Evolving Politics of Sodomy Reform

Once a critical mass of openly lesbian and gay persons such as Martha Shelley became visible and politically active, Kinsey's view that homosexuality is a tolerable sexual variation gained acceptance among professional communities of doctors, lawyers, and even prosecutors. The close connection between sodomy and homosexuality started to become a reason, as well as an obstacle, for sodomy law reform. In turn, the possibility of achieving reform through the political and legal process swiftly deradicalized the movement.

Diminished Police Enforcement of Sodomy and
Solicitation Laws Against Gay Men

In March 1970, New York's police raided the Snake Pit, a gay club located a few blocks from the Stonewall Inn, and arrested 167 people. Diego Vinales, a twenty-three-year-old Argentinean, realized that the arrest could lead to his deportation and broke free of his escorts at the police station. Leaping from a second-floor window, Vinales was impaled on a spiked iron fence, with six prongs embedded in his body. Miraculously, he survived. Shelley and her GLF colleagues conducted a vigil for him as he lay in a hospital, and gays all over the city mobilized new allies around this tragic accident. Representative Ed Koch wrote to the police commissioner, accusing him of making illegal arrests (the charges against virtually all the Snake Pit defendants were dismissed) and harassment of innocent people. Whitman Knapp, chair of the Commission on Police Corruption, charged that antihomosexual laws were a leading cause of police corruption in New York. Protesters associated with GLF and GAA "zapped" Mayor John Lindsay, embarrassing him at various public appearances. The commissioner resigned in September.[10]

After 1970, police beatings or harassment of gay people triggered detailed documentation, press coverage, and often protests, followed by meetings with the mayor's office and the human rights office, whose first chair, Eleanor Holmes Norton, was publicly pro-gay. Police officials became increasingly responsive to gay people's demands for respectful treatment. When Koch became mayor, in 1978, one of his first acts was a directive prohibiting sexual orientation discrimination by all municipal agencies, including the police department. Police Commissioner Robert McGuire established an Office of Equal Employment Opportunity to investigate discrimination complaints within the department, including sexual orientation claims. "By the end of the decade, serious police harassment of gay people had become uncommon in New York City. When it did occur the reaction was swift and strong."[11]

In May 1972, under pressure from gay activists, the District of Columbia Corporation Counsel agreed that the District's sodomy law could not be enforced against private activities between consenting adults. In response the police department stepped up enforcement of laws against public loitering and solicitation to commit sodomy. Assisted by ACLU lawyers, some of the men who were apprehended resisted the charges on constitutional grounds, and in early 1973, three judges threw out such arrests on that basis. The District's GAA staged a sit-in at police headquarters. When Frank Kameny orchestrated a lawsuit challenging both the sodomy law and the police practices, the latter abated almost immediately. After Congress granted the District home rule in 1975, and hence control over its own budget, the District's GAA persuaded the city council to defund the morals squad altogether. After that, police harassment of gay men cruising for sexual partners was more episodic.[12]

Police actions against gays in San Francisco had abated after 1965, but the flourishing of the gay subculture generated one last effort at suppression under Mayor Joseph Alioto. His police force arrested ninety-seven men for oral copulation in 1970 and 114 in 1971 (in striking contrast to the eleven men arrested in 1967, before Alioto's election). Unlike officials in Washington and New York, the Alioto administration scoffed at complaints by gay organizations—until gay groups helped elect maverick Richard Hongisto sheriff of San Francisco County in 1971. Immediately, arrests for consensual sodomy and even solicitation ceased. After 1972, arrests focused almost entirely on public or commercial sex, and police harassment eased. As gay people became more politically active in the city, the police force grew more gay-friendly. By 1981 San Francisco was recruiting gay men and lesbians to serve as police officers and was prosecuting straight youths for gay-bashing.[13]

The most dramatic turnaround came in Los Angeles, whose police department was the most aggressive sodomy and solicitation enforcement machine in the nation. As late as 1972, Police Chief Edward Davis refused even to talk with gay leaders about police harassment. "[O]pen and ostentatious merchandizing of the concept of homosexuality is a clear and present danger to the youth of our community," as Davis put it. "It's one thing to be a leper. It's another thing to be spreading the disease." As in the other cities, this attitude stimulated organized gay responses—publicity, zaps, criticisms by gay-friendly representatives. The turning point was the 1973 election of Burt Pines as district attorney, with critical gay support. Pines announced a new policy of prosecuting only "serious crimes" and not prosecuting lewdness cases that involved a lesbian or gay couple only holding hands, kissing, or dancing. Although the police resisted Pines's pro-gay policy, lewd vagrancy arrests fell off by fifty percent during his first year in office. Pines called for the hiring of openly gay police, the vice squad's budget was reduced in 1976, and a police liaison was finally named in 1981. The Los Angeles Police Department continued to have a deserved reputation for abuse, but by 1981 it was much less capable of harassing gay people.[14]

Policy changes were also notable in other large cities where gay people became politically salient, such as Boston, Chicago, Denver, Philadelphia, and Seattle. The results were more mixed, however, in southern cities such as Atlanta, Dallas, Houston, Memphis, and Richmond, where gay people were visible enough to be alarming but not well-organized as a political force.[15] To have a better idea of the national trend, consider the record of all the sodomy cases that resulted in a reported judicial decision during the twentieth century. Statistics for the 1970s demonstrate that there were more appeals of sodomy convictions than ever before—but the overwhelming majority of the cases involved rape scenarios, in which a man forced anal or oral sex on a woman (fifty percent of the total), another man (seven percent), or a minor (thirty-four percent). Figure 6.1 provides a graphic representation of the trends. Whereas a quarter of the reported sodomy cases before Stonewall had involved consenting male adults, only four percent did in the generation after Stonewall. Almost all those cases involved sexual activities in a public or quasi-public space, such as a theater, park, or tearoom. The changing nature of sodomy prosecutions owes something to the rise of gay power, but perhaps also to women's power. Women criticized police and prosecutors for neglecting crimes of violence against them, and so scarce police resources were directed away from spying and entrapping gay men, and toward apprehending and prosecuting straight men who were assaulting women and girls.

Ironically, once a significant number of lesbian and bisexual women came out of the closet after Stonewall, they too began to feel the bite of sodomy laws, although less through police harassment than through civil penalties. Federal, state, county, and municipal policies against the public employment of lesbians, gay men, and bisexuals also became more explicit. The largest employer in the country was the U.S. military, whose exclusion of gay people as presumptive

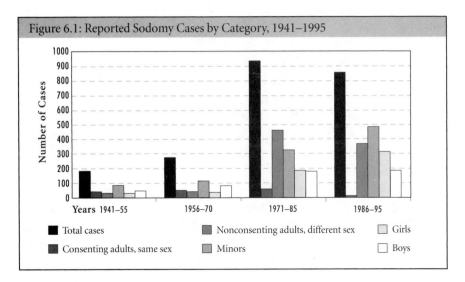

Figure 6.1: Reported Sodomy Cases by Category, 1941–1995

sodomites bore particularly hard on female soldiers, who were dismissed at twice or three times the rate of males. Gay or lesbian schoolteachers were unwelcome in most districts, and many of the litigated discharges involved women.[16]

Lesbian or bisexual women also felt discrimination in domestic issues. If a wife came out as a lesbian and her marriage was dissolved, as thousands were in the wake of Stonewall, there was often a custody battle. Angry husbands and even concerned grandparents argued that the mother was an immoral sodomite who would corrupt the children, and hundreds of mothers lost custody and even visitation rights for this reason. It was not until 1972 that an open lesbian, Camille Mitchell, was allowed to retain custody of her children in a contested case, and even then, Santa Clara County judge Gerald Chargin conditioned that decision on the mother's agreement not to bring a female partner into the home.[17]

Social and Medical Scientists as Allies

Before 1969 few doctors could say they knew a homosexual, apart from patients who had been driven to them by traumatic experiences. One of the most knowledgeable was Dr. Evelyn Hooker, who had engaged Mattachine Society members for a series of studies that demonstrated no discernible psychological differences between gay and straight men. In 1967–69, Dr. Hooker chaired a blue-ribbon task force sponsored by the National Institute of Mental Health (NIMH). Issued several months after Stonewall, the final report of the Task Force on Homosexuality found that none of the common stereotypes about homosexuals had any scientific foundation, and it endorsed Hooker's notion that homosexuality was a "social problem" *only* because of homophobia, the mental illness of bigots, and *not* because of anything inherently wrong with homosexuals. The task force recommended the repeal of state sodomy laws, not only because they were enforced abusively and had no positive effects, but also because of the collateral damage they inflicted on the lives of productive lesbian and gay citizens. "The existence of legal penalties relating to homosexual acts means that the mental health problems of homosexuals are exacerbated by the need for concealment and the emotional stresses arising from this need and from the opprobrium of being in violation of the law."[18]

The professional group most resistant to Dr. Hooker's arguments was the psychiatrists, many of whom continued to teach that homosexuality was a serious mental illness that manifested itself in narcissistic and predatory behavior. In 1970, the spring after Stonewall, gay activists confronted their opponents at the American Psychiatric Association's (APA) annual convention in San Francisco. Demanding that the APA remove the characterization of homosexuality as a psychiatric disorder from its diagnostic manual, activists heckled researchers such as Dr. Irving Bieber. "I've read your book, Dr. Bieber," yelled one protester, "and if that book talked about black people the way it talks about homosexuals, you'd be drawn and quartered and you'd deserve it." At the 1971 convention's plenary session in Washington, D.C., Frank Kameny seized the microphone to deliver a diatribe against the profession: "Psychiatry has waged a relentless war of extermination against us. You may take this as a declaration of war against you." Gay activists later sponsored their own panel, which made strong professional criticisms of psychiatry's views about homosexuality. Two years later the APA's Nomenclature Committee voted to drop homosexuality's classification as a disease in the standard diagnostic manual.[19]

These debates were as much about humanistic norms as about scientific fact. The norms that prevailed were those that had been advanced decades earlier by Alfred Kinsey and Evelyn Hooker: homosexual intercourse is for gay people an important feature of human flourishing and relationship building; homosexuality is a benign variation from the norm and poses no threat to heterosexuals. Although a declining number of social psychologists and psychiatrists continued to view homosexuality as a mental illness or sexual dysfunction, after 1973, medical science was officially hostile not only to consensual sodomy laws, but also to most state laws having a discriminatory impact on lesbians and gay men.

New Gay Legal Organizations and Allies

After graduating from Yale Law School, where he founded the film society, William Thom (born 1941) served in the military and then practiced law at a prestigious New York City firm. His best friend from law school introduced him to the thriving gay subculture. Bored with the routine matters he handled in private practice, Thom began providing legal advice and occasional representation to GAA and some individual gay clients. Through GAA, he met Cary Boggan. The cerebral Yankee and the sociable southerner believed that the street activism of Martha Shelley and the GAA zaps served a useful function, but that the practical day-to-day needs of lesbians and gay men were not being met.[20]

At a GAA meeting in 1971 Thom and Boggan proposed to create an organization that would provide legal assistance to gay people. In March 1972 they applied to the New York Supreme Court's Appellate Division for its approval of the Lambda Legal Defense and Education Fund. Patterned after the NAACP's Legal Defense and Education Fund, and copying the mission statement of the Puerto Rican LDEF, Lambda's goal was "to promote the availability of legal services to homosexuals" and, ultimately, to defend the rights of gay people to be treated with dignity and equity by the state. The judges rejected Lambda's application, partly because they saw no need for an organization to aid and abet presumptive lawbreakers. Lambda's first litigation victory was a successful appeal of this denial. The New York Court of Appeals required the lower court to register Lambda as a legal-assistance corporation. In 1973, Lambda commenced operations out of Thom's studio apartment on Forty-ninth Street. In its first decade most of Lambda's clients were lesbians and gay men arrested for sodomy-related crimes or penalized civilly because they were presumptive criminals.[21]

In separate petitions, Thom and Boggan asked the American Bar Association to take a public stance against consensual sodomy laws. In 1972, the ABA referred Thom's petition to a study committee within its Criminal Law Section. Although Thom and his allies presented police and psychiatric evidence that sodomy laws served no useful public purpose and had terrible effects on gay people, the committee did not make a recommendation. At the same time, Boggan and Haft were successfully pressing the same proposal within the ABA's Individual Rights Section. The section's report not only argued that such laws invaded people's private lives without sufficient public justification, but also took note of the new post-Stonewall equality claims. These laws "are most often applied against homosexuals, both in the enforcement of the statutes themselves and as a basis for discrimination against homosexuals on the ground that they are most likely violating the law." The section's resolution called on the states "to repeal all laws which classify as criminal conduct any form of noncommercial sexual contact between consenting adults in private, saving only those portions which protect minors or public decorum." In August 1973 the ABA debated and adopted this resolution at its annual meeting in Washington, D.C.[22]

At about the same time, Haft proposed that the ACLU establish a litigation project to protect the rights of sexual minorities, along the same lines as the ACLU's famous Women's Rights Project, run by Ruth Bader Ginsburg. This effort would translate gay liberationist ideas into constitutional challenges protecting gay people against discrimination and all Americans against prudish state regulations of their consensual sex. ACLU general counsel Norman Dorsen and legal director Aryeh Neier liked Haft's idea but urged her to define the project more broadly, in terms of privacy rather than just gay rights. The cash-strapped Union also required that she raise the money herself, which she did by calling on Hugh and Christie Hefner, the founder and president, respectively, of Playboy Enterprises. In one evening at the Playboy mansion in Chicago, the ACLU raised enough money to start the Sexual Privacy Project, a national task force aimed at eliminating laws regulating private sexual activities between consenting adults and "eliminating discriminatory practices which flow from such laws."[23]

Post-Stonewall Campaigns to Repeal Sodomy Laws: Success and Decline of the Model Penal Code Approach

Senator William Roden, a Republican, represented Boise in the Idaho legislature between 1961 and 1969. As a deputy prosecutor Roden had assisted in the prosecution of the men charged with "unnatural relations" with younger males in the famous "Boys of Boise" mania (chapter 3). In retrospect he believed the whole witch hunt was a "very unfortunate situation" for the state as well as for the homosexual defendants. In 1967, Senator Roden chaired the special subcommittee of Idaho's Legislative Council to consider revisions in the state criminal code; after he retired from the legislature, he was a special consultant to the subcommittee, which recommended adoption of the Model Penal Code, with minor modifications. The subcommittee members were aware that the new code would decriminalize consensual sodomy, a change Roden believed was justified. Although he could barely comprehend how two men or two women could take sexual pleasure in each other, Roden had met homosexuals who lived productive lives and saw no reason for the state to continue to brand them as presumptive criminals.[24]

As expected, the proposal faced opposition, but it came primarily from prosecutors who felt the new code as a whole was too lenient. The only legislator speaking out strongly against sex crime reform was Representative Wayne Loveless, a Mormon Democrat from Pocatello. "When you legalize homosexuality, lesbianism, adultery, fornication—you bring it out into the open," he argued. Supporters of sex crime reform countered that these laws were not enforced, but Loveless responded that repealing them would encourage open defiance of sexual mores: "At least under present law you keep it hid." These objections proved not to be an obstacle, however, and the new criminal code was adopted by large majorities in each chamber and was signed into law by Governor Cecil Andrus in March 1971, record time for such an ambitious overhaul.[25]

Idaho was the third state to decriminalize consensual sodomy, following the Illinois model: without publicly mentioning sodomy reform or homosexuals, pragmatic as well as liberal experts and legislators had pressed for full MPC adoption. Roden and his colleagues expected the people of Idaho to defer to their judgment about what activities should be subject to the criminal sanction. If these assumptions had held up, consensual sodomy laws would probably have disappeared in the 1970s, essentially replaced with laws making it a misdemeanor to loiter for purposes of homosexual solicitation—the MPC's concession to community standards of sexual and gender decorum. For several years after Stonewall, sodomy decriminalization indeed proceeded rapidly in many states. But America was changing, especially in the South and West, where middle-class white Americans increasingly believed that crime was out of control and blamed elites like Herbert Wechsler and Bill Roden for being too "soft on crime" as they humanized state criminal codes. An expanding minority was concerned about the growing influence of open homosexuals in the public culture. Radical activists like Martha Shelley scared them conservative.

Adopting the Model Penal Code: Colorado and Ohio Follow Illinois

Colorado, the fourth state to repeal its consensual sodomy law, followed the Illinois approach: the legislature established a Criminal Code Committee within the Legislative Council in 1963; advised by judges, law professors, and district attorneys, the committee drafted a proposed code, based largely on the Model Penal Code, in 1964; the proposed code was introduced into the legislature, where it was amended in minor respects and enacted in May 1971. During the process of committee drafting and legislative deliberation, homosexuality was not a concern, as there was little openly gay presence in the state. Even Denver, Colorado's bustling mile-high capital, had only a small, discreet community. A coalition of Protestant ministers asked the committee to criminalize adultery but made no mention of sodomy. Wondering why the ministers wanted to reinstate adultery but not fornication, Otto Moore, a former judge, quipped that he had a friend who had tried both and could not tell the difference.[26]

If legislators had worried about encouraging open homosexuality, the committee had provided plenty of cover. Following the MPC, the committee and the legislature made loitering in a public place "for the purpose of engaging in or soliciting another person to engage in prostitution or deviate sexual intercourse" a misdemeanor. Going beyond the MPC, the new code made it a crime for any person to make available a "facility" (like a bathhouse) to be used "for or in aid of deviate sexual intercourse." Most broadly, the public indecency crime included any "lewd fondling or caress of the body of another person" in a public place or "where the conduct may reasonably be expected to be viewed by members of the public." The committee justified this provision as aimed at homosexual kissing and caressing in public places, because it constituted a "gross flouting of community standards."[27]

The Colorado experience reveals that sodomy repeal did not necessarily entail deregulation of homosexual intimacies. For the mainstream community, this was an acceptable compromise in states whose legislators were eager for criminal code modernization and not particularly nervous about open lesbian and gay subcultures within their state. Between 1971 and 1974 six additional states decriminalized consensual sodomy, generally through enactment of the Model Penal Code. Others followed the New York approach of reducing consensual sodomy to a misdemeanor (see figure 6.2). None of the new repealing states was in the Roman Catholic Northeast, with its visible gay subcultures, or the Baptist South, with little lesbian or gay visibility but strong loyalty to traditional mores.

Lesbian and gay people had little or no public role in the repeal of statutes that declared them presumptive criminals. In Idaho and Colorado, most legislators were unaware that they were voting to legalize private homosexual conduct. When they were aware, they proceeded cautiously. In Delaware, for example, Republican senator Mike Castle of Wilmington, the main sponsor of the proposed criminal code in 1972, believed consensual sodomy should not be a crime but did not address the issue out of fear that decriminalization would sink his bill. He changed his mind only after conservative legislators objected that the state should not be spending taxpayers' money snooping into people's private lives.[28]

Just as all the other MPC states except Hawaii did, Delaware coupled sodomy repeal with a new crime for loitering to solicit homosexual sodomy. This double

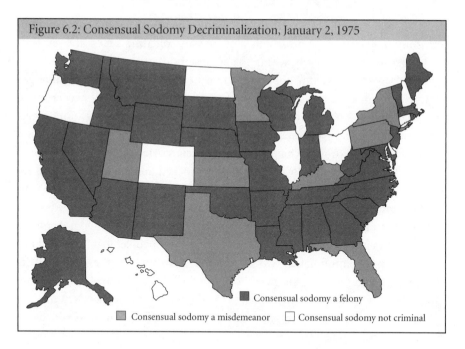

Figure 6.2: Consensual Sodomy Decriminalization, January 2, 1975

■ Consensual sodomy a felony

■ Consensual sodomy a misdemeanor   □ Consensual sodomy not criminal

edge of the MPC approach was exposed after Colorado's new law took effect, in July 1972. Denver police continued to arrest gay and bisexual men—no longer for sodomy, but rather for homosexual fondling or solicitation (crimes under the new state law) or "lewd acts," "indecent acts," or "behaving in a lewd, wanton, or lascivious manner" (all crimes under Denver's municipal code). The main effect of the revised law, clearly, was simply to change the category under which gay men were arrested. When gay activists Gerry Gerash, Jane Dundee, and Terry Mangan formed the Gay Coalition of Denver, the harassment got worse. Denver's vice squad imported a bus, dubbed the "Johnny Cash Special," which they parked in gay cruising areas, such as the State Capitol grounds. The bus driver would invite men to join him in a sexual adventure; when they accepted, undercover cops popped out of their hiding places in the back of the bus. Hundreds of men—literally, men by the busload—were arrested through this ruse. Arrests soared from sixty or seventy per month in 1971–72 to 125 in February 1973. "It's like they've gone on an arrest binge," said a local gay activist. "Like they figured out it might be their last chance."[29]

Assisted by the local ACLU, the Gay Coalition took the matter to court. Arapahoe County judge Irving Ettenberg declared both the state and the Denver antiloitering law unconstitutional. If private "deviate sexual intercourse" itself is legal, the judge reasoned, then asking someone else to join you in a private place must be legal as well. City judge Robert Commins ruled that the city could not constitutionally arrest or prosecute someone for soliciting unless the lewd act took place in public, namely, within the plain sight of other people.[30]

The Denver prosecutor announced that he would continue to charge gay men with homosexual solicitation, and the city council proposed new criminal laws that could be used to ensnare gay and bisexual men. At contentious meetings in October and November 1973, more than three hundred Gay Coalition speakers filled the council chambers, telling their stories of police entrapment, harassment, and brutality to an increasingly shocked audience. The council repealed the municipal lewd loitering and cross-dressing ordinances, and the Colorado Supreme Court invalidated the state antiloitering law. To settle the lawsuit that had been brought against it, Denver agreed that its police would not enforce criminal laws in a discriminatory manner against gay people; that "kissing, hugging, dancing, holding hands" would not be a basis for arrest, even under the state statute; and that the police would appoint a liaison with the Gay Coalition. Only after this settlement, in October 1974, did peace come to gay Denver.[31]

The experience of gay rights advocates was quite different in Ohio, which was the eighth state to repeal, on December 22, 1972. Similar to the codes adopted in other states, the new Ohio penal code decriminalized consensual sodomy but made "importuning" another person to commit "deviate sexual intercourse" a misdemeanor. As they had done in Colorado, gay rights activists and the ACLU challenged the new importuning law in court, maintaining that it violated the Freedom of Speech Clause of the First Amendment. Speaking to another person and inviting him to engage in mutually enjoyable, and legal, activities could not be squared with the Supreme Court's strong protection against state censorship of objectionable speech. The ACLU also argued that the law's terminology was so open-ended that it gave the police too much discretion to harass people they didn't like. The Ohio Supreme Court in 1979 upheld the importuning law against these constitutional attacks—but only after interpreting the law to cover sexual overtures only when it was clear that the overtures were unwelcome.[32]

Failure of the Illinois Approach: Pennsylvania and Michigan

Michigan and Pennsylvania resemble Illinois in many respects. All three states border the Great Lakes and have declining industrial and agricultural bases. Detroit and Philadelphia are economic hubs of Michigan and Pennsylvania, much as Chicago dominates Illinois's economy. All three cities had long-standing lesbian and gay subcultures, with corrupt police enforcing state sodomy and solicitation laws episodically but sometimes brutally. Like Illinoians, most Michiganders and Pennsylvanians lived in suburbs, small towns, and farms and had never met an openly homosexual person. The Roman Catholic Church was prominent in all three states but was not strongly involved in criminal code reform discussions, unless the topic of abortion came up. Both political parties were dominated by pragmatic liberals—Republicans like Michigan governor William Milliken (1969–83) and Democrats like Pennsylvania governor Milton Shapp (1971–79). If sodomy reform could succeed in Illinois, surely it could succeed in Pennsylvania and Michigan.

In neither case, however, was the effort successful. Pennsylvania's state bar association's Committee on Crime and Juvenile Delinquency worked with legislators, judges, and academics to develop a new penal code in 1967. University of Pennsylvania professor Louis Schwartz, advising the bar association's committee, strongly urged decriminalization of consensual sodomy. Prosecutors and other lawyers on the committee feared that sodomy deregulation would undermine the new code's likelihood of enactment, given legislative nervousness about Philadelphia's homosexual community. Therefore, the bar association's draft offered the legislature two alternatives: alternative A would have made "voluntary deviate sexual intercourse" a misdemeanor; alternative B would have made it a crime only if one of the participants was under age twenty-one. Sheldon Toll informed the legislature that the proposed penal code made no controversial policy judgments and therefore left the "death penalty, abortion, homosexuality, and wiretapping" to future deliberation. In December 1972 the legislature finally enacted the new penal code, choosing alternative A without much discussion.[33]

In 1965 the Michigan Bar Association established a criminal code revision commission of experts, including Professors Jerry Israel and A. J. George of the University of Michigan's School of Law. Unlike the Pennsylvania committee, the Michigan one followed the Model Penal Code's decriminalization of consensual sodomy, notwithstanding promotion-of-homosexuality concerns among some lawyers. The commission's 1968 report and draft formed the basis for a criminal code revision bill in 1969, but it went nowhere. The Detroit race riots that followed the assassination of Dr. Martin Luther King Jr. stimulated a law-and-order backlash in Michigan that precluded any serious consideration of criminal code liberalization.[34]

In 1971, State Representative Bob Traxler, a moderate Democrat from Bay City, introduced a modified version of the commission's proposal. The politically cautious bill would have made oral and anal intercourse between unmarried persons a misdemeanor, reduced from a felony. But Traxler was bothered that his bill left such an "archaic and irrelevant" crime in the code, one that had not been enforced for decades. When the House Judiciary Committee, which he chaired, marked up the bill, Traxler proposed to delete the consensual sodomy provision. Catholic representative Jim O'Neill objected that such deregulation would promote homosexuality. Traxler responded that his bill struck a balance by decriminalizing private homosexual conduct while regulating public gender-deviant conduct. Following the MPC, his bill made it a crime to loiter in a public place "for the purpose of engaging or soliciting another person to engage in prostitution, deviate sexual intercourse, or other sexual behavior of a deviate nature." Another provision made it an infraction for a person who is "masked or in any manner disguised by unusual or unnatural attire" to loiter with other similarly attired characters. With many members uncertain about its law enforcement consequences, the House passed the bill by a close margin.[35]

Unlike previous states, Michigan saw gay activists involved—but they opposed the revised Traxler bill. The Detroit Gay Alliance objected that the bill "actually increases the number of anti-gay laws ... and makes the enforcement of those state laws much easier. So actually it was a step backwards." Gay activists opposed any homosexual solicitation or cross-dressing crimes, but their opposition played no role in the fate of the bill. After it was passed by the House in October 1972, it went to the Michigan Senate, where it died in the Criminal Law Subcommittee. Senator James Flemming, a Catholic Republican and the subcommittee chair, felt that community values were sacrificed by the sex crime provisions and that the package as a whole was soft on crime, a sensitive concern in the wake of the Detroit riots. Senator Basil Brown, a liberal black Democrat from Detroit, was lukewarm on the bill, because he felt it would disadvantage defense attorneys. Together, these senators from opposite ends of the political spectrum killed the Traxler bill in that session. After Traxler himself won a special election for the U.S. House of Representatives, the Model Penal Code died in Michigan. When the legislature revised the sexual assault provisions of the criminal code in 1974, liberals and conservatives agreed to leave out sodomy reform.[36]

Success of the Illinois Approach, Then Regret: Idaho (Revisited)

After Idaho adopted the Model Penal Code, in March 1971, constituents and prosecutors expressed concern with the new code's provisions regulating firearm possession, bad checks, and even "rustling"—the theft of animals. The Church of Jesus Christ of Latter-day Saints (LDS) objected to the legalization of fornication, adultery, and "homosexuality." Like the Roman Catholics and Southern Baptists, the Mormons had long preached the sinfulness of engaging in nonmarital or nonprocreative sexual activities, and many LDS leaders believed that the state's criminal law ought to reflect these moral values. Once gun owners, prosecutors, ranchers, and Mormons came together, there was tremendous pressure on the legislature to revisit the new criminal code. Dozens of bills tinkering with it were introduced, but in January 1972 (weeks after the new code took effect) associations representing the police and prosecuting attorneys recommended that the legislature simply repeal the new code altogether.[37]

Although the state bar association, the judiciary committees in both chambers of the legislature, and eventually even the state supreme court defended the new code as a needed modernization, its critics enjoyed growing support from a wide range of citizens engaged, for the first time, in articulating their vision of the criminal code. Feelings ran high, and the attacks got personal. During House consideration of a bill to repeal the new code, Representative Loveless charged that it was devised by special interests favoring "liberalization of morality," and accused opponents of being "left-wing, Fabian socialists," strong language in Idaho. On February 23, the House voted 35–31 against repealing the new code. Given the comfortable margin and intense constituent pressure, two Democrats switched their votes, leaving a 33–33 tie that would have defeated the proposal. Three hours after the vote, however, the presiding officer announced that there had been a tabulation malfunction and that the original vote had been 34–31 against the proposal—so that the vote switches now left the repeal proposal with a 33–32 victory.[38]

In the Senate, legislators focused on the new code's decriminalization of sodomy, adultery, and fornication and its slightly stricter regulation of firearms. The Republicans, who controlled the Senate, were in a tough position: they wanted to defer to Senator Edith Klein Miller, the chair of the Judiciary Committee, who opposed repeal of the new code. The Republican leadership privately admitted that she was right on the merits, but gun owners, prosecutors and police, and the LDS were pressing for wholesale repeal. In March, most of the Republicans abandoned Klein Miller and joined the majority of Democrats in voting for repeal. Governor Andrus, a Democrat, signed the repeal legislation, which took effect on April 1, 1972.[39]

As the governor pointed out, Idaho would have no criminal law after April Fools' Day, and there was no time to develop a whole new code. Over Senator Klein Miller's objection that her colleagues' wishy-washiness was a "comedy of errors," the legislature in March reenacted the old code, without any serious debate on the merits. Essentially, it had been stampeded into criminal law unreform by the fears of the MPC's many critics. Roden was disgusted by the whole episode. In his view, the biggest difference between the old and new codes was sodomy reform, and the underlying reason for the legislators' volte-face was the fear they would be perceived as "promoting" homosexuality. "The code was repealed solely as the result of an emotional hysteria generated by some very right-wing church and political groups."[40]

From the LDS perspective, however, the Idaho experience was a popular response to the excessive liberalization of criminal law. Unlike lawyers such as Roden, ordinary citizens believed that criminal law should serve expressive purposes such as their own moral disapproval of sodomy. And the criminal law was the place to "draw the line" against the social pollution represented most starkly by the homosexuals. (Roden had added fuel to the fire when he told the *Advocate*, a gay journal, that sodomy reform would make Idaho a more congenial place for homosexuals.) Most Idaho voters probably agreed with Loveless's position that the state should not give the slightest encouragement to homosexuals. This moral stance was repeated in Montana, which in 1973 followed Kansas and Texas in revising its code to criminalize only homosexual sodomy; like Idaho, however, Montana made certain that homosexual sodomy remained a felony.[41]

Constitutional Challenges to State Sodomy Laws

Notwithstanding all the no promo homo rhetoric, actual enforcement of sodomy laws against consenting homosexuals within the home was almost unheard of in the 1970s. Eugene Enslin, the manager of the Tri-Massage Parlor and J.T.'s Bookstore on Mill Avenue in tiny Jacksonville, in eastern North Carolina, had attracted the attention of Detective Sam Hudson, who suspected that Enslin was a pimp for a female prostitution service. According to Enslin, the Jacksonville police had served him with eighty-four warrants for alleged illegalities in the massage parlor, none of which the magistrate sustained. Hudson accordingly devised a plan to entrap Enslin and put the parlor out of business. In return for having drug charges against him dropped, Herbert P. Morgan, a seventeen-year-old marine stationed at nearby Camp Lejeune, agreed to be Hudson's bait. On June 7, 1974, Morgan visited the massage parlor. "[W]earing a sleeveless sort of jacket, unbuttoned and his soft gut protrud[ing] over his belt," the marine engaged in friendly conversation with the proprietor. Behind some bushes on a hill overlooking Mill Avenue, Hudson and his men were watching with binoculars. This kind of trap was standard operating procedure for the police in apprehending prostitutes, and they usually urged the bait to make sure that the target gave him fellatio, so that the state could then charge her with a felony under the state crime-against-nature law.[42]

When Morgan asked Enslin for one of the masseuses to give him a massage with "extra excitement," Enslin told him he was too young; state rules barred licensed massage parlors from serving youths under age eighteen. Morgan left to confer with Hudson, who told him to be more direct; Hudson gave Morgan marked bills to pay Enslin. When Morgan asked Enslin if he could have sex for a fee, Enslin again said no. In the course of their conversation, Enslin told the marine that he enjoyed smoking "big, firm, juicy cigars," especially those attached to tall servicemen. After further coaching from Hudson, who revised his entrapment strategy, Morgan dropped into the bookstore shortly after 9:00 p.m. "Will you blow me?" Morgan asked. "Come in," said Enslin, as he led the tall former football player into a back room. There, Enslin twice fellated and twice sodomized the apparently willing Morgan. After the two men ejaculated, Morgan hurried back to his handlers. Enslin also departed, spending the remainder of the evening with friends. When he returned to Mill Avenue around midnight, Hudson arrested him. The state prosecuted Enslin, but not Morgan, for felonious sodomy.[43]

Enslin called his friend Frank Kameny, who brought the case to the attention of Marilyn Haft and Norman Smith, a local attorney who worked with the ACLU. These lawyers felt the case was the perfect vehicle for the ACLU's Privacy Project to challenge the constitutionality of state sodomy laws: the participants were adults (the age of consent in North Carolina was seventeen); the intercourse was consensual and private; and if there was any misconduct involved it was on the part of the state, whose agents solicited, coached, and funded a young man to have felonious sex. Within weeks of his arrest, the ACLU agreed to represent Enslin.[44]

At trial, the testimony of Enslin and Morgan established that the intercourse was private, consensual, and noncommercial. Hudson testified that this "was a deliberate and planned effort on my part using this 17-year-old prosecuting witness, Herbert Morgan, to set Mr. Enslin up so that I could prosecute him for homosexual conduct." This evidence established a violation of the state sodomy law, and the jury convicted. In a subsequent hearing Haft argued that the crime against nature could not constitutionally be applied to consensual private activities. Albert Klassen, a researcher for the Kinsey Institute, testified that consensual sodomy laws criminalize conduct that a large majority of heterosexuals enjoy and practice; that such laws have no effect on the desire of either gay or straight people to engage in prohibited conduct; that a medical consensus then existed to the effect that homosexuality is neither a disease nor a psychological defect, and that homosexuals pose no threat to society or its vulnerable members; and that the crime against nature had no other neutral justification as a matter of social policy. In her legal memoranda, Haft argued that the state law was inconsistent with three constitutional norms: the right of criminal defendants have to precise notice of what conduct constitutes a crime; the privacy right recognized in the contraception and abortion cases; and the equal protection of the laws that the state is supposed to ensure all persons. On September 26, 1974, the judge sentenced Eugene Enslin to a year in prison. The North Carolina Court of Appeals affirmed the conviction.[45]

At the same time that she was defending Enslin, Haft was in touch with Philip Hirschkop, an ACLU-affiliated attorney in northern Virginia who brought a class-action lawsuit challenging Virginia's crime-against-nature law. The representative plaintiff was Bill Bland, a resident of West Point, Virginia. Because he was asserting that he and his lover (Bruce Voeller, the founder of the National Gay Task Force) regularly committed felonious acts, Bland sued under a dummy name, John Doe. Hirschkop filed suit in the Eastern District of Virginia, and the trial was in Richmond, the old capital of the Confederacy. Like Haft, he rested his case on expert testimony and studies demonstrating that consensual sodomy was meaningful sexual expression for many Americans and essentially harmed no one. Speaking for a two-judge majority, Senior Judge Albert Bryan ruled that the state can promote "morality and decency" by punishing "homosexuality and adultery." Dissenting judge Robert Mehrige Jr. objected that enforcing sodomy laws against consenting adults violated the constitutional privacy right.[46]

Homosexuals and the Rule of Law: Vagueness, Privacy, and Equal Protection

The ACLU appealed both losses to the U.S. Supreme Court; Haft handled the *Enslin* petition, and Hirschkop handled *Doe*. The ACLU petitions were supported by an amicus brief from Lambda, drafted by Thom and Boggan. These briefs—landmarks in Supreme Court advocacy—argued that consensual sodomy laws represented an abrogation of the rule of law as applied to lesbians and gay men. Crime-against-nature statutes such as North Carolina's and Virginia's were so vague that they could be—and were—deployed against a wide range of activities by the police. They represented an intrusion into gay people's private lives, where police had no business snooping. Most of all, the presumptive criminality those laws laid on gay people rendered them susceptible to a limitless array of state discriminations. To transform productive Americans who did no harm to others into an outlaw class, a pariah group, was as deeply unconstitutional as apartheid had been. As Virginia and North Carolina argued, however, the Supreme Court would have to stretch some precedents and narrowly construe others if they chose to strike down these laws.

Procedural Due Process (Void for Vagueness). At the time of Stonewall, eighteen states made it a crime to commit "the abominable crime against nature," without elaborating on precisely what that term meant. It is a violation of due process for a legislature to criminalize conduct in language unclear to the ordinary citizen or for reasons unrelated to legitimate state objectives. In *Harris v. State* (1969) the Alaska Supreme Court ruled that crime-against-nature laws violated both features of this jurisprudence. Additionally the court invoked the MPC's libertarian philosophy as justification for clearing the decks. "[T]he widening gap between our formal statutory law and the actual attitudes and behavior of vast segments of our society can only sow the seeds of increasing disrespect for our legal institutions."[47]

If *Harris* had become the law of the land, almost half the nation's sodomy laws would have fallen. Following *Harris*, the Florida Supreme Court declared its crime-against-nature law void for vagueness in *Franklin v. State* (1971). *Franklin* did not apply to people convicted of the crime against nature before 1971. Two such inmates, Raymond Stone and Eugene Huffman, brought a federal habeas corpus action arguing that the Florida law violated the U.S. Constitution. The U.S. Court of Appeals for the Fifth Circuit agreed, but the Supreme Court rejected their vagueness claims in *Wainwright v. Stone* (1973). All nine justices joined an unsigned per curiam opinion drafted by Justice Byron White. On the same day, the Court also rejected vagueness challenges to Oklahoma's crime-against-nature law and Arkansas's buggery law.[48]

Justice White's rationale was that even vaguely worded crime-against-nature laws were constitutional if state courts had interpreted them to apply to particular activities, as they had in *Stone*. This idea was put to the test in the next case heard by the justices. Tennessee courts convicted Harold Locke of engaging in forcible cunnilingus with a female neighbor. Seeking a writ of habeas corpus, Locke argued that the crime-against-nature law was too vague. In another unsigned opinion by White, the Supreme Court disagreed. Although Tennessee had never applied its law to cunnilingus, its supreme court had in 1955 construed the crime-against-nature law to apply to fellatio. The Court reasoned that this was ample notice that the law also made oral sex on a woman a crime. Justices Brennan, Marshall, and Stewart objected that this chain of inference was too lengthy to ensure that citizens of the state were on proper notice. Apparently none of the justices was aware that, during the twentieth century, most American states had regulated fellatio even while few criminalized cunnilingus (chapter 2).[49]

By 1975, when *Enslin* and *Doe* were on appeal, the Supreme Court had repeatedly applied the void-for-vagueness doctrine in cases where police were enforcing laws in a racially discriminatory manner—but not when police were enforcing unclear statutes regulating sexual conduct. With the recent *Locke* decision, Hirschkop declined to challenge Virginia's law on vagueness grounds. Haft briefly argued that *Enslin* was different from *Stone* and *Locke*, both of which involved claims of forcible intercourse. Any citizen would have known that forcing someone else to have sex—whether sodomy or intercourse—is probably illegal, while most Americans would have had no clue as to whether it was a felony for consenting adults like Eugene Enslin and Herbert Morgan to engage in oral sex in a private bedroom.[50]

Substantive Due Process (Privacy Right). Reflecting the ACLU's post-1967 position, Haft and Hirschkop emphasized the right to privacy in their *Enslin* and *Doe* briefs. As originally articulated in *Griswold*, the privacy right seemed limited to sexual expression within marriage, but during its 1972 term the Supreme Court had extended its scope. In *Eisenstadt v. Baird* (1972) a narrow Court majority ruled that state anticontraception laws cannot discriminate against unmarried couples. In *Roe v. Wade* (1973) the Court ruled that the right protects a pregnant woman's choice of an abortion and, for most of the term of a pregnancy, bars all state regulation. Both precedents expanded the right recognized in *Griswold* beyond the marital context. As the Court said in *Eisenstadt*, "If the right of privacy means anything, it is the right of the *individual,* married or single, to be free from unwarranted governmental intrusion into matters so fundamentally affecting a person as the decision whether to bear or beget a child."[51]

Quoting this language, Haft read these decisions to recognize a gay person's "fundamental interest in living and acting in accordance with his inherent sexual orientation"—a delicate way of saying that homosexuals have the same kind of right to express themselves through consensual sodomy that heterosexuals have to express themselves through penile-vaginal intercourse (with or without pregnancy). Recalling Fowler Harper's argument in *Poe v. Ullman*, Haft read *Eisenstadt* to reflect the full thrust of the Freud-Kinsey philosophy: sexual expression is fundamental to human happiness, and the state cannot command individuals into a sexual conformity displeasing to them. If homosexual expression is a fundamental interest, the Court's precedents required the state to show that its regulation was justified by a compelling public interest, such as prevention of harm to third parties. As the MPC's authors had concluded, such a demonstration could not easily be made for consensual sodomy laws. In fact, their enforcement fomented precisely the kind of abusive police tactics involved in the Enslin case, a point emphasized by Thom and Boggan's amicus brief.[52]

Haft read the privacy cases as protecting *sexual autonomy* against state commandeering. Hirschkop read them as protecting intimate *spaces,* such as the home, against police intrusion. In addition to *Eisenstadt*, he relied on *Stanley v. Georgia* (1969), where the Supreme Court had overturned a conviction for possession of obscene materials within one's own home. Invoking the First Amendment as well as the right to privacy, *Stanley* held that Americans enjoy a "right to satisfy their intellectual and emotional needs in the privacy of [their] own home."

From this Hirschkop argued, in a very aggressive reading of *Stanley*, that "denial of the right of a homosexual to express himself in a private sexual matter is a substantial unconstitutional intrusion upon his fundamental First Amendment right to freedom of thought and expression."[53]

Equal Protection of the Law. The Court's precedents also required strict scrutiny when the state deployed a "suspect classification," such as race or ethnicity. The Warren and Burger Courts invalidated every law they reviewed that used a race-based classification that excluded racial minorities. Starting in 1970 the ACLU Women's Rights Project had been urging the Supreme Court to recognize sex as a suspect classification, because sex (like race) has traditionally been deployed to segregate men and women on the basis of stereotypes and not on public-regarding policy needs. Four justices had accepted this argument in 1973, and the Court had struck down several federal as well as state laws that classified according to sex. Haft asserted that sexual orientation was likewise a suspect classification, because it had traditionally been deployed to segregate and exclude gay and bisexual people on the basis of prejudice and stereotypes and not on public-regarding needs. Because crime-against-nature laws denied gay people their only means of sexual expression, while not so severely affecting straight people, they effectively discriminated on the basis of sexual orientation.[54]

Thom and Boggan made a simpler but more powerful argument: "The worst defect of the sodomy laws is that they serve as a pretext, socially and psychologically, for extensive discrimination and generally abusive conduct against gay people." Sodomy laws justified police harassment of gay people and their hangouts, the discharge of homosexuals from public as well as private employment, official refusals to protect gay people when victimized by assaults and other crimes, and deprivation of custody over or even contact with their children. "Law has been the means of opening the door to full participation in society for many minorities. Sodomy laws barricade that door against millions. It is time that these barricades were scrutinized by the Court." There was no precedent directly supporting this argument; it essentially rested on the plain language of the Constitution. With its extensive collateral effects, sodomy laws denied gay people "the equal protection of the law," and perhaps "any protection of the law."[55]

The Justices Ponder the Crime Against Nature

The audience for the ACLU and Lambda arguments was nine men, all born between 1906 and 1924. As a group they brought conservative judicial philosophies and virtually no understanding of homosexuality to the conference of February 20, 1976, at which they decided whether to accept review for the *Enslin* or

Doe cases. Very little was said at the justices' conference, but it is possible to figure out what was on their minds, and why each justice voted as he did. None was willing to agree with Lambda that homosexuals were a significant and worthy class of Americans that the Court should be protecting in the way it was protecting racial minorities and women. All thought the vagueness challenge was foreclosed by *Stone* and *Locke*.[56]

The most serious argument, from their point of view, was the privacy challenge. Haft emphasized *Eisenstadt*, which had been authored by Justice William Brennan (1906–1997). Although he was the Court's only Roman Catholic, Brennan was also a dyed-in-the-wool ACLU liberal and was receptive to Haft's reading of the privacy right to protect sexual choices. Hirschkop, meanwhile, emphasized *Stanley*, authored by Justice Thurgood Marshall (1908–1993), the former NAACP attorney who was the Court's other card-carrying liberal. *Eisenstadt* and *Stanley* reflected the individualistic, ACLU-friendly vision of the Constitution held by those two jurists, but by no one else on the Court. The other justices were much more reluctant to rule that community values cannot limit individual choice as a matter of constitutional law. As to the privacy claim, these justices would have focused on the unresolved status of *Roe v. Wade*.

Two justices had vigorously dissented in *Roe*. Byron "Whizzer" White (1917–2002), an All-America football star at the University of Colorado and Rhodes Scholar, was a Kennedy Democrat who believed that the Court should not override the democratic process unless required by constitutional text or by demonstrated insufficiency of that process. While White was willing to enforce the Equal Protection Clause aggressively to protect people of color and women against explicitly race- or sex-based discriminations, he was not willing to create a privacy right that had no basis in the Constitution. Having dissented in *Roe*, where he brutally argued that abortion enjoyed neither sympathy nor constitutional protection, White was not about to expand the right of privacy to include homosexual conduct.[57]

Also a *Roe* dissenter, William Rehnquist (1924–2005) was a conservative Republican who was just as incisive as White but was destined to greater influence because of his genial nature and his pursuit of a traditionalist agenda that became increasingly popular during his tenure. Two years after *Enslin*, the Court denied review to a lower-court decision ruling that the University of Missouri could not, consistent with the neutrality the First Amendment imposes on state universities, purge its campus of a student gay rights group. Dissenting from the Court's refusal to decide the appeal in *Ratchford v. Gay Lib* (1978), Rehnquist rejected the students' argument that they were engaged in protected speech and association. No, Rehnquist argued, their advocacy was tantamount to reprehensible conduct. If so, "the question is more akin to whether those suffering from measles have a constitutional right, in violation of quarantine regulations, to as-sociate together with others who do not presently have measles, in order to re-peal a state law providing that measles sufferers be quarantined. The very act of assemblage under these circumstances undercuts a significant interest of the state." Rehnquist suggested that "this danger [of contagion] may be particularly acute in the university setting where many students are still coping with sexual problems which accompany late adolescence and early adulthood." Although no friend of the homosexual, White declined to join this remarkable dissenting opinion.[58]

Chief Justice Warren Burger (1907–1995) had joined *Roe*, but without really accepting its rationale. Sharing Rehnquist's traditionalism but little of his charm, Burger was an unlikely vote to expand *Roe*'s right to privacy. This chief justice never voted for the Court to review decisions rejecting gay people's constitu-tional rights but was always a proponent of the Court's reviewing pro-gay deci-sions. In the few cases where the Court did consider a gay rights case, he not only invariably voted against the gay litigants but showed no respect for the rights of gay people. If any of the justices was personally invested in denying rights to gay people, it was the chief.[59]

With three justices unwilling to extend the *Roe* privacy right under any cir-cumstances and two willing to consider consensual sodomy within the *Roe* right, the balance of power within the Court fell with the author of *Roe*, Harry Black-mun (1908–1999), and with the two other midwestern justices who supported *Roe*, Potter Stewart (1915–1985) and John Paul Stevens (born 1920). All were sensitive to the rising tide of academic and popular criticism of *Roe*. Some critics assailed the justices for making value choices (when does life begin?) without either democratic legitimacy or constitutional support. Others charged that the privacy right opened up all state morals legislation to constitutional challenge. By rejecting privacy-based challenges to state sodomy laws, these centrists could demonstrate that they did not consider *Roe* to be an elastic precedent. Not least important, the midwestern jurists considered sodomy between two men at best distasteful, which was clearly Blackmun's view in *Enslin*. North Carolina's oppo-sition to certiorari argued that the case did not involve sex between consenting adults, because Enslin "performed the illegal act on a 17-year-old boy." Black-mun placed a check mark beside that statement, signifying that he agreed. An-other check noted agreement with the clerk's observation that the "pandering aspect of this case makes it a poor vehicle." The fact that sex took place between an older homosexual and a young marine apparently rendered it irrelevant that North Carolina's age of consent was seventeen and that the state had recruited Morgan, coached him, and sent him to entrap its target three times.[60]

The ninth justice, Lewis Powell of Virginia (1907–1998), was uncomfortable adjudicating or even discussing constitutional issues involving homosexuality. He almost always voted to deny review in homosexual rights cases, whatever the result in the lower courts. Like most southern gentlemen, Powell believed one's sex life was none of his or anyone else's business. For him, homosexuality was simply incomprehensible, as was homophobia. Although no more politically correct than White and Rehnquist, Powell thought the *Roe* dissents reactionary and was appalled at Rehnquist's injudicious dissent in *Ratchford*.[61]

The Supreme Court Votes in Enslin *and* Doe: *Quo Vadis?*

Given the importance of the issues presented, and the repudiation of sodomy laws by the country's leading legal and medical authorities, it is surprising that only Justice Brennan voted to take review in both *Enslin* and *Doe*. Signaling less interest to hear the cases, Justice Marshall voted to take the cases only if three other justices agreed (within the Court, this is known as a "join three" vote). Justice Stevens voted to take review in *Doe* but not *Enslin*. The six other justices voted to deny review in *Enslin* and to affirm the lower court in *Doe*, without further briefing from the parties or amici.[62]

Even though it was rendered without full briefing by the parties, *Doe* was technically binding on the lower federal courts. Just as *Locke* established that crime-against-nature laws do not violate the vagueness rules of the Due Process Clause, so *Doe* was read to establish that they do not violate the privacy features either. Marilyn Haft believed that the Equal Protection Clause ought to be understood as protecting gay people against pervasive discrimination, but a Court that allowed Sam Hudson to entrap Eugene Enslin with marine jailbait was not a Court that was likely to protect sodomites—presumptive criminals—against state discriminations.

Byron White would have told these people to go back to the political process and achieve their goals through persuasion. Gay rights groups were indeed pressing, sometimes successfully, for municipal ordinances prohibiting discrimination on the basis of sexual orientation in government and (sometimes) in private employment and accommodations. When Jimmy Carter was elected president in 1976, gay people were politically hopeful. Although a southern Baptist from rural Plains, Georgia, Carter emphasized the tolerant and inclusive features of evangelical Christianity. Little comprehending the lives and aspirations of gay people, President Carter appointed Midge Costanza as his liaison to the gay community. In 1977, Haft left the ACLU to work under Costanza in the White House, and the ACLU allowed the Privacy Project to lapse.

After the Supreme Court's decision denying his appeal, Eugene Enslin was contacted by a powerful North Carolina attorney, who told him that the Attorney General's Office was willing to look the other way if Enslin would just leave the state. Because that would mean forfeiture of the ACLU's bond, and because he did not trust the prosecutors in the least, Enslin rejected the offer and turned himself in that spring. He served five and one-half months in various state holding facilities, with the likes of a gentle giant nicknamed "Big Daddy" and a psychotic prisoner who shaved his head and called himself "Kojak." (When Kojak became violent, the guards would call Big Daddy, who would subdue him with a firm headlock.) Enslin stayed out of trouble and turned down all but one of the many requests for sex from his fellow inmates.[63]

CHAPTER SEVEN

Gay Civil Rights and a New Politics of Preservation, 1975–86

B ayard Rustin, the gay Quaker who was Dr. King's great strategist, taught that social change comes from the ground up and through a gradual process of peaceful insistence and persuasion. By 1972 Rustin was applying his civil rights experience to other social movements, urging women and minorities to press respectfully for the same things the Montgomery bus boycott demanded in the early 1950s: "the right to live in dignity, the right to resist arbitrary behavior on the part of authorities, the right essentially to be one's self in every respect, and the right to be protected under law." To achieve these goals, he believed, it was important to make common cause with one another and with labor unions. Rustin also made his case for minority rights in terms

Willie Brown

that could motivate mainstream society. If minorities only hurt themselves by violence and self-segregation, mainstream majorities posed terrible risks to the social order if they frustrated minorities by denying their legitimate claims. All groups are losers in a politics of anger; all might be winners in a truly democratic politics. Recalling the inclusive philosophy of Whitman's *Democratic Vistas*, Rustin put this challenge to Americans: "[I]f you want to know whether they are true democrats, . . . the question to ask is, 'What about gay people?' . . . The barometer for social change is measured by selecting the group which is most mistreated."[1]

Many alumni of the civil rights movement agreed with Rustin. One was Thurgood Marshall, the former NAACP Legal Defense Fund lawyer who as a Supreme Court justice had dissented from the Court's summary rebuff of gay rights in *Doe* and *Enslin* (1976). Another was William Lewis Brown Jr. (born 1934). Raised in Mineola, Texas, about eighty miles east of Dallas, "Willie" Brown worked as a field hand and shoeshine boy to earn money for food. In 1951 the seventeen-year-old took a train to San Francisco, carrying a cardboard suitcase and boundless ambition. During his schooling at the University of San Francisco, Brown became active in the local NAACP. At an NAACP convention he met Rustin, who was an inspiration for Brown's entire career. Like the tall, elegant Rustin, the diminutive, gregarious Brown combined a passion for civil rights with a cool, strategic mind, convinced that discrimination must be opposed, but not through empty protests or meaningless gestures. Civil rights was both an intellectual and a moral movement, seeking to convince Americans that racial variation was normal, and a political struggle, in which allies had to be recruited and battles picked carefully. After graduating from the Hastings law school (1958), Brown represented ordinary people whom no one else would take on, finding every possible legal means for them to win their cases. Some of his clients were closeted lesbian or gay educators who were threatened with losing their teaching licenses. Brown viewed their private lives as none of the state's business, and he worked hard to make sure the state did not deprive these decent people of their livelihoods.[2]

Just as Rustin had urged Dr. King and the Southern Christian Leadership Conference to focus on Congress (and not just the Supreme Court, as the NAACP had done), Brown realized that state antidiscrimination campaigns needed to focus on the legislature—and he was determined to become part of that. In 1964 he was elected to the California Assembly; he had many gay constituents, who were numerous in Haight-Ashbury and the Castro, the core of his district. Running for reelection in 1968, Brown attended a candidates' forum sponsored by the Society for Individual Rights. California's legislature was then contemplating revision of the state penal code, and while other candidates pledged general support for adoption of the Model Penal Code, Brown was always one step ahead. Speaking last, he announced that if reelected he would introduce a bill zeroing in on and repealing the laws making consensual sodomy and oral copulation criminal offenses. "The place went absolutely crazy," and other candidates joined his pledge. He won in a landslide.[3]

Another lesson of the civil rights movement was the importance of moral virtue in politics. For Dr. King and others, the moral edge of the movement came from their Christian faith; its centers were churches. Willie Brown was a proud product of the Mineola Colored Methodist-Episcopal Church, but most of the other civil rights alumni were Baptists, as exemplified by the Reverend Carey Pointer (born 1920). Reverend Pointer is a gentleman in all senses of the term— honorable, soft-spoken, kindhearted, courtly in his manner. A graduate of Leland

College and the Washington Baptist Seminary, Pointer has been a Baptist preacher in the District of Columbia metropolitan area for more than half a century. Since 1969, he has been pastor at the Providence Baptist Church, long located in Capitol Hill and now in Prince George's County, Maryland. He speaks most warmly of the Baptist Ministers Conference of Washington, D.C. (BMC). An assembly of black Baptist ministers, the BMC has for more than a century been a moral watchdog in the nation's capital. Long before King and Rustin organized protest marches, the BMC stood against racial segregation and other forms of discrimination. The Civil Rights Act and other milestones in the 1960s vindicated the BMC's moral leadership, but developments in the 1960s posed new challenges.[4]

Whereas Brown cheered lesbians and gay men as they emerged from their closets, Pointer feared that his community was threatened by them. Binding his community was a common faith, grounded in scripture. Leviticus and Romans contain clear admonitions against the "dishonorable passions" (Romans 1:26) that drive men and women to engage in immoral sexual practices, including sodomy and adultery. To be true to their fundamentalist faith, Baptists such as Pointer felt compelled to preach against these sinful practices. Until the late 1960s a preacher had little explaining to do in this area, because no one in the congregation was willing to raise the subject, except in discreet counseling. Of course, there were congregation members who engaged in immoral practices, and a number of choir directors and even preachers were obviously homosexual. But this was a matter for their own consciences.

Then things began to change for the worse, as people were no longer ashamed of committing adultery or sodomy, and young people engaged in sexual activities without considering any deeper meaning. Nothing good had come from the sexual revolution for Pointer's community: teenagers' lives were ruined by unwanted pregnancies; more children were born out of wedlock; sexual abuse of children and rape of adult women were epidemic, as were sexually transmitted diseases. Homosexual sodomy was, symbolically, the worst of these developments because it was a naked embrace of sex for pleasure and transgressed the most moral precepts. During the 1970s, ministers like Pointer tried to hold the line against society's moral decay—at the same time that leaders like Brown were trying to redefine the line of permissible sexual conduct. Although sodomy reform reached its crest in 1977, with almost half the states having repealed their statutes, the nation as a whole agreed with Pointer. Throughout the 1970s opinion polls found that more than two-thirds of the nation found sodomy immoral. Pointer's perspective gained ground in the late 1970s and early 1980s, through the advent of a new *politics of preservation.*

The politics of preservation was fueled by a renaissance of religious fundamentalism in the United States and in the world. Enclaves of Orthodox Jews,

Shiite Muslims, traditionalist Roman Catholics, and fundamentalist Protestants attracted new followers with their message that secular modernism and liberalism, which valued individual pleasure, were not only morally unworthy, but also threatened the integrity and even survival of society. A new generation of religious leaders were effective mobilizers of religious conservatives: Archbishop Marcel Lefebvre among Roman Catholics, the Reverends Jerry Falwell and Pat Robertson among Protestants, and the Ayatollah Khomeini among Muslims. If Reverend Pointer reflected the gentle charity of Christ, Falwell and Robertson were more in keeping with the judgmental vision of Saint Paul. Together these clerics and their Catholic counterparts revived Anthony Comstock's moralizing politics of the body. They created new forms of religion-based identity and achieved what the civil rights revolution had started: easing animosities among Protestants and Catholics and bringing black and white Christians together in common projects.[5]

Legislative Sodomy Reform Reaches Its Crest, 1975–79

Although there were nine sodomy law repeals (including the Idaho repeal that was immediately reversed) before 1975, notably unrepresented were the jurisdictions with the largest number of openly lesbian and gay citizens—New York, Massachusetts, Pennsylvania, the District of Columbia, Florida, Texas, and California. In the 1960s sodomy reform was possible only in states where the issue had not been homosexualized. California's Willie Brown was determined to address that matter. Introduced in 1969, Brown's sex crime reform bill decriminalized fornication, adultery, and consensual sodomy but imposed stricter regulation of forcible sex and sex with minors. With most legislators cringing at the mere mention of this politically combustible subject, Brown knew his bill had no chance of enactment, but raised it as a starting point for coalition-building within the legislature. Every year he reintroduced essentially the same bill, with growing support among legislators who were willing to admit, behind closed doors, that the state had no business regulating private sexual activities between consenting adults. In 1972 and 1973 the Committee on Criminal Justice reported the Brown bill to the Assembly, but in neither instance did it come to a vote, because Brown did not have the votes to pass it.[6]

    Brown's bill had little likelihood of being enacted during the administration of Governor Ronald Reagan (1967–75). The California Republican Party had grown increasingly traditionalist on social issues, and the Democrats feared religion-based criticism. One legendary minister traveled all around the state, attending legislators' home churches and denouncing them for objectionable votes; he would have decried a sodomy repeal vote as precipitating Armageddon. Despite such efforts, lawmakers were well aware that support for consensual sodomy laws was waning. According to a 1973 GOP poll, almost nine out of ten police and sheriff's department officers believed that oral copulation between consenting heterosexuals should not be a crime; about three-fifths said the same for consenting homosexual couples. The ACLU of Southern California conducted a constitutional guerrilla war against the state sodomy laws, regularly winning dismissals of criminal prosecutions from trial judges. The law enforcement community accepted the pragmatic and privacy critiques of sodomy laws originally advanced by Jeremy Bentham (chapter 4).[7]

Brown needed a window of opportunity, which came after the 1974 post-Watergate elections, when California Democrats won the governorship, fifty-five of the eighty Assembly seats, and twenty-five of the forty Senate seats. With a new infusion of young liberals, Brown called upon his colleagues to pass the measure. Initial opposition came from the California Peace Officers' Association, District Attorneys' Association, and State Sheriffs' Association. While acquiescing in the deregulation of private sexual activities among consenting adults—an important concession engineered by District Attorney Dick Eigelhart, a Brown friend—these groups objected to the bill's apparent deregulation of sex between prison inmates and public sexual solicitation by gay men. Brown immediately agreed to amend his bill to bar sodomy between prison inmates and, almost as quickly, obtained an opinion from the Legislative Counsel that his bill would have no effect on California's sexual solicitation laws. With those assurances in place, opponents lost their best practical arguments against the bill. Republican assemblyman Bruce Nestande (a closet moderate representing socially conservative Orange County) halfheartedly complained that Brown's bill would legalize "unnatural acts" and sanction "unnatural relationships," but legislators privately dismissed such arguments. With Brown beaming at the center of the action, his bill passed the Assembly with a 45–26 majority on March 6, 1975.[8]

Even with the assurances Brown procured, the fate of his bill seemed uncertain in the California Senate—not only because it was more evenly divided between the parties, but also because opposition became more intense after the Assembly vote. Senator Alfred Song, the Senate Judiciary Committee's chair, was appalled by some of the letters he received, including one complaining that the bill was supported by "Negroes and Jews." According to one fundamentalist, "[a] Jew looks ridiculous as a preacher of sex morality. Negro politicians have always been for the most part cynical and corrupt." Such openly bigoted appeals were exceptional, but most of the letters had little more influence, because they invoked only sectarian arguments (sodomy is a sin) or grotesque stereotypes (homosexuals are child molesters). Potentially more effective was the lobbying campaign led by David Depew, a lawyer from Alhambra who represented the Women's Christian Temperance Union. In April he lectured the Senate Judiciary Committee that the Brown bill would legalize "[h]omosexual activities and orgies in homes or apartments next to yours. . . . Since homosexual acts would be legal, pressure would be on to have such behavior as an accepted standard of decency and morality. The schools are now under pressure to teach homosexuality as a normal standard along with marriage." Depew's statement capitalized on the Gay is Good philosophy of California's gay rights organizations.[9]

Brown's bill had the perfect sponsor in the Senate—Majority Leader George Moscone, who was courting gay support for his campaign to be the next mayor of San Francisco. On May 1 the senators debated sex crime reform in their bordello-style chamber, with its plush red carpeting, pink walls, and faux-Corinthian columns. Pointing toward the motto carved in the frieze above the presiding officer, *Senatoris civitatis libertatem tueri* ("Senators must guard the liberty of the republic"), Moscone urged his colleagues to pass the bill for standard privacy reasons. Making consensual sodomy a crime did nothing to protect the most urgent victims of sex crimes (children and women assaulted without their consent), he argued, and only created opportunities for blackmail and abusive police practices.

The most outspoken opponent was Senator H. L. "Wild Bill" Richardson, who held up three thousand telegrams sent by voters opposed to this "horrendous liberalization." He denounced homosexuality as "an abomination, a perversion" that God punishes by death (Leviticus 20:13). Additionally, the Arcadia Republican challenged the notion that the bill's allowance of homosexuality could be confined to the private sphere. He warned that homosexuals spread venereal disease and therefore were a public health menace; courts would extend the bill's protections to "the beaches, the bushes, and the restrooms" (as California's high court had already done); and impressionable children would receive the message that "homosexuality is okay."[10]

Richardson's fellow Republicans and their leader, Senator George Deukmejian of Long Beach, were mildly embarrassed by this display of antihomosexual spleen, but they then made their own more subdued versions of Richardson's argument. The most impressive opponent was the towering Senator John Stull, a former naval captain from San Diego. "The Admiral" argued that deregulating sodomy would victimize "future generations of children who see that it's okay because it's legal." Senator Newton Russell worried that sexual liberalization would undermine the moral fiber of the community. Reminding his colleagues that Rome fell because it lost its moral compass, Russell feared the United States would similarly "go to hell." Senator Albert Rhodda of Sacramento, a former history professor, responded that the leading historians believed that Rome's decline owed more to its mixing religion and politics.[11]

Most legislators considered the no promo homo arguments irrelevant. The fate of the bill depended on how many legislators outside San Francisco and Los Angeles would be willing to risk losing votes in order to update the state's Warren-era sex crime laws. (Not a few legislators were astounded to learn that the oral sex they enjoyed with their wives or girlfriends was a felony. To reinforce this message, a few of the girlfriends were on hand for the vote.) The initial call of the roll left the bill short of a majority, but senators from both parties then appeared from their hiding places to cast votes. With the vote twenty to nineteen against the bill, at about 2:30 p.m., Senator Nate Holden, the state's second African-American senator, walked into the chamber to cast an "aye" that tied it. Richardson and Deukmejian wondered whether the bill would fail on a tie vote, as Lieutenant Governor Mervyn Dymally, a Democrat (and the first African American elected to the California Senate), was in Denver.[12]

Anticipating a possible tie vote, Brown had arranged for Dymally to be available, and Moscone telephoned the lieutenant governor. To prevent the Republicans from depriving him of a quorum, Moscone asked the presiding officer to lock the senators in their chamber while he phoned Dymally to return to Sacramento. As senators lounged at their mahogany desks and telephoned staff to cancel afternoon appointments, Dymally jetted into the San Francisco Airport, from which he was helicoptered to the State Capitol. At 7:47 p.m., he strolled into the chamber. Announcing that his vote would take the state "one step farther from *1984*," the lieutenant governor cast the twenty-first vote in favor of the bill. Willie Brown had achieved the greatest legislative triumph of his career. After the Assembly accepted the Senate's amendments, the Brown-Moscone bill went to Governor Edmund (Jerry) Brown Jr., who signed it into law without fanfare on May 6, 1975.[13]

California was the twelfth state to decriminalize consensual sodomy. In June, three more states followed. Washington's repeal, signed by Governor Dan Evans on June 30, went even further than California's. A gay-friendly legislator in the Willie Brown mold, Senator Pete Francis was open to arguments from Seattle's Dorian Society to deregulate sodomy solicitation as well as sodomy. Washington was only the second state (after Hawaii) to reject the Model Penal Code's compromise, which created a new crime of "loitering to solicit sodomy" in return for decriminalizing the underlying act.[14]

After June 1975 sodomy reform seemed like an idea whose time had come. By July 1, 1976 (when California's and Washington's reforms took effect), four additional states had repealed their consensual sodomy laws as part of a general criminal code revision; three states did so in 1977; two in 1978. Within a decade after the Stonewall riots, twenty-four states—almost half the states of the Union—had decriminalized consensual sodomy (though two states recriminalized it after a short period).* Thirteen states had reduced consensual sodomy to a misdemeanor, so that defendants were assured of serving little or no jail time.†

By January 1, 1979, the sodomy map of the United States looked completely different than it had before Stonewall. As seen in figure 7.1, almost ninety percent of the American people lived in the thirty-five states—just short of the three-quarters required to adopt a constitutional amendment, and about the same number that ratified the ERA—that had substantially decriminalized consensual sodomy. Had the liberal morality advanced by Walt Whitman and Alfred Kinsey completely triumphed over traditional morality? Had the sexual revolution confirmed that sex could be for pleasure alone, unconnected to marriage, procreation, or even relationships? Had women's equality rendered traditional gender roles so obsolete that homosexual relations were losing their power to disgust?

Traditionalists' Politics of Preservation, 1977–81

After the California legislature had acted, Senator Richardson and his allies formed a Coalition of Christian Citizens to overturn the so-called "Homosexual Freedom Act." "It's put the state on record that we approve of homosexuality," said Richardson. "I don't believe we do." He proposed that the voters should decide through a referendum, by which they could veto an act of the legislature. There had been no successful referendum in California since 1951, in part because the state constitution required signatures of five percent of the number of votes cast in the previous election—which entailed 312,404 signatures. Because

---

*After (1) Illinois, (2) Connecticut, (3) Idaho (revoked in 1972), and (4) Colorado, state sodomy repeals came in (5) Oregon (July 1971), (6) Hawaii (April 1972), (7) Delaware (July 1972), (8) Ohio (December 1972), (9) North Dakota (May 1973), (10) Arkansas (March 1975, revoked in 1977), (11) New Mexico (April 1975), (12) California (May 1975), (13) Maine (June 1975), (14) New Hampshire (June 1975), (15) Washington (June 1975), (16) Indiana (February 1976), (17) South Dakota (February 1976), (18) West Virginia (March 1976), (19) Iowa (June 1976), (20) Wyoming (February 1977), (21) Vermont (April 1977), (22) Nebraska (June 1977), (23) New Jersey (1978), and (24) Alaska (1978). See the Appendix for citations.

†States that by 1979 had reduced consensual sodomy to a misdemeanor were Kansas (1969, same-sex only), Florida (1971, by court decision), Pennsylvania (1972), Texas (1973, same-sex only), Utah (1973), Kentucky (1974, same-sex only), Alabama (1977), Arizona (1977), Arkansas (1977, same-sex only), Minnesota (1977), Missouri (1977, same-sex only), Nevada (1977, same-sex only), and Wisconsin (1977). See the Appendix for citations.

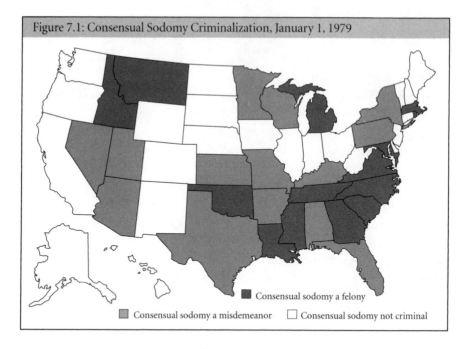

Figure 7.1: Consensual Sodomy Criminalization, January 1, 1979

■ Consensual sodomy a felony

■ Consensual sodomy a misdemeanor   □ Consensual sodomy not criminal

mainstream churches were unwilling to participate in the coalition, its underfunded petition drive failed. Simultaneously a legislative effort in New Hampshire to reverse that state's sodomy repeal—which had been unwittingly signed into law in 1975 by archconservative governor Meldrim Thomson—foundered when few of the state's organized religious groups insisted on recriminalization.[15]

Sodomy law revival did, however, find support in states where organized religion became involved. In 1975 the Arkansas legislature adopted the Model Penal Code, based on the recommendations of the state attorney general and criminal law experts. State Representative Bill Stancil, a former high school football coach from Fort Smith, was flabbergasted to learn that he had voted for sodomy repeal. Alerted to this ethical faux pas by Baptist preachers, he repented by introducing a bill to make "deviate sexual intercourse" a crime, but only if between persons of the same sex. Although a few legislators tried to stall the bill, no one dared oppose it, lest he be considered pro-homosexual. The Arkansas House voted for Stancil's measure, 66–2. Senator Milt Earnhardt, also representing Fort Smith, explained the bill to the Senate: "This bill is aimed at weirdos and queers who live in a fairyland world and are trying to wreck family life." The Senate passed the bill unanimously (25–0), and Governor David Pryor signed it on March 17, 1977.[16]

For the first time since the 1870s, fundamentalist Christians were becoming politically engaged in the politics of sex crime. Nothing better illustrates this development than the career of the Reverend Jerry Falwell Jr. (1933–2007). A Baptist preacher who in 1956 converted a Donald Duck Orange Juice bottling factory into the Thomas Road Baptist Church in Lynchburg, Virginia, Falwell preached to twenty-five hundred or more parishioners each Sunday, and to thousands more through telecasts of his *Old-Time Gospel Hour*. Hewing closely to scripture, his message was much like Pointer's, with one huge exception: reading Jesus to say that God created all human beings equal and cherished them in His love, Pointer preached that racial segregation was un-Christian, while Falwell preached that God made the races fundamentally different and admonished other preachers for getting politically involved in civil rights protests. He complained that the Civil Rights Act of 1964 committed the nation to "civil wrongs rather than civil rights." In 1967 Falwell created Lynchburg Christian Academy as a refuge for white parents who did not want to send their children to integrated public schools, though he later backed away from open segregation.[17]

Notwithstanding these differences, Falwell and Pointer came together in the 1970s over issues involving sexual morality—issues that also brought them into alliance with the Roman Catholic Church and the Church of Jesus Christ of Latter-day Saints, faith communities that Baptists had historically despised. State promotion of homosexuality through sodomy reform and antidiscrimination laws not only bound various religious groups in a common moral stance, but that stance brought them all into politics—a politics that changed the nature of religious faith in America.

The Politicization of Religion and New Traditionalist Identities

The United States has always hosted a multiplicity of religions, and animosity among them has been commonplace. This changed in the 1960s, as public life became more secular. The Supreme Court ruled that schools could not require prayer from students; states repealed their blue laws prohibiting business on Sundays; churchgoing declined. Yet modernism sparked a fundamentalist reaction that cut across the different denominations. Fundamentalism bills itself as a return to tradition, to fundamental natural truths about humanity that have stood the test of time. A resurgent fundamentalism split denominations and created cross-denominational alliances. No issue, with the exception of abortion, united fundamentalist Protestants, conservative Catholics, and Orthodox Jews more securely than homosexuality.[18]

The Roman Catholic Church has long followed a noninstrumentalist natural-law philosophy, valuing basic human goods. According to this philosophy, reproductive-type marital sex is good, not because it brings the partners delight or even because it perpetuates the human race (instrumentalist reasons), but instead because it actualizes a unique human communion between the man and the woman, a holy two-in-one-flesh union in the eyes of God. In His eyes, and in the view of many ancient philosophers as well, sexual pleasure that is nonmarital is an instrumental and therefore degrading use of the sacred human body. The church fathers taught that it is a serious sin. Under this moral theory, oral sex between two women or two men is deeply sinful, as it is by nature nonmarital.[19]

In the 1960s, Baptist fundamentalists like Carey Pointer and Jerry Falwell had little to do with the Roman Catholic Church. Many Baptists preached that Catholics were heathen because of their extravagant and unintelligible liturgies (Catholic Mass had until recently been delivered in Latin); their belief that Communion bread and wine actually become the blood and body of Christ (hence the fantastic charge that Catholics were "cannibals"); their disapproval of birth control, which resulted in large families; and their focus on community traditions rather than the authority of the biblical text and the one-to-one interaction between the believer and God. Fundamentalists also resented the Catholic Church's meddling in politics. (For this reason many Protestants voted against presidential candidate John F. Kennedy in 1960.) While Protestants saw birth control as a secular rather than religious issue, they agreed with Catholics that sex outside of marriage was wrong. Most fundamentalists felt it was degrading even to mention the crime against nature, and so they said virtually nothing about it.[20]

The women's rights movement and the sexual revolution had dramatic effects on faith in America. Mainstream Protestants and Reformed Jews liberalized their religions to accommodate new gender roles and sexual mores. The prevailing spirit held that we are all God's children, and God expects each of us to flourish in her or his own unique way. Accordingly, women became lay leaders in their churches, as well as pastors, priests, and rabbis. These religions endorsed family planning, with abortion tacitly and sometimes explicitly accepted. Some faiths cautiously welcomed open lesbians and gay men into their communities; gay-friendly caucuses formed in the Episcopalian, Methodist, Presbyterian, Quaker, Lutheran, Unitarian Universalist, and even Roman Catholic churches. In 1968 the Reverend Troy Perry founded the Metropolitan Community Church (MCC), aimed at gay people in Los Angeles. By 1976, there were almost one hundred MCC congregations and affiliates throughout the United States.[21]

Liberal Christians argued for gay-friendly readings of the Bible, suggesting, for example, that the sin of Sodom was not same-sex intimacy, but rather inhospitality and the threat of rape by the citizens against the visiting angels. Elsewhere in the Old Testament they found exemplars of same-sex commitment and even intimacy, as in the cases of Jonathan and David (1 Samuel 1:26) and Naomi and Ruth (Ruth 1:14–18). Since Christians consider the teachings of Jesus paramount, they pointed out that Jesus never disapproved of same-sex intimacy. Not only were His principles inclusive, but Jesus Himself showed special favor to Mary Magdalene, a fallen woman viewed with the same scorn by Jews that some fundamentalists reserve for homosexuals.[22]

Condemning "dishonorable passions" and "unnatural relations," Romans 1:26–27 was the hardest passage for gay-friendly Christians to assimilate. They maintained that Romans was best read as a rejection of sexual excess and infidelity, not as a blanket condemnation of same-sex intimacy within a committed relationship. In the first century there was no social or economic foundation for committed relations between two women or two men, and so their sex was likely to be pleasure-centered, "unnatural," and not spiritual. Romans 1:30–31 specifies the objects of Paul's outrage—"slanderers, haters of God, insolent, haughty, boastful, inventors of evil, disobedient to parents, foolish, faithless, heartless, ruthless." Because gay Christians were not haters of God, they escaped Paul's scorn, a reading that updated Romans 1:26–27 to modern circumstances. Fundamentalists objected that this was not a literal reading of the Bible, but in fact Paul never specifies what "unnatural relations" are, and the New Testament has almost nothing specific to say about sexual relations, even within marriage. A more valid objection is that Jews of the first century would have considered sexual relations between men or between women "unnatural"—but then the fundamentalist position is not that the Bible is God's word but that it is, instead, what God "meant" and whatever a specific community "would have understood" two thousand years ago. This is an odd position for a universal religion to take, for it ties God's word to the understanding of a particular human community. Moreover, the text and original meaning of 1 Timothy 6:1 are clearer—"Let all who are under the yoke of slavery regard their masters as worthy of all honor"—yet no Christian today believes that the verse justifies slavery.[23]

Many mainstream Protestants and Jews liberalized their beliefs along the foregoing lines, and similar ideas filtered into the post–Vatican II Roman Catholic Church and the post–civil rights Southern Baptist Convention. These denominations ultimately rejected the modern philosophy and, in the process, transformed fundamentalist Christianity itself. The turning points were the selection of Karol Wojtyla as Pope John Paul II in October 1978, and the election of Adrian Rogers as president of the Southern Baptist Convention in June 1979. John Paul II and his mentor, Josef Ratzinger (now Pope Benedict XVI), halted doctrinal innovation and rolled back the spiritual liberality opened up by

Vatican II. The new pope and his agents suppressed theological dissent in the United States on issues of sexual morality. Rogers was the first of an unbroken succession of fundamentalists selected to the Baptist presidency, which coincided with a series of moralistic proclamations.[24]

During this period of fundamentalist consolidation, the Roman Catholic Church and the Southern Baptist Convention created a countervision to the liberals' tolerance of homosexuality. Among Catholics, "new natural law" thinkers allied with Cardinal Ratzinger argued that homosexual relations are inherently nonmarital because they forsake the "two-in-one-flesh communion of persons" made possible by reproductive acts, and inherently immoral because they treat the body as a mere instrument of pleasure. It was a moral lie, and *not* tolerance, to say that homosexual relations could ever achieve the deep human good that reproductive-type relations might. The new natural law went beyond Comstockian fears of homosexual pollution and predation and represented itself as genuinely sympathetic to homosexuals. Like Saint Paul, the new natural-law theologians maintained that gay people themselves could flourish only by not acting on the alienating sexuality to which they were drawn. From that perspective, sodomy laws were actually doing gay people a favor by providing them with an incentive to refrain from degrading and self-alienating behavior.[25]

Fundamentalist Protestants as well as Catholics were receptive to this new interpretation of natural law. It made sense of scripture, especially the Letters of Saint Paul, and reflected a sophisticated philosophy that unashamedly retrieved an elemental norm—namely, that sex purely for pleasure was morally wrong. A culture that celebrated sex for pleasure—liberal culture—was one headed toward a formless polity that would inevitably decay. Embracing this philosophy, many Americans found a new political identity in the championing of *traditional family values* (TFV) as the basis for morality and for public policy, and in rejecting moral hedonism and political liberalism. This created new lines of identity-based alliances among religious fundamentalists. Longstanding doctrinal differences among conservative Protestants (such as Pointer and Falwell) and between Catholics and Protestants became less important once this political realignment occurred. By the 1990s the long-isolationist Southern Baptist Convention entered into an accord with the Roman Catholics and embraced the black Baptists in dramatic fashion.[26]

Most important, Protestant fundamentalists entered the political arena, which they had largely eschewed since the 1920s. In March 1972 Congress sent the Equal Rights Amendment to the states for ratification, and within three months, twenty (of the necessary thirty-eight) states had ratified. This alarmed Mrs. Phyllis Stewart Schlafly, a deeply religious wife and mother raising her six children in Alton, Illinois. The extravagantly coifed Republican activist was horrified at what she perceived to be the consequences of a constitutional amendment essentially eliminating sex-based classifications from American law. Women's colleges, special workplace protections for females, and wife-protecting alimony would be unconstitutional, as would women's exemption from the draft. In September 1972, Mrs. Schlafly founded STOP ERA. Three months later, the Supreme Court struck down state abortion restrictions in *Roe v. Wade* (1973). The morning Reverend Falwell read about *Roe*, he decided to bring his ministry into secular politics. *Roe* not only politicized millions of fundamentalists but gave black and white Baptists common cause with one another and with Catholics.[27]

While many religious Americans were uniting across denominational lines to oppose abortion and the ERA, they also became increasingly focused on homosexuality, especially after Stonewall brought thousands of flaunting gay people into the public culture. It was obvious to them that homosexual sodomy was the "unnatural relations" and homosexual attraction the "dishonorable passions" condemned in Romans 1:26–27. In the 1960s, fundamentalists had by and large followed the tolerant approach of Reverend Pointer, who believed that homosexuality should be left alone but not encouraged among the young and the weak of will. (In Romans 1:32, Paul criticized those "who know God's decree . . . but approve those who practice [unnatural acts].") In the 1970s, many fundamentalists followed a more aggressive script, which demonized homosexuals as embodying all the satanic features of sexuality unbound. The new generation of unclosetes homosexuals was more objectionable than mere sodomites, because they were shameless. Jerry Falwell and Tim LaHaye preached that they were the very "haters of God," the "foolish, faithless, heartless, ruthless" people Paul excoriated in Romans 1:30–31. The Southern Baptist Convention declared homosexuality an "abomination in the eyes of God," and their president announced that God created AIDS to reveal His displeasure with homosexuality.[28]

The Roman Catholic Church developed a theological basis for an approach more like Reverend Pointer's. Pope Paul VI's Declaration *Persona humana* (1975) condemned homosexual acts "as a serious depravity" and "intrinsically disordered." According to the official Catechism, men and women with homosexual tendencies are called, like other Christians, to live a life of chastity. The homosexual inclination is "objectively disordered" and homosexual practices are "sins gravely contrary to chastity." But such persons "must be accepted with respect, compassion and sensitivity. Every sign of unjust discrimination in their regard should be avoided." Within the Catholic Church the balance of sodomy-is-sinful rhetoric and don't-discriminate-against-homosexuals rhetoric shifted after 1978, with greater emphasis on the latter.[29]

Like Reverend Pointer and Cardinal Ratzinger, certain TFV individuals, in all denominations, rejected homosexuality and sodomy for reasons of sincere religious principle. Others demonized homosexuality based on prejudice and stereotypical thinking. Some traditionalists drew inspiration from both sources, in varying measures. For many traditionalists, aggressively antihomosexual rhetoric, sailing under the banner of natural law, satisfied the psychological needs of prejudiced people in a period of civil rights liberalization, when new moral lines were being drawn in public culture. The person disgusted by interracial intercourse and marriage was finding that his attitudes were no longer publicly tolerated, but his disgust with homosexual sodomy was both socially acceptable and just as emotionally fulfilling.[30]

By demonizing homosexuals as oversexed predators, the bigot—religious or otherwise—could reduce his anxieties about his own sexual urges. By disparaging homosexuals as a degraded Other, he could create a stable identity for himself as a heterosexual and, in the 1970s, as a person devoted to family and children. By attributing social decline to the homosexual agenda and the triumph of liberal sexuality, the bigot could find a manageable cure for complicated social problems and feel a sense of control over his own destiny. Such persons had previously deployed blacks, women, and Jews to satisfy their sentiments. Once racism, sexism, and anti-Semitism were less socially acceptable, by the 1970s, homophobia became an important all-purpose prejudice. Although the new natural law was itself not homophobic, its rhetoric appealed to homophobes because it singled out homosexual sodomy as uniquely sinful, even in ways heterosexual sodomy was not. As the eminent natural-law scholars Robert George and Gerard Bradley later put it, the state would be fully justified in criminalizing *only* homosexual sodomy, because "same-sex deviate acts can never occur within a marriage . . . or within any relationship that could ever lead to marriage," while heterosexual sodomy could obviously do so. Ironically, a philosophy that in principle condemned all nonprocreative intercourse had been re-presented, by its own leading lights, to justify antihomosexual policies that were supported, in truth, mainly by homophobes and heterohypocrites.[31]

Like earlier traditionalist campaigns, such as Anthony Comstock's (chapter 1), the TFV movement mobilized people's rejection of sexual variation and gender-bending, created images of social pollution by predatory "homosexuals and abortionists," and presented children, the family, and marriage as threatened by these new demons. Even though its earliest goals were defeat of the ERA (an effort in which they were immediately successful) and repudiation of *Roe* (in which they were not), the politics of preservation was increasingly devoted to stopping the homosexual agenda. This politics, which valorized woman as wife and mother, produced two of the most charismatic female political figures of the past century. One was Mrs. Schlafly, whose STOP ERA campaign added antihomosexual arguments to its women's rights arguments as the decade progressed. She warned Catholics, Protestants, and Orthodox Jews that the ERA would require homosexual marriage and promote a homosexual agenda harmful to children.[32] The other was Anita Bryant, the Florida Orange Juice Queen who briefly became the most admired and most reviled woman in America.

Anita Bryant's Save Our Children Campaign and the Moral Majority

By 1970 Florida was a multicultural state of almost 6.8 million. Another three million were added, mainly in Dade County (now Miami-Dade County), during the 1970s. Flocking to a climate that was sunny, hot, and humid all year long were anti-Castro refugees, retirees from the Northeast, and homosexuals. Despite being witch-hunted by the state in the 1950s and ignored by law reform commissions in the 1960s, gays were more numerous than ever in Dade County. In the post-Stonewall climate of activism, homosexuals formed a Gay Activists Alliance, the local NOW chapter formed a Lesbian Task Force, and gay motorcycle enthusiasts formed the Thebans. Lawyers successfully challenged Miami's cross-dressing and antihomosexual laws. For the first time in Miami, homosexuals became a significant and vocal political force.[33]

Even the Florida legislature took account of the growing homosexual community. In 1971 the Florida Supreme Court ruled that the crime-against-nature law was too vague to be enforced. Months later, Tampa senator Truett Ott introduced legislation to reinstate and better specify sodomy as a crime. The bill provoked a wild floor fight. Dade County legislators introduced an amendment to decriminalize all sexual activities between consenting adults; the Senate defeated it, 24–18. When Tampa senator David McLain proposed that penalties be limited to homosexual conduct, Ott successfully responded, "Deviant sex practices, in our society, are wrong, regardless of the sex involved." The Senate passed Ott's bill, but the House version omitted consensual sex crimes. Time ran out on the legislature before it could pass either version. In 1974, the legislature reached a similar stalemate and ultimately left the crime against nature out of the state code—but lewd and lascivious conduct (a misdemeanor) remained.[34]

In 1976 gay activist Bob Basker and entrepreneur Jack Campbell (the founder of Club Baths, a national chain of gay bathhouses) presided over the creation of the Dade County Coalition for the Humanistic Rights of Gays. Like Willie Brown they realized that homosexuals must become politically relevant in order to receive decent treatment from the government. Thirty-five coalition-backed candidates won positions in Dade County in the 1976 elections. One, Ruth Shack, took a seat on the Metro-Dade County Commission. Shack worked with Basker to introduce a bill in December 1976 to prohibit employment discrimination on grounds of sexual orientation. County and municipal employers would no longer be able to refuse to hire lesbian, gay, or bisexual people as firefighters, secretaries, or police officers.[35]

Or even as schoolteachers. This bothered Anita Bryant (born 1940), who lived in a thirty-four-room stucco mansion overlooking Biscayne Bay with her handsome husband, Bob Green, and their four children. Bryant was a former Miss Oklahoma whose trademark rendition of "Battle Hymn of the Republic" entertained thousands of American troops in Vietnam, President Johnson and his guests at White House functions, and the mourners at Johnson's funeral. The auburn-haired beauty had enjoyed great fame and fortune as the spokesperson for the Florida Citrus Commission since 1968. ("A day without orange juice is like a day without sunshine!") A Baptist who had accepted Jesus as her Savior at age eight, Bryant mixed religious disapproval of unnatural relations with some of her own idiosyncratic views about homosexuals. (In 1978 she told an interviewer that "homosexuals are called fruits" because they "eat the forbidden fruit of the tree of life," namely, sperm.) Bryant telephoned Ruth Shack, whom she had helped elect because Ruth's husband was her booking agent. "I expressed the valid fears we now felt of widespread militant homosexuals' efforts to influence children to their abnormal way of life." Shack told Bryant these fears were unfounded. "I grew up during the Holocaust. . . . I see this as a human rights issue."[36]

After a prayerful night Bryant wrote a letter to each commissioner, arguing that the antidiscrimination ordinance would not only violate God's biblical commandments, but would also "be infringing upon my rights, discriminating against me as a citizen and a mother to teach my children and set examples of God's moral code as stated in the Holy Scriptures. Also, you would be discriminating against my children's right to grow up in a healthy decent community." Her voice choking with emotion, Bryant made the same argument at the public hearing on January 18, 1977. Joining her were hundreds of Baptist parishioners and preachers, a representative of the Catholic archdiocese, and a leading Orthodox rabbi. Placards supported her stance with slogans such as, "God Says NO! Who Are You to Be Different?" and "Don't Legitimate Immorality for Dade County." Opponents prayed, wept, and jeered when supporters like Basker spoke. These witnesses apparently persuaded two commissioners to switch their votes: Neal Adams, an African-American Baptist minister, and Clare Oesterle, who sobbed after her own vote was cast. But Shack and born-again Christian Bill Oliver held firm; the commission voted five to three for the ordinance. Bryant was "aflame with indignation" that God's word had been disregarded. On the spot she and other citizens vowed to overturn the commission's action. Jubilant antidiscrimination supporters "dismissed Bryant as a joke, a cracker from Oklahoma who still lived in the pre-disco age."[37]

Dade County's charter provides that a law can be revoked if enough citizens petition for a referendum and then a majority of voters reject the law in the next election. Bryant found more than enough people to sign their names to her petition. She devoted the next four months to a campaign she called "Save Our Children," the premise of which was that the law should not give "special rights" to people who adhere to homosexuality (a lifestyle that is "immoral and against God's wishes"), especially teachers charged with children's education. "Public approval of admitted homosexual teachers could encourage more homosexuality by inducing pupils into looking upon it as an acceptable lifestyle." The debate was not one of gay rights versus discrimination, but of gay rights versus parents' and children's rights. This platform brought an unprecedented coalition of religious leaders under one political tent: Southern Baptist pastors, the Catholic archbishop of Miami, and Orthodox rabbis all endorsed the referendum and touted it from their pulpits. Governor Reuben Askew, a moderate Democrat, gave his support to the effort, proclaiming, "I would not want a known homosexual teaching my children."[38]

Nonetheless, Save Our Children's professional organizers realized, through their private polling, that most Dade County voters (especially women) supported the ordinance. Borrowing a page from Comstock's *Traps for the Young*, their campaign responded with charges that homosexuals were not just unacceptable role models, but were aggressive threats to children's innocence and the community's moral purity. In a *Miami Herald* ad, Save Our Children warned, "The recruitment of our children is absolutely necessary for the survival and growth of homosexuality. Since homosexuals cannot reproduce, they must recruit, must freshen their ranks." Another ad was more explicit, accusing predatory homosexuals of "outright seduction and molestation, a growing pattern that will predictably intensify if society approves laws granting legitimacy to the sexually perverted." On May 22, 1977, two weeks before the vote, Reverend Falwell addressed thousands of families at a Miami Convention Center rally, warning parents that "[s]o-called [gay] folks would just as soon kill you as look at you." These fantastic claims preyed on mothers' concerns for their children, as well as men's antihomosexual prejudices. Particularly extreme was Bryant's press release, "Why Certain Sexual Deviations Are Punishable by Death" (Leviticus 20:13). "As barnyard animals become restless, confused, and panicky just before a hurricane . . . [s]o too these vile beastly creatures evidently sense the coming judgment [of God]."[39]

The coalition underestimated the force of these charges, which incited a wave of antigay violence. "Kill a Queer for Christ" bumper stickers appeared, and volunteers were beaten up in front of the coalition's headquarters. Outside consultant Ethan Geto opted for an expensive media rather than grassroots campaign to defeat the referendum. Lesbian and feminist groups were not important in his strategy, and some feminists were irked by the sexism of the all-boys coalition leadership. Geto even directed Cuban-American activist Jesse Monteagudo to cease organizing within the Latino community, because it was "too conservative," and he did not want to rile its members. The *Miami Herald* switched its editorial stance, suggesting that the ordinance was "concocted, we suspect, by those more interested in flaunting their new deviate freedom than in preventing discrimination." Geto's expensive ads in the *Herald* were buried by news stories of homosexual molestation and call-boy rings.[40]

The traditionalists' own brilliant grassroots efforts and their neo-Puritan campaign of antihomosexual vilification, combined with the coalition's ineffectual response, were lethal for gay rights. On June 7 Dade County voters supported the referendum repealing the antidiscrimination ordinance by a more than two-to-one margin. The day after the vote, the Florida legislature barred homosexuals from adopting children, and Bryant further urged it to reinstate the old crime-against-nature felony (a plea the legislators ignored). She also created the Anita Bryant Ministries, a Miami-based counseling service to help homosexuals "convert," first to Christianity, and then to heterosexuality. Bryant announced that her allies would "carry our fight against similar laws throughout the nation that attempt to legitimize a lifestyle that is both perverse and dangerous to the sanctity of the family, dangerous to our children, dangerous to our freedom of religion and freedom of choice, dangerous to our survival as one nation, under God." True to her word, Bryant traveled from locale to locale preaching against antidiscrimination laws. Wichita, Kansas; St. Paul, Minnesota; and Eugene, Oregon immediately followed Dade County in repealing their gay rights ordinances by referenda.[41]

Yet Bryant's star plummeted after an oddball *Playboy* interview in May 1978, in which she admitted hostile feelings toward her husband and toward men generally. Following the loss of her orange juice contract, Bryant divorced Green and left Florida in 1980. Old allies shunned the divorcée, but built on her success. Like civil rights and gay rights movements before them, a new TFV movement in the late 1970s formed organizations and personal networks that enabled the traditionalist perspective to be heard in the public culture, to raise money for friends and against enemies, and to affect politics at every level of government. Such groups included the National Conservative Political Action Committee (NCPAC) run by Terry Dolan; the Christian Voice and the Religious Roundtable; Congressman John Ashbrook's American Conservative Union; and the Moral Majority, founded by Reverend Falwell in 1979. Denouncing President Carter as an advocate of "homosexuality" to southern Baptist and midwestern Catholic voters, these groups contributed to Ronald Reagan's election as president in 1980.[42]

The District of Columbia's Attempted Sodomy Repeal, 1981

Although gay and lesbian communities were shocked by the success of Save Our Children, Willie Brown's San Francisco continued to offer hope. George Moscone had been elected mayor after the sodomy repeal vote in 1975, and openly gay Harvey Milk was elected to the Board of Supervisors in 1977. But even in San Francisco, there were increased attacks on gay men in the year after Dade County. On the morning of November 17, 1978, former supervisor Dan White strolled into Moscone's office for a meeting about White's abrupt resignation the previous week. He fired four shots into the mayor at close range, two of them into his skull. White then filled his Smith & Wesson with hollow dum-dum bullets that explode on impact and walked past Dianne Feinstein's office toward Milk's. White invited Milk into the office he once occupied. He pulled out the gun and fired three dum-dums into Milk's arm and chest. As Milk fell to his knees, White fired two more shots into his head. At 11:20 a.m., Acting Mayor Feinstein announced the deaths of Mayor Moscone and Supervisor Milk. Dan White turned himself in five minutes later.[43]

One year earlier, in the wake of Dade County, Milk had filmed a video to be played in the event of his assassination. Acknowledging the anger many would feel, he urged that gays express themselves constructively. "I would like to see every gay doctor come out, every gay lawyer, every gay architect come out, stand up and let the world know. That would do more to end prejudice overnight than anybody could imagine." Galvanized by Milk's martyrdom and adopting the political strategy first implemented by Bayard Rustin, an estimated 75,000 gay men, lesbians, and bisexuals assembled for the first March on Washington for Lesbian and Gay Rights on October 14, 1979. Parading down Pennsylvania Avenue, they came out to the president, who was setting up a reception for Pope John Paul II, and they came out to Reverend Falwell, who denounced their shameless embrace of Sodom before he entered the White House to hobnob with the pope. Like Rustin sixteen years earlier, gay and lesbian leaders emphasized that the goal of the march was to petition the federal government to fulfill its constitutional duties of protecting them against hate-based violence and to assure them equal rights and opportunities.[44]

The march also energized the District's lesbian and gay activists, who were likewise following the Rustin approach of electing local allies to public office and building coalitions to achieve pro-gay legislation. In 1975 Congress had granted the District limited home rule, allowing its council to enact laws. One of the first was the Human Rights Act of 1977, prohibiting discrimination on the basis of sexual orientation (and race, etc.) in workplaces, public accommodations, and educational institutions. Instrumental in passing this landmark legislation, Frank

Kameny and the Gay Activists Alliance (GAA) also pressed for repeal of the 1948 statute making consensual oral and anal sex a felony. They worked with the District's Law Revision Commission to produce a Sexual Assault Reform Act that would create new penalties for sex between adults and minors and would decriminalize fornication, adultery, and consensual sodomy.[45]

The proposed liberalization did not meet with favor from the District's religious fundamentalists. The Civic and Social Activities Committee of the Baptist Ministers Conference (BMC) recommended that the BMC oppose the proposal. As Reverend Pointer (BMC president 1980–82) recalls, the Conference objected to lowering the age of consent to sixteen and to the decriminalization of fornication, adultery, and especially consensual sodomy. One fear was that the proposal would give "sexual predators free rein to molest school children"; a deeper fear was that the proposal would undermine traditional family values by withdrawing state disapproval of nonmarital sexual activities and by sending a message that homosexuality was acceptable. Pointer and his associates conveyed these objections to their political allies—Councilmembers John Ray, Wilhelmina Rolark, and Jerry Moore (a Baptist minister)—and pressed them during hearings by the council's Judiciary Committee in 1980 and 1981 (chaired by Ray).[46]

The Roman Catholic Archdiocese of Washington reached the same conclusion. By 1981 some American bishops would have preferred to remain on the sidelines, because they felt church opposition signaled antigay attitudes. This, however, was not the view of Archbishop James Aloysius Hickey (1920–2004). An Irish Catholic raised in the Michigan heartland, Hickey was an avid rule follower. At St. Joseph Seminary, there were "140 miserable rules to regulate our every small behavior," a colleague recalls. "James was the only one to keep all 140. He never talked in the library, and he always put his napkin back in the napkin holder." A strict and learned traditionalist, Hickey was a favorite of Pope John Paul II, who appointed him archbishop in 1980. After strongly reaffirming the church's position on birth control, adultery, and sodomy, Archbishop Hickey publicly opposed the Sexual Assault Reform Act, for the same reasons as the BMC.[47]

Opposition from both the BMC and the Catholic Church would once have been fatal to sex crime legislation in the District. But supporting the bill was a coalition of civil liberties and feminist groups, children's advocates, labor organizations, the bar association, and even NCPAC. GAA also had influential straight allies (council president David Clarke and Mayor Marion Barry) who were, like California's Brown, alumni of the civil rights movement and savvy politicians. With the city's sodomy law no longer enforced against consensual, private activities, police and prosecutors voiced no public objections. Even the BMC's closest legislative allies were ambivalent. Reverend Moore worried that the sodomy statute was a confusion of morality and law: "My personal view is that the [criminal] law should never attempt to legislate morality." For more than fifty years the pastor of the Nineteenth Street Baptist Church, the first African-American Baptist church in the District, Moore saw a shift in attitudes even among church-going blacks. Most of his younger parishioners were either supportive of sodomy reform, undecided, or opposed but not strongly.[48]

Councilmembers Moore and Ray were absent when the council voted for the Sexual Assault Reform Act; only Councilmember Rolark dissented. Mayor Barry signed it on July 21, 1981. But there was a catch: the District's home rule statute stipulated that laws adopted by the council could be vetoed by majority vote in either house of Congress. Shocked that the sex crime law passed almost unanimously over their opposition, Reverend Pointer and the BMC contemplated such an override petition. Reverend Cleveland Sparrow, BMC's secretary, was also the president of the Moral Majority in D.C. and suggested that the national organization might want to get involved. Reverend Pointer said amen to that idea.[49]

Sparrow contacted Reverend Falwell, who agreed with BMC and saw the sodomy issue as a means to expand his own constituency. On August 13 Falwell sent a mass mailing alerting Americans to the "massive homosexual revolution" that must be stopped. "The homosexuals are on the march in this country. Please remember, homosexuals do not reproduce! They recruit! And, many of them are after my children and your children. This is one major reason why we must keep the 'Old-Time Gospel Hour' alive!" Some of the money raised by appeals such as this financed a grassroots and lobbying effort to persuade the House of Representatives to veto the sex crime reform law. In September Falwell came to Washington to lead the campaign against this "perverted" law that would invite the wrath of God upon America. The Baptist ministers and Archbishop Hickey issued fresh public statements urging that Congress "not legitimize and encourage adultery, sodomy, fornication, homosexuality, seduction, and promiscuity," as Reverend Sparrow put it. Thousands from all over the country phoned or wrote their congressmen, objecting to the promotion of homosexuality. Neither the understaffed District government nor the fledgling lesbian and gay activist groups were even able to mount a response to this citizen crusade.[50]

Representative Philip Crane, a ramrod Illinois Republican associated with the Christian Voice, introduced House Resolution 208 to override the Sexual Assault Reform Act. The District of Columbia Committee, chaired by Representative Ronald Dellums of California, voted eight to three against the resolution. Normally, that would kill a measure, but the D.C. Home Rule Act enabled Crane to bring a House floor motion to discharge Resolution 208 from committee. Representative Stewart McKinney, the ranking Republican on the committee, moved to table Crane's motion. The House narrowly voted to table (106–98), until Crane demanded a roll-call vote, which yielded a huge margin (117–292) the other way. Crane's motion passed by an equally lopsided (279–126) vote, again after a voice vote against it.[51]

The House then debated the resolution. Representative Thomas Bliley of Virginia, a minority member of the committee, made the case: "This act, by specifically legalizing unusual sexual practices, would condone them. The moral and ethical traditions of this Nation do not condone acts such as sodomy and adultery." Few representatives dared speak out against the override. One liberal Democrat explained his silence: "How would you like to spend your goddamn campaign trying to explain how you're not in favor of people having sexual relations with animals?" An exception was McKinney, a moderate Republican from Connecticut. Noting that a dozen churches supported deregulation, he argued that "tolerating" was not the same as "endorsing homosexuality." Criminalization of consensual sex only invited abusive police practices. McKinney's opposition was politically brave, because he represented a competitive district in a Roman Catholic state, and because he was a closeted (married) gay man. Every other closeted gay representative was silent during the floor debate, and one of them (Steve Gunderson of Wisconsin) cast every roll-call vote with Crane.[52]

The House voted 281–119 to override the District's sex crime reform law. Voting for Resolution 208 were most Democrats as well as most Republicans—including Representatives Richard Cheney of Wyoming, Geraldine Ferraro of New York, Richard Gephardt of Missouri, Newt Gingrich of Georgia, Paul Simon of Illinois, Bob Traxler of Michigan, and Albert Gore of Tennessee. Three-quarters of the "no" votes came from members representing districts in the Northeast and the West Coast, where there were more openly gay people involved in civic life. Not a single African-American representative voted for the resolution, and Dellums was the leading speaker against it.[53]

The House's vote to reinstate the District's consensual sodomy law was a great victory for the BMC and the Moral Majority. As Reverend Pointer recalls it, Reverend Falwell sent his private airplane to Washington to fly Pointer and his BMC colleagues back to Lynchburg to celebrate. "He treated us like Kings and Princes—flew us down, entertained us lavishly, took pictures." It was a victory of traditional family values over homosexual equality.[54]

One striking irony is that the reform act Congress vetoed in the name of family values had as its primary focus protecting minors as well as adults from sexual aggression. The legislation represented years of expert study and legislative consensus building on legal issues involving sexual assault. At the same time that Philip Crane was reclaiming the District from homosexuals, his brother Dan

Crane (also a GOP representative from Illinois) was covering up a sexual affair he had had in 1980 with a teenage female page. Because he was married, this constituted misdemeanor adultery but was otherwise not criminal under D.C. law. After Dan Crane admitted this conduct in 1983, he was not prosecuted, though he was censured by the House. If the brothers Crane had not been successful in their veto campaign, Dan Crane's conduct might have fallen within a new felony that would have been added by the Sexual Assault Reform Act—having sex with a minor (under age eighteen) over whom he held a "position of responsibility" as her employer. The campaign by TFV Christians to reaffirm the criminality of homosexual sodomy also preserved a legal safe haven for powerful men to sexually harass young women under their supervision.[55]

Another irony is that the religious groups opposing sodomy reform included sexually active gay men within their own ranks; such men were tolerated, so long as they were discreet. For all their rhetoric, fundamentalist Protestants and Catholics were actually moving away from ridiculous stereotypes about homosexuality and toward recognition that gay people could have a place in the Christian republic. The line they drew was between the chaste Lynchburg, Virginia, homosexual who was genuinely ashamed of his "dishonorable passions," and the unrepentant San Francisco homosexual who "flaunted" his godless conduct. Even the closeted but sexually active homosexual was better than the flaunting one, because the latter tempted impressionable youth with the allure of sexual excitement. The new antihomosexual discourse did not need to rely on the myth of homosexuals as child molesters—although their fund-raising campaigns continued to do so—because the homosexual was naturally predatory in the same way Satan is: by offering temporary pleasure and the siren allure of Walt Whitman's "love of comrades," which the youth accepts at the price of his soul.[56]

One last irony was particularly tragic. In the House cloakrooms Representative Barney Frank, a Massachusetts Democrat, lobbied against Resolution 208, but a lot of colleagues told him, "Hey pal, you're right, but you know, nobody's being prosecuted, it's purely symbolic. It's not a big deal, right?" The Harvard Law School graduate bit his overeducated tongue. As a closeted gay man fearful that any sexual relationship with another man would ruin him, Frank felt that sodomy repeal was anything but symbolic politics. That Frank did not use his own life as a counterexample deprived his colleagues of information about his sexuality that might have affected their judgments. He was more correct than he realized. At the very moment when Frank was buttonholing his colleagues, medical researchers at the nearby National Institutes of Health were discussing an epidemic of immunological malfunctions among gay men. Doctors all over America were watching these men die agonizing deaths. Some were bisexual black men in the BMC congregations, others were Catholics, a few were priests. In July 1982 doctors named the new disease: acquired immune deficiency syndrome (AIDS).[57]

As the country learned about the spread of AIDS and its terrible consequences, the sodomy debate was revealed as having more-serious consequences than either Frank or Crane had guessed. Perhaps gay and bisexual men had something to learn from moral leaders such as Pointer and Hickey. The primary means of HIV (the virus associated with AIDS) transmission was discovered to be anal sex, the historic crime against nature. Romans 1:27 warned that "men committing shameless acts with men" would "receiv[e] in their own persons the due penalty for their error." Falwell characterized AIDS as God's judgment on homosexuals, while the Moral Majority generalized, "[W]hat gays do to each other makes them sick and, more and more frequently, dead!" Its newsletter urged a strong public response: "The gay chicken created by sexual liberation has come to roost in everybody's back yard, thus endangering everyone. His disease-ridden roost must be destroyed. Vigorous anti-sodomy laws can accomplish these necessary public health goals." In contrast to Falwell, Archbishop Hickey opened his churches to provide hospice and other care for people afflicted with AIDS. When his priest, the Reverend Michael Peterson, came to him dying of AIDS, Hickey offered compassion and assured him of God's forgiveness.[58]

Falwell notwithstanding, there was no evidence that sodomy laws actually served a public health function. Washington, D.C.'s sodomy law did not prevent it from having one of the highest HIV infection rates in the nation. In the 1980s medical professionals concluded that sodomy laws actually threatened their ability to deal with the epidemic, because they encouraged sexual secrecy and thereby impeded medical efforts to identify and inform potentially infected sex partners. More generally, the "don't ask, don't tell" approach to homosexuality contributed to the Reagan administration's refusal to create safer-sex education programs or to fund AIDS research at the levels recommended by medical experts. It was only after Dr. Michael Gottlieb of UCLA announced in July 1985 that Republican movie star and Reagan buddy Rock Hudson had AIDS that the media and the politicians started to create and fund serious AIDS programs.[59]

Meanwhile, men kept dying. One of them was Representative McKinney, who succumbed to pneumonia resulting from AIDS on May 8, 1987.

Political Impasse—Back to Court for Sodomy Reform

In 1983, the Supreme Court ruled that a one-house veto of agency rules violated the Constitution. Congress could create or negate law only through legislation adopted by both the House and the Senate and presented to the president. Although this decision made it clear that the House's 1981 veto of the District's sex crime reform law had no legal effect, Congress responded the next year with a statute confirming the earlier one-house override. Gay rights groups put up no resistance. Indeed, by the mid-1980s, sodomy reform was stalled or, some feared, dead.[60]

Legislative repeal campaigns had reached the point of diminishing marginal returns. For some years sodomy reform had been given a free ride because of the popularity of the Model Penal Code, but that free ride all but ended after California's freestanding sex crime reform legislation. Sodomy reform was possible in California because gay people there were well-organized and TFV groups were less prominent in politics. The states that had not legislated reforms were ones where the Southern Baptist Convention (the South and border states), the Church of Jesus Christ of Latter-day Saints (Utah, Idaho, Montana), and the Roman Catholic Church (New York, Massachusetts, Rhode Island, Michigan) retained a strong influence in local politics. Because it is much easier to block than to enact laws, gay people faced difficult odds in these states. No state legislature repealed its consensual sodomy law between 1978 and 1983. After Wisconsin repealed its sodomy law in 1983, no state would adopt a sodomy reform law for more than a decade—except for Tennessee, which in 1989 deregulated heterosexual sodomy but left homosexual sodomy a criminal misdemeanor.

A generation earlier, faced with even more daunting legislative roadblocks to repealing race-discriminatory laws in the South, the NAACP had asked federal courts to nullify such laws on constitutional grounds. That strategy met with legendary success, but *Doe* and *Enslin* suggested that Supreme Court justices were much less receptive to gay rights claims. With state legislative repeal and federal judicial review blocked for the time being, gay rights attorneys pressed for a third option—constitutional litigation in state courts. Gay rights attorneys, like women's rights counsel before them, found that state judges were often more receptive to their claims than state legislators.

Judicial Review of Consensual Sodomy Statutes: The Onofre Case

Ronald Onofre was a homosexual with incredibly poor judgment. A minister of the Universal Life Church, Onofre befriended and in 1976–77 enjoyed a sexual relationship with Russell Evans, a seventeen-year-old who probably had borderline intelligence. A friend noticed physical injuries Evans had allegedly sustained during anal intercourse, and helped him seek medical attention. At the friend's urging Evans filed criminal charges, and the Syracuse, New York, police arrested Onofre for forcible sodomy. To establish the consensual nature of their relationship, Onofre showed the police photographs of their oral and anal activities; Evans recanted his coercion claim. While Onondaga County dropped the forcible sodomy charges, it re-charged Onofre with violation of New York's *consensual* sodomy law. Given Onofre's own statements to the grand jury and the photographs proving "deviate sexual intercourse," Onofre's counsel Bonnie Strunk realized there was no defense to this charge—except to argue that the consensual sodomy law was unconstitutional. Rejecting this defense, the Onondaga County Court found Onofre guilty and sentenced him to a conditional discharge, with one year's probation.[61]

Conde Peoples III and Philip Goss were run-of-the-mill homosexuals who likewise ran into legal trouble. At 6:30 a.m. on November 28, 1978, two police officers patrolling Buffalo's Front Park observed an automobile parked on the side of the road. One officer approached the car and pointed a flashlight toward its interior, where he observed Peoples and Goss engaged in oral sex. The other officer observed Mr. Peoples's head rise from the lap of Mr. Goss. Although Peoples and Goss maintained that they were just masturbating each other, the police arrested them for consensual sodomy, and a jury convicted them. While neither man went to prison for the crime, Goss paid a $100 fine, and Peoples (the "active" partner), $200. Buffalo attorney Bill Gardner handled their case, as well as that of Mary Sweat, who was apprehended by the police for performing "oral sodomy" on a "male companion" she had flagged down in his Ford pickup truck.[62]

Strunk and Gardner contacted Lambda Legal, the litigation group created by Bill Thom and Cary Boggan. Margot Karle, the president of the Lambda board, agreed that these cases presented an opportunity to rid the state of its consensual sodomy law by reversing the burden of legislative inertia. This is exactly what had recently happened in Iowa and New Jersey: sensing that public support had declined, state judges declared that sodomy laws could not constitutionally be applied to private activities between consenting adults, and the Iowa and New Jersey legislatures had responded by rewriting their laws to exclude such activities.[63]

Because the Iowa and New Jersey decisions had extended *Griswold* to include same-sex intimacies, Lambda attorneys felt the time was coming when gay people would enjoy the same right to privacy as straight people, at least under state constitutions. Like the Lambda brief in *Enslin*, Karle and Strunk's brief on appeal emphasized *Eisenstadt*, which had invalidated a state restriction on contraceptives for unmarried couples, and *Stanley*, which had invalidated the seizure of obscene materials whose use was limited to the home. The *Onofre* brief also found support for a privacy-based right to engage in homosexual sodomy in the work of two leading constitutional scholars, NYU professor David Richards and Harvard professor Laurence Tribe. In *Onofre*, the challengers presented a second constitutional argument. Because New York defined "deviate sexual intercourse" to *exclude* activities between married persons, its consensual deviate sexual intercourse law discriminated against unmarried couples—exactly like the contraception statute the Supreme Court had struck down as a violation of equal protection in *Eisenstadt*.[64]

In January 1980 the Appellate Division invalidated the consensual sodomy law on both privacy and equal protection grounds. Onondaga County's district attorney appealed the reversal to the New York Court of Appeals; Gardner appealed the convictions of his clients as well, and their cases were consolidated with *Onofre*. For once, the odds favored Lambda. As the greatest common-law court in America, the New York Court of Appeals has long been a repository of reason and ecumenism. Because they served for lengthy terms, its judges were less susceptible to fears that they would be politically wounded for "promoting homosexuality." In *Onofre* the court was bombarded with amicus briefs supporting Strunk and Gardner. In addition to Lambda's excellent submission, there were briefs from the New York Civil Liberties Union, the New York City Bar Association, and Tom Coleman's National Committee for Sexual Liberties. Notable by his absence was New York attorney general Robert Abrams, a liberal Democrat who declined to defend the constitutionality of the consensual sodomy law. As if to seal the statute's doom, Pennsylvania's more-conservative Supreme Court struck down its consensual sodomy law soon after oral argument in *Onofre*.[65]

Judge Hugh Jones's opinion for the court in *People v. Onofre* (1980) found that the Fourteenth Amendment's Due Process Clause protects individual decisions involving sexual intimacy. Joined by the three most recent additions to the court (Sol Wachtler, Jacob Fuchsberg, and Bernard Meyer), Jones rejected the prosecutors' attempt to limit the right to marital and childbearing decisions. *Eisentstadt* could not be reconciled with a limitation to marital activities, and *Stanley* could not be reconciled with a limitation to childbearing decisions. Moreover, "no rational basis appears for excluding from the same protection decisions—such as those made by defendants before us—to seek sexual gratification from what at least once was commonly regarded as 'deviant' conduct, so long as the decisions are voluntarily made by adults in a noncommercial, private setting." Jones acknowledged that the arrests of Goss, Peoples, and Sweat were not in a "private setting," but ruled the sodomy law unconstitutional as to those defendants because of the discrimination against unmarried couples.[66]

The court's Catholic judges, Dominick Gabrielli and Lawrence Cooke, disagreed. They contrasted decisions relating to childbearing and family, which constituted the core cases for the right to privacy, with "deviant conduct," which had long been regulated by the state. "Scholars from Aquinas to Blackstone considered even consensual sodomy to be as heinous as the crime of rape." Because

"western man has never been free to pursue his own choice of sexual gratification without fear of State interference," it was wrong for the court to rule that it
was such "an integral part of our concept of ordered liberty" that it was now a
fundamental due process right. They also disputed the majority's equal protection analysis. The exclusion of married couples could be justified "on the theory
that the institution of marriage is so important to our society that even offensive
intimacies between married individuals should be tolerated," as *Griswold* itself
seemed to hold.[67]

Citing no state constitutional precedents, Judge Jones purposely grounded
his decision on the U.S. Constitution. Thus, Erie and Onondaga counties appealed to the U.S. Supreme Court to reverse, on the basis of *Doe* (chapter 6). Yet
when the justices met to discuss their petition on May 14, 1981, only Chief Justice Burger and Justice Rehnquist voted to take review in *New York v. Onofre*. An
important factor in that decision was probably a memorandum circulated to the
"certiorari pool" by Susan Lahne, a law clerk for Justice Blackmun. Most of the
justices were in the pool, and they would have learned from Lahne that twenty-
four states had by then decriminalized consensual sodomy. Other states might
follow, either by legislation or judicial review. "Further consideration of the matter in other forums will produce better understanding, and the Court should
delay taking this case to allow this full consideration." In a note to Justice Blackmun, Lahne added that Onofre's private conduct was surely a liberty protected
by the Constitution, "[y]et fighting for this result in this Court would be politically very difficult, [as] the heat of the Moral Majority would fall upon the
Court."[68]

Judicial Review of Sodomy-Solicitation Statutes: The Uplinger Case

Captain Kenneth Kennedy had been the commander of Buffalo's vice squad for
twenty years; it was his officers who arrested Conde Peoples, Philip Goss, and
Mary Sweat. A devout Catholic, Kennedy was appalled by the Court of Appeals's
decision in *Onofre*. The corner of North and Delaware streets downtown, and
LaSalle Park near the Niagara River, were hangouts where male homosexuals
cruised for sexual partners. According to Kennedy, this had become a public
safety issue. Men who worked or lived in these areas complained that they were
solicited, mothers complained that their boys were harassed, and homeowners
complained that solicitation and even sodomy were occurring on their property
or outside their windows. After *Onofre*, Kennedy instructed his officers that,
while they could not arrest these men for committing sodomy or attempted sodomy, they *could* arrest cruising homosexuals and prostitutes for violation of New
York's crime of "loiter[ing] or remain[ing] in a public place for the purpose of

engaging, or soliciting another person to engage, in deviate sexual intercourse or other sexual behavior of a deviant nature."[69]

At around 3:00 a.m. on August 7, 1981, Robert Uplinger was looking for a sex partner on North Street and invited an attractive Italian back to his apartment. What would you like to do for me? inquired the Italian. "I'll blow you," responded Uplinger, whereupon the Italian (Steven Nicosia of the vice squad) arrested him for solicitation to commit oral sex. Uplinger contacted Gardner, who agreed to represent him as another test case. As it had in the *Peoples* and *Sweat* cases, the Erie County court upheld Uplinger's conviction, and Gardner filed an appeal with the New York Court of Appeals. He was assisted by Abby Rubenfeld, a Tennessee lesbian who was the new legal director of Lambda (1982–88). Four months earlier one of Nicosia's vice colleagues had arrested Susan Butler for the same offense, and her counsel also filed an appeal. The Court of Appeals took both cases for review.

Uplinger's case was a challenge to the Model Penal Code's original compromise, whereby the state would decriminalize *private* consensual sodomy, but would leave *public* solicitation for the conduct a misdemeanor. Everywhere in the United States many more men were arrested each year for solicitation for deviate sexual conduct (Model Penal Code states) or lewd vagrancy (California) or disorderly conduct (pre-1967 New York) than for violation of sodomy laws. Most lewd vagrancy prosecutions involved one man's invitation to another adult male to commit oral copulation or sodomy, both felonies. But if the underlying activity was decriminalized, it was not clear that the solicitation law could any longer be constitutionally applied, or that it should be interpreted that broadly. The First Amendment protects speech generally and protects virtually any language that invites others to engage in lawful activities. While the state can make it a crime for you to negotiate with another person to defraud third parties, it cannot make it a crime for you to negotiate with that same person to go out drinking or to support gay rights. The state can, however, regulate speech that constitutes an invasion of another person's privacy or constitutes "fighting words" that threaten an immediate breach of the peace.

Once California had decriminalized consensual sodomy, the ACLU of Southern California and the National Committee for Sexual Liberties challenged that state's lewd vagrancy law in *Pryor v. Municipal Court* (1979). The defendant, Don Pryor, was arrested for soliciting an undercover Los Angeles cop to engage in oral intercourse, the same scenario that would later ensnare Robert Uplinger. In a brief authored by attorney Thomas Coleman, the Committee for Sexual Liberties demonstrated that the lewd vagrancy law was enforced almost exclusively, and often abusively, against gay and bisexual men soliciting other consenting adults for sexual liaisons. The court ruled that the statutory terms (solicitation for "lewd" or "dissolute" behavior) were hopelessly vague as well as broad, and gay defendants were basically left to the unpredictable sympathies of juries and prosecutors. Instead of striking the law from the books, though, the Court limited it to the few situations where it could be constitutionally applied—namely, solicitation of sexual conduct that would occur in a public place (public sex can be a crime), or sexual touching if the actor knows or should know of the presence of persons who would probably be offended by that kind of conduct (invasion of privacy or fighting words). The Ohio and Massachusetts supreme courts performed similar judicial surgery on their solicitation laws.[70]

Gardner and Rubenfeld asked the New York Court of Appeals to take the next step: invalidate New York's sodomy solicitation law as inconsistent with the *Onofre* privacy right. As in *Onofre*, Attorney General Abrams declined to defend the state law, and the court accepted Lambda's invitation. Construing the loitering statute as intended "to punish conduct anticipatory to the act of consensual sodomy," the Court of Appeals reasoned that "[i]nasmuch as the conduct ultimately contemplated by the loitering statute may not be deemed criminal, we perceive no basis upon which the State may continue to punish loitering for that purpose." The Erie County prosecutors felt that the court had not understood how necessary this antisolicitation law was to maintaining community order in a changing society, and in April 1983 sought review from the U.S. Supreme Court.[71]

The Court that received this petition was subtly different from the one that had denied review in *Onofre*. Already aware of the 1981 House override of the District's sodomy repeal, the justices were apprised that no state had repealed its consensual sodomy prohibition since 1977, and that no state court had followed *Onofre*. Chief Justice Burger and Justice Rehnquist voted to take review, as they had in *Onofre*. Justices White, Blackmun, and Sandra Day O'Connor (an Arizona Republican appointed in 1981 by President Reagan) each signaled a willingness to take review if three other justices voted that way, and so review was granted. Gary Born, a clerk in the Rehnquist chambers, produced the cert pool memorandum. He laid out Captain Kennedy's concerns for residential nuisances created by cruising homosexuals and concluded that the state could constitutionally "prohibit loitering and invitations to engage in sodomy." The memorandum was confident that the broad New York statute regulated an "insubstantial" amount of protected activity. Also, a privacy right, Born declared, "cannot extend to a situation in which someone asks a person he has known for ten minutes, on a public street, whether he wants to engage in sodomy." After the Court granted review, however, Born's analysis suffered a blow when New York attorney general Abrams filed an amicus brief conceding that the law was unconstitutional as applied to Uplinger.[72]

Chief Justice Burger launched the conference in *Uplinger* with an attack on *Onofre*. For 175 years no judge would have held that the Constitution protected homosexuals; *Onofre* represented a dangerous constitutional innovation that needed to be repudiated. Moreover, the loitering statute served the compelling state purposes of preventing "harassment" and protecting against the "risk to minors" posed by homosexuals. Justice White found the chief's speech irrelevant to the legal issues posed by the appeal, but he was inclined to reverse the lower court's decision and remand for reexamination of the state's antiharassment interest. Justices Brennan and Marshall questioned whether there was a federal constitutional holding to review and urged their colleagues to "DIG," or dismiss the writ of certiorari as improvidently granted. Because the lower court opinion was so ambiguous and the state attorney general supported its judgment, Justices Blackmun, Powell, and Stevens gave Brennan his majority. In an unsigned opinion handed down in May 1984, the Court dismissed the appeal. In one of his most emotional dissents, Burger accused the majority of violating judicial etiquette by dismissing a case that four justices believed required decision on the merits.[73]

Sodomy and Identity Speech: The Oklahoma Teachers' Case, 1985

The 1978 Briggs Initiative in California would have disqualified from public school employment anyone engaged in "advocating, soliciting, imposing or encouraging or promoting of private or public homosexual activity directed at, or likely to come to the attention of, schoolchildren and/or other employees." This was a milestone in the politics of preservation. Rather than repeal a standing gay rights law, Briggs sought to reaffirm a traditional state discrimination (against lesbian and gay teachers) that had been revoked by the California Supreme Court in the 1970s. The initiative also would have encoded the preservationist message of Save Our Children (which Senator Briggs had traveled to Miami to support): open homosexuality, per se, is a threat to children because its appeal is as alluring as its practice is ruinous.

Briggs had made explicit, more than anyone before him, the connection among "unnatural relations" (sodomy), "dishonorable passions" (homosexuality), and immoral hedonistic ideology (Gay is Good). He also went further than Anita Bryant in naming the culprits in America's moral pollution: it was not just homosexual schoolteachers who polluted public culture, but also their straight allies. The public-private line completely disappeared in the Briggs Initiative: even straight teachers who "encourag[ed] or promot[ed]" private homosexual activity must be discharged if such activity is "likely to come to the attention of schoolchildren." Willie Brown counseled gay activists that the possible impact on straights was Briggs's Achilles' heel. Former governor Reagan opposed the initiative for this very reason, and the well-funded opposition routed it by a two-to-one vote in November 1978.[74]

What would not play in California, however, did find a receptive audience in Baptist Oklahoma, Anita Bryant's home state. In 1978 a near-unanimous Oklahoma legislature enacted a statute stipulating that school boards could suspend or dismiss public school teachers or teachers' aides for either "public homosexual activities" (namely, "public" sodomy) or "public homosexual conduct." The law defined the latter as "advocating, soliciting, imposing, encouraging or promoting public or private homosexual activity in a manner that creates a substantial risk that such conduct will come to the attention of schoolchildren or school employees." The First Amendment protects "advocacy" even of illegal conduct except when the advocacy is "directed to inciting or producing imminent lawless action and is likely to incite or produce such action." In most cases, the First Amendment does not permit someone to be punished for advocating illegal conduct at some indefinite future time. Because the statute sought to suppress public debate on issues of sodomy and homosexuality, it was the kind of law the First Amendment was designed to thwart—but no one in the state was brave enough to challenge it.[75]

There were, however, national gay rights organizations willing to undertake such litigation. In addition to Lambda Legal, the pioneer was the National Gay Task Force (NGTF), which had been founded in 1973 by Bruce Voeller, the New York activist who served as its director until 1979. Claiming that its membership included several teachers in the Oklahoma public school system, NGTF sought a federal court declaratory judgment ruling that the statute violated the First Amendment. Representing NGTF were William Rogers, an Oklahoma City attorney affiliated with the local ACLU chapter, and Leonard Graff and Donald Knutson, the founders of National Gay Rights Advocates, operating out of San Francisco. The federal district judge upheld the statute by interpreting it narrowly, to allow discipline *only* when a teacher's pro-gay advocacy creates a "material and substantial disruption" in the classroom. A divided Court of Appeals rejected that gloss on the statute and ruled it unconstitutional because it reached constitutionally protected speech over a "substantial" range of circumstances. A dissenting judge argued that, because "[s]odomy is *malum in se*, i.e., immoral and corruptible in its nature," any teacher who promotes it in any way "is in fact and in truth *inciting* school children to participate in the abominable and detestable crime against nature."[76]

On appeal to the Supreme Court, six justices voted to grant review for *Board of Education v. National Gay Task Force* (1985). Representing NGTF before the Court, Professor Tribe argued that the Oklahoma law had a chilling effect on core political speech. The law authorized school boards to dismiss teachers who made public statements favoring sodomy reform, so long as there was a "substantial risk" that the testimony would come to the attention of schoolchildren, quite likely in a state where anything remotely pro-gay would create a stir. Although the school board promised it would enforce the statute only in extreme cases, Oklahoma attorney general Michael Turpen filed an amicus brief telling the Court that the statute reached "public advocacy of issues which are controversial" and "disruptive of the educational process." Turpen's brief underscored the amount of discretion that the law vested in local officials—so that a fearful teacher might refrain not only from testifying before the legislature, but also from any speech that some school board might construe to be "controversial." The purpose of the First Amendment's overbreadth doctrine, Tribe explained, is to invalidate laws whose breadth ensured that citizens would refrain from exercising their free speech rights. It was ridiculous to wait for teachers to be disciplined, because the intended effect of the law was to silence teachers completely, to enforce a regime in which even heterosexuals hid in the closet.[77]

As he did in every gay rights case during his tenure, Chief Justice Burger used every imaginable argument to reaffirm antigay discriminations. First, he insisted that the Task Force had no standing. Because NGTF's pleading stated, without rebuttal, that it represented Oklahoma teachers who were forfeiting their constitutional rights to speak, all the other justices but Rehnquist disagreed. Second, and most persuasively, Burger argued that the Court should ask the Oklahoma Supreme Court to interpret the statute and thereby resolve the dispute among the lower court judges. Surprisingly, only Rehnquist and O'Connor agreed with the chief justice on that point. Third, Burger argued that teachers' "subjective" fears of reprisals for pro-gay or gay-tolerant utterances were not sufficient to implicate the Court's stringent scrutiny for overbroad regulations. As Brennan, Marshall, Blackmun, and Stevens responded, this was an odd position to take in light of the Court's precedents, which had repeatedly warned that state efforts to instill subjective fear of reprisals were impermissible under the First Amendment. Only White and Rehnquist agreed with Burger on the merits; O'Connor took no position. In the end, four justices were prepared to affirm the Court of Appeals, and four to reverse on one or more of the grounds raised by the school board. Because Powell was recovering from cancer surgery, he did not participate in *NGTF*. Under such circumstances, the Court could have ordered reargument when Powell returned, but only the chief justice (determined to uphold the antihomosexual measure) supported this option. So the Court on March 28, 1985, announced, with no written opinion, that the lower court's judgment had been affirmed by an equally divided Court.[78]

Although the U.S. Supreme Court had managed to handle three explosive gay rights cases—*Onofre, Uplinger*, and *NGTF*—without providing any constitutional protection to gay people's private activities or speech, neither had it overturned lower court decisions providing such constitutional protections locally. Many gay rights and progressive lawyers misread these decisions and convinced themselves that there was now a potential majority of the Supreme Court to support the constitutional rule announced in *Onofre*. (There clearly was *not* such a majority.) But the defendant in a possible test case could not be someone like Robert Uplinger, a gay man soliciting other men in public, or Ronald Onofre, a mature man having an affair with a seventeen-year-old. Advocates realized that, for the sex-squeamish justices, the challenger would have to be a man or (better) a woman who was arrested for engaging in sodomy with a consenting adult in his or her own home. The search did not take long.

CHAPTER EIGHT

The Crime Against Nature on Trial, *Bowers v. Hardwick,* 1986

Michael Hardwick was an all-American boy. His parents, Billy Dale (Rick) and Kathleen (Kitty) Hardwick, already had three children (Patrick, Alice, and Susan) when Michael was born, on February 23, 1954. A veteran of World War II, the hard-edged Rick made a good living as a fireman and builder; he was both playful and emotionally unavailable. Kitty was devoted to her children and worked at home. Soon after Michael was born, the family moved into a large three-bedroom house in southwest Miami, right off Miller Road and Eighty-seventh Avenue. There were six or seven mango trees in the yard. From a young age, Michael would climb the trees, thump the fruit to determine which were ripe, and toss them down. He and his sister Susan sometimes piled them onto their little red wagon and tried to sell the ripe mangoes to neighbors (who of course had their own trees).[1]

Michael Hardwick, age 11 or 12

Miami was then one of the gayest cities in the United States. Starting in 1952, just before Michael was born, the city reacted to its new citizens with a stream of laws criminalizing cross-dressing, homosexual solicitation, and even serving liquor to homosexuals. The state government declared war on homosexuality, an effort that was orchestrated by the Johns Committee. In its final report, the committee explained the need for aggressive antihomosexual measures: "The homosexual's goal and part of his satisfaction is to 'bring over' the young person, to hook him for homosexuality." In fact, few homosexuals were recruited; most were homegrown in conventional households like the Hardwicks'. Kitty and Rick, a thoroughly heterosexual couple, raised a straight son (Patrick), a lesbian daughter (Alice), a straight daughter (Susan), and a gay son (Michael). As Kitty quips, "God gave me four kids—one of each."[2]

Michael was sensitive and deeply empathetic. "Even as a child, he was very compassionate, very caring, very tuned into people's feelings," his sister Susan recalls. One of his mother's friends told her, "Your son looks just like how Christ must have looked," referring to Mike's golden hair, which cascaded down his head like a waterfall. "There is such a glow about him." There was also a restlessness. Searching for a vocation and moving around the Southeast, Michael studied horticulture in college, opened a design business after graduating, lost his design profits investing in a health food store, and worked as a bartender at the Cove, an Atlanta gay bar. A popular bartender, he was in the prime of his life, the kind of man who turned heads when he walked into a room—tall, square-jawed, broad-shouldered. Michael had the consummate bartender's ability to make instant human contact. With his deep, raspy voice and penetrating blue-gray eyes that locked into his listener's, he was a captivating conversationalist.[3]

In 1981, when Michael Hardwick moved to Atlanta, Michael Bowers (born 1944) became attorney general of Georgia. Raised in a farmhouse in Jackson County, Georgia, Bowers was an ambitious and intelligent young man, graduating from West Point. After distinguished service in the Air Force, he earned a law degree from the University of Georgia. He joined the staff of Attorney General Arthur Bolton, who recommended Bowers as his replacement when he retired. Like Bolton, Bowers ran a professional office, staying out of partisan politics and making sure state agencies understood the requirements of the law. (For much of his tenure, the legislature refused to give Bowers a pay raise because he would not sacrifice the office's integrity on a variety of political matters.) Michael Bowers had much in common with Michael Hardwick. They were both young men of the New South—blue-eyed, handsome, well-mannered, and family-oriented.

The two men were brought together, as adversaries and Doppelgängers, in one of the great constitutional showdowns of the twentieth century.[4]

It all started on the morning of August 3, 1982.

Michael Hardwick's Lawsuit Against Michael Bowers

Once the headquarters for the Ku Klux Klan and the site of uncounted lynchings (such as Leo Frank's), Atlanta has a long history of prejudice-based violence.

After World War II, however, its civic leaders reinvented Atlanta as the "city too busy to hate." It became the first large southern city to integrate its police force (1948), its buses (1959), and its schools (1961). Underneath the city's racial peace and economic prosperity, however, old attitudes remained, and troubling new ones surfaced. In the wake of integration, whites fled the inner city for still-segregated suburbs, and Atlanta became the city "too busy moving to hate." In the 1970s, a novel minority, homosexuals, replaced people of color as the objects of open discrimination. As Bayard Rustin put it, homosexuals were the "new niggers." Michael Bowers embraced this new southern conservatism, in which the state excluded homosexuals (presumptive criminals) from most civic institutions, the way it had done to blacks before 1961, and white people lived in substantially segregated private enclaves, such as wealthy Buckhead. Michael Hardwick was a victim of this political philosophy.[5]

The Arrest of Michael Hardwick

As late as 1970, Atlanta homosexuals honored the southern tradition of utmost discretion, fitting comfortably in the roles of spinsters and confirmed bachelors sipping mint juleps as they gossiped and perused stories by Eudora Welty and Tennessee Williams. The Stonewall riots and Atlanta's booming economy brought thousands of younger, less-closeted lesbians and gay men into the city, replacing some of the white families fleeing to the suburbs. By 1981 Atlanta had dozens of restaurants and other businesses catering to a lesbian and gay clientele; a gay business guild; dozens of homophile political and community organizations, including minority associations; a flock of gay-oriented religious groups, with a religious council; and uncounted sport and social clubs offering fun and frolic in an atmosphere of southern hospitality. In 1979 the community founded the Atlanta Gay Center. The center's helpline referred lesbians and, especially, gay men with legal problems to attorneys willing to provide counsel.[6]

As homosexuals became more prominent in the urban culture, city government took notice. Even under pro–civil rights mayors Maynard Jackson (1974–82) and Andrew Young (1982–90), municipal officials were ambivalent about this subculture. In 1977, Police Commissioner Reginald Eaves announced that the police force would question all applicants about their participation in homosexual sodomy, and exclude all who answered yes. The policy was justified as necessary to preserve harmony within the department. As the city's first African-American police commissioner, Eaves explained, "I'm still fighting the feeling against hiring women and blacks." Although Chief of Police George Napper removed those questions in 1980, gay men complained that Atlanta police brutally harassed them in parks and bars. To confront abusive practices, a Lesbian/Gay Rights Chapter of the Georgia ACLU was created in April 1981. Its members met with Napper and Police Commissioner Lee Brown, Eaves's successor. Undercover vice cops were entrapping gay men into making sexual advances, while robberies, murders, and antigay violence were epidemic in the city.[7]

Napper assured gay citizens that the department was opposed to harassment and did not have a vice squad targeting them. "[I] will concede that there may be officers who are anti-gay. The official policy does not speak to that." But "[s]ome of the activities engaged in by gays are against the law," he reminded his audience. "To do it out of wedlock or with any style is also against the law," was the response. "It's not like the folks are out mugging or stealing things." Around Piedmont Park, Ansley Park (Hardwick's neighborhood), and other cruising areas, police would hassle suspected homosexuals and sometimes handcuff them, slap them around, and book them for activities that were either lawful or, at worst, minor infractions of park rules. According to witnesses, "[o]ne officer [said], 'we're going to get those [deleted] queers out of Piedmont Park yet.'" Another citizen reported that when he attended a symphony in the park the previous summer, straight couples were making love underneath blankets. "If it had been a gay couple as opposed to a heterosexual couple they would have been arrested." Commissioner Brown promised to address these concerns and instructed Napper and his deputies to initiate new training and other policies designed to reduce antigay violence and harassment by line officers.[8]

In July 1982 Michael Hardwick was helping redecorate the Cove, one of Atlanta's twenty-four gay bars and discos. He spent the night of July 4 designing and installing a lighting display. When he emerged from the bar early the next morning, he tossed a beer into the trash can next to the front door. Witnessing this act outside a known homosexual hangout, Officer Keith Torick leaped from his police car and ticketed Hardwick for drinking in public. Denying that he had even taken a swig outside the bar, Hardwick believed the officer "was just busting my chops because he knew I was gay." Although subject to a stream of citizen complaints for rudeness and roughness during his four years on the police force, the twenty-three-year-old Torick did not consider himself antigay. He had a homosexual friend or two and moonlighted as a security guard at the Bulldog Lounge, another Atlanta gay bar.[9]

Hardwick missed his court appearance for responding to the charge because Torick had written the wrong date at the top of the ticket, and Torick obtained an immediate warrant for his arrest. Subsequently Hardwick went to court, paid a $50 fine, and thought he had settled the matter. On August 3, 1982, Torick showed up at Hardwick's home, again in the morning, to arrest him. (At this point the warrant had been invalid for three weeks.) Later claiming the front door was ajar, Torick entered the apartment. A friend who had been sleeping on the living room couch pointed the officer to Hardwick's bedroom. "Officer Torick then came into my bedroom. The door was cracked, and the door opened up and I looked up and there was nobody there. I just blew it off as the wind and went back to what I was involved in, which was mutual oral sex," with a male friend visiting from North Carolina to apply for a teaching job. According to Hardwick, "About thirty-five seconds went by and I heard another noise and I looked up, and this officer is standing in my bedroom. . . . He said, My name is Officer Torick. Michael Hardwick, you are under arrest. I said, for what? What are you doing in my bedroom?" According to Torick, the schoolteacher then begged, "Please don't tell my wife. . . . I'll lose my teaching job." And Hardwick "rant[ed] and rav[ed] about how I had no right to be in his house, how he'd have my job. . . . I would never have made the case if he hadn't had an attitude problem."[10]

While Hardwick and the teacher dressed, Torick searched the room and confiscated a small amount of marijuana. Handcuffing the suspects together, the officer drove them downtown to be booked for violating the state sodomy law—a fact Torick broadcast to everyone in the station. "They should find what they're looking for here," snickered a jailer. He escorted Hardwick and his partner to a holding cell, where the guard taunted them: "Wait till they get ahold of you in the pit." What worried the prisoners the most, however, was a vague understanding that they were being charged with a serious crime. As its law was amended in 1968, Georgia defined sodomy to include any kind of oral sex. Such conduct, even between consenting adults, was a felony, punishable "by imprisonment for not less than one nor more than 20 years."[11]

The Tables Turn: Michael Hardwick versus Michael Bowers

Clint Sumrall of the Lesbian/Gay Rights ACLU chapter checked the local arrest docket every day, in search of a test case against the sodomy law. He excitedly brought Hardwick to the attention of John Sweet and Louis Levenson, lawyers working with the local ACLU. Sumrall contacted Hardwick, who brought his mother to meet with the ACLU representatives on August 5, 1982. Sweet and Levenson warned the Hardwicks of the risks. For a sodomy conviction, the law required a sentence of *at least* one year in prison, and perhaps as many as twenty. As Michael recalled, "[T]he judge could make an example out of me and give me twenty years in jail. My mom was saying, Do you realize I'll be *dead* before I see you again?" After pondering the matter for a few days, Hardwick, who had always been something of a laid-back party boy, "realized that if there was anything I could do, even if it was just laying the foundation to change this horrendous law, that I would feel pretty bad about myself if I just walked away from it." So he agreed to ACLU representation and pleaded guilty to the marijuana charge. But District Attorney Lewis Slaton then dismissed the sodomy charge, out of a belief that the sodomy law should not be applied to private activities between consenting adults; indeed, he had never brought such a prosecution. Moreover, given the expired warrant, the stream of citizen complaints against Torick, and the questionable validity of Torick's entry into the apartment, Slaton feared embarrassing publicity and, perhaps, a blot on his excellent record. (Serving as Fulton County DA from 1965 to 1996, Slaton won praise from civil libertarians for early integration of his office to include blacks and women.)[12]

Matters were out of Slaton's hands, however. On Valentine's Day, after the charges were dropped, Sweet and his associate Kathy Wilde filed a complaint in federal district court against Bowers, Slaton, and Napper. The named plaintiffs were Hardwick, described as a "practicing homosexual, who regularly engages in private homosexual acts and will do so in the future," and a married couple (John and Mary Doe) who desired to commit similar acts within their home. The complaint asked the court to declare the Georgia sodomy law unconstitutional as a violation of both the Due Process Clause's right of privacy and the First Amendment's rights of free expression and association.[13]

Meanwhile, Hardwick's arrest had generated considerable discussion among gay rights lawyers elsewhere. Abby Rubenfeld became Lambda Legal's legal director in January 1983. She knew from her law practice in Nashville that consensual sodomy laws were the legal basis for all manner of state antigay discriminations. Her goal was to coordinate the proliferating lesbian and gay legal groups in a unified challenge to state sodomy laws. Soon after the federal district court dismissed Hardwick's complaint in April 1983, Rubenfeld hosted a meeting of gay rights lawyers in the offices she shared with the New York Civil Liberties Union. Cooperating with Rubenfeld in giant conference calls (dubbed "sodomy calls") and in-person meetings were the Hardwick litigators: Burt Neuborne and Nan Hunter of the national ACLU, Tom Stoddard of the New York CLU, and Susan McGrievey of the ACLU of Southern California; Jay Kohurn and Leonard Graff from National Gay Rights Advocates (founded 1977); Roberta Achtenberg from San Francisco's Lesbian Rights Project (founded 1977); Kevin Cathcart of the Gay and Lesbian Advocates and Defenders in Boston (founded 1978); and Patrick Wiseman and Tom Coleman of the Texas Human Rights Foundation (founded 1979). In 1985 this group was formally named the Ad-Hoc Task Force to Challenge Sodomy Laws; in 1986, it became the Litigators' Roundtable.[14]

In these meetings the participants agreed with Rubenfeld that sodomy law reform should be a priority for their social movement, because "sodomy laws are the bedrock of legal discrimination against gay men and lesbians." Such a consensus might not have existed four years earlier. As Rosalyn Richter, Lambda's first managing attorney and legal director (1980–83), explained, many lesbians believed that a focus on sodomy reflected the male perspective that dominated the movement during the 1970s, when gay men enjoyed what they considered a golden age of sexual freedom. These frustrations eased in the 1980s, as straight men began to invoke sodomy laws as a way to deny child custody and even visitation to their wives who had come out as lesbian. Also, lesbians and gay men were thrown together even more closely than ever before to oppose what they considered the twin calamities of the decade—the Reagan administration and AIDS. As lesbians became caregivers for their male friends and gay men came to appreciate that the sexual golden age had ended, a new generation agreed with Richter and Rubenfeld that sodomy law reform should be a priority.[15]

Hardwick's case presented further strategic issues, however. Some lawyers felt that it would be better to attack a law that criminalized only same-sex sodomy, because both equal protection and privacy claims could be made, giving gays a double chance of a constitutional triumph. On the other hand, if an equal protection challenge alone was successful, most sodomy laws would remain in place. After much intracommunity discussion, Lambda and the ACLU both supported Hardwick's appeal to the Eleventh Circuit, the federal appeals court covering Georgia. Wilde's brief on appeal emphasized the right of sexual privacy, especially as the Supreme Court had articulated it to guarantee access to contraceptives for unmarried adults in *Eisenstadt v. Baird* (1972) and female minors in *Carey v. Population Services* (1977). These precedents recognized a broad right to make decisions regarding sexual partners without state interference. *Stanley v. Georgia* (1969) recognized a strong privacy right to carry on intimate activities in the home without state meddling, so long as third parties were not injured. Representing Lambda and Gay Rights Advocates, respectively, Rubenfeld and Graff also made an antidiscrimination argument: to the extent the Georgia sodomy law was applied solely against gay people, it denied gays the equal protection of the laws.[16]

Attorney General Bowers and his associates were confident that they would prevail. Because the Supreme Court had summarily affirmed the judgment upholding Virginia's consensual sodomy law in *Doe v. Commonwealth's Attorney* (1976), lower federal courts were not free to strike down Georgia's law. Wilde responded that the Supreme Court did not explain the basis for its *Doe* affirmance; Doe had not actually been arrested, and so the Court may have believed the challenger lacked standing. If *Doe* foreclosed lower courts from extending the right of privacy to consensual sodomy, the Court would have summarily reversed the New York Court of Appeals's decision in *Onofre*, which had relied on the federal privacy right (chapter 6). In an opinion by Judge Frank Johnson, the great Republican desegregation judge from Alabama, the Eleventh Circuit ruled that *Doe* was not dispositive for the reasons Wilde suggested and that *Eisenstadt* and *Stanley* established a right of privacy protecting Hardwick's personal life against Georgia's intrusion. Johnson also found that Hardwick had standing to sue, but the married couple did not. The court remanded the case for trial to determine whether Georgia could demonstrate a *compelling* state interest that could only be met by invading Hardwick's *fundamental* privacy right. No one thought the state could make such a showing.[17]

The Supreme Court Appeal: Michael Bowers v. Michael Hardwick

Attorney General Bowers was an odd defendant in the lawsuit, because his office had not enforced the sodomy law. Commissioner Napper was ultimately responsible for Officer Torick's arrest of Hardwick, and District Attorney Slaton was responsible for the decision to prosecute him. Bowers's office never objected to his inclusion, however, because Georgia law required him to defend state statutes against constitutional attack. Ironically, Bowers, the extra defendant, was the only one who appealed the Eleventh Circuit's judgment invalidating the state sodomy law. Michael Hobbs, a lawyer in the Public Safety Division of the Attorney General's Office who had been assigned to handle the case, filed a petition for review on July 25, 1985.[18]

In the Supreme Court's October 11 conference, Justice White advanced an excellent reason to take the case: it conflicted with another recent decision. In 1979 Don Baker, a Dallas gay activist and schoolteacher, had brought a federal lawsuit challenging the Texas Homosexual Conduct Law. Sitting en banc, the Fifth Circuit Court of Appeals had upheld the law against both federal privacy and equal protection attack the previous summer (chapter 10). An important role of the Supreme Court is to resolve conflicting interpretations of the Constitution or federal statutes among the lower courts. By 1985 there was a deep and growing division as to the constitutionality of consensual sodomy laws. State courts such as those in North Carolina and Texas upheld their laws, while the highest courts of New York and Pennsylvania had invalidated their laws on federal privacy and equal protection grounds. Now there was a split among federal judges. Clearly, the Supreme Court's summary affirmance in *Doe* had resolved nothing, and it was up to the Court to settle the matter for good, White argued.

Justice Rehnquist agreed; Chief Justice Warren Burger suggested he would vote for certiorari if three other justices did so ("join three"). But with four votes required to take review, the conference of October 11 denied the petition. On October 17 White circulated a draft dissent from the Court's denial.[19]

Surprisingly, the fourth vote came the next day, from the liberal Justice William Brennan. On reflection, Brennan thought White was right that the sodomy issue was ripe for decision. President Reagan had just won a landslide reelection, and new conservatives would surely join the Court in Reagan's second term. Brennan felt that there was a chance of striking down such laws with the current membership, so he voted for immediate review in a second conference on October 18. Sensing Brennan's strategy, Justice Thurgood Marshall also changed his vote, making four (two conservatives and two liberals), with the chief a probable fifth.[20]

Fearful that this case would become an occasion for the Court's antiabortion justices to undermine *Roe*, Justice Harry Blackmun and others within the Court cautioned the Brennan chambers. They believed that homosexuality and the rights of gay people were beyond the comprehension of the Brethren—including the pivotal justice, Lewis Powell. (Burger, White, Rehnquist, and O'Connor were likely votes to reverse.) Powell had told Blackmun, "'Harry, I've never known a homosexual in my life.' Well, when he said that, it happened there were two [homosexuals] in his chambers that very moment." This level of ignorance or denial made it unlikely that Powell would be eager to strike down the Georgia law, where the attorney general would trumpet "HOMOSEXUALS!" on every page of his brief. On October 23 Brennan withdrew his vote for review—but the next day Burger changed his join three to a firm vote to grant. Four was the magic number, and on November 4 the Court granted review in *Bowers v. Hardwick*.[21]

The Supreme Court Decides *Bowers v. Hardwick*

By the time the Court took his case, Hardwick had left Atlanta and returned to Miami. Wilde, with whom Hardwick had formed a close friendship, kept him well-informed of the progress of his case. His ever-expanding legal team was constructing a powerful constitutional argument against the Georgia sodomy law. The Supreme Court's 1985 term would be a landmark in the history of gay rights.

The Challengers' Strategy

Unlike Bowers and Hobbs, who treated the appeal as a routine matter of *following* precedent, Hardwick's legal coalition treated the appeal as an important civic moment when precedent would be *created*. To maximize their chances, Wilde and others urged that the Supreme Court case be handled by the savviest constitutional litigator in America—Harvard law professor Laurence Tribe, who had brilliantly handled the Oklahoma schoolteachers case the previous term. Tribe and David Richards had been the first prominent constitutional law scholars to argue that antigay policies, including sodomy laws, were constitutionally suspect. Wilde invited Tribe and his associate Kathleen Sullivan (soon to be appointed to the Harvard faculty) to a meeting of the Ad-Hoc Task Force to discuss legal strategy at the ACLU's offices on Forty-third Street in New York City.[22]

At the November 1985 meeting, the Texas lawyers argued that gay rights groups ought to urge the Court to take appeal in *Baker v. Wade* and consolidate it with the *Hardwick* appeal. Because the Texas sodomy statute regulated only homosexual conduct (chapter 10), there were equal protection as well as privacy problems under the Fourteenth Amendment. Because the natural-law tradition condemned sodomy without regard to the sex of its participants, challengers could argue that the only basis for the state discrimination was antigay animus. The Court had just struck down the application of a zoning law that shut down a home for the disabled in *Cleburne v. Cleburne Living Center* (1985). Justice White's opinion ruled that, even under the Court's most lenient standard of review, a "'bare ... desire to harm a politically unpopular group'" is not a legitimate state objective. The same principle could apply to same-sex sodomy laws such as that of Texas.[23]

Tribe warned that procedural problems made *Baker* an unlikely vehicle for a successful challenge. Because Baker had never been arrested, it was not clear whether he had standing to bring the case; because Texas attorney general Jim Mattox had withdrawn the state's appeal from the judgment invalidating the statute, it was also not clear whether the odd assortment of sheriffs had standing to pursue the appeal. More important, Tribe believed an equal protection challenge was a loser. The Court was unlikely to determine that sexual orientation was a "suspect classification" triggering strict scrutiny the way race and sex had, and he did not think the justices would extend *Cleburne*'s protection for the disabled, a group for whom the justices had sympathy, to homosexuals, whom the justices considered alien beings (or worse). Earlier that year, Justice Brennan had laid out an eloquent case for the Court to police antigay discrimination, and only Justice Marshall had joined him. Tribe thought the privacy theory was the only possible winner. With four justices completely unreceptive to gay rights claims, Justice Powell was necessary for a Court majority. As Tribe later put it, "The only hope of prevailing was to shift the Court's gaze from [homosexual] applications of the statute to application to couples of all sorts." An equal protection approach would focus the Court's attention on homosexuality, and risked losing the sex-squeamish Powell (and perhaps others) even on the privacy theory.[24]

After the presentations, every person in the room expressed an opinion. One by one, almost all the participants endorsed Tribe's position. Over the Texas lawyers' dissent, the consensus was to focus only on *Hardwick*, and to limit their challenge to the privacy right. Tribe and Sullivan were asked to represent the gay complainants in both *Hardwick* and *Baker*.[25]

Bowers's brief to the Supreme Court (written by Hobbs) framed the issue as whether gay people had a fundamental right to engage in "homosexual sodomy." This was an effective strategy because most of the reported consensual sodomy cases involved sex between two males, and more than sixty percent of the American people believed that homosexuality was an "unacceptable lifestyle" and that "homosexual conduct" was morally wrong. More than ninety-five percent told pollsters they would be unaccepting if their daughters or sons entered into "homosexual relationships." It is doubtful that most of these respondents believed that oral sex, per se, was immoral, because as many as three-quarters of them had engaged in this activity themselves with someone of the opposite sex. The combination of sexuality completely divorced from procreation *and* gender-role reversal was morally synergistic: however bad sodomy and cross-dressing were, "homosexual sodomy" was the worst by far, so bad that it was unmentionable as well as abominable. Most of the justices would share these attitudes.[26]

Acknowledging this high level of anxiety among older Americans, Tribe and Sullivan's brief sought instead to focus the justices' attention on "intimate sexual conduct in the privacy of the home." This characterization positioned Hardwick's conduct within the holdings of *Eisenstadt* (unmarried people have a right to contraceptives) and *Stanley* (obscene materials can be viewed within the home).[27] In response, Hobbs argued that the Court's privacy cases had protected activities relating only to marriage, decisions whether to bear children, and childrearing—*family*-based activities with no relevance to homosexuals. Tribe and Sullivan replied that this characterization did not explain *Stanley*; the narrowest principle covering both *Stanley* and *Eisenstadt* was that the state could not tell consenting adults how to comport their sex lives within the home. Even

Powell understood the sexual privacy right more broadly, to include "decisions concerning sexual relations."[28]

Hobbs's brief concluded with a defense of the state's constitutional discretion to create a moral framework, grounded in values held dear by the community, for family law. As Powell had also said, "[t]he State, representing the collective expression of moral aspirations, has an undeniable interest in ensuring that its rules of domestic relations reflect the widely held values of its people." The Court had invoked the discretion afforded by the Constitution to state accountability for public decency as a reason to uphold obscenity laws. The justices had just ruled that the state could prosecute consenting adults for the sale or consumption of obscene magazines or movies that appealed to "abnormal sexual appetites," which they contrasted with a "'good, old-fashioned, healthy' interest in sex." The epitome of old-fashioned, healthy sex is that practiced within marriage, and surely the state has wide discretion to create a legal regime affirming marriage as the only acceptable context for sexual activities. Sodomy laws worked with adultery and fornication laws to reinforce that pro-marriage and -family message.[29]

Hobbs then marred an otherwise well-crafted argument by asserting that Georgia could reasonably believe that homosexuality not only "epitomizes moral delinquency," but also leads to other "deviate practices such as sado-masochism, group orgies, or transvestism, to name only a few"; that homosexuality is usually practiced in public parks, with adolescents, and is accompanied by violence; and that homosexuality is pervasively linked to the transmission of AIDS. This may have been effective rhetoric, for it could mobilize the justices' personal disgust and fears of pollution, but it was morally questionable given that it rested on largely false stereotypes and exposed the state to charges of antigay prejudice. Most gay men had never been near an orgy, did not have sex in parks or with adolescents, and correctly considered unsafe sex, not sodomy, to contribute to HIV transmission. The American Public Health Association filed an amicus brief rejecting most of Hobbs's claims as factually erroneous, and arguing that sodomy laws actually undermine public health goals by inflicting psychological harm on gay people, discouraging safer-sex education, and impeding medical efforts to track people infected with HIV. Hobbs's list was outrageously wrong as regards sex between women. The incidence of public sex, affairs with teenagers, and AIDS among lesbians was much lower than rates for gay men, straight men, and even straight women. Indeed, a woman having sex with another woman was much less likely to be infected with a disease, molested, brutalized, or raped than a woman having sex with a man.[30]

If lesbians were utterly eclipsed by everyone's obsessive focus on gay men, the latter were ambiguously poised in Sullivan and Tribe's brief. You had to read that document very carefully to realize that Hardwick had actually been arrested for homosexual sodomy, and you would not know from it (or from the record transmitted to the Court) that he was a gay man. Because it seemed to push Hardwick's homosexuality into a constitutional closet, the brief raised a few eyebrows within the gayocracy. Many understood the post-Stonewall gay rights movement as pressing the view that sexuality is something to be celebrated and that homosexual expression is essential for the flourishing of lesbian and gay Americans. The Tribe and Sullivan brief, in contrast, seemed ashamed of Hardwick's conduct. But Abby Rubenfeld spoke for most gay rights leaders, and she thought the brief was the movement's best shot to win the case—and winning was essential. Her amicus brief for Lambda followed Tribe and Sullivan in pitching the equal treatment argument at a higher level of generality. Sodomy laws, she argued, "have damaging consequences beyond the invasion of privacy," for they "provide a basis for further, unjustified discrimination" and "injure the psychological well-being of millions of Americans." The justices would have certainly known that those "millions of Americans" referred to were for the most part lesbian and gay.[31]

Oral Argument: Privacy Triumphant?

Hardwick flew from Miami to Washington, D.C. to join his attorneys at the oral argument before the Supreme Court on March 31, 1986. Chief Justice Warren Burger announced the case and asked Michael Hobbs to begin. (Bowers was not in the courtroom.) Hobbs proceeded through his argument, speaking slowly in his soft, genial southern accent. In response to Justices O'Connor and Stevens, Hobbs conceded that the sodomy law could not constitutionally be applied to married couples. This was potentially troubling for his case, because *Eisenstadt* had invalidated a contraception law that discriminated against unmarried couples. Hobbs's answer would have been that *Eisenstadt* only concerned *heterosexual* activities, which could result in pregnancies, while this case was about *homosexual* sodomy. The major theme of his argument was that making homosexual sodomy a crime was essential to the long-standing and important program of encouraging Georgia residents to marry and form healthy families. Stevens wondered: If Hardwick was indeed guilty of having violated this very important public policy, why, then, did Lewis Slaton refuse to prosecute a case handed to him "on a silver platter"? Because there was no detailed factual record in the case, Hobbs could not answer the question. Earlier he had told the Court that the last consensual sodomy prosecution he could name occurred in the

1930s—a case that involved two women, whose conviction was overturned on appeal. Because the justices had shown interest in the bizarre operation of Georgia's consensual sodomy law, the dozens of lesbian and gay people in the courtroom felt hopeful at the end of Hobbs's argument.[32]

As they had with Hobbs, the justices immediately got to the point in Tribe's half-hour argument. In his honeyed Virginia whisper, Justice Powell asked what limiting principle there would be on a right of privacy that included sodomy. Tribe answered that the right would not necessarily apply outside the home. What about incest within the home? asked Powell and Burger. And adultery and polygamy within the home? chimed in Rehnquist. So where *do* you draw the line? wondered O'Connor. A less-experienced advocate would have been intimidated by the judicial tag-teaming, but Tribe immediately shifted ground to another limiting principle: the privacy right should not extend to physical intimacies that are harmful, the libertarian principle undergirding the Model Penal Code. Polygamy and incest could be regulated, because they harm wives and daughters. Hardwick's intimacy with another consenting adult harmed no one, and the fact that it took place in the home, a person's refuge, made it doubly immune from state intrusion. What is the *legal* basis for this conclusion? Powell gently inquired. Justice Harlan's *Poe* dissent specifically excluded homosexuality, adultery, and incest from the relationships traditionally valued in American history. Tribe answered that Harlan also recognized the "evolutionary character of the definition of those intimacies that are protected." The time had come for the Court to grapple with factual settings Harlan could not have imagined—such as one where a police officer serving an expired warrant walks into a man's bedroom and arrests him for engaging in the most private and most intimate behavior. If a line had to be drawn, Hardwick's case was a good place to draw it.[33]

When Tribe sat down after the most intense thirty minutes of his life, he was exhilarated, as were his client, his colleagues, and every lesbian and gay person in the courtroom. From their perspective Tribe had answered every question, made no mistakes, and surely persuaded Powell (perhaps also O'Connor) to affirm the Eleventh Circuit. After the argument several dozen lawyers joined Tribe, Sullivan, and their client for a triumphant lunch at the American Café on Massachusetts Avenue, a few blocks from the Court. The mood was ebullient. Even Tribe, who had always been cautious, felt five votes were in hand. After the meal Hardwick wandered off to see the city with Lambda lawyer Evan Wolfson, who had been his escort all day. Tribe asked where the client was. Rubenfeld quipped, "Michael is off exercising his constitutional rights." Wolfson and Hardwick spent a romantic afternoon at the Tidal Basin, but no crime against nature was committed. In the District, consensual sodomy could still bring you ten years in prison.[34]

Conference: Fighting for the Soul of Lewis Powell

Tribe's brilliant performance was less effective than his allies thought. Powell was sympathetic to Tribe's basic point, that applying sodomy laws to private activities between consenting adults was ridiculous, but he felt that Tribe lacked a defensible *constitutional* basis for striking down the statute. Having joined *Roe v. Wade*, Powell believed the Due Process Clause limits the state's ability to deprive people of fundamental liberties, but *Roe* had also taught the justice that substantive due process required a firm limiting principle—and Tribe had not provided him with one. Powell found "repellent" Tribe's emphasis on the home, "one of the most beautiful words in the English language. It usually connotes family, husband and wife, and children," not one-night stands. Tribe was reading too much into *Stanley*, which the Court had never expanded beyond its narrow facts: home possession of obscene movies. If the Court read *Stanley* broadly, Powell feared opening the courts to challenges for drug use and other unproductive activities. This would limit the states' ability to maintain or work toward the creation of decent communities. Tribe did not assuage Powell's doubts by his second limiting principle: that the privacy right does not protect activities that are nonconsensual or harm third parties. Did drug use within the home then have constitutional protection? Incest? When Tribe compared Hardwick's activities to "normal" marital intimacy, Powell felt an "emotional recoil from an argument that seemed to place homosexual sodomy on a par with the sexual intimacy between man and wife."[35]

Powell's doubts were fanned by Michael Mosman, the law clerk who worked on the Hardwick case. A graduate of Brigham Young Law School, Mosman was a devout Mormon, married with three children, and deeply committed to traditional family values. In his bench memorandum Mosman argued that Tribe's approach to the privacy right went well beyond the Court's precedents and had no limiting principle. The limiting principle suggested by the precedents was whether American history and tradition suggested an activity was off-limits to state regulation. "Homosexual sodomy" had no protection within the nation's traditions. "Personal sexual freedom is a newcomer among our national values, and may well be . . . a temporary national mood that fades. This may be reflected in the fact that in the 1970s twenty states decriminalized homosexual sodomy, while in the 1980s only two states have done so."[36] Powell felt the memo did not reflect a subtle understanding of the issue and sought out the views of his other law clerks. One was Cabell Chinnis, his liberal clerk. "I don't believe I've ever met a homosexual," Powell confided. Chinnis, who was gay, responded, "Certainly you have, but you just don't know that they are." As the clerk later told Powell's biographer, "[h]e couldn't understand the idea of sexual attraction between two men. It just had no content for him."[37]

The barely closeted Chinnis (few of his classmates at Yale Law School doubted his sexual orientation) wondered whether he should have come out to the justice. After all, many of Powell's recent law clerks had been gay or lesbian— including Paul Smith (1980 term), Mary Becker (1981 term), David Charny (1983 term), and Dan Ortiz (1984 term), as well as himself (1985 term). Other former clerks were probably closeted homosexuals; and the clerks believed that Powell's longtime secretary was a lesbian. (Two of Powell's law clerks, Charny and Ronald Carr [1974 term], would die of complications associated with AIDS after Powell's own death.) Powell made himself oblivious to all the homosexuals in his private circle. Not wanting to make his beloved boss uncomfortable, Chinnis did not come out to him but did make a passionate speech: "The right to love the person of my choice would be far more important to me than the right to vote in elections." Powell blandly responded, "That may be, but that doesn't mean it's in the Constitution."[38]

Powell turned to another law clerk, Bill Stuntz, for an answer to that last question. An evangelical Virginia Christian, also married with children, Stuntz accepted the importance of family and moral values in public discourse. But, also like Powell, Stuntz believed that fairness and decency were important moral values—and, unlike Powell, Stuntz knew gay people and could understand how they could form meaningful relationships that society should not be demonizing. Stuntz also had a fine lawyer's mind, and Powell asked him to develop a constitutional basis for overturning the Georgia law that was narrower than Tribe's privacy theory. Stuntz knew that the justice would not accept Lambda's equal protection theory. Powell thought the Court had already gone overboard on equal protection and was loath to write an opinion that called into question the various military- and family-law discriminations against gay people. Accordingly, Stuntz developed a theory grounded on the Eighth Amendment, which bars government from imposing "cruel and unusual punishments." Even if the state could constitutionally adopt laws discouraging extramarital or homosexual activities, it could not make private activities between consenting adults a serious crime, with *mandatory* jail time (one year in prison), as Georgia had done. This theory had case support. In 1962 the Court had ruled that the state could not criminalize the *status* of being a drug addict, and in 1968 five justices had opined that the state could not arrest an alcoholic for becoming drunk in his own home.[39]

On April 2, the justices discussed *Bowers v. Hardwick* at conference. Introducing the case, Warren Burger insisted the issue was a claimed right to engage in "homosexual sodomy," which had been regulated for five hundred years by Anglo-American law, and two hundred years in Georgia. "Our society has values that should be protected. Teachings of history and custom frown on and sanction its prohibition," as Harlan had recognized in his *Poe* dissent. There was no other way to limit the privacy right (and allow regulation of incest, for example) except through tradition, and tradition established that there was no fundamental right here. Reverse the Eleventh Circuit, demanded the chief justice. Speaking next, William Brennan countered that "this is not a case about homosexuality but is a case of privacy by consenting adults," and also a case about government intrusion into the home. There was surely a fundamental right here—but even if there was not, Hobbs had advanced no public-regarding reason for making this conduct a crime. Under the lenient scrutiny the Court applied to the discrimination against disabled people in *Cleburne*, there had to be a neutral *reason*. Send the case back to trial on that issue. Affirm the Eleventh Circuit.[40]

Byron White voted to reverse. This was an easy case for him, because neither history nor current opinion suggested that homosexual activity with a one-night stand had any connection to the family values protected in *Griswold*. Under such circumstances, courts should defer to legislative judgments—especially recent judgments (Georgia's law was updated in 1968) in accord with those of half the other states. Emphasizing *Stanley* and the context of the home, Thurgood Marshall and Harry Blackmun concurred with Brennan. Both justices knew gay people, including gay couples, and felt there were parallels between racism and homophobia. Blackmun, in particular, viewed White's deferential stance as a challenge to the ongoing validity of *Roe*, a precedent that Blackmun guarded with the ferocity of a tigress protecting her cub.[41]

With the votes three to two for affirming, Lewis Powell spoke, admitting, "I have mixed emotions." Certainly, "sodomy in the home should be decriminalized," and Georgia had not enforced the law against consenting adults for fifty years. Unwilling (like White) to concede any connection with family, Powell compared homosexuality to "drug addiction": the homosexual was addicted to sodomy the way others were addicted to drugs. The Court had held in *Robinson v. California* (1962) that sending someone to jail because he was a drug addict violated the Eighth Amendment. "If [we] accept [the] allegation that only acts of sodomy can satisfy this fellow [Hardwick], isn't that pertinent?" Powell was willing to affirm on the basis of this Eighth Amendment analysis. Blackmun quietly groaned, "Can this [rationale] possibly hold?"[42]

William Rehnquist responded that Powell's position was the "most extreme" of all. Because the state had never prosecuted much less imprisoned Hardwick,

Robinson could not resolve his case. Reverse. John Paul Stevens expressed sympathy for Powell's open-minded search for a mediating solution and had his own bombshell to toss into the discussion. "I have a bias" against homosexuality, Stevens announced, "but we have to live with this." The American Psychological Association tells us that homosexuality is not a mental illness. Why should homosexuals be treated differently from other Americans? Georgia tells us it could not constitutionally apply its sodomy statute to married couples, and *Eisenstadt* suggests it could not be applied to unmarried straight couples, either. If the sodomy statute could not be applied to married or unmarried straight couples, what *reason* supported its application to homosexuals? "Only prejudice supports the distinction," Stevens concluded. "This is a liberty case for me, and for homosexuals as well." That the conduct occurred in the home made no difference. Just as *Roe* protected women's freedom of sexual choice, so homosexuals had a constitutional freedom to make sexual choices in their lives.[43]

Although Stevens made five votes to affirm, Sandra Day O'Connor's vote was hardly irrelevant in light of Powell's rationale. Speaking without the emotion of her male colleagues, she expressed a reluctance to limit state morals regulation based on the unbounded privacy right. Following Harlan's admonition that substantive due process required guidance from the nation's legal history and traditions, she found it notable that "this prohibition [was in place] in 1787 and when the Fourteenth Amendment was adopted." She labeled Powell's Eighth Amendment compromise "a real risk and dangerous" for the Court's reputation. Reverse.[44]

As the senior justice in the five-to-four majority, Brennan assigned the case to Blackmun, who asked Pam Karlan to start work on an opinion for the Court. Karlan and her co-clerks started kicking around ideas. Their first approach was to start the opinion with a list of prominent homosexuals in history. Blackmun was famous within legal circles for having written *Flood v. Kuhn* (1972), where the Court upheld professional baseball's exemption from the antitrust laws. His opinion opened with an ode to baseball, which listed the game's greatest players—which generated rambunctious suggestions from other justices, who pitched their hometown favorites to be added to Blackmun's evolving list. The clerks assembled names for a similar group of Great Homosexuals—Leonardo da Vinci, Gertrude Stein, John Maynard Keynes, Sappho, and *Warren Earl Burger*, a dig at the Court's most obviously homophobic justice, and who had a creepy affection for their boss.[45]

Burger, meanwhile, sent Powell a private letter objecting to the Eighth Amendment theory. The chief justice noted that none of the parties or amici had briefed the issue; the Court was less likely to be on solid ground when it decided issues without full briefing (a point that Brennan had made in *Doe*, where the chief justice was willing to dismiss rights for gays without full briefing). He then rejected Powell's conclusion that sodomy laws were *status* crimes. "Hardwick merely wishes to seek his own form of sexual gratification," no different in kind than the gratification others seek through "incest, drug use, gambling, exhibitionism, prostitution, rape." In closing, Burger reminded Powell that April 13, 1986, would mark his thirtieth year on the federal bench. "This case presents for me the most far-reaching issue of those 30 years," the suggestion being that Powell should reconsider his position out of respect for Burger's long service. Powell circled this language and wrote, "Incredible statement!" Despite containing much "nonsense," Burger's letter deepened Powell's misgivings about his ability to make the Eighth Amendment theory work. In a memorandum to the Court on April 8, Powell reaffirmed his view that "in some cases it would violate the Eighth Amendment to imprison a person for a private act of homosexual sodomy," but not in Hardwick's case. Because he did not accept Tribe's privacy arguments, Powell's "bottom line" in *Bowers* was now to reverse.[46]

The next day the chief justice reassigned the opinion to White, who directed a law clerk to prepare the draft. Laboring to craft a relatively mild opinion, the clerk failed to meet the chamber's "nine-day rule" for drafting opinions—and White dashed off his own draft, which he circulated to the Court on April 21. Rehnquist and Burger joined it immediately; O'Connor joined after seeing the dissenting opinions in June. Initially Powell indicated he would join only the result and would write a separate opinion, thereby depriving White of a majority. But Mosman lobbied Powell not only to join White's opinion, but also to abandon completely the idea that homosexual sodomy was a "compulsion" protected by the Eighth Amendment. On May 21 Powell told Mosman he had changed his mind again. Unable to craft a suitable concurring rationale, Powell joined White's opinion.[47]

On June 30, 1986, the last day of the term, the Court announced its ruling in *Bowers v. Hardwick*. Byron White read the opinion for the Court. Sitting next to White, Harry Blackmun read a prepared statement summarizing his dissenting opinion. "[W]e grunted at each other, but walked off friends anyway," recalled Blackmun years later. Neither had any clue that his performance would inflame American law reviews more than any Supreme Court decision since their similar pas de deux (but with Blackmun delivering the opinion for the Court, and White dissenting) thirteen years before in *Roe*.

The Reaction to *Bowers v. Hardwick*

Justice White's opinion for the Court in *Bowers v. Hardwick* was brusque, simple, and historical. None of the Court's leading privacy precedents (none of which White had joined) went beyond decisions involving marriage, procreation, and childrearing. To *add* a protection for "homosexual sodomy" as a fundamental right, White reasoned, would require a showing that this liberty was "'deeply rooted in this Nation's history and tradition.'" Hardwick's attorneys had not made such a showing, nor could they, because proscriptions against "consensual sodomy" had "ancient roots." Sodomy was a crime in all thirteen states when they ratified the Bill of Rights in 1791, and in all but five of the thirty-seven states when the Fourteenth Amendment was added in 1868. "Against this background, to claim that a right to engage in such conduct is 'deeply rooted in this Nation's history and tradition' . . . is, at best, facetious." The Eleventh Circuit was therefore wrong to hold that Hardwick enjoyed a fundamental right to engage in homosexual sodomy. In a cursory concluding paragraph evaluating the claim that the state did not even have a "rational basis" for its law, White ruled that Georgia was within its constitutional discretion to criminalize sodomy to reflect "majority sentiments about the morality of homosexuality."[48]

Chief Justice Burger wrote a concurring opinion elaborating on White's historical discussion. Blackstone, the English commentator every American lawyer would have known at independence, described "'the infamous crime against nature' as an offense of 'deeper malignity' than rape." Sodomy was a capital crime until the nineteenth century. "To hold that the act of homosexual sodomy is somehow protected as a fundamental right would be to cast aside millennia of moral teaching."[49] Justice Powell's gentler concurring opinion suggested that a prison term for acts of consensual sodomy within the home would be subject to Eighth Amendment question, but Hardwick's case did not present that issue. "[F]or the reasons stated by the Court, I cannot say that conduct condemned for hundreds of years has now become a fundamental right."[50]

Joined by Justices Brennan, Marshall, and Stevens, Justice Blackmun filed a dissenting opinion that closely followed the Tribe and Sullivan brief. The case was no more about a fundamental right to homosexual sodomy than *Stanley* had been about a right to watch obscene movies. The statute made no such distinction; indeed, the state had expanded the law in 1968 to make certain that it included heterosexual as well as homosexual cunnilingus. Hardwick was only asking for the same right to be left alone that the state conceded to married couples and *Eisenstadt* assured unmarried straight couples. The Court's sexual privacy precedents guaranteed his freedom to make *decisions* regarding intimate relations, and its privacy-of-the-home precedents guaranteed his freedom against state intrusion into certain *places*. "[T]he right of an individual to conduct intimate relationships in the intimacy of his or her own home seems to me to be the heart of the Constitution's protection of privacy." Even if Hardwick had no fundamental right, however, Blackmun argued that antihomosexual "sentiment" could not provide the rational basis the Constitution requires for *any* statute, especially criminal laws. Certainly, the sectarian justifications emphasized by the state (and the chief justice) could not be a *neutral* reason that could justify "invading the houses, hearts, and minds of citizens who choose to live their lives differently."[51]

Justice Stevens wrote a separate dissenting opinion (joined by Brennan and Marshall, aging liberal Democrats who decided to let the Court's younger GOP justices speak for them). The Court was right to say that sodomy was long condemned by Anglo-American law—but the damnable conduct was *always* understood to apply to men and women, and to men or women with beasts, as well as to men and men. The crime against nature could be committed by married men with their wives. *Griswold* barred Georgia from prosecuting sodomy between married partners, as Hobbs conceded. *Eisenstadt* questioned the state's ability to discriminate against sodomy by unmarried heterosexuals. Could the state apply its broad statute *only* against homosexuals? Under the Constitution, there had to be "something more substantial than a habitual dislike for, or ignorance about, the disfavored group." That the state itself could not name a prosecution, even against homosexuals, for consensual sodomy since the 1930s suggested there was no such interest.[52]

Immediate Reaction to the Supreme Court's Decision

The press telephoned Kathy Wilde immediately after the Court announced its decision. She was surprised and "devastated" by the news, and she called Hardwick in Miami. He too had spoken to reporters. Also expecting a win, he was shocked by the judgment and poured out his heart to Wilde, who consoled him while he was consoling her. They both cried. When Hardwick read the opinions, he was astounded that the Supreme Court would dismiss his human rights claims as "at best, facetious," because King Henry VIII viewed his conduct as unnatural. He was angered by Burger's concurring opinion, especially its reference to Blackstone's view that the crime against nature is worse than rape. What kind of moral system was the Court willing to accept? Hardwick wondered. The chief moral lesson of the majority opinions, suggested by their obsession with "homosexual sodomy," seemed to be that the Constitution authorized homophobia and anti-gay discrimination.[53]

Lesbian and gay Americans read White's and Burger's dismissive opinions with similar shock and anger. The night the decision was announced, thousands filled the streets of San Francisco in spontaneous demonstrations protesting the decision. Smaller demonstrations occurred in New York and Washington, D.C. Hundreds of homosexuals and their friends wrote personal letters to the justices, in numbers greater than in any other case outside the abortion context. Arthur Wirth, the president of Parents and Friends of Lesbians and Gays, wrote Justice White, "If you knew our gay children personally I know that you would reject as wrong the idea that they are to be treated as pariahs, because that was the custom of the past." Individual gay persons and couples pleaded with the justices to understand that they lived decent, productive lives that little resembled the stereotypes suggested by the majority and concurring opinions. "As July Fourth approached, I did not feel terribly free," wrote Mark Fairchild of Whittier, California. Steven Cantor of Athens, Georgia, wrote Powell, begging him to reconsider his vote, because the Court's ruling will "encourage hateful, bigoted, and ignorant people to pursue [antigay] policies that have already destroyed—or at least terrified or harassed—many innocent people." Barbara Shor, a married woman, called her best friend and burst into tears after she read the New York Times account of the decision. "'All I can think to say to you is that, after my child, you are the person I love most in the world.' And my best friend, who is gay, said, 'Thank you. It helps. I just wish you'd tell that to Justice White.' And so I have," Shor wrote, in a letter mailed the next day.[54]

Father Robert Nugent, a Catholic theologian, wrote Blackmun praising his recognition that gay as well as straight people need protection for their expressions of sexuality and intimacy. "I regret that the Court's obsession with same-sex behavior has blinded them to the larger issues of human sexual interaction and intimacy which are distorted by such a narrow focus based on popular prejudices and even, at times, misreading of religious doctrines." The Reverend Kenneth Bastin, an evangelical Baptist, wrote the justices from the perspective of a cleric ministering to the needs of men dying of AIDS. He reported an upsurge of antigay violence following the Court's opinion. Everywhere he went, "I find appalling and irrational hatred and bigotry toward homosexual people as if it were they who created this deadly virus."[55]

Sorely disappointed, Laurence Tribe had a different public spin. "Despite the majority's disclaimers, [the decision] clearly extends to heterosexuals. Nothing in the approach of the majority opinion should make married people safe," he said the day the opinion came down. Bowers fueled a national conversation about state regulation of Americans' sexual practices. In George Orwell's 1984, Big Brother prohibited sexual pleasure and deployed cameras in everyone's home to enforce this rule. In Orwell's view, sexuality was a life force, a fundamental liberty pervasively threatening to despotic totalitarian governments, and so reactionary rulers suppressed sexuality as an exercise in despotic self-preservation. In Hardwick's case, Georgia looked like a bizarre amalgam of Big Brother and the Keystone Kops. If the police could barge into Hardwick's bedroom on trumped-up charges and cart him and his sexual partner off to jail, who in America was safe? Within days of the opinion, political cartoons appeared in hundreds of newspapers, depicting five justices (with varying resemblances to those in the *Bowers* majority) knocking at the doors of married couples, luridly peering through the windows of their bedrooms, and even making themselves at home in marital beds. Editorial writers took an equally critical stance.[56]

The Georgia authorities promptly reassured Atlanta residents that Big Brother had no interest in exposing *anyone's* sex lives. "What we said to the Supreme Court," Bowers announced, "was that if this law would have applied to a married couple, there would be significant constitutional difficulties." This was particularly reassuring to Keith Torick. Exhausted from citizen complaints and daily tussles with people he considered lowlifes, Torick had left the Atlanta police force in 1983. Soon thereafter, he interviewed for a job with the police department in Roswell, a gayfree, racially segregated zone twenty miles from the heart of Atlanta. Roswell required a polygraph test, which included the question "Have you ever broken the law?" Torick allegedly "flashed on the sodomy statute, which [he assumed] includes married couples, and asked that the question be rephrased as 'a serious undetected felony,' like robbing a bank. He passed." Georgia was filled with sodomites like Torick and his wife. Bowers reassured them that they were immune from the law.[57]

Bowers did not say whether heterosexual cohabiting or dating couples had anything to worry about. The Georgia Department of Corrections reported that only four of its 16,900 prison inmates in 1985 were in jail for sodomy, including two men for sodomy with a child and two women for sodomy with compensation. Even homosexuals should not worry too much. District Attorney Slaton reiterated that he would *not* prosecute Hardwick. Major J. E. Oliver, head of the Atlanta police's vice division, said: "If I walk into somebody's home with a warrant, say for narcotics, and [sodomy] is there, sure we'll charge them. But otherwise I don't see any reason to go into a house looking for sodomy." As the statement implied, sodomy arrests had long been, and would continue to be, confined to situations where consent was lacking or public sexuality created a nuisance.[58]

Bowers and Hobbs were certain that Tribe was wrong to find Big Brother lurking in the Supreme Court's decision and that Hardwick was wrong to be angered by it. From their point of view, the Court was merely reaffirming state authority to create a regulatory regime supporting marriage. The state did so by celebrating it and by showering married couples with many legal advantages and subsidies—but also by criminalizing nonmarital sexual expression. This is why Harlan had said that adultery, fornication, and homosexual sodomy were outside the protections of the privacy right he advanced in *Poe*. Even if unenforced, these laws represented important state symbols that suggested shameful conduct and even dishonorable passions that citizens should eschew. Bowers and Hobbs also agreed with the American Enterprise Institute's Bruce Fein, that the real punch line lay in civil exclusions. Under *Bowers*, "the government can say, 'We don't want to hire you because being a government employee sends a message to the public as to what kinds of people we approve of.'" Several years after the decision, Attorney General Bowers withdrew a job offer to Robin Shahar, a brilliant young lawyer, because she was planning to marry another woman. Although he did not believe Shahar should be subject to criminal sanctions, Bowers feared that her lesbian self-identification, which she flaunted through her wedding, made her a presumptive lawbreaker unsuited for service in a law enforcement office.[59]

Unlike the Georgia authorities, many fundamentalist Christians viewed *Bowers* as a great reaffirmation of moral values in American law. The night *Bowers* was handed down, Reverend Falwell appeared on *Larry King Live* to announce a moral renaissance in this country, where church and state would be partners in an enterprise to wean Americans from the soulless hedonism represented by homosexuality and other sins. Falwell's sentiments were expressed more brutally in letters to the Court. Matt Millen of Crown Point, Indiana, wrote Justice Blackmun a few days later: "You voted recently for queers having the freedom to practice their 'lifestyle' even privately. . . . No country has ever survived as a free country when sodomites were welcomed as normal." Carl Laurent wrote, "Does this mean you are homosexual? If so, this explains why you are also for murdering babies." Most blunt of all was Mrs. H. F. Mitchell of Homestead, Florida: "You are an old man and may die soon. If you don't repent, you will wake up in Hell." None of the anguished letters from homosexuals to White, Burger, and Powell was as mean-spirited as the letters Blackmun received from such Christians.[60]

Academic Critiques of *Bowers v. Hardwick*

As a decision by the U.S. Supreme Court firmly denying a fundamental constitutional right of gay people, *Bowers* was a landmark. But it was also significant as a statement by the Court's majority that the privacy right should not be further expanded. Indeed, the historical methodology deployed by Justice White's majority opinion could be, and soon was, deployed by the Reagan administration to urge the Court to reconsider *Roe*. Any decision of such importance would inevitably invite the closest scrutiny from law professors and commentators.

Progressive constitutional scholars, many of whom had been involved in the civil rights and women's rights movements, were predictably critical of the Supreme Court's decision—but so were some of the nation's most eminent conservatives, including Judge Richard Posner, a Chicago Law School law and economics scholar, and Reagan administration solicitor general Charles Fried. Posner and Fried believed that if you took the Court's privacy precedents seriously, they necessarily offered some protection for gays as well as straights, at least within their own homes. As Blackmun had argued, it was a retreat from privacy's libertarian bearings for the Court to have cabined the privacy right to decisions relating only to family, procreation, and childrearing. As Stevens had argued, it was a violation of equal protection for the Court to allow Georgia to focus only on homosexual sodomy, while assuring all its other citizens that the law did not apply to their conduct. Almost all law professors who wrote on the topic agreed with this criticism, and most went considerably further.[61]

The leading academic defender of the result and the methodology of *Bowers* was Judge (and former solicitor general) Robert Bork. Indeed, White's *Bowers* opinion closely tracked Bork's own decision in *Dronenberg v. Zech* (1984), which upheld the armed forces' exclusion of homosexuals on the ground that they are presumptive criminals (sodomites). Bork understood the Court's privacy precedents as judicial lawmaking unmoored to the Constitution. Like Powell, he looked for a limiting principle, which he found in original intent. Because sexual freedom was a relatively new development, and decidedly not recognized by American legal traditions, Bork was confident that the questionable privacy right should not be extended to "homosexual sodomy," exactly as the Court was to hold in *Bowers*.[62]

The original-intent story told by these judicial conservatives was, however, substantially wrong. White, Burger, and Bork treated the criminalization of "homosexual sodomy" as a phenomenon dating back to Roman times. As Stevens had said in *Bowers*, the crime against nature in both England and America always had applied to different-sex as well as same-sex couples, and even to married couples. If history was a reliable guide, then Georgia and the Court were wrong to assume that married couples could not be prosecuted. Professor Anne Goldstein demonstrated, further, that the concept of "homosexuality" or "homosexual sodomy" did not even exist until the late nineteenth century and that the conduct Hardwick was arrested for—oral sex—was *not* considered a crime against nature in England or the United States until the same period.[63]

So not only was White's opinion a slanted understanding of precedent, but it was also anachronistic history. As I demonstrated in a follow-up to Goldstein's

article, none of the aims of nineteenth-century sodomy laws supported their application against private activities between consenting adults. One purpose was
protection of the community against public indecency. In state codes sodomy
laws were typically listed with crimes against "public morals and decency"—
including bigamy and "open and notorious adultery"; printing or distributing
obscene literature; public indecency; "lewd and vicious cohabitation" or fornication; blasphemy or cursing in public places; and incest. Except for incest, the
other crimes involved actions outside the home that could be expected to disturb
the community. As we shall see, proof requirements for sodomy and incest made
it virtually impossible to prosecute any of those crimes if they were consensual
within the home.[64]

A second, and in practice the primary, purpose of nineteenth-century sodomy laws was protection of children, women, and weaker men against sexual
assault. Many codes listed sodomy as one of the "crimes against the person"—a
category that included rape, carnal knowledge of a girl, assault, and mayhem.[65]
This suggests that sodomy laws were understood as filling a regulatory gap as
regards nonconsensual sexual activity; in 1868 an adult male forcing himself
anally on a woman, girl, boy, or animal could only be prosecuted under sodomy
laws. All the model sodomy indictments reproduced in the leading collection
involved allegations of predation by an older man against a minor girl or boy.
Indeed, a man could not be convicted of sodomy based on the testimony of a
sexual partner who was his "accomplice." Conversely, the partner's testimony was
admissible if she or he was an unwilling participant or a minor (incapable of giving consent). This well-established proof requirement created an immunity for
sodomy within the home between consenting adults.[66]

As we saw in chapter 1, few Americans were arrested for the crime against
nature in the 1860s, and those who were arrested were men who engaged in anal
assaults on animals, children, women, or weaker men outside the home. In
short, White's originalist approach to the Fourteenth Amendment (applying it
only to strike down innovative laws that the framers in 1868 would probably
have found inconsistent with the rule of law) stood in stark contrast not only to
the Court's failure to follow an originalist approach in the contraception and
abortion cases, but also to White's own highly nonoriginalist approach (which
was not only dynamic, but wildly creative and ungrounded in any serious research) to the crime-against-nature laws he claimed the framers knew and approved. As a matter of *specific* intent, it would not have occurred to any framer
that the crime against nature could involve oral sex or could be prosecuted
against consenting adults without third-party witnesses. The framers of the
Fourteenth Amendment might have been willing to tolerate broadly applicable,
but unenforced, sodomy laws as a symbol of a public norm that held that sexual

pleasure was morally wrong unless procreative within marriage. But this third goal of crime-against-nature laws was one that *Griswold, Eisenstadt,* and *Roe* had firmly and repeatedly rejected.

The history suggests a larger normative problem with *Bowers,* and a possible normative defense. White's opinion rejustified the application of sodomy laws to consensual private conduct on the basis of an antihomosexual sentiment that was not only unknown to the 1868 framers, but was also a questionable modern justification for criminal sanctions. White defended this justification as the simple articulation of morality, but morality had also been the justification for laws criminalizing contraception (*Griswold*), abortion (*Roe*), and miscegenation or different-race marriage (*Loving v. Virginia,* 1967). By 1986 no one was willing to deny the validity of *Loving,* even though it had struck down a morals-based law that the framers of the Fourteenth Amendment firmly accepted. The reason that *Loving* is now uncontroversial is that the moral philosophy undergirding miscegenation laws is racism, which is no longer an acceptable moral stance. Because Americans since the 1920s have found consensual oral sex morally acceptable, the only form of sodomy they were willing to condemn was "homosexual sodomy," the natural focus of Bowers's brief and White's opinion. Depriving a small number of sodomites their freedom to do what the majority does with impunity cheapens morality-based legal regimes.[67]

Were there respectable moral arguments condemning homosexual but not heterosexual sodomy? Plato condemned same-sex sodomy for two interconnected reasons: it degrades the passive male partner to the status of a woman, and it is inherently nonprocreative. By 1986, preservation of rigid gender roles (man = inserter, woman = insertee) was no longer an acceptable justification for state policies under the Supreme Court's sex discrimination jurisprudence. Inspired by Plato's second reason, the best argument for criminalizing only homosexual sodomy is that its inevitable separation from procreative marital intercourse renders it a naked embrace of a philosophy of sex for pleasure alone. If that is allowed, or even encouraged, all moral distinctions in matters of sex between consenting adults would be obliterated. Plato also warned that a society recognizing no limits, especially sexual ones, would become formless and slip into inevitable decline. These kinds of concerns moved the majority justices in *Bowers.* Specifically, they worried that a broad reading of *Stanley* would protect drug use in the home, that an expansive understanding of *Griswold* would protect incest and adultery, and that new rights for homosexuals would associate the always vulnerable Court with condoning a hedonism without limits. Justice White's opinion reflected a quiet collective panic among the justices that their own legitimacy as guarantors of the rule of law would be imperiled if they did not announce firm limits to their jurisprudence of sexual liberty.[68]

Even under the foregoing philosophy, the question remained: Should the line be drawn at homosexual sodomy? Natural-law philosophy, the basis for Catholic doctrine and an inspiration for fundamentalist Protestants, not only condemns all sodomy, but also condemns antihomosexual discrimination. I am aware of no serious moral tradition that rejects oral and anal sex as immoral *only* if accomplished between persons of the same sex. Thus, Justice White's suggestion that homosexual sodomy can be a crime even if heterosexual sodomy is left unregulated appears to be more an expression of antihomosexual anxiety and prejudice than a serious statement of moral philosophy. This deep normative problem rendered *Bowers v. Hardwick* intellectually vulnerable from the very beginning.[69]

The Rule of Law as a Basis for Deregulating Consensual Sodomy

That the *Bowers* majority misunderstood almost everything—including moral philosophy as well as the legal history of the crime against nature—does not mean that the Georgia sodomy law was unconstitutional as applied to consenting activities within the home. But Lewis Powell and his clerk Bill Stuntz thought there was a case to be made—and one can be made. Its inspiration is Robert Bork. Although criticizing the privacy cases, Bork defended the Court's desegregation cases from originalist premises. Conceding that the framers did *not* believe that the Fourteenth Amendment immediately barred racial segregation, Bork argued that by 1954 it was clear that segregation, as applied, was inconsistent with the purposes of the Fourteenth Amendment. Chapter 1 of this book identifies its core purpose to be preservation of the rule of law in a democracy. Section 1 of the amendment advanced three principles essential to such a democratic rule of law: legality, liberty, and equality. The Georgia sodomy law, as enforced by Keith Torick and defended by Michael Bowers, was inconsistent with the Fourteenth Amendment's core purpose, understood through these three principles, and therefore unconstitutional under the originalist approach as applied by Bork.[70]

1. The Legality Principle. The notion that the state should exercise power predictably and neutrally, and only when authorized by law, applies with special force in criminal cases. The legality principle requires that criminal statutes give clear notice so that citizens know what conduct is illegal and police understand that they cannot apply the law selectively to terrorize particular citizens. Unlike the old crime-against-nature laws, the Georgia sodomy law, as updated in 1968, provided citizens with a sufficient description of the crime attributed to Hardwick—namely, fellatio. But in a society where three-quarters of the citizens engage in oral sex, the law could not be enforced against everyone—and so required the police to exercise discretion, which they inevitably used to harass despised minorities. Because consensual sodomy in Georgia carried with it a mandatory minimum sentence of a year in prison, and a maximum of twenty, that was a terrible discretion.[71]

In *Papachristou v. City of Jacksonville* (1972), the Supreme Court invalidated an ordinance making it a crime to be "vagabonds," "habitual loafers," and so forth. The police had arrested two interracial couples for driving around town— "loafing," under this ordinance. A unanimous Court ruled that the "archaic" law violated the Due Process Clause, because it "makes criminal actions which by modern standards are normally innocent," and was therefore mainly enforced mainly against "nonconformists." This was precisely the problem with the Georgia sodomy law, whose mandatory minimum penalty was greater than the maximum allowed under the *Papachristou* ordinance. Consensual activities within the home have, since colonial times, been legally "innocent," and the state's focus on "homosexual sodomy" alone was evidence that the brunt of its bar to consensual sex was borne by "nonconformists." Recall that Hobbs could identify only two instances between 1935 and 1985 when the Georgia law had been applied against consenting adults; the first case involved a lesbian couple whose conviction was overturned on due process grounds, and the second case was *Hardwick*. A *Papachristou*-based theory would have been a better legal basis for Powell's intuitions in *Hardwick*. An advantage of this theory is that it would have allowed the Court to dispose of the law on narrow grounds. If Georgia, or other states, really did want to conduct a moral campaign against consensual oral sex, the campaign would have to reach everyone, not just hapless homosexuals.[72]

2. The Liberty Principle. As historically understood, the liberty principle provides a possible foundation for a privacy jurisprudence that supports the *Bowers* dissents. Nineteenth-century America vigorously regulated sexual assaults and public conduct (including cross-dressing), but there is no evidence that the state officially enforced the crime against nature between consenting adults in the home. Nor did the state regulate reading obscene literature (analogous to the pornographic movie today) within the home, thereby providing historical support for *Stanley*. Although the state did regulate the public sale and advertisement of contraceptives, nineteenth-century statutes did not regulate their use by married couples within the home, thereby providing historical support for *Griswold*.

Does such an articulation also provide a suitable limit to the liberty principle, the question that troubled Justice Powell? The line between public and private is hard to draw without making controversial value judgments. Until the late twentieth century, a husband's forcing sex on his wife was considered a private matter, because it fell within the moral umbrella of marriage; today it is considered rape, a serious crime. The use of drugs and child pornography within the home might be considered public, either because private use contributes to a chain of production that harms third parties or creates addictions that create risks of harm to others. Incest and bestiality are equivocal; it is difficult to say that they have demonstrable public harms, but most Americans believe them unprotected by the privacy right. Questions like these tripped Tribe up at oral argument in *Bowers*, and for good reason: it is not a simple matter to answer persuasively.

The liberty principle can also be expressed in social and political terms. The pervasive regulatory state (unanticipated by the framers) threatens us as individuals in more ways than ever before, and the purpose of constitutional "liberty" is to mark off arenas of potential regulation that are least likely to serve public purposes and most likely to harm its targets' ability to flourish as individuals. The state can regulate these marked spaces only when it can demonstrate a tangible public need, such as protection of public health. Within this understanding, *Griswold* remains a paradigm case, because its complete ban of contraceptives was poorly linked to public purposes, such as preventing disease or premarital sex, while its potential effect was to undermine women's ability to control their own lives and plan their own families. While *Griswold* suggested the privacy line could be drawn around marriage, *Eisenstadt* backed away from such a line. Another precedent provides further illumination.

Although no one relied on it, *Skinner v. Oklahoma* (1942) is an even closer fit with *Bowers*. In 1934 Oklahoma provided for sterilization of men convicted of two or more crimes (including sodomy) involving "moral turpitude." As Victoria Nourse shows, this sterilization law was the apotheosis of that era's body politics—yet the Supreme Court struck it down. "The power to sterilize, if exercised, may have subtle, far-reaching and devastating effects. In evil or reckless hands it can cause races or types which are inimical to the dominant group to wither and disappear. There is no redemption for the individual whom the law touches. Any experiment which the State conducts is to his irreparable injury. He is forever deprived of a basic liberty." Sterilization is not the only state policy that can raise such concerns. The ability of the modern state to demonize sexual and gender minorities *and* to commandeer those people's bodies against their will is also a dangerous state assault on liberty. For sexually active women, state bars to contraception and abortion impede their ability to plan their lives as well as their families. For homosexuals, the crime against nature as presented by the *Bowers* Court was a state effort to commandeer their sexual lives, either forcing them into celibacy or the closet, to achieve highly symbolic or speculative goals.[73]

To be sure, Powell and White could not appreciate this parallel, because they understood homosexual sodomy to have no connection with family or other productive human relationships; it was, at best, an "addiction." Yet it was clear by 1986 that this was an outmoded attitude. Not only was there a largely undisputed medical consensus that human flourishing required sexual expression, including homosexual expression for many individuals, but there was a growing literature demonstrating that lesbians and gay men formed committed relationships whose intimacy involved the crime against nature. Powell and White were unaware of this literature, not because it went unmentioned in the case (it was prominently featured in amicus briefs), but because they were emotionally unable to assimilate it. Such a reaction is understandable for men of their generation, but it is an unacceptable basis for interpreting the Constitution.

3. The Anti–Class Legislation Principle. *Skinner* was an equal protection, and not just a liberty, case. As in *Papachristou*, the *Skinner* Court emphasized that the statute was aimed at the dispossessed and, as a matter of drafting, exempted white-collar criminals from its extreme sanction. Accordingly, *Skinner* illustrates how the legality, liberty, and equality principles of the Fourteenth Amendment overlap, and how they can work together to yield a verdict against particular state laws. *Bowers*'s focus on "homosexual sodomy" is deeply inconsistent with the anti–class legislation (equality) principle of the Fourteenth Amendment. Homosexual sodomy laws, in fact, are more profound intrusions into that principle than the Oklahoma sterilization law was.

In 1868 there was no social group of "homosexuals" (the term did not then exist); by 1986 homosexuals were a coherent social group, in large part because governments had declared their characteristic conduct to be the crime against nature and, based on that conduct, had imposed an array of civil penalties. In Georgia and other states of the South, the open homosexual as a presumptive felon could be excluded from:

- voting and jury service, if convicted of a crime of moral turpitude like sodomy or even solicitation (chapter 2);
- military service, under Reagan administration regulations excluding both sodomites and admitted homosexuals;
- remaining in the United States, if the homosexual was a noncitizen (chapter 5);
- opportunities to be municipal police officers or firefighters (chapter 10);
- state civil service jobs, including work in Attorney General Bowers's office;
- professional licenses, which could be denied or revoked on grounds of moral turpitude;

- housing, as leases often stipulated termination for immoral or felonious behavior (chapter 9);
- police protection against antigay violence;
- civil marriage, which involved more than one hundred associated legal benefits and duties also denied lesbian or gay couples (chapter 9);
- judicial enforcement of contractual promises or testamentary bequests to a committed lesbian or gay partner;
- adoption (chapter 11);
- raising one's own biological children, if a straight coparent wanted to punish the lesbian or gay coparent (chapter 11).

The openly gay person was, literally, rendered an outlaw. This regime was not nearly as oppressive as race-based apartheid had been in Georgia, because most homosexuals could avoid these exclusions by remaining in the closet or being discreet in their interactions with state officials. But such an *apartheid of the closet* did create a subordinate class potentially excluded from ordinary civic life and politically vulnerable, because of a stigmatizing trait (homosexuality) that is no more malignant than racial color. As Marilyn Haft and Cary Boggan first argued in *Enslin*, and Abby Rubenfeld and Roberta Achtenberg argued in *Bowers*, such a regime was a violation of the Fourteenth Amendment's anti–class legislation principle. This was a conclusion Powell would not have been comfortable supporting in 1986, but it is the strongest originalist indictment against consensual sodomy laws.[74]

Indeed, there was a potential constituency for this argument within the Supreme Court. Shortly before *Bowers*, the Oklahoma Court of Criminal Appeals ruled in *Post v. State* (1986) that its sodomy law could not constitutionally be applied to private activities between consenting adults of different sexes. Oklahoma asked the Supreme Court to review this determination on the ground that the privacy right did not protect extramarital *heterosexual sodomy* (its case) any more than it protected *homosexual sodomy* (the Georgia case). Burger, White, and Rehnquist, who lobbied very hard for the Court to take the *Bowers* appeal to stop judicial activism protecting *homosexuals,* had no interest whatsoever in stopping judicial activism protecting unmarried *heterosexuals.* Rejecting law clerks' suggestions that the Court should vacate the *Post* judgment and remand the case to Oklahoma courts in light of *Bowers,* a common course for the Court in such cases, these conservative justices voted to deny review altogether. So did the *Bowers* dissenters, for they agreed that straight as well as gay sodomites enjoyed the protection of the privacy precedents. Only Justice O'Connor raised any objection; at her behest, *Post* was carried over to the conference for October 10, 1986. In a memorandum reportedly circulated among the justices, she wondered whether *Bowers* swept more broadly than the Oklahoma court had surmised. Because there was no fundamental right to engage in any kind of sodomy, the state could regulate heterosexual as well as homosexual conduct that had been condemned by "millennia of moral teaching."[75]

O'Connor was right, of course. That none of her male colleagues was willing to agree underscores the rhetorical purpose of *Bowers*'s obsessive focus on homosexual sodomy. For some of the Brethren, it was important to create a constitutional as well as a moral distance between what degraded homosexuals do (homosexual fellatio) and what normal husbands and wives do (heterosexual fellatio), a firm differentiation that would have been threatened by reversing *Post*. O'Connor got the message from her conservative Brethren, and on October 10 she joined them in voting to deny review in *Post*.[76]

There was a related point O'Connor could have made, but did not. For states like Oklahoma and Georgia to reassure their straight and married citizens that the broadly written sodomy laws adopted by the legislature did not apply to "normal" people was a compromise of the rule of law, and one that linked the equality principle back to the legality principle. Justice Robert Jackson, Rehnquist's mentor, said it best: "[T]here is no more effective practical guaranty against arbitrary and unreasonable government than to require that the principles of law which officials would impose upon a minority must be imposed generally."[77]

In light of this intelligence, it is possible that there would have been a fifth vote to overturn consensual sodomy laws—not the applies-to-everyone law that Georgia had, but instead the homosexuals-only law that Texas had. Recall the choice the gayocracy made to separate the Georgia case from the Texas one. If the cases had been consolidated and heard together—which would have been difficult given the procedural problems with the Texas case—O'Connor might have provided a fifth vote to overturn the Texas law, which did on its face what the Oklahoma law did only by partial judicial invalidation. And if there had been a Court to strike down the Texas law, Powell might have been more willing to stick with his intuition that the Georgia law, too, was invalid.

If the Court had struck down both kinds of sodomy laws in 1986, however, Reagan-era America would have been appalled. The political scientist Nathaniel Persily and his colleagues maintain that public support for decriminalizing consensual sodomy had grown steadily until the early 1980s, when news reports repeatedly associated homosexual activity (indeed, the historic crime against nature, anal sex) with transmission of the virus causing AIDS. Once AIDS became associated with homosexual sodomy, Middle America became dramatically less willing to decriminalize such conduct. *Bowers* came to the Court just as the AIDS connection was peaking among mainstream Americans—precisely the *wrong* time for the Court to overturn all consensual sodomy laws under a vaguely defined privacy right. There would probably have been a popular backlash against the Court if it had invalidated all consensual sodomy laws, and perhaps even if it had just invalidated the seven homosexual-only laws.[78]

In terms of the Court's political capital, Justice Powell was right to search for a narrow basis to decide *Bowers*. While a narrow decision resting on *Papachristou* and *Skinner* would have been the most judicious resolution, it too might have generated a backlash, albeit probably a short-lived one. Politically, the safest resolution would have been for the Court to dismiss the case as not "justiciable," as it had done in the early contraception cases. Because Hardwick himself had not been prosecuted, the Court might have concluded that he lacked standing to challenge the Georgia sodomy law. Such a resolution would have avoided the academic firestorm that Justice White's dismissive opinion generated, while also avoiding the popular protest that would have accompanied an opinion by Justice Blackmun striking down all consensual sodomy laws as violating the privacy right.[79]

This is all speculation, of course.

What is not speculation is that few of its participants took pleasure from *Bowers v. Hardwick*. Retiring from the Court weeks after the decision, Warren Burger felt it was a fitting legacy for his leadership—but it turned out to be a disastrous legacy. *Bowers* is the most criticized Supreme Court decision of all time that *upheld* a law against constitutional attack. (Most of the decisions that have subjected the Court to criticism are those striking down laws, such as *Roe v. Wade*, which Burger also joined.)

Poor Byron White did not derive even temporary joy from denying Hardwick's constitutional claim. One Christmas soon after the decision was handed down, White and his wife dropped by an old friend's house for a yuletide party. He spotted the friend's son, whom he knew to be gay, and offered his hand in greeting. Furious at this jurist's public disrespect for "homosexuals," the son turned and walked away, leaving the stunned justice to ask the parents what was wrong with their son. Whizzer White, Yale Law School's Renaissance man, never understood the human reaction gay people had to his opinion. For him, Supreme Court cases were like football games, in which the losers accept defeat, and everyone prepares for the next match. White's brusque opinion not only fueled rage against the Court but also raised the stakes of the culture wars: traditionalists were now authorized by the Constitution to treat homosexuals like outlaws, a proposition deeply inconsistent with the Fourteenth Amendment, even when read conservatively. It is, nonetheless, tremendously unfair that the only majority opinion that history will remember from Byron White will be *Bowers*.[80]

William Brennan and Thurgood Marshall were appalled that their votes had enabled the case to get to the Court, at what turned out to be the worst time for the elderly justices to hear this sensitive issue. Harry Blackmun and John Paul Stevens were disappointed that their arguments had not persuaded more colleagues. Lewis Powell continued to have second (and third) thoughts about his vote. In a question-and-answer session after delivering the annual James Madison Lecture at NYU's law school in October 1990, a student asked if there were votes Powell would like to take back. Yes, he acknowledged—the vote in *Bowers*. This was no off-the-cuff remark, as Powell later confirmed that answer with a reporter: "When I had the opportunity to reread the opinions a few months later, I thought the [Blackmun] dissent had the better of the arguments."[81]

The winning counsel in one of the biggest constitutional cases of the century, Mike Hobbs, was pleased with his work. (Justice Powell's notes taken during oral argument describe Hobbs as a "*good lawyer*," a high compliment from the former president of the ABA. After Tribe, Powell wrote, "Torrent of words!") Laurence Tribe considers *Bowers* the most disappointing loss of his career, and William Stuntz, now Tribe's colleague at Harvard Law School, unfairly blames himself for not having developed a better theory to support Powell's intuition. Like Tribe and Stuntz, Kathy Wilde did a brilliant job seeking justice in Hardwick's case and laments the loss. That her side came so close to winning makes the disappointment keener.

Prosecutor Lewis Slaton and Police Commissioner George Napper, both of whom dropped out of the case as soon as they could, took no comfort in *Bowers*, because they thought the law was a relic of a past best unenforced. Although Hardwick and Bowers became celebrities, they regretted the glare of publicity, as both were rather private men. The attorney general surely regrets the fact that "gay rights" and "sodomy" will always be associated with his name, as generations of law students will read the case the Supreme Court has shorthanded as *Bowers*. His political career ended in 1998 when he resigned as attorney general to conduct a losing race for governor. After a decade of distinguished work in private practice, including representation of people of color who had been victims of race discrimination, Bowers was in 2006 voted a Leadership Award by the Atlanta Bar Association. Even this honor was soured, in small part, by objections from the Stonewall Bar Association that the award should not be granted because of his treatment of Hardwick and Shahar.

Back in his home area of Dade County, Florida, Michael Hardwick pursued a career as an "optical alchemist," or scenic designer for nightclubs. Working with chicken wire and papier-mâché, he created installations or fantasy spaces such as the "atomic garden" he later built for the Fort Lauderdale bar Squeeze: "In this place illuminated by black light, Hardwick's glowing green vines, with leaves as large as elephant ears, curl through purple-blue rafters. Sensuous flowers dot the vines. Giant red heliconias stand in a vase by the door. A phosphorescent green pterodactyl hovers overhead." Later, Hardwick created a twelve-foot-long Matisse-green winged lizard to hang over the bar itself. As his artistic work flourished, however, Michael became more personally reclusive. His experiences in Atlanta "had a chilling effect on me. I have not had a steady relationship since then," he wistfully recalled in 1990.[82]

CHAPTER NINE

The Lawyers and Sodomy Come Out
of Their Closets, 1986–2003

Ruth Harlow, Susan Sommer, and Suzanne Goldberg

R uth Harlow and Susan Sommer were roommates and best friends at Yale
Law School, graduating together in May 1986. Under Dean Guido Calabresi (1985–94), Yale had become the unquestioned top law school in America,
and one of the most gay-friendly, though many of the gay students were not out
of the closet. Some, like Harlow, did not realize they were lesbian or gay or bisexual until they were in law school. In a series of casual conversations, she came
out as a lesbian, to herself as well as to Sommer, in their second year at Yale. The
shy Harlow remained ambivalent about how "out" she should be professionally.
Having spent her childhood in Midland, Michigan, she felt that homosexuality
would do her legal career no good, an impression reinforced by news reports
about law firm conformity. Yet Harlow found the law school environment tremendously liberating. She and Donna Dennis (class of 1987) published the first
law review article on education law issues important for gay youth, and the law
school hosted an important conference on AIDS and the law, on the eve of *Bowers v. Hardwick*.[1]

To be sure, the situation was less open elsewhere. With exceptions such as the
University of Southern California and New York University, law schools in the

1970s and 1980s did not offer courses covering the interesting and pressing constitutional issues raised by state discrimination against gay people. Astoundingly, legal scholars and teachers who endlessly debated the right-to-privacy cases, especially *Roe v. Wade* (1973), said virtually nothing about consensual sodomy laws. While hundreds of law review articles argued about the constitutionality of affirmative action and various sex discriminations, few pages mentioned equal rights for sexual minorities. There were gay and lesbian professors at most major law schools in 1986, but only one was unequivocally out of the closet—Ohio State's prolific professor Rhonda Rivera.[2]

Handed down the month after Harlow and Sommer graduated, *Bowers* immediately transformed the constitutional law curriculum of Yale and every other law school in America. Justice White's (YLS class of 1946) opinion was an important statement that the privacy right must have strong limits; the limit he drew in *Bowers*, based on tradition, supported his dissent in *Roe*. Also raising the stakes in his *Bowers* dissent, Justice Blackmun (the author of *Roe*) wrote that White's opinion was a fundamental retreat from constitutional protection for our bodies, our homes, and our relationships—all Americans were now more open to government meddling. Justice Stevens's *Bowers* dissent posed the case in terms of the discriminations suffered by lesbian and gay Americans as a result of their perceived link to criminality. Did *Bowers* establish them as pariahs outside the normal protections of the rule of law? Ultimately, the case was about the conditions for democratic self-government itself. For all these intellectual reasons, as well as its inherent drama, *Bowers* was tremendously teachable. Rare was the student who emerged from a consideration of the case without a critical appreciation of the brutal rhetoric, the amateurish deployment of history, and the troubling consequences of *Bowers* for everyone's constitutional rights. In published articles and books, professors feasted on *Bowers* like famished dieters.[3]

The students matriculating at Yale in September 1987 included a particularly activist collection of lesbian, gay, and bisexual students who threw themselves into the campaign to defeat Judge Robert Bork's 1987 nomination to replace Lewis Powell on the Supreme Court. As a Yale law professor (1961–73, 1977–82), Bork had opposed the law school's addition of sexual orientation to its antidiscrimination policy in 1978, and as a judge he had authored *Dronenburg v. Zech* (1984), the roadmap opinion for an antihomosexual Constitution. Although an academic superstar, Bork found most of the Yale faculty and virtually all the students arrayed against his nomination, because of his hostility to the privacy right. In the public campaign against Bork's nomination, however, homosexuality remained in a political closet. The Senate Judiciary Committee rebuked the nominee instead for his principled critique of the contraception and other sexual privacy

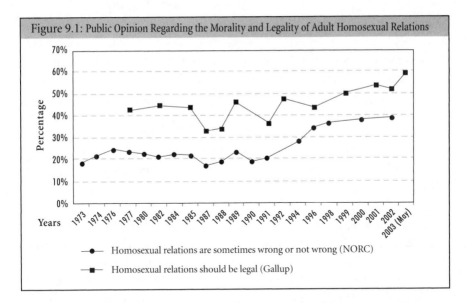

Figure 9.1: Public Opinion Regarding the Morality and Legality of Adult Homosexual Relations

precedents. Ordinary Americans believed that their right to be free from state snooping into their consensual practices was fundamental to the Constitution and opposed Bork by almost two-to-one margins. The Senate rejected his nomination by a 58–42 vote: "If the Bork hearings accomplished anything . . . it was the enshrinement of *Griswold* as 'a fixed star in our constitutional firmament.'"[4]

Did ordinary Americans believe that such privacy rights, this "fixed star," should be available to homosexuals? Not in 1987. The National Opinion Research Center (NORC) projected that eighty-two percent of Americans still considered homosexual relations "always" or "almost always wrong"; Gallup reported only thirty-three percent of its respondents willing to decriminalize "homosexual relations between consenting adults." In the next fifteen years, however, these numbers changed dramatically. By 2002 NORC estimated that fifty-eight percent of the population still believed that homosexual relations were "always" or "almost always wrong"; Gallup in May 2003 projected that sixty percent believed homosexual relations should be legal. Figure 9.1 plots the evolution of public attitudes according to these polls.[5]

What accounts for the striking change in attitudes? According to mainstream social scientists, the main reasons were higher levels of education and a shift toward a more liberal, pro-choice philosophy among Americans. Gay sociologists believe the numbers were driven by personal relationships with lesbians and gay men. In 1985 only twenty-two percent of Americans said they had a "friend or close acquaintance" who was gay or lesbian—but by 2000 fifty-six percent did. In the 1990s, homosexuality began to saturate public culture, with more positive and complex depictions of gay people showing up in the movies, on Broadway, in popular stories and novels, and even on television (*Will and Grace*, 1997). Perhaps the most important contributing factor was that Americans came to see homosexuals visibly cooperating in social, community, and even family relationships. Although some state prosecutors and religious leaders deployed AIDS as a metonym for homosexual promiscuity, more Americans came to appreciate that gay and bisexual men had changed their behavior after the epidemic's outbreak and had supported and nurtured those afflicted with the fatal disease. Unprecedented numbers of lesbians and gay men were also living together in openly committed relationships, often raising children born of the "lesbian baby boom" and a smaller "gayby" boomlet.[6]

Yet another reason for a softening of public attitudes toward homosexual sodomy is that heterosexual sodomy itself came out of its social closet. According to the 1994 NORC survey, 78.7 percent of American men and 73.1 percent of American women had received oral sex from different-sex partners; for one-quarter of the men and one-fifth of the women, this had occurred the last time they had had sex before participating in the survey. The following year, intern Monica Lewinsky fellated President Bill Clinton. This and subsequent episodes of oral sex in the Oval Office became a point of evidence in a sexual harassment lawsuit filed against the president by a former state employee, Paula Jones. Under oath, the president denied having "sexual relations" with "that woman," Lewinsky. In September 1998, Special Prosecutor Kenneth Starr provided Congress with strong evidence that the president had repeatedly engaged in oral sex with Lewinsky, evidence that Congress made public. The Starr Report was sensational in part because of its detailed and spicy descriptions of presidential sodomy and sexual kink. When parents objected that the Internet made this material available to their children, they were met with assurances that oral sex would come as no surprise to the youngsters, who had already discovered it on their own. By the time Clinton emerged from the scandal, after a House impeachment and Senate acquittal, it was a matter of public record that heterosexual sodomy was as American as baseball and chocolate donuts.[7]

In light of all these developments, was there any future for laws making "homosexual sodomy" a crime, as *Bowers* had suggested? In fact, post-*Bowers* repudiations of homosexual sodomy laws came even in the Baptist South, the Catholic Northeast, and the Mormon West. The 1994 NORC survey found that half of America's religious traditionalists had themselves engaged in oral sex, with one in ten admitting that they "always" did so; one in five said they had enjoyed anal sex. To be sure, their own violation of God's (supposed) command against nonprocreative sex was not why they abandoned the effort against homosexual sodomy laws. The apparent reason for this shift in attitude was that a new and bigger threat to traditional morality also emerged after *Bowers*. In the 1990s, the nation's sexual Maginot line shifted away from homosexual sodomy. By 2003, two-thirds of Americans believed that the state should not recognize same-sex marriage—while almost three-quarters said that the Supreme Court should overturn laws that make consensual homosexual, but not heterosexual, sodomy a crime.[8]

Sodomy Law Challenges Under State Constitutions

The year before *Bowers*, ACLU president Norman Dorsen had named Nan Hunter to head its new Gay and Lesbian Rights Project. Soon after *Bowers*, Sue Hyde joined the National Gay and Lesbian Task Force to focus on sodomy reform. Hunter, Hyde, and Abby Rubenfeld, the legal director of Lambda (1983–88), took from *Bowers* the lesson that the federal courts were not the best audience for gay rights claims. Any ruling based on the U.S. Constitution was reviewable by the same justices who had delivered *Bowers*. At the federal level, lesbian and gay lawyers focused on other pressing matters, such as AIDS policy and, relatedly, the Americans with Disabilities Act, which became law in 1990. At the state level, Hunter, Hyde, and Rubenfeld realized that repeal by legislatures was highly unlikely. The only hope for continued debate was legal challenges under state constitutions, which can add to rights guaranteed by the U.S. Constitution.[9]

Bootlegged Liquor and Gay Rights in Kentucky

In the fall of 1985 the Lexington, Kentucky, police department conducted an elaborate sting operation. A genteel bluegrass city, Lexington had one gay bar, Johnny Angel, located on Main Street at the center of town. (Its claim to fame in gay circles is that heartthrob Rock Hudson allegedly hung out there while he was dating another dashing star who had a farm nearby.) The sprawling parking lot behind Johnny Angel was a pickup spot where for several months undercover officers had struck up and recorded flirtatious conversations with men leaving the bar. If the suspect asked an officer if he wanted a blow job or to fuck—"deviate sexual intercourse" under Kentucky law—the officer would enthusiastically accept. Usually, the suspect would lead the officer to his house, but before they could enter another policeman would intervene and "scare" the decoy cop away. In January 1986, after a year of collecting names and addresses, the police arrested many of these men, charging most of them with solicitation to commit fourth-degree deviate intercourse. One was Jeffrey Wasson, a twenty-three-year-old nurse's assistant. Wasson had carried on a casual conversation with an undercover officer and, after what he considered aggressive "prodding" from the officer, had invited him to engage in private oral sex at his apartment.[10]

Unlike most of the others apprehended, Wasson asked his attorney, Ernesto Scorsone, to resist the charges. The son of immigrants from Palermo, Italy, Scorsone was himself gay (though not professionally out of the closet at that time) and was well-connected to Lexington's modest gay and lesbian community, which was energized by the flurry of arrests. All were eager to overturn the state's consensual sodomy law, which criminalized only homosexual "deviate intercourse." To litigate Wasson's case, the community enlisted the help of local attorney Shirley Weigand and Professor Carolyn Bratt of the University of Kentucky Law School, Scorsone's alma mater, located several blocks from Johnny Angel.[11]

The Kentucky Constitution of 1891 has a lengthy bill of rights, the first three of which read:

§1. All men are, by nature, free and equal, and have certain inherent and inalienable rights, among which may be reckoned: First, The right of enjoying and defending their lives and liberties. . . . Third, The right of seeking and pursuing their safety and happiness.

§2. Absolute and arbitrary power over the lives, liberty, and property of freemen exists nowhere in a republic, not even in the largest majority.

§3. All men, when they form a social compact, are equal.

Wasson's legal team relied on these provisions to ask Fayette County (Lexington) district judge Lewis Paisley to rule that the consensual sodomy law was unconstitutional. Although Kentucky's Constitution has no specific right of privacy, its courts had interpreted sections 1 and 2 broadly.[12]

The leading case was *Commonwealth v. Campbell* (1909). Police had arrested the defendant for carrying bootlegged liquor to his home for domestic consumption, which was a crime in "dry" Jefferson County. On the eve of Prohibition in this Baptist state, bootleggers were about as popular as homosexuals would be in the 1980s, but the Kentucky Court of Appeals overturned Campbell's conviction. Citing John Stuart Mill's treatise *On Liberty*, the court interpreted sections 1 and 2 to bar the state from regulating a citizen's pursuit of happiness in his own home, so long as he was not injuring other persons. "It is not within the competency of government to invade the privacy of a citizen's life. . . . [L]et a man therefore be ever so abandoned in his principles, or vicious in his practice, provided he keeps his wickedness to himself, and does not offend against the rules of public decency, he is out of the reach of human laws." In subsequent cases, the

Kentucky Supreme Court applied *Campbell* liberally, to bar the state from regulating immoral activities that occurred in the privacy of one's home.[13]

More daringly, Wasson's legal team also challenged the homosexual-only sodomy law on the ground that it violated the state equality guarantee. Recall that Hardwick's lawyers had kept homosexuality as closeted as they could. Scorsone, Bratt, and Weigand rejected that strategy, turning the hearing on the motion to dismiss into a tutorial on homosexuality. Working closely with the larger lesbian and gay community, they presented nine expert witnesses, all of them local except for Dr. Martin Weinberg of the Kinsey Institute. Without refutation from the state, the witnesses established the following propositions. First, the United States was unusual in the level of anxiety attached to same-sex intimacy; most cultures and many religions in world history have tolerated such intimacy, and some have celebrated it. Second, repressive state policies had no discernible effect on the incidence of homosexuality in a society—homosexuality was not a "choice," and there was no "cure" for it. Third, homosexual role models did not produce homosexuals; at most, they produced tolerance. Fourth, there was now a consensus among psychologists and medical researchers that homosexuality was not a disease or a mental illness. Fifth, homosexuals enjoyed meaningful and often committed relationships, and increasing numbers were raising children. Sixth, consensual oral or anal sex was important for the psychological flourishing of lesbians and gay men; sodomy laws sought to cut these citizens off from essential emotional outlets. Sodomy laws also retarded rather than assisted medical campaigns in controlling the AIDS epidemic.[14]

Perhaps displaying its own lack of enthusiasm for the law, the commonwealth called no witnesses. On October 31, four months after *Bowers* was announced, Judge Paisley ruled that the consensual sodomy law violated the state right of privacy. On appeal, Fayette Circuit Court judge Charles Tackett agreed with Judge Paisley and ruled that the law violated state equality guarantees as well.[15] On appeal to the Kentucky Supreme Court, however, the commonwealth was assured of three votes among the court's seven justices. Justices Donald Wintersheimer and Charles Reynolds were pro-life Roman Catholics who would be aghast at the lower courts' protection of both privacy and equality rights of homosexual sodomites. Justice Joseph Lambert (now the chief justice), a conservative Republican with larger political ambitions, was an almost certain third vote to read *Campbell*'s privacy right narrowly and to follow Judge Bork's reasoning that there were no equal protection rights for presumptive criminals.[16]

Assisted on appeal by Lexington lawyers Pam Goldman (who was the primary author of the appellate briefs) and Dean Bucalos, Scorsone rested his client's hopes on the state's libertarian tradition, best reflected in Justice Dan Jack

Combs, a former ACLU-affiliated lawyer from the east Kentucky mountains, and Justice Charles M. Leibson, a plaintiffs' tort lawyer from Louisville. Justice Thomas B. Spain usually voted with Leibson and Combs in civil liberties cases, as did Chief Justice Robert F. Stephens, who was from liberal Fayette County and would be particularly reluctant to reverse his friends on the bench there. But this likely coalition almost fell apart, twice. Just before oral argument, Leibson asked the parties whether he should recuse himself from the case, because his wife had contributed money to one of the organizations filing an amicus brief. If he was absent, the most that Scorsone could hope for was a 3–3 tie. And he did not realize that the chief justice's vote was uncertain, because Stephens feared public backlash. The court had already attracted criticism for requiring the legislature to equalize funding for local education. If the voters felt the court was promoting some "homosexual agenda" as well, its members would lose their reelection campaigns. Would this be *Bowers* revisited?[17]

Gay rights finally caught some breaks. In a gracious move, the commonwealth posed no objection to Justice Leibson's participation, and in the court's deliberations he persuaded the chief to go with his constitutional instincts. On September 24, 1992, Leibson delivered an opinion for the court accepting both constitutional claims. The court ruled that enforcement of morals legislation within the home was inconsistent with *Campbell* and the intent of the framers of the 1891 constitution. The constitutional framing debates accepted the precept laid out by Louis Brandeis's famous 1890 article on "The Right to Privacy," which Leibson (an alumnus of the Louis D. Brandeis School of Law at the University of Louisville) summarized: "[I]mmorality in private which does 'not operate to the detriment of others,' is placed beyond the reach of state action." The state argued that the court should follow *Bowers*, to which Leibson responded, "We view [*Bowers*] as a misdirected application of the theory of original intent." The homosexual conduct law also violated Kentucky's equality guarantees. "Certainly, the practice of deviate sexual intercourse violates traditional morality. But so does the same act between heterosexuals, which activity is decriminalized." The commonwealth defended the discrimination on grounds that "homosexuals are more promiscuous than heterosexuals" and are "more prone to engage in sex acts in public," assertions that Leibson termed "outrageous." Antihomosexual animus could not be the basis for state regulation. "'Equal Justice Under Law' inscribed above the entrance to the United States Supreme Court, expresses the unique goal to which all humanity aspires. In Kentucky, it is more than mere aspiration."[18]

In dissent, Justice Lambert argued that the *Campbell* rule was too broad, for it would disable the state from enforcing a whole range of morals-based rules. (Indeed, after his 1995 arrest for growing marijuana within his home for medical purposes, former justice Combs responded that the police raid was a violation of the *Wasson* privacy right.) Lambert also objected to the court's decision as placing the "imprimatur of Kentucky's highest court upon homosexual conduct."[19] The court's two Catholic justices expressed a broader basis for their dissent. *Campbell* must be read narrowly, and *Bowers* followed, because of the social nature of human communities. "The Mill theory of rugged individualism is flawed because 'No man is an island.'" Consensual sodomy "has an impact on other people and clearly has a ripple effect. Almost everything individuals do involves someone else. . . . 'Am I my brother's keeper?' The answer [is] 'Yes,'" especially in the modern era when our lives were more interconnected than ever before. "There is a vast difference between liberty and license. License, in this context, means an excessive undisciplined freedom constituting an abuse of liberty." Many Baptists agreed with these philosophical points, especially with respect to homosexuality.[20]

Wasson was a sensation within the state. *Wasson*'s lawyers and the majority justices received a bushel of hate mail. Preachers and politicians of both parties proposed a constitutional amendment to authorize the General Assembly to make consensual sodomy a crime. In the 1994 session, the Democratic House Caucus met in the same Supreme Court chamber where Scorsone the lawyer had won the *Wasson* appeal. The Caucus was persuaded that presenting such a constitutional amendment for popular vote would draw "the crazies" to the polls, which they thought would surely benefit the Republican Party. Some legislators were taken aback when they considered Scorsone's argument that future Legislatures might recriminalize consensual sodomy for everyone. (Scorsone represented Lexington in the legislature.) Behind closed doors, the Caucus voted to block and effectively kill the constitutional amendment. Scorsone believes that the vote would have come out differently if it had been public. In any event, the feared backlash never appeared; citizens were not quite as antihomosexual as the politicians believed. The crime against nature died a natural death.[21]

Wasson was also a sensation among gay rights lawyers. State judges almost never proclaim, as Leibson did, that a recent U.S. Supreme Court decision is simply *wrong*. *Wasson* suggested the utility of a new strategy for challenging sodomy laws in a period when legislatures and federal courts were unsympathetic. In 1987 the Michigan Organization for Human Rights (MOHR) filed suit in Wayne County Circuit Court to overturn Michigan's sodomy and gross indecency laws, as applied to private consensual activities. (Like the Georgia law, Michigan's carried a potential twenty-year prison sentence.) As the Kentucky lawyers had done, MOHR lawyers Helen Gallagher, David Piontkowski, and Paula Ettelbrick developed a detailed factual record at trial, demonstrating the harm of consensual sodomy laws, refuting the possible justifications (including public health and AIDS prevention), and arguing that such laws violated equality as well as privacy guarantees of the *state* constitution. The judge ruled the laws unconstitutional as applied to private consensual activities.[22]

In this wave of lawsuits, activists did not wait for men to be arrested for private consensual activities; instead, they sued for declaratory judgments that their laws violated state constitutional privacy and equality rights. In 1993 Linda Gryczan of the Women's Law Center in Helena filed a challenge to the Montana sodomy law, which made same-sex (but not different-sex) sodomy a felony. The following year Abby Rubenfeld filed a challenge to Tennessee's homosexual sodomy law, which had been created in 1989. (After serving as Lambda's legal director, Rubenfeld had returned to her home in Nashville.) Rubenfeld represented lesbian activist Penny Campbell and several John and Joan Does, who sued the governor for a decree declaring the sodomy law unenforceable. Less than a decade after *Bowers*, lesbian and gay rights attorneys and activists had sodomy laws on the defensive, or so it appeared.

Sodomy Reform and AIDS

Two weeks after *Bowers*, the Missouri Supreme Court upheld its same-sex sodomy law in *State v. Walsh* (1986). *Bowers* settled the privacy claim. As to the equal protection claim, the court agreed with the state that public health and AIDS prevention were a reasonable basis for criminalizing only homosexual sodomy. "[T]he General Assembly could reasonably have concluded that the general promiscuity characteristic of the homosexual lifestyle made [their deviate sexual intercourse] particularly deserving of regulation."[23]

Wasson's attorneys had refused to ignore AIDS at the hearing before Judge Paisley in the summer after *Bowers* and *Walsh*. Their last witness was Dr. Martin Raff, chief of the Section of Infectious Diseases at the University of Louisville. Although nearly three-quarters of the AIDS cases in the United States involved men who had sex with other men, AIDS was not, he insisted, a "homosexual disease." Worldwide, AIDS had mainly afflicted heterosexual populations; unprotected penile-vaginal intercourse remained the primary means of HIV transmission. The group with the lowest risk of infection is lesbians. Dr. Raff also testified that Kentucky's homosexual sodomy law had no rational relationship to anti-AIDS public health campaigns: HIV was not spread through oral sex, nor was it spread through condom-protected anal sex; HIV was spread through unprotected penile-vaginal as well as anal sex. Moreover, the sodomy law was actually an impediment to Kentucky's public health campaign. Doctors needed infected individuals to provide lists of their sexual partners, so they could be contacted and tested. Because they would be admitting to a crime under Kentucky law, men having sex with men were reluctant to come forward with this information. The only effective means of combating AIDS was public education, developed with the cooperation of gay communities.[24]

Without any evidence of its own, the commonwealth relied on AIDS prevention as a rational basis for the homosexual sodomy law. Amicus briefs filed by the American Public Health Association and by the American Psychological Association (and related groups) developed Dr. Raff's points in greater detail, and with reference to the medical consensus that existed, even more strongly, in 1990. Justice Leibson accepted this uncontroverted scientific consensus and added that AIDS prevention could not have been the goal of the legislature in 1974, years before anyone had heard of HIV and AIDS. In dissent, Justice Wintersheimer followed the commonwealth in concluding that public health was a rational basis for the state's criminalization of homosexual, and not heterosexual, sodomy. "[I]n the United States, AIDS is primarily a homosexual disease and 73 percent of all cases are among male homosexuals." Wintersheimer did not explain how AIDS could justify criminalization of sex between women.[25]

Following Scorsone's and Bratt's approach, Piontkowski and Ettelbrick in Michigan, Gryczan in Montana, and Rubenfeld in Tennessee developed detailed trial court records demonstrating that homosexual sodomy laws were not rationally related to AIDS prevention or other public health goals. The expert testimony in all these cases tracked that of Dr. Raff, for the facts about AIDS had changed little since 1986, with one exception: by 1992, new HIV infections in the United States were predominantly women infected by their male sexual partners and persons infected through intravenous drug use, not homosexuals. In the subsequent cases, counsel also developed the practical features of the public health argument in rich detail. Marybeth Frideres, from the Lewis and Clark County Health Department, testified in the Montana case that the homosexual sodomy law facilitated rather than slowed HIV infections by preventing clinics from providing safer-sex counseling to gay and bisexual men; by foreclosing realistic sex education campaigns, including those showing adolescents exactly how safer sex works; and by undermining the trust relationship between patients and health care providers. Among the organizations urging the repeal or nullification of the sodomy law were the American Public Health Association, the Montana Public Health Association, and the Montana Department of Health and Environmental Services.[26]

The trial judges in Michigan, Tennessee, and Montana accepted this evidence and ruled that their homosexual-only sodomy laws violated state constitutions. The Michigan attorney general did not appeal the Wayne County circuit judge's order. The state appealed and lost in the other two cases, *Campbell v. Sundquist* (1996) and *Gryczan v. State* (1997). Not a single judge in any of these states accepted public health or AIDS prevention as a basis for the state to make consensual (homosexual) sodomy a crime. These cases effectively ended the AIDS argument for sodomy laws. Following the leadership of Surgeon General C. Everett Koop, judges not only came to see AIDS as a public health problem to be addressed in practical ways, but came to regard gay men and lesbians as responsible sexual partners and caregivers, not sex maniacs.[27]

Homosexual Sodomy and Family

In a footnote he drafted but did not include in his *Bowers* concurrence, Justice Powell said, "[Homosexual] Sodomy is the antithesis of family." The ensuing decade would reveal many connections between sodomy and family. To begin with, homosexual sodomites were creating as well as raising children. The *Harvard Law Review* declared in 1989 that as many as "three million gay men and lesbians in the United States are parents, and between eight and ten million children are raised in gay or lesbian households." Although grossly exaggerated, such numbers dramatically informed Americans that lesbians and gay men not only raised children, but also made babies. Just as increasing numbers of straight couples were turning to new reproductive technologies, so were increasing numbers of gay people. The 1980s saw a lesbian baby boom, and the 1990s saw a smaller gayby boomlet among men. As Laura Benkov put it, lesbians and gay men were "reinventing the family."[28]

There was little the state could do to stop gays from having children, but it was sometimes called on to arbitrate custody disputes between parents when one came out and effectively ended the marriage. Southern and border states generally presumed *against* custody by the lesbian or gay parent, because of their presumed criminality. Ironically the antigay presumption came under heavier fire after *Bowers*. Some states abandoned the presumption, while others delinked it from sodomy laws. Rather than concluding that a lesbian parent should not have custody because she was a criminal, southern judges concluded that she was unfit because she was a "bad mother," or just a "bad person." But the evidence suggested otherwise: lesbians were usually capable parents, while their straight husbands were more often violent. By the 1990s even southern judges were increasingly willing to award custody to lesbian and gay parents. Outside the South, judges were not only fairer in custody hearings but were also willing to interpret state adoption statutes to allow gay persons to adopt the biological children of their same-sex partners. Such "second-parent adoptions" not only demonstrated that lesbians and gay men were raising children on their own, but that the law should recognize their family *units*—two parents, each with legal ties to the children they were raising together.[29]

Just as America was beginning to accept lesbian and gay parents, the issue of gay marriage hit the country, and hit it hard. Immediately after Denmark vested almost all the rights and duties of marriage in a new "registered partnership" institution for same-sex couples in 1989, gay and lesbian partners went to court in the District of Columbia and Hawaii to challenge their exclusion from civil marriage. In *Baehr v. Lewin* (1993) the Hawaii Supreme Court ruled that marriage law's exclusion of same-sex couples was a sex-based discrimination that could only be justified by a compelling state interest under the state ERA. Although the court remanded the case for proceedings allowing the state to advance justifications, *Baehr* unleashed a firestorm of debate about "homosexual marriage." Within three years seventeen states had adopted new statutes barring their judges from recognizing same-sex marriages in their jurisdictions. In 1996 Congress adopted the Defense of Marriage Act, which assured states they would not have to recognize out-of-state gay marriages and mandated that more than eleven hundred federal statutory and regulatory provisions using the terms "marriage" or "spouse" could never include same-sex couples married under state law.[30]

This public backlash had a surprising effect on the sodomy debate, as conservatives began to focus on homosexual marriage—and no longer private consensual sodomy—as the main threat to faith communities and traditional family values. Lest they seem simply prejudiced and reflexively antigay, some leading traditionalists openly suggested that sodomy laws could be dropped, so long as the polity prohibited same-sex marriage.[31]

In 1992 the District of Columbia Council considered a domestic partnership proposal that not only provided a registry, fringe benefits for city employees, and hospital visitation, but also spouse-like rights in cases where one's partner was incapacitated or died or was abusive. Although these few additional benefits would have cost the city almost nothing to implement, they raised immediate traditionalist opposition. Not only did the council fail to add the suggested benefits, but it changed the title of the bill to the "Health Care Benefits Extension Act." The bill was also expanded to include health care benefits for pairs of blood relatives, such as an elderly woman and her niece or nephew. After the council passed this desexualized law in 1992, Congress responded to complaints that the new law would "devalu[e] marriage" and "officially recognize and sanction homosexual unions" by prohibiting the District from funding the law.[32]

In 1993, on the heels of its humiliating treatment at the hands of Congress, the D.C. Council unanimously repealed its consensual sodomy law—the same law that the House had protected in its 1981 legislative veto (chapter 7). Not only was there no veto this time around, but there was not even a public effort to override the District. North Carolina senator Jesse Helms, a modern Comstock, drafted an override bill but was dissuaded from introducing it by Senators Robert Dole (the Senate GOP leader) and Alan Simpson (the GOP Senate Whip). Even conservative Republicans felt that consensual sodomy was no longer an issue they should be contesting, in part because their opposition to gays in the military, domestic partnership, and gay marriage was justified by the public stamp of approval those inclusions would connote for homosexuality. Especially in light of the bad odor surrounding *Bowers* and the rebuff suffered by Judge Bork, Republicans calculated that same-sex marriage was a much better wedge issue for them against a Democratic Party that had been rejuvenated by President William Clinton.

With Congress silent, the District's sodomy repeal took effect on July 1, 1994. On November 15, 1995, shortly after 10:00 p.m., Monica Lewinsky "performed oral sex" on the President of the United States in a room off the Oval Office. If this activity had occurred seventeen months earlier, it would have been a serious felony under District law. Lewinsky would have been astounded to know that, and even the wily president (yet another Yale Law School alumnus) would have been surprised. Unaware of their new freedom from felony prosecution, Clinton and Lewinsky repeated the crime against nature two days later and on at least seven subsequent occasions. In their penultimate sexual encounter, on February 28, 1997, the president gave the intern a special edition of Whitman's *Leaves of Grass*. Lewinsky described this as "the most sentimental gift he had given me." This was also the encounter that left presidential sperm on the intern's navy blue dress, evidence that ultimately compelled the president to confess his dalliance.[33]

The Supreme Court's Regime-Shifting Opinion in *Romer v. Evans* (1996)

In partnership with Don Knutson and Gerald McCrery, Matt Coles founded Gay Rights Advocates, the first gay rights law firm in San Francisco. He spent the 1980s working on gay rights and AIDS-related cases, projects that left him skeptical of the privacy right as the basis for overturning consensual sodomy laws. That right had no textual foundation in the Constitution, no discernible limits, and (in Coles's view) no conceptual core. In 1987, Coles joined the staff of the ACLU of Northern California and in 1995 succeeded William Rubenstein as the director of the ACLU's Lesbian and Gay Rights Project. During these first nine years with the ACLU, Coles played a central role in presenting the Supreme Court with an opportunity to invite lesbians, gay men, and bisexuals back into a Constitution that *Bowers* and *Dronenberg* seemed to say excluded them. In this effort, he received a huge boost from traditionalists and their lawyers in Colorado.[34]

Colorado's Amendment 2

While *Bowers* suggested that gay people should seek redress from the political rather than the judicial process, they found state political processes unresponsive in the South, because legislators feared that sodomy reform would tag them as friends of the "homosexual agenda" or even homosexual themselves. No southern or border-state legislature except West Virginia's had entirely decriminalized consensual sodomy. Five legislatures had decriminalized heterosexual sodomy but left homosexual sodomy a crime: Texas (1973), Kentucky (1974), Arkansas (1977), Missouri (1977), and Tennessee (1989). Courts invalidated heterosexual but not homosexual sodomy prosecutions in Maryland (1980) and Oklahoma (1986), without any reaction from their state legislatures. The politics of preservation was mighty powerful in the Baptist South.

Gay people did find the political process more amenable in urban areas, where they were concentrated. Between 1972 and 1992 they persuaded dozens of city and county councils to adopt ordinances prohibiting employers, public accommodations, and landlords from discriminating against employees, tenants, and patrons on the basis of their sexual orientation. Some of these antidiscrimination laws were revoked through popular referenda, such as the Save Our Children campaign in Dade County (1977). Between 1977 and 1993, local referenda revoking protections for gay people had a seventy-nine percent success rate, the highest for any significant category in American history.[35]

By the 1990s, however, municipal politics was comfortable enough with gay citizens that local referenda became practically unavailable as means by which traditionalists could overturn pro-gay legislation. Their next logical step, accordingly, was to attempt to overturn the ordinances through *state* referenda, in which gay-friendly urban voters could be swamped by traditionalist voters in the suburbs and rural areas. The first such successful campaign came in Colorado. Denver, its largest city and capital, is an economic center and transportation hub for the West; Boulder is a granola college town, home to the great University of Colorado (where Byron White had been an All-America football player). Aspen is a luxury resort; Colorado Springs is the headquarters for hundreds of religious organizations, including James Dobson's nationally influential Focus on the Family. This demography has yielded striking political contrasts. The 1992 election saw Colorado elect Ben Nighthorse Campbell (a moderate Democrat who later switched parties) to the Senate, narrowly cast its presidential votes for Democrat Bill Clinton while giving Independent Ross Perot almost a quarter of its votes, and amended the state constitution to limit gay rights.

Reflecting their sizable gay populations, Aspen (1977), Boulder (1987), and

Denver (1991) had adopted ordinances prohibiting sexual orientation discrimination in employment, public accommodations, and housing. In 1990 Governor Roy Romer had issued an executive order barring sexual orientation discrimination in state employment. Dobson and other religious leaders formed Colorado for Family Values (CFV) to override these directives. CFV drafted a state constitutional amendment, providing that no local or state governmental unit "shall enact, adopt or enforce any statute, regulation, ordinance or policy whereby homosexual, lesbian or bisexual orientation, conduct, practices or relationships shall constitute or otherwise be the basis of or entitle any person or class of persons to have or claim any minority status, quota preferences, protected status or claim of discrimination." The state certified this proposal as "Amendment 2" for the 1992 election.[36]

CFV's public campaign for Amendment 2 was a descendant of Anita Bryant's Save Our Children crusade, relying on the same panic-inducing stereotypes. According to CFV, gay men tended to be AIDS-infected; the average reported age of death for gay men was, allegedly, forty-two years old, and for lesbians forty-five years old. Before they died, these monsters molested children and were pushing educational materials that "try and convince children—maybe even your own—that they should consider homosexuality!" "To this angry, alienated minority, the family is the symbol of everything they attack." Finally, "special rights" for diseased and contagious homosexuals come at the cost of fundamental rights for normal people.[37]

Responding to this body politics, Colorado voters supported Amendment 2 by a 53.4 to 46.6 percent margin. As expected, Colorado Springs, the suburbs, and rural areas outvoted the more gay-friendly cities. This was exactly what Coles had been waiting for: an overreaching antigay measure. Amendment 2 was an unusually broad revocation of civil rights, for not only did it preempt local antidiscrimination laws, but it seemed to deny gay people "equal protection of the law" across the board. Say a bigoted official refused to issue driver's licenses to homosexual applicants. If homosexuals complained to an administrative supervisor or even a judge, Amendment 2 seemed to deny such officials authority to police discriminatory treatment, because the state "agency" (the bureau of motor vehicles) or "department" (the judiciary) would then be "enforc[ing]" a "policy whereby homosexual . . . orientation . . . shall . . . be the basis of . . . any . . . claim of discrimination." If a homophobic county decided to exclude homosexuals from juries, to deny them the right to vote, and to instruct police and fire departments not to provide them any assistance, the plain language of Amendment 2 precluded those homosexuals from seeking relief from Colorado courts. The country had seen nothing this broadly exclusionary since the slavery era.

Before Amendment 2 could take effect, the ACLU and local rights groups challenged it as a violation of the Equal Protection Clause. Because the measure was so unusual, it invited a number of different lines of attack. At various points in the litigation, ACLU lawyers (Rubenstein, Coles, and Harlow), the representative from Lambda (Suzanne Goldberg), and the local activists sharply disagreed with one another as to the best argument. One strategy was to insist that sexual orientation was a *suspect classification* for the state to use, and therefore Amendment 2 should be subject to strict scrutiny, requiring that the state show a compelling justification that could be met only by discriminating against gay people. Race was the model for suspect classifications, and all the lawyers agreed that sexual orientation was like race in being a trait that was irrelevant to a person's ability to contribute to society, yet had been the basis for pervasive discrimination in American history because of prejudice and stereotyping. Over the opposition of the outside attorneys, local activists later in the case presented evidence that sexual orientation was also like race in that it was immutable, the product of biological factors beyond anyone's control.[38]

At the beginning of the case, however, the local and national activists were in substantial agreement for an alternative approach: that Amendment 2 denied lesbians and gay men a "fundamental right to participate in the political process." In 1993 the Colorado Supreme Court accepted this argument, regarding democracy as an essential element of the Constitution. From this premise Chief Justice Luis Rovira deduced the further principle that "laws may not create unequal burdens on identifiable groups with respect to the right to participate in the political process absent a compelling state interest." Because Amendment 2 denied gay people a *fundamental right* of political participation, its discrimination against them required strict scrutiny and thus could only be sustained by compelling state interests. The court affirmed the trial judge's grant of a preliminary injunction postponing the effective date of Amendment 2 and remanded the case for trial to determine whether the state could justify Amendment 2's restrictions on the political process.[39]

On remand, the state trial judge heard evidence pertaining to community-based justifications for Amendment 2. The state's main argument was that tolerant Coloradans had decriminalized homosexuality but wanted a way to signal that homosexuality was morally inferior to heterosexuality. Their star witness was Oxford professor John Finnis, whose affidavit testified that the canonical thinkers of the Western tradition—from Plato to Thomas Aquinas—agreed that homosexual behaviors were morally defective because they could not allow partners to join in a human good, namely, procreation within marriage. Hence a state like Colorado that no longer criminalized homosexual sodomy for pragmatic reasons ought to be able to signal the moral inferiority of homosexuality to its citizens. The philosopher Martha Nussbaum disputed Finnis's general account, as well as his interpretation of Plato and other classical thinkers.[40]

The state also argued that "gay rights" did not deserve the same public investment as "civil rights" for racial minorities and for women. Unlike race and sex, homosexuality was a chosen "lifestyle" rather than an immutable trait, and homosexuals were economically more advantaged than most ordinary citizens. Not only did homosexuality not meet the traditional criteria for a protected classification, but adding this new category would "dilute" existing protections and undermine or dilute the respect most Coloradans accorded civil rights laws. Moreover, Colorado maintained that Amendment 2 protected the constitutional rights of free association held by traditionalists and religious minorities. The state believed that the Aspen and Boulder ordinances required religious landlords to share their houses with homosexual tenants and churches to hire homosexual clergy. Such ordinances "also affect familial privacy and the ability of parents to convey values to their children," because they would require school districts to hire homosexual teachers and staff. Finally, the state argued that Amendment 2 provided a useful statewide rule and deterred factionalism on the "deeply divisive issue of homosexuality," which threatened to "seriously fragment Colorado's body politic."[41]

The trial judge did not dispute the legitimacy of the state's interests but found Amendment 2 too loosely associated with them to justify the invasion of fundamental rights the Colorado Supreme Court had announced. (Few laws can meet the exacting requirements of strict scrutiny.) The Colorado Supreme Court affirmed the injunction barring the state from enforcing Amendment 2. Governor Romer, a moderate Democrat, vowed to appeal this result to the U.S. Supreme Court, and Attorney General Gale Norton, a conservative Republican, did so.[42]

Amendment 2 at the U.S. Supreme Court

Colorado brought in two of the nation's greatest appellate litigators to handle its petition for the Court to review the injunction—former U.S. solicitor general Rex Lee and his associate Carter Phillips, of Provo, Utah. In their excellent petition, they argued that the ACLU's theory was too broad. It is an axiom of constitutional law that state governments can remove entire topics from local governmental regulation. Thus, if the state electorate decides to make Colorado a "dry" state, where liquor cannot be sold, they can prevent "wet" majorities in Denver from enacting their preferences. While there were a few cases where the Supreme Court overturned referenda that blocked state efforts to remedy race-based discrimination, the Court had routinely upheld referenda taking other matters off the legislative agendas. In *James v. Valtierra* (1971), for example, voters amended the California Constitution to provide that a state public body could not develop low-rent housing projects without voter approval. Although the new rule had a disparate effect on racial minorities, the Court rejected the equal protection challenge under its ordinary rational-basis standard. Lee and Phillips argued that Amendment 2 was supported by much weightier community interests and actually advanced the civil rights of racial minorities.[43]

The state's dynamite petition was submitted to a Supreme Court that had been substantially reconstituted since *Bowers*. There were six new justices: Antonin Scalia, a brilliant and operatically aggressive conservative who replaced Rehnquist as associate justice when President Reagan promoted Rehnquist to chief justice in 1986; Anthony Kennedy, a friend of the Reagans' from Sacramento, named to the Court in 1988 after the Bork debacle; David Souter, a protégé of New Hampshire senator Warren Rudman, who replaced Justice Brennan in 1990; Clarence Thomas, a protégé of Missouri senator John Danforth, who replaced Justice Marshall in 1991; Ruth Bader Ginsburg, the pioneer litigator for women's rights whom President Clinton promoted to the Court when Justice White retired in 1993; and Stephen Breyer, Clinton's nominee to replace Justice Blackmun in 1994. The only holdovers from the *Bowers* Court were Rehnquist, Stevens, and O'Connor. Compared with the *Bowers* Court, the *Romer* Court was younger, more conservative, more Republican, and far more demographically diverse—a veritable rainbow coalition including two women, three Roman Catholics, two Jews, an Italian, an African American, a bachelor, and a Scandinavian.

On February 21, 1995, the Court announced it was taking review in *Romer v. Evans*. The challengers recognized that the grant meant trouble for their theory; the Court usually reverses the cases it hears. The ACLU attorneys were fairly confident that the Court was not ready to declare that sexual orientation was a suspect classification, but their brief on the merits emphasized another argument to supplement the political participation argument: Amendment 2 violated the Equal Protection Clause because it reflected "antipathy" to gay people. Direct evidence of antipathy included CFV's own ballot materials, which invoked false stereotypes of homosexuals as predatory and promiscuous and which thereby appealed to antigay prejudice. Less directly, Amendment 2's broad denial of gay people's rights was so unconnected with its alleged purposes that the justices should presume that its actual goal was antigay prejudice. The state's main asserted goal was conservation of scarce civil rights resources. CFV could have achieved this goal by simply preempting sexual orientation antidiscrimination laws, but their Amendment 2 seemed to sweep away ordinary legal protections for gay people as well. Amendment 2 also fell short of the goal. As the American

Bar Association argued in its first amicus brief in a gay rights case, "laws or policies that prohibit discrimination on the basis of sexual orientation would not be affected by Amendment 2 to the extent they confer protection on *heterosexuals.*" Thus, straight white men—the most advantaged group in Colorado—would retain "special rights" unaffected by Amendment 2. This suggested that Amendment 2's real agenda was to set gay people apart as a pariah class of citizens, a goal in conflict with the Fourteenth Amendment's purposes. A "scholars' brief" filed by Professor Tribe made a broader argument: by denying gay people access to state processes to challenge antigay discrimination and violence, Amendment 2 was a core violation of the Fourteenth Amendment's requirement that states not deny any group of persons the "equal *protection* of the law."[44]

At oral argument on October 10, 1995, Tribe's brief inspired the first question put to Colorado solicitor general Tim Tymkovich. In a querulous tone, Justice Kennedy wondered, "Here the classification seems to be adopted for its own sake," apparently to fence out a minority for all purposes. "I've never seen a case like this." Was there precedent for something this broad? Tymkovich responded with *Valtierra*, which Kennedy dismissed as only involving issues of low-income housing. Justice Ginsburg pressed Kennedy's point: there were many state policies low-income persons and their supporters could turn to to improve their situation; the *Valtierra* initiative took only one of them away from the local political process. Amendment 2, in contrast, barred gay people from petitioning local governments for *any* kind of measure that would improve their position.[45]

In her firm, gravelly voice, Justice O'Connor wondered aloud how far Amendment 2 actually reached. "[T]he literal language would indicate that, for example, a public library could refuse to allow books to be borrowed by homosexuals and there would be no relief from that, apparently." Other justices added their own examples. From Ginsburg: the early women's suffragists were able to obtain the right to vote in municipalities before they won it on the state or national level. "I take it from what you are arguing that if there had been a referendum that said no local ordinance can give women the vote, that would have been constitutional." From Stevens: "Would a homosexual have a right to be served in a restaurant?" Could there be redress for job discrimination or sexual harassment against gay employees? From Breyer: "So if a police department says there's been a lot of gay-bashing, it's our policy to stop it." If public officials or private citizens denied gay people library privileges, interfered with their right to vote, refused to serve them in restaurants or hire them, and even looked the other way when gays were assaulted, local governments apparently could not adopt policies protecting homosexuals from discrimination aimed at them because of their sexual orientation. Under the regime of Amendment 2, was there anything local officials could do to remedy antigay persecution?[46]

Tymkovich was overwhelmed by the hypotheticals, suggesting one answer, then retreating when the questioning justice pressed him into contradictions. Justice Scalia threw him a life raft by asking: Your argument is that laws of general application will still protect homosexuals, correct? All that Amendment 2 preempts are "special protection" by reason of homosexual status, right? So the library and the police could not breach their general obligations and carve out an excluded category of homosexuals. Tymkovich meekly agreed with Scalia's lucid exposition, but Breyer pointed out that Scalia was in fact rewriting Amendment 2, whose plain meaning would prevent a Colorado state court or police department from "enforc[ing]" a constitutional or administrative "policy whereby homosexual, lesbian or bisexual orientation" was "the basis of" a "claim of discrimination." Scalia responded to Breyer that routine enforcement of general library and police practices would not allow discrimination "against" homosexuals; the intent of Amendment 2 was, obviously, to prevent discriminations giving homosexuals "special" treatment other citizens did not receive.[47]

By the end, Tymkovich was irrelevant to the debate among the justices; a majority seemed to think that Amendment 2 left gay people in legal limbo. But the challengers' attorney, former Colorado Supreme Court justice Jean Dubofsky, ran into the same quandary: it was not clear how broadly Amendment 2 would be applied by the Colorado courts. Perhaps they would adopt a narrower interpretation or create exceptions to the broad language. Scalia posed another question: Was Dubofsky asking the Court to overrule *Bowers*? When she replied that no, she was not, Scalia pounced. Because Colorado could make homosexual conduct criminal, "[w]hy can't a state not take a step short of that and say, we're not going to make it criminal, but on the other hand, we certainly don't want to encourage it," as Amendment 2 did? This was the argument first made in *Dronenberg v. Zech* (1984), Judge Bork's opinion that Scalia had joined when he was a judge on the D.C. Circuit. Like Tymkovich, Dubofsky had no answer to the tough questions. The bench was hot that day, the lawyers cold.[48]

Because oral argument was dominated by confusion about the ambit of Amendment 2, there had been virtually no discussion of precisely what its shortcomings were as a matter of constitutional doctrine. None of the justices seemed persuaded by the Colorado courts, imposing strict scrutiny because Amendment 2 denied gay people a fundamental right to participate in the democratic processes. Kennedy was impressed by Tribe's argument that Amendment 2 denied a minority an unprecedented level of state protections, but he and his colleagues could not easily rest their judgment on such an argument when the scope of Amendment 2 remained unresolved. The Supreme Court has no authority to interpret state statutes and constitutions and considers itself bound by state supreme court interpretations. The Colorado Supreme Court had construed

Amendment 2 to do more than preempt local antidiscrimination laws but had said nothing determinative beyond that.

Romer was a case where conversations among the justices played a decisive role in the outcome. Rehnquist and Scalia, both charming, militant conservatives, had dominated the Court between 1986 and 1994, lobbying their colleagues to press constitutional doctrine toward Federalist Society values. After his appointment in 1994, Stephen Breyer changed the balance of the Court's internal discussions. Unlike the other centrists (Stevens, Ginsburg, Souter), Breyer was gregarious, schmoozing up his colleagues. O'Connor, especially, found in him a kindred spirit, because he was practical, with an uncanny ability to explain how institutions and processes *worked,* and how institutional operations played out with the legal arguments of a case. In *Romer* Breyer encouraged the other justices to focus on how Amendment 2 would seem to function in everyday governance. Once they started applying its broad language to hate crimes, discriminatory library lending, employment discrimination, and refusals to serve, the equality story developed by the challengers became more vivid and persuasive. It was apparent from the oral argument that Stevens, Kennedy, Souter, and Ginsburg were with him.[49]

At conference after argument, O'Connor cast her vote against Amendment 2. Having once served as majority leader in the Arizona Senate, she was the most politically sophisticated among the justices. Consistent with her vote in *Bowers,* she believed state legislatures had wide discretion to adopt morals-based laws, but Colorado's Amendment 2 presented a different case, as Justice Breyer helped persuade her. First, Georgia's sodomy law applied generally, to all its citizens, while Amendment 2 trained on an unpopular minority. As Scalia had once said, the Equal Protection Clause "requires the democratic majority to accept for themselves and their loved ones what they impose on you and me." Second, the Georgia law had been enacted, and revised, by the legislature after deliberation and input from experts—while the Colorado initiative had been voted directly by the people, after a campaign filled with open invocation of stereotypes and appeals to antigay prejudice. Third, Amendment 2 was simply too broad, however interpreted. It fenced off homosexuals from the rest of the population and denied them the ordinary process for seeking state remediation for an undetermined amount of antigay discrimination and violence. This, O'Connor concluded, was no longer politically acceptable in our pluralist democracy.[50]

Justice Stevens, the senior justice in the majority, assigned the opinion to Justice Kennedy. It was fitting that a Roman Catholic Republican appointed by President Reagan (and the man who got Judge Bork's seat) would write and announce the opinion for the Court. What was not known, outside the Washington Beltway, was that Kennedy had initially been blocked for the Bork seat by some of President Reagan's advisors, who felt he was pro-homosexual. As a lower-court judge, Kennedy had hired gay law clerks, one of whom had helped him draft an opinion upholding the armed services' exclusion of lesbian and gay soldiers but questioning the legitimacy of laws denying rights to gay civilians. The original replacement for Bork had been Judge Douglas Ginsburg, whose nomination sank under charges of illegal drug use. It was only after Ginsburg's nomination went up in smoke that Kennedy got the job.[51]

The Supreme Court's Decision in Romer v. Evans

Anthony Kennedy regards himself as the Court's political philosopher, and his approach to *Romer* was to outline a bold philosophical counterpoint to *Bowers*. The first line of Kennedy's opinion was a big bang: "One century ago, the first Justice Harlan"—in his famous dissent from the apartheid-sanctioning opinion in *Plessy v. Ferguson* (1896)—"admonished this Court that the Constitution 'neither knows nor tolerates classes among citizens.'" (*Romer* was announced on May 20, 1996, almost exactly one hundred years to the day after *Plessy*, which had been announced May 21, 1896.) Rejecting the Colorado notion that antidiscrimination laws give homosexuals, and only homosexuals, "special rights," Kennedy observed that "[t]hese are protections taken for granted by most people either because they already have them or do not need them; these are protections against exclusion from an almost limitless number of transactions and endeavors that constitute ordinary civic life in a free society." Moreover, "[i]t is a fair, if not necessary, inference from the broad language of the amendment that it deprives gays and lesbians even of the protection of general laws and policies that prohibit arbitrary discrimination in governmental and private settings," Kennedy concluded. "At some point in the systematic administration of these laws, an official must determine whether homosexuality is an arbitrary and, thus, forbidden basis for decision. Yet a decision to that effect would itself amount to a policy prohibiting discrimination on the basis of homosexuality, and so would appear to be no more valid under Amendment 2 than the specific prohibitions against discrimination the state court held invalid."[52]

This discussion established that Amendment 2 was both unprecedented and inconsistent with the core purpose of the Equal Protection Clause—namely, that no social group can be excluded from the "protection of the law." At this point, Kennedy had several doctrinal options. Like Tribe, he could have announced that it was a per se violation of the Equal Protection Clause; like the Colorado Supreme Court, he could have announced that it infringed a fundamental right and so triggered strict scrutiny; or he could even have applied some kind of heightened scrutiny because sexual orientation was a questionable classification.

Kennedy chose none of these options and, instead, followed the approach the ACLU and the ABA had argued: Amendment 2 was invalid because "its sheer breadth is so discontinuous with the reasons offered for it that the amendment seems inexplicable by anything but animus toward the class that it affects." This was, ultimately, a "status-based" law aimed at a class of citizens. Such laws violated the equal protection command that "'a bare . . . desire to harm a politically unpopular group cannot constitute a *legitimate* government interest.'"[53]

Six justices joined Kennedy's opinion, including three conservative Republicans. Three Republicans joined Scalia's dissenting opinion, whose rhetoric shocked the Supreme Court's staff and even some of Scalia's former law clerks. "The Court has mistaken a Kulturkampf for a fit of spite. The constitutional amendment before us here is not the manifestation of a 'bare . . . desire to harm' homosexuals, but is rather a modest attempt by seemingly tolerant Coloradans to preserve traditional sexual mores against the efforts of a politically powerful minority to revise those mores through use of the laws." The original *Kulturkampf* was Chancellor Bismarck's campaign to domesticate the Roman Catholic Church in Germany; it might generally connote a state-sponsored campaign to force a minority into conformity (chapter 3). This is far from tolerance, a fact brought to the attention of the Scalia chambers when it circulated the draft dissent. But the clerks said their boss was happy to stick with this unfortunate terminology. Indeed, Scalia identified the relevant precedent for Amendment 2: the anti-Mormon Kulturkampf the United States conducted in the late nineteenth century. To destroy the idea of polygamy, Congress not only made it illegal, but disenfranchised Mormon advocates of polygamy, excluded them from voting and serving on juries, and confiscated the property of the Church of Jesus Christ of Latter-day Saints. When Scalia emphasized that the Court upheld every one of these aggressive state actions, Kennedy responded that those decisions were wrong: both the Religion Clauses and the Equal Protection Clause were dead set against religion-based Kulturkampfs.[54]

Scalia also pressed the point he raised at oral argument: *Bowers* supplied the rational basis needed to sustain Amendment 2. "If it is constitutionally permissible for a State to make homosexual conduct criminal, surely it is constitutionally permissible for a State to enact other laws merely *disfavoring* homosexual conduct," or, put more provocatively, laws "merely prohibiting all levels of state government from bestowing *special protections* upon homosexual conduct." Kennedy had an obvious answer to this charge, that the Court was striking down Amendment 2 because it was overbroad and undifferentiated—but his opinion said nothing in response, thereby stranding *Bowers* in constitutional limbo. The Court's silence as to *Bowers* could not have been unintentional, and it gave gay rights lawyers hope that the reconstituted Court would be willing to reconsider *Bowers* if an appropriate case could be found.[55]

Post-*Romer* Sodomy Challenges, 1996–2002

Romer was that rare Supreme Court decision that successfully anticipated changes in public opinion before they were clear to other officials. Americans were coming to accept the fact that lesbians, gay men, bisexuals, and transgendered people had become a thriving group in America's pluralist landscape. If any doubt remained, the 2000 Census confirmed the existence of almost 600,000 Americans cohabiting with someone of the same sex; a disproportionate number of these were couples of color or different-race couples. One-third of the female couples, and one-fifth of the male couples, were raising children together.[56]

In the wake of *Romer*, therefore, it made sense for Lambda legal director Beatrice Dohrn (1993–2000) to focus the organization's attention on constitutional sodomy law challenges, even more than her predecessor, Paula Ettelbrick (1988–93), had done. A self-effacing former legal aid counsel, Dohrn nicely complemented the ACLU's gregarious Coles. Dohrn and Coles agreed to continue the state-by-state attack on sodomy laws, with the hope that success at the state level would motivate the U.S. Supreme Court to revisit *Bowers*. With limited resources, however, Lambda and the ACLU had to cooperate, so in May 1997 Dohrn and Coles divvied up the sodomy map. After victories in Tennessee and Montana, twenty-one states still criminalized consensual sodomy. In light of *Romer*, the six states that made only same-sex sodomy a crime seemed ripe for challenge. Lambda would take the lead in challenges to the Arkansas, Missouri, and Texas laws; the ACLU would take the lead in Kansas, Maryland, Oklahoma, and Puerto Rico (whose bizarre law banned anal and oral sex for all persons, and *any* homosexual activity or contact). The ACLU would challenge the all-sodomy Minnesota law, while Lambda would tackle Georgia's law. For each state, the non-lead organization would support the leader with amicus briefs and the like. The Rhode Island and Massachusetts sodomy laws would be left in the capable hands of Mary Bonauto, the chief litigator for Boston's Gay and Lesbian Advocates and Defenders (GLAD). Figure 9.2 reflects the division of responsibility reached by Coles and Dohrn.[57]

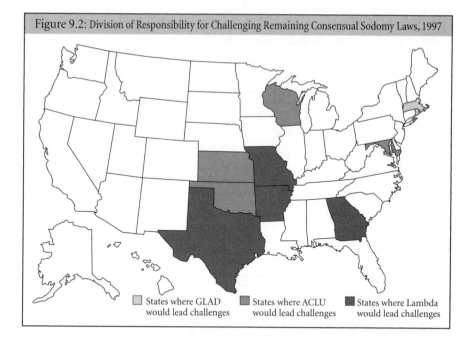

Figure 9.2: Division of Responsibility for Challenging Remaining Consensual Sodomy Laws, 1997

States where GLAD would lead challenges   States where ACLU would lead challenges   States where Lambda would lead challenges

Lambda Revisits the Georgia Sodomy Law, 1998

Lambda drew first blood, with the most unlikely challenger, Anthony San Juan Powell of Norcross, Georgia. Powell was a twenty-nine-year-old married man working for United Parcel Service. His wife's niece, seventeen-year-old Quashana Roland, came to stay with the Powells to help her aunt Gloria during the late stages of her pregnancy, and slept on the sofa in the Powells' living room. In the early morning of September 2, 1996, Anthony Powell joined Roland on the couch and began caressing her feet, then her thighs. When Powell pulled down her panties and began touching her vaginal area, Roland began to cry and placed her hands over her face. Powell performed oral sex on her, then penile-vaginal sex, and finally oral sex again, and then cleaned Roland's body with a paper towel. As she lay weeping on the couch, he apologized. Roland's mother reported the matter to the police, who arrested Powell. At his rape trial, Powell admitted that he had performed oral sex on Roland but claimed that he thought it was consensual, because she never said "no" and did not scream for help. The jury acquitted Powell of the rape charges but convicted him of consensual sodomy.[58]

There was nothing unusual in a prosecutor's using a state sodomy law to procure a conviction in a sexual assault case. In the decade after *Bowers*, there were almost nine hundred reported sodomy decisions, eighty-six percent of which involved different sexes, usually where the state charged a man with assaulting an adult or minor woman. In jurisdictions with general sodomy laws, some of the male-female rape cases included charges of consensual sodomy. As in *Powell*, juries would sometimes acquit the defendant of rape (because of conflicting testimony) but convict him of consensual sodomy. Like many other defendants, Anthony Powell was astounded to learn that consensual oral sex was a crime in Georgia, and that his "confession" ensured conviction of a serious felony.[59]

On appeal, Powell's public defender, Brenda Bernstein, argued that the judge should not have added the consensual sodomy count, for it violated the Georgia Constitution's right to privacy. Supporting Bernstein was Stephen Scarborough, a gay man in Yale's famous class of 1990 who had opened Lambda's southern regional office and helped found the Stonewall Bar Association of lesbian and gay lawyers in Atlanta. Lambda's amicus brief rehearsed the history of the privacy right under the Georgia Constitution. In *Pavesich v. New England Life Insurance Co.* (1905), the Georgia Supreme Court had ruled that its constitution's protection of "liberty" included "the right to live as one will, so long as that will not interfere with the rights of another or of the public." Georgia courts had applied the *Pavesich* right to prevent the state from imposing unwanted medical care on its citizens or forcing prisoners to end a hunger strike. Scarborough and Bernstein argued that consensual sex within the home fell within the core of *Pavesich*'s privacy right and thereby required a compelling state interest to justify its regulation. Under the Georgia precedents, the "anti-homosexual sentiment" mentioned in *Bowers* was insufficient.[60]

Represented by Michael Hobbs, as in *Bowers*, the state responded that *Bowers*'s historical discussion refuted the notion that sodomy fell within the state's traditions of privacy. The court had never applied *Pavesich* to intimate sexual activities, and Powell's case was not a promising factual setting for such an application. Yet the Georgia Supreme Court, with only one dissenting justice, struck down the state's consensual sodomy law in *Powell v. State* (1998). Chief Justice Robert Benham noted that state appellate courts in Montana, Tennessee, and Kentucky had interpreted their state constitutional privacy rights more broadly than *Bowers* had interpreted the federal right. Ritually announcing that the justices in no way meant to "condone" consensual sodomy, Benham nonetheless reasoned that consensual sodomy laws were inconsistent with the core principle of *Pavesich*. "Adults who 'withdraw from the public gaze' to engage in private, unforced sexual behavior are exercising a right 'embraced within the right of personal liberty.'" Two years later, a unanimous court interpreted the state law criminalizing sodomy solicitation to exempt solicitation to engage in private consensual activities (similar to *Wasson*).[61]

The days of the Georgia Supreme Court's being a bastion of apartheid were clearly gone. By 1998 the court was both pragmatic and relatively diverse, with

two African-American and two female justices. (The biggest groups *un*represented on the court were the Republican Party and the Roman Catholic Church.)
The last thing Atlanta wanted was a reputation as a center of homophobia. Reflecting the live-and-let-live philosophy of former Fulton County district attorney Lewis Slaton and Police Commissioner George Napper (unenthusiastic
defendants in *Bowers*), the court was not only willing to take the state out of
people's bedrooms, but was also *un*willing to leave the state in gay people's bedrooms, as the Oklahoma courts had done in a similar case immediately after
Bowers.[62]

Ironically, Michael Bowers played a role in *Powell*. In 1990 the attorney general had offered employment to Robin Shahar, a top alumna of Emory University's excellent law school. The following year Bowers revoked the offer when he
learned that she planned to marry another woman, a fact Shahar had disclosed
in her initial application. Shahar sued Bowers for unlawful discrimination but
lost before the Court of Appeals for the Eleventh Circuit in 1997. The judges accepted Bowers's representation that his office, dedicated to the enforcement of
Georgia's laws, could not employ a person who was violating one of those laws.
Later that year the *New York Times* reported that Bowers himself had been engaged in an adulterous affair during the period he was blackballing Shahar. Adultery is also a crime in Georgia; unlike sodomy, adultery is also condemned in the
Ten Commandments (it's number seven). The national publicity generated by
the Shahar case and Bowers's confession was humiliating for the state. *Powell*
was Atlanta's response, announcing to the world that Georgia's legal regime reflected sophisticated thinking, more advanced than that of its U.S. Supreme
Court superiors.[63]

The Roman Catholic Church Acquiesces: Sodomy Reform, 1998–2002

By 1998 thirty-four states had used the Model Penal Code as the basis for comprehensive criminal code reform. Two states that had not done so were Rhode
Island and Massachusetts—Roman Catholic in their faith and gay-friendly in
their politics. In 1989 Massachusetts became the first state to enact a comprehensive law barring discrimination based on sexual orientation by employers, public
accommodations, education, and housing. For fifteen years the church had held
up the antidiscrimination statute, on the ground that it would be viewed "by
many people as a step toward the legal approval of the homosexual lifestyle." Its
opposition softened in the late 1980s, in large part because lay attitudes had become more tolerant, but perhaps also because Pope John Paul II had made it
clear in 1986 that church condemnation of sodomy did not entail discrimination
against homosexuals. Some Catholic legislators found refuge in this distinction,

and they provided the margin of enactment in 1989.[64] Following doctrine, the church acquiesced in Rhode Island's equally comprehensive antidiscrimination law, enacted six years later. Although pro-life witnesses testified against the bill, it passed by large majorities and was signed by Republican governor Lincoln Almond.[65]

In both Massachusetts and Rhode Island, the reluctance of Catholic legislators made sodomy repeal more difficult than enactment of the comprehensive antidiscrimination law had been. Senator John Roney, the Providence Democrat who sponsored the antidiscrimination law, had also sponsored a sodomy-repeal bill every year since he came to the Senate, in 1993. Buoyed by the ho-hum reaction to that law, Roney persuaded the Democratic leadership to press for sodomy repeal in 1998. The police never enforced the law against purely consensual activities, and if they had done so they could have ensnared the entire Rhode Island legislature, warned Roney. Providence judge (now Rhode Island chief justice) Frank Williams declared the application of the law to consensual sodomy to be an equal protection violation, a move that put more pressure on the legislature. Gay rights activists proved once again to be an effective lobbying group, and the Church was surprisingly silent, perhaps because of publicity that Boston bishop Bernard Law (and others) had covered up sexual misconduct on the part of priests. Nonetheless, many Catholic legislators—including Senator Teresa Paiva-weed, the respected chair of the Judiciary Committee—voted against the bill, and Governor Almond declined to sign it. But neither did he veto it, and in June 1998 Rhode Island became the thirtieth state to decriminalize consensual sodomy.[66]

In Massachusetts GLAD's Mary Bonauto sought judicial abrogation of the crime-against-nature statute. The state conceded that the statute should not be interpreted to cover private activities between consenting adults. In *GLAD v. Attorney General* (2002), the court accepted the state's narrowing construction and thereby added Massachusetts to the sodomy-free states. Four years earlier, the Missouri Court of Appeals similarly acquiesced in the state's agreement that its homosexual conduct law, upheld against federal constitutional challenge in *Walsh*, properly applied only to public or nonconsensual activities. Because it arose in the context of a specific male-on-female prosecution and did not reach the state's highest court, the Missouri ruling did not cover the entire state.[67]

The ACLU's Matt Coles made certain that other judgments would be statewide. Maryland was a key target. Unlike the northeastern laws, Maryland's sodomy statute had been interpreted in a discriminatory manner, to regulate only homosexual sodomy when between consenting adults. After *Romer*, this was probably not a sustainable discrimination outside the South. Coles and Maryland ACLU attorneys represented Takoma Park mayor Bruce Williams and his life partner, the anthropologist Geoffrey Burkhart, in a class-action lawsuit against

Maryland governor Parris Glendening, whose beloved brother was a gay man. In October 1998, eight months after the lawsuit was filed, the Baltimore City Circuit Court ruled that Maryland's sodomy and unnatural practices laws could not constitutionally be applied to consensual homosexual sodomy. The ACLU and the Maryland attorney general stipulated that the class action benefiting from the judgment included all citizens of Maryland, not just those in Baltimore. A similar trial court judgment the ACLU procured in 2001 against Governor Jesse "The Body" Ventura ensured that the Minnesota sodomy law could not be applied to consensual activities anywhere in that state. Also in 2001, Arizona's legislature repealed its consensual sodomy law, with neither fanfare nor celebration.[68]

The fact that states as diverse as Catholic Rhode Island, Baptist Missouri, and Republican Arizona could agree on sodomy reform was strong evidence that Americans of many religious faiths had concluded that homosexuals should not be regarded as presumptive criminals. Once popular opinion had decisively changed, it had a snowball effect: while in 1981 pro-gay legislators and judges feared the "promoter of homosexuality" label, by 2001 antigay legislators and judges thought twice about resisting sodomy reform because they feared the "homophobia" label.

The Arkansas Sodomy Case

The post-*Bowers* gay legal activism reached even as far as Little Rock and Fayetteville, Arkansas. With no booming metropolis attracting lesbian and gay professionals and their families, Baptist Arkansas remained resolutely traditionalist. Yet there were many Arkansans—including Governor Bill Clinton (1979–81, 1983–93)—who counted gay people as friends and who believed that the South itself would profit from putting antigay violence and discrimination in the same historical trash can into which it had deposited apartheid. In 1991, 1993, and 1995, state senator Vic Snyder introduced bills to repeal the 1977 law making homosexual sodomy a misdemeanor. They died in committee, because legislators felt they would dig their political graves if they supported sodomy reform. Baptist ministers were watching them like hawks.[69]

Lesbian and gay Arkansans finally began to speak out for themselves. One of their leaders was Suzanne Pharr, a longtime counselor for rape and domestic violence victims. As a feminist theorist, Pharr had written the first book arguing that antihomosexual laws and policies were sex discrimination. She was also a founder of the Women's Project, which reported antigay as well as racist and misogynist violence and discrimination in Arkansas. In 1992 the Arkansas Advisory Committee to the U.S. Civil Rights Commission reported Pharr's testimony that lesbian and gay citizens were not only victims of discrimination and violence in Arkansas, but were brutalized by the very police who were charged with protecting the citizenry. "During a training session, [police] recruits described homosexuals as an abomination of God, that they do not want to deal with homosexuals for fear of getting AIDS, and that gay men and lesbians are attacked because 'Even chickens attack and kill deviants among themselves.'"[70]

As gay people and their supporters inched out of their closets, antihomosexual rhetoric and violence in the state escalated. In November 1992 the Arkansas State Baptist Convention adopted a resolution condemning "homosexual behavior as unnatural, perverted and destructive." Letters in Arkansas newspapers celebrated AIDS as a "purifier of the human race. It seems to eliminate the trash and dead wood from society: the sexually promiscuous, the drug addict, and the homosexual." Although they did not enforce the homosexual sodomy law against sex within the home, Little Rock police did harass men they thought to be gay if they lingered suspiciously in public parks. Every year the Women's Project published a *Women's Watchcare Network Log*, which reported antigay violence, discrimination, and rhetoric during the preceding year.[71]

In 1997 Lambda's Ruth Harlow and Beatrice Dohrn decided to make Arkansas their first test case. Its sodomy law was discriminatory and therefore vulnerable under *Romer*, and the state constitutional jurisprudence was promising. In autumn 1997 Lambda sent staff attorney Suzanne Goldberg to Arkansas (later joined by Susan Sommer, another Lambda attorney). An effective community organizer, Goldberg touched base with the Women's Project and set up a table at a community bakery in Little Rock to offer interested citizens opportunities to participate in the case. Some of them asked, "Are you just interested in 'model' plaintiffs—the feminine lesbians and the preppy white gay men?" Goldberg responded, "Absolutely not! We want people of all shapes, sizes, and colors. This is *your* lawsuit, if you want to participate." And a diverse group asked to be plaintiffs in the case: Elena Picado, a high school Spanish teacher raising two children with her life partner, April Armstrong; Randy McCain, a pastor; Bryan Manire, a school counselor; George Townsend, a nurse; Charlotte Downey, a lesbian who owned a bait-and-tackle shop; and computer wizards Robin White and Vernon Stokay.[72]

On January 19, 1998, Lambda filed a lawsuit in which these seven plaintiffs petitioned the state courts to declare the homosexual sodomy law a violation of the privacy and equality guarantees of the Arkansas Constitution. Although *Picado v. Bryant* would run into some procedural quagmires,[73] its constitutional strategy was a thoughtful synthesis of twenty-five years of sodomy litigation. The Lambda attorneys believed that a thorough trial record was necessary, both to persuade the trial judge and to create a helpful record for the Arkansas Supreme Court. Sommer procured affidavits from leading medical experts, historians, and local lawyers to create a strong record demonstrating that there was no medical support for old stereotypes about psychopathic homosexuals, that gay people were historically subject to discrimination, and that the discriminatory state encouraged and sometimes performed violent assaults on its gay citizens.[74]

Like Marilyn Haft and Cary Boggan in the 1970s, the Lambda attorneys also felt it was important (especially after *Romer*) to demonstrate the collateral effects of the homosexual sodomy law. Robin White, for example, testified that, as an open lesbian, she was a presumptive criminal who could be arrested at any time the police decided to target her. When she was a teenager, "Arkansas police maced and arrested me at the instigation of the family of a young woman with whom I was romantically involved." Under the terms of her lease, she could be thrown out on the street at the discretion of her landlord, because she regularly committed a state crime. White could be fired by her employer, a software development company; although she had a right not to be discharged because she was a woman, the company could defend its actions as antilesbian. Invoking the homosexual sodomy law, Arkansas would not provide relief for this kind of discrimination, nor would it provide legal protections for lesbian and gay relationships. The child welfare agency had barred lesbians from being foster parents. On the basis of the homosexual sodomy law, Arkansas courts had also presumed that lesbians were unfit mothers for their biological children and that heterosexual fathers should usually receive custody of those children.[75]

In 1998, Springdale, Arkansas, mayoral candidate Timothy Hill announced to an applauding audience, "Homosexuals are perverts. . . . I will do everything I can to keep them out of Springdale, including enforcing the sodomy law." He promised to post two signs at the city limits: "No fags in Springdale" and "Welcome to Springdale: Home of God-fearing, *armed* Christian citizens." Hill lost the race, but antigay violence was on the rise. Sophia Estes, a lesbian raising her family in Fayetteville, was beaten by coworkers, and her daughter was harassed by classmates. School officials denied responsibility for protecting the daughter, because the mother was "living in sin." The homosexual sodomy law left some homosexuals in a virtual state of nature, more *un*protected by the rule of law than the *Romer* justices felt gay people were in Colorado. Said White, "Singling out lesbians and gay men as criminals causes many heterosexuals in the State to believe that discriminating against us, denying us employment and housing, harassing us, and even beating us, are acceptable and justified."[76]

When Goldberg went on maternity leave in 1999, Sommer, Harlow's friend from law school, took over the *Picado* litigation. By joining Lambda, Sommer had come out of a closet herself—not as a lesbian (she married Stephen Warnke, another Yale law graduate, in 1988), but as an openly straight supporter of rights for gay people. This was another by-product of *Bowers*: after reading the opin-

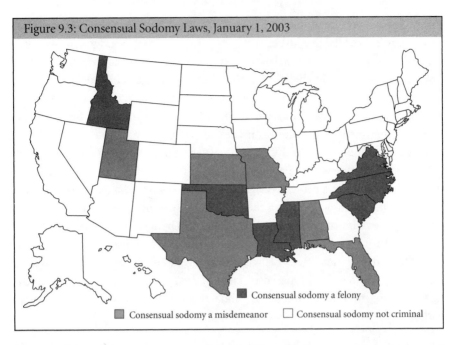

Figure 9.3: Consensual Sodomy Laws, January 1, 2003

Consensual sodomy a felony

Consensual sodomy a misdemeanor   □ Consensual sodomy not criminal

ions, straight students were angered by the Court's disrespectful and ignorant treatment of gay people. Sommer felt this outrage, and she has made a career of defending the rights of lesbians and gay men. In 2001 she persuaded circuit judge David Bogard to invalidate the homosexual sodomy law as a violation of both the privacy and equality protections of the Arkansas Constitution.[77]

Arguing the state's appeal, Sommer felt the Arkansas officials treated her and her clients with surprising respect. Attorney General Mark Pryor, the son of Governor David Pryor, who had signed the 1977 statute, was a rule-of-law moderate determined to defend the law without invoking antigay prejudice. On appeal the attorney general dropped the argument—which had shocked Sommer at trial—that homosexual relations were the moral equivalent of sex with animals. Nor did the state defend the antihomosexual discrimination as an anti-AIDS public health measure. Sommer pressed the Court to face the fact that the homosexual conduct law was objectionable because it meddled in people's homes and their private affairs *and* because it created an "accretion of legal affronts" having the intended effect of isolating homosexuals as a pariah class.[78]

Sommer won, narrowly. Writing for a majority of the Arkansas Supreme Court, Justice Annabelle Clinton Imber ruled that the Arkansas Constitution did protect sexual privacy, including homosexual conduct, as a fundamental right. Noting that nine states had invalidated their consensual sodomy laws on (either state or federal) privacy grounds, Imber followed *Wasson* (and declined to follow *Bowers*) to invalidate the homosexual sodomy law. She also ruled that the discriminatory feature of the law violated state constitutional guarantees of equal protection. Two of the five justices dissented from the court's judgment—not because they could find a rational basis for the law, but because they felt the plaintiffs did not have standing to challenge it until they were arrested or prosecuted.[79]

As figure 9.3 illustrates, the sodomy map of the United States changed dramatically after 1986. Handed down the day after the Fourth of July, 2002, *Picado* liberated the thirty-sixth state from the old regime. It was also a triumph for Lambda's litigation strategy. By careful lawyerly effort, Goldberg and Sommer had persuaded judges in a gay-anxious Baptist state that consensual sodomy within the home was a protected right *and* that a law has to have more justification than gay-bashing. Recalling the Puritan body politics of the 1690s, Justice Robert Brown said in his concurring remarks, "The idea of keeping a criminal statute on the books no one wants to enforce is perverse in itself. This brands the plaintiffs with a scarlet letter."[80] Having taken over as legal director of Lambda in 2000, Ruth Harlow was prepared to take the issue to the U.S. Supreme Court. Suzanne Goldberg had brought Lambda the perfect case almost four years earlier.

CHAPTER TEN

Sodomy Law at the Alamo,
Lawrence v. Texas, 2003

John Geddes Lawrence (born 1945) had been attracted to other men all his life. A heavyset man with a cowboy's weather-beaten furrowed face, Lawrence neither closeted nor flaunted his sexual orientation, and it involved him in remarkably few brushes with the law. As a Navy hospital corpsman third class, stationed in southeastern Virginia (1961–66), Lawrence frequented Norfolk and Virginia Beach gay bars and dated other Navy men. Although his intimacies with these men were felonies under state and military law, he was never arrested or harassed by the authorities. Soon after leaving the Navy with an honorable discharge, Lawrence

Tyron Garner and John Lawrence

returned to Texas to be near his mother and stepfather. After 1971 he lived in the Houston area. Because he was quiet and masculine, Lawrence was a virtual stranger to antihomosexual state or private policies until he was middle-aged. In the late 1980s Lawrence's close friend Michael was diagnosed with AIDS. When Michael fell ill with pneumonia, Lawrence took him to the emergency room. They missed the annual picnic at the hospital where they both worked. With his friend at his bedside, Michael died at 5:00 a.m. The hospital fired Lawrence at 8:00 a.m. "I think that was my first experience with 'homosexuality,'" Lawrence recalled.[1]

In 1987 John Lawrence moved to the Normandy, a gated apartment complex in east Houston. Nicely landscaped, with a split-level lagoon swimming pool and lavender crepe myrtle blooming much of the summer, the complex was a comfortable refuge where Lawrence could entertain his friends. Among them were Robert Eubanks and his lover, Tyron Garner. Eubanks came from Pasadena, a working-class suburb; a native of Houston's black ghetto, Garner was a younger man (born 1967) who had drifted from job to job and was still seeking a life vocation. On the evening of September 17, 1998, Eubanks, Garner, and Lawrence went out for a Mexican dinner and returned to the Normandy for more drinks and a relaxed evening. A little after 10:00 p.m. Eubanks announced that he and Garner were leaving—a proposition that was not acceptable to Garner. Lawrence said that Garner could stay if he wanted. At around 10:30 Eubanks left the apartment, saying he was going to pick up some snacks.[2]

Instead, Eubanks went to a pay phone and called the Harris County police. According to the police dispatcher, the caller claimed that "a black man was going crazy in the apartment and he was armed with a gun." The inebriated Eubanks was well aware that Garner had been arrested in the past for assault (once against a police officer), and that a complaint that an armed black man was threatening white residents of a gated apartment complex would provoke a prompt police response—as it did. Harris County deputy Joseph R. Quinn, a thirteen-year veteran, was the first to arrive on the scene, three minutes after he had been dispatched. He was joined by Deputy William Lilly and two other officers. Eubanks pointed the police team to Lawrence's second-floor apartment. With Quinn in the lead, the police entered the dwelling through its open front door, announced their presence, and then searched each room of the five-room unit. In the kitchen they found a thirty-six-year-old man later identified as Ramon Pelayo-Velez. After securing the living room and front bedroom, Lilly and Quinn moved to the back bedroom.[3]

There the door was open, and the lights were off. With their guns drawn, Lilly and then Quinn stepped into the room and announced their presence. Seeing two men together, Lilly "lurched back," and Quinn swiftly moved around him to enter the room in a crouched stance, his finger on the trigger and ready to fire. By their account, Quinn and Lilly witnessed Lawrence and Garner engaging in anal sex, and when the deputies pulled Lawrence off Garner, Lawrence responded angrily: "What the fuck are y'all doing?" Quinn says he replied: "You were close to being shot." Lawrence angrily demanded that the "jack-booted" thugs leave his apartment. Instead they handcuffed Lawrence, clad only in his underwear, and allowed Garner to pull up his pants. Both men were led into the living room, where Quinn took control of the situation and insisted that the two men be arrested for violating Texas's Homosexual Conduct Law. As he later told Dale Carpenter, "I think the totality of the circumstances where I think there's a guy with a gun and I almost have to shoot, that it warranted me giving them a citation. It was a lovers' triangle that could have got somebody hurt. I could have killed these guys over having sex. They were stupid enough to let it go that far."[4]

Other deputies soon arrived on the scene, including Sergeant Kenneth Adams. Quinn wanted to arrest all the homosexuals, but was uncertain what charges applied. He and Adams called Assistant District Attorney Ira Jones, who assured them that Section 21.06 covered homosexual activities within one's own home. At around 11:10 p.m. Quinn placed Lawrence and Garner under arrest. When Lawrence refused to accompany them, the officers dragged him down the concrete stairs outside his apartment, bruising and scraping his legs until they were bleeding. Garner went without incident. Both men were thrown into the backseat of a squad car. The officers also forcibly restrained Eubanks, whom they arrested for filing a false police report. They released Pelayo-Velez.[5]

The police drove off with the three perps, Lawrence still clad only in his briefs. According to Lawrence and Garner, they were driven around for almost two hours, finally arriving at the Harris County Jail, in downtown Houston, sometime after 1:00 a.m. on September 18. There they received orange jumpsuits and were taken to a holding cell, which they shared with as many as sixty other men. The police allowed them a telephone call, which Lawrence made to Lane Lewis, an activist friend. Lewis awoke Ray Hill, a grandfather figure to Houston's gay and lesbian activists. Hill and Lewis arranged for bond to be posted the next day; Lawrence and Garner were released around 1:00 a.m. on the morning of September 19 in the heart of downtown Houston—without money or even billfolds. Lawrence returned to his apartment, which the police had left unlocked and open to vandalism. Lawrence recalled, "It was the most humiliating experience I have ever gone through."[6]

Lawrence's travail was the beginning of the end of the Texas Homosexual Conduct Law, as well as the consensual sodomy laws in twelve other states. The process by which that occurred ultimately involved not just Lawrence and Garner, Quinn and Lilly, but also a wide array of local gay activists and attorneys, Lambda and other national gay rights organizations, Yale Law School, and the Republican Party of George W. Bush—who was governor of Texas when Lawrence and Garner were arrested and president of the United States when the Supreme Court overturned their convictions. The politics of criminal sodomy, which had become a politics of lies, racism, fag-bashing, and constant doses of denial, came to an end in 2003.

Homosexuals as Pariahs in Texas, 1973–95

Like Georgia, which generated the *Bowers* litigation, Texas is a southern state, where sexuality of any sort has been unspoken and sexual minorities best secluded in their magnolia closets. The exception to the southern look-the-other-way philosophy was, of course, interracial sexuality, which could still trigger violent outbursts. Unlike Georgia, Texas is also a frontier state, populated by tough and fiercely independent men and women. If the classic Georgian holder of power was the plantation owner, his Texas counterpart is the cowboy, the roughneck loner depicted in Annie Proulx's "Brokeback Mountain." By 1950, the cowboy was joined by the wildcatter, the gambler who staked all his money on drilling for oil in places the geologists had dismissed. In the twentieth century, the oil industry transformed Texas into a boom state, increasingly urban, with growing ghettos of rights-claiming homosexuals in Houston, Dallas, Austin, and San Antonio. As urban lesbian cowgirls and gay cowboys came out of their sagebrush closets, their tradition-bound neighbors in the ranches, suburbs, and small towns became plenty riled. The result was contentious and often bitter politics.[7]

Homosexuality as a Crime in Texas

As chapter 5 described, the Texas Bar's Committee on Revision of the Penal Code had decided in 1968 to propose that heterosexual sodomy be decriminalized and homosexual sodomy downgraded to a misdemeanor. The law professors advising the committee and at least two of its members (Dean Page Keeton and Judge Archie Brown) believed that gay people enjoyed constitutional rights to engage in private intimacies, but they bowed to the political reality that a criminal code branded as "promoting homosexuality" had little chance of passage in the legislature. Accordingly, the September 1970 draft of the proposed Texas Penal Code included Section 21.06, "Homosexuality," which made it a Class A misdemeanor for an individual to engage in "deviate sexual intercourse with another individual of the same sex." Notwithstanding the committee's caution and hard work, police and prosecutors assailed the code for having excessively lenient penalties for drug offenses, crimes of violence, and homosexual conduct. The legislature's imagination was seized by the notion that rising crime rates required more offenses, fewer defenses, and greater punishments.[8]

As Idaho citizens were to do the next year (chapter 6), ordinary Texans were reclaiming the criminal law from the experts, and commencing a decades-long process of racheting up criminal penalties. A reconstituted committee, filled with more prosecutors, proposed another draft code in October 1972. Like the 1970 version, the 1972 draft criminalized only "Homosexual Conduct" (Section 21.06) but reduced it from a Class A to a Class B misdemeanor. The Br'er Rabbit argument (that homosexuals would enjoy being in prison) continued to have force. Because prosecutors dominated its redrafting, the code's general approach was acceptable to hard-liners in the Sixty-third Session of the Texas Legislature. Marginalized in the revision process, the defense bar tepidly recommended that homosexual sodomy be decriminalized. "Realizing the facts of life, I don't really think this has any place in this Code," their representative testified before the Senate subcommittee. "But I'm not going to spend any time on it. We've recommended it be deleted simply because we think it's an anachronism, but uh. . . ." Dennis Milam, representing the National Organization for the Repeal of Sodomy Laws, testified more forcefully against the homosexual conduct provision before both House and Senate subcommittees, arguing that the provision was a needless intrusion into gay people's bedrooms and an unfair denigration of their lives. In executive session the House subcommittee reportedly debated the possibility of decriminalizing all consensual sodomy, but such a move was simply too controversial.[9]

The final witness before the Senate subcommittee was Frank Stovall, representing the Young Socialist Alliance. He argued that the homosexual conduct law implicated the same kind of privacy interests the Supreme Court had just protected against Texas's regulation in *Roe v. Wade* (1973). "It is a basic human right of every individual in this society to control his or her own body without any legal interference." Stovall stunned the subcommittee into silence by announcing his own homosexuality and, effectively, his own outlaw status: "Gays will not stop organizing and educating all over the country until every state has struck down these laws." Stovall was probably the first openly gay person to address the Texas Legislature. The Senate subcommittee reduced the penalty from a Class B to Class C misdemeanor, but only to eliminate the prosecutors' fantasy of gay men looking forward to time in all-male prisons, not to show an ounce of compassion for homosexuals.[10]

Ignoring fundamentalist objections that the proposed code repealed most sexual morality offenses (fornication, adultery, heterosexual sodomy, and bestiality), the Senate passed the reform bill by acclamation on May 16. On the floor of the House, the sponsors responded to the religious objection. If sex crimes were more broadly defined, the code would divert attention away from the most urgent problems—which they identified as rape, sexual abuse, and homosexuality. There was no recorded objection to this defense. On May 23, the proposed code, with only minor amendments, passed the House by a 114–27 vote. The Senate concurred in the House amendments the next day. Governor Dolph Briscoe, a teetotaling Baptist, signed the new Texas Penal Code into law on June 14, 1973.[11]

The new code revolutionized Texas's sodomy law. It differentiated among (1) coercive sodomy and (2) sodomy involving minors, both felonies, and (3) consensual sodomy, a Class C misdemeanor punishable by a $250 fine. When the new code took effect, several men who were in Ramsey Prison under the old felony law were released. One of those men was Alvin Buchanan, the hapless homosexual whose conviction had been the occasion for the first constitutional challenge to the old Texas sodomy law (chapter 5). More important, new Section 21.06 focused the crime of consensual sodomy only on homosexual sodomy. This was both a drastic narrowing of the state's consensual sodomy law (because it excluded heterosexual sodomy and also bestiality) and a significant broadening. For the first time in Texas's history, consensual oral sex between two women was marked as a crime.[12]

The irony of legalizing the crime against nature for the straight majority, while leaving it criminal for the lesbian and gay minority, did not sit well with Houston representative Craig Washington. As a freshman legislator, he did not challenge this decision in 1973, but during the Sixty-fourth Session (1975) he chaired a subcommittee with jurisdiction over the penal code. His subcommittee heard from representatives of the Texas Gay Task Force and the District and County Attorneys Association, urging repeal of Section 21.06. Realizing that the issue remained incendiary, Washington instructed the staff to add the Section 21.06 repeal provision (H.B. 759) to an omnibus penal code reform bill that the House would consider, literally, at the eleventh hour of the session. When the omnibus bill came to the floor for debate at 2:00 a.m. in May 1975, Representative Joe Spurlock of Forth Worth spotted the gambit and introduced an amendment to reinsert Section 21.06. Dallas representative Frank Gaston called a point of order: Was it true that only "homosexuals" could be counted to vote against the Spurlock amendment? The House erupted in laughter. Washington responded, "You can persecute people, Mr. Gaston, because you don't understand them. You can laugh about it, but that doesn't make it right." He added, "[I]f anybody thinks this applies to me, I invite them in[to] the restroom." More laughter. One representative seized a purse from Washington's desk and pranced around the floor of the chamber, sashaying and twirling the purse. "I debated on the merits, they debated on the prejudice," Washington recalls. The House reinserted Section 21.06 by a vote of 117–14.[13]

Gay people all over the state were outraged. As Houston activist Pokey Anderson stated, "I could have lived with being accorded less rights, but I couldn't live with being a joke on the floor of the Texas Legislature." House bills proposing deletion of Section 21.06 were introduced in the next sessions of the legislature (in 1977 and 1979) but died in committee. Texas politics was changing—but in complicated ways. At the same time that liberal Democrats were gaining important positions, conservative Democrats and Republicans were digging in on some issues, even as they abandoned others. With both Baptist Texas and gay Texas politically mobilized in the wake of the Dade County triumph of Anita Bryant's Save Our Children campaign in May 1977, the state was in for a rocky ride.[14]

Homo Resistance and the Texas Culture War

The Committee on Revision of the Penal Code and the Texas Legislature operated under the fanciful assumption that there were few homosexuals in the state, and that reaffirming homosexuality as a crime would keep them in the closet while discouraging new ones from immigrating. In fact, there were already pockets of open homosexuals in the state's major cities—Austin, the state capital and the home to the University of Texas; Houston, the fastest-growing major metropolitan area in America; Dallas, an oil-based boom city, and its stockyard twin, Fort Worth; San Antonio, the center of Mexican Texas. While open homosexuals would have been tarred and feathered in small towns, ranch communities, and even middle-size cities like Odessa and Midland, they could live comfortable lives in the big cities like Houston, as Lawrence and Garner had learned.

In 1973 Houston was the nation's sixth largest city. Thousands of its 1.2 million people were homosexuals, and sodomy laws did not prevent them from opening more than a dozen of gay and lesbian bars in the 1960s, most in the Montrose neighborhood of southwest Houston. Indeed, the biggest legal problem faced by lesbians was zealous police enforcement of Houston's 1861 ordinance making it a criminal offense to dress in the attire of the opposite sex. Soon after it opened, in June 1967, the Roaring Sixties was raided by police, who carted off twenty-five of the more "butch-looking" patrons for cross-dressing. Officers of the law also harassed and arrested gay men for public lewdness, indecency, and solicitation, but usually not consensual sodomy. Two years before Stonewall, Hill and Rita "Papa Bear" Wanstrom formed the Promethean Society to protest police abuses, and a pressure campaign at city hall was successful in reducing police enforcement of the cross-dressing law. In 1973, with police harassment of gay men on the rise, gay activists helped elect Fred Hofheinz mayor, initiating another period of relative calm. After a stint in Ramsey Prison for burglary (where he met Buchanan), Hill joined with Pokey Anderson and other activists to found the Houston Gay and Lesbian Political Caucus in 1975.[15]

Although its gay population kept growing—enough to support thirty bars and a Metropolitan Community Church—few Houston homosexuals were politically active. The city's lesbian and gay community took shape as a mass political force on June 17, 1977. Less than two weeks after her Dade County triumph (chapter 7), Anita Bryant was scheduled to entertain the Texas Bar Association at Houston's Hyatt Regency that night. Her appearance was leaked to gay activists in advance, and more than twelve thousand homosexuals from all over Texas showed up in Montrose, marching through the city to the Hyatt, where their chanting drowned out Bryant's booming voice. As lesbian activist Vivienne

Armstrong recalls, "it was an incredible, incredible event. It was electricity." It triggered community building unprecedented in the South. In 1978 activists held a Houston Town Meeting, where the lesbian and gay community decided to create institutions for a supportive subculture that would transcend that of the still-thriving lesbian and gay bars—including a counseling center, neighborhood patrols (the police could not be trusted to protect gays against violence), and a hotline for emergencies. That summer, Houston held its first Gay Pride Week, a series of celebratory events around the anniversary of the Stonewall riots. A coalition of organizations formed to protest the post-Bryant spurt in police harassment and arrests. In 1979 the Gay Political Caucus issued a detailed report on police misconduct, including perjured testimony, physical assaults on citizens, verbal abuse, selective enforcement of general laws, and a cover-up of the murder of a closeted homosexual. The caucus presented the report and its underlying evidence to the U.S. Civil Rights Commission and petitioned it to take action against the department (which it declined to do).[16]

The city government of Mayor Jim McConn and Police Chief Harry Caldwell was unreceptive to these complaints. Councilman Frank Mann lectured the caucus, "If all these homosexuals and queers left some of these young people alone then maybe they would steer clear of the police." (There was evidence, however, that police themselves had coerced youth to testify that they had been solicited by gay adults.) In 1979 Eleanor Tinsley ousted Mann from the council, in a campaign run by two politically savvy lesbian ex-nuns. Mayor McConn was the next to go, routed by City Comptroller Kathy Whitmire in the 1981 election. And then out went Caldwell, replaced by Lee Brown, the city's first African-American police chief. In 1984 Tinsley and Whitmire led the city council to adopt an ordinance barring municipal or private job discrimination because of sexual orientation. This would have allowed the dozens of closeted gay police officers to come out of their closets (theoretically), but the voters revoked the ordinance the next year, by a four-to-one margin. Although police harassment had abated, and the cross-dressing law was repealed, Houston's gay politics had only just scratched the surface.[17]

Everywhere in Texas, Section 21.06 reinforced gay-negative public attitudes, suggesting that homosexuals were essentially beyond the protection of the law. The most important role played by the code was to justify exclusion of open lesbians and gay men from sensitive public service jobs. No openly lesbian or gay police officer served in a major Texas city until the 1990s. In 1977, Dallas superintendent Dr. Nolan Estes announced that "any schoolteacher identified as a homosexual will be asked to resign immediately, regardless of whether the person has engaged in improper conduct. We're not going to have our young people exposed to that." When he became president of the Gay Political Caucus in 1979,

Navy veteran and schoolteacher Don Baker initiated a federal lawsuit challenging the constitutionality of Section 21.06. Federal judge Jerry Buchmeyer conducted a full-scale trial exploring the state's justifications for the law. Baker and his expert witnesses persuaded the judge that homosexuality was not a disease or mental disorder and that criminal sodomy laws, even when not seriously enforced against consensual conduct, "result in stigma, emotional stress, and other adverse effects" on gays. The judge asked Dallas district attorney Henry Wade how the allowance of heterosexual but not homosexual sodomy promoted the welfare of society. Wade testified, "I don't really know." Pressed further, he added, "I think the legislature wouldn't have passed it if there wasn't a public interest in it," but he still could not offer any justification.[18]

Judge Buchmeyer ruled the law unconstitutional, both because it violated Baker's right of privacy and because it discriminated against homosexuals without adequate justification. Texas attorney general Mark White filed an appeal, which was withdrawn by his successor, Jim Mattox, who concluded the law was unconstitutional. Also a defendant, District Attorney Danny Hill of Amarillo picked up the "appeal ball," and found a surprising amount of professional support. Traditionalists formed Alert Citizens of Texas to educate Texans about the public health dangers posed by homosexuality. Dallas Doctors Against AIDS defended the Homosexual Conduct Law as an important weapon in anti-AIDS campaigns. If Baker argued that Section 21.06 demeaned the lives of gay people, Dallas Doctors argued that homosexuals demeaned their own and those of others. Dr. Clem Mueller announced that homosexuals had deliberately spread the disease, for they refused to change their "lifestyles." "If the other people catch it it's their tough luck," he reported.[19]

The Fifth Circuit panel to which the case was assigned dismissed the appeal, on the ground that Hill did not have standing to defend a law the attorney general had abandoned. On August 26, 1985, the court of appeals, sitting en banc, voted to vacate the panel opinion and reverse Judge Buchmeyer. Nine judges (all but one appointed by Republican presidents Nixon and Reagan) joined the majority opinion, ruling that Baker's federal privacy claim was foreclosed by *Doe v. Commonwealth's Attorney* (1976) and that the state had sufficient reason to discriminate against "homosexual conduct" in light of moral objections that have "prevailed in Western culture for the past seven centuries." The majority ignored the public health arguments. Seven judges (all appointed by Democratic presidents Johnson and Carter) would have affirmed Judge Buchmeyer or dismissed the appeal on technical grounds.[20]

After Bowers: *The Morales Litigation*

Cofounder of the Texas Legal Rights Foundation and Baker's lawyer, Patrick Wiseman filed an appeal with the U.S. Supreme Court and urged the national gay litigation groups to make *Baker v. Wade* their test case. As chapter 8 indicated, Wiseman's plea was rejected, and the Supreme Court denied review in that procedurally complicated case. The Court's dismissive decision in *Bowers*, however, invigorated the gay rights movement in Texas. Activists were more determined than ever before to nullify Section 21.06, and they were encouraged by the election of progressive Democrat Ann Richards as governor in 1990. Even the U.S. Supreme Court seemed to smile on their community when, the year after *Bowers*, it unanimously overturned Ray Hill's conviction for disturbing the peace when he criticized a police officer for making a wrongful arrest.[21]

Wiseman, the tall Irishman who was the go-to lawyer for gay rights causes throughout Texas, was determined to nullify Section 21.06. Following the same approach as that of Ernesto Scorsone and Carolyn Bratt in Kentucky's *Wasson* litigation (chapter 9), he worked with the lesbian and gay community to create a detailed factual record supporting arguments that the homosexual conduct law was inconsistent with the Texas Constitution. His lead plaintiff was Linda Morales of Houston, a lesbian activist and labor leader. Onetime student body president at the University of Texas, Morales was a prominent feminist and founder of Houston's main women's support group, as well as a leader of the state's Mexican-American community. Other plaintiffs were John Thomas, executive director of the AIDS Resource Center in Dallas; Charlotte Taft, director of the Routh Street Women's Clinic in Dallas; Troy Doyal, former legal director of the Texas Human Rights Foundation; and Patricia Cramer of the Austin Lesbian and Gay Political Caucus. Because none of the plaintiffs had been arrested for violating Section 21.06, Wiseman's lawsuit was a civil one, seeking an injunction barring the attorney general from enforcing the law. Each plaintiff alleged that he or she feared arrest and the loss of civil rights because of her or his open homosexuality. "Having the law as part of the social and religious environment of Texas is unhealthy and wrong," said Thomas. "It makes a lot of gay men and women lie and hide. It's dehumanizing." On December 10, 1990, Austin district judge Paul Davis agreed, indicating the law was unconstitutional.[22]

Unlike his predecessor, the new Texas attorney general, Dan Morales (1991–99), gamely defended the statute on appeal. A Harvard Law School graduate, the ambitious Dan Morales (no relation to Linda) hoped that his Latino heritage and conservative political positions would enable him to move on to higher office. The attorney general not only maintained that the Texas Constitution permitted morals-based regulations (along the lines accepted in *Bowers*), but also that Wiseman's action could not be maintained in Texas's civil courts. Linda Morales and her colleagues would have to await a criminal prosecution before they could challenge the statute. Because Texas maintains two separate procedural systems—one for criminal prosecutions, one for civil cases—the Texas Supreme Court had created a general rule that judges on the civil side should not handle litigation directly challenging the constitutionality of criminal statutes. Wiseman responded that the court had created a huge exception to that rule in a 1969 case where it allowed a civil challenge to a Texas criminal statute barring fraternities and sororities in public secondary schools.[23]

The Austin Court of Appeals agreed with Wiseman on both points. Chief Justice Jimmy Carroll's opinion for the court in *State v. Morales* (1992) ruled that Section 21.06 violated the Texas Constitution. The Texas Supreme Court had recognized a broad constitutional privacy right, which Carroll applied to the Homosexual Conduct Law. "[W]e can think of nothing more fundamentally private and deserving of protection than sexual behavior between consenting adults in private." The constitutional injury was compounded by the legislature's effort to limit the crime to homosexual sodomy. Carroll then ruled that the state's only asserted interest—public morality—was not demonstrably served by the law, in part because other statutes already regulated sexual activities committed in public and in part because the state claimed that it never enforced Section 21.06. Attorney General Morales appealed to the Texas Supreme Court. While the appeal was pending, the Austin Court of Appeals followed *Morales* in *City of Dallas v. England* (1993). Dallas had refused to hire Mica England as a police officer because she was a lesbian, and therefore a presumptive criminal under Section 21.06. Because Section 21.06 was unconstitutional, Judge Bea Ann Smith ruled that the Dallas hiring policy was invalid. Probably revealing its acceptance of Judge Smith's ruling, Dallas mysteriously lost its chance to appeal when it filed a petition for rehearing en banc one day late.[24]

With *Morales* pending before it, dozens of letters poured into the Texas Supreme Court, warning that the lower-court opinions threatened the state with Armaggedon. Justices Raul Gonzalez and Nathan Hecht, religious conservatives, wanted to uphold Section 21.06 and set clear limits on the state privacy right, as *Bowers* had done. Justice Lloyd Doggett, a liberal Democrat, and Chief Justice Tom Phillips, a conservative Republican, wanted to affirm the lower courts, in defiance of the popular pressure. Justice John Cornyn, a pragmatic conservative, wanted to reverse the lower-court rulings, but without creating a divisive *Bowers*-like tempest in the courthouse. Although there were originally five justices willing to overturn Section 21.06, intense lobbying within the court persuaded one of them to switch to the Cornyn position as a compromise. Cornyn drafted an opinion for the five that accomplished the job of reversing the lower courts—not because they had misinterpreted the Texas Constitution, but because they had no jurisdiction over the dispute. The court held that civil courts had no jurisdiction to enjoin enforcement of criminal statutes, unless a plaintiff could show irreparable injury to her *property* interests. Thus, Mica England could sue Dallas, which had denied her a job and which relied on Section 21.06 as its only defense. But Linda Morales could not challenge the law, for she had not been prosecuted under the law or denied employment opportunities because of it.[25]

Patrick Wiseman passed away from cancer five years after the *Morales* litigation ended. A new generation of legal activists took his place. In 1996 Connie Moore, Rick Thompson, Charles Spain, and Mitchell Katine formed the Section on Sexual Orientation and Gay Interest Issues within the Texas Bar Association. Just as *Bowers* sprang thousands of lesbian and gay lawyers from their closets, so *Morales* inspired lesbian and gay lawyers in Texas to speak out. Values were changing. But in what direction?

The Lawrence and Garner Case Makes
Its Way to the U.S. Supreme Court, 1998–2002

Ray Hill knew that the *Morales* court was wrong when it said that Section 21.06 was *never* enforced. In the early 1980s Harris County law enforcement officers had arrested two men for having sex in a camper parked on state property near the San Jacinto monument celebrating Texas's war of independence from Mexico. While they were having intercourse, the sheet covering the entrance to the camper was lifted by a gust of wind, giving passersby a glimpse of the crime. The justice of the peace who handled the case tipped Hill off to the fact that this was a Section 21.06 prosecution. Although Hill tried to persuade the lawyer to use it as a vehicle to challenge the statute, the lawyer said, "Hell, no," in part because it was not in his clients' interest, and in part because he wanted to collect his legal fee.[26]

When he learned of the Lawrence and Garner arrest, Hill felt the community finally had a case that would satisfy the *Morales* requirement that direct challenges be brought only in defense of criminal prosecutions. Through their mutual friend Lane Lewis, Hill recommended that Lawrence and Garner contact Mitchell Katine, who was a law partner with one of Houston's finest criminal defense counsels, Gerry Birnberg. Rather than turning the case over to Birnberg, however, Katine called Suzanne Goldberg, the staff attorney at Lambda Legal with whom he had worked on an AIDS matter. Both attorneys understood that the events of September 17 offered the gay and lesbian community a rare opportunity to ask the U.S. Supreme Court to reconsider *Bowers*. Beatrice Dohrn, Lambda's legal director, was incredulous, and recalled, "This was too good to be true." Dohrn decided that Lambda should be involved from the very beginning and dispatched Goldberg to Houston. She and Katine explained the ramifications to Lawrence and Garner, neither of whom had any background in gay activism: this was a golden opportunity to get rid of Section 21.06, and perhaps all consensual sodomy laws in the country—but Lawrence and Garner would have to accept a misdemeanor conviction on their records. "I thought about it for a while," recalls Garner. "I wanted to fight this case. . . . I felt violated when [the] police intruded into [the] bedroom. I didn't realize the police could do this." Lawrence agreed, and these two friends officially became a "test case."[27]

All the participants were aware that while the case might reach the U.S. Supreme Court, the litigation train could stop at any point. The police could have confessed that they didn't really have the evidence needed to obtain a conviction under Section 21.06; prosecutors could have decided not to prosecute Lawrence and Garner; state judges could have dismissed charges on the ground that the law violated the Texas or U.S. Constitution. That none of these happened—and that the case did find its way to the U.S. Supreme Court—owed much to the complicated sociopolitical context of antihomosexual prejudice, good government, fundamentalist religion, and the triumph of the Republican Party in Texas.

Pissed-off Police Stick to Their Story

It was highly unusual for Texas police officers to arrest consenting adults for engaging in "deviate sexual intercourse" in their own homes. There would have been no constitutional case if the Harris County police had arrested Robert Eubanks for filing a false police report, and then left the Normandy. Why did they arrest Lawrence and Garner? The most apparent reason is that the officers were "pissed off." They had rushed to the scene of a potentially violent crime; they had stormed the apartment and had drawn their weapons—all they found was a homosexual "love triangle," as Quinn termed it.

Lilly and Quinn were disgusted by what they saw. Lilly "lurched back" when he saw Lawrence and Garner together and has refused to discuss what he saw in any detail. Quinn originally showed no such inhibition, telling Dale Carpenter that "Lawrence looked eye-to-eye at me," as he and Garner continued to engage in anal intercourse for "well in excess of a minute" after the officers turned on the light. (Carpenter says Quinn's after-the-fact account is filled with far-fetched statements like this.) As they were leaving the premises, Quinn cracked, "You have to wonder, 'What have we touched? Have we come into any contact with any fluids?'" He regaled Carpenter with this closing observation: "I made sure I doused myself with sanitizer," taken from his patrol car. This cleansing ritual is straight out of Leviticus.[28]

Ray Hill thinks that some of the officers were doubly disgusted by the interracial features of the coupling. If Quinn harbored racist feelings, they would have been mobilized by seeing intimacy between a black man and a white man, the most primitive form of American body politics, namely, miscegenation. For Lilly, an African-American Baptist, the encounter might have had yet another element of disgust, for the black man was (by his and Quinn's account) being penetrated by the white man. The combination of race and homosexuality was bound to produce profoundly disturbing feelings. Add to these speculations a fact on which Lawrence and Quinn agree: the uppity homosexual lashed out at the deputies, calling *them* ugly names and disrespecting *them*. This was not the way a social inferior was supposed to behave, especially when he had been apprehended in the course of his perversion. This inflamed reaction not only poured gas on the flames of Quinn's anger, but isolated John Geddes Lawrence in that room.

Were Quinn and Lilly disgusted enough to lie about what they saw in the bedroom? Hill thought so. Like homophobic police in New York, San Francisco, and Los Angeles earlier in the century (chapters 2–3), the Harris County deputies were reputed to adjust their version of the facts to fit spiteful rather than lawful agendas, or just to have fun with some queers. Hill had a more specific reason to think Quinn was lying. Justice of the Peace Michael Parrott told him that he would "not trust [Quinn] on a traffic ticket." Hill's theory was that Quinn arrested Lawrence and Garner in a fit of rage or passion. When he contacted a district attorney, as he did before making the arrest, he learned that they could not be convicted of violating Section 21.06 without evidence of penetration of one man's penis in the other man's orifice. Committed to hauling those homosexuals into jail, and having nothing else to charge them with, Quinn then retrofitted his story to the legal requirements. The equally disgusted Lilly went along to protect his partner but has clammed up since then.[29]

Old-Fashioned Republican Prosecutors Stick with the Homosexual Conduct Law

The Harris County District Attorney's Office is located on the corner of Franklin and San Jacinto streets in downtown Houston, across the street from the jail where Lawrence and Garner were held. The DA's Office is the product of Johnny B. Holmes Jr., one of the great prosecutors of the twentieth century. Longtime

DA Carol Vance (the most adamant antihomosexual voice on the Committee on Revision of the Penal Code in 1968) had run a good-ol'-boy police department, where favoritism was not unknown. When Vance retired, Holmes won the position as a good-government Republican. With his handlebar mustache and cowboy hat, Holmes appealed to the frontier sentiments of Texas politics. Firmly in favor of the death penalty, he sent hundreds of men to death row. On the other hand, he was a scrupulous believer in the rule of law who turned the DA's Office into a thoroughly professional operation. Holmes had no room for prejudice or stereotypes in his office; women, racial minorities, and even homosexuals worked effectively together to defend convictions of lawbreakers from all walks of life.

Respecting the rule of law also meant enforcing its boundaries, especially when overzealous police wanted to harass minorities. Early in Holmes's administration, a number of deputies who had been called to tone down a loud party found men dancing together, hugging and kissing, and cross-dressing. The officers filled a paddy wagon with homosexuals and brought them to jail. Applying Holmes's philosphy, Assistant DA Ira Jones refused to authorize charges, because the men had not violated Section 21.06. Jones insisted on applying Section 21.06 strictly—and the letter of the law did not apply to these defendants. Nor was Jones willing to stretch the law (disturbing the peace) to harass these men. He sent the homosexuals on their way, and the police learned their own lesson from the matter.[30]

When he learned of the Lawrence and Garner case, Holmes turned to his chief appellate lawyer, William J. Delmore III. Section 21.06 did apply to the conduct described in Quinn's affidavit accompanying the arrests, but the rule of law also required a prosecutor to ask himself: Can the statute be *constitutionally* applied here? Holmes gave Delmore about twenty minutes to come up with an answer. In that unrealistically brief period, Delmore found the Texas Supreme Court's decision in *Morales*, which left the issue unresolved, but did not come across the Austin Court of Appeals's decision in *England*, which would also have been on point.[31]

Delmore also did not see the opinion letter that Sarah Shirley had drafted for Attorney General Morales, following *England* to opine that Section 21.06 was unconstitutional. Immediately after *Morales*, Republican representative Harvey Hildebrand had formally requested an attorney general opinion on the constitutionality of the Homosexual Conduct Law. Following months of research and deliberation, Shirley drafted an opinion indicating that the law violated the Texas Constitution's privacy protections, which then went to Assistant Attorney General Jorge (George) Vega. Vega knew that, if his office released Shirley's letter, the Republicans would tag the attorney general as "pro-homosexual" and whisper that the unmarried Morales was "homosexual" himself. Wanting to protect his boss against partisan fag-bashing, Vega (who himself thought Section 21.06 was absurd) killed the letter administratively. It has never seen the light of day.[32]

Shirley's opinion might have stopped the Lawrence and Garner prosecution—but it remained locked in her drawer. Judge Bea Ann Smith's opinion in *England* might likewise have stopped the prosecution—but Delmore did not find it. Based on the information he did discover, Delmore opined that there was insufficient reason to conclude that Section 21.06 was unconstitutional. Thus assured, Holmes directed that the prosecution proceed and told the media, "We're supposed to presume that these laws are constitutional. If we say, 'Let this thing go away,' then we're not really complying with the law and I'm not comfortable with that. . . . But I've always said that the best way to get rid of a bad law is to enforce it."[33]

Goldberg was impressed with his scrupulousness, and she and Katine sought to follow the law as rigorously. The DA's Office arraigned Lawrence and Garner before Justice of the Peace Michael Parrott, who found the defendants guilty and assessed them fines of $125 apiece. Lambda appealed to Judge Sherman Ross of the criminal court. On December 16, Goldberg and Katine filed a motion to quash the complaint on the ground that Section 21.06 was a violation of the privacy and equality protections of the Texas and U.S. constitutions. At the same time, they were negotiating with prosecutor Angela Beavers. Consistent with Holmes's public stance, Beavers cooperated in the defense strategy of accepting punishment for the crime, while preserving all their constitutional objections for appeal. Pursuant to the plea negotiations, Judge Ross denied the motion and accepted pleas of no contest from each defendant at a hearing on December 22. The judge assessed each defendant a fine of $200 (the maximum statutory amount). Lambda appealed.[34]

New Republican Judges Stick with the No Promo Homo Philosophy

Just days before Lawrence and Garner's arraignment, George W. Bush was reelected governor of Texas with sixty-eight percent of the vote. He carried with him other Republicans, including Rick Perry as lieutenant governor, John Cornyn as attorney general, and Carole Keeton Rylander, Page Keeton's daughter, as comptroller. Three elements contributed to the Republicans' success. One was good government. Pragmatic Old Republicans like Holmes demonstrated that they could run local governments efficiently, without the unpredictability and corruption of some of the yellow-dog Democratic machines. John Cornyn impressed liberal Democrats with the efficiency he brought to the attorney general's office, after eight years of politicization under Dan Morales. A second element was the ability of Republicans to attract the votes of the conservative elements of rural Texas without alienating the growing Latino vote. The third element, and the one that most clearly distinguished New from Old Republicans, was their populist appeal to the politics of preservation (chapter 7). There was a big constituency for such appeals in Texas. The Reverend H. A. Criswell, pastor of Dallas's First Baptist Church, one of the nation's first megachurches, was a harbinger of the increasing participation of fundamentalists in politics. Criswell was president of the Southern Baptist Convention in 1969–70, and Texans held the presidency for ten of the next twenty-five years. By demonizing abortion and sodomy, Texas's Republican Party aggressively courted this politicized conservative constituency.[35]

For example, Phil Gramm won the 1984 Senate race in part by attacking his opponent, Lloyd Doggett (who as a Supreme Court justice would later try to overturn Section 21.06), for accepting contributions from homosexuals. Jim Mattox says that he was branded anti-family and pro-gay in every statewide campaign he ran against the Republicans, including the 1998 race for attorney general, won by John Cornyn (who had engineered the *Morales* majority that saved Section 21.06). In the 1994 governorship race, Bush publicly supported Section 21.06 as a "symbolic gesture of traditional values" and vowed to veto any bill repealing the Homosexual Conduct Law. His staff spread the word that Governor Ann Richards's administration was loaded with lesbians, whom even Democrats called the "Valkyries." Karl Rove, Bush's Rasputin, reportedly pushed a whisper campaign that the governor (separated from her heterosexual husband) was a lesbian.[36]

The Old Republican Party came into conflict with the New in *Lawrence v. State*. Chief Justice Paul Murphy, an Old Republican, presided at oral argument on November 3, 1999; with him were two younger Republicans, Justices J. Harvey Hudson and John Anderson. Representing Lawrence and Garner, Lambda's Ruth Harlow argued that the court should subject Section 21.06 to strictest scrutiny, either because it infringed on the defendants' constitutional privacy rights or because it denied them the equal protection of the laws. Bill Delmore conceded that the state could not meet such a standard, but maintained that neither constitution authorized strict scrutiny, essentially for the reasons outlined in *Bowers*. "Throughout history, there has been a historical, cultural and religious consensus that homosexual conduct is immoral. Only a majority of the electorate can determine whether that morality has changed."[37]

On June 8, 2000, the panel overturned the convictions and ruled that Section 21.06 violated the Texas Constitution—but not for Harlow's preferred reason. Anderson's opinion for the court ruled that Section 21.06 violated the Texas Equal Rights Amendment (ERA). The U.S. Supreme Court had held in *Loving v.*

Virginia (1967) that the state engaged in race discrimination when it penalized a black-white married couple because of the race of one partner (i.e., a black-black couple would have been left alone). By analogy, Section 21.06 was a *sex* discrimination, for it penalized a male-male couple because of the sex of one partner (i.e., a male-female couple would have been left alone). Because the ERA required courts to subject sex discriminations to strict scrutiny and Delmore had conceded that the law could not survive strict scrutiny, the Homosexual Conduct Law was invalid. Murphy joined this opinion, but Hudson disagreed, claiming that Section 21.06 discriminated only because of homosexuality. Such a discrimination was eminently reasonable, Hudson argued, as an exercise in the government's fundamental "responsibility of protecting virtue and restraining evil." "Considerable historical precedent" supported the legislature's categorization of "homosexual conduct" as "morally reprehensible."[38]

Justice Anderson's was the first majority opinion of an American appellate tribunal to accept the sex discrimination argument for gay rights. It was presented in *Lawrence* because it was a logical argument that associated feminist theory with gay rights (both were set against state-imposed gender roles). Dohrn and Harlow worried, however, that the argument was too powerful for risk-averse judges to accept. *Loving* was a different-race marriage case. If courts accepted the *Loving* analogy in the same-sex sodomy context, how could they deny it in the context of same-sex marriage? A plurality of the Hawaii Supreme Court had in 1993 accepted the sex discrimination argument as the reason to subject the state same-sex marriage bar to heightened scrutiny—but before the court had a chance to strike down the bar the Hawaii legislature and voters amended the state constitution to allow that discrimination. Congress adopted the Defense of Marriage Act (1996), and gay rights had been dealt a major setback.[39]

Whatever the policy consequences, the sex discrimination argument accepted by the court of appeals was entirely consistent with, and perhaps required by, the rule of law. Yet the New Texas Republican Party reacted with the ferocity of hornets whose nest has been disturbed. On June 16 the Republican platform condemned the ruling and reaffirmed that "homosexual behavior is contrary to the unchanging truths that have been ordained by God." The platform urged the voters to turn Republicans Anderson and Murphy out of office. Paul Murphy was particularly stung by these criticisms. He had been a GOP leader in rural Walker County back in the 1970s, when the Republicans were a nuisance party. "I paid my dues to the Republican Party, and that's why it hurt my feelings for them to rebuke me in their state platform," he sadly reflected. In March 2001 he resigned from the court after twenty years of service, just after the court of appeals, sitting en banc, voted seven to two (Murphy and Anderson) to reaffirm the constitutionality of Section 21.06.[40]

Also chock-full of New Republicans, the Texas Court of Criminal Appeals (the highest court in Texas for criminal cases) declined to review the court of appeals's decision. A few months later, the New Republicans swept the Texas off-year elections. Rick Perry won a full term as governor, the legislature went solidly Republican, and the GOP held every one of the twenty-nine statewide offices. Although Houston representative Debra Danberg had managed to bring a sodomy-repeal bill to the floor of the Texas House in 2001, she was turned out of office in the 2002 elections. The new no promo homo climate ensured that such a bill had no chance of success in the near future.

Liberty, Equality, and the Homosexual Conduct Law

Having succeeded Dohrn as Lambda's legal director in 2000, Harlow bore responsibility for deciding whether to petition the U.S. Supreme Court to review the Homosexual Conduct Law. Surely there was a Court majority that considered consensual sodomy laws a constitutional anachronism. The Centers for Disease Control and Prevention (CDC) had just established that ninety percent of Americans between the ages of fifteen and forty-four had engaged in heterosexual oral sex, and forty percent had engaged in heterosexual anal sex. Among young straights, sodomy was now almost as common as penile-vaginal sex. As the contraception cases had taught the country, the state cannot constitutionally criminalize conduct that everyone engages in and finds acceptable. The Texas statute, of course, was worse, for it criminalized sodomy only when engaged in by sexual minorities. (Six percent of the men and eleven percent of the women in the national CDC sample had engaged in homosexual oral or anal sex.)[41]

Harlow knew better than to rely entirely on abstract notions of fairness, however. She and her associates Susan Sommer and Patricia Logue consulted lawyers and academics familiar with the Supreme Court and with the larger LGBT community. Almost everyone agreed that this was the right time and *Lawrence* probably the right case for gay rights advocates to narrow or overturn *Bowers*. Finding virtual consensus in favor of proceeding, Lambda filed its appeal on July 16, 2002. Harris County filed a memorandum urging the Court not to take the case. The Supreme Court requested the views of Texas attorney general Cornyn, who declined to file a brief. On December 2, 2002, the Court granted review.[42]

Lambda's Constitutional Assault on the Homosexual Conduct Law

Even before review was granted, Harlow was orchestrating a campaign to present the Court with an array of briefs and arguments that were legally cogent and reflected both common values and diverse perspectives within progressive and LGBT communities. From the beginning, she relied on the advice of Bill Hohengarten, a brilliant and openly gay appellate attorney at Jenner & Block in Washington, D.C. With input from Paul Smith, a renowned appellate advocate at Jenner, and the Lambda attorneys, Harlow and Hohengarten created an impressive brief for Lawrence and Garner. Filed at the same time as that brief were fifteen amicus briefs supporting the case. Harlow and Sommer coordinated the amicus briefs, with three strategic considerations in mind.[43]

First, amicus briefs can deepen and expand arguments made by the main brief. Lambda's lead argument was that Texas's consensual sodomy law violated the federal right to privacy. "Being forced into a life without sexual intimacy would represent an intolerable and fundamental deprivation for the overwhelming majority [of Americans]." Yet such deprivations were permitted under *Bowers*, a precedent Lambda urged the Court to overrule. In general the Court is not eager to overrule constitutional precedents, as illustrated by the joint opinion of Justices O'Connor, Kennedy, and Souter in *Planned Parenthood v. Casey* (1992), reaffirming *Roe v. Wade* for reasons of stare decisis (the decision stands). Lambda's brief, however, argued that, unlike *Roe* or other foundational precedents, *Bowers* had not become "part of our national culture." Since *Bowers*, "the Nation has steadily moved toward rejecting second-class citizenship status for gay and lesbian Americans." Accordingly, "*Bowers* is an isolated decision," a "'doctrinal anachronism discounted by society.'"[44]

But, under the historical approach to substantive due process the Court had usually followed, was *Bowers* wrong? Lambda's main answer—that the Court sometimes followed evolving norms—would not be entirely satisfying to some justices. Three briefs provided historical depth to Lambda's argument. In an amicus brief drafted by the author of this book, the Cato Institute demonstrated that pre-twentieth-century crime-against-nature laws were aimed at, and exclusively applied to, nonconsensual or public activities. The vague laws in place in 1868, when the Fourteenth Amendment was adopted, targeted predatory and public anal sex by men against women, children, animals, and less-powerful men. American traditions protecting private consensual activities within the home were fully consistent with the sodomy laws the Reconstructionists knew— contrary to *Bowers*. Ten eminent social historians established that *Bowers*'s focus on "homosexual sodomy" was anachronistic, and Texas's Homosexual Conduct Law was a recent phenomenon in American law—much like Colorado's Amendment 2, struck down in *Romer*. The Kansas statute adopted in 1969 (chapter 5) was the first sodomy law in American history to criminalize homosexual sodomy alone. The ACLU's amicus brief, drafted by James Esseks with input from Matt Coles and Laurence Tribe, demonstrated that, even in the twentieth century, sodomy laws were applied almost entirely to police public sexuality, not consenting activities within the home. These three amicus briefs suggested that the "originalist" approach taken in *Bowers* did not, in fact, reflect the historical record. Also, the briefs presented a history-based account for the liberty right that Harlow was pressing in *Lawrence*. There was no tradition-based right for Americans to engage in "homosexual sodomy," because there was no such concept before the 1890s—but there was a strong and unbroken American tradition protecting people against police intrusion into consensual activities (including consensual sodomy) within the home.[45]

A subtler challenge for Lambda's liberty argument was to counter the perception, held by the *Bowers* majority and many Americans, that homosexuals as a group lay "outside" the great traditions of American life: the family, the church, and the community. The American Psychological Association filed an amicus brief demonstrating that LGBT Americans were normal people who formed lasting relationships with persons of the same sex and raised thousands of children within those relationships. Although Lawrence and Garner were not themselves a committed couple, millions of gay people did enjoy such relationships, and laws making their consummation a crime had no relevence to the "common welfare." Twenty-nine churches and gay-friendly groups within traditionalist denominations (such as the Catholics, Baptists, and Mormons) filed a brief demonstrating that many traditionalists strongly supported civil rights for gay people. In turn, many gays were people of faith. Tyron Garner, for example, worshipped at Joel Osteen's Lakewood Church; his large extended family, most of whom were Baptist, were supportive of his coming out of the closet in the context of the Texas sodomy litigation.[46]

Building on its privacy argument, Lambda also contended that the Homosexual Conduct Law violated the Equal Protection Clause. Section 21.06 imposed criminal liability upon "homosexual conduct" alone, and for no reason beyond "moral" and other objections to "homosexuality," contrary to *Romer*. More troubling, the law had discriminatory ripple effects, as it served as the justification for a host of antigay discriminations in employment, family law, and criminal law—an almost limitless array that made the Homosexual Conduct Law a closer fit to *Romer*'s Amendment 2. (The Homosexual Conduct Law had even been cited as a reason to impose the death penalty on Calvin Burdine, a gay man convicted of murder.) Finally, Lambda demonstrated some ways consensual sodomy laws created or reinforced a society that was hostile to gay citizens. Such laws encouraged antigay violence and served as reasons for the state not to devote resources against the most vicious hate crimes.[47]

The ripple effects of Section 21.06 were also explored in the amicus briefs, including those for the American Bar Association, the Cato Institute, the ACLU, and sixteen constitutional-law professors. (These briefs deepened the sodomy law attack originally developed in the *Enslin* case by Marilyn Haft and Cary Boggan [chapter 6].) Among the *legal* discriminations against gay people justified by sodomy laws in Texas were the following:

- a criminal code rule allowing promiscuity of a minor to be a defense to sex with that minor by an adult, but not if the sex was homosexual;
- open judicial disparagement of crimes against homosexuals, including one judge's questioning whether the law really made it a crime "to beat up a homosexual";
- exclusion of antigay violence from Texas's hate crime legislation;
- disqualification of gay people from public employment, including police officers and schoolteachers;
- potential disqualification of gay people from procuring state licenses to become doctors, nurses, athletic trainers, bus drivers, liquor sellers, and other occupations;
- denial of custody or visitation rights to gay parents (in neighboring states and possibly Texas);
- refusal of gay people's requests for adoption or foster parenting of parentless children (in neighboring states, and possibly Texas);
- exclusion of sexual orientation from state and local antidiscrimination laws;
- statutory requirements that state sex education programs introduce antigay messages.

The legal effects of the Homosexual Conduct Law were more demonstrably pervasive than the legal effects of the indecipherable amendment struck down in *Romer*. As Cato demonstrated, *Romer* had rejected the morality argument Texas was making as its main defense in *Lawrence*. Colorado had argued that Amendment 2 was justified as a signal that "tolerant" Coloradans did not "approve" of homosexuality even though they did not make it a crime. The Court had flatly rejected this defense.[48]

A second role that Harlow and Sommer played was as traffic cops. On the other side, defense of Section 21.06 attracted more than a dozen amicus briefs, few of which made legal arguments that had not already been capably made in Bill Delmore's brief for Harris County. Harlow worked to minimize such duplication of effort on her side. She also sought to marginalize the sex discrimination argument that had briefly prevailed with the Texas Court of Appeals. This proposition is controversial within the gay legal community. Suzanne Goldberg (now teaching law at Columbia) favors the argument, because of its formal elegance and its functional linkage of gay rights and feminism. Others disparage the argument as transvestic—dressing up gay rights in feminist garb. If so, the argument misses the basis of antigay discrimination—namely, that it is grounded on sexuality-based and not gender-based prejudice or stereotypes. But feminism and gay law actually are both opposed to discrimination because of sex, because it reinforces traditional gender roles. The deepest gender stereotyping is the notion that a woman cannot live a completely fulfilled life unless she marries a man and raises his children. That millions of women do lead fulfilling lives (often raising children) with other women poses a fundamental challenge. Harlow worried that it was too fundamental. If the sex discrimination argument was presented, Justice Scalia would have a field day at oral argument, suggesting that it required the Constitution to impose same-sex marriage on the country. Justices Kennedy and O'Connor might well be put off by that very logical possibility. Harlow felt that she could not prevent NOW from making the sex discrimination argument, but on the whole it was effectively out of the case.[49]

A third role Harlow played was political. She wanted the Supreme Court to recognize the diversity of the coalition against sodomy laws. It included not just the usual suspects—the ACLU, liberal law professors, feminists, homosexuals—but also a broader array of cultural and political actors. The ABA agreed to file an amicus brief, orchestrated by Mark Agrast and written by Beth Brinkman, arguing that the Homosexual Conduct Law was inconsistent with the *rule of law*, our nation's "commitment to evenhanded and neutral enforcement of rules that respect individuals as autonomous human beings." Not only did the conservative Cato Institute file an amicus brief, but so did the Republican Unity Coalition, former Wyoming senator (1979–97) Alan Simpson, and the Log Cabin Republicans. While the Old Republican Party stood with libertarian sodomy reform, the New Party largely stayed out of the case. There were no briefs from the Bush administration or even the Texas attorney general. Whereas twenty-nine churches and faith groups filed a brief supporting the challengers, no denomination filed in support of Harris County—not the Roman Catholic Church, not the Southern Baptist Convention, not the Church of Jesus Christ of Latter-day Saints.[50]

The primary briefs supporting the constitutional challenges were written by graduates of Yale Law School—Harlow, Sommer, Hohengarten, and Smith, authoring the Lambda brief; Agrast and Brinkman, the ABA's brief; Pam Karlan, writing for the sixteen constitutional scholars; and the author of this book (the Cato Brief). Spearheaded by Professor (now Dean) Harold Koh, Yale Law School's Lowenstein Human Rights Clinic submitted a brief informing the Court of developments in other countries. The justices themselves had said that it was "informative" to know how "foreign courts have applied standards roughly comparable to our own constitutional standards in roughly comparable circumstances," especially when "those opinions reflect a legal tradition that also underlies our own." One way for a judge to be more certain that she was not just reading her own views into the Constitution's liberty-protecting provisions was to see if judges elsewhere in the world were reaching the same normative judgment. By the time of *Lawrence* virtually all industrialized countries had decriminalized consensual sodomy, most of them generations earlier. Constitutional opinions in Europe had invalidated the few remaining consensual sodomy laws on grounds that they violated fundamental rights to privacy and human dignity. This comparative experience reinforced the powerful reasons for understanding the American Constitution to be supportive of privacy and even equality rights for gay people. The international brief was also suggesting to the Court that if the United States expected to maintain its world leadership in constitutional discourse, it should divest itself of embarrassing precedents like *Bowers*.[51]

Harris County and Section 21.06 at the Alamo

The Alamo is in San Antonio, but it is an apt metaphor for Harris County's doomed defense of Section 21.06. Like the legendary Alamo defenders, Bill Delmore conducted a spirited defense of Texas's law, against great odds. His brief led with the state's best argument—that stare decisis required the Court to follow *Bowers*. Without a strong historical case against *Bowers*, the precedent should not be overruled—and if it were, what tradition-based *legal* principle would replace it? This argument, however, did not take account of the Cato, historians', and ACLU briefs, which had been filed at the same time as Lambda's brief. Another problem was how to deal with *Romer*. Justice Scalia's *Romer* dissent said that this precedent was inconsistent with *Bowers*. Because Harris County was not asking the Court to overrule *Romer*, this created a dilemma that Delmore could not easily resolve.[52]

Moreover, Section 21.06 seemed inconsistent with equal protection, as understood in *Romer*. How was its focus on "homosexual sodomy" explicable by anything but antigay "animus"? Here Delmore had an ingenious answer. By 1973 it was apparent from *Griswold v. Connecticut* (1965) that Texas could not constitutionally regulate private consensual sodomy by married couples. In *Eisenstadt v. Baird* (1972) the Supreme Court extended *Griswold*'s privacy right to different-sex couples using contraceptives. Thus, "it is a reasonable inference from this context that the Texas Legislature's enactment of Section 21.06 in 1973 was not purposefully discriminatory against homosexuals, but was instead a reform of [prior law] in accordance with what then appeared to be the direction in which constitutional privacy law was heading." Hence, no animus, and Section 21.06 could withstand *Romer*. To be sure, the decision to limit the new penal code's sodomy prohibition to "homosexual conduct" was made by the Committee on Revision of the Penal Code in June 1968, years before *Eisenstadt*, and the actual reason the crime was limited was a no promo homo rationale that was more clearly prejudice-driven than the one the Court rejected in *Romer* (chapter 5). Ironically, none of the briefs supporting Lawrence and Garner (including Lambda's) made this response. So Delmore had a potentially winning argument on the equal protection issue. If stare decisis could save *Bowers* on the liberty issue, Harris County could win the case.[53]

Whatever hope Delmore entertained for winning was largely dissipated by the oral argument of March 26, 2003. Paul Smith spoke for Lawrence and Garner. A tall genial redhead, the once-married Smith was by now an open homosexual, and an experienced appellate advocate whom Harlow had personally asked to represent Lambda before the justices. The courtroom that day was packed with an estimated two hundred lesbians and gay men, including John Lawrence. What they saw was an exciting intellectual joust with Justice Scalia, who asked Smith twenty-three of the thirty-five questions posed to him. Scalia immediately insisted upon first principles: Isn't *Bowers* consistent with the framers' intent in 1868? Justice Ginsburg helpfully observed that *Eisenstadt* and other precedents had not considered original intent the primary focus. Smith agreed with Ginsburg and, in response to Scalia, offered the amici's evidence that nineteenth-century sodomy laws were never enforced against consenting adults in the home, and that the large majority of states had over the past forty years specifically rejected *Bowers*'s policy. Objecting to the relevance of recent shifts in public morality, Scalia riposted, "[S]uppose all the states had laws against flagpole-sitting at one time ... and then almost all of them repealed those laws. Does that make flagpole-sitting a fundamental right?" As ripples of astonished giggles responded to Scalia's striking analogy, Smith answered that the role of the activity in the "lives of real people" was the Court's focus in the abortion and contraception cases—a comment aimed at Justices O'Connor and Kennedy, each of whom recognized some of the lesbian and gay faces in the courtroom.[54]

Smith shifted to equal protection, which he believed to be the stronger claim. The point of morals-based rules is *generality* (it is wrong for human beings to do thus-and-so); by exempting almost everyone but despised homosexuals from its morality-based rule, Texas was revealing antigay animus rather than a genuine morals regime. Moreover, Texas had generalized its specific conduct-based rule to justify a wide array of status-based discriminations. Smith was asked whether some of those discriminations were not desirable. "If you prevail, Mr. Smith, and this law is struck down, do you think that . . . a State could not prefer heterosexuals to homosexuals to teach kindergarten?" In response to this invocation of a discredited antigay stereotype, the gallery roared with dismissive laughter. The justice continued: Can't the state legitimately fear that kindergarten "children might be induced to follow the path of homosexuality"? Smith dismissed the no promo homo justification; no justice pressed him to explain why. Instead, Ginsburg tossed him another softball: What about stare decisis? Smith responded with a crisp litany of reasons the Court should overrule *Bowers*. Smith did an excellent job—and as many as six justices were receptive to his arguments.[55]

Texas was represented by Charles Rosenthal, the new Harris County DA. The genteel prosecutor got off to a bad start, wasting several minutes insisting that there was nothing in the record to show that Lawrence and Garner were indeed "homosexuals." The justices looked at him as though he had lost his mind, and journalist Nina Totenberg (sitting off to the side in the press section) dropped her head onto her notepad; this fellow was hopeless, she seemed to be suggesting. Justice Breyer finally cut to the core issue: Why shouldn't we overrule *Bowers*? The challengers say the precedent got the history wrong, understated the constitutional value, and visited harms upon worthy Americans. "I would like to hear your—your *straight* answer to those points," Breyer insisted, to great laughter. Like Scalia, Breyer did not get his own joke, until Justice Thomas whispered an explanation. Breyer smiled, but Rosenthal seemed completely lost. Rambling, he lost his chance to argue for stare decisis.[56]

Breyer then asked what justification supported Section 21.06's discrimination against "homosexual" conduct. "[I]s this simply, 'I do not like thee, Doctor Fell, the reason why I cannot tell?'" Missing the point of the question, Rosenthal answered that the state had plenary authority to enact morals-based regulations. Breyer pursued this idea: "Could they say, for example, it is against the law at the dinner table to tell really serious lies to your family?" That law would be irrational, Rosenthal answered. Why? "It's very immoral," and more harmful than the conduct Texas was criminalizing, Breyer tartly riposted. A former Harvard law professor, Breyer felt that first-year students would have given better answers.[57]

As the argument concluded, the few sodomy law suporters in the courtroom had the same sinking feeling that Davy Crockett must have had as he saw the Alamo falling before his eyes, also in the month of March (1836). The siege of Section 21.06 was about to be concluded.

The Supreme Court's Decision:
From Homosexual Sodomy to Same-Sex Marriage

The *Lawrence* oral argument had featured one of the biggest mismatches in the history of the Court, but even if the balance had been reversed (with Rosenthal playing the starring role) the result would have been the same. Six justices were dead set against the Homosexual Conduct Law. John Paul Stevens had dissented in *Bowers* and was delighted that his position was going to be vindicated. Former Ivy League law professors Stephen Breyer and Ruth Ginsburg found the law a distasteful expression of antigay prejudice, worse even than the badly drafted Colorado law that had fallen in *Romer*. David Souter and Anthony Kennedy, the author of *Romer*, felt that the Court's privacy jurisprudence meant nothing if it allowed Harris County to invade the home in this way. Like their colleagues, they believed that *Bowers*'s openly antihomosexual rhetoric, textually echoed in the Texas law, had brought international disrepute to the Court. As the Cato brief suggested to them, *Bowers delenda est*. Even Sandra Day O'Connor, who had joined *Bowers*, felt that homosexual sodomy laws were unconstitutional. More than her colleagues, she had had her eyes opened by former law clerks who had come out as homosexual; at least one was raising a child. Perhaps regretting her vote in *Bowers*, she had no doubt that *Lawrence* should come out the other way. As she expected, the *Romer* dissenters—William Rehnquist, Antonin Scalia, and Clarence Thomas—defended the Texas law during the Court's conference, but only Scalia did so with any zeal.[58]

On June 26, 2003, the Court delivered its obituary for the Homosexual Conduct Law. Because it was the last day of the 2002 term, Court watchers knew that *Lawrence v. Texas* would be announced that morning. Justice Kennedy delivered the judgment of the Court, and the first sentence of his opinion teed up the issue in a favorable way: "Liberty protects the person from unwarranted government intrusions into a dwelling or other private places," and further "presumes an autonomy of self that includes freedom of thought, belief, expression, and certain intimate conduct." After working his way through the facts of the case, Kennedy got to the key legal issue—the continuing validity of *Bowers v. Hardwick*.[59]

The gasps and whispers were audible when Kennedy announced that *Bowers*'s framing of the issue as a "right of homosexuals to engage in sodomy" reflected "the Court's own failure to appreciate the extent of the liberty at stake. To say that the issue in *Bowers* was simply the right to engage in certain sexual conduct demeans the claim the individual put forward, just as it would demean a married couple were it to be said that marriage is simply about the right to have sexual intercourse." Most of the lesbian and gay people in the room were already in tears as Kennedy continued: The liberty claim is, properly put, an assertion of freedom from state control of personal relationships as well as private activities. "Having misapprehended the claim of liberty there presented to it," *Bowers* deepened its error by mangling the history. Closely following the Cato brief, Kennedy recounted the evolution of sodomy laws, from general proscriptions enforced exclusively against nonconsensual or public activities (nineteenth century), to laws frequently targeting homosexuals (mid-twentieth century). Once sodomy laws lost their exclusive focus on nonconsensual or public conduct, they came under increasing criticism, starting with the Model Penal Code and continuing with state supreme court constitutional repudiations in Arkansas, Georgia, Kentucky, Montana, and Tennessee, as well as constitutional invalidation by the European Court of Human Rights.[60]

Romer, too, was relevant to *Bowers*'s validity. Kennedy noted that the challengers were making equality as well as liberty claims, and suggested they "are linked in important respects." Thus, "[w]hen homosexual conduct is made criminal by the law of the State, that declaration in and of itself is an invitation to subject homosexual persons to discrimination both in the public and the private spheres." Hence *Romer*'s precept that antigay discrimination, for its own sake, was relevant to the Court's reevaluation of *Bowers*—as were the persistent criticisms of *Bowers*, from conservative Republicans like Reagan solicitor general Charles Fried and Reagan judge Richard Posner, and the different constitutional results reached by the European Court of Human Rights, as well as southern and western state courts (chapter 9). Kennedy concluded dramatically: "*Bowers* was not correct when it was decided, and it is not correct today. It ought not to remain binding precedent. *Bowers v. Hardwick* should be and now is overruled." No one could remember a case where the Supreme Court had announced that one of its precedents had been wrong *when it was decided*. To hear a conservative Republican jurist denounce *Bowers* as "demeaning" was emotionally overpowering for the gays in court. For some, it was the first time in their lives they felt they were acceptable citizens of the United States.[61]

The chief justice announced that Justice O'Connor concurred in the Court's judgment. Declining to overrule *Bowers*, which she had joined, O'Connor's separate opinion (not read that morning) applied *Romer* to sustain Lambda's equal protection claim. "Moral disapproval of this group [homosexuals], like a bare desire to harm the group, is an interest that is insufficient to satisfy rational basis review under the Equal Protection Clause. 'A legislative classification that threatens the creation of an underclass'" cannot be sustained. Ruth Harlow and her Lambda colleagues readily understood that *Lawrence* might be a double victory for gay rights—not only extending the privacy right to bar consensual sodomy laws, but also (implicitly) extending *Romer* to bar antigay discriminations grounded on nothing more than moral disapproval. Surely, the five justices who joined Kennedy's opinion for the Court—all of whom had joined *Romer*—agreed with O'Connor's analysis.[62]

With the stroke of a judicial pen, the Homosexual Conduct Law was no longer enforceable, either in a criminal prosecution or as the foundation for civil discriminations. On June 30, the lesbian and gay community in Houston staged a mass rally to celebrate *Lawrence v. Texas*; similar rallies were held in forty other cities. Ray Hill remarked, "Well, children, it's been a long hunt." There had not been so many Houston homosexuals in one place since 1977, when they had marched against Anita Bryant. Linda Morales reminded the community of the activists (such as Patrick Wiseman) who did not live to see this day, and of the need to continue to engage in political activism on behalf of civil rights for all minorities. Deborah Bell, the president of NOW in Houston, urged the audience to embrace the "right to love" and to complete the "unfinished civil rights agenda."[63]

Texas conservatives shed few tears for the passing of their Homosexual Conduct Law. Joseph Quinn, the arresting officer, was philosophical: "It's not illegal for a man and woman to do that, so under the equal protection [of the law], I figured they'd rule like they did." Governor Perry immediately announced that Texas would comply with the Court's decision. Delmore was not surprised by the ruling. He had the satisfaction of having represented the state capably, and with a southern graciousness that impressed his adversaries. Senator Cornyn lost no sleep. When he was attorney general, one of his best attorneys was a lesbian who had represented the state brilliantly in the *Morales* litigation. Responding to inquiries about *Lawrence*, President Bush's press secretary said, "[T]he Administration did not file a brief in this case. . . . And this is now a state matter."[64]

Many conservatives did not share the Bush administration's blasé attitude. Although most of the law clerks for the justices were elated by the opinions in *Lawrence*, a vocal minority of religious clerks (including one in Kennedy's own chambers) were not. The day the decision was announced, they held a prayer meeting in the Court, imploring God to forgive the justices for elevating sexual license to a constitutional right. Justice Scalia's dissenting opinion, also read to the gallery on June 26, spoke for them. He lambasted his colleagues for their judicial activism—not only striking down a law adopted by the elected legislature, but doing so in the face of contrary precedent (*Bowers*), without sufficient basis in the legal traditions of the country, and, most galling of all, with reference to "foreign moods, fads, or fashions." Based on elite country-club Old Republican values, "the Court has taken sides in the culture war, departing from its role of assuring, as neutral observer, that the democratic rules of engagement are observed." The Reverend Pat Robertson denounced the "tyranny of a nonelected oligarchy," unaccountable judges who "can change the moral fabric of the nation." He announced a prayer initiative, petitioning "our Lord to change the Court. . . . One justice is 83 years old, another has cancer, and another has a heart condition. Would it not be possible for God to put in the minds of these three judges that the time has come to retire?" Several clerks in the Scalia chambers said amen to that.[65]

Scalia's charge of judicial activism was unfair. Except for *Bowers*, the Court has generally not followed an originalist approach in its privacy cases—and *Bowers* revealed how original-meaning jurisprudence can be just as result-oriented and less constraining than a jurisprudence based on precedent. As a matter of original meaning, moreover, there is much to be said for Justice Kennedy's and, especially, Justice O'Connor's opinions. As chapter 1 demonstrated, the Fourteenth Amendment's framers meant to protect people's substantive rights "to pursue and obtain happiness and safety; subject nonetheless to such restraints as the government may justly prescribe for the general good of the whole"; even when the state can bar happiness-conferring activities, it cannot discriminate through "class legislation." Consensual sodomy is essential to the pursuit of happiness for gay people; the originalist inquiry is whether the government may "justly" determine that the "general good" requires that their intercourse be deemed criminal, while leaving the same conduct by different-sex couples alone. That inquiry should be informed by the history of state regulation. Unlike the *Bowers* Court, the *Lawrence* Court engaged in a serious fact-based inquiry into precisely what American states had actually criminalized for two hundred years and concluded that private and consensual activities had not traditionally been the basis for state regulation. Although Justice Scalia rejected the Court's history, he did not actually dispute these pertinent historical facts: not a single reported sodomy case that the framers would have known about involved conduct in the home or consensual activities; oral sex between men was not a crime against nature anywhere in the United States until 1879 and was not criminal in most states until the twentieth century; oral sex between women was not a crime against nature until well into the twentieth century and was never clearly a crime in many states; sodomy laws had never until 1968–69 even mentioned "homosexual sodomy," the focus of *Bowers* and the Texas statute. If the crime against nature was abominable, surely it was abominable for all, and the state could not justly demonize a minority for conduct regularly engaged in by the majority.[66]

Scalia was correct in asserting that American history was not replete with the same kind of affirmative protection for private adult (homosexual) intimacy as for marriage and childrearing. But that mode of argument would have defeated the privacy claims in *Eisenstadt* and *Roe*, and perhaps even *Griswold*, superprecedents that anchor the privacy right now foundational to American constitutional law. Scalia criticized the *Lawrence* Court for overruling *Bowers*, but had himself pronounced *Bowers*'s obituary after *Romer*. Because the *Lawrence* parties treated *Romer* as an unquestioned precedent, stare decisis strongly supported the approach taken by Justice O'Connor, who followed *Romer* without overruling *Bowers*. Indeed, for that reason, the O'Connor opinion can be considered the strongest as a matter of traditional conservative law-finding. There is a broader point that suggests a stare decisis case for Justice Kennedy's opinion as well. Like *Brown* (which overruled the apartheid-era precedents) and unlike *Casey* (which reaffirmed *Roe*), *Lawrence* was conforming constitutional law to a new sociopolitical reality: lesbian, gay, bisexual, and transgendered Americans were productive citizens, and it was no longer reasonable to treat them as presumptive outlaws.[67]

Justice O'Connor's concurring opinion epitomized the responsible rule of law, for it scrupulously followed precedent, hewed closely to the original purpose of the Fourteenth Amendment, and struck down a discrimination that had no fact-based defense. (Given the prejudice- and stereotype-based motives for the antihomosexual discrimination, discussed in chapter 5 and this chapter, the case for O'Connor's result is even stronger.) While more venturesome, Justice Kennedy's opinion for the Court was no less law-following than Justice Scalia's dissent: both relied on one precedent and dismissed another, and each opinion was historically connected to a substantive account of the Fourteenth Amendment's purpose. Kennedy's opinion achieves its greatest cogency when understood in light of the larger purposes of the rule of law—that is, to assure productive American citizens that the state will not lightly invade their personal relationships and will not isolate them as a class of outlaws. *Lawrence* rightly connects Texas's invasion of Lawrence's home and personal relations with its larger project of setting all homosexuals apart from the normal operation of the law, precisely the defect *Romer* identified in Colorado's Amendment 2. By extending an olive branch to a social group subject to intense state violence and discrimination between 1935 and 1961, Justice Kennedy dramatically established that the rule of law protects the unpopular minority (*Lawrence*) as well as the mainstream (*Griswold*, *Eisenstadt*, and *Roe*).

Justice Scalia's best points addressed the scope of *Lawrence*: What principle now defined constitutional *liberty* or told the state what regulations it could justly place on private sexual relations? Scalia claimed that *Lawrence* spelled the end of morals-based legislation—not just sodomy laws, but also laws against fornication, adultery, bigamy, adult incest, bestiality, obscenity, and masturbation. What antihomosexual discriminations survived *Lawrence* and *Romer*? Scalia claimed that these precedents constitutionalized the entire "homosexual agenda," which entailed invalidation of all state discriminations against homosexuals, including state and national bars to same-sex marriage. The American Society for the Defense of Tradition, Family, and Property decried *Lawrence* as "America's moral 9/11," and the following chapter will explore whether *Lawrence* has had the radical effect attributed to it by Justice Scalia.[68]

At a press conference on June 26, John Lawrence said this: "We never chose to be public figures or to take on this fight, but we also never thought we could be arrested in this way. We're glad that not only this ruling lets us get on with our lives but that it opens doors for gay people all across this country to be treated equally." The decision in *Lawrence v. Texas* did open doors for gay people to claim rights to equal treatment—but at the same time it opened doors for religious conservatives to reaffirm traditional family values. The Federal Marriage Amendment, which a backbencher had introduced to amend the Constitution to bar same-sex marriage earlier that year, suddenly became a major plank in the New Republican Party. The culture wars had moved on to a new front.

CHAPTER ELEVEN

American Public Law After *Lawrence*

Steven Lofton (born 1957) met his life partner, Roger Croteau (born 1955), when they were both earning advanced degrees in nursing. After 1983 the two men lived together in a committed relationship; for most of that period, their home was Miami, Florida. In 1988, when both were working with AIDS patients, a dying mother asked Lofton if he would be willing to become a foster parent to her baby. The couple agreed to care for the baby, Frank. The same year,

Steve Lofton, Roger Croteau, and their children

they became foster parents to HIV-infected baby girls they named Ginger and Tracy. Lofton quit his job to work full-time with these three children. For Lofton this meant not only caring for their substantial medical needs, but creating a loving family environment for the children, and bringing joy and stability to their young lives. Bert joined the family in 1992. Ginger died of complications associated with AIDS in 1995; every bit of happiness she had known had originated with her two dads and three brothers.[1]

By 1994 Bert had seroconverted under his parents' care. This was a wonderful development for the family of two white men and their three black children, but it also made Bert "adoptable." A caseworker urged Lofton to petition for adoption, but it was denied by the state, because a 1977 Florida law prohibited "homosexuals" from adopting children. Gay men could be foster parents, but they could not have the permanent rights of adoptive parents. The couple turned to the ACLU, which brought a lawsuit challenging the constitutionality of Florida's adoption rule. *Lawrence* was decided while their case was on appeal to the U.S. Court of Appeals for the Fifth Circuit. The ACLU argued that *Lawrence* recognized a broad liberty interest for gay people to create relationships productive for them and their loved ones. The state could invade that liberty only for serious community reasons, which Florida was not able to produce in support of its adoption ban. Additionally, *Lawrence* reinforced the rule of *Romer v. Evans* (1996) that state policies grounded on antigay "animus" were unconstitutional. The 1977 adoption ban was added days after Anita Bryant's Dade County triumph and reflected her politics of antihomosexual disgust and contagion (chapter 7). Its discrimination could not stand.[2]

Ironically, the ACLU found support in Justice Scalia's *Lawrence* dissent. Texas had defended its regulation of private sexuality on grounds of traditional morality—which the Court rejected as a rational basis. The same reasoning, Scalia argued, could apply to *any* state discrimination against homosexuals. Scalia also read *Lawrence* to announce the end of *all* morals-based legislation, including laws against obscenity, child abuse, and so forth. Agreeing with Scalia's broad readings of *Lawrence*, the ACLU maintained that Florida's antihomosexual discrimination, like Texas's, violated the Constitution because it was a liberty-infringing morals regulation and reflected antigay "animus" (the *Romer* term) rather than a rational basis.[3]

Some constitutional scholars agree with Scalia's conclusions about the broad sweep of *Lawrence*. Randy Barnett, for example, reads *Lawrence* to codify John Stuart Mill's libertarian philosophy of government into the Due Process Clause: the state may not deny me any freedom unless I am harming a third party. Laurence Tribe reads *Lawrence* to "advanc[e]" an "equality-based and relationally situated theory of substantive liberty." Most lesbian or gay constitutional scholars have not read *Lawrence* as broadly as Barnett or Tribe. Perhaps the Constitution should be read that broadly, but the Supreme Court has not announced such a broad reading.[4]

What brought *Bowers* tumbling down was not the triumph of a constitutional liberalism, but instead the confluence of opinion among (1) sexual prochoice liberals, (2) relationals who understood that gay people formed families and committed unions, and (3) pragmatic traditionalists who believed the legal line should be drawn at gay marriage rather than homosexual criminality. Anthony Kennedy, the author of *Lawrence*, recognized all three of these reasons—as did his opinion for the Court. For all its progay rhetoric, Kennedy's opinion did not hold that Americans have a "fundamental" liberty right to engage in sexual activities with consenting partners. Nor did he or Justice O'Connor state that homosexuality is a "suspect classification" that renders problematic all antigay discriminations. While the justices overturned the prior regime, which was based on discriminatory traditionalism, they did not commit themselves to either a complete sexual liberalism or what Scalia calls the "homosexual agenda."[5]

Reflecting the combined power of sexual liberals and relationals, and acquiescence from pragmatic traditionalists, the Court committed the Constitution to an important principle—that there is a *tolerable* range of sexual variation that the state cannot persecute, either through criminal prohibitions or pervasive civil exclusions. *Lawrence* acknowledged that lesbian, gay, bisexual, and transgendered people are normal, functioning human beings who have much to add to the community. As *Romer* held, Florida could not exclude Lofton and Croteau from access to routine governmental services, including the state police and the judiciary, to protect their home and family from danger. *Lawrence* held that Florida could not charge the two men with "unnatural and lascivious" conduct (a misdemeanor still on its statute books) for intimacy in their own bedroom. Did *Lawrence* also preclude Florida from criminalizing fornication, adultery, and bestiality, as Justice Scalia believed? *Romer* and *Lawrence* called into question state exclusions of LGBT persons from responsible positions in education, law enforcement, and public health. Could Florida still discriminate against gay people like Lofton who want to adopt foster children they raised? Could it deny state marriage licenses to same-sex couples like Lofton and Croteau?[6]

In the short term *Lawrence* did not radically change the legal landscape. Lofton and Croteau, for example, did not prevail in their constitutional challenge to Florida's bar to adoption by gay people. In the longer term, *Lawrence* will likely have greater bite against broad and harmful antigay discriminations than it will against state regulations of sexual behavior. This prediction is grounded not on *Lawrence*'s own logic but rather on this book's themes. Individual and community morality will continue to draw from reservoirs of disgust that people feel toward certain sexual practices and to require the enforcement of law-based ethical lines. *Lawrence* will channel arguments for regulating sexual behavior away from religious natural-law models, and toward the effects of such conduct on other persons and toward what kinds of behavior the state ought to be encouraging. If LGBT persons continue to assimilate into mainstream America and to form families, constitutional as well as political support for antigay discriminations will erode.

Lawrence as a Regime Shift in Constitutional Law: Tolerable Sexual Variation as the New Baseline

Read with *Romer*, *Lawrence* repudiated not only the specific holding of *Bowers*, but also its philosophy—that states are free to treat homosexuality and its associated conduct as a malign (dangerous) variation from the norm, heterosexuality. But *Lawrence* and *Romer* did not go as far as gay liberal lawyers would read the

Constitution, that is, for the proposition that states must treat homosexuality as a benign (good) variation, normatively indistinguishable from heterosexuality. *Lawrence* treated homosexual conduct with careful respect, but also considerable moral distance. Contrast Justice Douglas's opinion for the Court in *Griswold v. Connecticut* (1965), protecting the right of married couples to use contraceptives. Douglas concluded with a lavish ode to heterosexual marriage as "intimate to the degree of being sacred. It is an association that promotes a way of life, not causes; a harmony in living, not political faiths; a bilateral loyalty, not commercial or social projects. Yet it is an association for as noble a purpose as any involved in our prior decisions." Kennedy's opinion in *Lawrence* concluded on a flatter note: "The case does involve two adults who, with full and mutual consent from each other, engaged in sexual practices common to a homosexual lifestyle." This is the language of both tolerance and moral distance. Heterosexuals have "sacred" and "noble" marriage; homosexuals have a "lifestyle."[7]

Lawrence established that the states must treat homosexuality and same-sex intimacy as a tolerable variation, but left the states free to suggest that there is still a preferred norm, heterosexuality or marriage or whatever. Thus, Florida could not treat Lofton and Croteau as common criminals. But *Lawrence* did not require Florida to abandon all morals-based regulations, nor did *Lawrence* nullify all antigay discriminations. The distinction between tolerable and benign variation helps us to situate *Romer* and *Lawrence* in our constitutional history and to understand how much of a regime shift these decisions represented. Two complementary analogies come to mind: *Roe v. Wade* (1973) and *Brown v. Board of Education* (1954).[8]

Like *Lawrence*, *Roe* protected the freedom of Americans to make sexual choices but took no moral position on the value of those choices. The pro-life movement vigorously maintained that *Roe* was wrongly decided and that abortion was a malignant moral choice—essentially murder. That countermovement was not able to persuade Americans that the fetus is a human person; most Americans have agreed that an abortion is a tolerable moral choice, such that the state cannot make it a crime. But many have agreed with the critics that abortion is not a benign or good moral choice, such that the state must support or "promote" it. In *Maher v. Roe* (1977), the Supreme Court ruled that it is not unconstitutional for state Medicaid programs to exclude abortions even if they fund childbirths. The Court interpreted *Roe* as protecting a woman against "unduly burdensome interference with her freedom to decide whether to terminate her pregnancy"—a freedom from state "compulsion" that did not at the same time entitle women to have their abortions paid for by the state. "There is a basic difference between direct state interference with a protected activity and state encouragement of an alternative activity consonant with legislative policy." The state has wide latitude not to promote abortion by funding it; this is a policy issue best left to the democratically elected legislators.[9]

Maher encouraged pro-life activists to press for laws discouraging abortion as a choice. Such laws required that abortions be performed only after doctors obtain the written consent of their patients, and that the consent be informed by pro-life information the doctors were required to provide. The Supreme Court rebuffed their early efforts but acquiesced in *Planned Parenthood v. Casey* (1992). The joint opinion, delivered by Justices O'Connor, Kennedy, and Souter (also the core in *Lawrence*), reaffirmed the "essential holding" of *Roe*, but applied *Maher*'s undue burden test to uphold a state law requiring waiting periods, informational disclosures, and (for minors) parental consent before exercising one's choice to have an abortion.[10]

It is only in retrospect that *Brown* has been understood as representing the triumph of the NAACP's norm of benign racial variation. Chief Justice Warren's *Brown* opinion focused on the importance of public education as a training ground for citizenship and the dignitary harms visited on black schoolchildren who were the obvious targets of segregation. Warren said nothing about race as a presumptively inadmissible classification across the board. Immediately after *Brown* the Court had an opportunity to take that step. In *Naim v. Naim* (1954) Virginia courts upheld that state's law making different-race marriage a crime. The Supreme Court remanded the case for the state court to reconsider in light of *Brown*. Virginia stuck to its original position, which was that different-race marriage would yield a "mongrel race," diluting white purity. There could have been no clearer rejection of the idea that racial variation is benign, yet the Supreme Court allowed the decision to stand. The apparent reason was the furious reaction in the South to *Brown* and the equivocal support the Court was receiving from Congress and the president. It was not until *Loving v. Virginia* (1967) that the Court repudiated *Naim*—after all states but those in the South had repealed their miscegenation laws.[11]

Romer and *Lawrence* accomplished for LGBT people roughly what *Brown* accomplished for people of color and *Roe* accomplished for women: to establish homosexuality as a tolerable sexual variation, which (like race) the state cannot make the basis for a regime of criminalization or general exclusion. Like abortion, homosexual sodomy is tolerable conduct that the state cannot make a crime. What comes next for gay people is not completely predictable. Parallel to the claims made by people of color, LGBT communities maintain that homosexuality is a benign sexual variation and that homosexual sodomy is benign conduct—in other words, Gay is Good and not just Tolerable. *Loving* offers gay people hope that this moral vision will prevail. Parallel to the claims made by pro-life supporters, TFV communities and their legal representatives argue that homosexuality and homosexual conduct are either bad or unfortunate variations from an excellent norm, procreative marriage or just heterosexuality: Gay is God Awful and, at best, Unfortunate. *Casey* offers traditionalists hope that this moral vision will prevail.

Thus, Justice Scalia was wrong to conclude that the *Lawrence* constitutionalized the "homosexual agenda" and, further, precluded the states from adopting regulations reflecting and trying to influence public morality. In the short term the Constitution may tolerate some regulations whose justification is, essentially, no promo homo. If that is so, what constitutional principles enable us to determine which morals regulations and which antigay discriminations have survived *Lawrence*? To answer this question we need to return to the Fourteenth Amendment's history and ongoing legacy.

The twin goals of Reconstruction, explored in chapter 1, were *reunification* of the nation and *integration* of the former slaves into national and state communities. Starting from those aims, the Fourteenth Amendment assured not only the freed slaves but all Americans certain rights that states had to respect. Its constitutionalized rule of law did not, however, absolutely bar the states from regulating people's activities. States could deprive people of certain liberties—so long as they followed "due process of law" and did not deny "equal protection of the law." The Fourteenth Amendment did not define these key terms, and our constitutional history has not given them rigid content. Moreover, even when these requirements have suggested firm libertarian or inclusionary requirements, their judicial implementation has often been cautious if not downright lethargic. The Supreme Court is the "least dangerous branch," as Alexander Hamilton said. Its ability to remedy rights violations depends critically on a certain level of political support outside its corridors.[12]

Before 1933 most accounts of judicial review assumed that the Supreme Court had no role to play in the operation of the democratic process. Responding to the NAACP's stream of criminal procedure and voting cases, the New Deal Court suggested that it was prepared to be a referee for the political process, not only (1) when it violated the Constitution's clearly specified rights (such as those in the First Amendment), but also (2) when local political elites sought to lock in their power by excluding minorities from participation or (3) when laws were motivated by "prejudice against discrete and insular minorities" such that the ordinary political process could not be relied on. The Supreme Court should not be eager to apply libertarian and egalitarian protections against statutes that were the product of a normally functioning democratic process, one in which all relevant groups participated freely (even if with unequal success). Aggressive judicial interpretation of the open-textured Fourteenth Amendment, under this theory, should be exceptional, limited to cases involving self-perpetuating majorities and minorities that were systematically excluded.[13]

Such a representation-reinforcing theory of judicial review suggests one good reason why *Lawrence* was right to interpret the Fourteenth Amendment to invalidate the Texas Homosexual Conduct Law. The law imposed unique disabilities on a ghettoized minority that had been demonized in the Texas political process. Before 1973 Texas made it a felony for anyone to engage in consensual sodomy. By 1973 it was apparent to legislators that oral sex in particular was widespread in the state, but almost no one would admit to such conduct, for religious reasons. Because there were few openly gay people in the state, their interests could be entirely ignored. Under such circumstances, it was a natural but unfair compromise to do what the Committee on Revision of the Penal Code proposed in 1968 and the Legislature enacted in 1973—limit the sodomy crime to "homosexual conduct." Its intended effect was to signal that open homosexuals could be denied an indeterminate range of state benefits and thereby to confine the homosexual minority to their closets. This is both arbitrary and undemocratic. "[T]here is no more effective practical guaranty against arbitrary and unreasonable government than to require the principles of law which officials would impose upon a minority must be imposed generally."[14]

The foregoing account is a response to Scalia's charge that the Court should have left the matter to the Texas Legislature. This argument also lends particular support to Justice O'Connor's proposition that the Texas law be invalidated on equal protection grounds. O'Connor's point can likewise be made against general sodomy laws, not just those that discriminate on their face. The Georgia Attorney General's Office told the *Bowers* Court that its general sodomy law could not be applied to married couples, and told the people of Georgia that the law would never be applied to consensual conduct between adults of different sexes. Under these circumstances Justice Stevens's *Bowers* dissent cogently argued that Georgia's general sodomy law violated the anti–class legislation principle of the Fourteenth Amendment.[15]

There is another way of thinking about judicial review that supports Kennedy's broader opinion. In addition to local lock-ins and prejudice-based discriminations, a third problem with pluralist democracy is that its stakes can get too high. This is a particular problem when groups hate or demonize one another—the classic culture war. In the modern regulatory state, dominant social groups will deploy governmental apparatus to persecute hated minorities. A brutal example is the Kulturkampf, when the state seeks to erase a minority or coerce it into conformity through a campaign of terror, with criminal prosecutions and forfeitures for disobedience. Less extreme examples involve interference with the minority's institutions or harassment of individuals in the minority.[16]

It is dangerous for the state to take sides so decisively in culture wars. By persecuting or harassing minorities, the state embitters the minority, creates dangers for the majority, and destabilizes the democracy. Angry minorities, or some of them, will tend to go outside the political process to vent their anger against the majority, or the state itself. Violence becomes a stronger possibility. The nightmare result is the game of "chicken," where each group keeps raising the stakes of the conflict, with disastrous results for both sides (and the general public).[17] If the escalation is not stopped, the game of "chicken" can destroy the conditions for democracy itself, a fact understood by our founding fathers. In 1791 religion was at the center of the kind of identity-based politics we now call culture wars. The Religion Clauses of the First Amendment (1791) limit the federal government's involvement in such private feuds. The government can neither interfere with the free exercise of minority religions nor establish one official religion. From the polity's point of view, the Religion Clauses insist on a *jurisprudence of tolerance.* Reconstruction extended this jurisprudence to the states.[18]

The Religion Clauses provide a useful model for applying the open-textured language of the Fourteenth Amendment to modern culture clashes: the Supreme Court should discourage heavy-handed state interventions raising the stakes of politics, already high when there is a private culture war. *Lawrence* and *Romer* illustrate this precept. In both cases the Court overturned laws that represented policies that marginally (at best) benefited the public but stigmatized and broadly excluded the homosexual minority from a wide range of state services. This stakes-lowering precept protects traditionalists, as well. In *Hurley v. Gay, Lesbian, Bisexual Irish of Boston* (1995), a unanimous Supreme Court ruled that a Massachusetts law barring sexual orientation discrimination by public accommodations could not constitutionally be applied to the Boston St. Patrick's Day Parade. The parade organizers sought to present a traditionalist point of view, and the presence of an openly lesbian, gay, and bisexual marching group would detract from that point of view. Accordingly the Court held that the law, as applied, violated the First Amendment. In *Dale v. Boy Scouts of America* (2000) a divided Court extended *Hurley* to invalidate the application of a similar antidiscrimination laws to the Boy Scouts. The Court majority found that the Boy Scouts were an expressive association whose normative "no promo homo" message would be undermined by the presence of an openly gay man as an assistant scoutmaster.[19]

A Supreme Court that decided *Dale* and *Hurley* was not a Court that had accepted the "homosexual agenda." But a Court that decided *Romer* and *Lawrence* as well as *Hurley* and *Dale* was a Court that had taken a role in managing culture clashes. The question then becomes: What constitutional limits does the Fourteenth Amendment impose on the states? To answer this question, start with generally applicable morals regulations, and then turn to discriminatory employment and family law regulations. In the process, however, the observant reader should think beyond Scalia's old-fashioned dichotomy between morals legislation (such as the Texas sodomy law) versus the libertarian presumption (such as that reflected in the Model Penal Code).

Criminal Law After *Lawrence*: Beyond Sectarian Morals Regulation

Every regime shift threatens a slippery slope. Once a prior normative understanding has been called into constitutional question by the Court, once-settled issues are subject to rethinking and relitigation. For example, *Griswold*, the contraception case, opened the Constitution to abortion and sodomy challenges. Its sexual privacy principle *could* be applied more broadly, and it was in the interest of freshly energized social groups (women and gays) to develop social scripts supporting an extension of that right. Once women (in the 1970s) and gay people (1990s) became established political forces and important audiences for Supreme Court opinions, the Court felt it should accommodate their scripts and their constitutional arguments. Likewise, the antidiscrimination right advanced by *Brown* for people of color was extended to sex and sexual orientation discrimination (the 1970s and 1990s, respectively).[20]

Echoing Lord Patrick Devlin's critique of the Wolfenden Report four decades earlier, Justice Scalia charged that *Lawrence* would mean the end of all laws regulating immoral conduct—specifically including fornication, adultery, adult incest, bigamy, obscenity, bestiality, prostitution, and even masturbation. Don't believe it. The truth is, there is no newly energized social group poised to exploit the constitutional opportunities allegedly created by *Lawrence*. The United Kingdom did not descend into moral chaos after it decriminalized consensual sodomy in 1967, and neither will the United States. Post-*Lawrence* litigation will, however, weed out some kinds of morals laws, while strengthening others by forcing them to modernize their justifications.[21]

Kansas makes it a serious crime for anyone to have oral or anal sex with a fourteen- to sixteen-year-old minor; punishment for a first offense is 55 to 60 months in prison, with a range of 89 to 100 months for a second offense and 206 to 228 months for a third offense. On February 16, 2000, Matthew Limon, who had just celebrated his eighteenth birthday, asked fourteen-year-old M.A.R. if he could perform oral sex on the younger boy; M.A.R. agreed. When he asked Limon to stop, Limon did so. The incident eventually came to the attention of the police, and Limon was prosecuted for sodomy with a minor. Because he had two previous convictions, he was sentenced to 206 months (over seventeen years) in prison, followed by sixty months of post-release supervision. The U.S. Supreme Court vacated state appellate decisions affirming Limon's sentence, and remanded his case for reconsideration in light of *Lawrence*. Did the U.S. Constitution require reversal of the conviction?[22]

Most Morals Legislation Survives the Libertarian Presumption

It is a canard to say that *Lawrence* invalidated all state morals legislation. Indeed, Kennedy's opinion accepted the libertarian idea, derived from the moral philosophy of Jeremy Bentham and John Stuart Mill (chapter 4), that the state ought to prohibit citizens from engaging in activities harming other persons. As the Model Penal Code reflected, the libertarian "harm" principle has long been the most popular justification for the criminal sanction. But as the harm principle has become more popular, it has also become more diluted, so that today it can justify punishment of a wide array of sex crimes, including most on Scalia's list.[23]

Adultery, for example, may harm third parties as a matter of law, biology, and economics. When a married man has intercourse with someone other than his wife, he has not only violated his wife's legal right to his fidelity, but he has usually imposed significant emotional costs upon her, as well as introducing the possibility of sexually transmitted diseases. Adultery also puts at risk the welfare of the marital children, because sexual infidelity can be linked to marital troubles and divorce, either of which carries with it harm to the children. Although half the states have, like Texas, repealed their criminal adultery laws, there are good libertarian defenses for the legislation that remains in place in twenty-five of them (as of 2005). Some of the same consequentialist arguments can be invoked to justify state laws prohibiting bigamy.[24]

Every state bars promulgation of obscene materials, and all but one (Nevada) make prostitution a crime.[25] *Lawrence* poses little threat to these statutes; Kennedy's opinion explicitly distinguished public from private conduct. Obscenity laws usually speak to public displays of lewdness, or traffic in such displays, and so are limited to situations where third parties or children will be exposed to unwanted sexual images. Recall that the Supreme Court in *Stanley v. Georgia* (1969) ruled it unconstitutional for the state to apply obscenity laws to private viewing of pornography within the home, but the result would have been different if Mr. Stanley had been distributing these materials to neighbors or the public. Child pornography, in particular, is also regulated because of the harmful effects on children participating in its production. Likewise, illegal prostitution is usually limited to public solicitation of sex for compensation. Antiprostitution laws are sometimes also justified by the harm sex work allegedly brings to women and their children.[26]

While adultery, antiprostitution, and obscenity laws were originally inspired by religious principles, they survived *Lawrence* because their justifications have been modernized.[27] From a religious perspective, a husband's extramarital dalliances are immoral because they violate the natural law (or God's rule) of no sex outside of marriage. In the modern era this conduct is considered even more powerfully immoral because of its catastrophic effects on a particularly vulnerable third party, in addition to its infraction of natural law. Even bestiality laws might be sustained under a libertarian philosophy. Studies suggest that bestiality is linked to sexual assault on children; if accurate, that could serve as a respectable modern rationale. Twenty-five states make it a crime to have intercourse with an animal in private. Prosecutions still occur, though not often. Because sex-with-animals people have not united into a coherent social group, there will be little *Lawrence*-based pressure to invalidate these laws.[28]

In a libertarian regime, consent is essential for regulating sexual activities. If a man forces himself sexually on a woman, the activity is deemed to be rape, completely unprotected from state regulation, not fornication, possibly protected under the libertarian philosophy. Indeed, one might argue that the state has an obligation, not just the discretion, to protect its citizens against sexual assaults. Our society has rationally concluded that young persons are not mature enough to consent to sexual relations with others. While the "age of consent" differs from state to state, all states have decided that fourteen is too young. That was the age of Limon's sexual partner, and so most libertarian theories would support Kansas's regulation of Limon's sex with M.A.R. Under the Eighth Amendment one might object to the seventeen-year sentence Limon received, but the ability of the state to protect underage youth against sexual experience with older persons is well-established. There is enormous evidence of the possible harm such encounters pose for youth.[29]

Another potentially relevant factor for a harm analysis is the institutional context of sexual activity. Lawrence and Garner's arrest was particularly outrageous because they were in the confines of Lawrence's home. Limon's case involved sexual activity within a residential school for developmentally disabled youth, where he and M.A.R. were living. Even within most liberal frameworks, state institutions have substantial discretion to regulate sexual interactions that undermine the institution's ability to do its job. The more totalizing the state institution, the greater the discretion. Hence, prisons can prohibit inmates from having consensual sex with other inmates, not only because they would be doing it on state property and in quasi-public settings, but also because such rules might be necessary to assure order within the prison. The national armed forces have a similarly broad discretion, which justifies their rules against sex between an officer and a subordinate, as well as against barracks sex. On the other hand, sexual activities by service personnel off-base and with civilians implicates *Lawrence*, as several military courts have held. Although the state did not rest its prosecution on the institutional context of Limon's encounter with M.A.R., it is relevant to the constitutional analysis. Through appropriate criminal statutes, the state has substantial authority to regulate sexual conduct of minors under its care and supervision. In short, *Lawrence* created little doubt as to Kansas's authority to criminalize Matthew Limon's conduct with M.A.R.

Community Norms: History and Beyond History

Even under Scalia's broad reading, *Lawrence* did not constitutionally deregulate sexual activities that harm third parties, including public activities. Hence, *Lawrence* did not disable states from regulating adultery, bigamy, promulgation of obscene materials, bestiality, and sex with minors. That reduces Scalia's list of assertedly deregulated activities to adult incest, fornication, and masturbation in private places. An Ohio court has suggested that "protecting the family unit" is a post-*Lawrence* state interest justifying incest laws, but in a case where the daughter denied that her father's advances were consensual. Ought the court's dicta be generalized?[30]

Lawrence did not constitutionalize the libertarian philosophy and its harm principle as the *only* basis for criminal penalties. Consider the structure of Justice Kennedy's opinion. It opened with an examination of the weightiness of the "liberty" interest asserted by Lawrence and Garner. Kennedy associated consensual sodomy with gay people's freedom to form "personal relationships" within the "confines of their homes." Later in his opinion he also noted the many civil discriminations Texas and other states justified by reference to their homosexual sodomy laws. What was significant to the Court was not only the liberty of Lawrence and Garner to avoid arrest, but also the related freedoms curtailed by their sodomy conviction, and the liberties denied en masse to a coherent and productive social group.[31]

Kennedy next considered the ongoing history of sodomy regulation. He concluded that the crime against nature was not enforced against private consensual activities in nineteenth-century America; that such enforcement occurred only episodically in the twentieth century; that the focus on "homosexual sodomy" did not appear until the last third of the twentieth century; and that this recent focus has been overridden by the counterfocus represented by the Model Penal Code. The historical discussion suggested that the considered moral judgment of the community, today as well as over time, has been skeptical that consensual sodomy within the home should be a crime.[32]

Finally, Kennedy analyzed state interests that might justify the significant liberty deprivations Texas's law visited upon homosexuals. As *Romer* suggested, antihomosexual animus could not be posited as such a legitimate interest. Nor could private religious beliefs, standing alone, justify such a far-reaching and novel deprivation of liberty. Kennedy acknowledged that many Americans have disapproved of sodomy because of "religious beliefs" and ethical concerns—but the majority could not "use the power of the State to enforce these [sectarian] views on the whole society." Texas was never able to articulate a neutral state interest, even one rooted in a nonsectarian moral tradition. That the state also disclaimed any intention of enforcing the law sealed its doom.[33]

Kennedy's opinion artfully combined a sophisticated understanding of liberty, history, and neutral state policy choices. His analysis can be generalized: most immediately vulnerable under *Lawrence* are morals laws that (1) represent significant liberty deprivations for members of a politically mobilized social group, (2) criminalize behavior that has not been historically targeted and is not today widely criminalized, and (3) serve no neutral state interest, including but not limited to protecting public spaces and third parties. When the state creates new discriminations burdening important liberties of a traditionally disadvantaged group, it must present a serious public purpose that is factually grounded and not just speculative.[34]

Under this kind of analysis, private masturbation is an easy call. Sex researchers tell us that almost everyone finds this activity satisfying (without demonstrable harm); historically and today, masturbation has been considered a crime only if practiced in front of third parties, generally children; it is hard to think of a neutral state interest for regulating this activity, much less actually enforcing it. Fortunately for most Americans, there are no laws making private masturbation (not involving minors) a crime. Scalia's invocation of masturbation as a crime is a lavender herring.[35]

Private fornication also fits within this hard-to-regulate core, though not as snugly. Traditionally, fornication was only a crime when it was open and scandalized the community. Most states have decriminalized fornication, there is little evidence of third-party harms, and most Americans consider the right to fornicate important to their lives, or formative experiences in their youths. In *Martin v. Ziherl* (2005) the Virginia Supreme Court extended *Lawrence* to rule its fornication law unconstitutional. Kristopher Joseph Ziherl defended the statute on the grounds that it protected public health and encouraged heterosexual couples to engage in procreative activities only within marriage. The public health justification was undermined by the facts of the case: Muguet Martin was suing Ziherl for transmitting genital herpes to her during their two-year sexual relationship; Ziherl's main defense was that Martin could not recover for harm sustained during the commission of a crime (fornication). Because Virginia never enforced its fornication law, the only deterrent to men infecting their sexual partners with STDs would be tort lawsuits such as Martin's. Ironically, then, public health would best be served by removing the criminal law impediment, as the court did. Ziherl's other justification, state encouragement of procreation only within marriage, was weightier. Fornication poses significant risks of producing nonmarital children, and the state might conclude that it wants to encourage childrearing within marriage. Yet Justice Elizabeth Lacy's opinion for the court reasoned that *Lawrence* reflected a judgment that this plausible justification for fornication laws was not sufficient to impose criminal penalties on consenting adults for conduct that is important to their meaningful relationship.[36]

The Virginia justices could have distinguished *Lawrence*, on the ground that a fornication law could promote marriage and childbirth within marriage. Under traditional rational basis analysis, that justification would usually suffice. Yet they read *Lawrence* to be inconsistent with the fornication law. *Ziherl* followed the suggestion made in Justice O'Connor's concurring opinion in *Lawrence*: "We have been most likely to apply rational basis review to hold a law unconstitutional ... [where] that challenged legislation inhibits personal relationships," and not economic matters. O'Connor provided an edge to the approach outlined above: when the state makes personal relations between consenting adults criminal or otherwise penalizes them, it bears a burden of showing that the penalty actually serves a neutral state interest. When economic regulations are evaluated, the statute can be saved by hypothesizing various state interests and imagining plausible connections. When "personal relationships" are regulated, especially through criminal sanctions, the state interest must be more tangible and there must be evidence that the regulation actually serves the state interest. Admittedly, this is more than traditional rational basis review has demanded. But this is what *Lawrence* demanded, and before it *Romer* and *Casey*. In all three cases, the Court applied rational basis review, yet with greater bite than it has applied to pure economic regulations.[37]

Conversely, laws criminalizing conduct that (1) is not fundamental to the lives of socially productive Americans, (2) has been historically criminalized and continues to be the source of fresh legal prohibitions, and (3) is discernibly contrary to the public interest, neutrally defined, are easy calls in the other direction: the state has substantial freedom to criminalize. Most of the items on Scalia's list (adultery, etc.) fall within this category of easily permissible state regulation. The hardest call is adult incest, especially sex between first cousins and siblings by affinity (marriage) rather than blood. Although adult incest between siblings is criminal everywhere, many states do not include siblings by affinity, and most do not make it a crime for first cousins to have sex. If the reported cases are any guide, these statutes are almost never enforced in cases involving consensual intercourse.[38] The harm of adult incest seems speculative but plausible: if close relatives (cousins) or people raised together (siblings by affinity) could engage in sex once they became adults, the family as a sexually safe place would be undermined. Also, there are none of the collateral consequences for adult incestophiles that *Lawrence* found troubling for homosexual sodomy laws. And no social movement has formed to persuade America that adult incest is acceptable. In large part because the social and normative stakes of adult incest among cousins or siblings by affinity are so low, *Lawrence*'s jurisprudence of tolerance does not require that these statutes violate the Fourteenth Amendment.[39]

Scalia's list is a poor guide to *Lawrence*'s ramifications for criminal law—not just because it's overstated, but also because it's obsolete. Fornication and even adultery do not stir the moral imagination today the way they did forty years ago, when Lord Devlin created his antecedent to Scalia's list. We have already entered a brave new world of hypersexuality, where the key questions are not whether two adults can engage in consensual private intercourse, but how we balance individual pleasure seeking with possible harm to the individual or third parties, and what sexual activities we want to encourage and how. Cutting-edge issues include the following:

- *sexual nondisclosure or fraud,* where a partner does not disclose that he is infected with the HIV virus or another sexually transmitted disease;[40]
- the use of *sex toys,* such as dildos, vibrators, clamps, and other erotic stimulators;[41]
- the *infliction of pain* as an erotic activity among consenting adults, including flogging, spanking, piercing, and fisting, all of which pose risks of physical injury to at least one partner;[42]
- *self-destructive sexual behavior,* including self-mutilation, barebacking (HIV-risky, unprotected anal intercourse), possibly group sex;[43]
- *cybersex,* including sexual chat rooms, violent sexual imagery, sexual threats and cyber-rapes, simulated images of nude children or sex with children, and for-pay erotic sites, as well as escort services;[44]

• *sexual play among minors,* including prepubescent children's games of "house," dating by early teens, hooking up by high schoolers, mock rapes and date rapes by youths.[45]

Lawrence provides little basis for judicial monitoring of laws regulating the foregoing activities, partly because the activities arguably violate the harm principle as well as natural law, and partly because there is no social movement agitating for freedom to carry out such behaviors. To the extent the judiciary monitors state regulation of the current cutting edge of sexuality, it will tend to do so under the First Amendment, which has been a sharp limit on state regulation of child pornography, for example.[46]

Yet *Lawrence* ought to be an occasion for states to abandon sectarian religious justifications for their sex crime statutes and focus instead on religion-neutral reasons, including a historically grounded public morality. This reading gives *Lawrence* an additional constitutional edge, as a prophylactic rule informed by the Anti-Establishment Clause of the First Amendment. It might not, per se, be considered a state establishment of religion to codify the Levitical crimes, as the New Haven Colony once did, but allowing states like Texas to codify sectarian rules embraced by religious majorities might create the conditions for a de facto establishment of a religion-based orthodoxy. *Lawrence* can be read as creating a prophylactic rule for criminal law that makes such a situation less possible.[47]

Lawrence should also be an occasion for the sex-regulatory state to move beyond the Model Penal Code. Sodomy, fornication, and masturbation ought not be considered crimes, not just because such a regime is unconstitutional, but because it is misfocused. After *Lawrence*, state courts should clear away some of these obsolete laws, as Virginia did in *Ziherl*. More important, state legislatures should focus on new issues of sexual risk, predation, and danger and should approach those issues from a perspective reflecting the diversity of the population. In particular they need to avoid scapegoating sexual minorities. It is an unproductive approach to public safety and health issues—and after *Romer* and *Lawrence* it's often going to be unconstitutional as well.

Discriminatory Criminal Laws

Another potential legacy for *Lawrence* would be to sweep away state criminal laws that openly discriminate, as Texas's law did. Indeed, the primary constitutional issue litigated in Matthew Limon's case was not the due process legitimacy of making sex with M.A.R. a crime, but rather Kansas's discriminatory punishment regime. Limon's prison sentence was seventeen years. The state had a "Romeo and Juliet" exception to this high level of punishment, but only if the defendant was less than nineteen years old, the age difference was less than four years, and the teenagers were of the "opposite sex." Limon met the first two criteria but not the third. Under the Romeo-and-Juliet exception, punishment for a first or second offense was presumptively probation; punishment for a third offense was no more than fifteen months in prison. Because there was no Romeo-and-Mercutio exception, the sex of one's partner made a big difference in Kansas (and Texas, by the way). Was that constitutional?[48]

On remand the Kansas Court of Appeals ruled that it was. Two of the three judges affirmed Limon's sentence, on the ground that the state could punish teen "homosexual sodomy" more severely than "heterosexual sodomy" because "there are certain health risks [e.g., HIV transmission] more generally associated with homosexual activity than with heterosexual activity, especially among males." Until teenagers were old enough to make their own choices, the state ought to have substantial leeway to signal greater disapproval of homosexual activity by an older teen with a younger one. In *Limon v. State* (2005) the Kansas Supreme Court rejected this rationale and found the discrimination unconstitutional under *Romer* and *Lawrence*. First, there was no evidence that disease prevention was the reason the Kansas legislature penalized homosexual sodomy between consenting teens so much more severely than heterosexual sodomy. Indeed, when the legislature was deliberating in 1999, neither the sentencing commission that proposed a youth exception for statutory rape penalties nor prosecutors opposing the proposal made any distinction between heterosexual and homosexual conduct. The only public health concerns raised by prosecutors were that teenage women would be infected or impregnated by teenage males. The youth exception became gendered in conference committee, but with no expressed reason—just as Kansas had done thirty years earlier when it had enacted the nation's first homosexual-only sodomy law (chapter 5).[49]

Assume that the discrimination was actually a public health measure. As Justice Marla Luckert's opinion for the Kansas Supreme Court stressed, a second problem was that the discrimination was "one of those seemingly paradoxical situations where the classification is both over- and under-inclusive." It was overinclusive (covering activities having no connection with the disease-prevention goal) because most homosexual activity among teenagers did not pose the risks the lower court hypothesized. Sex between girls posed virtually no risk of HIV transmission; lesbians of all ages were the lowest AIDS- or STD-risk group, yet their intercourse received the most draconian punishment Kansas meted out. The antihomosexual discrimination was underinclusive (missing its goal) because it substantially deregulated HIV-risky heterosexual anal sex and penile-vaginal sex leading to pregnancy (the latter was, ironically, the main health concern raised in 1999). As in *Romer*, the lack of connection between the discriminatory classification (homosexual conduct) and the public health goal (disease prevention) was so pronounced that the judges were left with the inference that the classification was irrational or prejudiced.[50]

Third, the medical consensus was that criminalizing sodomy was not a rational approach to containing STDs, especially AIDS (chapter 9). Not only did Kansas's homosexual sodomy laws deflect attention from the essential public health safer-sex campaigns (use a condom, save your life), but they defeated sex education goals by closeting sexual discussion and undermined AIDS containment by making sexual partners harder to trace. The public health justification for Kansas's discrimination was profoundly irrational. Also unfounded was the argument one lower-court judge inverted—namely, the state's interest in channeling impressionable adolescents into heterosexuality and away from homosexuality.[51]

Although *Lawrence* created no liberty protection for sex between teenagers, *Romer* provided a framework for evaluating a criminal law regime, like Kansas's, that discriminated against homosexual sodomy. Like Amendment 2, struck down in *Romer*, Kansas's discriminatory Romeo-and-Juliet exception was unprecedented in American law, and had an even more powerfully negative effect on gay teens than Amendment 2 had, for it potentially sent them to prison for seventeen years. And like Amendment 2, the discrimination was so ill-fitted to serve the state interests attributed to it that the inference is inescapable that it was motivated by antihomosexual "animus." The *Limon* court was entirely correct to hold that Kansas's discrimination violated *Romer*. The discrimination was also inconsistent with the O'Connor opinion in *Lawrence*, which argued that Texas's Homosexual Conduct Law violated the Equal Protection Clause. Kansas's Romeo-and-Juliet discrimination was more serious than Texas's.[52]

Other criminal laws discriminate against gay people, albeit without the drastic consequences of Kansas's law. Ohio, for example, makes it a misdemeanor to "solicit a person of the same sex to engage in sexual activity with the offender," if the invitation is offensive. Early on, the Ohio Supreme Court interpreted the law to apply only when the invitation was so offensive as to constitute "fighting words," which would provoke a breach of the peace. Before *Lawrence* the court ruled that the statutory discrimination between offensive homosexual solicitations and offensive heterosexual ones was a content regulation of speech, invalid under the First Amendment. *Lawrence*'s jurisprudence of tolerance lends support to that result. The state has some discretion to regulate public solicitations, certainly those constituting fighting words and others that create public nuisances, but it must exercise that discretion evenhandedly. The state might be able to show that different-sex cruising and solicitation poses less risk of breaching the peace or creating nuisances than cruising by men of other men, but *Lawrence* and *Romer* arguably require the state to make such a showing and not just an assertion. Moreover, the state would have to justify the inclusion of woman-on-woman cruising to sustain a criminal law applicable to same-sex solicitation generally.[53]

A different case is posed by statutes that simply make the solicitation of sodomy a crime. Although the New York Court of Appeals struck down the law in *Uplinger v. State* (1983), most courts have upheld similar ones. After *Lawrence*, courts should limit such statutes to solicitations to commit sodomy that are *not* constitutionally protected. While the invitations of Robert Uplinger (chapter 7) and Jeffrey Wasson (chapter 9) to undercover cops to return home with them to engage in sodomy would be constitutionally protected by the First and Fourteenth amendments, an invitation to have sex in a public restroom, park, or adult theater would usually not be protected. Most important, municipalities wanting to regulate public nuisances created by nocturnal male cruising for sex partners can regulate the nuisance directly through laws prohibiting public indecent exposure, unwelcome harassment, trespassing, and disorderly conduct (carefully defined).[54]

What if the state makes it a crime only to solicit for (unprotected) sodomy or prostitution, but leaves solicitation to engage in fornication, adultery, and other different-sex activities legal? In the wake of *Lawrence*, this is an approach followed in some southern states. Such a scheme would not be a direct discrimination, but would probably have a disparate impact on homosexual and bisexual men, especially if the law were enforced with a sharper eye for the gay guy. For example, police officers rarely arrest men soliciting women to have sex in the backseat of a car, while departments still invest resources to send plainclothes officers into gay bars or public toilets to await solicitation from male patrons. Neither *Lawrence* nor *Romer* renders practices having gay-discriminatory effects constitutionally questionable, if police are enforcing constitutional statutes. State courts may interpret their state constitutions more liberally than the Supreme Court is willing, or able, to construe the U.S. Constitution. Given the previous analysis of the new directions sex crimes and their enforcement are taking, the discriminatory application of otherwise neutral laws may become a minor cutting edge of criminal law litigation at the state level.[55]

Discriminations After *Lawrence*: Beyond the "Homosexual Agenda"

Justice Scalia's biggest fear was that *Lawrence* would force the entire "homosexual agenda" on an unwilling populace. Despite the almost obsessive attention to this notion by religious conservatives, it is one that is virtually meaningless to the people who supposedly sponsor it. Americans who are erotically attracted to persons of the same sex are as diverse in their viewpoints as Americans attracted to persons of a different sex. The Republican Party, including current senators and governors, is filled with practicing homosexuals who support antigay discriminations and no promo homo policies. Many gays in the military opposed efforts of lawyers to end the presidential exclusion of gay people from the armed forces. Many lesbian feminists and most "queer" theorists oppose same-sex marriage. "Post-queer" youth assail any kind of agenda that would assimilate gender-benders and other minorities into the mainstream. Although most lesbian and gay lawyers applaud *Lawrence* for ridding the nation of consensual sodomy laws, they are not of one mind as to what should come next.[56]

Steve Lofton and Roger Croteau scoff at the fact that people tag them as gay, and stop at that definition. "It's a small part and it's a perfectly wonderful part of who we are. But it's not who we are," says Croteau. "My only agenda now is to raise the kids well. To give them a normal healthy childhood." Theirs is perhaps a "children's agenda." From Lofton and Croteau's point of view, American public law should get beyond its obsession with a "homosexual agenda" and focus on the genuine needs and welfare of families and children. That is a noble goal, one where liberals and traditionalists might find common ground. Do *Lawrence* and *Romer* advance that project?[57]

Public Education: No Promo Homo?

In 2007, three of Lofton and Croteau's children attended the Metropolitan Learning Center in Portland, Oregon, where several teachers are gay. Like Anita Bryant of yesteryear, some parents cared about these educators' homosexual orientation, especially if it became a matter of public record. Recall the *Lawrence* oral argument: If consensual sodomy were no longer a crime, would the state have to allow homosexuals to teach kindergarten? Lawrence and Garner's attorney had a quick answer to that question (yes), but under close doctrinal analysis it is more complicated.[58]

Traditionally, most states have conditioned teachers' licenses and jobs on assurances that applicants were not committing "immoral conduct" or crimes of "moral turpitude," such as the crime against nature. Teachers who admitted homosexual conduct—or whose homosexual orientation was somehow leaked to the public—often lost their licenses or were discharged. Between 1969 and 1978 the California Supreme Court discouraged and then barred such discharges, in judicial opinions that spurred the Briggs Initiative of 1978. Outside of California, however, federal as well as state judges usually found a way to uphold school board discharges of lesbian, gay, or bisexual schoolteachers. One reason supporting the majority view was that gay schoolteachers were presumptive lawbreakers and, for that reason, inappropriate role models for impressionable students. *Lawrence* removed that justification for public school policies against gay teachers.[59]

Another reason for such educational policies was suggested by the question in *Lawrence*—parental fear that "children might be induced to follow the path of homosexuality" if they had homosexual role models as teachers. (This question was an echo of then Justice Rehnquist's claim in 1978 that homosexuality was infectious, like measles, and homosexuals might be quarantined.) Neither *Lawrence* nor *Romer* resolved this issue. On the merits, it is questionable. There is no generally accepted "cause" for one's sexual orientation, but none of the leading theories (those with empirical support) maintains that homosexuality is the result of inspiration from role models, much less kindergarten teachers. Although there is an audience for the belief that homosexuality can be reversed by "reparative therapy," reparative therapists have not established any scientific basis for believing that role models are responsible for influencing a sexual orientation. Even before *Lawrence*, courts found the role model rationale too tenuous to support a general exclusion of LGBT individuals from schoolteaching. Underlying the role model rationale is often the fear that the homosexual teacher will prey on vulnerable children. The "vampire lesbian" and "predatory homosexual" stereotype is simply untrue: men sexually involved with or married to women are the predominant predators against children, including boys.[60]

Nor did *Lawrence* speak to the main reason for allowing such discharges, namely, institutional efficiency. Under the Supreme Court's precedents, public institutions—from prisons and the armed forces to schools—are granted a substantial discretion to censor speech and even to discriminate in their membership, so as to preserve their ability to carry out their public purposes. While the state cannot discriminate against gay people in voting, access to police protection, and public education, it might be able to discriminate by refusing to have openly gay persons as voting registrars, police officers, and teachers. The Supreme Court has repeatedly supported school administrator discretion to take action to maintain an orderly learning environment and to be responsive to parental interests. If a principal had good reason to believe that an openly lesbian or gay teacher would disrupt the learning environment or undermine the community's confidence in the school, lower courts have allowed some discrimination, and it is not clear that the Supreme Court would require otherwise.[61]

To be sure, the state cannot exclude people of color or women from these positions of public trust, but only because the Supreme Court has constitutionally recognized that race and sex (unlike sexual orientation) are suspect classifications. Because racial and gender variation is culturally recognized as *benign*, while sexual variation is only *tolerable* under *Lawrence*, there is room for state agencies to exclude sexual minorities under *Lawrence/Romer*. This does not mean, however, that the state has a constitutional free pass to discriminate. Most schools in the United States tolerate LGBT staff and teachers; few have blanket exclusions. Under some state constitutions (like Oregon's), where sexual orientation has been established as a suspect classification, any kind of public employment discrimination would probably be invalid.[62]

Parenting

Even more important than a good education are the rights Lofton and Croteau would like to have as legal (adoptive) parents of their children. Oregon law would allow them to adopt Wayne and Ernie, and any gay-based adoption ban would presumptively violate Oregon's Constitution. Not only did Florida refuse to allow these parents to adopt Frank, Tracy, and Bert, but the state periodically sent them letters updating them on the state's efforts to take Bert away and deposit him with approved (nonhomosexual) parents. After *Lawrence* a federal court of appeals upheld Florida's law excluding LGBT people from adopting children in *Lofton v. Secretary of Department of Children & Family Services* (2004).[63]

Judge Stanley Birch's *Lofton* opinion found *Lawrence* inapposite. Whatever additional bite the Due Process Clause had for Lawrence and Garner's liberty to engage in private sexual activities did not apply to Lofton and Croteau's desire to adopt Frank, Tracy, and Bert. The Supreme Court has ruled that no one has a constitutional liberty interest in adopting children, and Birch set the bar that the state needed to meet quite low. Modernizing the justification for its antigay discrimination, Florida declined to attribute a morality-based reason and instead defended its policy as a reasonable signal by the state that it considered husband-and-wife households to be the best environments for rearing children, most of whom would be heterosexual when they grew up. The antihomosexual rule was "designed to create adoptive homes that resemble the nuclear family as closely as possible." Judge Birch accepted the state's position that "disallowing adoption into homosexual households, which are necessarily motherless or fatherless and lack the stability that comes with marriage, is a rational means of furthering Florida's interest in promoting adoption by marital families."[64]

Although the *Lofton* panel was unanimous, six of the twelve participating judges voted for the entire Court of Appeals for the Eleventh Circuit to hear the case. This is the same court that upheld Attorney General Bowers's refusal to employ an open lesbian in his office. In her dissent from the denial of rehearing, Judge Rosemary Barkett (once a Florida Supreme Court justice) made three important points, any of which should have invalidated the adoption discrimination. First, she argued that *Romer* required a different outcome. Like Colorado's Amendment 2, Florida's law was an innovative antigay discrimination, the first of its kind in the United States. As of 2007, no other state statute had singled out *all* lesbians and gay men as a class unfit to adopt children.[65] Like that of Colorado, Florida's discriminatory classification was underinclusive. If the state goal were to encourage adoption within marital households, one would expect the state either to bar adoption by single people or, at least, to create a presumption favoring adoption by married people. Florida did neither. Its discrimination was also overinclusive. Many gay and lesbian households—not just Lofton-Croteau, but others who joined in the class action—were among the *best* environments for childrearing, even under the state's rationale. Florida also argued that "dual-gender parenting" was important for shaping a child's "sexual and gender identity and in providing heterosexual role modeling." But under that rationale, it was just as bad for single heterosexuals as for single homosexuals to adopt. In Miami-Dade County, where Lofton and Croteau lived, forty percent of the adoptions from foster care were to single people.[66]

Second, the Florida statute had a feature the *Romer* justices did not know that Amendment 2 had—an open appeal to antigay animus. *Romer* inferred Colorado's animus from Amendment 2's over- and underinclusion, but Barkett found Florida's animus clearly in its legislative history, which followed the ferociously antigay script Anita Bryant had written in Dade County (chapter 7). Senator Curtis Peterson introduced the adoption proposal during the Save Our Children campaign, and legislative supporters publicly referred to the campaign as one that had galvanized constituent interest in protecting children from homosexuals. At the House committee hearing on May 19, 1977, the sponsor asserted that the "majority of the committee supports Ms. Bryant." When the bill was passed by the Senate on May 31, Senator Peterson underscored its message for homosexuals: "We're really tired of you. We wish you'd go back into the closet." Echoing the Save Our Children constitutionalism, Senator Peterson continued, "The problem in Florida is that homosexuals are surfacing to such an extent that they're beginning to aggravate the ordinary folks, who have a few rights of their own." Governor Reuben Askew, who had endorsed Bryant's politics, signed the bill into law on June 8, the day after Dade County revoked its antidiscrimination ordinance.[67]

Third, Barkett argued that the court took too narrow a view of the constitutional *liberty* at stake. Birch was correct that, under the Supreme Court's decisions, Lawrence and Garner had a stronger liberty interest than Lofton and Croteau, but he overlooked the liberty interests of the children. Because Florida allowed gay men to be foster parents, and because Lofton and Croteau were the only people willing to care for an HIV-infected black baby, they were the only parents Bert had ever known, and removing him from that household would have been emotionally devastating. Florida's adoption discrimination left Bert and others like him in legal limbo and exposed them to the harmful risk of being taken from their psychological family. Considering Florida's policy from the perspective of the children, as Lofton and Croteau did, there was a commanding liberty interest, the statutory discrimination was historically novel and currently isolated, and the state's justifications were speculative and greatly over- and underinclusive. Under the *Lawrence/Romer* framework, this was a statutory discrimination that should have been laid to rest. Under the rule of law that lower-court judges are supposed to deduce from Supreme Court jurisprudence, Rosemary Barkett had the better arguments.[68]

The Supreme Court denied review in *Lofton*, probably to allow the country to simmer down after *Lawrence*. Perhaps, too, the adoption issue was not yet ready for the Court's consideration. Several states were considering antigay adoption bans, and the results of their deliberations might be relevant to the Court's decision whether to remove this as a contested arena from the culture wars. If other states fail to follow Florida's broad approach, the Court ought to be receptive to future challenges.[69]

Likewise, the Supreme Court in an appropriate case ought to consider the constitutionality of antigay presumptions followed by some southern states in adjudicating disputes between two legal parents for child custody or visitation. An explicit presumption against custody or visitation by a lesbian or gay parent ought to be vulnerable under *Lawrence*, both because a biological parent has a fundamental liberty interest in her or his children, and because the child's best interests must not be neglected in order to serve some political symbolism. As Florida did in defending its adoption law, most states have already modernized the justifications for their discriminatory policies. In *Bottoms v. Bottoms* (1995), the Virginia Supreme Court (over objections from Justice Lacy and two colleagues) transferred a child from its lesbian mother to its maternal grandmother. The court's reliance on the fact that "[c]onduct inherent in lesbianism" was a felony in Virginia would be disallowed under *Lawrence*. But the main grounds for the court's transfer were the trial judge's findings that Sharon Bottoms was a bad mother and that "living daily under conditions stemming from active lesbianism practiced in the home may impose a burden upon a child by reason of the 'social condemnation' attached to such an arrangement."[70]

As the U.S. Supreme Court subsequently ruled in another case, *Bottoms* was wrongly decided because it slighted the fundamental liberty of the biological parent.[71] The trial judge's findings might also have been questioned under *Romer* and *Lawrence*. Although the Supreme Court does not sit to review the neutrality of state trial judges, state appellate courts have a constitutional obligation to do so, and to overturn prejudice-based findings of fact. Indeed, southern appellate courts have been performing this valuable function, with one huge recent exception—the Alabama Supreme Court. In *Ex parte D.W.W.* (1998), the trial judge granted custody of two minor children to a straight father while imposing highly restrictive visitation conditions on the lesbian mother. An intermediate appeals court removed the restrictions. The Alabama Supreme Court unanimously affirmed the custody order and (by a split vote) reinstated the restrictions, on the basis of exactly the same mix of reasons *Bottoms* had invoked (lesbians were criminals, she was a bad mother, society would disapprove). What made *D.W.W.* remarkable was that the record revealed a father who had driven drunk with the children in the car, threatened the mother and the children with extreme violence, neglected the children's education, and once locked his son in the clothes dryer. Decisions like *D.W.W.* are a core violation of the Fourteenth Amendment—lawless in their barely concealed antigay prejudice, willing to sacrifice the liberty and perhaps even the lives of children, and blatantly and even proudly discriminatory. While it is likely that decisions like *Bottoms* and *D.W.W.* will disappear, if they do recur and the lesbian or gay parent petitions the U.S. Supreme Court for review, it is essential that the Court take one of these cases and explain to outlier jurists the unconstitutionality of such decisions.[72]

Marriage

Justice Scalia's biggest fear is that *Lawrence* now requires the states to recognize same-sex marriage. Steve Lofton and Roger Croteau would be delighted. In early March 2004, Multnomah County, Oregon, started issuing marriage licenses to same-sex couples. At the dinner table that night, Frank wondered whether his dads intended to take advantage of this new legal option. This question alarmed Bert, who thought his dads *were* married. Frank explained that the state would not let them get married, but this hardly satisfied Bert. Tracy chimed in, "I think you *should* get married!" Lofton and Croteau didn't care so much, for their friends and family considered them "married" already. (Lofton and Croteau had been one another's life partner for more than twenty years.) But like everything else in their lives, they did it for the children. On Monday, March 8 (a school holiday), the couple and their five kids trotted down to the county courthouse and got hitched. That night, they went out for a celebratory dinner. In April 2005, the Oregon Supreme Court nullified their marriage, on the grounds that the county went beyond the authorization of state law.[73]

Did *Lawrence* require Oregon to reinstate Lofton and Croteau's marriage, as a federal constitutional matter? There is much to say, under the Court's equal protection precedents, for same-sex marriage. A state's refusal to recognize the committed relationship of two men is an open discrimination based on sex (usually an unacceptable basis for discrimination) that denies a limitless array of legal rights and duties to lesbians and gay men, as well as many bisexuals and transgendered persons. State justifications for continuing the discrimination tend to be speculative or symbolic reasons that cannot be the basis for state denials of fundamental rights to any citizens, or for state discriminations based on quasi-suspect classifications like sex. Indeed, state justifications for denying marriage rights to same-sex couples—signaling traditional family values and protecting old-fashioned marriage—are not hugely different from those Colorado advanced in *Romer* or Harris County suggested in *Lawrence*. And in both cases, the Court ruled the justifications did not even constitute a rational basis, a much easier test than the heightened scrutiny required when fundamental liberties are infringed or suspect classifications deployed. Indeed, *Lawrence* and its generally favorable public reception probably emboldened Chief Justice Margaret Marshall and her colleagues on the Massachusetts Supreme Judicial Court, who interpreted their state constitution to require same-sex marriage four months after *Lawrence*.[74]

Nonetheless, the case for same-sex marriage is not one that a jurisprudence of tolerance can impose on the states as a federal constitutional matter. Even after Massachusetts started issuing marriage licenses to same-sex couples in May 2004, the other forty-nine states have continued to limit marriage to one man and one woman, as of 2007. Forty-four states have statutes or constitutional amendments barring recognition in those states of same-sex marriages validly entered elsewhere; most such measures have been adopted in the last ten years, after full opportunity for public participation. The majority of citizens would be disturbed by recognition of same-sex marriages in their states; for many the limitation of marriage to people of different sexes is at the core of their religious identities. *Roe v. Wade* was a more compelling case for constitutional intervention on the part of the Supreme Court, for abortion reform had more support in the United States in 1973 than same-sex marriage had in 2007. Court-enforced same-sex marriage would be even more incendiary to the body politic than *Roe* was a generation ago.[75]

The jurisprudence of tolerance counsels that the Supreme Court do little about this issue for the time being. Either rejecting or endorsing the constitutionality of same-sex marriage bars would immediately raise the stakes of national politics. Same-sex marriage not only remains divisive, but divides in ways that cut to the core of people's identities. Under these circumstances, the Court's best strategy is to leave the matter to the states, those famous laboratories of experimentation. Indeed, this is the very approach the Court took, with success, in the right-to-die case, *Washington v. Glucksberg* (1997). Although the chief justice's opinion for the Court rejected any constitutional right to die, five justices took the position that the matter was not ripe for complete resolution and pronounced themselves open to future claims. Meanwhile, the states remain free to recognize a right to die, and their experience (and experience from abroad) will provide valuable information for other states and for the courts in future cases.[76]

Like the right to die, same-sex marriage is an issue that would benefit from state experimentation. Prompted by a state supreme court decision, Vermont's legislature debated this issue in 2000 and revealed its population to be open to recognition of lesbian and gay "civil unions" (an institution Connecticut's legislature joined in 2005). In 2003 California extended its statewide domestic partnership law to provide almost all the benefits and obligations of marriage to same-sex couples.[77] Interpreting her state constitution to require recognition of same-sex marriages, Massachusetts chief justice Margaret Marshall opened her opinion in *Goodridge v. Department of Public Health* (2003) with a quotation from *Lawrence*: "Our obligation is to define the liberty of all, not to mandate our own moral code." She also followed *Lawrence* in linking constitutional liberty and equality as overlapping justifications for opening up marriage to lesbian and gay couples, and in ruling that the antigay discrimination failed rational basis review. Three dissenting justices argued that their colleagues were pressing constitutional liberty and equality principles far beyond *Lawrence*.[78]

Although Marshall invoked *Lawrence*'s principles at key points in her own opinion, no one (not even Scalia) believes that the U.S. Supreme Court would apply the Fourteenth Amendment this broadly. Marshall's opinion reached well beyond the jurisprudence of tolerance. So long as the politics of preservation retains a strong following, neither judges nor legislators would dare adopt same-sex marriage as a constitutional policy. But by 2003 Massachusetts had moved beyond the politics of tolerance. The state had not only adopted a broad antidiscrimination law protecting gay employees, tenants, and users of public accommodations, but most municipalities and the state chief executive had adopted measures providing employment benefits to the "domestic partners" of lesbian and gay government workers. These legal developments were made possible by, and then facilitated, the flourishing of an openly LGBT culture in the state. This culture had persuaded many citizens that homosexuality is not just a tolerable variation, but is benign and ought to make no difference in the state's treatment of a person. That normative shift, in turn, made *Goodridge* possible. And the durability of that shift will determine whether it survives. At the time of the writing of this book, most citizens did not support the campaign to override the court's decision through a constitutional amendment, and the legislature killed it in 2007.[79]

The conditions that made *Goodridge* a plausible interpretation of the Massachusetts Constitution are absent in most other states—certainly in Georgia, Kentucky, Arkansas, Texas, and Florida, but also in such states as Illinois, the first to repeal its consensual sodomy law, and other early repealers such as Colorado and Ohio. Decisions requiring same-sex marriage by either their state supreme courts or the U.S. Supreme Court would raise the stakes of politics in such states. The resulting turmoil would be catastrophic not only for traditionalists and judges, but also for gay people. In other states, mainly those of New England, the Northeast, and the West Coast, there may be sufficient support for state recognition of lesbian and gay relationships—not marriage, but a legal instrument like Vermont's civil unions or New Jersey's domestic partnerships. Even in these states, the legacy of *Lawrence* should not be revolutionary in the short term. These changes have been coming from legislatures as well as judges, as they did in Vermont. Although Oregon's courts have not insisted on same-sex marriage as a matter of constitutional right, Oregon in 2007 created a new "domestic partnership" institution for same-sex couples.[80]

Was *Goodridge* therefore wrong? A great virtue of federalism is that it offers *conditions for falsification*. Proposals to change a long-standing national rule—such as the limitation of marriage to different-sex couples—are at a triple disadvantage: citizens embrace the status quo because they are used to it, feel advantaged by it, and fear the consequences of change. Federalism ameliorates this third, and most unfair, advantage of the status quo. Before Massachusetts legalized same-sex marriage in 2004, almost any kind of fantastic justification was made to stop this legal innovation. The most popular was a "defense of marriage" argument: same-sex marriage would further undermine "traditional marriage," an institution already under attack by liberalizations such as no-fault divorce and cohabitation rules. Now that same-sex marriages are being celebrated in Massachusetts, Americans will have an opportunity to see for themselves whether these claims hold up. Thus far, the sky has not fallen.[81]

Steve Lofton and Roger Croteau have not become married spouses or even domestic partners under Oregon law, nor are they legal parents under Florida law. Yet they are not sexual outlaws who can be jailed as Alice Mitchell was in the 1890s and Bayard Rustin in the 1950s. Nor are they rebels who will lose their jobs because of gender-bending, as Walt Whitman did in the 1860s or Pauli Murray in the 1930s. They are not poster boys for the homosexual agenda, nor advocates seeking the end of morals legislation. They are simply health professionals who spend most of their time cooperating, creating, and caregiving.

The adult relationship the state will not recognize has not only given these men great joy, but it has enabled Lofton to devote all his time to the rearing of five children. The adult-child relationships the state will not recognize have not only saved the lives of these children, but have also enabled them to live rich lives and to enrich the lives of others. While the body politics of antihomosexual disgust and contagion, inaugurated by Anita Bryant a generation ago and perfected by her traditionalist heirs, has denied legal rights to this eclectic family, it has not managed to destroy it. Conversely, even a gay-friendly Constitution would not solve all of Lofton and Croteau's life challenges. For example, a liberal reading of *Lawrence* would not give them back what they would most desire: Ginger, Lofton and Croteau's twinkling daughter and their kids' cheerful sister, who died of complications associated with AIDS in 1995.

CHAPTER TWELVE

Lawrence and Popular Constitutionalism

America has traveled a long distance between the Civil War amendments to the Constitution and *Lawrence v. Texas*. As chapter 1 illustrates, no one in 1868 would have thought that crime-against-nature laws violated the new Fourteenth Amendment. The "crime against nature" had a clear meaning in 1868: unnatural anal assault against a woman, girl, boy, animal, or subordinate man by a more powerful man. Prosecuting men for this infraction would have been no more a denial of fair warning, liberty, or equal protection than prosecuting a rapist or child molester.

The Fourteenth Amendment's language had not changed by 2003, but everything else had. By then, the con-stitutional text had been enriched—

Michael Hardwick during his period as an artist, when he was in his late thirties

or expanded, depending upon your perspective—by Supreme Court precedents applying the Fourteenth Amendment guarantees of fair notice, liberty, and equal protection to state laws or policies affecting women and people of color. The legal meaning of sodomy or the crime against nature had also expanded to include oral sex and other nonprocreative forms of sexual pleasure, at the same time that these activities were becoming almost universal among Americans over the age of fourteen. And, most important, the crime against nature had by 2003 come to have a social meaning closely linked to homosexuality, a concept unimaginable in 1868. This social fact effectively narrowed the focus of the crime against nature and created a class of Americans whose fate was linked to its demise. Over the course of a generation, from *Enslin* to *Lawrence*, those Americans made their case, with ultimate success.

As the last chapter demonstrated, *Lawrence* was neither the end of constitutional debate nor a victory for anything-goes sexual liberty or the Gay is Good "homosexual agenda." It is, however, a turning point in the debate. Off the table now are laws making private consensual sodomy a crime or stigmatizing presumptive sodomites with a broad array of state discriminations. More important, *Lawrence* gives us an opportunity to reflect on the *process* of constitutional change that this book has documented. Reflecting on the process helps us clarify our thoughts, and our disagreements, about the nature of constitutionalism and the mechanisms for change. *Lawrence* is not only a defensible but an exemplary operation of the process of constitutional change. Not only should progressives, liberals, and gay rights advocates applaud *Lawrence*, but so should traditionalists, conservatives, and family values advocates. Conversely, gay people should understand that the ultimate meaning and significance of *Lawrence* will and ought to be determined by the nation's larger constitutional culture, which commits them to an ongoing debate with traditionalists and others.[1]

Three Theories of Constitutional Change

Legal scholars and judges have fiercely debated about how constitutional law changes and what mechanisms for change are legitimate. Some newspapers and commentators present this process as a debate between a static and a living Constitution. While the debate between the majority and dissenting justices in *Lawrence* can be understood in that way, it is simply wrong. Under any sensible theory, the Constitution is an evolving document. The only serious debate should involve what the criteria for its evolution ought to be. Should it be linked to original meaning or purposes, as Justice Scalia's *Lawrence* dissent assumed? Should it follow new political consensuses, as some commentators read the *Lawrence* majority? Or should constitutional evolution reflect the deep compromises reached by contending understandings in our pluralist constitutional culture? This last criterion best captures the Court's jurisprudence, but none of them has or ought to have a monopoly on our thinking about constitutionalism. Each theory enriches our understanding of the meaning of *Lawrence v. Texas*.

Formal Constitutionalism: Evolution Through
Common-Law Purposive Reasoning

Formal constitutionalism seeks to understand the Constitution as a document establishing the structure of our representative democracy and the core values useful for that democracy to operate. Article V provides a mechanism for adding language to the Constitution, and thus for updating the document to address problems that arise in the course of history. Unfortunately, the supermajority requirements of Article V have never been easy to meet; the Fourteenth Amendment itself was possible only because radical Republicans conditioned southern state readmission to the Union on it, and the Equal Rights Amendment failed by just a few states. But it is clear that Article V is not the only mechanism by which the Constitution has evolved.[2]

Given the difficulty of the amendment process and the open-textured command of some of the Constitution's critical provisions (such as the Due Process and Equal Protection clauses), the primary mechanism for constitutional evolution has been through interpretation. Contrary to media claims, dynamic constitutional interpretation is neither avoidable nor has it been driven mainly by liberal judges. Because the two-hundred-year-old document must be applied to new situations that its framers could not have foreseen, it is no surprise that neither the Constitution's text nor its original meaning contains clear guidance for restraining the government when it adopts drastic measures against suspected terrorists, creates regulations for the sale of handguns, or enforces sodomy laws against private activities between consenting adults. Whether it is Bush 43 administration lawyers Jay Bybee and John Yoo admonishing statutory efforts to interfere with executive authority to order the torture of persons suspected of terrorism, or Reagan-appointed Justice Antonin Scalia creating a nontextual freedom for state sheriffs from being commandeered by congressional gun control programs, interpreters applying the Constitution to novel contexts will invariably be updating the document.[3]

"Changed circumstances" is the reason constitutional text and original meaning do not easily resolve the question faced by the *Lawrence* Court. The Cato and other historiographical briefs established that *Bowers v. Hardwick* got almost all the historical evidence wrong: in 1868, there was *no* concept of "homosexuality," the crime against nature did *not* include sex between women and did *not* target gay men, consensual activities within the home were *not* prosecuted in any reported case the framers could have known, and so on. The statute in *Lawrence* was even more distant from the world of the framers. As Justice Kennedy reasoned for the majority, a law criminalizing *only* "homosexual conduct" as the Texas law did was until 1969 an unprecedented kind of criminal prohibition, not only singling out a minority for conduct everyone else engaged in, but also effectively rendering them presumptive outlaws and therefore subject to an indefinite array of potential civil disabilities. This was, literally, a violation of the Fourteenth Amendment's textual admonition that the state cannot deny to any person "the equal protection of the laws," and was inconsistent with original meaning, namely, avoidance of "class legislation" that denied a social group ordinary legal protections and left it in a state of nature. Abandoning the erroneous *Bowers* claim that states made "homosexuality" a crime in 1868, Justice Scalia's dissenting opinion had no definitive textualist or original meaning argument against this judgment. His best attempt was a practical one: if the Fourteenth Amendment protects "homosexuals" against state criminalization, then it is harder to draw the line against laws punishing other despised groups—polygamists, incestophiles, masturbators, and persons attracted to different-race partners.[4]

The last item is an addition to Scalia's list, left out of the justice's collection, probably because the Court struck down state laws prohibiting sexual cohabitation between persons of different races in *McLaughlin v. Florida* (1963). Four years later, the Court invalidated different-race marriage bans in *Loving v. Virginia* (1967). From the perspective of the framers of the Fourteenth Amendment—all but a few of whom expressed open disgust at interracial sexuality—there is no persuasive defense of these decisions. Yet in this post-Bork era, even Justice Scalia does not dare criticize these "activist" Warren Court decisions, nor has he argued for overruling the equally nonoriginalist Burger Court decisions invalidating pervasive legal sex-based discriminations. (The 1868 framers consciously declined to address women's exclusions but were not as adamant about them as about interracial sexuality.) Even *Brown v. Board of Education* (1954) is hard to defend under an original-meaning theory of reading the Constitution's text, yet originalists such as Judge Bork defend it on the ground that it updates the original understanding after circumstances had changed.[5]

If an original-meaning approach to the Constitution (the formalist theory most people have heard of) is always going to be dynamic, once circumstances have changed, the originalist must then make a choice between accepting the status quo (racial segregation, consensual sodomy laws) *or* exercising judgment to strike down an objectionable law (*Brown*, *Lawrence*). These dynamics do not mean that such choices are unguided or unconstrained. For the many problems that the constitutional text does not specifically address, the primary sources of guidance are constitutional principles, the purposes of particular provisions, and precedents handed down by prior and differently constituted Courts. A devout Catholic and conservative Republican, a friend of the Reagans from Sacramento,

Anthony Kennedy found that these sources supported the constitutional claims of two men whose lives were quite different from his—in contrast to Justice Scalia, who was certain that these sources confirmed the validity of sodomy laws traditionally supported by his Catholic Church and recently championed by his Republican Party.

As chapter 1 demonstrated, the Fourteenth Amendment's framers meant to protect people's substantive rights "to pursue and obtain happiness and safety; subject nonetheless to such restraints as the government may *justly* prescribe for the general good of the whole." Consensual sodomy is essential to the pursuit of happiness for gay people such as Lawrence and Garner; the originalist inquiry is whether the government may "justly" determine that the "general good" requires that their intercourse be judged criminal, while leaving the same conduct by different-sex couples alone. That inquiry should be informed by the history of state regulation. Unlike the *Bowers* Court, the *Lawrence* Court engaged in a serious, fact-based inquiry into precisely what American states had actually criminalized for two hundred years and concluded that private and consensual activities had not *traditionally* been the basis for state regulation. As this book has demonstrated in some detail, once sodomy became associated with homosexuality in the course of the twentieth century, states began to enforce those laws more aggressively and sometimes explicitly targeted only "homosexual conduct," as Texas did. But if the crime against nature is abominable, surely it is abominable for all, and the state cannot justly demonize a minority for conduct regularly engaged in by the majority.[6]

The original purposes of the Equal Protection Clause are also illuminating. Even when the state can bar happiness-conferring activities, it cannot discriminate through "class legislation," which the Senate sponsor of the amendment defined as "the injustice of subjecting one caste of persons to a code not applicable to another." As documented in chapter 10, the *Lawrence* Court was confronted with undisputed evidence that Texas and neighboring states deployed their homosexual sodomy laws to deny lesbians, gay men, and bisexuals an elastic range of civil rights, including those extending to basic rights of family formation, contracting, and property ownership. This massive discrimination against a productive class of citizens informed both Justice Kennedy's opinion for the Court and Justice O'Connor's opinion concurring in its judgment.[7]

The primary legal constraint on judicial interpretation is stare decisis, the notion that courts must follow and faithfully apply previous precedents. In our system constitutional precedent is important not only because public and private institutions rely on it to arrange and plan their affairs, but also because it reflects a collective wisdom arrived at over a period of time. That is, differently situated justices in different eras have shared their judgments about how to apply the Fourteenth Amendment. A robust interpretation is one that can find support in earlier analyses from a range of authors. Justice Scalia criticized the *Lawrence* Court for overruling *Bowers*, but had himself pronounced *Bowers'* obituary after *Romer v. Evans* (1996), where the Court interpreted the Fourteenth Amendment to strike down a state initiative denying lesbians and gay men an indefinite array of rights ensured others. Because the *Lawrence* parties treated *Romer* as an unquestioned precedent, and even Justice Scalia did not argue for overruling it, stare decisis cut both ways. As regards the Texas Homosexual Conduct Law, *Romer* demanded one answer and *Bowers* another. Given the unquestioned status of *Romer* and Justice Scalia's earlier concession that it was inconsistent with *Bowers*, it was clear the earlier precedent had to be overruled, a judgment made easier by the fact that *Bowers* was a departure from the Court's earlier privacy precedents (the contraception, abortion, regulation of the home, and other pre-*Bowers* cases). Stare decisis provided even stronger support to the approach taken by Justice O'Connor, who followed *Romer* without overruling *Bowers*. Justice O'Connor's concurring opinion epitomized the rule-of-law values of formal constitutionalism, for it scrupulously followed precedent, hewed closely to the original purpose of the Fourteenth Amendment, and struck down a discrimination that had no fact-based defense. Although Justice Scalia lampooned her approach, he did not deny that it was she, perhaps alone, who rigorously satisfied the demands of original meaning and stare decisis.[8]

For frequently litigated issues such as equal protection and due process liberty, even the most formal theories of constitutional interpretation ultimately amount to common-law constitutionalism, where original constitutional principles and purposes are applied, case by case, to new problems or even to old problems in light of new circumstances. This was exactly what the framers of the Constitution of 1789 envisioned, and they were confident that this would be a workable method for elaborating on the elegant but open-ended document they crafted. The analysis above follows the framers' understanding that case-by-case adjudication would develop constitutional principles prudently and slowly. The analysis in the next section follows their suggestion that the Supreme Court, as the "least dangerous branch," would be least likely to usurp power from the political branches of government, a factor that also contributes to our understanding of *Lawrence*.[9]

Polycentric Constitutionalism: Evolution Through Institutional Consensus

Common-law constitutionalism can operate outside the courts. During the War-ren Court era (1953–69), southern states challenged the primacy of the Supreme Court as the final word in constitutional interpretation. Although we now dis-miss that challenge as racist, it reflected practices endorsed by some of the found-ing generation (especially Thomas Jefferson and James Madison). The intense southern opposition to *Brown* directly motivated the Court's timid "all deliber-ate speed" implementation in *Brown II* (1955). It was not until the Great Society (1963–69), when liberals controlled all three branches of the federal government, that the Court put more than nominal pressure on the states to implement *Brown*. During the Reagan administration (1981–89) the Department of Justice argued that the executive department was entitled, indeed obliged, to interpret the Constitution on its own. Thus, the Reagan administration treated *Brown* and *Loving* as settled constitutional interpretations, but challenged the validity of *Roe v. Wade* (1973) and the Court's post-*Roe* abortion jurisprudence. Although the Court did not overrule *Roe*, it has upheld most state restrictions on abortion choices since then.[10]

Many scholars have argued that constitutionalism is *polycentric* in the ways illustrated by the above examples. The Supreme Court is not the only institutional speaker responsible for interpreting the Constitution. State judges, legislators and governors, Congress, and the president take the same oath to support the Consti-tution that the justices take, and they have some interpretive advantages in a rep-resentative democracy such as ours. (The Constitution starts: "We the People . . .") Political officials are more in touch with popular opinion regarding some consti-tutional principles and purposes, for they are more numerous, have much greater diversity in background, and are accountable through the pressures of reelection. Because formal constitutionalism is concerned with applying open-textured con-stitutional provisions such as "liberty"and "equal protection of the laws" and of-ten falls back on general principles such as federalism and equal citizenship, judges ought to be interested and might be influenced by inputs as well as consensus on these issues from other branches of government.[11]

The key concept of polycentric constitutionalism is that the ambiguities con-fronting formal constitutionalism can be ameliorated by factual and normative contributions from other branches and should presumptively be resolved in fa-vor of an institutional consensus, if there is one. For some of the same reasons they follow their own precedents, justices should be particularly open to the con-sidered views of state judges on issues such as liberty, equality, and free speech. Any consensus there reflects a broader sample of thoughtful officials whose job it is to enforce a rule of law. If both the president and Congress agree or acquiesce to the same norm, such as equality for women in the 1970s or caution on abortion in the new millennium, that agreement is some indication that We the People are at rest on the issue—surely of significance when the formal legal factors provide competing arguments rather than interpretive closure. If the Court rebuffs the consensus view of state and other federal officials, it can expect second-guessing, resistance, and perhaps even reprisals from the political branches. If there is no institutional consensus, the Court should proceed cautiously and resolve as little as possible, common-law style.

Consider an example. Virginia's antimiscegenation law first came to the Supreme Court in 1955, right on the heels of *Brown*. After remanding the case to Virginia's Supreme Court (which reaffirmed its statute notwithstanding *Brown*), the Court ultimately dismissed the appeal. There was insufficient basis in constitutional principle for ducking the case, but the Supreme Court rightly feared that striking down such a law risked a firestorm of protest—not just from the South (already in revolt over *Brown*), but also from northern and western states. Large majorities of Americans believed that miscegenation was unacceptable. Thirty of the forty-eight states had antimiscegenation laws at the end of World War II; the *Brown*-weary Eisenhower administration and Congress were hostile to judicial activism on this issue. Attitudes changed in the next half-generation, in large part because more white Americans associated with people of color in the armed forces and other public venues. Many Americans who had found interracial sex objectionable became at least ambivalent, and sometimes ashamed, about their feelings. All but sixteen states (in the South) repealed their antimiscegenation laws by the time the Supreme Court decided *Loving* in 1967. Not coincidentally, President Lyndon Johnson and the Great Society Congress had thoroughly renounced apartheid and expressed a national consensus that race-based distinctions were strongly disfavored in the law. It is only the circumstances of this polycentric institutional support for race-blind marriage that can explain the Supreme Court's unanimous decision in *Loving*.[12]

A polycentric approach to constitutionalism also helps us understand and even reconcile the Supreme Court's decisions in *Bowers* and *Lawrence*. When the justices were deliberating the ambit of the privacy right in *Bowers*, twenty-four states had decriminalized consensual sodomy in private places, while twenty-six had declined to do so. The highest courts in fifteen of these twenty-six states had upheld their consensual sodomy laws against right to privacy challenges since 1962. President Reagan and the Republican-controlled Senate were perceived as uninterested in or hostile to sodomy reform, and the Democratic-controlled House of Representatives had in 1981 voted 281–119 to override the District of Columbia's attempted sodomy reform. After more than a generation of pressure from supporters of the Model Penal Code and half a generation of insistence by openly gay citizens, there was no agreement on this issue, a lack of consensus that was confirmed by opinion polls. Under these circumstances, it is understandable that Justice Powell thought twice about reading the privacy principle broadly enough to protect "homosexual sodomy."[13]

The country's negative reaction to *Bowers* and the Senate's decisive rejection of Judge Bork's nomination to replace Justice Powell established that the right to privacy had deeper public support than some of the justices suspected. More important, public attitudes toward homosexual sodomy decisively changed in the 1990s. By 2003 half the *Bowers* states had abandoned their consensual sodomy laws, leaving only thirteen in place (fewer than the number of antimiscegenation laws in place when the Court decided *Loving*); the District had quietly repealed its law in 1993, with Senate Republican leaders quashing proposals to override that decision this time around. Judicial decisions in such traditionalist states as Arkansas, Georgia (the *Bowers* state), Kentucky, Missouri, Maryland, (Catholic) Massachusetts, Minnesota, Montana, (Catholic) Rhode Island, and Tennessee had announced that consensual sodomy laws violated state constitutional privacy guarantees. (In the same period, decisions in Kansas, Louisiana, and Texas rejected such challenges.) Although the Bush 43 administration was no friend to the gay or lesbian American, the president made it clear that his focus was preventing gay marriage and that he had no interest in the Supreme Court's disposition of Texas's Homosexual Conduct Law. Following the lead of the Roman Catholic Church and the Southern Baptist Convention, the conservative Republican Texas attorney general declined to defend the statute (notwithstanding an invitation from the Court). However controversial sodomy reform had been in 1986, it was virtually a consensus deal in 2003. Even the Court's fiercest traditionalist, Antonin Scalia, concentrated his fire on gay marriage, not sodomy reform.[14]

When the Court announced its judgment in *Lawrence v. Texas*, it read the constitutional principles and its precedents to accord with the national consensus that the state ought not make consensual sodomy a crime. This consensus reflected not only inputs from conservative as well as liberal academic critics of *Bowers*, state legislators and judges, Congress and the Bush 43 administration (implicitly), but also constitutional courts in Europe. *Lawrence* is defensible but still debatable along formal constitutional lines. Under a polycentric constitutionalism, doubts about how to read precedent and constitutional principles should have been resolved against the Texas Homosexual Conduct Law, exactly as the Court did.

Popular Constitutionalism: Evolution Through Social Movement Debates

A third cluster of theories about constitutional change might be categorized as *popular constitutionalism*. This diverse assortment of theories maintains that our nation's constitutional culture exists not only outside and often prior to Supreme Court opinions, but also outside and often prior to other organs of federal and state governance. We the People participate in the articulation of constitutional culture, and we do so through institutions such as the media, the Internet, workplaces, unions, churches, civic associations, social clubs, family reunions, and the like. In this view the primary engine for constitutional change is social movements. Social movements arise when many persons simultaneously accept a norm, organize subcultural mores and institutions around that norm, and finally engage in political activism to entrench that norm in our constitutional culture. Social movements include not just the classic identity-based movements (the civil rights, women's, and gay rights movements), but also the temperance movement of the late nineteenth and early twentieth centuries, the environmental movement that took off after Earth Day in 1970, and the traditional family values movement of the 1970s and beyond (chapter 7).[15]

Social movements decisively affected the evolution of constitutional doctrine in the twentieth century. The imperial First Amendment, the due process privacy right, an Equal Protection Clause with bite, expansive criminal procedure rights, death penalty jurisprudence, and voting rights doctrine emerged case by case from social movement–based lawsuits and amicus briefs. The justices adjudicating those lawsuits and reading those briefs had themselves been vetted by movement leaders and political allies. The Supreme Court was responsive to social movement efforts to constitutionalize their normative claims but always filtered those claims through their own legalistic and political values. Moreover, movement claims were subject to refutation and resistance from competing social movements. Thus the pro-choice movement supporting abortion on demand was countered by a pro-life movement dedicated to banning abortions; the women's rights movement supported the ERA, which was blocked by Phyllis Schlafly's STOP ERA movement.[16]

The gay rights movement (chapters 5–10) is one such normative social movement—but so is the traditional family values movement (chapters 7–8), which stands in opposition to much of the "homosexual agenda." While the popular press call their debate a "culture war," a term Justice Scalia darkly translated as "Kulturkampf" in *Romer*, the clash between these movements has been an ongoing debate over the content of America's constitutional culture. That culture finds expression at the water cooler, in church pulpits and pews, on television shows, in classrooms, at PTA meetings, in town gatherings, in phone calls to legislators and talk show hosts, and so on. Their debate goes to the role of government in our society and its proper regulation of sexuality. Recall, from chapter 1, that similar debates accompanied the birth of the Fourteenth Amendment, namely, between traditionalists and feminists.

In the 1870s Anthony Comstock and his allies argued that the state is responsible for creating conditions supportive of the moral flourishing of its citizens, including ethical leadership and education emphasizing marriage, sex for procreation, and long-established gender roles. Comstock's philosophy of sexuality and gender was traditionalist, and his political philosophy was communitarian. Although the two philosophies are conceptually distinct, they have complemented each other throughout American history. They constitute common ground among such otherwise disparate figures as FBI director J. Edgar Hoover and Governor Earl Warren, Chief Justice Warren and Justice Antonin Scalia, Anita Bryant and Pope Benedict XVI.[17]

Another way of rationalizing the modern regulatory state focuses more on choice-based individual flourishing. This kind of liberal theory might be associated with early feminists such as Elizabeth Cady Stanton and Susan B. Anthony. A classical expression of this theory came from the poet Walt Whitman, who asserted a positive understanding of government, "not merely to rule, to repress disorder, &c., but to develop, to open up to cultivation, to encourage the possibilities of all beneficent and manly outcroppage, and of that aspiration to independence, and the pride and self-respect latent in all characters." The role of law, "higher than the highest arbitrary rule, [is] to train communities through all their grades, beginning with individuals and ending there again, to rule themselves." Although political liberalism is perfectly consistent with traditionalist philosophies of sexuality and gender role, Stanton, Anthony, and Whitman were pathfinding in their insistence that political liberalism be linked to a liberal philosophy of gender equality and sexuality as a source of pleasure and sociability. Such a synthesis captures the understanding of the activist state held by such diverse Americans as Franz Boas and his students Ruth Benedict and Margaret Mead, Alfred and Clara Kinsey, Bayard Rustin, and Justices Thurgood Marshall and Ruth Bader Ginsburg.[18]

As this book has documented, American constitutional culture has changed significantly since 1868. A debate over the crime against nature that would have been inconceivable in 1868 gained traction in the latter half of the twentieth century. The Supreme Court's decision in *Lawrence* was a dramatic point in the specific debate, and in the more general debate between liberal and traditionalist philosophies, but the mechanisms for normative change were on the whole *not* judicial opinions. They were feminist speeches and tracts as well as traditionalist responses, Whitmanesque poetry and literature, classes in social anthropology, newspaper headlines and editorial pages, workplace interactions, military boot camps and trysts in the trenches, speakeasies and bars, published surveys of Americans' sexual practices, deliberations of criminal code reform commissions and state legislatures, medical conferences and journals, district attorney and mayoral elections, lesbian and gay bar cultures and regulatory struggles, individual "coming out" stories and the reactions of family and friends, church and Sunday school services, city council meetings and popular referenda or initiative campaigns, feminist and gay consciousness-raising groups, Bible study groups (including Metropolitan Community Churches), and openly gay-themed literature, movies, and television shows. So long as these thousand points of light agreed that the state should make consensual sodomy a crime and consider "homosexuals and other sex perverts" presumptive criminals, there was nothing for legislatures or courts to do about sodomy laws, except determine how broadly they should be written and how vigorously they should be enforced. Only after liberals, pragmatists, and even some traditionalists had come to an overlapping consensus that consensual sodomy should not be a crime and homosexuals accepted as presumptively lawful citizens, only *then* did individual state legislatures repeal their consensual sodomy laws, state supreme courts strike them down, and ultimately the U.S. Supreme Court strike down the remnant. This is the deep story of *Lawrence*, from the perspective of our national constitutional culture.

The story of the rise, decline, and fall of the crime against nature in America is not about the triumph of a liberal perspective, nor about the perils of traditionalism. Instead, it is about a dialogue between these points of view and their respective constituencies. The constitutional conversation about consensual sodomy laws was a *practical* conversation, in which fact and norm interacted in complex and unpredictable ways. Competing norms ought to be, and under our federalist arrangement often are, given opportunities to prove themselves through local application and feedback. The American system of trial-and-error experimentation has worked surprisingly well. To conclude, let us examine some practical lessons the history of the crime against nature has for popular constitutionalism generally, and perhaps for the same-sex marriage debate more specifically.

Three Lessons for Traditionalist Communitarians

As attorney general, Mike Bowers faithfully defended what he called "homosexual sodomy" laws for morality-expressing communitarian reasons. He was disappointed by the Supreme Court's decision in *Lawrence*, a decision he had not read when he was interviewed for this book in January 2004. One thesis of

Dishonorable Passions is to persuade tolerant conservatives like him that we are well rid of consensual sodomy laws. The communitarian argument favoring such criminal laws starts with the proposition that homosexual sodomy is not a worthy aspiration for American citizens, because it elevates pleasure seeking above more deeply productive activities such as creating marital families. To promote family values, the state should express disapproval through misdemeanor criminal law and various civil exclusions. Is there a persuasive response, within the premises of a traditionalist communitarianism, to this argument? There are three responses to which this book contributes.[19]

1. Sodomy as a Human Good. At the same time the twentieth century was incorporating oral sex into the crime against nature, fellatio and cunnilingus were gaining popularity as an important feature of marriage bonds. By the 1920s married couples (and increasing numbers of unmarried female-male ones) found oral sex not only enjoyable, but an intimacy that helped cement their marital vows and deepen their commitments to their families. Americans' interest in oral sex steadily increased throughout the century, until it is now a standard part of most people's intimate repertoire. For some couples, it is the activity that best promotes the human goods of intimacy and mutual commitment. To be sure, straight couples typically understand oral sex to be foreplay rather than the main event. More important, some traditionalists make a distinction between heterosexual and homosexual sodomy: only the former can be tied to procreative, "productive" sexuality; the latter is more tied to "pleasure" and is ultimately "sterile."[20]

An increasing number of communitarians believe, for good reasons, that homosexual sodomy can also be the foundation for basic human goods such as marriage and family. Indeed, the basis for such a position was the decision in *Bowers v. Hardwick*—not the Supreme Court's decision, but that of Judge Frank Johnson for the court of appeals. Johnson suggested that marriage, whose intimacy forms the core of the privacy right, was constitutionally important "because of the unsurpassed opportunity for mutual support and self-expression." For homosexuals, the crime against nature can "serv[e] the same purpose as the intimacy of marriage." Michael Hardwick believed this, but his lawyers chose to avoid the idea because they (correctly) suspected that it would have been beyond the comprehension of Justice Lewis Powell, whose vote was necessary to affirm Johnson's result. Professor Michael Sandel and other communitarian philosophers believe this is a persuasive response to arguments for the crime against nature: lesbians and gay men have formed families and communities that have deepened their own lives and enriched the larger communities, even those unfriendly to them. For many traditionalists the fact that about one in four lesbian and gay Americans is raising children within partnered relationships has been a reason to oppose antigay discrimination and the criminalization of consensual sodomy. Justice Anthony Kennedy, a traditionalist public figure deeply interested in developing a nonpartisan public good, made this a key feature of his opinion for the Court in *Lawrence v. Texas* (2003): "To say that the issue in *Bowers* was simply the right to engage in certain sexual conduct demeans the claim the individual put forward, just as it would demean a married couple were it to be said that marriage is simply about the right to have sexual intercourse."[21]

This book offers various stories that illustrate the point that Sandel and Kennedy are making. Inspired by various sexual perversions and "dishonorable passions," Walt Whitman created the first great body of American poetry (chapter 1). More ambiguously partnered, Jane Addams redefined the notion of "charitable" activities; her feminist-dominated Hull House was the classic good neighbor, transforming the working-class community in which it was situated (chapter 2). Ruth Benedict and Margaret Mead, sexual and intellectual partners and life friends, revolutionized American anthropology, inspired by the synergy of their intertwined lives (chapter 2). The bisexual Alfred Kinsey created a brilliantly creative community in Bloomington, Indiana, including his wife, his fellow researchers and their families, and long-term links with closeted homosexuals all over the Midwest (chapter 4). Today, Steven Lofton and Roger Croteau's life partnership is a model for Americans of all orientations, as these nurses have given six HIV-positive children a chance to live and participate in a world that remains anxious about homosexuality, disease, and black skin color (chapter 11).[22]

While these are not necessarily representative stories of American sodomites, they are, with the possible exception of Addams's partnership with Mary Rozet Smith, examples of productive relationships between same-sex couples founded upon and deepened by the crime against nature. This history also supports arguments by scholars such as Carlos Ball and Andrew Koppelman that lesbian and gay families are evidence that sodomy can be a foundation for genuine human goods. As the country's ferocious debate over same-sex marriage indicates, most Americans do not agree with this proposition, and it remains officially irreconcilable with Roman Catholic doctrine. In an interview, Bowers candidly expressed skepticism on this score, especially when the topic of gay marriage came up, but he agreed that his then thirteen-year-old grandson will probably understand this matter very differently.[23]

2. Paradoxes of State Sex Regulation. The best is often the enemy of the good. One lesson of our nation's experiment with Prohibition (1920–33) is that it is disastrous for a polity to criminalize activities in which nearly everyone engages. It may be the case, as temperance advocates maintained, that consumption of alcohol is a sin against God, creates terrible medical and addiction risks for many people, endangers public safety, and offers temptations for the young. Nonetheless, it was a mistake for the nation to ban alcohol, for it turned us into a nation of lawbreakers. An equally bad alternative would have been to ban alcohol only for a minority group, such as Irish Americans, who were denigrated by the mainstream as the worst of a besotted populace. America's ban against oral sex in Kinsey's era was our Sexual Prohibition, and the Texas Homosexual Conduct Law bore the same defect as the hypothetical Prohibition for Irish Only.

Why were Prohibition and Kinsey-era Sodomy Prohibition such failures, even from a communitarian perspective? Why are Prohibition for Irish Only and the Homosexual Conduct Law equally bad ideas, even for those who genuinely believe that the Irish are natural alcoholics and homosexuals sexually and morally sterile? Consider this question: What kind of polity does a particular regulatory regime help to construct? This book's account of the decline and fall of the crime against nature suggests that (Homosexual) Sodomy Prohibition helps create a polity that most traditionalists would not want to live in.[24]

A state that criminalizes sexual conduct most citizens enjoy is vesting great and inevitably corrupting authority in its police force. The history of consensual sodomy laws is a history of municipal corruption similar to the corruption engendered by Prohibition. Armed with the authority to arrest any part of the populace they were willing to invest resources in detecting, police all over America used that authority to enrich themselves with bribes, to bully and harass people they did not like, and to brutalize and even rape citizens who were harming no one else. If this was a power routinely exercised by the police, the office was bound to become more attractive to the thug, the bigot, and the political hack. By corrupting the police force, sodomy laws, like Prohibition, threatened to undermine the rule of law itself.[25]

Moreover, crime-against-nature laws contributed to a politics of scapegoating and group anger. The police tended to enforce generally worded sodomy statutes against people they found disgusting or degenerate—not only homosexuals, but also cross-dressers, African Americans, and Mexican, Puerto Rican, and other Latino Americans. From a communitarian perspective the worst sin of scapegoating is that it needlessly fractures community and diverts public resources away from genuine community problems. In the period 1947–61, for example, the public was concerned that adult men were abusing children, but when that concern was translated into greater enforcement and penalties for the crime against nature, the public value was lost (chapter 3). Thus, the many anti-homosexual laws Governor Earl Warren signed between 1943 and 1953 (chapter 3) not only affected the choices of responsible lesbians and gay men, an objection to such laws from a liberal point of view, but also detracted from serious public deliberation about how to help children (especially girls) being molested within their own homes by grandparents, stepparents, fathers, uncles, and maternal boyfriends, an objection to such laws from a *communitarian* as well as liberal point of view. By demonizing homosexuality, traditionalists run the risk of believing they are addressing issues of responsible sexuality, when in fact they are mainly diverting attention away from serious problems.[26]

As Kinsey demonstrated half a century ago (chapter 4), the crime against nature, even when it was felonious everywhere, had no discernible effect on the incidence of oral and anal sex within the population. At the height of the criminalization of sodomy, everyone seemed to be committing the crime against nature; Americans were all sodomites. Nor is there any reason to believe that these laws had a salutary educational effect on the young. If anything, they taught teenagers that oral and anal sex were activities best pursued secretively, without discussion with parents and other authority figures. As the "Boys of Boise" scandal revealed (chapter 3), these laws sometimes helped turn juvenile delinquents into hustlers but otherwise seemed to have no effect on sexual activities even in small-town Idaho.

Indeed, the obsessive attention given to the crime against nature in the twentieth-century United States may have helped *create* more "perverted" Americans. Sexual preferences, fantasies, and orientations are not consumer choices. Attraction to a sexual object is not like selecting a pair of shoes. Indeed, there is significant evidence that modern sexual feelings are more likely to be a reaction against, rather than adherence to, lines insisted upon by society and the state. Notwithstanding overwhelming state signals that sodomy is disgusting and homosexuality is predatory, Ruth Benedict (chapter 2), Bayard Rustin (chapter 3), Frank Kameny (chapter 5), Martha Shelley (chapter 6), and millions of other Americans found themselves attracted to persons of the same sex. If anything, the state's obsession about the exotic perversion of homosexuality contributed to their homosexual feelings. Moreover, the state's draconian enforcement of sodomy laws opened many closet doors, pushing Kameny (after his 1956 arrest) and Shelley (after the 1969 Stonewall riots) into the public eye as openly homosexual Americans.[27]

Even heterosexuals are subject to this phenomenon. For many straight persons sexual excitement depends in part on transgressing social or even legal boundaries. Just as many gay and bisexual men have found sex in public restrooms and steamrooms erotic in part because it is illegal, so many straight men and women are turned on by the idea of sex in an elevator, an airplane restroom, automobiles, and other quasi-public places. All of this constitutes illegal public indecency, yet the legal as well as social risk of discovery actually heightens the sexual attraction for many people. As David Cole has said, "the sex drive is itself

shaped by the regulatory lines we draw and precisely by the excitement that tran-
gressing those taboos promises." Hence, "sexual expression to some extent will
always elude society's desperate attempts to regulate it, because sexual expression
transforms whatever taboo is imposed into a fetish."[28]

3. The Communitarian Case for Tolerance and Equal Treatment. Although a
moral traditionalist and political communitarian, Bowers understood that both
tradition and community to demand state tolerance and even equal treatment
for sexual minorities. At no point in his tenure as attorney general (1981–97) did
he advocate enforcement of the sodomy law against private homosexual activities. Today he is perfectly happy that Georgia's sodomy law cannot be applied to
consensual private activities, though he believes that judges reached this result
through a creative rather than strictly legal interpretation of the Georgia and
U.S. constitutions. He now says this: "Of all the constitutional rights, the most
important is the idea of equality under the law." Thus, Bowers believes that the
state should not discriminate against homosexuals and regrets the way he handled Robin Shahar's application for employment with his office in the 1990s.
The essence of this latter point is widely shared by Americans of all moral per-
suasions. Since 1977 strong and growing majorities have told pollsters that homosexuals should not face job discrimination. A recent Gallup poll (May 2006)
reports that eighty-nine percent of respondents said that "homosexuals should
have equal rights in terms of job opportunities."[29]

Mike Bowers, a thoughtful traditionalist, is a pointed contrast to the antigay
bigot, including religious bigots. The latter may consider themselves traditionalists, but religion in their case is a self-serving justification for anger, fears, and
status anxiety. Rejecting the perspective of the bigot, a genuine communitarian
(or a genuine Christian) recognizes the worth of fellow citizens, including those
he finds strange and even immoral, and sees the wisdom in Whitman's idea that
all social groups must "be placed, in each and in the whole, on one broad, primary, universal, common platform." A politics of tolerance is not just idealistic,
it is practically essential for the polity to thrive. A democratic community such as
ours integrates and accommodates various social, economic, and ideological
groups, and at key moments even gets them all to join together for important
national projects (like World War II). This system of mutual tolerance and cooperation is threatened when the system becomes embroiled in bitter disputes that
drive salient, productive groups away from engagement in pluralist politics. It is
particularly dangerous for the state to take sides so decisively in culture wars. By
persecuting or harassing minorities, the state embitters the minority, creates
dangers for the majority, and destabilizes the democracy.[30]

The Religion Clauses provide a useful model for managing the culture clash between traditional family values citizens and their lesbian and gay neighbors. Just as the Free Exercise Clause prevents the government from meddling in the private affairs of or discriminating against minority religions, so a politics of tolerance prevents feuding culture groups from using the government as an instrument of persecution or discrimination. Just as the Anti-Establishment Clause prohibits the government from creating an official state religion, so the politics of tolerance prevents the government from announcing that one cultural group has prevailed and now dictates orthodoxy for all. This is a principle that both liberals and communitarians ought to support. An honest traditionalist like Mike Bowers can appreciate *Lawrence*'s holding that the state cannot invade gay people's private homes if he recalls that the same Court ruled in *Boy Scouts of America v. Dale* (2000) (chapter 11) that the state also cannot invade traditionalists' private associations and clubs to impose gay-friendly policies. From a communitarian point of view, such a politics of tolerance is a workable system, even when there is pervasive distrust or ill will between the groups. If the legislative process cannot stay its hand, the judicial process should set limits, as the Supreme Court did in both *Lawrence* and *Dale*.[31]

Three Lessons for Gay Rights Liberals

San Francisco's José Sarria and Washington, D.C.'s Frank Kameny read *Lawrence* as a constitutional vindication of their motto, Gay is Good, and a vindication of the Stonewall philosophy that sex for pleasure is not only morally permissible, but constitutionally required. As chapter 11 reveals, this is not what the Court actually said in *Lawrence*. The rhetoric and reasoning deployed by Justice Kennedy's majority opinion, and Justice O'Connor's concurring opinion, did not enshrine Bentham's liberal philosophy (the state can regulate only when the actor is harming third parties) in the Constitution, nor do they invalidate the thousands of sexual orientation discriminations in American law. The state can no longer legislate gay people as outlaws, but neither must it treat sexual variation as completely benign or neutral. Gay may be Good, but the Constitution does not impose that norm upon homo-anxious states.

While gay rights supporters, especially lawyers, cannot dispute the foregoing analysis, they certainly can regard *Lawrence* as the first step in an inevitable progression of judicial decisions recognizing the homo-equality idea that Lambda and the ACLU have been pressing for several decades. The Supreme Court has trod this path before. In *Reed v. Reed* (1971) the Court for the first time in its history overturned a state sex discrimination as unconstitutional, but in an opinion that concluded, without much reasoning, that Idaho's discrimination lacked a rational basis—the same conclusion the Court reached in *Lawrence*. Over the next five years the Court evaluated a number of sex discriminations under this vague standard, until it ruled in *Craig v. Boren* (1976) that sex discriminations should be subjected to quasi-strict scrutiny, and in most instances sex discriminations have been invalidated. There are now very few open sex discriminations in American law, and twenty years from now sexual orientation discriminations may be just as sparse.[32]

That explicitly antigay discriminations by the state will melt away is certainly the way Michael Hardwick would have understood *Lawrence*. But this book's history suggests that such a process will not be inevitable, and will not occur as the result of constitutional decisions by the Supreme Court. Indeed, one of the lessons of *Dishonorable Passions* is that a gay rights liberalism unmoored from family and kin would be doomed constitutional politics. Consider some lessons that gay rights liberals themselves should draw from *Lawrence*.

1. Winning in Court Is Less Important than Persuading Your Neighbors. Within the lesbian and gay community, there was much despair after *Bowers* (chapter 8) and much elation after *Lawrence* (chapter 10). Some historians are now reexamining this history, and their analysis suggests that a victory in *Bowers* would have produced a public backlash against gay people. Perhaps, but a narrow opinion striking down the Georgia sodomy law that was so bizarrely applied as to violate the fair warning and evenhanded enforcement principles of *Papachristou v. City of Jacksonville* (1972) might not have stirred antigay sentiment and would have given rise to an important debate at the state level: Are we really serious about criminalizing consensual sodomy? This latter point is the key one. In a democracy, We the People are ultimately responsible for value choices, and the primary audience for Gay is Good claims ought to be our neighbors and our legislators, not (just) our judges.[33]

One way that *Bowers* contributed to gay rights was that it forced the LGBT community to return to the states. At the state level, rights-based liberal arguments grounded in abstract notions of privacy or equality were subordinated to community-based arguments grounded in the experience of groups of citizens whose fates were linked. Even when post-*Bowers* sodomy nullification came through state constitutional litigation (as in Kentucky and Arkansas) rather than state legislation (as in Rhode Island and Arizona), success was a process in which activists engaged in grassroots community organizing, presented detailed evidence that consensual sodomy laws disrupted good lives and undermined public health, and preserved constitutional victories against override by popular referenda.[34]

Conversely, *Lawrence* could undermine gay rights. In the months after the Supreme Court's decision, Americans alarmed by Justice Scalia's insistence that constitutionalized homo equality meant that same-sex marriage would soon be foisted upon them by the Rehnquist Court briefly changed their minds about sodomy reform. Whereas sixty percent of respondents in May 2003 believed that adult homosexual relations ought to be legal, only fifty-one percent said the same thing in July, right after *Lawrence*. That lower figure was consistent through the end of the year, after the Massachusetts Supreme Judicial Court relied on *Lawrence* to require that state to recognize same-sex marriages. After it became apparent, through the passage of time if nothing else, that the Rehnquist Court had no interest in gay marriage, other than avoiding the subject, public opinion returned to pre-*Lawrence* levels.[35]

A more profound way that *Lawrence* might undermine gay rights is by lulling gay people into believing that the culture war has been won, or that victory is just around the corner after more constitutional litigation. But constitutional rights can easily be diluted or evaded entirely if activists do not have a grassroots political strategy in place to reinforce their constitutional victory. And, perhaps, a great deal of luck. Thus *Brown* has had less bite for people of color and *Roe* less bite for women because those decisions stimulated powerful resegregationist and pro-life countermovements, which have negated the positive effect of those great constitutional "triumphs." To date, *Lawrence* has not inspired a sodomy-revival movement, in part because the sodomy issue was overripe by the time the Court finally settled it and in larger part because traditionalists' focus had moved on to same-sex marriage.[36]

2. The Politics of Disgust and Contagion Remains a Powerful Force. Gay rights advocates tend to view the overruling of *Bowers v. Hardwick* as a product of the inevitable liberalization of American constitutional law. This book should dispel such an optimistic view. It took seventeen years for a similar case (sodomy by consenting adults within the home) to reach the Court, and *Lawrence* could, indeed should, have been derailed at various points. J. R. Quinn should not have arrested John Lawrence and Tyron Garner. William J. Delmore III should have told the district attorney that the Homosexual Conduct Law probably violated the Texas Constitution. The Texas judges should have overturned the conviction, perhaps through a narrowing interpretation of the Homosexual Conduct Law. Any one of these actions would have stopped the case before it reached the U.S. Supreme Court.

It was likewise hardly inevitable that the Court the case reached would have been hospitable to the constitutional claims Lambda was making. If Judge Bork, the author of *Dronenberg v. Zech* (1985), had publicly disavowed his criticism of *Griswold*, or if his former colleagues on the Harvard faculty had not exposed Judge Douglas Ginsburg's recreational drug use in 1987, either man would have been confirmed to replace Justice Powell; Anthony Kennedy would not have been nominated to the Supreme Court, and overruling *Bowers* would have required the vote of Sandra Day O'Connor, a *Bowers* participant who disapproved of overruling precedent. If the first Bush administration had enjoyed more reliable reconnaissance as regards David Souter's libertarian streak and had nominated a social conservative to the Court in 1991, as they would do the following year with Clarence Thomas, there would have been at most four votes (Stevens, O'Connor, Ginsburg, Breyer) to invalidate Colorado's Amendment 2 in *Romer* or the Texas Homosexual Conduct Law in *Lawrence* under the Equal Protection Clause.

Luck aside, Lambda did not prevail in *Lawrence* because the United States or its Supreme Court had become either morally or politically liberal between 1986 and 2003. As a cultural and political matter, Lambda prevailed because *relationals,* Americans who believe that sex is moral if within a relationship, joined *liberals* and some pragmatic *traditionalists* in condemning consensual sodomy laws as measures that should be politically out of bounds. To repeat: the United States has not become a nation of moral liberals generally, and certainly not as regards homosexuals. Notwithstanding the sexual revolution and Stonewall, a majority of Americans have never endorsed the proposition that sex for pleasure is morally worthy. In 2004 fifty-seven percent of Americans believed that homosexual relations are "always wrong," about the same number as those saying abortion is always wrong, and almost double the number who say premarital sex is always wrong.[37]

Indeed, matters are even worse: a significant minority of Americans is affirmatively prejudiced against homosexuals—they are homophobic, not just homo-anxious. Contrary to conventional liberal wisdom, homophobes are not dysfunctional cretins. For the most part they are fairly decent people (even to homosexuals), and their antigay prejudice actually serves emotional needs, helping them deal with their own unacceptable sexual feelings, which they can displace onto the homosexual; with their obsessional concern that hallowed lines are not blurring; and with anxiety about their own stable and superior identities (chapter 1). But one does not have to be a homophobe to believe that homosexuality is disgusting and should be firmly discouraged, lest it pollute our children, public culture, and cherished institutions such as the family. Mike Bowers, for example, supports *both* state tolerance and equal treatment for gay people *and* a variety of "no promo homo" policies in public education and family law.[38]

In short, the body politics of disgust and contagion remains a powerful force in American culture and government. As oral sex has become commonplace, disapproval of homosexual conduct has eased a bit; as most Americans have come to accept sex outside of marriage, homosexual relationships are not as objectionable as they were in the 1950s. Note again the contingent nature of "progress" for homosexuals. If the original crime against nature, anal sex, had not expanded in the early twentieth century to assimilate oral sex, the disapproval of sodomy would be much higher today. Unlike oral sex, anal sex is much less practiced by Americans, including gay men and especially lesbians, than oral sex. Among teens, oral sex is the most frequent form of sexual intercourse; indeed, many high school and college students do not consider oral sex "intercourse" at all.[39]

The history of sodomy reform offers strong lessons for the same-sex marriage movement. The most significant is that the law (including constitutional law announced by judges) will not change until public attitudes change. So long as most Americans believed that homosexuality was a *malignant* variation from the norm (compulsory heterosexuality), even liberals in the ACLU could support the crime against nature as a normative regime. Once most Americans came around to the view that homosexuality was a *tolerable* variation from the norm (strongly preferred heterosexuality), most liberals and increasing numbers of relationals supported sodomy repeal. Even nonhomophobic traditionalists could acquiesce in *Lawrence*, once the line separating disapproved homosexuality and cherished traditions shifted from the crime against nature to marriage. With almost all the states explicitly disapproving gay marriage and many adopting other explicitly antigay laws, the repeal or nullification of consensual sodomy laws could not reasonably be read as "promoting homosexuality." If most Americans ultimately come around to the view, held by Dr. Kinsey and most gay activists, that homosexuality is a *benign* variation and that there is no single norm for human relations, then state recognition of same-sex marriages will be inevitable, for the same reason that disapproval of different-race marriages faded away (namely, we came to see racial variation as completely benign).[40]

Under this analysis, constitutional law is hardly irrelevant, because it may under certain circumstances reverse the burden of inertia in a political system. Thus, today most people in Georgia could live with a draconian sodomy law so long as they believed it would not be enforced against them, but almost as many of them are willing to live with no consensual sodomy law. When public opinion is not strongly engaged with issues like this, constitutional decisions can safely protect minority groups, like gay people, against unfair treatment. It is not clear that either Georgia or the United States would have acquiesced in a Supreme Court decision striking down all consensual sodomy laws in *Bowers v. Hardwick* (1986), at the apex of people's association of AIDS with homosexual sodomy. But in 1998, the Georgia Supreme Court reversed the burden of inertia in *Powell v. State*: citizens of Georgia were not demanding that their legislature reformulate the crime against nature, but neither were they energized to override the court when it struck down the law as applied to consensual activities (chapter 9). For the most part the southern states whose miscegenation laws were overturned in *Loving v. Virginia* (1967) were the jurisdictions most affected by *Lawrence*—which led to much less disapproval than *Loving* had.[41]

But these circumstances are not present for issues like gay marriage in states like Georgia, where antihomosexual sentiment is fully engaged. Large majorities in Georgia believe that a marriage sealed by homosexual conduct is not only disgusting, but a sacrilege disrespecting the integrity of their religious identities and, for some, the stable line between man and woman. Because it involves long-standing cultural lines being crossed, traditionalist and most relationalist citizens of Georgia believe that gay marriage will destroy the institution of marriage—not because there is an ounce of evidence to indicate that is the case (the experience in Europe, Canada, and Massachusetts is that gay marriage has no negative effect), but because they feel the homosexualization of marriage is a pollution per se. In contrast, citizens in states like Massachusetts, Vermont, and California do not consider homosexual conduct as threatening. (Reasons for this greater acceptance include larger numbers of openly lesbian and gay persons and families; lower rates of fundamentalist Protestantism; and higher rates of non-marital cohabitation.) In those states judges have greater discretion to interpret their state constitutions to require same-sex marriage (as Massachusetts has), or civil unions (as Vermont has), or domestic partnerships (as California has). This discretion does not exist for judges in the South, Midwest, and Rocky Mountains, nor would judges in those states have any inclination to require same-sex marriage even if they could.[42]

3. Homosexuality and Community. *Lawrence* should also be understood as a challenge for gay people. Recalling an old-fashioned conception of citizenship as entailing obligations as well as freedoms, *Lawrence* should stir LGBT people to commit themselves to families, communities, and institutions (including religious ones) from which they have been alienated because of sodomy laws, social stigma, and other disabilities. Gay people should not use *Lawrence* as a bludgeon to force states and municipalities to abandon discriminatory policies, but instead should invoke *Lawrence* as an invitation for governments at all levels to rethink their policies, with input from gay people as well as from traditionalists.

This deployment of *Lawrence* requires a longer-term strategy, involving appeals to agencies and legislatures more than to judges. But it is a superior strategy, in part because it yields deeper normative change and because a judges-only strategy reads more into *Lawrence* than judges are able, or willing, to do on their own.[43]

Philosophical liberals, such as John Rawls and Richard Posner, have tended to underestimate the importance of family and community values to the government's role in structuring legal rights and responsibilities. Most gay rights activists have accepted, even applauded this approach, but a new generation of gay or gay-friendly thinkers—such as the law professors Carlos Ball and Chai Feldblum, the philosophers Stephen Macedo and Michael Sandel, the anthropologist Kath Weston, and journalists like Bruce Bawer and Jonathan Rauch—maintain that gay people ought to understand themselves as family members and actors interacting with communities. This is strategically important. To the extent that gay people are perceived this way by mainstream Americans, they will be less vulnerable to the politics of disgust and contagion. But it is also normatively important. As early as Walt Whitman (*Leaves of Grass*) and Susan B. Anthony ("Homes of Single Women"), key liberal thinkers have argued that sexual freedom and gender equality require community (chapter 1). Theirs was a different kind of community from that envisioned by traditionalists (husband-wife marriages with children), and that is the challenge *Lawrence* and the same-sex marriage movement pose to LGBT Americans: What kind of community, what understanding of family, do you stand for?[44]

The story of the decline and fall of the crime against nature offers, at first glance, few affirmative models for this kind of reconstruction. Most of the famous litigants suffered tragic lives after their encounters with the law: Clive Michael Boutilier (chapter 5) tried to commit suicide after his deportation to Canada and died broken and alone in 2003. After serving five and one-half months in jail for committing the crime against nature, Eugene Enslin (chapter 6) returned to manage the massage parlor and adult bookstore in Jacksonville, North Carolina, where he originally got into trouble. The city finally closed down the establishment for minor rule infractions, and Enslin left town. Since 1995, he has lived in New Bern, North Carolina, where his main source of support has been federal disability payments; his best friend is a sick puppy he inherited from a neighbor. Although John Lawrence continues to live the good life in Houston, his friend Tyron Garner (chapter 10) died on September 11, 2006, of meningitis. Because he died in poverty, his lawyer, Mitchell Katine, appealed to the lesbian and gay community to raise money for a proper funeral. The community that raised $750,000 to finance the sodomy law litigation contributed $200 (half from Katine) to bury Garner. On October 18 the family surrendered his body to the state for cremation, "an unceremonious fate that most often befalls the indigent or the forgotten."[45]

What of Michael Hardwick, the most famous of all the gay defendants in the jurisprudence of sodomy? Recall from chapter 8 that he found his life vocation as an optical alchemist (a designer of installations for gay nightclubs and discotheques) in South Beach, Miami-Dade County, after the Supreme Court's unsettling decision in his case. This vocation might have become his vindication, but within a year of the Court's decision, Hardwick discovered he had thrush around his neck. By 1989, his immune system was severely compromised, and his once-athletic body grew frail. Although he continued to produce art and cavort with his big white Lab, Jumbo, Hardwick's body wasted away. In 1990, Michael's sister Susan Browning Chriss moved him to Archer, Florida (outside of Gainesville), where she, their sister Alice, and their mother, Kitty, all lived. They shared caregiving duties for their cherished brother, whose body shrank to sixty-five pounds. On June 13, 1991, Michael Hardwick died of complications associated with AIDS. His brother, Patrick, and his mother took his ashes to Bonita Springs Beach, Florida, where Kitty Hardwick tearfully sprinkled them into the Gulf of Mexico.[46]

Throughout the litigation Michael Hardwick had probably been carrying within his body the virus that not only brought him an early death, but that epitomized for many Americans the problem with homosexuality. As the Moral Majority put it in 1983, AIDS and homosexuality were a "Moral Time Bomb." Just as HIV was a Trojan horse in the body, so homosexuality was a Trojan horse in society—infecting it and then destroying it from within. Thankfully, even most fundamentalists do not subscribe to the Moral Majority's antihomosexual rhetoric, but it does reflect an undercurrent of American culture. What sense should the LGBT community and America make of Michael Hardwick's life and death? What is his legacy for the larger community?[47]

One lesson is the importance of family. Many of the sodomites in this book formed committed relationships with loved ones, relationships cemented by what was then the crime against nature. These include Ruth Benedict and Margaret Mead (chapter 2), whose intertwined lives transformed American anthropology, and Bessie Smith and Ma Rainey (chapter 2), whose intertwined lives created the blues and transformed American music; Bayard Rustin (chapter 3) and his life partner Walter Neagle, who now preserves Rustin's extraordinary collection of African art and Christian relics and the documents surrounding his remarkable civil rights activism; Alfred and Clara Kinsey (chapter 4), whose sodomy-saturated marriage was the foundation for scientific work that transformed American sexology and law, as well as producing three successful children; Del Martin and Phyllis Lyon (chapters 4–5), whose life partnership forged the

Daughters of Bilitis, the first lesbian rights group and an inspiration for the feminist movement of the 1960s; Willie Brown (chapter 7) and his wife, whose marriage sustained one of the great political careers in American history; Paula Ettelbrick and Suzanne Goldberg (chapters 9–10), whose relationship synergistically fueled the careers of both women as legal rights activists and produced two children; and Steve Lofton and Roger Croteau (chapter 11), whose long-term union (briefly a state-sanctioned marriage) has centered on the nurturing of the six HIV-positive children of color for whom they have been foster parents. There are millions of productive Americans today, straight as well as gay, for whom the old crime against nature is an important emotional foundation for committed relationships and family.

It would be a mistake to think that Michael Hardwick was not just as committed to family as these others, and as those Americans whose just as excellent marriages do not include sodomy. Although he never formed a life partnership with another man, he touched the lives of the men who were his lovers. His lasting relationships were with his mother and his two sisters, Susan Browning Chriss and Alice Hardwick Ahehr. Michael was in the hospital room for the birth of Susan's daughter Jasmine, was a loving uncle to Alice's daughter Jessica, and was a mentor for Susan's son, Robert Hardwick Weston. Robert grew up in a household where it was never a secret that his glamorous uncle was gay, and when his own homosexual orientation became clear to him it was not the traumatic experience that it was for women and men of his parents' generation. Uncle Michael taught Robert much about the life of the mind, thinking for oneself and learning from one's past mistakes without becoming bitter about them.[48]

I met Robert at Café Raffaella, in New York City's West Village, and was impressed with his easy acceptance of homosexuality, his brilliance, and his seriousness as a Ph.D. student in German Studies at Columbia University (he has recently earned the Ph.D.). We discussed the *Lawrence* opinion, especially Justice Scalia's dissent. Weston was fascinated by Scalia's extravagant rhetoric and his charge that the majority opinion was simply an exercise in elitist political correctness. This charge was "degrading, belittling [to] gay people's lives" in its treatment of the majority's reasoning as some kind of political game; Weston was disappointed that the dissenters did not engage the majority more deeply on the history of the crime against nature, the morality of a law focusing just on "homosexual sodomy," and the connection between liberty and equality suggested by the majority and concurring opinions. While not a lawyer, Weston appreciated Justice Kennedy's insistence that the issue be framed in a fair and neutral way. The *Bowers* Court stacked the deck, not just because it focused only on "homosexual sodomy," but more importantly because it treated human lovemaking as an abstract series of acts having no connection to people's lives.[49]

I concluded our interview with this: How would Uncle Michael have reacted to Justice Kennedy's opinion? Robert thought his reaction would have been "bittersweet," filled with both joy and regret. "Michael Hardwick would have found much consolation in the way Justice Kennedy's opinion in *Lawrence* vindicated his struggle." He did not say exactly what Michael's struggle was, but one way of putting it is this: his uncle struggled so that young homosexuals like Robert could live their lives without shame, could focus on productive activities such as his German studies and his own long-term relationship with another man, and could even imagine having families of their own.[50]

APPENDIX

The Evolution of State Sodomy Laws, Colonial Times to *Lawrence v. Texas* (2003)

State	Early Statutory Criminalizations of Crime Against Nature and Its Solicitation	Expansion of the Crime Against Nature to Include Oral Sex, Masturbation, etc.
Alabama	1841 Alabama Penal Code § 7 ("crime against nature")	*Woods v. State,* 64 So. 508 (Alabama Court of Appeals, 1914) (fellatio is a crime against nature); *Brown v. State,* 22 So. 2d 45 (Alabama Supreme Court, 1945) (cunnilingus); 1955 Alabama Acts No. 397 (new crime of "indecent liberties" with minors)
Alaska	Act of March 3, 1899, 30 Stat. 1253 (crime of "sodomy")	1915 Alaska Laws chap. 22 (adding "unnatural carnal copulation by means of the mouth"). But see 1971 Alaska Laws chap. 32, interpreted as legalizing oral sex in *Spencer v. State,* 514 P.2d 14 (Alaska Supreme Court, 1973)
Arizona	Arizona (Terr.) Code chap. 10, § 48 (1865) ("crime against nature"); 1951 Arizona Laws chaps. 110–111 (loitering near schoolyard or public toilet)	1913 Penal Code § 280 (crime against nature expanded to include fellatio [repealed 1951]); 1917 Arizona Laws chap. 2 (new misdemeanor: "lewd or lascivious act," including cunnilingus); 1939 Arizona Laws chap. 13 (indecent liberties with minors); *State v. Mortimer,* 467 P.2d 60 (Arizona Supreme Court, 1970) (mutual masturbation is criminal lewdness)
Arkansas	Arkansas Penitentiary Act, December 17, 1838, § 4 ("sodomy, or buggery," death penalty); 1848 Arkansas Penal Code § 9 (sodomy or attempted sodomy by whites, 5–21 years prison; death penalty for blacks until 1873); 1953 Arkansas Acts No. 94 (loitering near schoolyard)	*Strum v. State,* 272 S.W. 359 (Arkansas Supreme Court, 1925) (fellatio is a crime against nature); 1953 Arkansas Acts Nos. 48 and 94 (new crimes of "indecent liberties" with and exposing minors, "indecency")
California	1850 California Statutes chap. 99, § 48 ("infamous crime against nature," 1 year–life in prison); 1855 California Statutes chap. 82 ("assault to commit sodomy"); 1903 California Statutes chap. 89 ("lewd vagrancy," anti-solicitation law, periodically updated); 1929 California Statutes, page 697 (loitering near schoolyard)	1901 California Statutes chap. 201 ("lewd acts" in presence of minor); 1903 California Statutes chap. 201 (criminalizing any act that outrages public decency, frequently updated); 1915 California Statutes chap. 586 ("fellatio" and "cunnilingus"; invalidated 1919), superseded by 1921 California Statutes chap. 848 (new crime: "oral copulation"); 1929 California Statutes page 697 (child molestation)

Expansive Consequences of Committing the Crime Against Nature and Its Solicitation	Contraction of the Crime Against Nature, as Regards Consensual Activities
1967 Alabama Acts No. 506 (sex offender registration law for sodomites et al.)	Reduced to misdemeanor, 1977 Alabama Acts No. 607, § 2318. Invalidated, *Lawrence v. Texas*, 539 U.S. 558 (2003)
	Crime against nature clause invalidated, as applied to consensual activities, *Harris v. State*, 457 P.2d 638 (Alaska Supreme Court, 1969). Consensual "sodomy" entirely decriminalized, 1978 Alaska Laws chap. 166, § 121
1951 Arizona Acts chap. 105 (registration with sheriff for crimes against nature and lewd acts); ibid., chap. 134 (sodomy penalty 5–20 years in prison)	Consensual sodomy reduced to misdemeanor, 1977 Arizona Laws chap. 142, § 67. Consensual sodomy and lewd or lascivious acts decriminalized, 2001 Arizona Laws chap. 382
	Decriminalized, 1975 Arkansas Acts No. 280. Recriminalized, only for same-sex partners, as misdemeanor, 1977 Arkansas Acts No. 828. Invalidated, *Jegley v. Picado*, 80 S.W.3d 332 (Arkansas Supreme Court, 2002)
1909 California Statutes chap. 720 (sterilization for imprisoned "moral or sexual perverts"); 1941 California Statutes chap. 106 (castration of "sex perverts"); 1945 California Statutes chap. 138 (expanding 1939 sexual psychopath law to allow indefinite civil commitment for dangerous sex perverts); 1947 California Statutes chap. 1124 (sex offender registration law for sodomy, oral copulation, [later] lewd vagrancy); 1952 California Statutes, 1st Extr. Sess., chap. 23 (teaching certificates withdrawn for same three crimes)	1950 California Statutes, 1st Extr. Sess. chap. 56 (creating misdemeanor alternative for oral copulation crime; new enhanced penalties for nonconsensual oral sex added 1952). Consensual sodomy and oral copulation decriminalized, 1975 California Statutes chap. 71, § 7

State	Early Statutory Criminalizations of Crime Against Nature and Its Solicitation	Expansion of the Crime Against Nature to Include Oral Sex, Masturbation, etc.
Colorado	1861 Colorado Laws chap. 297, § 46 ("crime against nature"); 1939 Colorado Laws chap. 97 ("solicitation of any unnatural carnal copulation")	1905 Colorado Laws, page 181 (indecent liberties with minors); 1939 Colorado Laws chap. 97 ("carnal copulation per os"); *Gilmore v. People*, 467 P.2d 828 (Colorado Supreme Court, 1970) (cunnilingus)
Connecticut	Act of December 1, 1642, § 7 ("man lying with man," capital crime); 1672 General Laws page 9; *State v. Trumbley*, 197 A.2d 944 (Connecticut Supreme Court, 1964) (applying lewdness statute to homosexual solicitation)	1925 Connecticut Laws chap. 66 (exposure of minors to indecency). Consensual oral sex never clearly a crime, but 1919 Connecticut Acts No. 77 (new "lewdness" crime), may have applied to oral sex
Delaware	Act for the Advancement of Justice etc., chap. XXII, § 5 (1719) ("sodomy, buggery," capital crime); 1826 Delaware Laws chap. 362 (reducing penalty to three years in prison)	*State v. Maida*, 96 A. 207 (Delaware Supreme Court, 1915) (fellatio); 1947 Delaware Laws chap. 81 (indecent liberties with minors)
District of Columbia	Act of March 3, 1901, 31 Stat. 1189 (recognizing common law crimes); Act of August 14, 1935, 49 Stat. 651 (crime to invite a person to go somewhere for "prostitution or any other immoral or lewd purpose"); Act of June 9, 1948, § 104, 62 Stat. 347 ("sodomy," 1–10 years in prison; sexual solicitation of minors)	Act of June 9, 1948, § 104, 62 Stat. 347 (sodomy includes placing or taking "into his or her mouth or anus the sexual organ"; new crime of indecent liberties with minors); Public Law Nos. 83–85, § 202(a)(1), 67 Stat. 97 (1953) (criminalizing any indecent sexual proposal or exposure, including those in private places)
Florida	Act of March 5, 1842, § 1, pamp. 20 ("buggery or sodomy"); 1868 Florida Laws chap. 1637(8), § 17 ("crime against nature")	1917 Florida Laws chap. 7361 (new misdemeanor: "unnatural and lascivious acts"); 1951 Florida Laws chaps. 26 and 580 (indecent liberties or lewd acts with minors)
Georgia	Charter of June 20, 1732 (common law in force, apparently including "buggery" as a capital crime); 1816 Georgia Penal Code § 61 ("sodomy," also "carnal knowledge"); 1968 Georgia Acts No. 1157 (new crime of soliciting another person to commit the crime against nature)	*Herring v. State*, 46 S.E.2d 876 (Georgia Supreme Court, 1904) (fellatio); *Comer v. State*, S.E.2d (Georgia Supreme Court, 1917) (cunnilingus), overruled in 1963 but reinstated by 1968 Georgia Acts No. 1157 (expanding sodomy to include any kind of oral sex); ibid. (new crime of "lewd caresses or indecent fondling"); 1950 Georgia Laws page 387 (indecent liberties with or sexual solicitation of minors)

Expansive Consequences of Committing the Crime Against Nature and Its Solicitation	Contraction of the Crime Against Nature, as Regards Consensual Activities
1953 Colorado Laws chap. 89 (indefinite civil commitment on conviction of sodomy etc.)	Decriminalized, 1971 Colorado Laws chap. 121
	Decriminalized, 1969 Connecticut Acts No. 828, § 214
	Decriminalized, 58 Delaware Laws chap. 497 (1972)
Act of June 9, 1948, 62 Stat. 347 (indefinite civil commitment of sex deviants upon petition to court); Executive Order 10405, S8(a)(1)(iii) (1953) ("sexual perversion" as a basis for investigation and purge from federal civil service)	Decriminalized, D.C. Act No. 4-69 (1981), but U.S. House of Representatives vetoed. House Resolution 208 (1981), 127 Cong. Rec. 22, 778–79 (1981). Decriminalized, Act of December 28, 1994, § 501(b), 42 D.C. Reg. 62
1951 Florida Laws chap. 29881 (potential indefinite civil commitment if charged or convicted of sodomy, lewdness, and other sex crimes with minors); 1959 Florida Laws chap. 404 (teaching certificate revoked for "moral misconduct," i.e., homosexuality).	Crime against nature (if consensual) invalidated, *Franklin v. State*, 257 So. 2d 21 (Florida Supreme Court, 1971), and decriminalized, 1974 Florida Laws chap. 74-121. Unnatural and lascivious acts (if consensual) invalidated, *Lawrence v. Texas*, 539 U.S. 558 (2003)
1968 Georgia Acts No. 1157 (penalty for sodomy, 1–20 years in prison, harshest regime in nation)	Consensual sodomy application upheld against constitutional attack, *Bowers v. Hardwick*, 478 U.S. 186 (USSC, 1986). Invalidated, as applied to consensual sodomy, *Powell v. State*, 510 S.E.2d 18 (Georgia Supreme Court, 1998)

State	Early Statutory Criminalizations of Crime Against Nature and Its Solicitation	Expansion of the Crime Against Nature to Include Oral Sex, Masturbation, etc.
Hawaii	1850 Hawaii (Terr.) Penal Code § 11 ("sodomy" or "crime against nature"); 1949 Hawaii Laws No. 139 (loitering in public place for purpose of "committing a crime against nature or other lewdness")	*Territory v. Wilson*, 26 Haw. 360 (Hawaii Supreme Court, 1922) (fellatio)
Idaho	1864 Idaho (Terr.) Laws chap. 3, § 45 ("crime against nature")	*State v. Altwatter*, 157 P.2d 256 (Idaho Supreme Court, 1916) (fellatio); 1949 Idaho laws chap. 214 (indecent liberties with minors); *State v. Limberhand*, 788 P.2d 857 (Idaho Supreme Court, 1990) (masturbation in public toilet)
Illinois	Laws of Northwest Territory, Act of July 14, 1795 ("sodomy" a capital offense); 1819 Illinois Penal Code § 20 ("crime against nature")	1907 Illinois Laws page 266 ("indecent liberties" with a minor, expanded in 1915 to criminalize lewd acts in presence of minor); *Honselman v. People*, 48 N.E. 304 (Illinois Supreme Court, 1897) (fellatio is a crime against nature), but *People v. Smith*, 101 N.E.2d 957 (Illinois Supreme Court, 1913) (cunnilingus is not)
Indiana	1881 Indiana Acts No. 37, § 100 ("crime against nature," which includes enticing a minor "to commit masturbation")	Ibid. (enticing minors "to commit masturbation"); *Glover v. State*, 101 N.E.2d 629 (Indiana Supreme Court, 1913) (fellatio); *Young v. State*, 141 N.E.2d 309 (Indiana Supreme Court, 1923) (cunnilingus)
Iowa	1892 Iowa Acts chap. 39 ("carnal copulation")	1902 Iowa Acts chap. 148 ("carnal copulation in any opening of the body except the sexual parts"), applied to fellatio in *State v. Magruder*, 101 N.W. 646 (Iowa Supreme Court, 1904); 1907 Iowa Acts chap. 173 (indecent liberties with minors)
Kansas	1855 Kansas (Terr.) Statutes chap. 53, § 7 ("crime against nature"); 1868 Kansas General Statutes chap. 31, § 1868 (same); 1969 Kansas Laws chap. 180, § 21-4108 (misdemeanor solicitation "for immoral purposes")	*State v. Hurlbert*, 234 P.2d 945 (Kansas Supreme Court, 1915) (fellatio); 1955 Kansas Laws chap. 195 (indecent liberties with minors, updated 1957, 1959); 1990 Kansas Laws chap. 149 (male-female cunnilingus), overriding *State v. Moppin*, 783 P.2d 878 (Kansas Supreme Court, 1989); 1991 Kansas Laws chap. 86 (all cunnilingus)

Expansive Consequences of Committing the Crime Against Nature and Its Solicitation	Contraction of the Crime Against Nature, as Regards Consensual Activities
	Decriminalized, 1972 Hawaii Laws No. 9, § 1300
1925 Idaho Laws chap. 194 (sterilization of "moral degenerates and sexual perverts"); 1993 Idaho Laws chap. 155 (registration of sodomites and other sex offenders)	Decriminalized, 1971 Idaho laws chap. 143, but recriminalized 1972 Idaho Laws chap. 336. Invalidated. *Lawrence v. Texas*, 539 U.S. 558 (2003)
1938 Illinois Laws page 28 (early sexual psychopath law, authorizing indefinite civil commitment of persons charged with sodomy or other sex offenses; narrowed in 1955 to include only those charged with sex crimes against children)	Decriminalized, 1961 Illinois Penal Code § 35-1 (1961 Illinois Laws page 2044)
1907 Indiana Acts No. 215 (sterilization of "confirmed criminals"); 1949 Indiana Acts No. 124 (indefinite civil commitment for persons charged with or convicted of sodomy or other specified sex crimes)	Decriminalized, 1976 Indiana Acts No. 148, § 24
1911 Iowa Laws chap. 129 (sterilization of inmates who are "moral or sexual perverts"; invalidated 1914); 1929 Iowa Laws chap. 66 (sterilization of "moral degenerates or sexual perverts who are a menace to society"); 1955 Iowa Laws chap. 121 (indefinite civil commitment for persons with "propensities toward the commission of sex crimes")	Invalidated for different-sex copulation, *State v. Pilcher*, 242 N.W.2d 348 (Iowa Supreme Court, 1976). Decriminalized for all consenting couples, 1976 Iowa Acts No. 1245, chap. 4, § 526
1913 Kansas Laws chap. 305 (sterilization for "habitual criminals"); 1953 Kansas Laws chap. 185 (indefinite civil commitment for persons committing offenses involving "perversion or mental aberration")	Decriminalized for different-sex "deviate sexual intercourse," misdemeanor for same-sex activities, 1969 Kansas Laws chap. 180, § 21-3505. Invalidated, *Lawrence v. Texas*, 539 U.S. 558 (2003)

State	Early Statutory Criminalizations of Crime Against Nature and Its Solicitation	Expansion of the Crime Against Nature to Include Oral Sex, Masturbation, etc.
Kentucky	Kentucky Constitution, 1792, § 8 ("buggery"); An Act to Amend the Penal Laws, 1798, § 4 ("sodomy"); 1968 Kentucky Acts chap. 105, § 8(1)(c) (schoolyard loitering); 1974 Kentucky Acts chap. 36 (loitering to solicit "deviate sexual intercourse")	1948 Kentucky Acts chap. 36 (indecent liberties with minors); 1974 Kentucky Acts chap. 406, § 90 ("deviate sexual intercourse," including fellatio and cunnilingus), overriding *Poindexter v. State*, S.W. (Kentucky Supreme Court, 1909)
Louisiana	1805 Louisiana Acts chap. I, § 2 ("crime against nature"); 1982 Louisiana Acts No. 703 (solicitation for crime against nature felony if for pay)	1896 Louisiana Acts No. 69, applied to fellatio in *State v. Vicknair*, 28 So. 273 (Louisiana Supreme Court, 1900); 1912 Louisiana Acts No. 202 (indecent liberties with minors); *State v. Murry*, 66 So. 963, 965 (Louisiana Supreme Court, 1914) (dicta) (crime against nature covers cunnilingus); 1942 Louisiana Acts No. 43 (exposing minors to indecency)
Maine	1821 Maine Laws chap. 5 ("crime against nature")	1913 Maine Laws chap. 62 (indecent liberties with minors); *State v. Cyr*, 198 A. 743 (Maine Supreme Court, 1938) (fellatio); *State v. Townsend*, 71 A.2d 517 (Maine Supreme Court, 1950) (cunnilingus); *State v. Pratt*, 116 A.2d 924 (Maine Supreme Court, 1955) (mutual masturbation is not a crime against nature)
Maryland	Declaration of Rights, 1776, § 3 (adopting common law, including buggery as capital crime); 1793 Maryland Laws chap. 57, § 10 ("sodomy" 7 years hard labor for free men, death for slaves); 1920 Maryland Laws chap. 739 (soliciting for "any unnatural sexual practice")	1916 Maryland Laws chap. 616 (new crime of "unnatural or perverted practices")
Massachusetts	1641–1642 Capital Lawes of New England [Mass. Bay] § 8 ("man lyeth with mankind," capital crime); Act Against Sodomy, 1785; 1805 Massachusetts Acts chap. 133 (penalty for "crime against nature" reduced to 1–10 years in prison); 1915 Massachusetts Acts chap. 180 (crime to resort to saloon etc. for "immoral solicitation")	1886 Massachusetts Laws chap. 329 (sexual solicitation of minors, also 1898 law); 1887 Massachusetts Acts chap. 436 (new crime: "unnatural and lascivious acts"), confirmed in *Commonwealth v. Dill*, 36 N.E. 472 (Massachusetts Supreme Judicial Court, 1894) (fellatio); 1955 Massachusetts Laws chap. 763, § 4 (indecent liberties with minors)

Expansive Consequences of Committing the Crime Against Nature and Its Solicitation	Contraction of the Crime Against Nature, as Regards Consensual Activities
	Decriminalized for different-sex "deviate sexual intercourse," misdemeanor for same-sex activities, 1974 Kentucky Acts chap. 406, § 90. Invalidated, *Commonwealth v. Wasson*, 842 S.W.2d 487 (Kentucky Supreme Court, 1992)
1992 Louisiana Acts No. 388 (registration for sex offenders, including those convicted of consensual sodomy)	1962 Louisiana Acts No. 60 (new "aggravated crime against nature" if forcible or with minor, but consensual sex left a felony). Invalidated, *Lawrence v. Texas*, 539 U.S. 558 (2003)
	Decriminalized, 1975 Maine Laws chap. 499, § 5
1951 Maryland Laws chap. 13 (indefinite civil commitment for persons charged with crime who represent threat to society)	Unnatural practices law inapplicable to consensual different-sex activities, *Schochet v. State*, 580 A.2d 176 (Maryland Court of Appeals, 1980). Unnatural practices law invalidated as to all consensual activities, *Williams v. Glendening*, No. 9803 6031 (Baltimore Circuit Court, October 15, 1998) (statewide consent decree); ibid. (January 19, 1999) (same for consensual sodomy)
1947 Massachusetts Acts chap. 683 (indefinite civil commitment for persons whose "habitual course of misconduct in sexual matters" is evidence of inability to control "sexual impulses"; updated in 1954 to add conviction of crime as a trigger)	Unnatural acts law construed to exclude consensual activities, *Commonwealth v. Balthazar*, 318 N.E.2d 478 (Massachusetts Supreme Judicial Court, 1974). Same for crime against nature law, *GLAD v. Attorney General*, 763 N.E.2d 38 (Massachusetts Supreme Court, 2002)

State	Early Statutory Criminalizations of Crime Against Nature and Its Solicitation	Expansion of the Crime Against Nature to Include Oral Sex, Masturbation, etc.
Michigan	1816 Penal Code § 4 ("sodomy"); Michigan Revised Statutes title 30, chap. 158, § 16 ("crime against nature"); 1931 Michigan Public Acts No. 328, §448 (soliciting to commit any "lewd or immoral act"); 1935 Michigan Public Acts No. 174 (sexual solicitation of minors)	1903 Michigan Public Acts No. 198 ("gross indecency" between males); 1939 Michigan Public Acts No. 148 ("gross indecency" between females); 1952 Michigan Public Acts No. 73 (indecent liberties with minors)
Minnesota	Minnesota (Terr.) Revised Statutes chap. 108, § 13 (1851) ("crime against nature"); 1929 Minnesota Laws chap. 181 (schoolyard loitering)	1921 Minnesota Laws chap. 224 ("carnally knows by the mouth"); 1927 Minnesota Laws chap. 394 (indecent liberties with minors; updated 1929, 1967); *State v. Blom*, 358 N.W.2d 63 (Minnesota Supreme Court, 1984) (sodomy law includes cunnilingus)
Mississippi	1839 Mississippi Laws page 162, § 20 ("crime against nature")	1942 Mississippi Code § 2413 ("unnatural intercourse"); *State v. Davis*, 79 S.W.2d 432 (Mississippi Supreme Court, 1955) (fellatio)
Missouri	Missouri Revised Statutes article 7, § 7 (1835) ("crime against nature"); Act of March 7, 1845, article VIII, § 7	1911 Missouri Laws page 198 (oral copulation law), applied in *State v. Katz*, 181 S.W.2d 425 (Missouri Supreme Court, 1916) (fellatio), but not in *State v. Wellman*, 161 S.W. 795 (Missouri Supreme Court, 1913) (cunnilingus); 1949 Missouri Laws, page 249 (indecent liberties with minors); 1977 Missouri Laws page 687, § 566.090 (illegal "deviate sexual intercourse" includes mutual masturbation)
Montana	1864–1868 Montana (Terr.) 1st Legislative Assembly, Criminal Practice Acts chap. 4, § 44 ("crime against nature")	1913 Montana Laws chap. 59 (indecent liberties with minors; updated 1939 and 1959); *State v. Guerin*, 152 P. 747 (Montana Supreme Court, 1915) (sodomy law covers fellatio)
Nebraska	1858 Nebraska (Terr.) Criminal Code § 48 ("crime against nature"); 1929 Nebraska Laws chap. 70 (felony of attempting to commit sodomy)	1913 Nebraska Laws chap. 69 ("carnal copulation"); 1951 Nebraska Laws chap. 82 (indecent liberties with minors)

Expansive Consequences of Committing the Crime Against Nature and Its Solicitation	Contraction of the Crime Against Nature, as Regards Consensual Activities
1935 Michigan Acts No. 88 (indefinite civil commitment for persons convicted of "indecent crimes"; updated 1937 to target "sex degenerates" and "sex perverts") (invalidated and reenacted in 1939)	Invalidated for Wayne County, *Michigan Organization for Human Rights v. Kelly*, No. 88-815820 CZ (Wayne County Circuit Court, July 9, 1990). Invalidated statewide, *Lawrence v. Texas*, 539 U.S. 558 (2003)
1939 Minnesota Laws chap. 369 (indefinite civil commitment for any person considered "irresponsible for his conduct with respect to sexual matters")	Penalty reduced to misdemeanor level (one year), 1977 Minnesota Laws chap. 130, § 4. Invalidated, *Doe v. Ventura*, No. MC 01-489 (Minneapolis District Court, May 15, 2001) (statewide class action)
1987 Mississippi Laws chap. 465 (sexual offender registry); 1995 Mississippi Laws chap. 595 (sexual offender registration law)	Invalidated, *Lawrence v. Texas*, 539 U.S. 558 (2003)
1949 Missouri Laws page 252 (indefinite civil commitment for any person accused of a sex crime, especially those with a history of "sexual deviation")	Decriminalized for different-sex, misdemeanor for same-sex, 1977 Missouri Laws page 687, § 566.090. Invalidated for Western District Court of Appeals, *State v. Cogshell*, 997 S.W.2d 534 (Missouri Supreme Court, 1999). Invalidated statewide, *Lawrence v. Texas*, 539 U.S. 558 (2003)
1989 Montana Laws chap. 293 (registration of sex offenders)	Decriminalized for different-sex, felony for same-sex sodomy, 1973 Montana Laws chap. 513. Invalidated *Gryczan v. State*, 942 P.2d 112 (Montana Supreme Court, 1997)
1929 Nebraska Laws chap. 163 (sterilization law expanded to include inmates who were "moral degenerates or sexual perverts"); 1949 Nebraska Laws chap. 294 (civil commitment for "sexual misconduct")	Decriminalized, 1977 Nebraska Laws (L.B. 38), § 328

State	Early Statutory Criminalizations of Crime Against Nature and Its Solicitation	Expansion of the Crime Against Nature to Include Oral Sex, Masturbation, etc.
Nevada	1861 Nevada (Terr.) Laws chap. 28, § 45 ("crime against nature"); 1912 Nevada Revised Laws § 6459; 1967 Nevada Laws chap. 523, § 439 (loitering around public toilets); 1979 Nevada Laws chap. 384 (enticing minor to engage in crime against nature)	*Ex parte Benites*, 140 P. 436 (Nevada Supreme Court, 1914) (sodomy law covers fellatio); 1915 Nevada Laws chap. 32 (misdemeanor for boys to hang around dens of vice); 1925 Nevada Laws chap. 24 (indecent liberties with minors; updated 1947 and 1961); *Sheriff v. Dearing*, 510 P.2d 874 (Nevada Supreme Court, 1973) (cunnilingus)
New Hampshire	Act of March 16, 1679 ("man lye with mankind," capital offense); Acts for the Punishment of Certain Crimes, 1791 ("crime against nature"); 1812 New Hampshire Laws pages 5–6, § 5 (crime against nature penalty reduced to 1–10 years hard labor)	1899 New Hampshire Laws chap. 33 (new crime: "unnatural or lascivious acts"), applied to fellatio in *State v. Vredenburg*, 19 A.2d 414 (New Hampshire Supreme Court, 1914)
New Jersey	Act of May 30, 1668 ("buggery" and "sodomy," capital offenses); New Jersey Constitution, 1776, § 22 (incorporating common law, including buggery); 1796 New Jersey Laws ("crime against nature," up to 21 years hard labor); 1930 New Jersey Laws chap. 205 (misdemeanor for soliciting lewd or lascivious acts)	1898 New Jersey Laws chap. 235, § 113 (assault to commit sodomy); ibid., § 20 (misdemeanor to conceal sodomy); ibid., § 37 (conspiracy to commit sodomy); 1906 New Jersey Laws chap. 71 (new crime: "private lewdness or carnal indecency"), applied to cunnilingus in *State v. Morrison*, 96 A.2d 723 (New Jersey Supreme Court, 1953); 1945 New Jersey Laws chap. 242 (indecent liberties with minors)
New Mexico	Law of July 12, 1851, § 18 (adopting common law crimes, including buggery); 1876 New Mexico (Terr.) Laws chap. 34 ("sodomy")	1949 New Mexico Laws chap. 140 (indecent liberties with minors; updated 1963); 1963 New Mexico Laws chap. 303, § 9-6 ("deviate sexual intercourse," defined to include oral sex), applied to cunnilingus in *State v. Putnam*, 434 P.2d 77 (New Mexico Supreme Court, 1967)
New York	Duke of York's Law, March 1, 1665, § 6 (lying with men); 1691–1776 (buggery, capital offense); 1796 New York Laws chap. 30 (penalty reduced to 14 years hard labor); 1900 New York Laws chap. 281 (soliciting for "immoral purposes"; periodically updated); 1923 New York Laws chap. 642 (loitering for purposes of soliciting men for "crime against nature or other lewdness"); 1954 New York laws chap. 519 (schoolyard loitering)	1886 New York Laws chap. 31, § 303 (revised "crime against nature" law applies to anyone who "carnally knows any male or female person in any manner contrary to nature," or voluntarily submits to such carnal knowledge); 1927 New York Laws chap. 383 (indecent liberties with minors; updated 1929, 1933, 1937, and 1950)

Expansive Consequences of Committing the Crime Against Nature and Its Solicitation	Contraction of the Crime Against Nature, as Regards Consensual Activities
Nev. Rev. Laws, 1861–1912, vol. 2, page 1812, § 6293 (sterilization of "habitual criminals"); 1961 Nevada Laws chap. 147 (registration of sex offenders, including sodomites); 1967 Nevada Laws chap. 211, § 78 (reduce sodomy penalty from 1 year–life in prison to 1–6 years)	Decriminalized for different-sex, misdemeanor for "deviate sexual intercourse" between persons of same sex, 1977 Nevada Laws chap. 598, § 17. Decriminalized entirely, 1993 Nevada Laws chap. 532, § 26
1949 New Hampshire Laws chap. 314 (indefinite civil commitment for persons upon petition to court or criminal charge of sodomy, unnatural acts, attempts to commit the same, and other specified sex crimes)	Decriminalized for married couples, misdemeanor for different-sex couples, 1971 New Hampshire Laws chap. 518, § 632:2. Decriminalized entirely, 1975 New Hampshire Laws chap. 302 (rape reform package)
1898 New Jersey Laws chap. 235, § 110 (immunity for murder of any person attempting to commit sodomy); 1911 New Jersey Laws chap. 190 (sterilization for persons with "confirmed criminal tendencies"; invalidated 1913); 1950 New Jersey Laws chap. 207 (indefinite civil commitment for persons committing sodomy or another sex crime *and* crime involves violence or a minor)	Private lewdness law limited to non-consensual activities, *State v. Dorsey*, 316 A.2d 689 (New Jersey Supreme Court, 1974). Consensual sodomy law invalidated, *State v. Ciufini*, 395 A.2d 904 (New Jersey Court of Appeals, 1978), and decriminalized, 1978 New Jersey Laws chap. 95, § 2C:98-2
	Decriminalized, 1975 New Mexico Laws chap. 109, § 8
1950 New York Laws chap. 525 (civil commitment for persons convicted of forcible sodomy, sodomy with a minor, and other non-consensual sex crimes)	Consensual sodomy reduced to misdemeanor, 1950 New York Laws chap. 525, § 15. Invalidated, *People v. Onofre*, 415 N.E.2d 936 (New York Court of Appeals, 1980)

State	Early Statutory Criminalizations of Crime Against Nature and Its Solicitation	Expansion of the Crime Against Nature to Include Oral Sex, Masturbation, etc.
North Carolina	Act of April 14, 1778 (adopting common law crimes, including buggery, capital offense); Act of December 1836, § 6 ("crime against nature"); 1868 North Carolina Laws chap. 167 (penalty reduced to maximum of 60 years in prison); 1979 North Carolina Laws chap. 873 (interfering with "free passage" for purposes of violating prostitution or sodomy laws)	*State v. Fenner*, 80 S.E. 970 (North Carolina Supreme Court, 1914) (fellatio); 1955 North Carolina Laws chap. 764 (indecent liberties with minors)
North Dakota	Dakota (Terr.) Law of April 28, 1862, chap. 9, § 47 ("buggery"); 1877 Dakota (Terr.) Penal Code § 346 ("crime against nature"); 1973 North Dakota Laws chap. 117, § 12.1-31-01(6) (misdemeanor, "loitering in a public place for the purpose of soliciting sexual contact")	1895 North Dakota Penal Law chap. 32, § 7186 (sodomy applies to anyone who "carnally knows any male or female person by the anus or by or with the mouth"), applied to cunnilingus in *State v. Nelson*, 163 N.W. 278 (North Dakota Supreme Court, 1917); 1923 North Dakota Laws chap. 167 (indecent liberties with minors; updated 1951 and 1953)
Ohio	Act of February 14, 1805 (common law crimes, perhaps including buggery; repealed 1806); 82 Ohio Laws, S.B. 508, page 241 (1885) ("carnal copulation against nature"); 129 Ohio Laws, page 1670 (1961) (solicitation to engage in "an unnatural sex act"; updated 1965 and 1972; invalidated 2002); 130 Ohio Laws, page 659 (1963) (sexual solicitation of minors)	86 Ohio Laws, H.B. 779, page 251 (1889) (sodomy redefined to include "carnal copulation in any opening of the body, except sexual parts"; prison up to 20 years), applied to fellatio in *Franklin v. State*, 33 Ohio C.C. 21 (Ohio Court of Appeals, 1910), but not cunnilingus, *State v. Forquer*, 58 N.E.2d 696 (Ohio Supreme Court, 1944); 121 Ohio Laws, page 557 (1953) (indecent liberties with minors)
Oklahoma	1890 Oklahoma (Terr.) Laws chap. 25, § 2196 ("crime against nature" up to ten years in prison); 1943 Oklahoma Laws chap. 39 (sexual solicitation)	*Ex parte DeFord*, 168 P. 58 (Oklahoma Court of Criminal Appeals, 1917) (fellatio); *Roberts v. State*, 47 P.2d 607 (Oklahoma Court of Criminal Appeals, 1935); 1943 Oklahoma Laws chap. 39 (lewdness); 1951 Oklahoma Laws, page 60 (indecent liberties with minors; updated 1955)
Oregon	Act of December 22, 1853, chap. 11, § 12 ("sodomy or the crime against nature"; prison 1–5 years); 1953 Oregon Laws chap. 641 (sexual solicitation of minors); 1971 Oregon Laws chap. 743, § 119 ("accosting for deviate purposes"; invalidated 1981 and repealed 1983)	1913 Oregon Laws chap. 21 (sodomy redefined to include "sexual perversity" and "osculatory relations with the private parts of any man, woman, or child"; prison 1–15 years), applied to fellatio in *State v. Start*, 132 P. 512 (Oregon Supreme Court, 1913), and masturbation, *State v. Brazell*, 269 P. 884 (Oregon Supreme Court, 1928), and cunnilingus, *State v. Black*, 366 P.2d 323 (Oregon Supreme Court, 1961)

Expansive Consequences of Committing the Crime Against Nature and Its Solicitation	Contraction of the Crime Against Nature, as Regards Consensual Activities
1919 North Carolina Laws chap. 281 (sterilization of state-institutionalized persons if improving their "moral condition"; invalidated and reenacted 1933)	Reduced penalty for consensual sodomy to three years in prison, 1993 North Carolina Laws chap. 539. Invalidated, *Lawrence v. Texas*, 539 U.S. 558 (2003)
1927 North Dakota Laws chap. 263 (expand sterilization law to include "habitual criminals, moral degenerates, and sexual perverts")	Decriminalized, 1973 North Dakota Laws chap. 113
118 Ohio Laws, page 686 (1939) (indefinite civil commitment for dangerous persons convicted of felonies; amended 1945 to limit triggering offenses to sodomy and five other crimes; amended 1951 to include misdemeanors in which "abnormal sexual tendencies are displayed"); 130 Ohio Laws, page 658 (1963) (state registry for sodomites and other sex criminals)	Decriminalized, 1972 Ohio Laws, H.B. 511, pages 1906–1911
1933 Oklahoma Laws chap. 46 (sterilization of "habitual criminals"; revised 1935 to limit sterilization to "felonies involving moral turpitude")	Invalidated for consensual activities between different-sex partners, *Post v. State*, 715 P.2d 1105 (Oklahoma Court of Criminal Appeals, 1986). Invalidated for all consensual activities, *Lawrence v. Texas*, 539 U.S. 558 (2003)
1917 Oregon Laws chap. 279 (sterilization of "habitual criminals, moral degenerates, and sexual perverts" whose "offspring would probably become a social menace"; invalidated 1923, revised and reenacted 1923 and 1925); 1953 Oregon Laws chap. 641 (indefinite civil commitment for persons convicted of sex offense, including sodomy, involving a minor)	Decriminalized, 1971 Oregon Laws chap. 743, § 432

State	Early Statutory Criminalizations of Crime Against Nature and Its Solicitation	Expansion of the Crime Against Nature to Include Oral Sex, Masturbation, etc.
Pennsylvania	Penn's Great Law, December 7, 1682 ("sodomy," six months' hard labor); Act of November 27, 1700 (life imprisonment for whites; capital offense for blacks); Act of May 31, 1718 (capital offense for all); Act of September 15, 1786 (ten years' hard labor); 1860 Penn. Laws No. 374, § 33 (assault or solicitation to commit sodomy)	1879 Pennsylvania Laws No. 156 (sodomy includes "carnal knowledge" by "penetrating the mouth of [another] person"), applied to fellatio in *Commonwealth v. Smith*, 14 Luz. L.R. 362 (Pennsylvania Superior Court, October 26, 1885), and cunnilingus in *Commonwealth v. Donahue*, 136 Pa. Super. 306 (1939)
Rhode Island	Providence Plantation Code, 1647 ("sodomy," capital offense); An Act to Reform the Penal Laws, 1798, § 8 (penalty of three years' hard labor; life for second offense)	*State v. Milne*, 187 A.2d 136 (Rhode Island Supreme Court, 1962) (crime against nature includes fellatio); *State v. McParlin*, 422 A.2d 742 (Rhode Island Supreme Court, 1980) (cunnilingus); 1980 Rhode Island Laws chap. 279 (loitering for indecent purposes)
South Carolina	Act for the Punishment of the Vice of Buggery, 1712 (capital offense); An Act to Amend the Criminal Law, 1869 (eliminating death penalty; 1872 mandatory five years in prison)	1953 South Carolina Laws chap. 48 (indecent liberties with minors; updated 1964). The South Carolina buggery statute was never applied to fellatio by an authoritative South Carolina Supreme Court decision, and the Court ruled that cunnilingus was *not* included in *State v. Nicholson*, 89 S.E.2d 876 (1955)
South Dakota	Dakota (Terr.) Law of April 28, 1862, chap. 9, § 47 ("buggery," one year to life in prison); 1877 Dakota (Terr.) Penal Code § 346 ("crime against nature," 1–10 years)	*State v. Whitmarsh*, 128 N.W. 580 (South Dakota Supreme Court, 1910) (sodomy law covers fellatio); 1950 South Dakota Laws chap. 3 (indecent liberties with minors)
Tennessee	1829 Tennessee Acts chap. 23, § 17 ("crime against nature," 5–15 year prison)	*Fisher v. State*, 277 S.W.2d 340 (Tennessee Supreme Court, 1955) (crime against nature includes fellatio); *Locke v. State*, 501 S.W.2d 826 (Tennessee Supreme Court, 1973) (cunnilingus)
Texas	1859 Texas General Laws chap. 74 ("crime against nature," 5–15 years in prison); 1950 Texas Laws chap. 8 (sexual solicitation of minors)	1943 Texas Laws chap. 112 (expanding crime against nature to include "carnal copulation . . . in an opening of the body, except the sexual parts"; indecent liberties with minors); ibid., chap. 154 (vagrancy expanded to include lewd conduct); 1950 Texas Laws chap. 12 (indecent liberties with minors)

Expansive Consequences of Committing the Crime Against Nature and Its Solicitation	Contraction of the Crime Against Nature, as Regards Consensual Activities
1951–1952 Pennsylvania Laws No. 495 (indefinite civil commitment if convicted of sodomy, solicitation, etc.); 1953 Pennsylvania Laws No. 50 (doubled sentence [20 years] for sodomy with minor)	Decriminalized for married couples, 1972 Pennsylvania Laws No. 334, § 3101, and different-sex partners, reduced to misdemeanor for same-sex partners, ibid., § 3124. Invalidated, *Commonwealth v. Bonadio*, 415 A.2d 47 (Pennsylvania Supreme Court, 1980)
1961 Rhode Island Laws chap. 176 (potential indefinite civil commitment for persons charged with being lewd, lascivious, indecent, etc., *and* having been convicted of a crime)	Decriminalized, 1998 Rhode Island Laws chap. 24
1994 South Carolina Laws No. 497 (sex offender registry)	Buggery penalty lowered to five years. 1993 South Carolina Laws No. 184. Invalidated, *Lawrence v. Texas*, 539 U.S. 558 (2003)
1950 South Dakota Laws chap. 27 (potential indefinite civil commitment for persons convicted of sex with minors)	Decriminalized, 1976 South Dakota Laws chap. 158, § 22-8
1957 Tennessee Public Acts chap. 288 (potential indefinite civil commitment for persons who in the "course of misconduct in sexual matters has evidenced a general lack of power to control his sexual impulses")	Decriminalized for different-sex partners, misdemeanor for same-sex partners (up to 30 days in jail), 1989 Tennessee Public Acts chap. 591. Invalidated, *Campbell v. Sundquist*, 926 S.W.2d 250 (Tennessee Court of Appeals, 1996) (appeal denied)
	Decriminalized for different-sex partners, misdemeanor for same-sex partners, 1973 Texas Laws, chap. 399, § 21.06. Invalidated, *Lawrence v. Texas*, 539 U.S. 558 (2003)

State	Early Statutory Criminalizations of Crime Against Nature and Its Solicitation	Expansion of the Crime Against Nature to Include Oral Sex, Masturbation, etc.
Utah	1876 Utah (Terr.) Penal Code tit. 21, § 144 ("crime against nature," up to 5 years in prison; up to 10 years for assault to commit the crime against nature)	1923 Utah Laws chap. 13 (crime against nature expanded to include acts committed "with either the sex organs or the mouth"; 3–20 years in prison)
Vermont	Acts and laws, 1779 (common law in force, possibly including buggery crime); see *State v. LaForrest,* 45 A.2d 225 (Vermont Supreme Court, 1899)	1937 Vermont Public Acts No. 211 ("copulating the mouth of one person with the sexual organ of another," 1–5 years in prison; also new crime of indecent liberties with minors)
Virginia	Act of May 24, 1610 (military code, "sodomie," capital offense); Act of March 23, 1661 (English law in effect, "buggery"); Act of December 10,1792 (same); Act of January 25, 1800 (penalty reduced to 1–10 years for free persons; death for slaves [discrimination ended 1860])	1916 Virginia Public Acts chap. 295 (adding "carnal copulation" between partners of the same sex to the buggery law); 1924 Virginia Public Acts chap. 358 (buggery statute revised to make any kind of "carnal knowledge" a felony); 1958 Virginia Public Acts chap. 163 (indecent liberties with minors; updated 1960)
Washington	1893 Washington Laws chap. 139 ("crime against nature," 10–14 years in prison); 1961 Washington Laws chap. 65 (sexual solicitation of minors)	1909 Washington Laws chap. 249, § 204 (crime against nature updated to include sexual activity "with mouth or tongue"), applied to fellatio in *State v. Bestoles,* 283 P. 687 (Washington Supreme Court, 1930); 1955 Washington Laws chap. 127 (indecent liberties with minors). See also *State v. Olsen,* 258 P.2d 810, 811 (Washington Supreme Court, 1953) (dictum: sodomy law covers cunnilingus)
West Virginia	West Virginia Constitution, 1863, article XI, § 8 (retaining criminal laws of Virginia, including "buggery," 1–5 years in prison)	West Virginia Code, 1931, chap.149, § 12 ("carnal knowledge by the anus or the mouth," 1–10 years in prison), applied to cunnilingus by West Virginia Attorney General, Opinion No. 170 (January 13, 1956)
Wisconsin	1839 Wisconsin (Terr.) Statutes § 14 ("sodomy" or "crime against nature," 1–5 years in prison); 1849 Wisconsin Revised Statutes chap. 139, § 15; 1977 Wisconsin Laws chap. 173 (misdemeanor vagrancy to "solicit another to commit a crime against sexual morality")	Act of August 20, 1897, 1898 Wisconsin Statutes § 4591 (crime against nature includes "penetration of the mouth . . . by the organ of any male person"), inapplicable to cunnilingus, *Garred v. State,* 216 N. W.2d 496 (Wisconsin Supreme Court, 1927); 1897 Wisconsin Laws chap. 198 (indecent liberties with minors; updated 1915 and 1925); 1955 Wisconsin Laws chap. 696 (crime against nature changed to "sexual perversion," expanded to make cunnilingus a crime)

Expansive Consequences of Committing the Crime Against Nature and Its Solicitation	Contraction of the Crime Against Nature, as Regards Consensual Activities
1925 Utah Laws chap. 82 (sterilization for inmates with "habitual [degenerate, added 1929] sexual criminal tendencies"); 1951 Utah Laws chap. 22 (potential indefinite civil commitment for persons convicted of sodomy and other sex crimes)	Consensual sodomy reduced to misdemeanor (up to 6 months in county jail), 1969 Utah Laws chap. 244 (exemption for married couples, 1973). Invalidated, *Lawrence v. Texas*, 539 U.S. 558 (1973)
1943 Vermont Public Acts No. 100 (potential indefinite civil commitment for persons guilty of "gross immorality" *and* "considered dangerous to public welfare"; amended in 1945 to require conviction of specified sex crime)	Oral copulation law repealed, 1977 Vermont Public Acts No. 51, § 2
1950 Virginia Public Acts chap. 463 (potential indefinite civil commitment for persons convicted of crimes involving "sexual abnormality"); 1975 Virginia Public Acts chap. 14 (rare post-1969 state law *increasing* the penalty for sodomy, from three years in prison to five years)	Invalidated, *Lawrence v. Texas*, 539 U.S. 558 (2003)
1909 Washington Laws chap. 249 (sterilization for "habitual criminals," updated in 1921 to include "moral degenerates and sexual perverts"; invalidated 1942); 1947 Washington Laws chap. 273 (potential indefinite civil commitment for persons convicted of the crime against nature or "any disorderly conduct involving a sex offense")	Decriminalized, 1975 Washington Laws chap. 260, § 9A.92.010
1957 West Virginia Laws chap. 43 (potential indefinite civil commitment for persons charged with incest and the crime against nature)	Decriminalized, 1976 West Virginia Laws chap. 43
1913 Wisconsin Laws chap. 693 (sterilization of inmates); 1947 Wisconsin Laws chap. 459 (potential indefinite civil commitment for persons considered dangers to society; amended by Sexual Deviate Act, 1951, to require conviction of specified sex crimes); 1958–1959 Wisconsin Laws chap. 583 (state driver's license cannot be issued to persons convicted of the crime against nature)	Reduced to misdemeanor, 1977 Wisconsin Laws chap. 173, § 92. Decriminalized, 1983 Wisconsin Laws chap. 17, § 5

State	Early Statutory Criminalizations of Crime Against Nature and Its Solicitation	Expansion of the Crime Against Nature to Include Oral Sex, Masturbation, etc.
Wyoming	1890 Wyoming Laws chap. 73, § 87 ("crime against nature," including enticing a minor to masturbation)	1890 Wyoming Laws chap. 73, § 87 (crime against nature includes oral sex and masturbation with minor); 1957 Wyoming Laws chap. 220, § 8 (indecent liberties with minors)

Sources: State-by-state review of penal codes and sodomy cases; William N. Eskridge Jr., *Gaylaw: Challenging the Apartheid of the Closet* (Cambridge, MA: Harvard University Press, 1999), 328–51; George Painter, *The Sensibilities of Our Fathers: The History of Sodomy Laws in the United States*, available at www.sodomylaws.org/sensibilities.

Expansive Consequences of Committing the Crime Against Nature and Its Solicitation	Contraction of the Crime Against Nature, as Regards Consensual Activities
1951 Wyoming Laws chap. 25 (potential indefinite civil commitment of persons convicted of sodomy, liberties with a minor, and other specific sex crimes)	Decriminalized, 1977 Wyoming Laws chap. 70, § 3

Notes

Archival Sources and Abbreviations

ACLU Papers Papers of the American Civil Liberties Union, Princeton University, Mudd Library, Princeton, New Jersey

AEI Polls (2006) AEI Studies in Public Opinion, "Attitudes About Homosexuality and Gay Marriage" (compiled by Karlyn Bowman and updated October 27, 2006), available at www .aei.org/publications/pubID.14882,filter.all/pub_detail.asp

ALI Archives American Law Institute Archives, University of Pennsylvania School of Law, Biddle Law Library, Special Collections

Atlanta Archives Atlanta [Georgia] Historical Center, Kenan Research Center, Atlanta, Georgia, Manuscript Series 773, on Lesbians, Gay Men, Bisexuals, and Transgendered People in Atlanta

Blackmun Papers Papers of Justice Harry A. Blackmun, Library of Congress, Madison Building, Washington, D.C., Manuscript Collection

Brennan Papers Papers of Justice William J. Brennan (access by special permission), Library of Congress, Madison Building, Washington, D.C., Manuscript Collection

Cal Leg History California Governor's Chaptered Bill Files (Microfilm), California State Archives, Sacramento, California

CCA California Court of Appeals

COF Papers New York City's Committee of Fourteen Collection, New York Public Library, Manuscript Division

CSC California Supreme Court

Douglas Papers Papers of Justice William O. Douglas, Library of Congress, Madison Building, Washington, D.C., Manuscript Collection

Fisher Papers Notes and Papers of Eugene Fisher, Reporter for the *Sacramento Bee*, Folder CD1 002 060 in Archives for the City of Sacramento, California

Fla Leg History Florida Legislative Research Service, Tallahassee, Florida

Hand Papers Papers of the Honorable Learned Hand, Harvard Law School Library, Special Collections, Cambridge, Massachusetts

Harlan Papers Papers of Justice John M. Harlan, Princeton University, Mudd Library, Princeton, New Jersey

Johns Papers Papers of the Florida Legislative Investigation Committee (the "Johns Committee," after its Chair, Senator Charley Johns), Florida State Archives, Tallahassee, Florida, Record Group 000940, Series 1486

Keeton Papers W. Page Keeton Papers, Tarlton Law Library, University of Texas, Rare Books and Special Collections, Austin, Texas

Kinsey Archive Kinsey Institute for Research in Sex, Gender, and Reproduction Archive, Indiana University, Bloomington, Indiana

MMR *Moral Majority Report*, May 1981–September 1987, Contemporary Issues Pamphlet Collection, MS 81-07, Wichita State University Libraries, Department of Special Collections

MSW-FBI FBI Files on the Mattachine Society of Washington, File Number HQ 100-403320, Serial 106, part of the FBI's FOIA release files on the general topic of homosexuality and gay rights

Murray Papers Papers of Pauli Murray, Hollis Library, Radcliffe College, Manuscript Collection, Cambridge, Massachusetts

Niebuhr Papers Papers of Reinhold Niebuhr, Library of Congress, Madison Building, Manuscript Collections, Washington, D.C.

NORC (1994) National Opinion Research Center, National Health and Social Science Survey, reported in Edward O. Laumann, John H. Gagnon, Robert T. Michael, and Stuart Michaels, *The Social Organization of Sexuality: Sexual Practices in the United States* (Chicago: University of Chicago Press, 1994)

NYC Magistrates Annual Reports of the New York City Magistrates' Courts, available on microfilm at New York Public Library, *ZAN-10223

NY Leg History New York Public Library, Social Sciences Building, New York City, Microfiche Collection of Bill Jackets Compiled for the Governor's Consideration of Statutes Enacted by the Legislature

NYPL New York Public Library

NYSSV Papers Post Office Records for the New York Society for the Suppression of Vice (Comstock Society), Library of Congress, Madison Building, Manuscript Collections, Washington, D.C.

Painter, *Sensibilities* George Painter, *The Sensibilities of Our Fathers: The History of Sodomy Laws in the United States*, available at www.sodomylaws.org/sensibilities

Police Reports (Atlanta) Annual Reports of the Department of Police for the City of Atlanta, in Papers of Herbert Jenkins, Atlanta Historical Center, Kenan Research Center, Atlanta, Georgia

Police Reports (Baltimore) Annual Reports of the Board of Police Commissioners of the City of Baltimore, Enoch Pratt Free Library, Baltimore, Maryland

Police Reports (Boston) Annual Reports for the Police Commissioners/Board of Police/Police Commissioner (title changes over time) of Boston, Boston Public Library, Boston, Massachusetts

Police Reports (Chicago) Annual Reports of the Board of Police, in the Police Department, to the Common Council of the City of Chicago, Police Archives, Chicago, Illinois

Police Reports (Cincinnati) Annual Reports of the Chief of Police to the Mayor of Cincinnati, Cincinnati Public Library, Cincinnati, Ohio

Police Reports (Cleveland) Annual Reports of the Cleveland [Ohio] Police Department, Microfilm

Police Reports (DC) Annual Reports of the Metropolitan Police Department for the District of Columbia, Martin Luther King (Public) Library, Washington, D.C.

Police Reports (Florida) Annual Report of the Attorney General of the State of Florida, Florida State University Law Library, Tallahassee, Florida

Police Reports (LA) Annual Reports of the Police Department of the City of Los Angeles, Police Archives, Pasadena, California

Police Reports (Minneapolis) Annual Reports of the Minneapolis Department of Police, Minneapolis Public Library, Minneapolis, Minnesota

Police Reports (Nashville) Annual Reports of the City Treasurer et al., Nashville Public Library, Nashville, Tennessee

Police Reports (NYC) Annual Reports for the New York City Police Department, New York Public Library, New York City

Police Reports (Philadephia) Annual Reports of the Chief of Police for the City of Philadelphia, Philadelphia Free Library, Philadelphia, Pennsylvania

Police Reports (Richmond) Annual Message and Accompanying Documents of the Mayor of Richmond to the City Council, Richmond Public Library, Richmond, Virginia

Police Reports (South Carolina) Reports of the Attorney General to the General Assembly of South Carolina, Columbia, South Carolina

Police Reports (San Francisco) San Francisco Municipal Reports, Published by the Board of Supervisors, San Francisco Public Library, San Francisco, California

Police Reports (St. Louis) Annual Reports for the Board of Police Commissioners of the City of St. Louis, St. Louis Public Library, St. Louis, Missouri

Powell Papers Papers of Justice Lewis A. Powell Jr., Washington & Lee University School of Law Library, Special Collections, Lexington, Virginia

RSV *The Holy Bible, Containing the Old and New Testaments*, Revised Standard Version by the National Council of Churches (New York: Thomas Nelson & Sons, 1946/1952)

Rustin (FBI) Federal Bureau of Investigation, Surveillance File for Bayard Rustin, FOIA File, FBI Headquarters, Washington, D.C.

Searcy Papers Papers of Seth S. Searcy III, Records of the Texas Committee for Criminal Law Reform, Tarlton Law Library, University of Texas, Austin, Texas

Suitland Archives National Archives, United States of America, Suitland, Maryland

TLRS Texas Legislative Research Services, Audio-Tape Collection of Committee and Floor Debate of the Texas Legislature, Austin, Texas

USCCAN *United States Code Congressional and Administrative News*, published annually by the West Publishing Company, St. Paul, Minnesota

USSC United States Supreme Court

Warren History The Earl Warren Oral History Project, University of California at Berkeley, Bancroft Library, Berkeley, California

Warren Papers Papers of Governor Earl Warren, California State Archives, Sacramento, California

Wechsler Papers Papers of Herbert Wechsler, Columbia University School of Law Library, Special Collections, New York City, New York

Whitman Archive www.whitmanarchive.org, created by Professors Ed Folsom (University of Iowa) and Kenneth M. Price (University of Nebraska–Lincoln)

Whitman (LOA) *Walt Whitman: Complete Poetry and Collected Prose*, selected and edited by Justin Kaplan (New York: The Library of America, 1982)

Wilson Papers Papers of Professor Paul E. Wilson, Kansas State Historical Society, Topeka, Kansas

Introduction

1. I owe the points in text to conversations with Len Becker, Ian Ayres, and Jed Shugerman.

2. James A. Morone, *Hellfire Nation: The Politics of Sin in American History* (New Haven, CT: Yale University Press, 2003) (recurrence of Puritan themes throughout American history); Robert H. Bork, *Slouching Towards Gomorrah: Modern Liberalism and American Decline* (New York: ReganBooks, 1996), positing a general cultural decline in our country because liberalism has allowed pleasure-seeking Americans to ignore natural rules.

3. Sir William Blackstone, *Commentaries on the Laws of England*, vol. 1 (Oxford: Clarendon Press, 1765), 215; chapters 1–2.

4. On the deployment of sodomy laws to crimes against minors, see, e.g., *Territory v. Mahaffrey*, 3 Mont. 112 (Montana Supreme Court, 1878) (oral sex on a fourteen-year-old boy); *Honselman v. People*, 48 N.E. 304 (Illinois Supreme Court, 1897) (similar); 1881 Indiana Statutes 195–96, § 100 (enticing minors "to commit masturbation"); 1890 Wyoming Statutes chap. 73, § 87 (same); 1897 Michigan Public Acts No. 95 (separate crime of sodomy with boys).

5. Saint Augustine, *De bono conjugali (On the Good of Marriage)*; Richard Mather and William Thompson, *An Heart-Melting Exhortation Together with a Cordiall Consolation Presented in a Letter from New-England* (London: A.M., 1650) (quotation in text, citing 1 Cor. 6:9–10; Gal. 5:20–21). I owe the Mather and Thompson reference to George Fisher, "Alcohol Monogamy: The Drug War's Moral Roots" (draft, 2006), chap. 2.

6. Randall Kennedy, *Interracial Intimacies: Sex, Marriage, Identity, and Adoption* (New York: Pantheon, 2003); Irving C. Rosse, "Sexual Hypochondriasis and Perversion of the Genetic Instinct," *Journal of Nervous and Mental Disease* 17 (1892): 795 (African Americans introduced cross-dressing and other perversions into America).

7. Paul Rozin, "Disgust," in Michael Lewis and Jeannette M. Haviland-Jones, eds., *Handbook of Emotions* (New York: Guilford, 2000), 642 (quotation in text); William Ian Miller, *The Anatomy of Disgust* (Cambridge, MA: Harvard University Press, 1997), 98–101 (sexuality and disgust); Martha C. Nussbaum, *Hiding from Humanity: Disgust, Shame, and the Law* (Princeton, NJ: Princeton University Press, 2004), 89 (pursuing Rozin's themes).

8. On the enforcement of sodomy laws, see chapter 1 (colonial enforcement) and William N. Eskridge Jr., *Gaylaw: Challenging the Apartheid of the Closet* (Cambridge, MA: Harvard University Press, 1999), 375, appendix C2 (reported cases, 1885–1995).

9. Mary Douglas, *Purity and Danger: An Analysis of the Concepts of Pollution and Taboo* (New York: Praeger, 1966), 123–24; Courtney Megan Cahill, "Same-Sex Marriage, Slippery-Slope Rhetoric, and the Politics of Disgust: A Critical Perspective on Contemporary Family Discourse and the Incest Taboo," *Northwestern University Law Review* 99 (2005): 1543, which applies Douglas's social pollution idea to incest taboos.

10. Plato, *The Republic*, trans. Allan Bloom (New York: Basic Books, 2d ed., 1991), II.561c–d (first quotation in text); ibid., 563d (second quotation). See Arlene W. Saxonhouse, "Democracy, Equality, and *Eide*: A Radical View from Book Eight of *The Republic*," *American Political Science Review* 92 (1998): 280; Scott T. Fitzgibbon, "The Formless City of Plato's *Republic*," *Issues in Legal Scholarship* 5 (2004–5): article 5, www.bepress.com/ils/iss5 (viewed November 2006), which applies Saxonhouse's reading of Plato to argue against same-sex marriage as reflecting an "ideology of licentiousness," the worst kind of formlessness.

11. William Ian Miller, *The Anatomy of Disgust* (Cambridge, MA: Harvard University Press, 1998), 194–95 (first quotation in text); ibid., 250–51 (second quotation); Douglas, *Purity and Danger*, 41–57 (Levitical rules as community-building).

12. William Stacy Johnson, *A Time to Embrace: Same-Gender Unions in Religion, Law, and Politics* (Grand Rapids, MI: Eerdmans, 2006), 131–33. On the fundamental distinction between man and woman and the destabilizing nature of cross-gender presentation, see Marjorie Garber, *Vested Interests: Cross-Dressing and Cultural Anxiety* (New York: Routledge, 1992); Elisabeth Young-Bruehl, *The Anatomy of Prejudices* (Cambridge, MA: Harvard University Press, 1996).

13. See, for example, Robert George, *In Defense of Natural Law* (Princeton, NJ: Princeton University Press, 2002).

14. On the tendency to fetishize minor sexual differences, see Mary Anne Case, "Couples and Coupling in the Public Sphere: A Comment on the Legal History of Litigating for Lesbian and Gay Rights," *Virginia Law Review* 79 (1993): 1662–63.

15. David Johnson, *The Lavender Scare: The Cold War Persecution of Gays and Lesbians in the Federal Government* (Chicago: University of Chicago Press, 2004).

16. The observation that the crime against nature had as its primary effect blackmail and police corruption originates with Jeremy Bentham, "On Paederasty" (unpublished, 1785), discussed in chapter 3.

17. On the complicated relationship between sexual fetishes and legal lines and social taboos, see the introduction to Michel Foucault, *History of Sexuality*, vol. 1, trans. Robert Hurley, (New York: Vintage, 1978), 104–6; David Cole, "Playing by Pornography's Rules: The Regulation of Sexual Expression," *University of Pennsylvania Law Review* 143 (2000): 143–77.

18. See John D'Emilio, *Sexual Politics, Sexual Communities: The Making of a Homosexual Minority in the United States, 1940–1970* (Chicago: University of Chicago Press, 1983), for the early homophile politics of toleration; William N. Eskridge Jr., "Body Politics: *Lawrence v. Texas* and the Constitution of Disgust and Contagion," *Florida Law Review* 57 (2005): 1011–29, for the politics of preservation.

19. The best introduction to our nation's constitutional structure and its intended protection of liberty is Akhil Reed Amar, *America's Constitution: A Biography* (New York: Random House, 2005).

20. On the modernization of justification for preserving traditional status distinctions, see Reva Siegel, "'The Rule of Love': Wife Beating as Prerogative and Privacy," *Yale Law Journal* 105 (1996): 2117–21, 2175–88.

Chapter One: American Body Politics and the Crime Against Nature, 1861–81

1. "Leaves of Grass," *Saturday Review*, March 15, 1856, 393–94; Whitman Archive (Criticism) (quoting a description of Whitman from the Brooklyn *Daily Times*).

2. [First Poem, Untitled], *Leaves of Grass* (1855), Whitman (LOA), 46 (first quotation in text), 50–51 (second), reprinted and revised as "Song of Myself," §§ 21, 24, *Leaves* (1860).

3. "A Woman Waits for Me," *Leaves* (1891–92), Whitman (LOA), 258–60.

4. Whitman, "In Paths Untrodden," *Leaves* (1860), Whitman (LOA), 268.

5. Elizabeth Cady Stanton, "Address to the Legislature of New York on Women's Rights," February 14, 1854, reprinted in Ellen Carol DuBois, ed. *The Elizabeth Cady Stanton–Susan B.*

Anthony Reader, rev. ed. (Boston: Northeastern University Press, 1992), 44–52; see Ellen Carol DuBois, *Feminism and Suffrage: The Emergence of an Independent Women's Movement in America, 1848–1869* (Ithaca, NY: Cornell University Press, 1978).

6. Theodore Stanton and Harry Stanton Blatch, eds., *Elizabeth Cady Stanton as Revealed in Her Letters, Diary and Reminiscences* (New York: Harper & Brothers, 1922), 210 (Stanton's diary entry for September 6, 1883, commenting on Whitman's celebration of female sexuality). See Lois Banner, *Elizabeth Cady Stanton: A Radical for Women's Rights* (Boston: Little, Brown, 1980); Sherry Ceniza, *Walt Whitman and Nineteenth-Century Women Reformers* (Tuscaloosa: University of Alabama Press, 1998) (feminist theory influenced the 1860 edition of *Leaves*).

7. On Whitman's male relationships, see Justin Kaplan, *Walt Whitman: A Life* (New York: Simon & Schuster, 1980); Gary Schmidgall, *Walt Whitman: A Gay Life* (New York: Dutton, 1997); Charley Shively, *Calamus Lovers: Walt Whitman's Working Class Camerados* (San Francisco: Gay Sunshine, 1987). On Anthony's female relationships, see Katharine Susan Anthony (no relation), *Susan B. Anthony: Her History and Her Era* (New York: Doubleday, 1954); Kathleen Barry, *Susan B. Anthony: A Biography of a Singular Feminist* (New York: New York University Press, 1988).

8. Lillian Faderman, *To Believe in Women: What Lesbians Have Done for America—A History* (New York: Houghton Mifflin, 1999), 22–30, reads Anthony as a lesbian, unpersuasively. Most modern critics believe Whitman to have engaged in sexual activities with men. See sources in note 7 above; Martin Duberman, *About Time: Exploring the Gay Past* (New York: Meridian, 1991), 109–120 (persuasive evidence that Whitman engaged in oral sex and intimate touching).

9. The Puritans presented the classic defense of their regime just as the social conditions for its flourishing were disappearing. See Perry Miller, *The New England Mind: The Seventeenth Century,* 2d ed. (Cambridge, MA: Harvard University Press, 1954); Morone, *Hellfire,* 55–99 (see introd., n. 2).

10. Act of 1533, 25 Henry VIII, chap. 6 (England), discussed in François Lafitte, "Homosexuality and the Law," *British Journal of Delinquency* 9 (1958): 8–14. On European regulation, see Louis Crompton, *Homosexuality and Civilization* (Cambridge, MA: Harvard University Press, 2003), 196–204, 362–66.

11. Sir Edward Coke, *The Third Part of the Institutes of the Laws of England* (London, 1677), 58–59; *Stafford's Case,* 77 Eng. Rep. 1318 (1607) (anal intercourse between men); *Rex v. Wiseman,* 92 Eng. Rep. 774 (1716) (anal intercourse between a man and a girl); *Rex v. Jacobs,* 168 Eng. Rep. 830 (1817) (oral intercourse between a man and a boy *not* embraced within the statute).

12. Caroline Bingham, "Seventeenth-Century Attitudes Toward Deviant Sex," *Journal of Interdisciplinary History* 1 (1971): 447–68; Louis Crompton, "Homosexuals and the Death Penalty in Colonial America," *Journal of Homosexuality* 1 (1976): 277–93. Primary documents are collected in Jonathan Ned Katz, *Gay/Lesbian Almanac: A New Documentary* (New York: Harper & Row, 1983), 66–133.

13. *For the Colony in Virginea Brittania: Lawes Divine, Morall, and Martiall,* ed. David H. Flaherty (Charlottesville: University of Virginia Press, 1969); Katz, *Gay/Lesbian Almanac,* 29 (the Cornish case); William E. Nelson, "The Common Law in Colonial America: The Chesapeake and New England, 1607–1660, Part I" (draft, 2005)(excellent overview of sex crime law in colonial Virginia).

14. For the texts of Pennsylvania's statutory prohibitions, see Katz, *Gay/Lesbian Almanac,*

119–20 (1682 statute), 121 (1693), 122–23 (1700), 125 (1706), 130 (1718). On nonenforcement, see William E. Nelson, "Government by Judiciary: The Growth of Judicial Power in Colonial Pennsylvania," *SMU Law Review* 59 (2006): 44–45.

15. Primary documents are in Katz, *Gay/Lesbian Almanac*, 76–78 (1641 *Capitall Lawes*), 78–87 (ministers' opinions as to "sodomitical" practices), 91 (Rhode Island's sodomy law), 101–2 (New Haven's sodomy law), 118–19 (New Hampshire's sodomy law), 121–22 (new Massachusetts buggery law). See also ibid., 85–86 (1642 Massachusetts prosecution of female intimacy as "unseemly practices"), 92–93 (1649 Plymouth prosecution of female intimacy as "lewd behavior"); William E. Nelson, "The Common Law in Colonial America: The Chesapeake and New England, 1607–1660, Part II" (draft, 2005); Robert F. Oaks, "'Things Fearful to Name': Sodomy and Buggery in Seventeenth-Century New England," *Journal of Social History* 12 (1978): 268–81.

16. The figure for executions draws from Katz, *Gay/Lesbian Almanac*, and Nelson, "Common Law in Colonial America [I & II]." The description of Plaine's case is from John Winthrop, *History of New England from 1630 to 1649*, ed. James Savage (New York, 1853), 324, reprinted in Jonathan Ned Katz, *Gay American History* (New York: Avon, 1976), 34–35.

17. On Anna Plaine, see the marriage and death records in the New Haven Archives.

18. Nelson, "Government by Judiciary," 44 (quotation in text). On the Puritan obsession with sexual purity, see, e.g., Katz, *Gay/Lesbian Almanac*, 82–84 (Reverend Thomas Shepard, Massachusetts), 86–87 (William Bradford, Plymouth), 94–100 (Reverend Michael Wigglesworth, Massachusetts).

19. Ibid., 127–28 (Mingo's case); Randolph Trumbach, "Sodomitical Subcultures, Sodomitical Roles, and the Gender Revolution of the Eighteenth Century: The Recent Historiography," in Robert Purks MacCubbin, ed., *'Tis Nature's Fault: Unauthorized Sexuality During the Enlightenment* (Cambridge: Cambridge University Press, 1985), 109–21.

20. Katz, *Gay/Lesbian Almanac*, 104–31 (state-by-state account of decapitalizing sodomy); William E. Nelson, *Americanization of the Common Law: The Impact of Legal Change on Massachusetts Society, 1760–1830* (Cambridge, MA: Harvard University Press, 1975), 89–110.

21. Appendix (state-by-state description of early American sodomy laws); Blackstone, *Commentaries*, (see introd., n. 3) ("infamous crime against nature").

22. On the limited reach of nineteenth-century sodomy laws, see Joel Prentiss Bishop, *Commentaries on the Criminal Law*, vol. 2, 2d ed. (Boston: Little, Brown, 1859), § 1028; Joseph Chitty, *A Practical Treatise on the Criminal Law*, vol. 2 (New York: Banks, Gould & Co., 1847), 49; Robert Desty, *A Compendium of American Criminal Law* (San Francisco: Bancroft-Whitney, 1887), 143; John May, *The Law of Crimes* (New York, 1881), § 210; Francis Wharton, *A Treatise on the Criminal Law of the United States*, 2d ed. (Philadelphia: J. Kay and Brother, 1852), 443.

23. Act of March 21, 1801, chap. 58, 1801 New York Laws 97 (criminalizing rape, burglary, robbery, and the "abominable and detestable crime against nature"); John D. Cushing, ed., *The Earliest Laws of the New Haven and Connecticut Colonies, 1636–1673* (New Haven, 1977), 18 (1656 sodomy law). All the sample sodomy law indictments listed in Chitty, *Criminal Law*, 48–50, involved allegations of predation by an adult man against a minor girl or boy.

24. Bishop, *Criminal Law*, vol. 2, 688: "Unlike rape, sodomy may be committed between two persons both of whom consent: so husband and wife can perpetrate this offense together: so can two men, or a boy and a man." But sodomy required corroboration if the partner was a willing accomplice. Wharton, *Criminal Law*, 443.

25. *Davis v. Maryland*, 3 H.&J. 154 (Maryland Court of Appeals, 1810); Katz, *Gay American*

History, 40–42 (expanded record in *Davis*); Jonathan Ned Katz, *Love Stories: Sex Between Men Before Homosexuality* (Chicago: University of Chicago Press, 2002), 402–6 (listing 105 sodomy cases); William N. Eskridge Jr., "*Hardwick* and Historiography," *University of Illinois Law Review* 1999, 655–57. According to Katz, the only example of a reported case where the sodomy conviction of a possibly consensual encounter was upheld was *Snow v. State*, 111 Mass. 411 (1873), but the record suggests there was no consent: the defendant allegedly imposed himself over the objections of a "boy."

26. *Medis v. State*, 11 S.W. 112 (Texas Court of Criminal Appeals, 1889).

27. Katz, *Love Stories*, 45–55 (quotations in text, from the *Whip*'s stories); Timothy J. Gilfoyle, *City of Eros: New York City, Prostitution, and the Commercialization of Sex, 1790–1920* (New York: Norton, 1992), 135–38 (male prostitution); Michael Lynch, "New York Sodomy, 1796–1873" (unpublished manuscript, 1985), discussed in John D'Emilio and Estelle B. Freedman, *Intimate Matters: A History of Sexuality in America* (New York: Harper & Row, 1988), 123.

28. Police Reports (San Francisco) 1860–1880 (San Francisco arrest statistics); Nan Alamilla Boyd, *Wide-Open Town: A History of Queer San Francisco to 1965* (Berkeley: University of California Press, 2003), 25–29 (quotation in text); Susan Stryker and Jim Van Buskirk, *Gay by the Bay: A History of Queer Culture in the San Francisco Bay Area* (San Francisco: Chronicle Books, 1996), 8–21; Allan Bérubé, "Lesbians and Gay Men in Early San Francisco" (San Francisco Gay History Project, no date).

29. George Napheys, *The Transmission of Life: Counsels on the Nature and Hygiene of the Masculine Function* (Philadelphia: David McKay, 1898 [1871]), 29. The sodomy arrest statistics are compiled by the author from Police Reports (Atlanta), Police Reports (Boston), Police Reports (Chicago), Police Reports (Cincinnati), Police Reports (Cleveland), Police Reports (Philadelphia), and Police Reports (Richmond) for the years 1865–80. For other contemporary complaints of rampant sodomy, see George Thompson, *City Crimes* (Boston, 1849) (predatory older sodomites in Boston).

30. U.S. Department of the Interior, Census Office, *Report of the Defective, Dependent, and Delinquent Classes of the Population, as Returned at the Tenth Census* (Washington, D.C.: Government Printing Office, 1880), 506–9, 516–17, 562–63, reprinted in Katz, *Gay American History*, 57–58.

31. Katz, *Love Stories*, 48–53 (quotations from *Whip*).

32. On state prohibitions as *normalizing*, see Georges Canguilhem, *On the Normal and the Pathological*, trans. Carolyn R. Fawcett (Boston: D. Reidel Publishing Co., 1978 [1966]); Michel Foucault, *Discipline and Punish: The Birth of the Prison*, trans. Alan Sheridan (New York: Pantheon, 1977 [1975]), 182–84, and *Abnormal: Lectures at the Collège de France, 1974–1975*, trans. Graham Burchell (New York: Picador, 2003).

33. David A. J. Richards, *Women, Gays, and the Constitution: The Grounds for Feminism and Gay Rights in Culture and Law* (Chicago: University of Chicago Press, 1998).

34. Whitman, "I Sing the Body Electric," *Leaves* (1881), Whitman (LOA), 250–58, an expanded version of [Fourth Poem, Untitled], *Leaves* (1855), Whitman (LOA), 118–24; Whitman, "Native Moments," *Leaves* (1860), Whitman (LOA), 265–66 (quotations in text). For Whitman's celebration of sex for pleasure, see "Song of Myself," § 11, ibid., 197–98 (oral sex and masturbation among bathers); "Once I Pass'd through a Populous City," ibid., 266 (fornication).

35. Walt Whitman, *Democratic Vistas* (1870), in Whitman (LOA), 955 (quotation in text);

Elizabeth Cady Stanton, *The Woman's Bible* (New York: European Publishing Co., 1898). On the NWSA, see Rogers M. Smith, *Civic Ideals: Conflicting Visions of Citizenship in United States History* (New Haven, CT: Yale University Press, 1997), 315.

36. Elizabeth Cady Stanton, "Speech to the McFarland-Richardson Protest Meeting" (1869), reprinted in *Stanton-Anthony Reader*, 125–30; ibid., 129 (first quotation in text); Susan B. Anthony, "Homes of Single Women," October 1877, reprinted ibid., 146–51; ibid., 148–49, 151 (subsequent quotations in text). On feminist claims of "self-ownership," see Jill Elaine Hasday, "Contest and Consent: A Legal History of Marital Rape," *California Law Review* 88 (2000): 1417–27.

37. Rufus W. Griswold, *Criterion* 1 (November 10, 1855): 24; Jerome M. Loving, "Whitman and Harlan: New Evidence," *American Literature* 48 (1976): 219–22.

38. James C. Mohr, *Abortion in America: The Origins and Evolution of a National Policy, 1800–1900* (Oxford: Oxford University Press, 1978); Reva B. Siegel, "'The Rule of Love': Wife Beating as Prerogative and Privacy," *Yale Law Journal* 105 (1996): 2117–2208.

39. On distinctions and relationships between feminism and free love, see Hasday, "Contest and Consent," 1413–27, 1444–51.

40. NYSSV, Reel 1, Container 1, *Arrest Records*, "Patrick Bannon" (March 5, 1872). On Comstock and his society, see Anna Louise Bates, *Weeder in the Garden of the Lord: Anthony Comstock's Life and Career* (Lanham, MD: University Press of America, 1995); Nicola Kay Beisel, *Imperiled Innocents: Anthony Comstock and Family Reproduction in Victorian America* (Princeton, NJ: Princeton University Press, 1997); Heywood Broun and Margaret Leech, *Roundsman of the Lord* (New York: A & C Boni, 1927).

41. On Comstock's campaign against the free lovers, see Bates, *Weeder in the Garden of the Lord*, 69–80, 125–49; Beisel, *Imperiled Innocents*, 76–102. On the censorship of *Leaves* in Boston, see Bates, *Weeder*, 143–44; Betsy Erkkila, *Whitman the Political Poet* (New York: Oxford University Press, 1989), 308–13.

42. Morone, *Hellfire Nation*, 191–200 (nativism and racism, 1850–70); [David Croly], *Miscegenation: The Theory of the Blending of Races Applied to the American White and Negro* (New York: H. Dexter Hamilton, 1864).

43. Mary Douglas, *Purity and Danger: An Analysis of the Concepts of Pollution and Taboo* (New York: Praeger, 1966); Morone, *Hellfire Nation*; Victoria Nourse, *In Evil or Reckless Hands: Science, Crime, and Constitution in New Deal and War—The History of* Skinner v. Oklahoma (manuscript, 2006); Elisabeth Young-Bruehl, *The Anatomy of Prejudices* (Cambridge, MA: Harvard University Press, 1996).

44. Griswold, Review (first quotation in text); Juliette [a.k.a. Calvin] Beach, "Leaves of Grass," New York *Saturday Press*, June 2, 1860, 2, in Whitman Archive (Critics) (second quotation); [William Dean Howells], "A Hoosier's Opinion of Walt Whitman," New York *Saturday Press*, August 11, 1860, 2, in Whitman Archive (Critics) (remaining quotations).

45. Anthony Comstock, *Traps for the Young* (Boston: Funk and Wagnalls, 1883), chaps. 10, 13 (first quotations in text); NYSSV, *Sixth Annual Report, 1880*, 11 (second quotation in text); Bates, *Weeder in the Garden of the Lord*, 153 (third quotation, from a Comstock article).

46. Jonathan Haidt, "The Emotional Dog and Its Rational Tail: A Social Intuitionist Approach to Moral Judgment," *Psychological Review* 108 (2001): 814 (quotation in text); Joshua Greene and Jonathan Haidt, "How (and Where) Does Moral Judgment Work?" *Trends in Cognitive Sciences* 6 (2002): 517–23 (neutral bases for social intuitionist theory of how we form moral judgments).

47. Young-Bruehl, *Anatomy of Prejudices*, 219–30, 363–77; ibid., 230 (quotations in text). Comstock's diaries (now destroyed) suggested to his first biographers that he could not "will out from his mind all erotic fancies, and so he turned all the more fiercely upon the ribaldry of others." Broun and Leech, *Roundsman of the Lord*, 27.

48. William Ian Miller, *Anatomy of Disgust* (Cambridge, MA: Harvard University Press, 1999), 194–95; Joseph R. Gusfield, "On Legislating Morals: The Symbolic Process of Designating Deviance," *Southern California Law Review* 56 (1968): 54–73. On obsessives, see Young-Bruehl, *Anatomy of Prejudices*, 210–19, 274–81, 343–63; ibid., 214 (quotation in text); also Pierre Schlag, "The Aesthetics of American Law," *Harvard Law Review* 115 (2002): 1061–65, who discusses the law's obsession with classifications and grids.

49. Griswold, Review (first quotation in text); Anonymous, "Leaves of Grass," *Literary Gazette*, July 7, 1860, 798–99 (second quotation).

50. NYSSV, *First Annual Report, 1875,* 10–11 (quotation in text); Report of Anthony Comstock, Twenty-five Consecutive Years a Special Agent or Inspector of the Post Office Department [1897], in NYSSV Papers, Reel 2, Container 8 (data reported in text); Beisel, *Imperiled Innocents*, 49–75.

51. Reverend James Monroe Buckley, introduction, *Traps for the Young*, 2 (first quotation in text); Comstock, *Traps for the Young*, 135–36 (second quotation); ibid., 159 (third quotation); NYSSV, *Third Annual Report, 1877*, 8-9 (fourth quotation).

52. Beisel, *Imperiled Innocents*, 68–71; NYSSV, *Sixth Annual Report, 1880*, 26 (quotation in text).

53. Young-Bruehl, *Anatomy of Prejudices*, 230–38, 281–98, 377–85; ibid., 283 (first quotation in text); ibid., 385 (second quotation).

54. Whitman, "Song of Myself," § 1, *Leaves* (1881), Whitman (LOA), 188 (first quotation); ibid., § 15, Whitman (LOA), 200–203 (list of Americans Whitman celebrates); ibid., § 21, Whitman (LOA), 207 (second quotation).

55. Carroll Smith-Rosenberg, *Disorderly Conduct* (New York: Oxford University Press, 1985).

56. Broun and Leech, *Roundsman of the Lord*, 112, quoting Comstock's (now destroyed) diary, April 15, 1873.

57. See Daniel Mark Epstein, *Lincoln and Whitman: Parallel Lives in Civil War Washington* (New York: Random House, 2004).

58. Most useful in my own understanding of the Fourteenth Amendment, from the perspective of its framers, are Akhil Reed Amar, *The Bill of Rights: Creation and Reconstruction* (New Haven, CT: Yale University Press, 1998); Michael Kent Curtis, *No State Shall Abridge: The Fourteenth Amendment and the Bill of Rights* (Durham, NC: Duke University Press, 1986); William E. Nelson, *The Fourteenth Amendment: From Political Principle to Judicial Doctrine* (Cambridge, MA: Harvard University Press, 1988); Jacobus tenBroek, *The Anti-Slavery Origins of the Fourteenth Amendment* (Berkeley: University of California Press, 1951).

59. Brief of the Cato Institute as *Amicus Curiae* in Support of Petitioners, *Lawrence v. Texas*, Docket No. 02-102 (USSC), appendix 1 (reproducing all state sodomy laws, 1868); ibid., appendix 2 (summarizing reported nineteenth-century sodomy decisions); *Wainwright v. Stone*, 414 U.S. 21 (USSC, 1973) (per curiam) (Florida's crime-against-nature law constitutional, because court decisions lent sufficient determinacy to the crime).

60. Act of June 19, 1812, § 5, New Hampshire Laws, made it a crime if a "man lye with mankind," but was not included in the New Hampshire General Statutes of 1843, 1851, or 1867.

State v. LaForrest, 45 A. 225 (Vermont Supreme Court, 1899), ruled that Vermont's adoption of the English common law in 1779 included the 1533 buggery law.

61. Blackstone, *Commentaries*, vol. 1, 123–24, 125–29 (initial quotations in text); *Corfield v. Coryell*, 6 F.Cas. 546, 552 (Circuit Court for the Eastern District of Pennsylvania, 1823) (no. 3230) (last quotation). See also Albert W. Alschuler, "Rediscovering Blackstone," *University of Pennsylvania Law Review* 145 (1996): 28–36. On the libertarian metaphilosophy of the nineteenth-century Constitution, see Nelson, *Americanization of the Common Law*, 89–110; Ronald Hamowy, "Preventive Medicine and the Criminalization of Sexual Immorality in Nineteenth Century America," in Randy E. Barnett and John Hagel III, eds., *Assessing the Criminal: Restitution, Retribution, and the Legal Process* (Cambridge, MA: Ballinger, 1977), 35–97.

62. *Congressional Globe*, 39th Cong., 1st Sess. 1088–89 (1866) (first quotation in text); ibid., 2766 (Senator Howard) (second quotation); *Railway Express Agency, Inc. v. New York*, 336 U.S. 106, 112 (USSC, 1949) (Jackson, J., concurring) (third quotation). See also Nelson, *Fourteenth Amendment* (thorough examination of the framers' articulation of a general equality principle).

63. Contrast *Yick Wo v. Hopkins*, 118 U.S. 356 (USSC, 1886), striking down a San Francisco laundry licensing scheme enforced only against Chinese laundries.

64. Elizabeth Cady Stanton, Susan B. Anthony, and Matilda Joslyn Gage, eds., *History of Woman Suffrage*, vol. 2 (New York: Fowler & Wells, 1882) 90 et seq. (feminist petitions protesting the gendered language in the proposed Fourteenth Amendment); ibid., 269–312 (debate at the New York Convention, which voted to ratify without protections for women); ibid., 313–44 (feminists' lack of success in procuring the franchise under the Fifteenth Amendment); Stanton, "Address to the Legislature," 51 (quotation in text).

65. *History of Woman Suffrage*, vol. 2, 409 et seq. (Minor's 1869 speech); ibid., 510 (Stanton's 1872 speech); Adam Winkler, "A Revolution Too Soon: Woman Suffragists and the 'Living Constitution,'" *NYU Law Review* 76 (2001): 1473–89 (the evolution of Minor's argument, 1869–71).

66. Whitman, *Democratic Vistas*, 968 (first quotation in text); ibid., 979 (second quotation), 946–47 (remaining quotations). Whitman understood male adhesiveness as the great glue binding America together. Ibid., 949, 981–82 footnote.

67. Ibid., 940–41 (balance between individualism and community); ibid., 929 (first quotation, invoking Mill's *On Liberty*); ibid., 942 (second quotation).

68. Ibid., 949 (quotations in text).

69. Winkler, "Revolution Too Soon," 1489–91 (House Judiciary Committee rejected feminist constitutional arguments; majority report written by Representative Bingham, drafter of Fourteenth Amendment), 1504–18 (judicial rejection as well, *Bradwell v. Illinois*, 83 U.S. 130 [USSC, 1872]; *United States v. Anthony*, 24 F.Cas. 829 [Circuit Court for the Northern District of New York, 1873]; *Minor v. Happersett*, 88 U.S. 162 [USSC, 1874]).

70. Comstock, *Traps for the Young*, 215–23 (broad constitutional vision of federal government empowered to act broadly in the public interest); NYSSV, *Third Annual Report, 1877*, 7–8 (quotation in text; emphasis in original).

71. Comstock, *Traps for the Young*, 199 (first quotation in text); ibid., 198 (second quotation); NYSSV, *Fifth Annual Report, 1879*, 11 (third quotation).

72. *Bradwell*, 83 U.S. 141 (Bradley, J., concurring); Beisel, *Imperiled Innocents*, 71–75 (mothers have primary responsibility for protecting youth).

Chapter Two: **From the Sodomite to the Homosexual, 1881–1935**

1. Letter from John Addington Symonds to Walt Whitman, February 7, 1872, excerpted in Katz, *Gay American History*, 515–16 (first quotations in text); letter from Symonds to Whitman, August 3, 1890, reprinted in ibid., 524–26 (second Symonds quotations in text); draft letter from Whitman to Symonds, August 19, 1890, reprinted in ibid., 527 (Whitman quotations in text).

2. On the 1881–82 censorship of *Leaves*, see Betsy Erkkila, *Whitman the Political Poet* (New York: Oxford University Press, 1989), 308–13; Kenneth M. Price, *To Walt Whitman, America* (Chapel Hill: University of North Carolina Press, 2004), 30–33.

3. My account of Mitchell and Ward is taken from Lisa Duggan, *Sapphic Slashers: Sex, Violence, and American Modernity* (Durham, NC: Duke University Press, 2002), 9–119.

4. Cf. ibid., 14–31 (linking the lynching narrative of black men assaulting white women with the sapphic slasher narrative of vampire lesbians assaulting white women).

5. W. C. Rivers, "Walt Whitman's Anomaly" (1913), reprinted in Duberman, *About Time*, 106–9; William Lee Howard, *The Perverts* (New York: G. W. Dillingham, 1901). For similar links among feminism, masculine women, and sexual perversion, see Howard, "Effeminate Men and Masculine Women," *New York Medical Journal* 71 (1900): 686–87; Havelock Ellis, *Sexual Inversion* (New York: F. A. Davis Co., 3d ed., 1915), 261–63.

6. *Fourteenth Census of the United States Taken in the Year 1920* (Washington, D.C.: Government Printing Office, 1921), 1:78.

7. Carroll Smith-Rosenberg, *Disorderly Conduct: Visions of Gender in Victorian America* (New York: Knopf, 1985), 176.

8. "The Subjective Necessity for Social Settlements," in Henry Adams, ed., *Philanthropy and Social Progress* (New York: Crowell, 1893), 1–26; see Victoria Bissell Brown, *The Education of Jane Addams* (Philadelphia: University of Pennsylvania Press, 2004), 263–70; Jean Bethke Elshtain, *Jane Addams and the Dream of American Democracy: A Life* (New York: Basic Books, 2002), 94; Louise W. Knight, *Citizen: Jane Addams and the Struggle for Democracy* (Chicago: University of Chicago Press, 2005), 252–59.

9. On Boston marriages, see the History Project, *Improper Bostonians: Lesbian and Gay History from the Puritans to Playland* (Boston: Beacon, 1998), 57–84; Knight, *Citizen*, 217–18; R. W. B. Lewis, *The Jameses: A Family Narrative* (New York: Farrar, Straus & Giroux, 1991). Compare Faderman, *Believing in Women*, 119–32, who claims Addams as a lesbian, with Elshtain, *Addams and Democracy*, 9–14, 23, who seems appalled at the suggestion, with Brown, *Education of Jane Addams*, 11, 361–62 note 60, 387 note 40, who considers Addams's female relationships critical to her mission but is agnostic as to their sexual nature.

10. Nancy Sahli, "Smashing: Women's Relationships Before the Fall," *Chrysalis* 8 (1979): 17–27.

11. Smith-Rosenberg, *Disorderly Conduct*, 172–81. On the crisis of masculinity, see Joe L. Dubbert, "Progressivism and the Masculinity Crisis," *Psychoanalytic Review* 61 (1974): 443–55; Anthony Rotundo, *American Manhood: Transformations in Masculinity from the Revolution to the Modern Era* (New York: Basic Books, 1993).

12. Duggan, *Sapphic Slashers*, 128 (quotation in text), and generally, 123–55.

13. Whitman, "Once I Pass'd Through a Populous City," *Leaves* (1860 edition) (quotation in text); Gilfoyle, *City of Eros*, 58–59, 119–26, 161–78. See Ruth Rosen, *The Lost Sisterhood: Prostitution in America, 1900–1918* (Baltimore: Johns Hopkins University Press, 1982); Judith

Walkowitz, *Prostitution and Victorian Society: Women, Class, and the State* (New York: Cambridge University Press, 1980).

14. Katy Coyle and Nadiene Van Dyke, "Sex, Smashing, and Storyville in Turn-of-the-Century New Orleans," in John Howard, ed., *Carryin' On in the Lesbian and Gay South* (New York: NYU Press, 1997), 54–72; Gilfoyle, *City of Eros*, 181–91 (Comstock episode). For contemporary sources identifying oral sex (and other perversions) by male as well as female sex workers, see, e.g., Vice Commission of Chicago, *The Social Evil in Chicago: A Study of Existing Conditions* (Chicago: Gunthorp-Warren Printing, 1911), 39, 73, 295–98; *Report of the Hartford Vice Commission* (Hartford, CT, 1913), 37; Committee of Fifteen, *The Social Evil, with Special Reference to Conditions Existing in the City of New York* (New York: G. P. Putnam's Sons, 1912), 6–9, 62–63; *Report of the Vice Commission of Maryland* (Baltimore, 1915), 1:102–3 and 429, 2:91, 3:144 ("perversions" practiced by male and female prostitutes); Vice Commission of Philadelphia, *A Report of Existing Conditions, with Recommendations* (Philadelphia, 1913), 5; Committee of Eighteen Citizens, *The Social Evil in Syracuse* (Syracuse, NY, 1913), 19–21, 34, 67–80.

15. Gilfoyle, *City of Eros*, 138–41, quoting Whitman.

16. *The Social Evil [NYC]*, 227 (listing cities with active antivice societies in 1906); Eskridge, "Regulation, 1880–1946," 1112–20 (statistics in the South); Police Reports (St. Louis). On the purity movement generally, see Barbara Meil Hobson, *Uneasy Virtue: The Politics of Prostitution and the American Reform Tradition* (Chicago: University of Chicago Press, 1990); David J. Pivar, *Purity Crusade: Sexual Morality and Social Control, 1868–1900* (Westport, CT: Greenwood, 1973), and *Purity and Hygiene: Women, Prostitution, and the "American Plan," 1900–1930* (Westport, CT: Greenwood, 2002); Rosen, *Sisterhood*.

17. On the original object of Whitman's "Populous City," see Emory Holloway, "Walt Whitman's Love Affairs," *Dial* 69 (1920): 473–83. On gay/fairy subcultures in New York, see Ralph Werther (a.k.a. Jennie June and Earl Lind), *The Female-Impersonators* (New York: Medico-Legal Journal, 1922); George Chauncey Jr., *Gay New York: Gender, Urban Culture, and the Making of the Gay Male World, 1890–1940* (New York: Basic Books, 1994), 33–45 (Paresis Hall), 47–63 (fairies), 99–127 (middle-class "queers").

18. San Francisco Lesbian and Gay History Project, "'She Even Chewed Tobacco': A Pictorial Narrative of Passing Women in America," in Martin B. Duberman et al., eds., *Hidden from History: Reclaiming the Gay and Lesbian Past* (New York: NAL Books, 1989), 183–89; Stryker and Van Buskirk, *Gay by the Bay: A History of Queer Culture in the San Francisco Bay Area* (San Francisco: Chronicle Books, 1996) 18.

19. G. Frank Lydston, "Clinical Lecture: Sexual Perversion, Satyriasis and Nymphomania," *Medical and Surgical Reporter* 61 (1889): 253–58, 281–84, excerpted in Jonathan Ned Katz, *Gay/Lesbian Almanac: A New Documentary* (New York: Harper & Row, 1983), 213; *The Social Evil in Chicago*, 295–98.

20. Xavier Mayne (a.k.a. Edward Stevenson), *The Intersexes: A History of Similsexualism as a Problem in Social Life* (Rome, 1908), 640 (appendix C) (list in text). For my supplement, see Vice Commission of Maryland, *Report*, 1:423–25 ("sexual orgies" among men in Baltimore); Gary L. Atkins, *Gay Seattle: Stories of Exile and Belonging* (Seattle: University of Washington Press, 2003), 3–33; Lillian Faderman and Stuart Timmons, *Gay L.A.: A History of Sexual Outlaws, Power Politics, and Lipstick Lesbians* (New York: Basic Books, 2006), 14–30; Painter, *Sensibilities*, "Oregon" (Portland); Sharon R. Ullman, "'The Twentieth Century Way': Female Impersonation and Sexual Practice in Turn-of-the-Century America," *Journal of the History of Sexuality* 5 (1995): 573–600 (Long Beach).

21. Werther [Lind], *Female-Impersonators*, 24–25 (quoting Comstock). See also sources in notes 14, 17, 18, and 20 above.

22. Nathan G. Hale Jr., *Freud and the Americans: The Beginnings of Psychoanalysis in the United States, 1876–1917* (New York: Oxford University Press, 1971), 34–97. See also Lillian Faderman, *Surpassing the Love of Men: Romantic Friendship and Love Between Women, from the Renaissance to the Present* (New York: Morrow, 1981).

23. The quotations in text are from Richard von Krafft-Ebing, *Psychopathia Sexualis, with Especial Reference to Antipathic Sexual Instinct: A Medico-Forensic Study* (New York: Arcade Publishing, 1998) (reprint of the Franklin S. Klaf translation of the twelfth German edition), 8–9, 28, 35–36. See also ibid., 188–307, for discussion of "Antipathic Sexuality" and other topics relating to same-sex intimacy. Alice Mitchell's case study is at 388–91.

24. George M. Beard, *Sexual Neurasthenia, Its Hygiene, Causes, Symptoms, and Treatment* (1884), 106–7 (first quotation in text); James G. Kiernan, "Insanity: Sexual Perversion," *Chicago Medical Recorder* 3, no. 3 (May 1892): 185–210 (second and fourth quotations); Charles H. Hughes, "Alice Mitchell, the 'Sexual Pervert' and Her Crime," *Alienist and Neurologist* 14, no. 4 (July 1892): 554–57 (third quotation). See also George F. Shrady, "Perverted Sexual Instinct," *Medical Record* 26 (1884): 70; P. M. Wise, "Case of Sexual Perversion," *Alienist and Neurologist* 4 (1883): 87–91.

25. James Weir Jr., "The Effects of Female Suffrage on Posterity," *American Naturalist* 29 (September 1895): 819 (first and second quotations in text); Edward Carpenter, *The Intermediate Sex: A Study of Some Transitional Types of Men and Women* (London: George Allen & Unwin, 1908), reprinted in Donald Webster Cory, ed., *Homosexuality: A Cross Cultural Approach* (New York: Julian Press, 1956), 175–76 (third quotation); Ellis, *Sexual Inversion* (1915), 262 (fourth quotation). See generally Lillian Faderman, *Odd Girls and Twilight Lovers: A History of Lesbian Life in Twentieth-Century America* (New York: Columbia University Press, 1991), 45-48.

26. Ellis, *Inversion*, 320–21; Theodore H. Kellogg, *Treatise on Mental Diseases* (New York: William Wood & Co., 1897), 197–98; G. Frank Lydston, *The Diseases of Society (The Vice and Crime Problem)* (Philadelphia: J. B. Lippincott, 1904), 37 (quotations in text), as well as 308–9, 372–73 (tracing the influence of degenerate classes on the development of perversion in Chicago, Paris, and London).

27. The racist features of degeneration theory were first noted in Katz, *Gay American History*, 63–67, 75–76; Katz, *Gay/Lesbian Almanac*, 179–387 (reproducing primary documents). See also Siobhan B. Somerville, *Queering the Color Line: Race and the Invention of Homosexuality in American Culture* (Durham, NC: Duke University Press, 2000); Duggan, *Sapphic Slashers*, 156–79; Jennifer Terry, *American Obsession: Science, Medicine, and Homosexuality in Modern Society* (Chicago: University of Chicago Press, 1999), 27–119.

28. Irving C. Rosse, "Sexual Hypochondriasis and Perversion of the Genetic Instinct," *Journal of Nervous and Mental Disease* 17 (1892): 795; C. H. Hughes, "Postscript to a Paper on 'Erotopathia'—An Organization of Colored Erotopaths," *Alienist and Neurologist* 14, no. 4 (October 1893): 731–32, and "Homo Sexual Complexion Perverts in St. Louis: Note on a Feature of Sexual Psychopathy," *Alienist and Neurologist* 28 (November 1907): 487–88. The Hughes articles are excerpted in Katz, *Gay American History*, 42–43, 48–49.

29. Lydston, *Diseases*, 395; Correspondence, "Sexual Crimes Among the Southern Negroes [etc.]," *Virginia Medical Monthly* 20 (May 1893): 105–8 (Letter from Dr. Hunter McGuire, March 11, 1893), 108–25 (Letter from Dr. Frank Lydston, March 16, 1893); Duggan, *Sapphic*

Slashers, 32–46, as well as 158–63 (the raced as well as gendered account of degeneracy theory accepted by Americans).

30. [John Addington Symonds], *A Problem in Modern Ethics* (London, 1896), reprinted in Cory, *Homosexuality*, 71–79, 93–98; Ellis, *Sexual Inversion* (1915), 354; (draft) letter from Walt Whitman to John Addington Symonds, August 19, 1890, reprinted in Katz, *Gay American History*, 527.

31. *Tenth Census of the United States, 1880* (Washington, D.C.: Government Printing Office, 1888), 21:506; *Eleventh Census of the United States, 1890* (Washington, D.C.: Government Printing Office, 1895), 4:18. For sodomy laws in each listed jurisdiction, see appendix of this book.

32. Faderman and Timmons, *Gay L.A.*, 30–31; *Gay Girls Guide to the M.S. and the Modern World* (Fall 1957), 19, in *One* Archives.

33. 1879 Pennsylvania Public Laws No. 156 (law quoted in text). See appendix of this book for references for other state laws noted in text.

34. An Act to make further provision for the Protection of Women and Girls, the suppression of brothels etc., 48 & 49 Victoria 69, clause 11 (U.K. 1885) (the Labouchere Amendment); F. B. Smith, "Labouchere's Amendment to the Criminal Law Amendment Bill," *Historical Studies [Australia]* 17 (1976): 165 (legislative background and Labouchere's own murky motives); see appendix of this book (references for American state laws).

35. "Publicity Is Needed and Then More Publicity," *L.A. Times*, November 26, 1914, II:8; Fisher Notes and Papers; Faderman and Timmons, *Gay L.A.*, 30–37.

36. 1915 California Statutes chap. 586. The California Supreme Court struck down the statute for using obscure Latin terms, and the legislature replaced the 1915 law with one making "oral copulation" a felony. 1921 California Statutes chap. 848.

37. *Honselman v. People*, 48 N.E. 304 (Illinois Supreme Court, 1897); see appendix of this book (references for other state court opinions noted in text).

38. *Prindle v. State*, 21 S.W. 360 (Texas Court of Criminal Appeals, 1893); see appendix of this book (references for state court opinions noted in text).

39. 1886 New York Laws chap. 31 (expanding the definition of the crime against nature); 1895 North Dakota Penal Law chap. 32, § 7186. In a 1917 lecture, Dr. Alfred Herzog opined that the 1886 law covered cunnilingus because there was "penetration" of a woman's sexual organ by another person's tongue. *Medico-Legal Journal* 34 (November/December 1917): 1–3.

40. 1896 Louisiana Laws, Act 69, interpreted in *State v. Murry*, 66 So. 963, 965 (Louisiana Supreme Court, 1914); 1913 Oregon Laws chap. 21. The Louisiana law was probably a response to New Orleans's thriving prostitution trade, see Coyle and VanDyke, "Sex, Smashing, and Storyville." Oregon's law was a response to the Portland YMCA oral sex epidemic in 1912. Painter, *Sensibilities*, "Oregon."

41. *State v. Smith*, 101 N.E.2d 957 (Illinois Supreme Court, 1913) (cunnilingus is not a crime against nature, even though fellatio is); 1903 Michigan Public Acts No. 198 ("gross indecency" between males); *State v. Wellman*, 161 S.W. 795 (Missouri Supreme Court, 1913) (1911 amendment to crime-against-nature law criminalized fellatio but not cunnilingus); *Ex parte Benites*, 140 P. 436 (Nevada Supreme Court, 1914) (same); *Garred v. State*, 216 N.W. 496 (Wisconsin Supreme Court, 1927) (same).

42. *Comer v. State*, 94 S.E.2d 314 (Georgia Court of Appeals, 1917) (applying Georgia's "carnal knowledge" language to both female-on-male fellatio and male-on-female cunnilingus); 1916 Virginia Public Acts chap. 295 ("carnal copulation" added to buggery law, but only as to same-sex partners; extended to different-sex partners in 1924 Virginia Public Acts chap. 358).

43. Charles G. Chaddock, "Sexual Crimes," in Allan McLane Hamilton and Lawrence Godkin, eds., *A System of Legal Medicine* (New York: E. B. Treat, 1894), 2:525–72; ibid., 543–44 (quotations in text); W. Travis Gibb, "Indecent Assault Upon Children," in ibid., 1:649–57. See Philip Jenkins, *Moral Panic: Changing Concepts of the Child Molester in Modern America* (New Haven, CT: Yale University Press, 1998), 28–31.

44. 1897 Wisconsin Laws chap. 198; 1907 Illinois Laws 266; 1915 Illinois Laws 368; Eskridge, *Gaylaw*, appendix A3, 342–51 (cataloging indecent liberty and contributing-to-delinquency laws).

45. Jenkins, *Moral Panic*, 42–43 (early sterilization proposals and nationwide statutory craze); 1911 Iowa Laws chap. 129 (sterilization of inmates who are "moral or sexual perverts"), invalidated 1914, and replaced by 1929 Iowa Laws chap. 66 (sterilization of "moral degenerates or sexual perverts who are a menace to society").

46. 1901 California Statutes 201 (codified Penal Code § 288); 1905 California Statutes 74 (§ 273f); 1907 California Statutes 756 (§ 273g); 1929 California Statutes 697 (§ 647a).

47. 1909 California Statutes chap. 720 (original sterilization law), expanded by 1937 California Statutes chap. 369, § 6624; California State Department of Mental Hygiene, Statistical Research Bureau, *Sterilization Operations in California State Hospitals for the Mentally Ill etc., 1909–1960* (implementation of sterilization law); see Daniel Kevles, *In the Name of Eugenics: Genetics and the Uses of Human Heredity,* rev. ed. (Cambridge, MA: Harvard University Press, 1995); Victoria Nourse, *In Evil or Reckless Hands: Science, Crime and Constitution in New Deal and War—The History of* Skinner v. Oklahoma (draft, 2006).

48. See Police Reports (Boston) 1880–1900; Mathew Michael, "Analysis of the Adoption of Oral Sex Laws on Sodomy Arrests for Selected Cities" (August 1997).

49. Police Reports (NYC) 1901–1930; Police Reports (Boston) 1889–1930; Police Reports (St. Louis) 1874–1921.

50. Between 1881 and 1900, D.C. police arrested twenty-seven people for sodomy; sixteen of the twenty-seven were people of color, four were white, and seven were racially unidentified. Between 1901 and 1920, D.C. police arrested twenty-three people for sodomy: seventeen people of color, six whites. See Police Reports (DC) 1881–1920. For Maryland's less racially slanted enforcement, see Police Reports (Baltimore) 1906–21. Other sources discussing southern arrest rates report similarly disproportionate rates for people of color. For instance, Duggan, *Sapphic Slashers,* 63 (fifty-one percent of the men arrested in Memphis were black, seventy-seven percent of the women).

51. 1900 New York Laws chap. 281, adding New York Code of Criminal Procedure (NYCCP) § 887(9) (recodified in 1910 New York Laws chaps. 381–82); Katz, *Gay American History,* 72–73 (reproducing portions of the Mazet Committee report).

52. 1915 New York Laws chap. 285, and 1919 New York Laws chap. 502, both amending NYCCP § 887(4). On the committee's involvement, see "Legislation," Committee of Fourteen Bulletin #725 (February 15, 1915), in COF Papers.

53. 1881 New York Laws chap. 442, creating NYCCP § 887(7), applied in *People v. Luechini,* 136 N.Y.S.2d 319 (Supreme Court, Erie County, 1912). See generally *People v. Archibald,* 296 N.Y.S.2d 834 (Appellate Division, 1968) (history of cross-dressing law).

54. F. H. Whitin, "Sexual Perversion Cases in New York City Courts, 1916–1921," Bulletin

#1480, Committee of Fourteen (November 13, 1921), in COF Papers, Box 87; 1923 New York Laws chap. 642 (adding New York Penal Law § 722[8]), and Bill Jacket for this law, NYPL.

55. California Statutes 1903, chap. 89, amending California Penal Code § 647(5) (now superseded) (lewd vagrancy); ibid., chap. 201, adding § 650 1/2 (now § 650.5) (public indecency). On enforcement against sexual minorities, see Arthur H. Sherry, "Vagrants, Rogues and Vagabonds—Old Concepts in Need of Revision," *California Law Review* 48 (1960): 557–73; Note "Use of Vagrancy-Type Laws for Arrest and Detention of Suspicious Persons," *Yale Law Journal* 59 (1950): 1351–64.

56. For enforcement of criminal laws against gender-benders and homosexuals in the early twentieth century, see Atkins, *Gay Seattle*, 3–33; Chauncey, *Gay New York*; Faderman and Timmons, *Gay L.A.*, 30–37, 44–47.

57. On Reverend Kent and his investigation, see Lawrence R. Murphy, *Perverts by Official Order: The Campaign Against Homosexuals by the United States Navy* (New York: Harrington Park Press, 1988), as well as the Navy's files for the investigation, the two courts of inquiry, and the two trials of Reverend Kent, NA, Record Group 125, Records of Proceedings of Courts of Inquiry etc., Suitland Archive.

58. Murphy, *Perverts*, 10, 26–29, 32–33, 77–80, 97–103. For the court-martial proceedings for fifteen of the sailors, see ibid., 62–64.

59. Ibid., 97–117 (arrest and state trial), 121–51 (federal trial).

60. Record of Proceedings on a Court of Inquiry Convened at the U.S. Naval Training Station, Newport, Rhode Island, January 22, 1920, at 741, in Record Group 125, Records of Proceedings of Courts of Inquiry, Boards of Investigation, and Boards of Inquest, No. 10821-1, Suitland Archive (quotation in text); U.S. Senate Committee on Naval Affairs, *Alleged Immoral Conditions at Newport (R.I.) Naval Training Station* (1921), 29.

61. The Articles of War (1916), article 93, made only "assault with intent to commit sodomy," and not sodomy itself, a court-martial offense 39 Stat. 619, 650–70. The 1917 *Manual for Courts-Martial* ¶ 443, limited sodomy to its common-law definition and explicitly said that "penetration of the mouth" was not sodomy. The Articles of War (1920), article 93, included sodomy as a court-martial offense, 41 Stat. 787, and the 1921 *Manual for Courts-Martial* ¶ 443 defined sodomy to include oral sex.

62. Second Court of Inquiry Transcript, 1360 (Charles Zipf's testimony, quoted in text); ibid., 1956 (second quotation in text). On Zipf, see Murphy, *Perverts*, 22–33, 121–25, 140–42, 222–24 (including a photograph).

63. Sigmund Freud, "The Sexual Aberrations," in *Three Essays on the Theory of Sexuality*, trans. and rev. by James Strachey (New York: Basic Books, 1962 [4th ed., 1920]), 1–2 (aim versus object); ibid., 15–28 (perversions and pathology). On the reception of Freud in America, see Hale, *Freud and the Americans, 1876–1917*; Nathan G. Hale Jr., *The Rise and Crisis of Psychoanalysis in the United States: Freud and the Americans, 1917–1985* (New York: Oxford University Press, 1995), 13–22.

64. Freud, "The Sexual Aberrations," 16–19; ibid., 16 (quotation in text). Alexander Glage suggested to me this more radical reading of Freud.

65. Ibid., 4; Letter from Dr. Sigmund Freud to an American Mother (April 9, 1935), reprinted in Katz, *Gay/Lesbian Almanac*, 506–7 (concluding that homosexuality "is assuredly no advantage but it is nothing to be ashamed of, no vice, no degradation, it cannot be classified as an illness; we consider it to be a variation of the sexual function, produced by a certain arrest of sexual development"). See also George Fisher, *Drugs* (draft, 2006), who argues that Americans accept alcohol in moderation because of its accepted links to sociability and even good health, while they reject drugs (except marijuana) because their only purpose seems to be pleasure.

66. Christina Simmons, "Companionate Marriage and the Lesbian Threat," *Frontiers* 4, no. 3 (Fall 1979): 54–59; see Hale, *Freud and the Americans, 1917–1985*, 57–100. For examples of works extolling marital pleasure but rejecting homosexuality, see Floyd Dell, *Love in the Machine Age: A Psychological Study of the Transition from Patriarchal Society* (New York: Farrar, 1930); Margaret Sanger, *Happiness in Marriage* (New York: Brentano's, 1926).

67. NORC (1994), 106–7 (quotation in text).

68. Boyd, *Wide-Open Town*, 38–62 (San Francisco); Chauncey, *Gay New York*; Don Paulson and Roger Simpson, *An Evening at the Garden of Allah* (New York: Columbia University Press, 1996) (Seattle); Ina Russell, ed., *Jeb and Dash: A Diary of Gay Life, 1918–1945* (Boston: Faber and Faber, 1993) (Washington); Stuart Timmons, *The Trouble with Harry Hay: Founder of the Modern Gay Movement* (Boston: Alyson, 1990), 38–94 (Los Angeles); David Johnson, "Gay Male Culture on Chicago's Near North Side in the 1930s," in Brett Beemyn, ed., *Creating a Place for Ourselves: Lesbian, Gay, and Bisexual Community Histories* (New York: Routledge, 1997).

69. George W. Henry, *Sex Variants: A Study of Homosexual Patterns* (New York: Paul B. Hoebner, 1941). My references will be to the one-volume 1948 edition. For detailed background, see Terry, *American Obsession*, 178–267.

70. Henry, *Sex Variants*, 255 (Gene S.); Chauncey, *Gay New York*, 179–205.

71. *Jeb and Dash*, 17–18 (first quotation in text), 33 (associating his love for Dash with Ellis's *Sexual Inversion*, 1921), 61 ("Calamite"), 65 (second quotation). "Jeb Alexander" is a pseudonym chosen by the man's family when they allowed some of his diaries to be published.

72. Henry, *Sex Variants*, 34 (Donald H., married to a lesbian), 156 (Eric D., married to a bisexual woman), 253–55 (Gene S., desiring to marry), 299 (Archibald T., desiring to marry), 311 (Dennis C., desiring to marry a lesbian), 389 (Rafael G., desiring to marry so long as he can have homosexual affairs on the side), 408 (Max N., married to a lesbian), 459 (Leonard R., living with a lesbian), 485 (Percival G., noting that many of his bisexual friends marry rich women and have affairs with boys), 495 (Rudolph von H., married); Timmons, *Harry Hay*, 49–94 (Hay's many affairs with men), 95–114 (married to Anita Platky but continued to have sexual relations with men).

73. *Jeb and Dash*, 150 (the 1928 Christmas party). On Randall's marriage to a woman, see ibid., 90–91, 100.

74. Chauncey, *Gay New York*, 151–77, 207–67, 301–29. See also Boyd, *Wide-Open Town*, 38–62 (San Francisco); Faderman and Timmons, *Gay L.A.*, 39–69; Johnson, "Gay Male Culture on Chicago's Near North Side."

75. For a sense of the sexual variety reported by the sex variants, see, e.g., Henry, *Sex Variants*, 70–71 (Tracy O., sixty-nine fellatio, sleeping naked with another man, no anal sex), 136–41 (Michael D., mutual fellatio, passive anal sex, and domination scenarios), 178 (Salvatore N., kissing and affection from older men, no anal or oral sex), 225–28 (Paul A., kissing and body contact, active oral sex, no "sodomy"), 236–37 (Theodore S., mutual masturbation, sixty-nine, fellatio; hates "sodomy"), 265 (James D., "soul-kissing," fellatio, "sodomy"), 287 (Walter R., rough sex and being dominated), 362–63 (Leo S., kissing, rimming, perhaps passive sodomy).

76. Eskridge, *Gaylaw*, appendix A3, 342–51 (state-by-state survey of criminal laws protecting minors against exposure to adult sexuality).

77. Timmons, *Harry Hay*, 35–36; Eskridge, *Gaylaw*, appendix C3, 375 (reported sodomy cases). There are thirty-six reported sodomy cases for California from 1920 to 1946: eight involved rape, twenty-five involved children and adolescents (eighteen boys, seven girls), and three involved consensual adult male sex.

78. Between 1921 and 1942, D.C. police arrested sixty people for sodomy. Twenty-seven were people of color, twenty-four were white, nine have no racial identification, Police Reports (DC) 1921–1942.

79. See Police Reports (Chicago) 1920–30; Police Reports (NYC) 1920–30; *Report of the Mayor's Committee for the Study of Sex Offenses* (New York, 1940), 66 (reporting that ninety percent of the sodomy law arrests in the 1930s were for sex with minors); Henry, *Sex Variants*, 364 (Leo S.).

80. *Jeb and Dash*, 62–64.

81. Henry, *Sex Variants*, 474 (Peter R.). See Chauncey, *Gay New York*; Faderman and Timmons, *Gay L.A.*, 44–47.

82. Henry, *Sex Variants*, 57 (Sidney H.), 94 (Norman T.), 154 (Eric D.), 338 (Irving T.), 409 (Max N.). See also ibid., 115 (Nathan T., who resisted blackmail and was robbed and beaten), 444 (Victor R., whose parents hired a detective to expose his affair with a sailor), 483 (Percival G., who refused to succumb to blackmail).

83. Faderman, *Odd Girls*, 48–57; Lois W. Banner, *Intertwined Lives: Margaret Mead, Ruth Benedict, and Their Circle* (New York: Alfred A. Knopf, 2003), 95–154.

84. Banner, *Intertwined Lives*, 179–89, 226–34.

85. Katharine Bement Davis, *Factors in the Sex Life of Twenty-two Hundred Women* (New York: Harper & Row, 1928), 12–37 (contraception and abortion), 38 (importance of sexual relations to the success of a marriage), 297–328 (homosexual experiences of women who were married). See also Terry, *American Obsession*, 122–58 (analyzing the Davis and other sex surveys of the 1920s).

86. Davis, *Factors*, 238–96 (homosexual experiences of twelve hundred unmarried, college-educated women); Faderman, *Odd Girls*, 65–67 (lesbian-themed plays and books); Banner, *Intertwined Lives*, 252–54.

87. Banner, *Intertwined Lives*, 122; *Thompson v. Aldredge*, 200 S.E. 799 (Georgia Supreme Court, 1939); Police Reports (NYC) 1911–40; Police Reports (Boston) 1921–35; Police Reports (Baltimore) 1917–45.

88. Harvey Warren Zorbaugh, *The Gold Coast and the Slum: A Sociological Study of Chicago's Near North Side* (Chicago: University of Chicago Press, 1929) (quotation in text). On the butch-femme bar culture for working-class lesbians, see Elizabeth Lapovsky Kennedy and Madeline D. Davis, *Boots of Leather, Slippers of Gold: The History of a Lesbian Community* (New York: Routledge, 1993); Roey Thorpe, "The Changing Face of Lesbian Bars in Detroit, 1938–1965," in Beemyn, *Place for Ourselves*. 165–82.

89. Boyd, *Wide-Open Town*, 68–69; Faderman, *Odd Girls*, 79–81, 105–12 (listing lesbian bars in the 1930s).

90. Duggan, *Sapphic Slashers*, 9–46.

91. *Hunter v. Underwood*, 471 U.S. 222 (USSC, 1985) (examining the racist motivations of Alabama's law disenfranchising men convicted of sodomy and other crimes of moral turpitude); Jeff Manza and Christopher Uggen, *Locked Out: Felon Disenfranchisement and American Democracy* (New York: Oxford University Press, 2006), 41–68.

92. Steven A. Reich, ed., *Encyclopedia of the Great Black Migration* (Westport, CT: Greenwood, 2006), 351; A. B. Christa Schwarz, *Gay Voices of the Harlem Renaissance* (Bloomington:

Indiana University Press, 2003). See also Anne Elizabeth Carroll, *Word, Image, and the New Negro: Representation and Identity in the Harlem Renaissance* (Bloomington: Indiana University Press, 2005); David Levering Lewis, *When Harlem Was in Vogue* (New York: Knopf, 1981); Cheryl A. Wall, *Women of the Harlem Renaissance* (Bloomington: Indiana University Press, 1995).

93. Angela Y. Davis, *Blues Legacies and Black Feminism: Gertrude "Ma" Rainey, Bessie Smith, and Billie Holliday* (New York: Pantheon, 1998), 3–41.

94. Faderman, *Odd Girls*, 74–77 (quotations in text); Sarah Lieb, *Mother of the Blues: A Study of Ma Rainey* (Amherst: University of Massachusetts Press, 1981), 17–18 (Rainey's arrest).

95. Schwarz, *Gay Voices*, 120–41 (Nugent), 48–67 (Cullen), 68–87 (Hughes), 88–119 (McKay). See generally Thomas H. Wirth, ed., *Gay Rebel of the Harlem Renaissance: Selections from the Work of Richard Bruce Nugent* (Durham, NC: Duke University Press, 2002), 1–61.

96. Schwarz, *Gay Voices*, 6–24.

Chapter Three: **The Antihomosexual Kulturkampf, 1935–61**

1. Jervin Anderson, *Bayard Rustin: Troubles I've Seen* (New York: HarperCollins, 2000), 155 (Rustin's conversation with his grandmother); Daniel Levine, *Bayard Rustin and the Civil Rights Movement* (New York: Rutgers University Press, 2000), 14 (Rustin's apparent sexual initiation, at age fourteen). The best account of Rustin's life is John D'Emilio, *Lost Prophet: The Life and Times of Bayard Rustin* (New York: Free Press, 2003). See also Ed Edwin, interview with Bayard Rustin, in *The Reminiscences of Bayard Rustin* (Alexandria, VA, 2003); Devon W. Carbado and Donald Weise, "The Civil Rights Identity of Bayard Rustin," *Texas Law Review* 82 (2004): 1134–95.

2. D'Emilio, *Lost Prophet*, 79–96; Henry Seidel Canby, *Walt Whitman, An American* (Boston: Houghton Mifflin, 1943), 201–2 (quotations in text). Canby denied that Whitman was a homosexual, concluding that he was pan-erotic. Ibid., 186–206. Contrast Emory Holloway, *Free and Lonesome Heart* (New York: Vantage, 1960), 16, 55–56, who interpreted Whitman as bisexual, and Richard Chase, *Walt Whitman Reconsidered* (New York: William Sloane Associates, 1955), 48, who interpreted Whitman's sexuality as undeveloped.

3. D'Emilio, *Lost Prophet*, 191–92; 109 *Congressional Record* 14837–38 (August 13, 1963) (reproducing Rustin's arrest sheet and newspaper articles reporting some details of his arrest).

4. D'Emilio, *Lost Prophet*, 198–248 (Rustin's reemergence in the civil rights movement after the Pasadena arrest); ibid., 237 (quotation in text); *Brother Outsider: The Life of Bayard Rustin*, PBS documentary, 2003.

5. Taylor Branch, *Pillar of Fire: America in the King Years, 1963–1965* (New York: Simon & Schuster, 1998), 242–43; D'Emilio, *Lost Prophet*, 369.

6. Estelle Freedman, "'Uncontrolled Desires': The Response to the Sexual Psychopath, 1920–1960," *Journal of American History* 74 (June 1987): 83–107; Police Reports (Atlanta), 1890–1932; Police Reports (Baltimore) 1890–1940; Police Reports (Boston) 1890–1935; Police Reports (Chicago) 1890–1935; Police Reports (St. Louis) 1890–1940; William N. Eskridge Jr., "Law and the Construction of the Closet: American Regulation of Same-Sex Intimacy, 1871–1946," *Iowa Law Review* 82 (1997): 1112–21. For child-molestation laws, see William N. Eskridge Jr., *Gaylaw: Challenging the Apartheid of the Closet* (Cambridge, MA: Harvard University Press, 1999), 342–51. For the post–World War II panic, see Robert Corber, *Homosexuality in*

Cold War America: Resistance and the Crisis of Masculinity (Durham, NC: Duke University Press, 1997); George Chauncey Jr., "The Postwar Sex Crime Panic," in William Graebner, ed., *True Stories from the American Past* (New York: HarperCollins, 1993), 160–78.

7. *Report of Mayor's Committee for the Study of Sex Offenders* (New York City, 1939), 39–41 (New York City averages in 1930s); Eskridge, *Gaylaw*, appendix C1, 374 (sodomy arrests in twelve major cities).

8. Alfred C. Kinsey, Wardell B. Pomeroy, and Clyde E. Martin, *Sexual Behavior in the Human Male* (Philadelphia: W. B. Saunders, 1948), 392 (quotation in text); Alfred C. Kinsey, Wardell B. Pomeroy, Clyde E. Martin, and Paul Gebhard, *Sexual Behavior in the Human Female* (Philadelphia: W. B. Saunders, 1953), 280–81, 286, 419, 453. For a skeptical analysis, see David Allyn, "Private Acts/Public Policy: Alfred Kinsey, the American Law Institute and the Privatization of American Sexual Morality," *Journal of American Studies* 30 (1996): 405–28.

9. Kinsey et al., *Human Female*, 361, 399 (table 100). *Human Female* does not report data for the incidence of anal sex for women (either with men or with animals).

10. For surveys of booming homosexual subcultures and bars, 1930s–'50s, see Gary L. Atkins, *Gay Seattle: Stories of Exile and Belonging* (Seattle: University of Washington Press, 2003), 3–33; Brett Beemyn, ed., *Creating a Place for Ourselves: Lesbian, Gay, and Bisexual Community Histories* (New York: Routledge, 1997) (Chicago and Detroit); Nan Alamilla Boyd, *Wide-Open Town: A History of Queer San Francisco to 1965* (Berkeley: University of California Press, 2003); Lillian Faderman, *Odd Girls and Twilight Lovers: A History of Lesbian Life in Twentieth-Century America* (New York: Columbia University Press, 1991), 79–81, 105–112; Elizabeth Lapovsky Kennedy and Madeline D. Davis, *Boots of Leather, Slippers of Gold: The History of a Lesbian Community* (New York: Routledge, 1993).

11. J. Edgar Hoover, "How *Safe* Is Your Youngster?" *American Magazine*, March 1955, 19, 99–103, and "How Safe Is Your Daughter?" *American Magazine*, July 1947, 32. On Hoover's obsessive interest in homosexuals, see Richard Hack, *Puppetmaster: The Secret Life of J. Edgar Hoover* (Beverly Hills: New Millennium Press, 2004), 224–26, 243–44, 268–78; and the sex lives of Rustin and King, see ibid., 312–39. See also Anthony Summers, *Official and Confidential: The Secret Life of J. Edgar Hoover* (New York: Putnam, 1993), which speculates about Hoover's own sexual proclivities.

12. Glen Elder Jr., *Children of the Great Depression: Social Change and Life Experience* (Chicago: University of Chicago Press, 1974); also Andrew J. Cherlin, *Marriage, Divorce, Remarriage*, rev. ed. (Cambridge, MA: Harvard University Press, 1992), 6–43; Nancy F. Cott, *The Grounding of Modern Feminism* (New Haven, CT: Yale University Press, 1987), 145–211.

13. Elaine Tyler May, *Homeward Bound: American Families in the Cold War Era* (New York: Basic Books, 1988); also Cherlin, *Marriage*, 18–19, 35–43; Steven Mintz and Susan Kellogg, *Domestic Revolutions: A Social History of American Family Life* (New York: Free Press, 1998), 133–201; John Modell, *Into One's Own: From Youth to Adulthood in the United States, 1920–1975* (Berkeley: University of California Press, 1989), 213–61.

14. Reverend James Monroe Buckley, Introduction, Anthony Comstock, *Traps for the Young* (Boston: Funk and Wagnalls, 1883), 2.

15. Report of Lieutenant Colonel Birge Holt and Captain Ruby Herman to the Acting Inspector General of the Army, July 29, 1944, in Suitland Archives, Record Group 159 (Office of Inspector General), File 333.9 (Third WAC Training Center). See Leisa Meyer, *G.I. Jane: Sexuality and Power in the Women's Army Corps During World War II* (New York: Columbia University Press, 1996), 173–76.

16. Nicola Kay Beisel, *Imperiled Innocents: Anthony Comstock and Family Reproduction in Victorian America* (Princeton, NJ: Princeton University Press, 1997) (Comstock's crusades caught on in cities with large flows of immigrants, such as New York and Boston, but not in other cities without such flows, such as Philadelphia); Steven A. Reich, ed., *Encyclopedia of the Great Black Migration* (Westport, CT: Greenwood, 2006), 351–52; Daniel M. Johnson and Rex R. Campbell, eds., *Black Migration in America* (Durham, NC: Duke University Press, 1981), 78, 129.

17. Dal McIntire, "Tangents," *One,* April 1960, 15 (the Bodenheimer story).

18. *Mayor's Report,* 81–83 (New York data); Police Reports (DC) 1953–75; Walter Rapaport and Karl M. Bowman, *Final Report on California Sexual Deviation Research* (Sacramento, 1954), 101–2, 110 (San Francisco and California breakdowns by race); also Manfred S. Guttmacher, "The Homosexual in Court," *American Journal of Psychiatry* 112 (1955–56): 591–98 (half of those charged with sodomy in Baltimore were black men); David Johnson, "Gay Male Culture on Chicago's Near North Side in the 1930s," in Beemyn, *Place for Ourselves.*

19. *Latinos in New York* (South Bend, IN: Notre Dame University Press, 1996), 7–12; Rudolfo O. de la Garza et al., eds., *The Mexican American Experience: An Interdisciplinary Anthology* (Austin: University of Texas Press, 1985), 13–17; Rapaport and Bowman, *California Sexual Deviation Research,* 101.

20. On the harsher treatment of black sodomy defendants, see Guttmacher, "Homosexual in Court," 597 (Baltimore); Eskridge, *Gaylaw,* 87–88 (differential treatment of white and black sodomy defendants in Oklahoma); James T. Sears, *The Lonely Hunters: An Oral History of Lesbian and Gay Southern Life, 1948–1968* (Boulder, CO: Westview Press, 1997), 21–22 (Florida episode described in text).

21. On the companionate marriage norm, 1920–60, see, e.g., Mintz and Kellogg, *Domestic Revolutions,* 107–31, 175–201; Modell, *Into One's Own,* 249–59.

22. For detailed accounts of antihomosexual campaigns, see Allan Bérubé, *Coming Out Under Fire: The History of Gay Men and Women in World War II* (New York: Free Press, 1990); David Johnson, *The Lavender Scare: The Cold War Persecution of Gays and Lesbians in the Federal Government* (Chicago: University of Chicago Press, 2004) (federal civil service witch hunts); Sears, *Lonely Hunters,* 48–108 (Florida's Johns Committee).

23. Hoover, "How Safe Is Your Daughter?" 32 (first two quotations in text); *People v. Babb,* 229 P.2d 843, 845–46 (CCA, 1951) (third quotation); *Sultan Turkish Bath, Inc. v. Board of Police Commissioners, Los Angeles,* 337 P.2d 203, 208 (CCA, 1959) (fourth quotation). See also Dr. Carlton Simon (nationwide police consultant), "Homosexuals and Sex Crimes" (International Association of Police Chiefs, September 1947) (depicting homosexuals as diseased, addicted to marijuana, and predatory).

24. Florida Legislative Investigation Committee, *Homosexuality and Citizenship in Florida* (Tallahassee, January 1964), in Johns Papers, Box 1, Folder 21, discussed in William N. Eskridge Jr., "Privacy Jurisprudence and the Apartheid of the Closet, 1946–1961," *Florida State University Law Review* 24 (1997): 747–52.

25. Subcommittee on Investigations of the Senate Committee on Expenditures in the Executive Departments, "Interim Report: Employment of Homosexuals and Other Sex Perverts in Government" (1950) (Hoey Committee Report), 4 (all the quotations in text); Johnson, *Lavender Scare,* 101–18.

26. Johns Committee, *Homosexuality and Citizenship,* 9–10 (quotations in text).

27. War Department Regulations Nos. 1–9, Standards of Physical Examination During Mobilization § 20(93)(h) (1942) ("Sexual Perversions," a subcategory of "Psychoses, Psychoneuroses, Personality Disorders") (first quotation in text), discussed in Bérubé, *Coming Out Under Fire*, 19–20; Chaplain's Presentation to WAVE Recruits, 2 (second quotation), reprinted as appendix 23 to Report of the Board Appointed to Prepare and Submit Recommendations to the Secretary of the Navy for the Revision of Policies, Procedures and Directives Dealing with Homosexuals (1957), the "Crittenden Report."

28. Police Reports (NYC) 1946–65; Police Reports (LA) 1942, 1948; Police Reports (SF) 1946–54; Police Reports (Atlanta) 1946–61; Police Reports (Cleveland) 1946–61; Police Reports (DC) 1951–61; Police Reports (Richmond) 1946–61; S.C. Att'y Gen. Reports, 1954–55 to 1973–74 (South Carolina prosecutions for sodomy peak 1958–63); Eskridge, *Gaylaw*, appendix C2, 375 (reported sodomy cases).

29. Eskridge, *Gaylaw*, appendix C2, 375; Police Reports (DC) 1953–70. For one marital sodomy case, see *People v. Doggett*, 188 P.2d 792 (CCA, 1948), where photos of the couple came into the hands of police.

30. NYC Magistrates, 1951–62 (separately reporting felonious sodomy, involving force or minors, and misdemeanor sodomy, involving consenting adults). For examples of prosecutions for consensual sodomy in private places, see, e.g., *Faber v. State*, 152 P.2d 671 (Arizona Supreme Court, 1944) (two men engaged in fellatio in the home); *People v. Jordan*, 74 P.2d 519 (CCA 1937) (oral sex party in a private home); *Martin v. People*, 162 P.2d 597 (Colorado Supreme Court, 1944) (homosexual prosecuted for sodomy in his home when he complains that his sexual partners robbed him); *People v. Livermore*, 155 N.W.2d 711 (Michigan Supreme Court, 1967) (two women in a camping tent); *In re Latham*, 168 Ohio St. 14 (Ohio Court of Appeals, 1958) (consensual sodomy in private place); *State v. Edwards*, 412 P.2d 526 (Oregon Supreme Court, 1966) (police arrest cohabiting male partners for sodomy in their "marriage").

31. For examples of prosecutions of men for oral sex with experienced and willing teenage boys, see, e.g., *People v. Williams*, 12 Cal.App.2d 207 (CCA, 1936); *People v. Walker*, 198 P.2d 534 (CCA, 1948); *People v. Milo*, 201 P.2d 556 (CCA, 1949).

32. George Chauncey Jr., *Gay New York* (New York: HarperCollins, 1994), 182–83 (LaGuardia crackdown); Jim Kepner, *Rough News, Daring Views: 1950's Pioneer Gay Press Journalism* (New York: Haworth Press, 1998), 49–55 (Miami panic), 169–70 (Chicago, Santa Monica panics).

33. Editorial, *Idaho Statesman*, November 3, 1955, 4 (first quotation in text); John Gerassi, *The Boys of Boise: Furor, Vice, and Folly in an American City* (New York: Macmillan, 1966); ibid., 71 (second quotation); Dal McIntire, "Tangents," *One*, January 1956, 12.

34. Editorial, *Idaho Statesman*, November 29, 1955, 4 (boys "infected" by homosexuals); Gerassi, *Boys of Boise*, 79 (Koelsch quotation); ibid., 25 (Blaine quotation).

35. Ronald J. Ross, "Enforcing the *Kulturkampf* in the Bismarckian State and the Limits of Coercion in Imperial Germany," *Journal of Modern History* 56 (1984): 456–82.

36. The account of the Glucoft affair is taken from front-page articles in the *Sacramento Bee*, November 15–19, 1949. A week later, the rape and murder of Josephine Yanez, seventeen months old, reinforced the flames ignited by the Glucoft murder. *Sacramento Bee*, November 21, 1949, 1.

37. G. Edward White, *Earl Warren: A Public Life* (New York: Oxford University Press, 1982), 67–77 (Japanese Americans as "foreign threats"); ibid., 101–5 (Warren's progressive philosophy); ibid., 112–26 (Warren's anti-Communism). On Warren's "quite bigoted" attitude toward Japanese Americans, see Interview of Merrill Farnham Small, Departmental Secretary under Governor Warren, 1972, in Warren History, 41–43.

38. Small Interview, 61, describing effeminate Beach Vasey and Warren's abuse of him; Bernard Schwartz, *Super Chief: Earl Warren and His Supreme Court—A Judicial Biography* (New York: NYU Press, 1983), 250–54 (Warren's puritan sexual attitudes; quotations in text). Neither Schwartz's nor any other biography of Warren says anything about the governor's antihomosexual attitudes or crusade. E.g., Ed Cray, *Chief Justice: A Biography of Earl Warren* (New York: Simon & Schuster, 2000); Leo Katcher, *Earl Warren: A Political Biography* (New York: McGraw-Hill, 1967).

39. Allison Varzally, "Romantic Crossings: Making Love, Family, and Non-Whiteness in California, 1925–50," *Journal of American Ethnic History* 23 (2003): 3–54, especially 4–7.

40. "Warren Calls for Drive On Sex Criminals," *Sacramento Bee*, November 22, 1949, 1; H. P. Gleason, *Summary Report: Governor's Law Enforcement Agencies' Conference on Sex Crimes Against Children* (Sacramento, December 7, 1949); *Preliminary Report of the Subcommittee on Sex Crimes of the Assembly Interim Committee on Judicial System and Judicial Process* (Sacramento, 1950). Letters from concerned mothers, parent-teacher associations, and various groups, demanding that the state respond aggressively to the sex crime menace can be found in Warren Papers, Administrative Files, Department of Justice, Item 204 (Folder on Sex Crimes, 1949); ibid., Legislative Files, First Extraordinary Session 1949, Item 417 (Folder on Criminal Laws on Sex Crimes).

41. Act of June 9, 1948 (Miller Act), Public Law No. 80-615, § 104, 62 Stat. 346, 347, adding a new sodomy law to the District's penal code; Senate Report No. 1377 (incorporating H.R. Report No. 1787), 80th Congress, 1st Session (1948), reprinted in 1948 *USCCAN* 1717 (quotation in text, one of the two justifications for the legislation).

42. 1945 California Statutes chap. 934 (adding sodomy to the repeat offender law); 1949 California Statutes, Extraordinary Session chap. 14 (January 6, 1950) (expanding recidivism enhancement law to include oral sex and toilet loitering convictions); ibid., chap. 15 (doubling the penalties for sodomy); 1950 California Statutes, First Extraordinary Session chap. 28 (April 26, 1950) (adding sodomy and oral copulation to the habitual offender law, imposing mandatory life in prison for a third conviction); 1952 California Statutes, First Extraordinary Session chap. 23 (April 17, 1952) (possible life sentence for sodomy; mandatory minimum sentence for forcible oral sex and oral sex with a minor). The post-1948 laws originated with the Governor's 1949 Law Enforcement Agencies' Conference. Gleason, *Summary Report*, 8–11.

43. Letter from Assemblyman H. Allen Smith to Governor Earl Warren, April 11, 1950, in Cal Leg Hist for 1950 California Statutes, First Extraordinary Session chap. 56.

44. 1950 New York Statutes chap. 525, § 15 (creating three crimes: consensual sodomy, forcible sodomy, and sodomy with minors), discussed in chapter 4.

45. See, e.g., Miller Act of 1948, § 104, 62 Stat. 347 (sodomy in Washington includes taking another person's sex organ "into his or her mouth"); 1943 Texas General Laws chap. 112 (making it a crime to use one's "mouth on the sexual parts of another human being for the purpose of having carnal copulation").

46. See, e.g., 1947 California Statutes chap. 730 (crime to "molest" any child); 1943 Florida Laws chap. 21974 (crime to fondle a girl "in a lewd, lascivious, or indecent manner"); 1951 Florida Laws chap. 26580 (same for fondling a boy). Other states accomplished this regulatory expansion in one statute, covering both boys and girls—including Arizona, Delaware, Georgia, Idaho, Illinois, Kentucky, Louisiana, Minnesota, Missouri, North Carolina, Texas, and Washington. See Eskridge, *Gaylaw*, 342–51 (appendix A3).

47. 1949 California Statutes, First Extraordinary Session chap. 14 (January 6, 1950).

48. 1947 California Statutes chap. 730 (June 14, 1947), expanded by 1949 California Statutes, First Extraordinary Session chap. 14 (January 6, 1950).

49. 1947 California Statutes, Extraordinary Session chap. 1124 (July 7, 1947) (requiring registration of persons convicted of sodomy, oral copulation, and various crimes against children); Letter from Director of Corrections Richard McGee to Governor Warren, July 2, 1947, in Cal Leg Hist for chap. 1124 (first quotation in text); Memo from Beach Vasey to Governor Warren, July 3, 1947, in ibid. (Warren's annotation quoted in text); 1949 California Statutes, Extraordinary Session chap. 13 (January 6, 1950) (expanding registration requirement to persons convicted of lewd vagrancy). The state law was patterned on Los Angeles Municipal Registration Law, L.A. Code chap. V, § 52.39(a) (1945). On federal proposals for national registration, see "Are You or Have You Ever Been a Homosexual?" *One*, April 1953, 5–8.

50. 1949 California Statutes, Extra Session chap. 12 (January 6, 1950) (information-sharing law); 109 *Congressional Record* 14838 (August 13, 1963) (Senator Thurmond, inserting Rustin's booking slip into the *Record*).

51. Public Law No. 83-85, § 202(a)(1), 67 Stat. 90, 92 (1953); House Report No. 83-514, 83rd Congress, First Session (1953), 4; House Report No. 82-538, 82d Congress, First Session (1951), 19, 516; 99 *Congressional Record* 6207 (1953); Note, "Private Consensual Homosexual Behavior: The Crime and Its Enforcement," *Yale Law Journal* 70 (1960): 635 (appendix listing statutes making it a crime to invite someone of the same sex back to one's home for sexual purposes).

52. 1941 California Statutes chap. 106 (castration law for sex perverts).

53. Doreen Marie Drury, "'Experimentation on the Male Side': Race, Class, Gender, and Sexuality in Pauli Murray's Quest for Love and Identity, 1910–1960" (Ph.D. dissertation, Boston College, Department of History, December 2000), 205–10. Murray developed a good relationship with her therapist, ibid., 220–21.

54. Eskridge, *Gaylaw*, 42–43 (description of early sexual psychopath laws); 1939 California Statutes chap. 447, § 5500, amended by 1945 California Statutes chap. 138; *People v. Barnett*, 166 P.2d 4 (CSC, 1946) (early application of psychopath law to treat a sexual "invert").

55. Eskridge, *Gaylaw*, 354–55 (appendix B1, listing state sexual psychopath statutes); *Ex parte Stone*, 197 P.2d 847 (CSC, 1948) (requiring more than a sex offense charge to justify commitment as a sexual psychopath); Letter from Director of Mental Hygiene Lawrence Kolb to Governor Earl Warren, July 25, 1949, in Cal Leg Hist for 1949 California Statutes chap. 1325 (signed by the governor three days later). See also 1955 California Statutes chap. 757 (confirming that sexual psychopaths could be detained indefinitely).

56. Paul Tappan, *The Habitual Sex Offender: Report and Recommendations of the Commission on the Habitual Sex Offender* (New Jersey, 1953), 28–29; Elias S. Cohen, "Administration of the Criminal Sexual Psychopath Statute in Indiana," *Indiana Law Journal* 32 (1957): 450–56. For other useful surveys on the application of these laws to adults engaged in homosexual activities with other adults, see Rapaport and Bowman, *California Sexual Deviation Research*; *Report of the Governor's Study Commission on the Deviated Sex Offender* (Michigan, 1951); Henry M. Baker, "Sex Offenders in a Massachusetts Court," *Journal of Psychiatric Social Work* 20 (1950): 102–7; Domenico Caporale and Deryl F. Harmann, "Sexual Psychopathy—A Legal Labyrinth of Medicine, Morals, and Mythology," *Nebraska Law Review* 36 (1957): 350–51; G. Donald Niswander, "Some Aspects of 'Sexual Psychopath' Exams in New Hampshire," *New Hampshire Bar Journal* 4 (1962): 68ff.; Bernard Glueck, *Final Report: Research Project for the Study and Treatment of Persons Convicted of Crimes Involving Sexual Aberrations* (New York, 1952–55).

57. John LaStala, "Atascadero: Dachau for Queers?" *Advocate*, April 26, 1972, 11, 13 (first-hand account from former inmate); Rob Cole, "Inside Atascadero: Life, Liberty, and the Pursuit of Treatment," *Advocate*, October 11, 1972, 5; Rudolph Buki, "A Treatment Program for Homosexuals," *Diseases of the Nervous System* 25 (1964): 304–7.

58. On police techniques for gathering evidence of homosexual offenses, see Richard C. Donnelly, "Judicial Control of Informants: Spies, Stool Pigeons, and Agent Provocateurs," *Yale Law Journal* 60 (1951): 1091–1131; Harold Jacobs, Note, "Decoy Enforcement of Homosexual Laws," *University of Pennsylvania Law Review* 112 (1963): 259–84; Frank Wood Jr., "The Homosexual and the Police," *One*, May 1963, 21–22.

59. Police Report (Philadelphia) 1950, 31 (morals squad activity); Marc Stein, *City of Sisterly and Brotherly Loves: Lesbian and Gay Philadelphia, 1945–1972* (Chicago: University of Chicago Press, 2000); Kepner, *Rough News*, 377–85.

60. On aggressive police tactics, see Wood, "Homosexual and the Police," 21–22, as well as Lillian Faderman and Stuart Timmons, *Gay L.A.: A History of Sexual Outlaws, Power Politics, and Lipstick Lesbians* (New York: Basic Books, 2006), 75–97; Laud Humphreys, *Tearoom Trade: Impersonal Sex in Public Places* (Chicago: Aldine, 1970); Jess Stearn, *The Sixth Man* (Garden City, NY: Doubleday, 1961), 168; John Howard, "The Library, the Park, and the Pervert," in *Carryin' On in the Old South* (New York: NYU Press, 1997), 107–20 (police toilet spying and park surveillance in Atlanta, 1950s); Charles K. Robinson, "The Raid," *One*, July 1960, 26. The example in the text is from *People v. Earl*, 31 Cal. Rptr. 76 (CCA, 1963).

61. See Dal McIntire's [Jim Kepner's] "Tangents" column for these issues of *One*: December 1955 (Baltimore); April/May 1956 (Redwood City); April 1959 (Philadelphia); October/November 1957 (Tampa); December 1961 (San Francisco), all but the last reprinted in Kepner, *Rough News*, 86–87, 119–20, 203, 329–31. The Yuga ball raid is discussed in Jim Loughery, *The Other Side of Silence—Men's Lives and Gay Identities: A Twentieth-Century History* (New York: Henry Holt, 1998), 275–76.

62. Police Reports (NYC) 1930–61 (sodomy arrests and degeneracy arraignments); Police Reports (LA) 1940 and 1948 (sodomy, sex perversion, and lewd vagrancy arrests).

63. See Painter, *Sensibilities*, "South Carolina" (examination of South Carolina Attorney General's reports, 1946–61).

64. The thirty percent lower limit reflects the portion of sodomy arraignments in New York between 1951 and 1962 that were misdemeanors (therefore consensual) and not felonies (forcible or with minors): 688 out of 2,265. NYC Magistrates, 1951–62. The forty-five percent upper limit reflects a survey of sodomy complaints filed with or by the District of Columbia police: there were 999 complaints, 888 of which involved same-sex sodomy, 433 same-sex sodomy between an adult and a male minor, and therefore 455 same-sex sodomy between two adults. Police Reports (DC) 1950–69. Only twenty percent of the reported sodomy cases in the West National Reporter System for 1941–55 involved consenting activities), but that reflects the strong bias against taking a public appeal by those charged with the less serious form of sodomy.

65. For New York City, yearly arrests for sodomy ranged between 100 and 200; arrests for disorderly conduct–degeneracy were typically ten to twenty times those figures, and arrests for toilet loitering were five to ten times higher. See Police Reports (NYC) 1946–65. Los Angeles area prosecutions for the early 1960s suggest a multiplier of twenty. Jon Gallo et al., "The Consenting Adult Homosexual and the Law: An Empirical Study of Enforcement and Administration in Los Angeles County," *UCLA Law Review* 13 (1966): 643–832, found 439 sodomy cases in Los Angeles courts for a three-year period (1962–64), or 146 cases per year; for the period May 1964–April 1965, the study found 2,994 men prosecuted for homosexual misdemeanors (lewd vagrancy, public indecency, obscenity). Ibid., 799. Taking into account that the 439 cases involved more than 439 defendants and that the sodomy/oral perversion sample was taken from a larger countywide jurisdiction, factors that cut in different directions, one is left with about twenty charges for homosexual solicitation or expression for every charge of sodomy.

66. Leslie Feinberg, *Stone Butch Blues* (Ithaca, NY: Firebrand Books, 1993), 5–12, 33–37, 52–53, 61–63 (New York). For other first-person accounts of brutal police harassment of lesbians, see Kennedy and Davis, *Boots of Leather* (Buffalo); Eric Marcus, *Making History: The Struggle for Gay and Lesbian Equal Rights, 1945–1990, an Oral History* (New York: HarperCollins, 1992), 8 (Los Angeles).

67. Sears, *Lonely Hunters*, 24–26 (account of "Rose Levinson," a pseudonym).

68. Hoey Committee Report, appendix (civil service discharges, 1947–50); Bérubé, *Coming Out Under Fire*, 262, 354 note 14 (discharges of homosexuals from the armed forces, 1947–50). The 1949 Defense Department policy was implemented in Army Regulation 635-443 (January 12, 1950); SECNAV Instruction 1620.1 (December 10, 1949); Air Force Regulation 35-66 (January 12, 1951).

69. 96 *Congressional Record* 5699 (April 25, 1950) (Senator Wherry) (first quotation in text); ibid., 4528 (March 31, 1950) (Representative Miller) (second quotation); Jack Tait and Lee Mortimer, *Washington Confidential* (New York: Crown, 1951), 44 (third quotation). On the association of homosexuality and Communism, see Johnson, *Lavender Scare*, 30–38; John D'Emilio, "The Homosexual Menace: The Politics of Sexuality in Cold War America," in *Passion and Power: Sexuality in History* (Philadelphia: Temple University Press, 1989), 227–32.

70. Letter from James Hatcher, Civil Service Commission, Investigations Division, to Donald Webster Cory, May 3, 1951, reprinted in Cory, *The Homosexual in America* (New York: Greenberg, 1951), 269; John D'Emilio, *Sexual Politics, Sexual Communities* (Chicago: University of Chicago Press, 1970), 44. According to the Commission's personnel director, "persons about whom there is evidence that they have engaged in or solicited others to engage in homosexual or sexually perverted acts with them without evidence of rehabilitation are not suitable for Federal employment." Memorandum from D. J. Brennan Jr. to W. C. Sullivan, December 24, 1963, "Re: Mattachine Society of Washington," MSW-FBI.

71. D'Emilio, *Sexual Politics*, 45–46; Allan Bérubé and John D'Emilio, "The Military and Lesbians during the McCarthy Years," *Signs* 9 (1984): 759–74 (Kessler and other incidents in text); Jackie Cursi, "Leaping Lesbians," *Lesbian Ethics*, Fall 1986, 81–83 (quotation in text). For annual discharge rates, see Colin J. Williams and Martin S. Weinberg, *Homosexuals and the Military: A Study of Less Than Honorable Discharge* (New York: Harper & Row, 1971), 46–53.

72. Public Law No. 82-414, § 212(a)(4), 66 Stat. 163, 182 (1952) (repealed 1990); House Report No. 82-1365, 47 (1952), reprinted in 1952 *USSCAN* 1653, 1701 (quoting original McCarran bill); Senate Report No. 82-1137, 9 (1952); *Ex parte Benites*, 140 P. 436 (Nevada Supreme Court, 1914) (McCarran, J.).

73. Johnson, *Lavender Scare*, 166. Eisenhower's original exclusion of homosexuals from federal employment is Executive Order No. 10,450, § 8(a)(1)(iii), 18 *Federal Register* 2489, 2491 (April 29, 1953), codified at 3 C.F.R. 936, 938 (1949–1953); D'Emilio, *Sexual Politics*, 44. His security clearance order is Executive Order 10,865, 25 *Federal Register* 1583–84 (February 20, 1960), codified at 3 C.F.R. 398 (1959–1963), and Department of Defense Directive No. 5220.6, § VI.P (December 7, 1966).

74. *One, Inc. v. Olesen*, 241 F.2d 772 (USCA, Ninth Circuit, 1957) (agreeing with Post Office that *One* contained obscenity), summarily reversed, 355 U.S. 371 (USSC, 1958); Rodger Streitmatter, *Unspeakable: The Rise of the Gay and Lesbian Press in America* (Boston: Faber & Faber, 1995), 32 (homophile press flourished notwithstanding harassment).

75. Exclusions for engaging in "immoral conduct" are found in California Education Code §§ 13202, 13209 (certificates for state teachers), 24306(a) (state college employees) (West 1960); California Government Code § 19572(l) (civil service workers) (West 1954). The Warren-era amendments are 1951 California Statutes chap. 872 (June 4, 1951) (arrest notification); 1952 California Statutes, Extraordinary Session chap. 23 (April 17, 1952). For an early application, see *Sarac v. State Board of Education*, 57 Cal. Rptr. 69 (CCA, 1957).

76. 1959 Florida Laws chap. 59-404 (new revocation standard); 1961 Florida Laws chap. 61-396 (new expedited procedure); Florida Legislative Investigation Committee, *Homosexuality and Citizenship*, 10; Deposition of [Deponent Blacked Out], Florida Legislative Investigation Committee, February 6, 1959, in Johns Papers, Box 7; Report of the Florida Legislative Investigation Committee to the 1959 Session of the Legislature (April 13, 1959), in Johns Papers, Box 1, Folder 21; Florida Legislative Investigation Committee, Staff Memoranda, July–September 1964, in Johns Papers, Box 1, Folder 6 (final documentation of Johns Committee–backed removals).

77. Mark Hawes, Chief Counsel, "Investigation of Homosexual Activities in State Institutions" (February 2, 1959), in Johns Papers, Box 1, Folder 14; Memorandum from William Tanner, Security Officer, to Dr. Gordon Blackwell, President, University of Florida, January 31, 1961, 19–20, in Johns Papers, Box 1, Folder 13; Florida Legislative Investigation Committee, "Report: Investigation of University of South Florida" (1962), in Johns Papers, Box 1, Folder 22. Depositions of University of Florida students can be found in Johns Papers, Box 6, Folders 138–57, and Box 7, Folders 1–8. See also D'Emilio, *Lost Prophet*, 29 (Rustin's expulsion); Drury, "Pauli Murray's Quest," 161–66 (Murray's near expulsion).

78. *In re Boyd*, 307 P.2d 625 (CSC, 1957) (lawyer disbarred, lewd vagrancy); *McLaughlin v. Board of Medical Examiners*, 111 Cal. Rptr. 353 (CCA, 1973) (doctor, fondling of decoy policeman); Marcus, *Making History*, 57 (hairdresser, lewd vagrancy), 149–51 (lawyers and teachers, copulation and lewd vagrancy); Wood, "Homosexual and the Police," 21–22 (doctor, lewd indecency).

79. Sears, *Lonely Hunters*, 32.

80. *Stoumen v. Reilly*, 234 P.2d 969 (CSC, 1951) (overturning Black Cat's license revocation); 1955 California Statutes chap. 1217 (broad anti–gay bar law, quoted in text), invalidated in *Vallerga v. Department of Alcoholic Beverage Control*, 347 P.2d 909 (CSC, 1959); *Kershaw v. Department of Beverage Control*, 318 P.2d 494 (CCA, 1957).

81. *One Eleven Wines & Liquors, Inc. v. Division of Alcoholic Beverage Control*, 235 A.2d 12 (New Jersey Supreme Court, 1967) (New Jersey's aggressive regulation, starting in 1941); 1949 Texas General Laws chap. 543 (license revocation for places where sexual solicitations occur); 1956 Virginia Acts chap. 521 (license revocation for bars becoming "a meeting place" for "homosexuals" et al.). See Bérubé, *Coming Out Under Fire*, 356 note 31 (1948 Michigan rule barring licensed establishments from serving drinks to homosexuals); Chauncey, *Gay New York*, 335–54 (New York's investigations to delicense homosexual hangouts).

82. Susan Stryker and Jim Van Buskirk, *Gay by the Bay: A History of Queer Culture in the San Francisco Bay Area* (San Francisco: Chronicle Books, 1996), 31; Hal Call, "Why Perpetuate This Barbarism?" *Mattachine Review*, June 1960, 14.

83. Fred Fejes, "Murder, Perversion, and Moral Panic: The 1954 Media Campaign Against Miami's Homosexuals and the Discourse of Civic Betterment," *Journal of the History of Sexuality* 9 (2000): 305–47.

84. Ibid., 315–16 note 36; Miami Ordinance No. 45-86 (making female impersonation a crime); Miami Ordinance No. 51-35 (prohibiting bars from serving or allowing homosexuals to congregate); Miami Ordinance No. 55-21 (cross-dressing and lewd act); Bureau of Public Information, "Miami Junks the Constitution," *One*, January 1954, 16, 18–19; Lyn Pedersen, "Miami Hurricane," *One*, November 1954, 6.

85. Pedersen, "Miami Hurricane," 6; Lyn Pedersen, "Miami's New Type of Witch Hunt," *One*, April–May 1956, 6–7 (quotation in text).

86. Eskridge, "Apartheid of the Closet," 730–33 (Tampa and Miami police investigations, 1957–60); Sears, *Lonely Hunters*, 32–33 (Levinson's law practice).

87. On the precise parallels between the antihomosexual Nazi laws of 1933–45 and the antihomosexual American laws of 1935–61, see Eskridge, "Apartheid of the Closet," 766–70.

88. On the Whitman Bridge's naming, see Stein, *Sisterly and Brotherly Loves*, 138–54; ibid., 138, 144 (quotations in text).

Chapter Four: The Case(s) Against Sodomy Laws, 1935–61

1. Alfred C. Kinsey, "Biological Aspects of Some Social Problems" (draft, April 1, 1935), 21, discussed in James H. Jones, *Alfred C. Kinsey: A Public/Private Life* (New York: W. W. Norton, 1997), 305–9; Jonathan Gathorne-Hardy, *Alfred C. Kinsey: Sex the Measure of All Things* (London: Chatto & Windus, 1998), 121–22.

2. The quotations in the text are from Kinsey's lectures on "Biologic Bases of Society" and "Individual Variation," both in the Kinsey Institute Archive. On the marriage course, see Jones, *Kinsey*, 322–36; Gathorne-Hardy, *Kinsey*, 120–33.

3. On the contrast between expressive and utilitarian theories of criminal law, see Jerome Michael and Herbert Wechsler, *Criminal Law and Its Administration: Cases, Statutes, and Commentaries* (Chicago: Foundation Press, 1940), 10–11.

4. William Blackstone, *Commentaries on the Laws of England*, vol. 4 (Oxford: Clarendon Press, 1765) 125–26; Jeremy Bentham, *Theory of Legislation*, ed. by C. K. Ogden (New York: Harcourt Brace, 1931 [1821]) (appendix on "Offenses Against Taste," added by the editor from Bentham's notes, 1814–16). See David Lieberman, *The Province of Legislation Determined: Legal Theory in Eighteenth-Century Britain* (Cambridge: Cambridge University Press, 1989).

5. Jeremy Bentham, "On Paederasty" (written 1785, annotated 1816). As deciphered by Louis Crompton, the full text is published in the *Journal of Homosexuality* 3 (1978): 389–405; ibid., 4 (1978): 91–107. Page references will be to the *Journal*.

6. Bentham, "On Paederasty," 94–98 (antipathy), 389–90 (distinguishing between consensual and forcible sodomy); John Stuart Mill, *On Liberty* (New York: Prometheus Books, 1986 [1859]), chap. 4 (the libertarian presumption).

7. Bentham, "On Paederasty," 94–102; Louis Crompton, *Byron and Greek Love: Homophobia in Nineteenth-Century England* (Berkeley: University of California Press, 1985), chap. 7 (Bentham's post-1785 notes on sodomy laws).

8. Crompton, *Byron*, 44–45 (quoting Bentham); note 5 above.

9. Havelock Ellis, *Studies in the Psychology of Sex: Sexual Inversion*, 3d ed. (New York: F. A. Davis Co. 1915), 354 (quotation in text); ibid., 346–55 (the complete argument against consensual sodomy laws). For a similar argument against sodomy laws, see Richard von Krafft-Ebing, *Psychopathia Sexualis, with Especial Reference to the Antipathic Sexual Instinct: A Medico-Forensic Study* (New York: Arcade Publishing, 1998) (reprint of the Franklin S. Klaf translation of the twelfth German edition), 384–88.

10. See Xavier Mayne [Edward Stevenson], *The Intersexes: A History of Similisexualism* (Rome, 1908), 66–71; Magnus Hirschfeld, *The Homosexuality of Men and Women* (New York: Prometheus Books, 2000) (translation and reprint of the 1920 German edition), 923–52, 979–1005.

11. Ruth Benedict, *Patterns of Culture* (New York: Houghton Mifflin, 1934); Margaret Mead, *Sex and Temperament in Three Primitive Societies* (New York: W. Morrow & Co., 1935). See generally Lois W. Banner, *Intertwined Lives: Margaret Mead, Ruth Benedict, and Their Circle* (New York: Alfred A. Knopf, 2003), 285–376. For a demonstration that most cultures tolerated or accepted consensual sodomy, see Clellan S. Ford and Frank A. Beach, *Patterns of Sexual Behavior* (New York: Harper & Row, 1951), 130–31.

12. On Benedict's and Mead's knowledge of the sexologists, see Banner, *Intertwined Lives*, 119–23. On their fear of exposure as homosexuals, see ibid., 266–73 (late 1920s), 378–80 (1930s), 428–30 (threat of exposure in summer 1939).

13. Karl M. Bowman, "Psychiatric Aspects of the Problem," *Mental Hygiene* 22 (1938): 10–20; Joseph Wortis, "Sex Taboos, Sex Offenders and the Law," *American Journal of Orthopsychiatry* 9 (1939): 554–64.

14. On the rise and fall of the marriage course and Kinsey's early techniques in taking sexual histories, see Jones, *Kinsey*, 337–65, 397–411. On the outside financial support, see ibid., 417–64.

15. Alfred C. Kinsey, Wardell B. Pomeroy, and Clyde E. Martin, *Sexual Behavior in the Human Male* (Philadelphia: W. B. Saunders, 1948), 5.

16. Kinsey, *Human Male*, 325–26 (quotation in text). This conclusion was based upon two to three thousand psychological tests that Kinsey had earlier dismissed as unreliable. Gathorne-Hardy, *Kinsey*, 260–61. On Kinsey as a moral crusader deploying science to assault traditional morality, see Paul Robinson, *The Modernization of Sex: Havelock Ellis, Alfred Kinsey, and William Masters and Virginia Johnson* (Ithaca, NY: Cornell University Press, 1989); Jones, *Kinsey*, 465–66, 518–33.

17. Kinsey, *Human Male*, 639 (quotation in text); ibid., 650–51, based on the data in tables 141–50 and figures 162–70. Kinsey manipulated the presentation in "Homosexual Outlet" to maximize the shock of so much homosexual conduct, but it is unclear whether he slanted the sample to ensure an unrepresentative number of homosexual men. Jones, *Kinsey*, 369–90, suggests that Kinsey's regular trips into Chicago's gay bar culture to obtain sex histories skewed his sample, as did the many histories from sex offenders in prison. Wardell B. Pomeroy, *Dr. Kinsey and the Institute for Sex Research* (New Haven, CT: Yale University Press, 1982), observes that no one group materially affects the total numbers; the incidence of homosexual behavior remains about the same when prisoners are excluded from the calculations. Gathorne-Hardy, *Kinsey*, 280–82, notes that Kinsey's approach had a minuscule refusal rate; once Kinsey found a sample, he got everyone's interview. Kinsey's methodology—the face-to-face interview—ensured more truthful and complete answers than have ever been achieved either before or since his survey. Ibid., 283–86; Jones, *Kinsey*, 352–65.

18. For instance, Albert Deutsch, ed., *Sex Habits of American Men: Symposium on the Kinsey Report* (New York: Prentice-Hall, 1948) (collection of favorable reactions, from a wide array of scientific and religious perspectives); William Cochran, Frederick Mosteller and John Tukey, "Statistical Problems of the Kinsey Report," *Journal of the American Statistical Association* 48 (December 1953): 573 et seq.

19. Alfred C. Kinsey, Wardell B. Pomeroy, Clyde E. Martin, and Paul Gebhard, *Sexual Behavior in the Human Female* (Philadelphia: W. B. Saunders, 1953), 8–21 (critique of sexual psychopath and other sex crime laws), 474–75 (incidence of homosexual attraction and behavior among females in the sample).

20. Reinhold Niebuhr, "Sex and Religion in the Kinsey Report," *Christianity and Crisis*, November 2, 1953, 138 (first quotation in text); Letter from Jackson Tolby to Reinhold Niebuhr, September 13,1953, in Niebuhr Papers, Box 26 (second quotation); Billy Graham, "The Bible and Dr. Kinsey," *Moody Monthly*, November 1953, 13 (third quotation). On the critical reaction to *Human Female*, see Jones, *Kinsey*, 701–37; Gathorne-Hardy, *Kinsey*, 394–402.

21. Jones, *Kinsey*, 727–37 (federal investigation and Rockefeller Foundation defunding of Kinsey's institute). The foundation's board had come within two votes of accepting John Foster Dulles's proposal to defund Kinsey in 1951, ibid., 649–51.

22. For instance, Morris Ploscowe, *Sex and the Law* (New York: Prentice-Hall, 1951) (survey of the nation's hodgepodge of sex crimes).

23. Michael and Wechsler, *Criminal Law and Its Administration*, 10–11.

24. "Memoranda on Legislative Bills Vetoed," in *Public Papers of Governor Thomas E. Dewey* (New York, 1947), 254–56 (veto message for Senate Bill No. 2790, April 7, 1947). Dewey's anti-blackmail campaign is described in Ploscowe, *Sex and the Law*, 209–10.

25. Letter from Morris Ploscowe to Charles Breitel, Counsel to the Governor, March 31, 1947, in the "Bill Jacket" for Senate Bill No. 2790, NYPL(Law); William N. Eskridge Jr., *Gaylaw: Challenging the Apartheid of the Closet* (Cambridge, MA: Harvard University Press, 1999), 85–86 (surveying New York and D.C. cases where judges narrowly construed antihomosexual crime statutes). In 1951, Ploscowe advocated decriminalizing consensual sodomy. Ploscowe, *Sex and the Law*, 213.

26. 1950 New York Laws, chap. 525, § 15, revising New York Penal Code § 690 (forcible sodomy and sodomy with a minor remain felonies; all other sodomy, namely, that between consenting adults, is reduced to a misdemeanor); Letter from Charles J. Tobin, Secretary, New York State Catholic Welfare Committee, to Lawrence E. Walsh, Counsel to the Governor, April 4, 1950, in the "Bill Jacket" for Senate Bill No. 3372 (originally No. 2830), NYPL(Law).

27. For references to and discussion of the sex-crime study commissions of 1949–59, see William N. Eskridge Jr., "Privacy Jurisprudence and the Apartheid of the Closet, 1946–1961," *Florida State University Law Review* 24 (1997): 703–17, 773–77.

28. Telephone interview with Francis Allen, February 27, 2004; Letter from Francis Allen to William Eskridge, June 25, 2004.

29. *Report of the Illinois Commission on Sex Offenders to the 68th General Assembly of Illinois* (Springfield, March 15, 1953), 2 and 8–9 (quotations in text). The same recommendation to decriminalize private consensual sodomy was made by Paul Tappan, *The Habitual Sex Offender: Report and Recommendations of the Commission on the Habitual Sex Offender* (Trenton, NJ, 1953); Karl Bowman, California Department of Mental Hygiene, *Final Report on California Sexual Deviation Research* (Sacramento, 1954); Bernard Glueck, *Research Project for the Study and Treatment of Persons Convicted of Crimes Involving Sexual Aberrations, Final Report* (Albany, NY, 1955).

30. Herbert Wechsler, "The Challenge of a Model Penal Code," *Harvard Law Review* 65 (1952): 1097–1133 (synthesizing memoranda Wechsler had written for the ALI).

31. Louis Schwartz, book review (Kinsey, *Human Male*), *University of Pennsylvania Law Review* 96 (1948): 914–18; ALI, Minutes of the Ninetieth Meeting of the Council, March 11–14, 1953, 11, in Hand Papers, Box 120, Folder 7.

32. Associate Reporter Louis B. Schwartz, "Article 207—Sexual Offenses," Section 207.5, Submitted to the Criminal Law Advisory Group of the ALI (January 7, 1955), in ALI MPC Archive, Box 5602, Item 1.

33. Ibid., 137–38 (quotations in text from Schwartz's comment on "Deviate Sexual Gratification").

34. Ibid., 142 (explanation for retaining public homosexual solicitation as a crime); Louis B. Schwartz, "Morals Offenses and the Model Penal Code," *Columbia Law Review* 63 (1963): 669, 675 (subsequent elaboration by the associate reporter).

35. The Criminal Law Advisory Committee consisted of thirty-two members, including nine law professors and six non-law academics. Its membership was overwhelmingly northeastern (twenty-two members); only two were from the South. The American Law Institute Council had forty-one members, with no law professors. Fourteen were from the South and seven from the Midwest and Rockies. Hand Papers, Box 120, Folder 18.

36. The quotations in the text are from Model Penal Code § 213.2, Commentary (Philadelphia: ALI, 1980) (Official Draft and Revised Comments), 372. The Minutes of the Ninetyfourth Meeting of the Council, March 16–20, 1955, at 18, ALI Archive, Box 8016, Item 19, do not reveal the reasons given by the council. On the different moral philosophies of the judges who opposed Schwartz's position, see William C. Burris, *Judge John J. Parker and the Constitution* (Bessemer, AL: Colonial Press, 1987) (traditionalist); Gerald Gunther, *Learned Hand: The Man and the Judge* (New York: Alfred A. Knopf, 1994), 573–638 (liberal). See also Hand Papers, Box 88, Folder 36 ("discreet" sex for pay ought to be legal).

37. Reporter Schwartz's next draft was ALI, Model Penal Code, Tentative Draft No. 4 (April 25, 1955), 91–93 ("Sodomy and Related Offenses"), in ALI MPC Archive, Box 5607, Item 13. His "Special Note Re Consensual Sodomy Between Adults," ibid., 276–91, is almost verbatim his original comment on § 207.5.

38. The exchange between Parker and Hand is reported in Proceedings of the Thirtysecond Annual Meeting of the American Law Institute (May 18–21, 1955), 128–29.

39. Ibid., 130 (quotation in text). Afterward, Hand congratulated Parker for being "in such good form" at the meeting. Letter from Hand to Parker, June 17, 1955, in Hand Papers, Box 94, Folder 2. When Parker died, his family asked Hand to be an honorary pallbearer. Telegram, March 18, 1958, in Hand Papers, Box 94, Folder 2.

40. Model Penal Code, Official Draft and Explanatory Notes (Philadelphia: ALI, 1962); Proceedings of the Thirty-ninth Annual Meeting of the American Law Institute, May 1962, at 155. A revised version has been published as Model Penal Code and Commentaries (Official Draft and Revised Comments) (Philadelphia: ALI, 1980). The comment on § 213.2 (Deviate Sexual Intercourse by Force or Imposition) follows Professor Schwartz's 1955 comment but updates it significantly. Ibid., 357–76.

41. Illinois State and Chicago Bar Associations' Joint Committee to Revise the Illinois Criminal Code, "Committee Foreword," to Tentative Final Draft of the Proposed Illinois Revised Criminal Code of 1961 (Chicago: Burdette Smith Co., 1960), 3–6; Charles H. Bowman,

"The Illinois Criminal Code of 1961 and Code of Criminal Procedure of 1963," *University of Michigan Journal of Law Reform* 4 (1971): 461–75.

42. Home Office and Scottish Home Department, *Report of the Committee on Homosexual Offenses and Prostitution* (London: Her Majesty's Stationery Office, September 1957) (the Wolfenden Report). Like the MPC, the Wolfenden Report followed Benthamite premises, ibid., 9–10, with a formal bow to Kinsey, ibid., 11–20. Following Mill's presumption of the importance of "individual freedom of choice and action in matters of private morality," ibid., 24 (¶ 61), the committee by a near-unanimous vote proposed that "homosexual behaviour between consenting adults in private should no longer be a criminal offense." Ibid., 25 (¶ 62). The Wolfenden Report was a sensation in the United States as well as in the United Kingdom.

43. Letter from Francis A. Allen to William N. Eskridge Jr., June 25, 2004 (quotations in text); telephone interview with Francis Allen, February 27, 2004. On Chicago police harassment and blackmail of homosexuals, see David K. Johnson, "Gay Male Culture on Chicago's Near North Side in the 1930s," in Brett Beemyn, ed., *Creating a Place for Ourselves: Lesbian, Gay, and Bisexual Community Histories* (New York: Routledge, 1997), 112–13.

44. Joint Committee, Tentative Final Draft, 239 (opening commentary for Article II, Sex Crimes) (first quotation in text); ibid., 242 (commentary to proposed § 11-2, Deviate Sexual Conduct) (second quotation); ibid., 255–56 (commentary to proposed § 11-9(a)(4), Public Indecency) (final quotations). See generally Morris J. Wexler, "Sex Offenses Under the New Criminal Code," *Illinois Bar Journal* 51 (1962): 152–58.

45. On the legislative history of the Illinois code, see Charles H. Bowman, "The Illinois Criminal Code of 1961 and Code of Criminal Procedure of 1963," *University of Michigan Journal of Law Reform* 3 (1971): 461–71.

46. Interview with Frank Allen, Gainesville, Florida, March 17, 2005; Letter from Dr. Charles Bowman, June 15, 1964, in Florida State Archives, Tallahassee, Florida, series 1486, carton 2 (summarizing Illinois's experience with sodomy reform to a Florida official who had inquired) (quotations in text); Bowman, "Illinois Code," 468–71.

47. Allen interview (quotation in text). On the Daley machine, see Milton L. Rakove, *We Don't Want Nobody Nobody Sent: An Oral History of the Daley Years* (Bloomington: Indiana University Press, 1979), especially the interview with Abner Mikva, ibid., 318–29.

48. Telephone interview with Dawn Clark Netsch, February 19, 2004 (first quotation in text); telephone interview with Abner Mikva, January 21, 2004 (second quotation). See generally Charles H. Bowman, "The Illinois Criminal Code, 1961," *Illinois Bar Journal* 50 (1961–62): 34–40.

49. Stuart Timmons, *The Trouble with Harry Hay: Founder of the Modern Gay Rights Movement* (Boston: Alyson, 1990), 132–38 (quotations in text).

50. Harry Hay, Preliminary Concepts: International Bachelors' Fraternal Order for Peace & Social Dignity (1950), reprinted in Will Roscoe, ed., *Radically Gay: Gay Liberation in the Words of Its Founder* (Boston: Beacon, 1996), 63–76. On Mattachine, see Timmons, *Harry Hay*, 139–56.

51. Donald Webster Cory [Edward Sagarin], *The Homosexual in America: A Subjective Approach* (New York: Greenberg, 1951); James [Barr] Fugaté, "Release from the Navy Under Honorable Conditions," *Mattachine Review* 1:3 (May 1955): 42 (quotation in text).

52. Marvin Cutler, ed., *Homosexuals Today: A Handbook of Organizations and Publications* (Los Angeles: One, 1956), 22 (committee's public statement, quoted in text); Dale Jennings, "To

Be Accused Is to Be Guilty," *One* 1:1 (January 1953): 10–13 (second and third quotations); Timmons, *Harry Hay*, 163–71.

53. John D'Emilio, *Sexual Politics, Sexual Communities* (Chicago: University of Chicago Press, 1981), 75–91.

54. Cory, *Homosexual in America*, 54 (quotation in text).

55. "Daughters of Bilitis—Purpose," *Ladder* 1:1 (October 1956): 4 (Purpose #4). On the many DOB/Mattachine distinctions, see Phyllis Gorman, "The Daughters of Bilitis: A Description and Analysis of a Female Homophile Social Movement Organization, 1955–1963" (M.A. thesis, Ohio State University, 1985).

56. Nan Alamilla Boyd, *Wide-Open Town: A History of Queer San Francisco to 1965* (Berkeley: University of California Press, 2003), 171–76; Eskridge, "Privacy Jurisprudence," 706–7, 771–72.

57. "Your Rights in Case of Arrest," *One,* January 1954, 14; *One,* March 1961, 4–5; see Eskridge, "Privacy Jurisprudence," 703, 783–91; Martin Meeker, "Behind the Mask of Respectability: Reconsidering the Mattachine Society and Male Homophile Practice, 1950s and 1960s," *Journal of the History of Sexuality* 10:1 (2001): 79–116.

58. "A Report from the Legal Director, Mattachine Society," *San Francisco Mattachine Newsletter*, no. 31 (December 1955) (first quotation in text); [Louis Schwartz], January 1955 Draft of [MPC] Article 207 (Sexual Offenses), 137–38 (second quotation in text). Schwartz's language is repeated in March 1955 Draft of [MPC] Article 207 (Sexual Offenses), 132–33; MPC, Tentative Draft No. 4 (April 1955), 278 (the draft accepted by the ALI).

59. 1961 California Laws chap. 560, §§ 1–2.

60. Brief for Appellants, 29-31, *Poe v. Ullman* (USSC 1960 Term, No. 60), appeal dismissed on ripeness grounds, 367 U.S. 497 (USSC 1961) (Planned Parenthood's argument, penned by Professor Fowler Harper [an old friend of Kinsey] advocating a constitutional right of sexual privacy).

61. On the proliferation of lesbian and gay bars after 1945, see Lillian Faderman, *Odd Girls and Twilight Lovers: A History of Lesbian Life in Twentieth-Century America* (New York: Columbia University Press, 1991), 159–87; Arthur Leonard, "The Gay Bar and the Right to Hang Out Together," in *Sexuality and the Law: An Encyclopedia of Major Legal Cases* (New York: Garland Publishing, 1993), 191–96. For specific cities, see Gary L. Atkins, *Gay Seattle: Stories of Exile and Belonging* (Seattle: University of Washington Press, 2003), 55–67; Boyd, *Wide-Open Town*, 68–101 (San Francisco's lesbian bars), 129–46 (gay bars); Daneel Buring, *Lesbian and Gay Memphis: Building Communities Behind the Magnolia Curtain* (New York: Garland Publishing, 1997); Lillian Faderman and Stuart Timmons, *Gay L.A.: A History of Sexual Outlaws, Power Politics, and Lipstick Lesbians* (New York: Basic Books, 2006), 175–93; James T. Sears, *Lonely Hunters: An Oral History of Lesbian and Gay Southern Life, 1948–1968* (Boulder, CO: Westview Press, 1997), 12–47 (Miami); Brett Beemyn, "A Queer Capital: Race, Class, Gender, and the Changing Social Landscape of Washington's Gay Communities, 1940–1955," in *Place for Ourselves*, 183–209; Roey Thorpe, "The Changing Face of Lesbian Bars in Detroit, 1938–1965," ibid., 165–81.

62. Elizabeth Lapovsky Kennedy and Madeline Davis, *Boots of Leather, Slippers of Gold: The History of a Lesbian Community* (New York: Routledge, 1993). On the butch-femme roles, see Joan Nestle, "Butch-Femme Relationships, Sexual Courage in the 1950s," *Heresies* 2 (1981): 21–24; Esther Newton, "The Mythic Mannish Lesbian: Radclyffe Hall and the New Woman," *Signs* 9 (1984): 557–75.

63. For first-person accounts of the lesbian-affirming bar culture, see Leslie Feinberg, *Stone Butch Blues* (Ithaca, NY: Firebrand Books, 1993); Kelly Hankin, *The Girls in the Back Room* (Minneapolis: University of Minnesota Press, 2002).

64. On Kinsey's frequent forays into Chicago's gay bars in 1939–40, see Jones, *Kinsey*, 370–86. At precisely the same time, June 1939, when Kinsey started his monthly trips to Chicago, he presented a lecture on "Variation" that argued that society's intolerance of sexual variation imposed needless emotional harm on countless individuals. Ibid., 365–67. What he encountered in Chicago deepened his sense of injustice.

65. On Sarria and the Black Cat, see Boyd, *Wide-Open Town*, 20–24, 56–62, 144–46; Sherri Cavan, "Interaction in Home Territories," *Berkeley Journal of Sociology* 4 (1963): 17–32.

66. Michael R. Gorman, *The Empress Is a Man: Stories from the Life of José Sarria* (New York: Haworth Press, 1998), 162 (quoting Sarria).

67. Boyd, *Wide-Open Town*, 59 (quotation in text).

68. George Dorsey, *Christopher of San Francisco* (New York: Macmillan, 1962), 187; Del Martin, "Editorial: The Homosexual Vote," *Ladder* 4:10 (July 1960): 4–5; John D'Emilio, "Gay Politics, Gay Community: San Francisco's Experience," *Socialist Review* 55 (January/February 1981): 77–104 (placing the Christopher-Wolden campaign in a broader political context).

69. Boyd, *Wide-Open Town*, 209, quoting from Allen Brown, "The Question Man—Should We Discourage Gay Bars?" *San Francisco Chronicle*, August 6, 1960.

70. Boyd, *Wide-Open Town*, 212 (quotation in text); Guy Strait, "The Nightengale," *San Francisco News*, December 23, 1963, 4 (describing Sarria's campaign and his Gay is Good platform).

71. Allen interview.

Chapter Five: **Homo Equality and Sodomy Reform, 1961–69**

1. The account of Kameny's arrest and its consequences is taken from an interview with Dr. Franklin E. Kameny, Washington, D.C. (Northwest), January 17, 2004; Petitioner's Brief, *Kameny v. Brucker* (Supreme Court, 1960 Term, No. 676), 6–9; Respondent's Brief, ibid., 3–4 and note 4.

2. The quotations in the text are from Petitioner's Brief, *Kameny*, 24–29. For background, see David K. Johnson, *The Lavender Scare: The Cold War Persecution of Gays and Lesbians in the Federal Government* (Chicago: University of Chicago Press, 2003).

3. Petitioner's Brief, *Kameny*, 32, 34–35, 37, 49, 56 (quotations in text). See Evelyn Hooker, "The Adjustment of the Male Overt Homosexual," *Journal of Projective Techniques* 21 (1957): 18–31; Hooker, "Male Homosexuality in the Rorschach," *Journal of Projective Techniques* 22 (1958): 33–54.

4. *Kameny v. Brucker*, 365 U.S. 843 (USSC, 1961) (denying Kameny's petition for review); the Brennan Papers record no votes for Kameny's petition.

5. John D'Emilio, *Sexual Politics, Sexual Communities: The Making of a Homosexual Minority in the United States, 1940–1970* (Chicago: University of Chicago Press, 1985). For particular cities, see Gary L. Atkins, *Gay Seattle: Stories of Exile and Belonging* (Seattle: University of Washington Press, 2003), 81–128; Nan Alamilla Boyd, *Wide-Open Town: A History of Queer San Francisco to 1965* (Berkeley: University of California Press, 2003), 194–236; Lillian Faderman and Stuart Timmons, *Gay L.A.: A History of Sexual Outlaws, Power Politics, and Lipstick Lesbians* (New York: Basic Books, 2006); Johnson, *Lavender Scare*, 147–209 (Washington, D.C.);

James Sears, *The Lonely Hunters: An Oral History of Lesbian and Gay Southern Life, 1948–1968* (Boulder, CO: Westview Press, 1997) (Florida); Marc Stein, *City of Sisterly and Brotherly Loves: Lesbian and Gay Philadelphia, 1945–1972* (Chicago: University of Chicago Press, 2000).

6. Seymour Krim, "Revolt of the Homosexual," *Mattachine Review*, May 1959, 4–5, 9 (quotation in text); Charles Taylor, "The Politics of Recognition," in Amy Gutmann, ed., *Multiculturalism* (Princeton, NJ: Princeton University Press, 1994), 25–73; Nancy Fraser, "Rethinking Recognition," *New Left Review*, May/June 2000, 107–21.

7. Johnson, *Lavender Scare*, 182–83; interview with Dr. Franklin E. Kameny, Washingon, D.C. (Northwest), January 17, 2004.

8. Constitution of the Mattachine Society of Washington, art. II, § 1(a)–(c) (1962); news release from the Mattachine Society of Washington, D.C. (August 1962) (on file with the FBI, FOIA File HQ 100-403320 (Mattachine Society) § 6, Serial No. 90X).

9. Hugo Black Jr., *My Father: A Remembrance* (New York: Random House, 1975), 128 (quotations in text); Kameny interview.

10. *Mattachine Review*, September 1963, 4–10 (reprinting documents discussed in text); *Amending District of Columbia Charitable Solicitation Act: Hearings Before Subcomm. No. 4 of the House Comm. on the District of Columbia*, 88th Congress, 2d Session (1964) (hearings where Rep. Dowdy confronted MSW and its allies); "Dowdy Says Gays Behind Conviction," *Advocate*, May 10, 1972, 4 (quotation in text).

11. Telephone interview with Dr. Franklin E. Kameny (by Michael Gottlieb), October 29, 2004.

12. 109 *Congressional Record* 13968–75 (August 2, 1963) (Senator Thurmond's original charges that the March on Washington was headed by Communists and subversives); ibid., 14454–63 (August 7, 1963) (more of the same); ibid., 14836–44 (August 13, 1963) (Thurmond attacks Rustin as a "sex pervert"); see John D'Emilio, *Lost Prophet: The Life and Times of Bayard Rustin* (New York: Free Press, 2003), 338–58.

13. Kameny telephone (Gottlieb) interview.

14. Simone de Beauvoir, *The Second Sex* (New York: Random House, 1953 [English translation of the 1949 French edition]); Betty Friedan, *The Feminine Mystique* (New York: Dell, 1963). See generally Margaret Simons, *Beauvoir and* The Second Sex: *Feminism, Race and the Origins of Existentialism* (Lanham, MD: Rowman & Littlefield, 1999); Maribel Morey, "A Displaced American Feminist in Paris" (NYU School of Law, 2004).

15. *Mattachine Society of Philadelphia Newsletter*, March 1961, 1–2 (understanding lesbians and gay men as a "minority" group); *Janus Society Newsletter*, January 1962, 1–2 (principles of the renamed association). See Stein, *Sisterly and Brotherly Love*, 206–19.

16. *Janus*, February 1964, 2. See Stein, *Sisterly and Brotherly Love*, 226–58 (Janus Society under Polak's domination); Rodger Streitmatter, *Unspeakable: The Rise of the Gay and Lesbian Press in America* (Boston: Faber & Faber, 1995) (detailed account of Polak's roller-coaster career as the publisher of *Drum* and homoerotica).

17. Nancy Love, "The Invisible Sorority," *Philadelphia Magazine*, November 1967, 66–71, 84–93; A.B. & C.F., *Homophile Action League Newsletter*, November 1968, 1–2; Stein, *Sisterly and Brotherly Love*, 274–81 (the raid on Rusty's and radicalization of DOB); chapter 6, on Pennsylvania's demotion of consensual sodomy to a misdemeanor.

18. Louisiana enacted a comprehensive revision in 1942; Wisconsin in 1955; Illinois in 1961; Minnesota and New Mexico in 1963; New York in 1965; Georgia in 1968; Connecticut and Kansas in 1969. By 1969, study commissions were working on comprehensive new criminal codes, all patterned on the Model Penal Code, in Alaska, California, Colorado, Delaware, Florida, Hawaii, Idaho, Iowa, Kentucky, Maine, Maryland, Massachusetts, Michigan, Montana, New Hampshire, New Jersey, Ohio, Oregon, Pennsylvania, Rhode Island, Texas, Vermont, and Washington. See Herbert Wechsler, "Status of Substantive Penal Law Revision" (April 1971), in Keeton Papers, Box K26, Folder 5.

19. 1967 Minnesota Statutes chap. 507, revising § 609.293(5) (consensual sodomy punishable by up to one year in prison); see Maynard E. Pirsig, "Proposed Revision of the Minnesota Criminal Code," *Minnesota Law Review* 47 (1963): 417–63.

20. Minutes of the Advisory Committee to the Florida Investigative Comm., June 29–30, 1964, in Johns Papers, Box 1, Folder 15, reprinted in William N. Eskridge Jr., "Privacy Jurisprudence and the Apartheid of the Closet," *Florida State University Law Review* 24 (1997): 829–33 (appendix 6).

21. Ibid., 832–33 (recommendations and justifications of Judge Lamar Weingart's legal group). The Advisory Committee's final proposals are reprinted in ibid., 834–35. In 1965–67, the legislature considered but did not act on the committee's proposed sex crime law. For the possibly effective opposition of the state's tiny homophile group, see Sears, *Lonely Hunters*, 222–34.

22. Temporary State Commission on Revision of the Penal Law and Criminal Code, *Proposed New York Penal Law* (New York: Edward Thompson Co., 1964).

23. Telephone interview with the Honorable Richard Bartlett, March 19, 2004.

24. Catholic Welfare Committee, Memorandum with Respect to the Proposed New York State Penal Code (1964), discussed in note, "Deviate Sexual Behavior: The Desirability of Legislative Proscription?" *Albany Law Review* 30 (1966): 291–94; Bartlett telephone interview.

25. John Sibley, "Assembly Passes a Total Revision of the Penal Law," *New York Times*, June 4, 1965, 1, 20 (first quotation in text); Bartlett telephone interview (second quotation).

26. John Sibley, "Senate Accepts Ban on Adultery," *New York Times*, June 10, 1965, 43.

27. 1965 New York Laws chap. 1038 (amendment to new penal code recriminalizing consensual sodomy as a Class B misdemeanor). The letters for and against the sodomy amendment are in the "Bill Jacket" for A.I. 4973, Pr. 5148 (Volker), 1965 New York Laws, Microfilm NYPL(SS). See also 1965 N.Y. Laws chap. 1030, codified at N.Y. Penal Code § 240.35(3) (creating new crime of loitering to solicit "deviate sexual intercourse").

28. Bill Beardemphl, editorial, *Vector* 1:3 (February 1965): 6 (quotation in text); Joint Legislative Committee for Revision of the Penal Code, *Penal Code Revision Project, Tentative Draft No. 1—Division 11: Crimes Against Sexual Morality, Public Decency, and the Family* (Berkeley: University of California Press, 1967), 61–76. On SIR's principles and activities, see Boyd, *Wide-Open Town*, 213–16, 227–31; D'Emilio, *Sexual Politics*, 190–91.

29. On the New Year's day raid, see Eric Marcus, *Making History: The Struggle for Gay and Lesbian Equal Rights, 1945–1990—An Oral History* (New York: HarperCollins, 1992), 136–65 (interviews with the participants). On the outraged response, see Council of Religion and the Homosexual, "A Brief of Injustices: An Indictment of Our Society in Its Treatment of the Homosexual," *Citizens News* 4 (May 1965): 16; Boyd, *Wide-Open Town*, 231–36.

30. "The Consenting Adult Homosexual and the Law: An Empirical Study of Enforcement and Administration in Los Angeles County," *UCLA Law Review* 13 (1966): 799 (arrest statistics); see ibid., 673–85 (excellent summary of California's antihomosexual criminal laws, 1966); Faderman and Timmons, *Gay L.A.*, 154–58 (increased gay activism, 1967–68).

31. D'Emilio, *Sexual Politics*, 198; "U.S. Homophile Movement Gains National Strength," *Ladder*, April 1966, 4 (quoting the conference's resolutions).

32. Clark Polak, "The Failure," *Drum*, September 1965, 4 (quotation in text).

33. *Poe v. Ullman*, 367 U.S. 497 (USSC, 1961) (plurality opinion of Frankfurter, J., dismissing the appeal for lack of justiciability); ibid., 509 (Brennan, J., concurring the judgment); Brief for Appellants, *Poe* (USSC 1960 Term, Nos. 60–61) (Harper's brief). See David J. Garrow, *Liberty and Sexuality: The Right of Privacy and the Making of* Roe v. Wade (New York: Macmillan, 1994), 152–95.

34. *Poe*, 367 U.S., 515 (Douglas, J., dissenting) (quotation in text); see ibid., 514–15 (Douglas's linkage of constitutional protection for speech and liberty to the precepts implicit in a free society, an antitotalitarian principle).

35. Ibid., 542, 546 (Harlan, J., dissenting) (quotations in text). See Norman Dorsen, "The Second Mr. Justice Harlan: A Constitutional Conservative," *NYU Law Review* 44 (1969): 249–71.

36. Brief and Appendices for Planned Parenthood Federation of America, Inc. as *Amicus Curiae*, 8–9, *Griswold* (1964 Term, No. 496) (quotations in text); see Brief for Appellants, 62–65, ibid.; Garrow, *Liberty and Sexuality*, 196–269.

37. Conference Notes for *Griswold v. Connecticut* (1964 Term, No. 496), in Douglas Papers, Box 1347 (Argued Cases, Cert. & Conf. Memos); Conference Notes for *Griswold*, in Brennan Papers, Box I: 114, Folder 1; *Griswold v. Connecticut*, 381 U.S. 479, 482–85 (USSC, 1965) (Justice Douglas's labored recognition of a right of privacy teased out from the "penumbras" of the Bill of Rights); ibid., 485–86 (traditional protection of marital privacy).

38. *Griswold*, 381 U.S., 497 (Goldberg, J., joined by Warren, C.J., and Brennan, J., concurring), quoting *Poe*, 367 U.S., 553 (Harlan, J., dissenting) (quotation in text); *Griswold*, 381 U.S., 499–502 (Harlan, J., concurring in the judgment); ibid., 502–7 (White, J., concurring in the judgment); ibid., 507–27 (Black, J., dissenting); ibid., 527–31 (Stewart, J., dissenting).

39. "ACLU Position on Homosexuality" (January 7, 1957), in ACLU Papers, Box 1127, Folder 7, and reprinted in *Mattachine Review*, March 1957, 7. For an early example of ACLU homo-anxiety, see David Rabban, *Free Speech in Its Forgotten Years* (New York: Cambridge University Press, 1997), 302–10.

40. Allan Bérubé and John D'Emilio, "The Military and Lesbians During the McCarthy Years," *Signs* 9 (1984): 749–75 (ACLU attorneys sometimes represented lesbians witch hunted by the armed forces); *Vallerga v. Department of Alcoholic Beverage Control*, 347 P.2d 909–14 (CSC, 1959) (accepting the Lowenthals' ACLU argument that the First Amendment protects homosexuals' freedom of association).

41. Letter from David Carliner, Chairman ACLU-NCA, to Professor Norman Dorsen, February 7, 1964, ACLU Papers, Box 1011, Folder 5 (first quotation in text); ACLU Board Minutes, December 13, 1965, ibid., Box 1127, Folder 18 (second quotation); ACLU Board Minutes, November 16, 1966, ibid., Box 1127, Folder 22 (final quotation).

42. "ACLU Statement on Homosexuality" (August 31, 1967), in ACLU Papers, Box 1127, Folder 18.

43. Letter from Franklin E. Kameny, MSW, to Lynn Rosner, ACLU, September 17, 1967, and letter from Alan Reitman, Associate Director, ACLU, September 25, 1967, both in ACLU Papers, Box 1127, Folder 25.

44. *State v. Rhinehart*, 424 P.2d 906 (Washington Supreme Court, 1967). On Rhinehart's case, see Atkins, *Gay Seattle*, 85–88, 102–3, 220. On the Dorian Society, see ibid., 108–28.

45. *Buchanan v. Batchelor*, 308 F. Supp. 729, 735 (U.S. District Court, Northern District of Texas, 1970) (Dallas arrest statistics); James T. Sears, *Rebels, Rubyfruits, and Rhinestones: Queering Space in the Stonewall South* (New Brunswick, NJ: Rutgers University Press, 2001), 55–56 (Circle of Friends and the Buchanan litigation); Joyce Murdoch and Deb Price, *Courting Justice: Gay Men and Lesbians v. the Supreme Court* (New York: Basic Books, 2001), 158–61 (Buchanan).

46. *Buchanan v. Batchelor*, 308 F. Supp. 729 (U.S. District Court, Northern District of Texas, 1970) (three-judge court), vacated and remanded, 401 U.S. 989 (USSC, 1971).

47. Motion of the North American Conference of Homophile Organizations to File a Brief as *Amicus Curiae* and Brief *Amicus Curiae, Wade v. Buchanan* (USSC, 1969 Term, Nos. 289–90), 3 (quotation in text).

48. *Wade v. Buchanan*, 401 U.S. 989 (USSC, 1971) (vacating Judge Hughes's ruling that the Texas sodomy law violated the right to marital privacy); *Buchanan v. Texas*, 405 U.S. 930 (USSC, 1972), denying review to *Buchanan v. State*, 471 S.W.2d 401 (Texas Court of Criminal Appeals, 1971). On the *Buchanan* litigation and the fate of its participants, see Garrow, *Liberty and Sexuality*, 398–99; Murdoch and Price, *Courting Justice*, 158–61.

49. Petitioner's Brief, 6–9, 15, *Schlegel v. United States* (USSC, 1969 Term, No. 1257) (quotations in text); Petitioner's Brief, 5, *Adams v. Laird* (ibid., No. 1258) (incorporating the reasons given in *Schlegel*). The *Schlegel* brief, 17–18, also invoked the antidiscrimination principle of the Civil Rights Act of 1964.

50. Respondent's Brief, *Adams v. Laird* (USSC, No. 69-1258) (quotation in text); *Schlegel v. United States*, 397 U.S. 1039 (USSC, 1970) (denying the ACLU's petition for review); *Adams v. Laird*, 397 U.S. 1039 (USSC, 1970) (same).

51. 8 U.S.C. § 1212(a)(4) (excluding aliens "afflicted with psychopathic personality"). The facts of Boutilier's case are taken from the Record on Appeal in *Boutilier v. INS*, 387 U.S. 118 (USSC, 1967), and Marc Stein, "*Boutilier* and the U.S. Supreme Court's Sexual Revolution," 33–34 (draft, 2002), to be published as a chapter in *The U.S. Supreme Court's Sexual Revolution?* (forthcoming).

52. See Pub. L. No. 89-236, § 15(b), 79 Stat. 911, 919 (Oct. 5, 1965), codified at 8 U.S.C. § 1182(a)(4) (the same provision excluding aliens on grounds of psychopathic personality).

53. Brief of the Homosexual Law Reform Society of America, *Amicus Curiae*, in *Boutilier* (USSC 1966 Term, No. 440); *Boutilier*, 387 U.S., 121–23 (Clark, J., for the Court); see William N. Eskridge Jr., "Gadamer/Statutory Interpretation," *Columbia Law Review* 90 (1990): 609–81.

54. Conference Notes for *Boutilier* (1966 Term, No. 440), in Douglas Papers, Container 1391.

55. For evidence of the *Boutilier* justices' acceptance of antigay stereotypes, see *Manual Enterprises, Inc. v. Day*, 370 U.S. 478, 490 (USSC, 1962) (plurality opinion of Harlan, J.) (referring to male homosexuals as "unfortunate persons" and their erotic materials as "tawdry"); ibid., 519 (Clark, J., dissenting) (vigorously disparaging homosexuals); Black, *My Father*, 128 (Black, viewing homosexuals as subhuman); chapter 4 (Warren's antihomosexual record as governor of California); *Boutilier*, 387 U.S., 127 (Douglas, J., dissenting) (quotation in text).

56. Helen Gurley Brown, *Sex and the Single Girl* (New York: Random House, 1962). On the liberalization of sex as pleasure, see Catherine S. Chilman, *Adolescent Sexuality in a Changing American Society* (Washington, D.C.: Department of HEW Publication No. 79-1426 [NIH], 1979), as well as David Allyn, *Make Love Not War: The Sexual Revolution—An Unfettered History* (Boston: Little, Brown, 2000); Ann Ferguson, *Sexual Democracy: Women, Oppression, Revo-*

lution (Boulder, CO: Westview Press, 1991), chap. 4. On the demographic consequences of greater sexual liberalism, see Beth Bailey, *From Front Porch to Back Seat: Courtship in Twentieth-Century America* (Baltimore: Johns Hopkins University Press, 1988); Andrew J. Cherlin, *Marriage, Divorce, Remarriage*, rev. ed. (Cambridge, MA: Harvard University Press 1992); Steven Mintz and Susan Kellogg, *Domestic Revolutions: A Social History of American Family Life* (New York: Free Press, 1997); John Modell, *Into One's Own: From Youth to Adulthood in the United States, 1920–1975* (Berkeley: University of California Press, 1989); Kevin White, *Sexual Liberation or Sexual License? The American Revolt Against Victorianism* (Chicago: Ivan R. Dee, 2000).

57. William H. Masters and Virginia Johnson, *Human Sexual Response* (Boston: Little, Brown, 1966); John Heidenry, *What Wild Ecstasy: The Rise and Fall of the Sexual Revolution* (New York: Simon & Schuster, 2000), 17–39.

58. Simone de Beauvoir, *The Second Sex*; Morey, "American Feminist in Paris." See generally Catherine MacKinnon, *Toward a Feminist Theory of the State* (Cambridge, MA: Harvard University Press, 1989), 83–154 (consciousness raising); Milton Viorst, *Fire in the Streets: America in the 1960s* (New York: Simon & Schuster, 1979) (Black Power and antiwar anger).

59. Phyllis Lyon, "Del Martin," in Vern L. Bullough, ed., *Before Stonewall: Activists for Gay and Lesbian Rights in Historical Context* (New York: Harrington Park Press, 2002), 165. On the ambivalent and evolving relationship between lesbians and organization feminists, see Alice Echols, *Daring to Be Bad: Radical Feminism in America, 1967–1975* (Minneapolis: University of Minnesota Press, 1989).

60. Marcus, *Making History*, 187–90 (Rivera's story, in his own words); Martin Duberman, *Stonewall* (New York: Plume/Penguin, 1993), 20–24, 65–71 (interview-based account of Rivera's early life); Eldridge Cleaver, *Soul on Ice* (New York, 1968), 103 (quotation in text). See Amy Abugo Ongiri, "We the Family: Miscegenation, Black Nationalism, Black Masculinity, and the Black Gay Cultural Imagination," in Kostas Myrsiades and Linda Myrsiades, eds., *Race-ing Representation: Voice, History, and Sexuality* (New York: 1998), 233–36.

61. Floris W. Wood, ed., *An American Profile—Opinions and Behavior, 1972–1989* (Detroit: Gale Research Inc., 1990), 586–87. This study breaks down respondents by age; one may identify boomer children (ages 18–29 in 1973) and parents (ages 42–59 in 1973).

62. David R. Reuben, *Everything You Always Wanted to Know About Sex* (*But Were Afraid to Ask)* (New York: David McKay, 1969), 129–51; Eric Marcus, *Making History: The Struggle for Gay and Lesbian Rights 1945–1990—An Oral History* (New York: HarperCollins, 1992), 166–73 ("Dear Abby"); Douglas Auchincloss, "The Gay Crowd," in Joe David Brown, ed., *Sex in the '60s: A Candid Look at the Age of Mini-Morals* (New York: Time-Life, 1968), 65–66 (quotation in text).

63. *Report of the Commission to Revise the Criminal Statutes* (Hartford, 1967), 129. The commission was strongly critical of the existing state sodomy law, on grounds of its vagueness and indeterminate scope, its unconstitutional (*Griswold*) application to married couples, and its needless intrusion into private conduct not causing harm to others. Ibid., 134–35.

64. Hearing of the Judiciary and Government Functions Committees (Assembly and Senate), March 25, 1969, *Connecticut Joint Standing Committee Hearings (Judiciary)*, 2–9 (testimony of David Borden); ibid., 14–16 (testimony of John Williams, for the Caucus of Connecticut Democrats); ibid., 17–19 (testimony of Donald Holtman, for the Connecticut Civil Liberties Union); ibid., 33–34 (testimony of Sergeant Roach, quoted in text).

65. Telephone interview with the Honorable David Borden, May 16, 2006.

66. Connecticut General Assembly (Senate), *Proceedings 1969*, vol. 13:7, 3522 (Senator Lyddy) (quotation in text). For other senatorial statements supporting the Lyddy amendment, see ibid., 3526 (Senator Lipton), 3526–27 (Senator Caldwell), 3527–28 (Senator Dupont), 3534 (Senator Finney), 3538 (Senator Stanley), 3539 (Senator Amenta). The amendment lost on a stand-and-be-counted vote, with nineteen senators opposed. Ibid., 3541–42. See also Scott T. Fitzgibbon, "The Formless City of Plato's *Republic*," *Issues in Legal Scholarship* 5 (2004–5): article 5, www .bepress.com/ils/iss5/ (viewed November 2006), which nicely conceptualizes Lyddy's objection.

67. 1969 Connecticut Public Acts No. 828, effective January 1, 1971.

68. W. Page Keeton and William G. Reid, "Proposed Revision of the Texas Penal Code," *Texas Law Review* 45 (1967): 402 (quotation in text). See also Page Keeton and Seth S. Searcy III, "A New Penal Code for Texas," *Texas Bar Journal* (December 1970): 980–92 (summary of the committee's work). My understanding of the work of Texas's Committee on Revision of the Penal Code has been enriched by telephone interviews with Fred Cohen, June 16, 2004; Joel J. Finer, June 8, 2004; William G. Reid, April 14, 2004; and Seth S. Searcy III, April 16, 2004.

69. W. Page Keeton and Michael T. Johnson, "Preliminary Draft: Report on Sexual Offenses" (June 7, 1968), 29–31, in Keeton Papers, Box K30, Folder 1.

70. Texas Penal Code Revision Project, *Summary of Minutes*, June 28, 1968, 30, in Searcy Papers.

71. Ibid., 30; Keeton and Johnson, "Preliminary Draft," 31.

72. Minutes of June 28 meeting, 30–32 (quotations in text). Subsequent interviews with eight of the nine voting committee members, as well as Dean Keeton, are reported in Randy Von Beitel, "The Criminalization of Private Homosexual Acts: A Jurisprudential Case Study of a Decision by the Texas Bar Penal Code Revision Committee," *Human Rights* (ABA's Section of Individual Rights and Responsibilities) 6 (Fall 1976): 23–72.

73. The Kansas committee's working drafts decriminalized fornication in 1966, Wilson Papers, Box 4.1; cohabitation in 1967, ibid.; and adultery in 1968. Ibid., Box 6.1. See Doyle E. White and Paul E. Wilson, "A New Criminal Code for Kansas" [speech, 1968], 20–21 (quotation in text), also in the Wilson Papers. Dianne Rosell provided these references.

74. Ibid., Box 10.3 (Senate Bill 9, § 21-3505, Senate Committee's 1968 redraft of the consensual sodomy provision); Letter from John C. Weeks, Kansas Revisor of Statutes, to Senator Steadman Ball, December 23, 1968, in ibid., Box 9.3 (reporting on redraft to § 21-3505 along lines directed by Senator Ball). For perspective on Kansas's political pragmatism in the late 1960s, see Craig Miner, *Kansas: The History of the Sunflower State, 1854–2000* (Lawrence: University of Kansas Press, 2002).

Chapter Six: **The Crime Against Nature After Stonewall, 1969–75**

1. David Carter, *Stonewall: The Riots That Sparked the Gay Revolution* (New York: St. Martin's Press, 2004), 67–88.

2. Carter, *Stonewall*, 129–205; Bruce Voeller, "Stonewall Anniversary: Assessing the Activist Years," *Advocate*, July 12, 1979, 30 (quotation in text); see also Martin Duberman, *Stonewall* (New York: Dutton, 1993), 181–212. For contemporary accounts of the Stonewall riots, see Dick Leitsch, "First Gay Riot: Police Raid on N.Y. Club Sets Off First Gay Riot," *Advocate*, September 1969, 3; Lucian Truscott IV, "Gay Power Comes to Sheridan Square," and Howard Smith, "Full Moon Over the Stonewall," both in *Village Voice*, July 3, 1969, 1.

3. Carter, *Stonewall*, 175–77 (quotations describing the battles between police and queers), 182–94 (second night of rioting); Truscott, "Gay Power" (quoting graffiti).

4. On Ginsberg's reaction, see Carter, *Stonewall*, 195–200; David Carter, ed., *Spontaneous Mind: Selected Interviews, 1958–1996* (New York: HarperCollins, 2001), 259–72, 303–42 (interviews with Ginsberg). On Shelley and the GLF, see Dudley Clendinen and Adam Nagourney, *Out for Good: The Struggle to Build a Gay Rights Movement in America* (New York: Simon & Schuster, 1999), 28–32; Eric Marcus, *Making History: The Struggle for Gay and Lesbian Equal Rights, 1945–1990—An Oral History* (New York: HarperCollins, 1992), 175–86 (Shelley's first-person account).

5. Martha Shelley, "Gay Is Good," in Karla Jay and Allen Young, eds., *Out of the Closets: Voices of Gay Liberation* (New York: NYU Press, 2d ed., 1992 [1972]), 32–34 (first two quotations in text); Elaine Herscher, "Gay Celebration: Ex-Members Mark Liberation Front's 30th-Birthday," *San Francisco Chronicle*, April 16, 1999, A22 (quoting Shelley). On GLF groups elsewhere, see, e.g., Lillian Faderman and Stuart Timmons, *Gay L.A.: A History of Sexual Outlaws, Power Politics, and Lipstick Lesbians* (New York: Basic Books, 2006), 174–80.

6. For instance, Carl Wittman, "A Gay Manifesto," in *Out of the Closets*, 330–41. See Gayle Rubin, "Thinking Sex: Notes for a Radical Theory of the Politics of Sexuality," in Carole S. Vance, ed., *Pleasure and Danger: Exploring Female Sexuality* (Boston: Routledge & Kegan Paul, 1984), 267–319. On the post-Stonewall radical ideology, see Toby Marotta, *The Politics of Homosexuality* (Boston: Houghton Mifflin, 1981); Kay Tobin and Randy Wicker, *The Gay Crusaders* (New York: Paperback Library, 1972); Donn Teal, *The Gay Militants* (New York: Stein & Day, 1971).

7. Shelley, "Gay Is Good," 34 (quotation in text). On the critique of compulsory heterosexuality, see Radicalesbians, "The Woman-Identified Woman," in *Out of the Closets*, 172–76; Adrienne Rich, "Compulsory Heterosexuality and Lesbian Existence," *Blood, Bread, and Poetry: Selected Prose, 1979–1985* (New York: W. W. Norton & Co., 1986), 23–75. See Alice Echols, *Daring to Be Bad: Radical Feminism in America, 1967–1975* (Minneapolis: University of Minnesota Press, 1989).

8. Huey Newton, "A Letter from Huey Newton to the Revolutionary Brothers and Sisters About the Women's Liberation and Gay Liberation Movements," *Black Panther*, August 21, 1970, 5 (quotations in text); Marc Stein, *City of Sisterly and Brotherly Loves: Lesbian and Gay Philadelphia, 1945–1972* (Chicago: University of Chicago Press, 2000), 330–40. Arguing that the Panther leadership was ambivalently homoerotic is Alice Walker, "Black Panthers or Black Punks? They Ran on Empty," *New York Times*, May 5, 1993, A23.

9. Telephone interview with Marilyn Geisler Haft, February 11, 2004.

10. "Homosexuals Hold Protest in 'Village' After Raid Nets 167," *New York Times*, March 9, 1970, 29; "Koch Accuses Police Here of Harassing Homosexuals," *New York Times*, March 26, 1970, 30; David Burnham, "Knapp Says Laws Spur Police Graft: Lindsay Appointee Explains Objectives of Inquiry," *New York Times*, June 7, 1970, 65; Frank J. Prial, "Protest March by Homosexuals Sparks Disturbance in 'Village,'" *New York Times*, August 30, 1970, 49.

11. Steven A. Rosen, "Police Harassment of Homosexual Women and Men in New York City 1960–1980," *Columbia Human Rights Law Review* 12 (1980–81): 188 (quotation in text).

12. Cade Ware, "Cruise News," *Gay Blade*, January 1973, 1; Ware, "Gay Sit-In at Police Chief's Office," *Gay Blade*, April 1973, 1; "D.C. Judges Balk at Sodomy Convictions," *Advocate*, April 25, 1973, 5; "D.C. Sodomy Accord Totters," *Advocate*, September 12, 1973, 3; David K.

Johnson, "'Homosexual Citizens': Washington's Gay Community Confronts the Civil Service," *Washington History*, Fall/Winter 1994–1995, 44. See Clendinen and Nagourney, *Out for Good*, 109–24.

13. "Four-Year Sex Arrest Climb Traceable to S.F. Mayor?" *Advocate*, August 30, 1972, 12; Sasha Gregory-Lewis, "Building a Gay Politic: The San Francisco Model," *Advocate*, October 8, 1975, 27–32. See Clendinen and Nagourney, *Out for Good*, 148–63.

14. On Los Angeles's easing of sodomy-solicitation arrests, compare "LAPD Chief Compares Gays, Lepers," *Advocate*, January 5, 1972, 7 (Davis quotation in text), with Joel Tlumak, "No Police Agreement: Pines Eases Gay Prosecutions," *Advocate*, May 22, 1974, 1, and "Hollywood Lewd Busts Off 48%," *Advocate*, October 9, 1974, 5, and Faderman and Timmons, *Gay L.A.*, 214–18 (police harassment decline in long term due to gay political activism).

15. Chapters 8 (Atlanta) and 10 (Dallas and Houston); Gary L. Atkins, *Gay Seattle: A Stories of Exile and Belonging* (Seattle: University of Washington Press, 2003), 193–206; Daneel Buring, *Lesbian and Gay Memphis: Building Communities Behind the Magnolia Curtain* (New York: Garland, 1997); Stein, *Lesbian and Gay Philadelphia*.

16. On government employment discriminations against gay people, see Rhonda R. Rivera, "Our Straight-Laced Judges: The Legal Position of Homosexual Persons in the United States," *Hastings Law Journal* 30 (1979), 799–955; William N. Eskridge Jr., "Challenging the Apartheid of the Closet: Establishing Conditions for Lesbian and Gay Intimacy, Nomos, and Citizenship, 1961–1981," *Hofstra Law Review* 25 (1997), 911–30.

17. Rivera, "Straight-Laced Judges," 883–904; Nan D. Hunter and Nancy D. Polikoff, "Custody Rights of Lesbian Mothers: Legal Theory and Litigation Strategy," *Buffalo Law Review* 25 (1976): 691–733; Sasha Gregory, "Gay Mother Wins Children's Custody," *Advocate*, July 19, 1972, 6 (Camille Mitchell's case).

18. U.S. National Institute of Mental Health, Task Force on Homosexuality, Final Report (Washington, D.C., October 10, 1969), 4, 18 (quotations in text); interview with Professor Stanton Wheeler (member of the task force), Yale Law School, New Haven, CT, March 14, 2005.

19. Ronald Bayer, *Homosexuality and American Psychiatry: The Politics of Diagnosis* (Chicago: University of Chicago Press, 1981), 103–07 (the 1971 APA convention); ibid., 115–21, 129–38 (the campaign to delist homosexuality as a disease); Gary Alinder, "Gay Liberation Meets the Shrinks," in *Out of the Closets*, 141–45; Richard D. Lyons, "Psychiatrists, in a Shift, Declare Homosexuality No Mental Illness," *New York Times*, December 16, 1973, 1.

20. Interview with William Thom, New York City (Gramercy Park), December 15, 2004.

21. *In re Thom*, 350 N.Y.S.2d 1 (Appellate Division, First Department, 1973), allowing Lambda to register, on remand from *In re Thom*, 301 N.E.2d 542 (New York Court of Appeals, 1973), reversing 337 N.Y.S.2d 588 (Appellate Division, 1972); Thom interview; Ellen Ann Andersen, *Out of the Closets and into the Courts: Legal Opportunity Structure and Gay Rights Litigation* (Ann Arbor: University of Michigan Press, 2005), 1–2, 30–32.

22. Haft telephone interview; Report No. 2 of the ABA, Section of Individual Rights (1973); Thomas Coleman, "Nation's Lawyers Call for Consent Laws," *Advocate*, August 29, 1973, 1; Brief of the ABA as *Amicus Curiae, Lawrence v. Texas* (USSC, No. 02-102), 3–6.

23. ACLU Papers; Haft telephone interview; interview with Norman Dorsen, New York City (Upper West Side), June 2004; Rob Cole, "ACLU Launched on Major Gay Rights Project," *Advocate*, Nov. 21, 1973, 18.

24. Telephone interview with William Roden, February 13, 2004; "Idaho Sex Reform: Adult Consent Law Adopted; Nation's Third," *Advocate*, June 22, 1971.

25. "House Passes Criminal Code Revision Which Opponents Claim Weakens Laws," *Idaho Statesman*, February 27, 1971, 10; "Senate Passes, 23–11, Revised Crime Code," *Idaho Statesman*.

26. 1971 Colorado Session Laws chap. 121 (decriminalizing consensual sodomy but not adultery); Legislative Council, *Preliminary Revision of Colorado's Criminal Laws*, Research Publication No. 98 (Denver, November 1964), 42–43 ("deviate sexual intercourse" criminal only if accomplished by force or upon a minor), and *Criminal Laws and Indeterminate Sentencing*, Research Publication No. 113 (Denver, November 1966) (committee's first bills introduced into legislature focus on sentencing and sanity testing, with substantive criminal code reform coming later); Carroll E. Multz, "The New Colorado Criminal Code," *Colorado Lawyer*, November 1971, 1–4 (summary of new code by a primary drafter); telephone interview with Carroll E. Multz, April 14, 2004 (story of the ministers' proposal and Moore's quip).

27. 1971 Colorado Session Laws chap. 121, revising Colorado's Criminal Justice Code §§ 40-9-113(c) (loitering to solicit for deviate sexual intercourse), 40-7-208 (facility for aiding in deviate sexual intercourse), 40-7-301(d) (lewd fondling); Legislative Council, *Preliminary Revision*, 72–73 (explaining the rationales for these crimes).

28. "Delaware May Get Consent Law," *Advocate*, March 16, 1971, 4; "Consent Sex Code Signed in Delaware," *Advocate*, August 2, 1972, 1.

29. "Denver Daily Takes Hard Look at Cops' Treatment of Gays," *Advocate*, May 23, 1973, 16; "Dilemma in Denver: As Laws Fall, Arrests Soar," *Advocate*, March 28, 1973, 15 (quotation in text).

30. "Denver Sex Laws Hit by New Court Ruling," *Advocate*, April 11, 1973, 2; Joan White, "Judge Rules Homosexual Act Not Lewd If Done Privately," *Denver Post*, March 23, 1973, 16.

31. Norm Udevitz, "Council Passes Criminal Code on Preliminary Reading," *Denver Post*, November 20, 1973, 3 (Councilmember Irving Hook and Gay Coalition persuade council to drop antigay provisions from proposed municipal code); Lee Anderson, "Denver Free: Months of Legal and Political Maneuvering Pay Off as Police Chief Signs Accord to Halt Harassment," *Advocate*, November 6, 1974, 3; *People v. Gibson*, 521 P.2d 774 (Colorado Supreme Court, 1974); Jerry Gerash, "The Origins of the [Gay Community] Center—How and Why It Came About" (October 2001).

32. "Baptists Hit Proposed Ohio Consent Code," *Advocate*, May 10, 1972, 4; "Gay Sex Legalized—Ohio Law Reform," *Advocate*, January 30, 1973, 1, 17; *State v. Phipps*, 389 N.E.2d 1128 (Ohio Supreme Court, 1979), upholding against constitutional attack but narrowly interpreting Ohio's new homosexual solicitation law, Revised Code §2907.07(B).

33. See Hearing on Senate Bill No. 455 (Proposed Criminal Code) Before the Joint House and Senate Judiciary Committees and the House Law and Order Committee of the Pennsylvania Legislature, Testimony of Genevieve Blatt, Vice-Chair of the Bar Association's Committee on Crime and Juvenile Delinquency, September 30, 1971 (Pennsylvania State House Library, Harrisburg); ibid., Testimony of Sheldon B. Toll, Reporter for the Bar Association Committee (quotation in text); Comment, "Revision of the Law of Sex Crimes in Pennsylvania and New Jersey," *Dickinson Law Review* 78 (1973): 73–114. The proposed penal code was enacted on December 22, 1972. See 1972 Pennsylvania Laws 334.

34. Interview with Professor Jerry Israel, Gainesville, Florida, March 17, 2005.

35. Telephone interview with former representative J. Robert Traxler, May 17, 2005.

36. Traxler telephone interview; "Michigan Gays Attack Bill Legalizing Same-Sex Acts," *Advocate*, October 10, 1972, 2 (quotations in text); "Law Reform Push Fails in Michigan," *Advocate*, January 3, 1973, 3; "Michigan Snafu: Sodomy Repeal Awaits a Spark," *Advocate*, July 3, 1974, 9; 1974 Michigan Public Acts No. 266 (revised sexual assault law).

37. The account of the reaction against the new Idaho Criminal Code and its eventual repeal is taken from articles in the *Idaho Statesman* reporting the 1972 session of the legislature. Jamal Greene did the underlying research into the newspaper's archives.

38. Jerry Gilliland, "Criminal Code Reform Bill Bounced Back to Committee," *Idaho Statesman*, February 15, 1972, 12 ("Fabian socialists" charge), and "House Votes 33–32 to Repeal Idaho's New Criminal Code," *Idaho Statesman*, February 24, 1972, A1 (House vote).

39. John Corlett, "Bill to Repeal Criminal Code Sent to Andrus," *Idaho Statesman*, March 4, 1972, 1.

40. 1972 Idaho Laws chap. 336, reenacting Penal Code § 18-6605; "Idaho Repeals New Consenting Adults Code," *Advocate*, May 10, 1972, 3; Roden interview (quotation in text). For one of many articles making fun of the reenactment of the old code, see Richard Charnock, "Return to Old Crime Code Revives Archaic Idaho rulings," *Idaho Statesman*, March 16, 1972, B9.

41. 1973 Montana Laws chap. 513, adding Penal Code §§ 45-2-10(20), 45-5-505 (deviate sexual intercourse, defined to include only activities between persons of the same sex, a felony).

42. Statement from Eugene Enslin to the ACLU, May 22, 1976, in ACLU Papers, Box 1367, Folder 2; telephone interview with Eugene Willard Enslin, December 17, 2006.

43. The account in text is largely taken from the Enslin ACLU statement and the 2006 Enslin telephone interview, which are consistent with Morgan's and Hudson's testimony at trial, except that Morgan claimed that Enslin only fellated him. See Record on Appeal, *Enslin v. North Carolina* (USSC, No. 75-897), 8.

44. Haft telephone interview.

45. *State v. Enslin*, 214 S.E.2d 318 (North Carolina Court of Appeals, 1975); *Enslin* Supreme Court Record.

46. *Doe v. Commonwealth's Attorney*, 403 F. Supp. 1199 (U.S. District Court, Eastern District of Virginia, 1975) (three-judge court); ibid. (Mehrige, J., dissenting).

47. *Harris v. State*, 457 P.2d 638, 644–46 (Alaska Supreme Court, 1969).

48. *Franklin v. State*, 257 So. 2d 21 (Florida Supreme Court, 1971) (per curiam) (invalidating crime-against-nature law); *Thomas v. State*, 326 So. 2d 413 (Florida Supreme Court, 1975) (upholding misdemeanor conviction for oral sex as an "unnatural and lascivious act"); *Wainwright v. Stone*, 414 U.S. 21 (USSC, 1973), reversing 478 F.2d 390 (Fifth Circuit, 1973); *Canfield v. State*, 414 U.S, 991 (USSC, 1973), dismissing appeal for 506 P.2d 987 (Oklahoma Court of Criminal Appeals, 1972); *Connor v. State*, 414 U.S. 991 (USSC, 1973), dismissing appeal for 490 S.W.2d 114 (Arkansas Supreme Court, 1972).

49. *Rose v. Locke*, 423 U.S. 48, 50–52 (USSC, 1975) (per curiam) (the Court's reasoning), reversing 514 F.2d 570 (U.S. Court of Appeals for the Fifth Circuit, 1975); ibid., 53–59 (Brennan, J., dissenting); ibid., 59–60 (Stewart, J., dissenting).

50. Petition for a Writ of Certiorari, *Enslin v. North Carolina* (USSC, No. 75-897), 16–17 (Haft's void-for-vagueness argument).

51. *Eisenstadt v. Baird*, 405 U.S. 438, 445 (USSC, 1972) (quotation in text). For in-depth

Notes

discussion of the background of *Eisenstadt* and *Roe v. Wade*, see David J. Garrow, *Liberty and Sexuality: The Right to Privacy and the Making of* Roe v. Wade (New York: Macmillan, 1994), 389–599.

52. *Enslin* Petition, 11–14 (Haft's privacy arguments); Brief of Lambda Legal Defense and Education Fund, Inc. as *Amicus Curiae* in Support of Petition for a Writ of Certiorari, *Enslin v. State* (USSC, No. 75-897), 7–9 (Thom and Boggan's argument that enforcement of consensual sodomy laws comes only through abusive police practices such as those in this case).

53. Jurisdictional Statement, *Doe v. Commonwealth's Attorney* (USSC, No. 75-896), 7–8, 11, relying upon *Stanley v. Georgia*, 394 U.S. 557, 565 (USSC, 1969). For an update of Hirschkop's argument, see David Cole and William N. Eskridge Jr., "From Hand-Holding to Sodomy: First Amendment Protection of Homosexual (Expressive) Conduct," *Harvard Civil Rights–Civil Liberties Law Review* 29 (1994): 319–51.

54. *Enslin* Petition, 14–16. Haft also argued that singling out Enslin constituted an equal-protection violation. Ibid., 17–18.

55. Lambda *Amicus, Enslin* (No. 75-897), 10–12 (all quotations in text). The ACLU and Lambda made similar arguments in their briefs seeking rehearing of the Court's refusal to grant review, and there they were joined by the Brief of the National Gay Task Force as *Amicus Curiae* in Support of Petition for Rehearing, *Enslin* (No. 75-897).

56. The justices' decision whether to grant certiorari in *Enslin* was entirely discretionary. As a formal matter, *Doe* fell within the Court's mandatory jurisdiction, but the Court frequently dismissed even mandatory appeals, effectively asserting discretion over these cases as well. Today, the Court has complete discretion as to both kinds of cases.

57. Dennis J. Hutchinson, *The Man Who Once Was Whizzer White: A Portrait of Justice Byron R. White* (New York: Free Press, 2002) (White's underappreciated judicial philosophy, emphasizing the primacy of the democratic process); Mary Ann Glendon, "Partial Justice: Jurisprudence on the Supreme Court," *Commentary*, August 1994 (similar); *Ward v. Illinois*, 431 U.S. 767, 771–72 and notes 3–5 (USSC, 1977) (White, J.) (upholding state censorship of materials depicting "abnormal" sex and equating same-sex intercourse and foreplay with rape and sadomasochism).

58. *Ratchford v. Gay Lib*, 434 U.S. 1080 (USSC, 1978) (Rehnquist, J., dissenting from the denial of certiorari to *Gay Lib v. University of Missouri*, 558 F.2d 848 (U.S. Court of Appeals for the Eighth Circuit, 1977)); ibid., 1084 (quotation in text).

59. I agree with the argument for Burger's personal homophobia in Joyce Murdoch and Deb Price, *Courting Justice: Gay Men and Lesbians v. The Supreme Court* (New York: Knopf, 2001), 148–49. Tim Flanagan, Burger's official biographer, responds, "What we would identify as gay bashing today was not part of his makeup. One thing about Warren Burger that is not widely appreciated is that he rarely said anything negative or unkind about anyone." Ibid., 320 (quoting Flanagan). Flanagan misses the point. Most homophobes are nice people. Their problem is their own confused sexuality, which they take out on homosexuals as scapegoats. For a glimpse at the possibly sexual investment Burger had in Harry Blackmun, see Linda Greenhouse, *Becoming Harry Blackmun* (New York: Random House, 2005), 25–30 (Burger's hysterical reaction when Blackmun declined his invitation for the two middle-aged men to spend several weeks together, just the two of them, on an extended date in Europe).

60. See Justice Blackmun's marked-up copy of his law clerk's preliminary memo on *Enslin*, Blackmun Papers, Box 844, Folder 4. The queasiness Blackmun apparently had for homosexual "pandering" helps explain his willingness to join Rehnquist's *Ratchford* dissent.

61. John C. Jeffries Jr., *Lewis Powell, Jr.* (New York: Charles Scribner's Sons, 1994), 511–12, 528–29; conversations and interviews with assorted former law clerks of Justice Powell.

62. *Doe v. Commonwealth's Attorney*, 425 U.S. 901 (USSC, 1976) (per curiam) (summarily affirming 403 F. Supp. 1199 (U.S. District Court for the Eastern District of Virginia, 1975); *Enslin v. State*, 425 U.S. 901 (USSC, 1976) (denying review). The justices' votes in *Enslin* and *Doe* are recorded in the Blackmun Papers, Box 675, Folder 5. In addition to general biographical treatments for individual justices, I have relied on memoranda from law clerks for Justices Marshall, Powell, and Blackmun for the account in the text.

63. Enslin telephone interview.

Chapter Seven: **Gay Civil Rights and a New Politics of Preservation, 1975–86**

1. Bayard Rustin, "Feminism and Equality" (1970), in Devon W. Carbado and Donald Weise, eds., *Time on Two Crosses: The Collected Writings of Bayard Rustin* (San Francisco: Cleis Press, 2003), 237–38; Rustin, "From Montgomery to Stonewall" (1986), in ibid., 273 (first quotation in text); Rustin, "The New 'Niggers' Are Gays" (1986), in ibid., 275 (second quotation).

2. Interview with William Brown, San Francisco (Embarcadero), January 10, 2005; James Richardson, *Willie Brown: A Biography* (Berkeley: University of California Press, 1996).

3. Brown interview; interview with Phyllis Lyon and Del Martin, San Francisco (Noe Valley), January 10, 2005.

4. Telephone interview with the Reverend Carey E. Pointer, Prince George's County, Maryland, May 22, 2004; David L. Chappell, *A Stone of Hope: Prophetic Religion and the Death of Jim Crow* (Chapel Hill: University of North Carolina Press, 2004).

5. Gabriel A. Almond, R. Scott Appleby, and Emmanuel Sivan, *Strong Religion: The Rise of Fundamentalisms Around the World* (Chicago: University of Chicago Press, 2003) (a synthesis of studies compiled by the University of Chicago's Fundamentalism Project); Bruce A. Lawrence, *Defenders of God: The Fundamentalist Revolt Against the Modern Age* (San Francisco: Harper & Row, 1989). For "inside fundamentalism" accounts, see Nancy Taton Ammerman, *Southern Baptists Observed: Changing Perspectives on a Changing Denomination* (Knoxville: University of Tennessee Press, 1993); Jerry Falwell, ed., *The Fundamentalist Phenomenon: The Resurgence of Conservative Christianity* (Garden City, NY: Doubleday, 1981).

6. My history of the California sex crimes reform bill is taken from the file of documents maintained by the Senate Judiciary Committee for A.B. 489, CalLRS (1975 session of the California legislature) in Sacramento (the "Senate Committee File"), as well as the Brown interview.

7. "Police Opinion Questionnaire Completed—Here Are the Results," *Law Enforcement Journal*, July 1973 (copy available in the Assembly's Republican Caucus File for AB 489). Some of the unreported trial court opinions are discussed in "Ruling Hits California's Oral Sex Law," *Advocate*, October 11, 1972, 1; "San Diego Judge Strikes Felony Oral Copulation Law," *Advocate*, April 11, 1973.

8. Letter from California Peace Officers' Association et al. to Honorable Willie Brown Jr., February 28, 1975 (in Senate Committee Files) (objecting to Brown's bill, mainly because it would allow sexual solicitation); Letter from George H. Murphy, Legislative Counsel of California, to Honorable Willie Brown Jr., March 5, 1975 (opining that Brown's bill would have no effect on the state's sexual solicitation provisions); "Assembly Passes Bill to Decriminalize Sex Acts," *Los Angeles Daily Journal*, March 10, 1975, 3 (reporting arguments made by supporters and opponents, as well as final vote).

9. Letter from Wyn Rummler to Honorable Alfred H. Song, Senate Judiciary Committee, March 28, 1975 (Senate Committee File); David A. Depew, "Analysis of AB-489" [for the Senate Judiciary Committee], April 1975 (rated "X" by its author) (Senate Committee File) (leading testimony against the Brown bill); "Consenting Sex Acts Legality Bill Gains," *Sacramento Bee*, April 16, 1975 (reporting testimony and vote of Senate Judiciary Committee).

10. Richardson's arguments are recounted in Johanna Neuman, "Battle Over Consenting Sex Rages, Ends in Draw," *Los Angeles Daily Journal*, May 2, 1975, 1, 20; "Sex Bill Passes in Historic Senate Tie-Breaker," *Advocate*, May 21, 1975, 4.

11. "Battle Over Consenting Sex," 1, 20; Doug Dempster, "State Senate Passes Sex Acts Bill," *Sacramento Bee*, May 2, 1975, A1, A3.

12. Brown interview.

13. Brown interview; interview with former Lieutenant Governor Mervyn Dymally, (East) Los Angeles, February 24, 2007; telephone interview with Dymally, January 17, 2005; Jerry Gillam, "Dymally Breaks Tie, Senate OK's Sex Measure," *Los Angeles Times*, May 2, 1975, 1, 31.

14. "Washington Reforms Pass Senate Panel; Success Predicted," *Advocate*, April 11, 1973, 3; Randy Shilts, "Sodomy Repeal Signed by Washington Governor," *Advocate*, July 30, 1975, 5.

15. On the California sodomy recriminalization campaign, see "Church Group Starts Move to Upset Sex Law," *Sacramento Bee*, May 19, 1975; "Battle Lines Form in Sex Bill Referendum Fight," *Advocate*, June 18, 1975, 4; "Consenting Adult Sex Law Repeal Attempt Short of Signatures," *Los Angeles Daily Journal*, July 23, 1975. On the New Hampshire bill to create a new crime of "lewd" behavior between persons of the same sex, see Randy Shilts, "Legislative Report—Sodomy and Gay Rights Hit 12 State Houses," *Advocate*, March 9, 1977, 17–18.

16. "Arkansas Reinstates Most Bills Marking Time," *Advocate*, April 20, 1977, 36 (quotation in text); Bill Clinton, *My Life* (New York: Knopf, 2003), 247–48 (account of the 1977 law by the man who was Arkansas's attorney general in 1977).

17. Jerry Falwell, *Strength for the Journey: An Autobiography* (New York: Simon & Schuster, 1987), 290 (quotation in text). Reverend Falwell says that he knew racial segregation was wrong but declined to say anything against it (ibid., 298). Thomas Road was (token) integrated in 1968, and the private academy in 1969 (ibid., 298–99). Yet militant segregationist governors Lester Maddox (Georgia, 1967–71) and George Wallace (Alabama, 1963–67, 1971–79) were featured speakers on *The Old-Time Gospel Hour*. I attended services at Thomas Road on March 14, 2004, and was struck by racial diversity within the choir and the dearth of black faces in the congregation.

18. On resurgent fundamentalism and its ecumenical possibilities, see Robert Wuthnow, *The Restructuring of American Religion* (Princeton, NJ: Princeton University Press, 1988).

19. On Roman Catholic natural law, see Germain Gabriel Grisez, *Living a Christian Life* (Quincy, IL: Franciscan Press, 1993), and its early application to same-sex relations, Bernadette J. Brooten, *Love Between Women: Early Christian Responses to Female Homoeroticism* (Chicago: University of Chicago Press, 1996).

20. Nancy Taton Ammerman, *Baptist Battles: Social Change and Religious Conflict in the Southern Baptist Convention* (New Brunswick, NJ: Rutgers University Press, 1990); Robert Andrew Baker, *The Southern Baptist Convention and Its People, 1607–1972* (Nashville: Broadman Press, 1974). On traditional anti-Catholic and anti-Semitic views among Protestant fundamentalists, see George M. Marsden, *Fundamentalism and American Culture: The Shaping of Twentieth-Century Evangelicalism, 1870–1925* (New York: Oxford University Press, 1980); Will

Herberg, *Protestant, Catholic, Jew: An Essay in American Religious Sociology* (Garden City, NY: Anchor, 1960).

21. Faderman and Timmons, *Gay L.A.*, 162–65, 258–67 (MCC); "*Advocate* Survey— Religion: A Guide to the Spiritual Mainline," *Advocate*, October 6, 1976, 18–19.

22. For gay-friendly readings of the Bible, see Derrick Sherwin Bailey, *Homosexuality and the Western Christian Tradition* (London: Green, 1955); William Stacy Johnson, *A Time to Embrace: Same-Gender Unions in Religion, Law, and Politics* (Grand Rapids, MI: Eerdmans, 2006); John J. McNeill, S.J., *The Church and the Homosexual*, 4th ed. (Boston: Beacon, 1993); Eugene F. Rogers Jr., *Sexuality and the Christian Body: Their Way into the Triune God* (Malden, MA: Blackwell, 1999), 17–66; see generally Arlene Swidler, ed., *Homosexuality and World Religions* (Valley Forge, PA: Trinity Press, 1993).

23. Brooten, *Love Between Women*, 215–302; Rogers, *Sexuality and the Christian Body*, 20–21. Compare Mark D. Smith, "Ancient Bisexuality and the Interpretation of Romans 1:26–27," *Journal of the American Academy of Religion* 64 (1996): 223–56 (traditionalist reading), with Daniel Helminiak, "Ethics, Biblical and Denominational: A Response to Mark Smith," ibid. 65 (1997): 855–59, and Dale B. Martin, "Heterosexism and the Interpretation of Romans 1:18–32," *Biblical Interpretation* 3 (1995): 332–55 (gay-friendly readings).

24. On Pope John Paul II's and Cardinal Ratzinger's roles in halting liberal reform, see John L. Allen Jr., *Cardinal Ratzinger: The Vatican's Enforcer of the Faith* (New York: Continuum, 2000); David France, *Our Fathers: The Secret Life of the Catholic Church in an Age of Scandal* (New York: Broadway Books, 2004). On the fundamentalist takeover of the Southern Baptist Convention, see Oran P. Smith, *The Rise of Baptist Republicanism* (New York: NYU Press, 1997), 52–67, 164–71; ibid., 215–31 (Southern Baptist Convention resolutions and pronouncements, many of them stridently antihomosexual).

25. John M. Finnis, "Law, Morality, and 'Sexual Orientation,'" *Notre Dame Law Review* 69 (1994): 1063–69; Robert P. George, *In Defense of Natural Law* (New York: Oxford University Press, 1999); Robert P. George and Gerard V. Bradley, "Marriage and the Liberal Imagination," *Georgetown Law Journal* 84 (1995): 301–20. For a discussion of natural law and sexual morality, see Frederick Liu, "Marriage, Moral Values, and the U.S. Senate: The 'Deliberative Deficit' in American Democracy" (senior thesis, Princeton, 2005), 56–57.

26. Smith, *Baptist Republicanism*, 181–85 (the short-lived 1994 "Evangelicals and Catholics Together" accord); ibid., 185–90 (the 1995 resolution renouncing racism and making common cause between white and black Baptists).

27. Carol Felsenthal, *The Sweetheart of the Silent Majority: The Biography of Phyllis Schlafly* (Garden City, NY: Doubleday, 1981), 232–42 (Schlafly's reaction to the ERA); Falwell, *Strength for the Journey*, 334–47 (Falwell's shocked reaction to *Roe*). See Donald T. Critchlow, *Phyllis Schlafly and Grassroots Conservatism: A Woman's Crusade* (Princeton, NJ: Princeton University Press, 2005); Jerome L. Himmelstein, *To the Right: The Transformation of American Conservatism* (Berkeley: University of California Press, 1990).

28. Didi Herman, *The Antigay Agenda: Orthodox Vision and the Christian Right* (Chicago: University of Chicago Press, 1997), 25–59 (fundamentalists' construction of homosexuals in the 1960s); ibid., 60–91 (1970s); Smith, *Baptist Republicanism*, 171, 218–31 (Baptists' increasingly strident antihomosexual proclamations in 1985–97). For an early published example of the more aggressive antigay discourse, see Tim F. LaHaye, *The Unhappy Gays: What Everyone Should Know About Homosexuality* (Wheaton, IL: Tyndale House, 1978).

29. Congregation for the Doctrine of the Faith, Declaration *Persona humana* 8 (December 29, 1975) (citing Romans 1:24–27, 1 Corinthians 6:10, 1 Timothy 1:10); *Catechism of the Catholic Church*, Nos. 2358 & 2396. This philosophy was reaffirmed by Cardinal Ratzinger in Congregation for the Doctrine of the Faith, *Letter on the pastoral care of homosexual persons* (October 1, 1986); Congregation for the Doctrine of the Faith, *Considerations regarding proposals to give legal recognitions to unions between homosexual persons* (June 3, 2003).

30. The psychological needs served by "prejudice"—dealing with one's own "dirty" sexual feelings, which generate *hysterical* prejudices; distancing oneself from the Other, which generates *narcissistic* prejudices; and explaining one's own failures by reference to conspiracies, which generate *obsessional* prejudices—are explicated in Elisabeth Young-Bruehl, *The Anatomy of Prejudices* (Cambridge, MA: Harvard University Press, 1996), 200–52, discussed in chapter 1.

31. Professors Robert George and Gerard Bradley authored the Brief for the Family Research Council, Inc. and Focus on the Family as *Amici Curiae* Supporting Respondent, in *Texas v. Lawrence*, 539 U.S. 558 (USSC, Docket No. 02-102); see ibid., 3–4 (quotation in text).

32. On Mrs. Schlafly's antihomosexual arguments against the ERA, see Critchlow, *Schlafly*, 225, 229; Felsenthal, *Sweetheart of the Silent Majority*, 273–74, 289–90.

33. James T. Sears, *Rebels, Rubyfruit, and Rhinestones: Queering Space in the Stonewall South* (New Brunswick, NJ: Rutgers University Press, 2001), 119–30, 226–45.

34. "Florida Sodomy Law Dies in Legislative Deadlock," *Advocate*, May 10, 1972, 2 (failure of legislation to reinstate the crime against nature; discussion of proposed amendments); Act of May 31, 1974, Act No. 74-121, § 1, 1974 Fla. Laws 372 (recodification, with no crime-against-nature provision).

35. Sears, *Rebels, Rubyfruit*, 229–33; Clendinen and Nagourney, *Out for Good*, 291–95.

36. "Bryant's Boyfriend Tells All," *Advocate*, May 3, 1978, 7 ("why homosexuals are called fruits"); Anita Bryant, *The Anita Bryant Story: The Survival of Our Nation's Families and the Threat of Militant Homosexuality* (Old Tappan, NJ: Fleming H. Ravell Co., 1977), 13–15 (Bryant's shock at learning of the proposed gay rights ordinance); Sears, *Rebels, Rubyfruit*, 234 (Shack's response to Bryant).

37. Bryant, *Anita Bryant Story*, 16–26 (Bryant's quotations in text); Sears, *Rebels, Rubyfruit*, 233–36 (account of the January 18 meeting, and "cracker" quotation).

38. Bryant, *Anita Bryant Story*, 117 (quotations in text); see also Joe Baker, "Anita . . . With the Smiling Cheek," *Advocate*, April 20, 1977, 6.

39. Baker, "Anita," 6 (first quotation); Clendinen and Nagourney, *Out for Good*, 304 (second quotation); ibid., 306 (Falwell quotation); Sears, *Rebels, Rubyfruit*, 372 note 63 ("Deviations Are Punishable by Death"). Bryant objected that some of her statements were distorted. She gave one example. The media quoted her as saying that homosexuals were "garbage." Instead, "I said, 'If [children] are exposed to homosexuality, I might as well feed them garbage.'" Bryant, *Anita Bryant Story*, 27.

40. Sears, *Rebels, Rubyfruit*, 236–45 (critical account of Geto's strategy).

41. Bryant, *Anita Bryant Story*, 131–38. On the unusual success of antigay referenda between 1974 and 1993, see Barbara S. Gamble, "Putting Civil Rights to a Popular Vote," *American Journal of Political Science* 41 (1997): 245–69.

42. Anita Bryant, *A New Day* (Nashville: Broadman Press, 1992) (Bryant's account of her downfall); Perry Deane Young, *God's Bullies: Native Reflections on Preachers and Politics* (New York: Holt, Rinehart and Winston, 1982), 88–105 (interconnected institutions of the New Right); Falwell, *Strength for the Journey*, 356–66 (Moral Majority); Jeffrey L. Brudney and Gary

W. Copeland, "Evangelicals as a Political Force: Reagan and the 1980 Religious Vote," *Social Science Quarterly* 65 (1982): 1072–79; Stephen D. Johnson and Joseph B. Tammey, "The Christian Right and the 1980 Presidential Election," *Journal of the Scientific Study of Religion* 21 (1982): 123–31.

43. Randy Shilts, *The Mayor of Castro Street: The Life and Times of Harvey Milk* (New York: St. Martin's Press, 1982), 262–72.

44. Ibid., 275–77 (the Milk video). On the 1979 march, see Clendinen and Nagourney, *Out for Good*, 398–409.

45. On the background of the District's sodomy reform law, see *Sexual Assault Reform Act of 1981 (Council Act No. 4-69): Hearing and Disposition Before the House Committee on the District of Columbia*, 79th Congress, 1st Session (September 24, 1981), 1–6; ibid., 111–25 (reprinting the D.C. Council's committee report).

46. Telephone interview with the Reverend Carey E. Pointer, May 22, 2004.

47. Laura Sessions Stepp, "The Cardinal's Rule," *Washington Post* Magazine, May 21,1989, W20 (Hickey's conservative rule; quotation in text from Reverend Bernard Kirchman, Hickey's classmate).

48. Telephone interview with Reverend Jerry A. Moore Jr., June 9, 2004 (quotations in text). The proposed District of Columbia Sexual Assault Reform Act of 1981, D.C. Act No. 4-69, is summarized and its supporters listed in *House D.C. Hearing*, 5–6, 111–15; and 127 *Congressional Record* 22768–69 (October 1, 1981).

49. Telephone interview with Reverend Cleveland Sparrow, June 10, 2004; Pointer telephone interview.

50. Letter from Archbishop James A. Hickey, July 16, 1981, reprinted in *House D.C. Hearing*, 74, and 127 *Congressional Record* 22762–63 (October 1, 1981); ibid., 22769 (Rep. Stewart McKinney) (quoting Falwell); fund-raising letter from Jerry Falwell, August 13, 1981 (quotation in text); "House Denies D.C. Sex Bill 4–69," *Moral Majority Report (MMR)*, October 19, 1981, 4 (quoting Sparrow's letter); Keith B. Richburg, "Falwell and Moral Majority Declare War on City's 'Perverted Act,'" *Washington Post*, September 10, 1981, C9.

51. 127 *Congressional Record* 22753 (October 1, 1981) (Crane defeats McKinney's motion to table his motion to discharge, 117–292); ibid. (Crane's motion to discharge passes, 279–126); ibid. (Crane's motion to limit debate passes 106–66, then after Dellums's objection there was no quorum, 253–141).

52. 127 *Congressional Record* 22766 (October 1, 1981) (Rep. Thomas Bliley) (first quotation in text); ibid., 22749 (Rep. Bliley) (similar); ibid., 22767 (Rep. Mark Siljander) (similar); ibid., 22767–69 (Rep. Stewart McKinney) (third quotation); Michael Isikoff and Howie Kurz, "DC Sex Bill Explodes Land Mine on Home Rule Battlefield," *Washington Post*, October 26, 1981, A1 (second quotation).

53. 127 *Congressional Record* 22778–79 (October 1, 1981) (roll-call vote on House Resolution 208). Cheney and Gephardt were parents of lesbian daughters; Cheney's wife had just written a racy lesbian romance, *Sisters*. Gingrich's sister is a lesbian. Ferraro and Gore are prominent liberals whom the Democrats nominated for national office. Simon was a liberal Democrat from the first state to decriminalize consensual sodomy. Traxler was the floor manager for Michigan's proposed sodomy repeal in 1971–73.

54. See generally Robert Wuthnow, *The Restructuring of American Religion: Society and Faith Since World War II* (Princeton, NJ: Princeton University Press, 1988).

55. Dan Crane was not the only representative engaging in sexual activities with pages. At the same time, Representative Gerry Studds was engaged in sexual relations with a male page. The Moral Majority's executive vice president responded, "Both men did grave wrongs. One man publicly repented. The other 'came out of the closet' and marched in a parade thereafter with no trace of repentance. I think this makes a difference," and so conservatives were to rally around the adulterous Representative Crane, even as they condemned the unrepentant Representative Studds. Dr. Ron Godwin, "A Proper Response to Immorality," *MMR*, October 1983, 9, 18.

56. Pointer interview (homosexuals in BMC); Young, *God's Bullies*, 132–52 (homosexuals in the Christian Right). On the important moral distinction between the repentant, ashamed homosexual and the unashamed, flaunting one, see Cardinal Humberto Medeiros, "Pastoral Care for the Homosexual," in John Gallagher, ed., *Homosexuality and the Magisterium: Documents from the Vatican and U.S. Bishops, 1975–1985* (Mt. Rainier, MD: New Ways Ministry), 12–21; Archbishop James A. Hickey, "Letter on Homosexuality," ibid., 94–96; Falwell, *Strength for the Journey*, 371 (Moral Majority position); Jerry Falwell, *Listen America!* (Garden City, NY: Doubleday, 1980), 182–86.

57. Interview with Representative Barney Frank (by Michael Gottlieb), the Capitol, Washington, D.C., November 8, 2004; Randy Shilts, *And the Band Played On: Politics, People, and the AIDS Epidemic* (New York: St. Martin's Press, 1987), 85–98 (medical concern about diseases affecting gay men, August–October 1981), 171 (naming AIDS).

58. Dr. Ron Godwin, "AIDS: A Moral and Political Time Bomb," *MMR*, July 1983, 2 (first quotation in text); Dr. Paul Cameron, "Homosexuality: A Deathstyle, Not a Lifestyle," *MMR*, September 1983, 7 (second quotation).

59. Shilts, *The Band Played On*, 575–601 (Rock Hudson outed as person with AIDS, and the aftermath).

60. Public Law No. 98-473, § 131(b), 98 Stat. 1837 (October 12, 1984) (amending the D.C. Home Rule Act to require action by both chambers of Congress, and presentment to the president, in order for Congress to override a D.C. Council law); ibid., § 131(k) (nullifying previous D.C. Council laws, such as the 1981 Sexual Assault Reform Act, which had been one-house-vetoed under the original Home Rule Act); Sandra Evans, "Conferees Amend Home-Rule Legislation Change; Prevents Overturning of Criminal Convictions," *Washington Post*, October 11, 1984, C7 (background for 1984 statute).

61. The facts in Onofre's case are those established at the trial court hearings, reprinted in the Record on Appeal, *People v. Onofre*, 51 N.Y. 476 (New York Court of Appeals, 1980). Compare Petition for Writ of Certiorari, *State v. Onofre*, Docket No. 80-1634 (USSC), 4–5, which depicted Evans as a "mentally retarded youth," with Brief in Opposition, ibid., 2, which objected to that characterization and demonstrated that it had no support in the Record.

62. The facts in the *Peoples/Goss* and the *Sweat* cases are those established at the trial in the two cases, reprinted in the Record on Appeal, *People v. Onofre*, 51 N.Y. 476 (New York Court of Appeals, 1980). Compare Petition for Writ of Certiorari, *State v. Onofre*, No. 80-1634 (USSC), 2–3.

63. The discussion of the role of Lambda in the *Onofre* litigation is drawn from the briefs they filed in the case, and from an interview with the Honorable Rosalyn H. Richter, New York City (Chelsea), September 20, 2004. Richter joined Lambda during the *Onofre* litigation and was Lambda's first executive director (1980–82). For judicial decisions triggering legislative sodomy reform, see *State v. Pilcher*, 242 N.W.2d 348 (Iowa Supreme Court, 1976) (striking down the consensual sodomy law, codified by 1976 Iowa Act No. 1245, chap. 4, § 526); *State v.*

Ciufini, 395 A.2d 904 (New Jersey Supreme Court, 1978) (same, codified by 1978 New Jersey Laws chap. 95, § 2C:98-2).

64. David A. J. Richards, "Unnatural Acts and the Constitutional Right to Privacy: A Moral Theory," *Fordham Law Review* 45 (1977): 1282–1348; Laurence Tribe, *American Constitutional Law* (Mineola, NY: Foundation Press, 1978), 941–48. Accord, Harry H. Wellington, "Common Law Rules and Constitutional Double Standards: Some Notes on Adjudication," *Yale Law Journal* 83 (1973): 221–311; J. Harvie Wilkinson III and G. Edward White, "Constitutional Protection for Personal Lifestyles," *Cornell Law Review* 62 (1977): 563–625.

65. *Commonwealth v. Bonadio*, 415 A.2d 47 (Pennsylvania Supreme Court, 1980), ruling that the state could not constitutionally apply its consensual sodomy (misdemeanor) law to oral sex by a female sex club performer and a male in the audience. *Bonadio* applied privacy and equal protection rights much more broadly than *Onofre* would a few months later.

66. *People v. Onofre*, 415 N.E.2d 937, 940–41 (New York Court of Appeals, 1980) (quotation in text). Rejecting the majority's privacy analysis, Judge Matthew Jasen concurred in its result on the equal protection ground (ibid., 944).

67. Ibid., 944–50 (Gabrielli, J., dissenting).

68. Justice Blackmun's Certiorari Tally Sheet for *New York v. Onofre* (No. 80-1634), in Blackmun Papers, Box 689, Folder 7; Preliminary Memorandum, from Susan G. Lahne, re: *New York v. Onofre* (No. 80-1634) and *New York v. Peoples* (No. 80-1710), 9 and handwritten addenda, Blackmun Papers, Box. 943, Folder 6 (quotations in text).

69. New York Penal Code § 240.35(3), added by 1967 New York Statutes chap. 791, § 42 (quotation in text); Joint Appendix, *State v. Uplinger* (USSC, No. 82-1724), 7–30 (Kennedy's concerns about public order). Kennedy's conclusion that cruising homosexuals disrupted public order is sharply disputed in Rhonda Copelon's Brief *Amicus Curiae* of Center for Constitutional Rights and National Lawyers Guild, in *Uplinger* (No. 82-1724).

70. *Pryor v. Municipal Court*, 599 P.2d 636 (CSC, 1979); Brief of *Amicus Curiae* National Committee for Sexual Civil Liberties, *Pryor* (L.A. 30901). See also Barry Copilow and Tom Coleman, "Enforcement of Section 647(a) of the California Penal Code by the Los Angeles Police Department" (unpublished, 1972); Toy, "Update: Enforcement of Section 647(a) of the California Penal Code by the Los Angeles Police Department" (unpublished, 1974), which established that state enforcement of the lewd vagrancy law targeted male homosexuals. *Pryor*, 599 P.2d at 644 n.8.

71. *Uplinger v. State*, 447 N.E.2d 62 (New York Court of Appeals, 1983).

72. Blackmun Papers, Box 696, Folder 4 (certiorari votes for *Uplinger*); Powell Papers, *New York v. Uplinger* File (similar listing); Preliminary Memorandum from Gary Born, re *New York v. Uplinger* (No. 82-1724), June 1, 1983, in Blackmun Papers, Box 402, Folder 10; Brief *Amicus Curiae* of the Attorney General of the State of New York, *Uplinger* (No. 82-1724).

73. *People v. Uplinger*, 467 U.S. 246 (USSC, 1984) (dismissing the writ as improvidently granted). The views of the justices in conference are based upon the notes in the Brennan Papers, Box I: 627, Folder 1 (*New York v. Uplinger*, No. 82-1724); Powell Papers, *New York v. Uplinger* File; Blackmun Papers, Box 696, Folder 4.

74. Clendinen and Nagourney, *Out for Good*, 385–90. On the novel discourse of the Briggs Initiative, see Nan D. Hunter, "Identity, Speech, and Equality," *Virginia Law Review* 79 (1993): 1695–1706; Jane S. Schacter, "The Gay Civil Rights Debate in the States: Decoding the Discourse of Equivalents," *Harvard Civil Rights–Civil Liberties Law Review* 29 (1994): 283–317.

75. Oklahoma Statutes title 70, § 6-103.15(A)(2) (definition of "public homosexual conduct"); *Brandenburg v. Ohio*, 395 U.S. 444, 447 (USSC, 1969) (quotation in text). In *Brandenburg*, the Court overturned a conviction of KKK members who called for suppression of minority races but not immediate lawless actions against them.

76. Clendinen and Nagourney, *Out for Good*, 188–98, 533 (NGTF and the Oklahoma litigation); *National Gay Task Force v. Board of Education*, 729 F.2d 1270 (U.S. Court of Appeals for the Tenth Circuit, 1984); ibid., 1276 (Barrett, J., dissenting) (quotation in text).

77. Brief for Appellee, *NGTF* (No. 83-2030), 11–22; Brief of the State of Oklahoma as *Amicus Curiae*, ibid., 3, 22 (quotation in text). The attorney general saw the law as a means to reduce "strife within a school system," ibid., 3–4, a position the school board essentially repudiated. Reply Brief of Appellant, ibid., 2–3 note 3.

78. *Board of Education of Oklahoma City v. NGTF*, 470 U.S. 903 (U.S. Supreme Court, 1985). The justices' conference discussions are taken from the notes made by Justices Brennan and Blackmun, which coincide perfectly. Brennan Papers, Box I:661, Folder 4 (*Board of Education v. NGTF*, No. 83-2030); Blackmun Papers, Box 699, Folder 5 (ibid.).

Chapter Eight: **The Crime Against Nature on Trial,** *Bowers v. Hardwick*, **1986**

1. Interview with Kathleen Blalock Hardwick (Michael's mother), Archer, Florida, March 2005; telephone interview with Kathleen Blalock Hardwick, March 20, 2004; telephone interview with Susan Browning Chriss (Michael's sister), October 6, 2006.

2. Chapter 3 (Miami's and Florida's antihomosexual Kulturkampfs); Kathleen Hardwick telephone interview.

3. Telephone interview with Susan Browning Chriss, January 2004 (quotations in text); interview with Robert Hardwick Weston (Susan Chriss's son), New York City (West Village), January 22, 2004; interview with Evan Wolfson, New York City (Chelsea), January 13, 2004.

4. Interview with Michael Bowers, Atlanta (Buckhead), January 4, 2004.

5. Kevin M. Kruse, *White Flight: Atlanta and the Making of Modern Conservatism* (Princeton, NJ: Princeton University Press, 2005), 19–41; Bayard Rustin, "The New 'Niggers' Are Gays" (1986), in Devon W. Carbado and Donald Weise, eds., *Time on Two Crosses: The Collected Writings of Bayard Rustin* (San Francisco: Cleis Press, 2003), 275.

6. B. Newman, "What's Cookin' in Atlanta—Southern Style," *Advocate*, January 22, 1981, 20–21 (quotation in text); Atlanta Archives, Series II (original records of various lesbian and gay legal groups, starting in 1979).

7. "Gay Police: Controversy Heats Up," *Advocate*, October 5, 1977, 12 (1978 policy); Lesbian/Gay Rights Chapter Meeting [with Commissioner Brown and Chief Napper], September 22, 1981, in Atlanta Archives, Series II, Subseries 6, Box 1, Folder 5.

8. September 22 meeting (quotations in text); Police/Community Action Agreement, November 3, 1981 (Commissioner Brown's proposed new policies to reduce police harassment of gays).

9. Art Harris, "The Unintended Battle of Michael Hardwick," *Washington Post*, August 21, 1986, C4 (Hardwick's and Torick's conflicting accounts of the citation); telephone interview with Kathy Wilde, February 13, 2004 (the Cove).

10. Peter Irons, *The Courage of Their Convictions* (New York: Free Press, 1988), 394–96 (Hardwick's account of his arrest); Harris, "Unintended Battle," C4 (accounts by both Hardwick and Torick).

11. Irons, *Courage of Their Convictions*, 395; Harris, "Unintended Battle," C4; Georgia Code § 16-6-2 (1984) (sodomy law and penalty).

12. Irons, *Courage of Their Convictions*, 395–96 (quotations in text); Kathleen Hardwick interview; Susan Browning Chriss interview.

13. Complaint, *Hardwick et al. v. Bowers et al.*, Civil Action No. C83-0273A (U.S. District Court for the Northern District of Georgia, filed February 14, 1983), reprinted in Joint Appendix, *Bowers v. Hardwick* (USSC, No. 85-140), 2–7.

14. On the Ad-Hoc Task Force and the "sodomy calls," see telephone interview with Abby Rubenfeld, February 13, 2004; interview with Nan D. Hunter, Brooklyn, New York, December 13, 2004; Ellen Ann Andersen, *Out of the Closets and into the Courts* (Ann Arbor: University of Michigan Press, 2005), 40–42.

15. *Lambda Update*, February 1984, 3 (quotation in text); interview with the Honorable Rosalyn Richter, New York City (Chelsea), September 2004; Andersen, *Out of the Closets*, 84–86; Patricia A. Cain, "Litigating for Lesbian and Gay Rights: A Legal History," *Virginia Law Review* 79 (1993): 1584–89.

16. *Carey v. Population Services International*, 431 U.S. 678 (USSC, 1977) (striking down state bar to making contraceptives available to minors); Brief of Plaintiffs-Appellants, *Bowers v. Hardwick* (U.S. Court of Appeals for the Eleventh Circuit, No. 83-8378); Brief of Joint *Amicus Curiae* Lambda Legal Defense and Education Fund, Inc. and National Gay Rights Advocates in Support of Plaintiffs-Appellants, ibid.

17. *Doe v. Commonwealth's Attorney*, 425 U.S. 901 (USSC, 1976) (per curiam); *Bowers v. Hardwick*, 760 F.2d 1202 (U.S. Court of Appeals for the Eleventh Circuit, May 21, 1985); see ibid., 1206–7 (standing), 1207–10 (*Doe*), 1210–13 (privacy violation). Arguing that the appeal was governed by *Doe*, Judge Phyllis Kravitch dissented. Ibid., 1213–16.

18. Letter from Michael E. Hobbs, Deputy Attorney General, Georgia, to William N. Eskridge Jr., March 7, 2005.

19. Justice White's dissent from denial of certiorari can be found in the Powell Papers, Supreme Court Files, O.T. 1985, *Bowers v. Hardwick*, Docket No. 85-140.

20. The tally sheets for the certiorari votes in *Bowers v. Hardwick* are in the Brennan Papers, Box I:693, Folder 4, and Blackmun Papers, Box 702, Folder 8. Memoranda among the justices can be found in Blackmun Papers, Box 451, Folder 7, and Powell Papers, Supreme Court Cases, *Bowers v. Hardwick*, Docket No. 85-140. Details of Justice Brennan's strategy come from an interview with Professor Larry Kramer, New York City (West Village), October 1993. (Kramer clerked for Brennan during the 1985 term; the documents are consistent with his account.)

21. The Justice Harry A. Blackmun Oral History Project (recorded 1994–95), 369, in Blackmun Papers (quotation in text); Kramer interview. The memoranda from Brennan and Burger changing their votes are in the Blackmun Papers, Box 451, Folder 7.

22. Telephone interview with Laurence Tribe, February 17, 2005.

23. Interview with Nan D. Hunter, Brooklyn, New York, December 2004; interview with Matt Coles, New York City (Chelsea), December 29, 2004; *Cleburne v. Cleburne Living Center*, 473 U.S. 432 (USSC, 1985).

24. Hunter interview; Tribe telephone interview; *Rowland v. Mad River School District*, 470 U.S. 1009 (USSC, 1985) (Brennan, J., dissenting from the denial of certiorari); Laurence H. Tribe, "The 'Fundamental Right' That Dare Not Speak Its Name," *Harvard Law Review* 117 (2004): 1951–52 (quotation in text).

25. Hunter interview.

26. Brief of Petitioner, *Bowers v. Hardwick* (USSC, No. 85-140), 2–4, 18–34 (repeated emphasis on "homosexual sodomy" and "rights of homosexuals"). The Roper Center for Public Opinion Research provided my assistant, Daniel Bird, with its data for 1985–86. Respondents in September 1985 answered that homosexuality is "basically wrong" (62%–31%). About ninety-five percent of the respondents in March 1985 answered that they would be "unhappy" if their adult daughter or son announced she or he was engaged in a "homosexual relationship."

27. Brief for Respondent, ibid., 2 (Georgia is one of nineteen states to make all sodomy a crime), 7–19 (emphasis on "intimate sexual conduct" in the "home").

28. Compare Brief for Petitioner, ibid., 19–20 (Bowers's argument), with Brief for Respondent, ibid., 9–16 (Tribe and Sullivan's reply). See *Carey v. Population Services International*, 431 U.S. 678, 711 (USSC, 1977) (Powell, J., concurring in the judgment).

29. *Zablocki v. Redhail*, 434 U.S. 374, 399 (USSC, 1978) (Powell, J., concurring in the judgment) (first quotation in text); *Brockett v. Spokane Arcades, Inc.*, 472 U.S. 491, 507 (USSC, 1985) (second quotation); ibid., 499 (third quotation); Brief for Petitioner, *Bowers v. Hardwick*, 31–34, 37–39.

30. Compare Brief for Petitioner, ibid., 36–37 (degraded practices allegedly associated with homosexuality, including AIDS), and Brief of David Robinson Jr., ibid., 29–39 (recognizing that a constitutional right to commit sodomy would encourage HIV-risky behavior and speed the AIDS epidemic), with Brief of *Amici Curiae* American Psychological Association and American Public Health Association, ibid., 19–30 (refuting associations of homosexuality with degraded practices and arguing that sodomy laws retard medical efforts to research HIV and to slow down the AIDS epidemic).

31. Brief *Amicus Curiae* on Behalf of the Lambda Legal Defense and Education Fund, Inc. [et al.], ibid., 25–30. Roberta Achtenberg and Mary Dunlap made the antigay discrimination point even more explicitly in Brief *Amicus Curiae* for Lesbian Rights Project [and other feminist groups], ibid., 21–27.

32. The discussion of the oral argument in *Bowers v. Hardwick* is based upon the audiotape of the argument reproduced in *The Supreme Court's Greatest Hits*, developed by Jerry Goldman (Chicago: Northwestern University Press, 1999) (DVD). The transcript is available from the Supreme Court and from Philip B. Kurland and Gerhard Caspar, eds., *Landmark Briefs and Arguments of the Supreme Court of the United States*, vol. 164 (Washington, D.C.: University Publications of America, 1987), 633–57. See also Hobbs letter to Eskridge; *Thompson v. Aldredge*, 187 Ga. 467 (1939), in which the Georgia Supreme Court ruled that oral sex between two women was not "sodomy" covered by the criminal law.

33. Transcript of Oral Argument in *Bowers v. Hardwick*, March 30, 1986.

34. Rubenfeld telephone interview; Wolfson interview; D.C. Code § 22-502 (1981) (oral and anal sex felonious in the District).

35. Telephone interview with Professor William J. Stuntz, February 15, 2005 (general analysis in text); Memorandum from Justice Lewis Powell to Mike Mosman, March 31, 1986, in Powell Papers, *Bowers v. Hardwick* File, 6 (first quotation in text); John C. Jeffries Jr., *Justice Lewis F. Powell, Jr.* (New York: Charles Scribner's Sons, 1994), 515 (second quotation). In *Zablocki v. Redhail*, 434 U.S. 374 (USSC, 1978), Powell refused to join an opinion articulating a right to marry, for he saw no limiting principle and feared such a right might lead to same-sex marriage. Ibid., 399.

36. Memorandum from Michael Mosman to Justice Lewis Powell, March 29, 1986, 11–12 (quotation in text), in Powell Papers, *Bowers v. Hardwick* File. Mosman followed up his argument with another post–oral argument memorandum assailing Tribe for "condescendingly" (Powell wrote "yes!" in the margin) "dismiss[ing] the state's interest in legislating some moral principle" and for offering no limiting concept for his own moral theory. Memorandum from Mike Mosman to Justice Lewis Powell, March 31, 1986, ibid.

37. Jeffries, *Powell*, 521.

38. Ibid., 522. In a presentation to a Gaylaw reading group in Washington, D.C., Dean Jeffries opined that Chinnis would probably not have "changed Powell's mind" if he had come out, but that the conversation would have been different.

39. Stuntz telephone interview; Memorandum from Bill Stuntz to Justice Lewis Powell, re: *Robinson/Powell* Argument in *Bowers v. Hardwick* (no date), in Powell Papers, *Bowers v. Hardwick* File (one of the Stuntz memos). Stuntz reports that one of his memos is missing from the Powell Papers. The cases are *Robinson v. California*, 370 U.S. 660 (USSC, 1962), and *Powell v. Texas*, 392 U.S. 514 (USSC, 1968) (statements of four dissenting justices and of Justice White, who concurred in the judgment).

40. The chief justice's remarks are taken from Brennan Papers, Box I:693, Folder 4; Blackmun Papers, Box 451, Folder 9; Powell Papers, *Bowers v. Hardwick* File. Brennan's remarks are taken from the Blackmun Papers and the Powell Papers.

41. David D. Meyer, "Justice White and the Right of Privacy: A Model of Realism and Restraint," *Catholic University Law Review* 52 (2003): 915–57; William E. Nelson, "Deference and the Limits on Deference in the Constitutional Jurisprudence of Justice Byron R. White," *University of Colorado Law Review* 58 (1987): 347; David A. J. Richards, *The Case for Gay Rights: From* Bowers *to* Lawrence *and Beyond* (Lawrence: University Press of Kansas, 2005), 83–85, 193 note 25 (personal account of Blackmun's acquaintance with gay couples).

42. The quotations in the text are from Brennan Papers, Box I:693, Folder 4; Blackmun Papers, Box 451, Folder 9.

43. The quotations in the text are from Brennan Papers, Box I:693, Folder 4; Blackmun Papers, Box 451, Folder 9. In Blackmun's notes, Stevens suggested that the Court should simply declare the Georgia law unconstitutional, rather than remand to the lower courts for a trial on the state's justifications.

44. The quotations in the text are from Brennan Papers, Box I:693, Folder 4; Blackmun Papers, Box 451, Folder 9.

45. Telephone interview with Professor Pamela Karlan, February 14, 2004.

46. Letter from Chief Justice Warren E. Burger to Justice Lewis F. Powell Jr., April 3, 1986, in Powell Papers, *Bowers v. Hardwick* File (quotations in text, including Powell's annotations); Lewis F. Powell Jr., Memorandum to the Conference, re 85–140 *Bowers v. Hardwick*, April 8, 1986, in Blackmun Papers, Box 451, Folder 7 (quoted in text).

47. Memorandum from Justice Lewis F. Powell Jr. to Mike Mosman, May 21, 1986, in Powell Papers, *Bowers v. Hardwick* File; Memorandum from Mike Mosman to Justice Lewis Powell, June 12, 1986, ibid.

48. *Bowers v. Hardwick*, 478 U.S. 186, 192 (USSC, 1986), quoting *Moore v. City of East Cleveland*, 431 U.S. 494, 503 (USSC, 1977) (plurality opinion of Powell, J.). The other quotations in the text are from *Bowers*, 478 U.S., 192, 194, 196. White's opinion distinguished *Stanley* as involving only First and Fourth Amendment rights, and not relevant to a general privacy right. Ibid., 195–96.

49. *Bowers*, 478 U.S., 196–97 (Burger, C.J., concurring).

50. Ibid., 197–98 (Powell, J., concurring); ibid., 198 note 2 (quotation in text).

51. Ibid., 199–214 (Blackmun, J., dissenting); ibid., 208 (first quotation in text); ibid., 213 (second quotation).

52. Ibid., 214–20 (Stevens, J., dissenting); ibid., 219 (quotation in text).

53. Wilde telephone interview; Robert Weston interview.

54. Letter from Arthur G. Wirth to Justice Byron White, July 25, 1986, in Blackmun Papers, Box 452, Folder 6; Letter from Mark Scott Fairchild to Justice Harry Blackmun, July 18, 1986, in Blackmun Papers, Box 452, Folder 2; Letter from Steven Cantor to Justice Lewis Powell, August 11, 1986, in Blackmun Papers, Box 452, Folder 1; Letter from Barbara Shor to Justice Byron White, July 2, 1986, in Blackmun Papers, Box 452, Folder 5.

55. Letter from Reverend Robert Nugent, S.D.S., to Justice Harry Blackmun, July 1, 1986, in Blackmun Papers, Box 452, Folder 4; Letter from Reverend Kenneth A. Bastin to Justice Harry Blackmun, June 15, 1987, in Blackmun Papers, Box 452, Folder 1.

56. Jim Galloway, "High Court Upholds State Sodomy Law," *Atlanta Journal Constitution*, July 1, 1986, A1 (quotation in text).

57. Tracy Thompson, "Homosexuals Fear Sodomy Ruling Will Have Far-Reaching Effect," *Atlanta Journal Constitution*, July 6, 1986 (Bowers quotation); Harris, "Unintended Battle of Michael Hardwick," C4 (account of Torick's lie-detector test).

58. Thompson, "Homosexuals Fear" (prison statistics); Galloway, "High Court" (Oliver statement).

59. Bowers interview; Hobbs telephone interview; Thompson, "Homosexuals Fear" (Fein quotation); *Shahar v. Bowers*, 114 F.3d 1097 (U.S. Court of Appeals for the Eleventh Circuit, en banc, 1997).

60. Letter from Matt Miller to Mr. Harry A. Blackmun, July 5, 1986; Letter from Carl Laurent to Justice Blackmun, July 5, 1986; Letter from Mrs. H. F. Mitchell to Justice Harry Blackmun, August 23, 1986. All these letters, and others like them, are in the Blackmun Papers, Box 452, Folders 8–9.

61. Charles Fried, *Order and Law: Arguing the Reagan Revolution*—A Firsthand Account (New York: Simon & Schuster, 1991), 81–84; Richard A. Posner, *Sex and Reason* (Cambridge, MA: Harvard University Press, 1992), 341–50, chapter 10 note 3; Earl Maltz, "The Prospects for a Revival of Conservative Activism in Constitutional Jurisprudence," *Georgia Law Review* 24 (1990): 645 note 95, citing thirty-three law review articles critical of *Bowers*.

62. *Dronenberg v. Zech*, 731 F.2d 1388 (U.S. Court of Appeals for the District of Columbia Circuit, 1984) (Bork, J.), which drew from White's dissent in *Moore v. City of East Cleveland*, 431 U.S. 494 (USSC, 1977), and in turn probably influenced White's opinion in *Hardwick*. (White had a photographic memory, and could have recalled whole pages, with citations, from Bork's opinion as he wrote his own.)

63. *Bowers*, 478 U.S., 214–16 (Stevens, J., dissenting); Anne Goldstein, "History, Homosexuality, and Political Values: Searching for the Hidden Determinants of *Bowers v. Hardwick*," *Yale Law Journal* 97 (1988): 1073–1103.

64. William N. Eskridge Jr., "*Hardwick* and Historiography," *Illinois Law Review* 1999: 631–702; see Ronald Hamowy, "Preventive Medicine and the Criminalization of Sexual Immorality in Nineteenth Century America," in Randy Barnett and John Hagell III, eds., *Assessing the Criminal* (Cambridge, MA: Ballinger, 1977), 39–41.

65. Arkansas, California, Georgia, Illinois, Kentucky, Louisiana, New York, and North Carolina most clearly fit the pattern in the text, but other states explicitly linked proof requirements for sodomy and rape. For instance, Illinois General Laws chap. 30, div. V, § 38; Oregon General Laws chap. XLVIII, § 216.

66. Joseph Chitty, *A Practical Treatise on Criminal Law*, vol. 2 (1836), 48–50 (collection of model sodomy indictments). On the evidence rule that consenting partners could not testify without independent corroboration, see Francis Wharton, *Treatise on the Criminal Law of the United States*, 2d ed. (1852), 443; Francis Wharton, *A Treatise on Criminal Law*, vol. 1, 8th ed., (1880), 512.

67. *Bowers*, 478 U.S., 200–205 (Blackmun, J., dissenting); *Loving v. Virginia*, 388 U.S. 1 (USSC, 1967); Richards, *Case for Gay Rights*, 81–83.

68. Plato, *Laws*, Book VIII, 835d–842a (condemning nonprocreative sex); Plato, *The Republic*, II.561c–d (when traditional moral lines blur, society becomes formless); Peter Brown, *The Body and Society: Men, Women, and Sexual Renunciation in Early Christianity* (New York: Columbia University Press, 1988), 382–83 (similar ideas among early Christians). For an over-the-top psychoanalysis of a panicked Court along these lines, see Kendall Thomas, "Corpus Juris (Hetero)sexualis: Doctrine, Discourse, and Desire in *Bowers v. Hardwick*," *GLQ* 1 (1993): 33ff.

69. For current natural-law theory's condemnation of both sodomy and antihomosexual prejudice, see, e.g., Cardinal Josef Ratzinger, Congregation for the Doctrine of the Faith, *Letter on the pastoral care of homosexual persons* (October 1, 1986).

70. Robert H. Bork, "Neutral Principles and Some First Amendment Problems," *Indiana Law Journal* (1971): 12–15; Robert H. Bork, *The Tempting of America: The Political Seduction of the Law* (New York: Free Press, 1990), 75–82.

71. *McBoyle v. United States*, 283 U.S. 25 (USSC, 1931) (due process requires notice to the citizenry as to what conduct is criminal); *Cox v. Louisiana*, 379 U.S. 559, 579 (USSC, 1965) (due process regulates selective enforcement of vague statutes).

72. *Papachristou v. City of Jacksonville*, 405 U.S. 156, 161–62, 163–64, 170 (USSC, 1972) (quotations in text); see *Smith v. Groguen*, 415 U.S. 566, 575–76 (USSC, 1974).

73. *Skinner v. Oklahoma*, 316 U.S. 535 (USSC, 1942); Victoria Nourse, *In Evil or Reckless Hands: Science, Crime, and Constitution in New Deal and War—The History of* Skinner v. Oklahoma (manuscript, 2006). For arguments that the privacy cases should protect gay people against state commandeering of their bodies or their lives, see Kenneth L. Karst, *Belonging to America: Equal Citizenship and the Constitution* (New Haven, CT: Yale University Press, 1989), 201–6, 226–27; Jed Rubenfeld, "The Right of Privacy," *Harvard Law Review* 102 (1989): 737–807.

74. On the civil discriminations against admitted homosexuals or convicted sodomites, see Nan D. Hunter et al., *The Rights of Lesbians and Gay Men: The Basic ACLU Guide to a Gay Person's Rights*, 3d ed. (Carbondale: Southern Illinois University Press, 1992); Rhonda R. Rivera, "Our Straight-Laced Judges: The Legal Position of Homosexual Persons in the United States," *Hastings Law Journal* 30 (1979): 799–955.

75. Preliminary Memorandum from David Leitch (Rehnquist clerk) on *Oklahoma v. Post*, August 1, 1986, in Blackmun Papers, Box 1083, Folder 5 (the cert pool memo, urging that the Court vacate and remand to reconsider in light of *Bowers*); Conference List for October 10, 1986, in Marshall Papers, Box 406, Folder 6 (O'Connor's request that *Post* be relisted); telephone interview with Professor Chai R. Feldblum, February 17, 2005, who clerked for Justice Blackmun during the 1986 term and read the O'Connor memorandum. I have not been able to locate that memorandum in the Blackmun Papers, however.

76. *State v. Post*, 479 U.S. 890 (USSC, October 14, 1986), denying review to *Post v. State*, 715 S.W.2d 1105 (Oklahoma Court of Criminal Appeals, 1986); see *Hinkle v. State*, 771 P.2d 232 (Oklahoma Court of Criminal Appeals, 1989) (reaffirming *Post* and distinguishing *Bowers* as involving only "homosexual sodomy").

77. *Railway Express Agency, Inc. v. New York*, 336 U.S. 106, 112 (USSC, 1949) (Jackson, J., concurring) (quotation in text).

78. Patrick Egan, Nathaniel Persily, and Kevin Wallsten, "Gay Rights," in Persily et al., ed., *Public Opinion and Constitutional Controversy* (New York: Oxford University Press, forthcoming 2008), figure 5 (media coverage of AIDS and homosexual conduct runs parallel to public opinion favoring criminalization of such conduct).

79. See Alexander M. Bickel, *The Least Dangerous Branch: The Supreme Court at the Bar of Politics* (New Haven, CT: Yale University Press, 1962), arguing that the "passive virtues" (postponing decision of political issues) enable the Court to conserve its needed political capital. Compare *Poe v. Ullman*, 367 U.S. 497 (USSC, 1961) (dismissing contraception law challenge because the lack of enforcement rendered the issue not "ripe" for the Court's decision); *Tileston v. Ullman*, 318 U.S. 44 (USSC, 1943) (dismissing contraception law challenge because the physician was not directly harmed and therefore lacked "standing").

80. For varying assessments, compare Dennis J. Hutchinson, *The Man Who Once Was Whizzer White* (1998) (White was willing to protect the rights of unmarried fathers but not homosexuals); Meyer, "Realism and Restraint" (although poorly informed, White was applying a consistent jurisprudence of restraint in *Bowers* and other cases); Kate Stith, "Byron R. White, Last of the New Deal Liberals," *Yale Law Journal* 103 (1993): 21–22 (similar).

81. Anand Agneshwar, "Ex-Justice Says He May Have Been Wrong," *National Law Journal*, November 5, 1990, 3; Jeffries, *Powell*, 530.

82. Jill Young Miller, "The Metamorphosis of Michael," *Miami Sun-Sentinel*, September 10, 1989, E1, E4 (first quotation in text); Tracie Cone, "Landmark by Design," *Miami Herald*, December 17, 1990, C1–2 (second quotation).

Chapter Nine: **The Lawyers and Sodomy Come Out of Their Closets, 1986–2003**

1. Francis J. Flaherty, "The Homosexual Lawyer," *National Law Journal*, August 2, 1982, 1; Lynn Miller, "The Legal Closet: Many Gay Law Students and Lawyers Are Coming Out and Speaking Out. But Many More Are Hiding Out," *Student Lawyer*, February 1988, 13; interview with Ruth Harlow, New York City (Midtown), November 22, 2004; telephone interview with Susan Sommer, March 14, 2005. See Derek B. Dorn, "Sexual Orientation and the Legal Academy: The Experience at Yale" (YLS SAW, June 2002), 109–45 (experiences of lesbian and gay Yale law students, 1979–86).

2. The first comprehensive surveys of gay people's constitutional rights were E. Carrington Boggan, Marilyn G. Haft, Charles Lister, and John P. Rupp, *The Rights of Gay People: The Basic ACLU Guide to a Gay Person's Rights* (New York: Discus Books, 1975) (periodically updated by the ACLU); Rhonda R. Rivera, "Our Straight-Laced Judges: The Legal Position of Homosexual Persons in the United States," *Hastings Law Journal* 30 (1979): 799–955.

3. Academic criticisms of *Bowers* include William N. Eskridge Jr., *Gaylaw: Challenging the Apartheid of the Closet* (Cambridge, MA: Harvard University Press, 1998), 149–73; Kenneth L. Karst, *Belonging to America: Equal Citizenship and the Constitution* (New Haven, CT: Yale University Press, 1989), 201–6, 226–27; Richard A. Posner, *Sex and Reason* (Cambridge, MA: Harvard University Press, 1992), 341–50; David A. J. Richards, *The Case for Gay Rights* (Lawrence: University Press of Kansas, 2005), 73–87; Eve Kosofsky Sedgwick, *The Epistemology of the Closet* (Berkeley: University of California Press, 1990), 6–7; Laurence Tribe, *American Constitutional Law* (Mineola, NY: Foundation Press, 2d ed., 1988), 1421–35; Anne Goldstein, "History, Homosexuality, and Political Values: Searching for the Hidden Determinants of *Bowers v. Hardwick*," *Yale Law Journal* 97 (1988): 1073–1103; Sylvia Law, "Homosexuality and the Social Meaning of Gender," *Wisconsin Law Review*, 1988, 187–235; Frank Michelman, "Law's Republic," *Yale Law Journal* 97 (1988): 1493–1537; Rhonda R. Rivera, "Our Straight-Laced Judges Twenty Years Later," *Hastings Law Journal* 50 (1999): 1179–98; Jed Rubenfeld, "The Right of Privacy," *Harvard Law Review* 102 (1989): 737; Kendall Thomas, "Beyond the Privacy Principle," *Columbia Law Review* 92 (1992): 1431–1516.

4. Dorn, "Experience at Yale," 142–77; Senate Judiciary Committee, *Report on the Nomination of Robert H. Bork*, Executive Report No. 100-7, 100th Congress, 1st Session (October 13, 1987); Gary McDowell, "Congress and the Courts," *Public Interest* (Summer 1990): 100 (quotation in text). See Ethan Bronner, *Battle for Justice: How the Bork Nomination Shook America* (New York: W. W. Norton, 1990); *Cardozo Law Review* 9 (1987): 1–509, collecting essays and original documents relating to the Bork nomination.

5. AEI Polls (2006); see Alan S. Yang, "The Polls—Trends: Attitudes Toward Homosexuality," *Public Opinion Quarterly* 61 (1997): 477–501 (seventy percent of Americans believed homosexual conduct is immoral).

6. Jeni Loftus, "America's Liberalization in Attitudes Toward Homosexuality, 1973 to 1998," *American Sociological Review* 66 (2001): 762–82; Gregory M. Herek and Eric K. Glunt, "Interpersonal Contact and Heterosexuals' Attitudes Toward Gay Men: Results from a National Survey," *Journal of Sex Research* 30 (1993): 239–44; Daniel E. Klein et al., "Changes in AIDS Risk Behaviors Among Homosexual Male Physicians and University Students," *American Journal of Psychiatry* 144 (1987): 742–47; William N. Eskridge Jr., *The Case for Same-Sex Marriage: From Sexual Liberty to Civilized Commitment* (New York: Free Press, 1996); Gina Kolata, "Lesbian Partners Find the Means to Be Parents," *New York Times*, January 30, 1989, A13, as corrected by Nan D. Hunter, "Lesbian Parents Prove to Be in No Way Inferior," *New York Times*, February 13, 1989, A20.

7. NORC (1994), 98–99; *The Starr Report: The Findings of Independent Counsel Kenneth W. Starr on President Clinton and the Lewinsky Affair* (New York: Public Affairs, 1998); Tamar Lewin, "Teen-Agers Alter Sexual Practices, Thinking Risks Will Be Avoided," *New York Times*, April 5, 1997, A8 (soaring incidence of oral sex among teens). For evidence that the oral and anal sex numbers are now even higher, see William D. Mosher et al., "Sexual Behavior and Selected Health Measures: Men and Women 15–44 Years of Age, United States, 2002," in Centers for Disease Control and Prevention, *Advance Data*, No. 362 (Atlanta, September 15, 2005), 1–56.

8. NORC (1994), 532–33; AEI Polls (2006) (2003 Gallup poll on same-sex marriage and Harris Interactive poll on overturning homosexual sodomy law).

9. Nan D. Hunter, "Life After *Hardwick*," *Harvard Civil Rights–Civil Liberties Law Review* 27 (1992): 531–54; interview with Nan D. Hunter, New York City (Brooklyn Heights), December 2004; interview with Paula Ettelbrick, Montreal, Canada (Centre Ville), July 28, 2006; telephone interview with Abby Rubenfeld, February 13, 2004.

10. Record on Appeal, *Commonwealth v. Wasson*, File No. 90-SC-558-TG (Kentucky Supreme Court); interview with Ernesto Scorsone, Lexington, Kentucky, December 8, 2006. The establishment is still operating, now under the name "Bar, Inc." But high above the bar, in the back, is "Johnny Angel" in purple lights.

11. Telephone interview with Ernesto Scorsone, March 7, 2005; Scorsone Lexington interview.

12. Letter from Ernesto Scorsone to William N. Eskridge Jr., August 25, 2005.

13. *Commonwealth v. Campbell*, 117 S.W. 383, 385–86 (Kentucky Court of Appeals, 1909) (quotation in text), followed in *Commonwealth v. Smith*, 173 S.W. 340 (Kentucky Court of Appeals, 1915) (consumption of beer in the back room of an office); *Hershberg v. City of Barboursville*, 133 S.W. 985 (Kentucky Court of Appeals, 1911) (cigarette smoking in one's own home).

14. Transcript of Hearing on Motion to Dismiss, *Commonwealth v. Wasson*, Fayette District Court, 1986; Scorsone Lexington interview.

15. Judge Tackett originally dismissed the appeal, but the court of appeals directed him to decide the case on the merits. *Commonwealth v. Wasson*, 785 S.W.2d 67 (1990). On June 8, 1990, Judge Tackett issued his decision on the merits. The attorney general filed an appeal with the court of appeals, and Scorsone asked the Kentucky Supreme Court to transfer the case to its final jurisdiction. The court did so on October 15, 1990.

16. My description of the Kentucky Supreme Court is drawn from off-the-record interviews with several court watchers in Lexington and at the University of Kentucky's excellent School of Law, which I visited on December 6–8, 2006.

17. Scorsone Letter; Scorsone Lexington interview. See Jennifer DiGiovanni, "Justice Charles M. Leibson and the Revival of State Constitutional Law: A Microcosm of a Movement," *Kentucky Law Journal* 86 (1998): 1009–et seq., for analysis of the Leibson-led liberal interpretation of the Kentucky Constitution. Leibson was on the court from 1983 to 1995; Stephens was chief justice from 1983 to 1998.

18. *Commonwealth v. Wasson*, 842 S.W.2d 487, 494–96 (Kentucky Supreme Court, 1992), analyzing the framing debates and Louis D. Brandeis and Samuel D. Warren, "The Right to Privacy," *Harvard Law Review* 4 (1890): 193–220; *Wasson*, 842 S.W.2d, 497 (criticism of *Bowers*), 499 (second quotation in text), 501 (remaining quotations).

19. Ibid., 503–9 (Lambert, J., dissenting); ibid., 509 (quotation in text); Jamie Lucke, "Combs Says Drug Searches Were Like 'Gestapo,'" *Lexington Herald-Leader*, September 4, 1995.

20. *Wasson*, 842 S.W.2d, 509–20 (Wintersheimer, J., dissenting); ibid., 517 (first quotation in text); ibid., 519 (second quotation, citing a Catholic religious treatise).

21. Mark R. Chellgren, "House Democrats Won't Put Sodomy Amendment on Ballot," Associated Press, March 22, 1994; Scorsone Lexington interview.

22. *Michigan Organization for Human Rights v. Kelly*, Docket No. 88-815820 CZ (Wayne County Circuit Court, 1990); interview with Paula Ettelbrick, Montreal, Canada (Centre Ville), July 28, 2006.

23. *State v. Walsh*, 713 S.W.2d 508, 512–13 (Missouri Supreme Court, July 15, 1986) (quotation in text). Justice Donnelly's opinion made clear that the court was not addressing the law's constitutionality under the Missouri Constitution. Ibid., 513.

24. Dr. Raff's testimony is in the Record on Appeal to the Kentucky Supreme Court in *Wasson*, Docket No. 90SC-558-TG, and is discussed in Brief for Appellee [Wasson], ibid., 4–5, 30–33, and in Brief for Brief for Movant [Commonwealth], ibid., 42–43. For literature supporting

Dr. Raff's testimony, see J. L. Denser, *AIDS and the Heterosexual* (Silver Spring, MD: 1991); Larry Gostin, "The Interconnected Epidemics of Drug Dependency and AIDS," *Harvard Civil Rights–Civil Liberties Law Review* 26 (1991): 113–84; Tomas J. Philipson and Richard A. Posner, *Private Choices and Public Health: The AIDS Epidemic in an Economic Perspective* (Cambridge, MA: Harvard University Press, 1993).

25. Compare *Wasson*, 842 S.W.2d at 501 (Leibson, J., for the court), with ibid., 517 (Wintersheimer, J., dissenting).

26. Centers for Disease Control and Prevention, *HIV/AIDS Surveillance Report* (Atlanta, October 1993), 6–8 (tables 3–5); George A. Conway, "Trends in HIV Prevalence Among Disadvantaged Youth," *Journal of the American Medical Association* 269 (1993): 2887–89; *Gryczan v. State*, Docket No. BDV-93-1869 (Montana District Court, Lewis and Clark County, February 16, 1995), 14–15.

27. *Campbell v. Sundquist*, 926 S.W.2d 250 (Tennessee Court of Appeals 1996, review denied); *Gryczan v. State*, 942 P.2d 112 (Montana Supreme Court, 1997); C. Everett Koop, "Surgeon General's Report on Acquired Immune Deficiency Syndrome" (Washington, D.C.: HHS, 1986). The death of the AIDS argument did not mean that gay-friendly lawyers always won their challenges, especially in the Deep South. For instance, *State v. Baxley*, 656 So.2d 973 (Louisiana Supreme Court, 1995).

28. Powell Papers, Supreme Court—Case Files, *Bowers v. Hardwick*, O.T. 1985, Docket No. 85-140 (Powell's draft footnote); Editors of the *Harvard Law Review, Sexual Orientation and the Law* (Cambridge, MA: Harvard University Press, 1989), 119; Lewin, "Lesbian Partners Find the Means to Be Parents"; Marla Hollandsworth, "Gay Men Creating Families Through Surro-Gay Arrangements: A Paradigm for Reproductive Freedom," *American University Journal of Gender and the Law* 3 (1995): 183–246; Laura Benkov, *Reinventing the Family: Lesbian and Gay Parents* (New York: Crown, 1994).

29. William N. Eskridge Jr. and Nan D. Hunter, *Sexuality, Gender, and the Law*, 2d ed. (New York: Foundation Press, 2003), 1165–88 (custody cases), 1210–26 (second-parent adoption cases); Nancy Polikoff, "This Child Does Have Two Mothers: Redefining Parenthood to Meet the Needs of Children in Lesbian-Mother and Other Nontraditional Families," *Georgetown Law Journal* 78 (1990): 459–575.

30. *Baehr v. Lewin*, 852 P.2d 44 (Hawaii Supreme Court, 1993); William N. Eskridge Jr., *Equality Practice: Civil Unions and the Future of Gay Rights* (New York: Routledge, 2002), 22–42 (backlash against *Baehr*). States immediately adopting new laws refusing to recognize out-of-state same-sex marriages included Alaska (1996), Arizona (1996), Delaware (1996), Georgia (1996), Idaho (1996), Illinois (1996), Kansas (1996), Louisiana (1996), Michigan (1996), Missouri (1996), North Carolina (1995), Oklahoma (1996), Pennsylvania (1996), South Carolina (1996), South Dakota (1996), Tennessee (1996), and Utah (1995). On DOMA, Public Law No. 104-199, 110 Stat. 2419 (1996), see Andrew Koppelman, *The Gay Rights Question in Contemporary American Law* (Chicago: University of Chicago Press, 2002).

31. E.g., Richard A. Posner, *Sex and Reason* (Cambridge, MA: Harvard University Press, 1992), 310–14; John M. Finnis, "Law, Morality, and 'Sexual Orientation,'" *Notre Dame Law Review* 69 (1994): 1049–76.

32. See *D.C. Health Care Benefits Extension Act of 1992*, Law 9-114, 39 D.C. Reg. 2861 (codified at *D.C. Code* §§ 36-1401 to 36-1408) (D.C.'s domestic partnership law); 138 *Congressional Record* 27407 (1992) (statement of Rep. Bliley, criticizing the law, quoted in text); 139 *Congressional Record* 17031 (1993) (statement of Sen. Lott, also quoted in text); Public Law No. 102-

382, tit. I, 106 Stat. 1422, 1422 (1992) (forbidding the District from funding the domestic partnership law). Every D.C. appropriations law between 1992 and 2003 contained similar language.

33. *Starr Report*, 50–54 (November 15 and 17 encounters), 79 (the Whitman gift). On subsequent oral sex episodes, see ibid., 54–55, 56–60, 66–69, 78–81.

34. Interview with Matt Coles, New York City (Chelsea), December 29, 2004.

35. Barbara S. Gamble, "Putting Civil Rights to a Popular Vote," *American Journal of Political Science* 41 (1997): 245–58.

36. See generally Stephen Bransford, *Gay Politics vs. Colorado and America: The Inside Story of Amendment 2* (Denver: Sardis Press, 1994) (inside account of Amendment 2).

37. "Colorado for Family Values, Equal Rights—Not Special Rights!" (1992) (the official ballot materials distributed to voters as an explanation of the proposed amendment, quoted in text), reprinted in Robert F. Nagel, "Playing Defense," *William and Mary Bill of Rights Journal* 6 (1997): 191–99 (appendix A); Bransford, *Gay Politics vs. Colorado*, 36–40, appendix C. Compare Hans A. Linde, "When Initiative Lawmaking Is Not 'Republican Government': The Campaign Against Homosexuality," *Oregon Law Review* 72 (1993): 19–45 (describing similar Oregon antigay initiative).

38. Lisa Keen and Suzanne B. Goldberg, *Strangers to the Law: Gay People on Trial* (Ann Arbor: University of Michigan Press, 2000), 35–38, 43–73.

39. *Evans v. Romer*, 854 P.2d 1270 (Colorado Supreme Court, 1993), cert. denied, 510 U.S. 959 (USSC, 1993) (first Amendment 2 decision).

40. Brief for Petitioners, *Romer v. Evans* (USSC, No. 94-1039), 41–43; ibid., 42 (quotation in text); see Daniel Mendelsohn, "The Stand: Expert Witnesses and Ancient Mysteries in a Colorado Courtroom," *Lingua Franca*, September/October 1996, 34ff.

41. Petitioners' Brief, *Romer*, 44–48 (quotations in text); Joint Appendix, *Romer*, 197–98 (Mansfield's testimony, cited in Petitioner's Brief, 47); Timothy M. Tymkovich et al., "A Tale of Three Theories: Reason and Prejudice in the Battle over Amendment 2," *University of Colorado Law Review* 68 (1997): 287–333 (defense of Amendment 2 by counsel on appeal). See Keen and Goldberg, *Strangers to the Law*, 133–57; Richard F. Duncan, "Who Wants to Stop the Church: Homosexual Rights Legislation, Public Policy, and Religious Freedom," *Notre Dame Law Review* 69 (1994): 393–445.

42. *Romer v. Evans*, 882 P.2d 1335 (Colorado Supreme Court, 1995) (affirming trial judge's injunction against Amendment 2), affirmed, 517 U.S. 620 (USSC, 1996).

43. Petition for Certiorari, *Romer v. Evans* (USSC, No. 94-1039), 14–16, 21–22, 39–48; *James v. Valtierra*, 402 U.S. 137 (USSC, 1971).

44. Brief for Respondents, *Romer v. Evans* (USSC, No. 94-1039), 35–50; Brief for the American Bar Association as *Amicus Curiae* in Support of Respondents, ibid., 4 (quotation in text); Brief of Laurence H. Tribe, John Hart Ely, Gerald Gunther, Philip B. Kurland, and Kathleen M. Sullivan, as *Amici Curiae* in Support of Respondents, ibid. (the "scholars' brief"). Mark Agrast was the coordinator and Ruth Harlow the primary author of the ABA brief, a project in which I assisted. For an earlier assertion of this kind of argument, see William N. Eskridge Jr. and Philip P. Frickey, "The Supreme Court, 1993 Term—Foreword: Law as Equlibrium," *Harvard Law Review* 108 (1994): 92–95.

45. Transcript of the Oral Argument in *Romer v. Evans* (USSC, No. 94-1039), 1–2 (Kennedy's initial questions), 7 (Ginsburg). The transcript is reprinted in Gerald Gunther and Gerhard Casper, eds. *Landmark Briefs and Arguments of the Supreme Court of the United States:*

Constitutional Law, 1995 Term Supplement, vol. 248 (Washington, D.C.: University Publications of America, 1997), 1151–84. My analysis of the oral argument is also informed by my listening to a tape recording, and conversations with persons who attended the argument.

46. Transcript of *Romer* Argument, 3, 7, 10, 15 (quotations in text).

47. Ibid., 9, 15 (quotations in text). Scalia was probably right about voter "intent," given the ballot materials discussed in Tymkovich et al., "Tale of Three Theories," 290–98. But Breyer was right about the plain meaning of Amendment 2, a criterion that Scalia says must always be dispositive. Antonin Scalia, *A Matter of Interpretation* (Princeton, NJ: Princeton University Press, 1997).

48. Ibid., 22, 30 (Scalia's questions to Dubofsky); Linda Greenhouse, "U.S. Justices Hear, and Also Debate a Gay Rights Case," *New York Times*, October 11, 1995, A1.

49. The generalizations about the internal dynamics of the *Romer* Court are based upon several confidential interviews with Court personnel.

50. See generally Joan Biskupic, *Sandra Day O'Connor: How the First Woman on the Supreme Court Became Its Most Influential Justice* (New York: Ecco, 2005); Sandra Day O'Connor and H. Alan Day, *Lazy B: Growing Up on a Cattle Ranch in the American Southwest* (New York: Random House, 2003).

51. Al Kamen and Ruth Marcus, "Record Contrasts with Bork's; Kennedy Appears to Be Less Ideologically Driven," *Washington Post*, November 9, 1987, A1; *Beller v. Middendorf*, 632 F.2d 788 (U.S. Court of Appeals for the Ninth Circuit, 1980) (Kennedy, J.), cert. denied, 454 U.S. 855 (USSC, 1981) (denying right of gay people to serve in the military but questioning antigay civilian discriminations).

52. *Romer v. Evans*, 517 U.S. 620, 623 (USSC, 1996), quoting *Plessy v. Ferguson*, 163 U.S. 537, 559 (USSC, 1896) (Harlan, J., dissenting) (first quotation in text); *Romer*, 517 U.S., 631 (second quotation); ibid., 630 (third quotation).

53. *Romer*, 517 U.S., 631, 634–35, quoting *Department of Agriculture v. Moreno*, 413 U.S. 528, 534 (USSC, 1973) (quotations in text).

54. *Romer*, 517 U.S., 636 (Scalia, J., dissenting) (the Kulturkampf konnection); ibid., 648–51 (invoking the Court's anti-Mormon decisions); ibid., 634 (Kennedy's response). On the anti-Mormon Kulturkampf, see Sarah Barringer Gordon, *The Mormon Question: Polygamy and Constitutional Conflict in Nineteenth-Century America* (Chapel Hill: University of North Carolina Press, 2002); William N. Eskridge Jr., "A Jurisprudence of 'Coming Out': Religion, Homosexuality, and Collisions of Liberty and Equality in American Public Law," *Yale Law Journal* 106 (1997): 2411–30.

55. *Romer*, 517 U.S., 641 (quotation in text). For arguments that *Romer* could not be reconciled with *Bowers*, see Robert H. Bork, *Slouching Towards Gomorrah* (New York: ReganBooks, 1996), 112–14 (disapproving); Eskridge, *Gaylaw*, 150–51, 209–11 (approving); Ronald Dworkin, "Sex, Death, and the Courts," *New York Review of Books*, August 8, 1996, 48–50 (approving); Lino Graglia, "*Romer v. Evans*: The People Foiled Again by the Constitution," *University of Colorado Law Review* 68 (1997): 409–28 (disapproving); Thomas Grey, "*Bowers v. Hardwick* Diminished," ibid., 373–86 (approving). Developing Kennedy's response is Lynn Baker, "The Missing Pages of the Majority Opinion in *Romer v. Evans*," ibid., 387–408.

56. Tavia Simmons and Martin McConnell, *Married Couple and Unmarried-Partner Households: 2000* (Washington, D.C.: U.S. Census, February 2003); M. V. Lee Badgett and Marc A. Rogers, *Left Out of the Count: Missing Same-Sex Couples in Census 2000* (Amherst, MA: Institute for Gay and Lesbian Strategic Studies, 2003).

57. Interview with Beatrice Dohrn, New York City (Chelsea), December 14, 2004; Coles interview; Harlow interview; *Christensen v. State*, 468 S.E.2d 188 (Georgia Supreme Court, 1996); *Sawatzky v. Oklahoma City*, 906 P.2d 785 (Oklahoma Court of Criminal Appeals, 1995); *Topeka v. Movsovitz*, Docket No. 77,372 (Kansas Court of Appeals, April 24, 1998) (unreported decision).

58. Brief of Appellee [District Attorney, Gwinnett County, Georgia], *Powell v. State*, Docket No. S98 AO 755 (Supreme Court of Georgia), 1–3 (summarizing the trial record).

59. Eskridge, *Gaylaw*, 375 (appendix C3) (different-sex sodomy cases, 1986–95); Joyce Murdoch, "Laws Against Sodomy Survive in 24 States," *Washington Post*, April 11, 1993, A20 (providing examples of consensual sodomy charges in heterosexual rape cases).

60. Brief of *Amici Curiae* Lambda Legal Defense and Education Fund, Inc. [et al.], *Powell*, relying on *Pavesich v. New England Life Insurance Co.*, 50 S.E. 68, 70 (Georgia Supreme Court, 1905) (quotation in text); *State v. McAfee*, 385 S.E.2d 651 (Georgia Supreme Court, 1989) (summarizing post-*Pavesich* cases); telephone interview with Steven Scarborough (YLS class of 1990), April 12, 2005.

61. *Powell v. State*, 510 S.E.2d 18 (Georgia Supreme Court, 1998); ibid., 24 (quotation in text); *Howard v. State*, 527 S.E.2d 194 (Georgia Supreme Court, 2000).

62. Tom Wolfe, *A Man in Full* (New York: Farrar, Straus & Giroux, 1998).

63. *Shahar v. Bowers*, 114 F.2d 1097 (U.S. Court of Appeals for the Fifth Circuit, en banc, 1997); Kevin Sack, "Georgia Candidate for Governor [Bowers] Admits Adultery and Resigns Commission in Guard," *New York Times*, June 6, 1997, A1. In the summer of 1998, I had dinner with one of the (majority) justices in *Powell*. I asked the justice what folks in Georgia thought about the Shahar case and the attorney general's adulterous affair. Knowing that I am gay, the justice rolled his eyes at the Shahar case and said (roughly) this about the affair, "You know, Bill, I think what shocked people the most was that it went on for *so-o lo-o-ong!*" A few months later, he and his colleagues struck down the state's consensual sodomy law.

64. Act of November 15, 1989, *1989 Massachusetts Acts* chap. 516, codified in *Massachusetts General Laws* chaps. 151B, 272; letter from Gerald D'Avolio, Executive Director, Massachusetts Catholic Conference, to the Committee on Commerce and Labor, March 24, 1988, quoted in Peter C. Cicchino et al., Comment, "Sex, Lies, and Civil Rights: A Critical History of the Massachusetts Gay Civil Rights Bill," *Harvard Civil Rights–Civil Liberties Law Review* 26 (1991): 594. The church's antidiscrimination stance is laid out in Congregation for the Doctrine of the Faith, *Letter on the pastoral care of homosexual persons* (October 1, 1986).

65. *Rhode Island General Laws* §§ 11-24-1 to -8 (2006); interview with John Roney, Providence, Rhode Island, June 11, 2004.

66. *1998 Rhode Island Laws* chap. 24; *State v. McGovern*, Docket No. W1/97-0053 (B)(C) (Providence Superior Court, 1998); Roney interview.

67. *Gay & Lesbian Advocates & Defenders v. Attorney General*, 763 N.E.2d 38 (Massachusetts Supreme Judicial Court, 2002), expanding *Commonwealth v. Balthazar*, 318 N.E.2d 478 (Massachusetts Supreme Judicial Court, 1974) (interpreting the state's lascivious conduct law to be inapplicable to consensual oral sex); *State v. Cogshell*, 997 S.W.2d 534, 537 (Missouri Court of Appeals, Western District, 1999) (the state acquiesced in the reversal of defendant's conviction for consensual sodomy).

68. *Schochet v. State*, 580 A.2d 176 (Maryland Court of Appeals, 1990) (sodomy law cannot be constitutionally applied to consensual heterosexual sodomy), extended to consensual homosexual sodomy in *Williams v. State*, 1998 Extra LEXIS 260, Civil Docket No. 9803 6031/CC-1059 (Baltimore City Circuit Court, October 15, 1998); *Doe v. Ventura*, 2001 WestLaw 543734, Civil Docket No. MC 01-489 (Hennepin County District Court, May 15, 2001) (class-action judgment that sodomy law could not be applied to consensual activities anywhere in Minnesota); *2001 Arizona Session Laws*, 382.

69. The bills to repeal the homosexual sodomy law were Senate Bill 125, 78th Arkansas General Assembly (1991); Senate Bill 565, 79th Arkansas General Assembly (1993); Senate Bill 378, 80th Arkansas General Assembly (1995).

70. Arkansas Advisory Committee to the U.S. Commission on Civil Rights, *Civil Rights Issues in Arkansas, 1991–92: A Summary Report* (September 1992), 5 (describing Pharr's findings and report on police training); Suzanne Pharr, *Homophobia: A Weapon of Sexism* (Inverness, CA: Chardon Press, 1988).

71. *1992 Women's Watchcare Network Log*, 19–20.

72. Interview with Suzanne Goldberg, New York City (Columbia University), December 16, 2004.

73. The Arkansas Supreme Court ruled in *Bryant v. Picado*, 996 S.W.2d 17 (1999), that the case should have been filed in the circuit court, the court of general jurisdiction. On remand, the Pulaski County Circuit Court dismissed the attorney general from the lawsuit. Order of February 9, 2000, *Picado v. Jegley*, CV 99-7048 (Circuit Court of Pulaski County). The court certified a class of prosecuting attorneys as defendants in Order of June 12, 2000, ibid.

74. Before the Pulaski County Circuit Court, Goldberg presented affidavits from psychologists Nicholas DeMara and John Gonsiorek; historian George Chauncey Jr.; and Little Rock lawyer David Ivers.

75. Affidavit of Robin White, *Picado v. Jegley*, CV 99-7048 (Pulaski County Circuit Court, filed November 2000); *Thigpen v. Carpenter*, 730 S.W.2d 510 (Arkansas Court of Appeals, 1987) (presumption against child custody for lesbian mothers).

76. White Affidavit, ¶ 10 and Exhibit D (Springdale mayor's race); ibid., ¶ 23 (violence against Estes and her daughter); ibid., ¶ 24 (quotation in text).

77. E-mail from Ruth Harlow to William Eskridge, September 4, 2005; *Picado v. Jegley*, CV 99-7048 (Pulaski County Circuit Court, March 23, 2001) (order granting summary judgment to the challengers).

78. Interview with Susan Sommer, New York City (Wall Street), January 27, 2004 (account of the oral arguments before the circuit and supreme courts).

79. *Jegley v. Picado*, 80 S.W.3d 332 (Arkansas Supreme Court, 2002). Three justices joined Justice Imber's majority opinion, and two joined the dissenting opinion. Ibid., 356–60 (Thornton, J., dissenting).

80. Ibid., 354 (Brown, J., concurring).

Chapter Ten: **Sodomy Law at the Alamo,** *Lawrence v. Texas*, 2003

1. Interview with John Geddes Lawrence and Mitchell Katine, Houston, June 23, 2004.

2. Lawrence interview; telephone interview with Tyron Garner, Houston, June 24, 2003.

3. Probable Cause Affidavit filed by Deputy Joseph R. Quinn, September 17, 1998, reprinted as an appendix to the Petition for a Writ of Certiorari, *Lawrence v. Texas*, Docket No. 02-102 (USSC, filed July 2, 2002), 129a.

4. Dale Carpenter, "The Unknown Past of *Lawrence v. Texas*," *Michigan Law Review* 102 (2004): 1464, 1481–83 (detailed account of arrest, based upon interviews with Deputies Quinn and Lilly); ibid., 1486–87 (reprinting Quinn's police report). I have made corrections based upon my separate interviews with Lawrence and Garner.

5. Ibid., 1483–84 (Carpenter's account, based upon interviews with Quinn, Lilly, Jones, and Adams). Since Carpenter's interviews, the police officers have become unavailable for comment about the case.

6. Lawrence interview (quotation in text); Garner telephone interview (the holding cell); telephone interview with Ray Hill, April 15, 2005.

7. Texas Bix Binder, *Don't Squat With Yer Spurs On: A Cowboy's Guide to Life* (Salt Lake City: Cobbs-Smith, 1992); Roger M. and Diana Davids Olien, *Oil in Texas: The Gusher Age, 1895–1945* (Austin: University of Texas Press, 2002).

8. State Bar Committee on Revision of the Penal Code, *Texas Penal Code: A Proposed Revision* (St. Paul, MN: West, October 1970), 162–63 (§ 21.06, "Homosexual Conduct"); Randy Von Beitel, "The Criminalization of Private Homosexual Acts: A Jurisprudential Case Study of a Decision by the Texas Bar Penal Code Revision Committee," *Human Rights* (ABA's Section of Individual Rights and Responsibilities) 6 (Fall 1976): 23–72 (interviews with Dean Keeton, Judge Brown, and other committee members); Dean Page Keeton, "The Proposed Penal Code: A Reply to Its Critics" (March 1, 1971), in Keeton Papers, Box K26, Folder 7 (testimony before the joint legislative committee considering the new penal code).

9. State Bar Committee on Revision of the Penal Code, *Texas Penal Code: A Proposed Revision* (October 1972), § 21.06; Senate Subcommittee on Criminal Matters, Hearings on SB 34 [the proposed Texas Penal Code], February 20, 1973, Sixty-third Session, Texas Legislature, TLRS (audiotaped testimony of Frank Maloney, representing the Criminal Defense Lawyers Association) (quotation in text); ibid. (testimony of Dennis Ray Milam, representing the National Organization for the Repeal of Sodomy Laws); Von Beitel, "Private Homosexual Acts," 34 (House subcommittee's executive session); telephone interview with Dain Whitworth [lobbyist for the Texas District and County Attorneys Association in 1973], April 16, 2004.

10. Senate Subcommittee on Criminal Matters, Hearings on SB 34 [the proposed Texas Penal Code], February 20, 1973, Sixty-third Session, Texas Legislature, TLRS (testimony of Frank Stovall, representing the Young Socialist Alliance).

11. House Floor Debate on SB 34, May 19, 1973, Sixty-third Session, Texas Legislature, TLRS.

12. Telephone interview with Ray Hill, April 15, 2005 (account of Alvin Buchanan's release from Ramsey Prison).

13. Rob Shivers, "Lone Star Solons Defeat Sodomy Reform," *Advocate*, August 13, 1975, 5 (first quotation in text); telephone interview with Craig Washington, May 5, 2004 (second quotation); Pokey Anderson, "Taxation Without Representation," *Pointback Times*, 1:5 (August 1975).

14. E-mail from Pokey Anderson to William N. Eskridge Jr., June 12, 2006 (quotation in text).

15. Hill telephone interview; James T. Sears, *Rebels, Rubyfruit, and Rhinestones: Queering Space in the Stonewall South* (New Brunswick, NJ: Rutgers University Press, 2001), 48–58, 165–76; Scott P. Anderson, "Houston: Hot Spot of the South," *Advocate*, September 17, 1981, 18–21.

16. Hill telphone interview (the Bryant march and its community-building effects); The

Dallas Gay & Lesbian Community, *Finding Our Voice* (Dallas: KERA-TV 2000) (Armstrong quotation); "Police Ambush Public Sex," *Advocate*, May 31, 1978, 11 (police activity after the Bryant visit).

17. "Houstonians Testify on Antigay Violence," *Advocate*, August 9, 1979, 9–10 (quotation in text); Anderson, "Houston: Hot Spot," 18 (Tinsley election); William K. Stevens, "Houston Accepts New Political Force," *New York Times*, November 2, 1981, A16 (gays become politically salient); "Houston Gets Progay Mayor, City Council," *Advocate*, December 24, 1981, 9; Joe Baker, "2 Rights Laws Barely Pass Houston, Tex., City Council," *Advocate*, July 24, 1984, 10; Joe Baker, "Antigay Houston Vote: 4 to 1," *Advocate*, February 19, 1985, 7.

18. Dallas Gay & Lesbian Community, *Finding Our Voice* (documentary, KERA-TV, 2000) (detailed account of the Estes flap); *Baker v. Wade*, 553 F. Supp. 1121, 1126–31 (U.S. District Court for the Northern District of Texas, 1982) (testimony of Baker and his medical experts); ibid., 1131–34 (testimony of Wade and other defense witnesses).

19. "Texas Backs Out of Sodomy Appeal but New Foes Will Take Up Case," *Advocate*, April 28, 1985, 8; "Sodomy Laws—Protecting the Public," *Moral Majority Report*, September 1983, 8–9 (Alert Citizens of Texas; quotations in text). For an inside-the-Attorney-General's-Office account of the *Baker* appeal, see David Richards, *Once Upon a Time in Texas: A Liberal in the Lone Star State* (Austin: University of Texas Press, 2002), 231–33.

20. *Baker v. Wade*, 769 F.2d 289 (U.S. Court of Appeals for the Fifth Circuit, en banc, 1985), reversing 553 F. Supp. 1121 (U.S. District Court for the Northern District of Texas, 1982) (Judge Buchmeyer).

21. *Houston v. Hill*, 482 U.S. 451 (USSC, 1987), ruling that the First Amendment prevented Houston from making it a crime for a citizen to criticize a police officer for making an arguably unlawful arrest.

22. Telephone interview with Linda Morales, June 2005; UPI, "State Judge Declares Texas Sodomy Law Unconstitutional," December 10, 2000 (quotation in text); Guillermo X. Garcia, "Judge Declares Anti-Sodomy Law Unconstitutional," *Austin American-Statesman*, December 11, 1990, A1.

23. *Passel v. Fort Worth Independent School System*, 440 S.W.2d 61 (Texas Supreme Court, 1969), appeal dismissed, 402 U.S. 968 (USSC, 1971).

24. *State v. Morales*, 826 S.W.2d 201, 204 (Texas Court of Appeals, Austin, 1992) (privacy violation, applying *Texas State Employees Union v. Texas Department of Mental Health & Mental Retardation*, 746 S.W.2d 203 (Texas Supreme Court, 1987)); ibid., 205 (asserted state interest in public morals not served by §21.06); *City of Dallas v. England*, 846 S.W.2d 957 (Texas Court of Appeals, Austin, 1993) (appeal dismissed for procedural reasons); interview with Edward Tuddingham (Mica England's attorney), Austin, Texas, May 8, 2004.

25. *State v. Morales*, 869 S.W.2d 941, 943–48 (Texas Supreme Court, 1994); cf. ibid., 942 note 5 (distinguishing *England*, where the plaintiff was complaining about an injury to her property entitlements). Joined by Chief Justice Tom Phillips and Justices Lloyd Doggett and Rose Spector, Justice Robert Gammage dissented on the ground that plaintiffs alleged irreparable injury to their personal rights, and that was enough under equity principles and Texas precedent. Ibid., 949–54. My account of the Texas Supreme Court's decision-making process is based upon conversations with court insiders and knowledgeable observers.

26. Hill telephone interview. See also Carpenter, "Unknown Past of *Lawrence*," 1474 (same story from Carpenter's interview with Hill).

27. Interview with Beatrice Dohrn, New York City (Chelsea), December 14, 2004 (first quotation in text); Katine interview; Lawrence interview; Garner telephone interview (quotation in text). I have also drawn from interview with Ruth Harlow, New York City (Midtown), November 22, 2004; interview with Suzanne Goldberg, New York City (Columbia University), December 2004.

28. Carpenter, "Unknown Past of *Lawrence v. Texas*," 1482 (quoting from his interview with Quinn); ibid., 1484 (same).

29. Hill telephone interview; William N. Eskridge Jr., *Gaylaw: Challenging the Apartheid of the Closet* (Cambridge, MA: Harvard University Press, 1999), 87 (pattern of police perjury and harassment because of anti-gay disgust). See also Carpenter, "Unknown Past of *Lawrence v. Texas*," 1490–1508, which is probably inspired by Hill's skepticism and engages in a detailed critique of Quinn's account.

30. Carpenter, "Unknown Past of *Lawrence v. Texas*," 1474–75.

31. Interview with William J. Delmore III, Houston (Harris County DA's Office), June 23, 2004.

32. The Texas attorney general issues opinion letters resolving legal or constitutional issues not authoritatively resolved by the Texas courts. State legislators regularly put such questions to the attorney general, who by law is supposed to respond within a specified period of time. The account in the text is based upon personal and telephone interviews with several Texas government officials in July 2004.

33. Delmore interview; R. A. Dyer, "Two Men Charged Under State's Sodomy Law," *Houston Chronicle*, November 5, 1998 (Holmes quotation in text).

34. Interview with Angela Beavers, Houston (Harris County DA's Office), June 23, 2004; Hearing Transcript, Motion to Quash the Complaints, December 22, 1998, reprinted in *Lawrence* Petition, Appendix F, 111a–16a; Defendants' Motion to Quash Complaint/Information, December 16, 1998, ibid., Appendix G, 117a–25a.

35. Michael Barone and Grant Ujifusa, *The Almanac of American Politics, 2000* (Washington, DC: National Journal, 1999), 1516–17; Robert A. Calvert et al., *The History of Texas* (Wheeling, IL: Harlan Davidson, 3d ed., 2002), 457–60; Richards, *Liberal in the Lone Star State*, 203–11, 249–52; Oran P. Smith, *The Rise of Baptist Republicanism* (New York: NYU Press, 1997), 40–41, 48–50, 62–64, 82–85.

36. Telephone interview with James Mattox, May 5, 2004; David Elliott, "Bush Promises to Veto Attempts to Repeal Sodomy Law," *Austin American-Statesman*, January 22, 1994, B3; Carl M. Cannon et al., *Boy Genius: Karl Rove, The Architect of George W. Bush's Remarkable Political Triumphs* (New York: Public Affairs, 2005), 72–75 (Rove's lesbian-bashing whisper campaign against Ann Richards).

37. Nathan Koppel, "Anti-Sodomy Law Challenged: Texas Presents Unique Test Case," *Law News Network*, November 9, 1999, available at www.sodomylaws.org/usa/texas35.htm (viewed June 14, 2004).

38. *Lawrence v. Texas*, Docket Nos. 14-99-001909-CR & 14-99-00111 (Fourteenth Court of Appeals, Texas, June 8, 2000), majority opinion, 5–9; ibid., dissenting opinion, 5–8 (rejecting the sex discrimination argument), 9–11 (rational basis for Section 21.06 in morality; quotations in text). The June 8 opinion is attached as appendix D to the Petition for Certiorari, *Lawrence v. Texas* (USSC, No. 02-102), 80a–106a.

39. E-mail from Ruth Harlow to William N. Eskridge Jr., September 4, 2005; Andrew Koppelman, *The Gay Rights Question in Contemporary American Law* (Chicago: University of Chicago Press, 2002), 53–71 (classic articulation of the sex discrimination argument for gay rights);

William N. Eskridge Jr., *Equality Practice: Civil Unions and the Future of Gay Rights* (New York: Routledge, 2002), 22–42 (Hawaii decision and national backlash).

40. Alan Bernstein, "Texas Republicans Target One of Their Own: Plan to Put Political Pressure on Sodomy-Law Judge Fizzles," *Houston Chronicle*, July 3, 2000 (Republican Party reaction to Justice Anderson's opinion); videotape of Symposium on *Lawrence v. Texas*, South Texas College of Law, Remarks of former chief justice Paul Murphy, February 2004; *Lawrence v. State*, 41 S.W.3d 349 (Texas Court of Appeals, Fourteenth Circuit, en banc, 2001) (reaffirming the constitutionality of Section 21.06).

41. William D. Mosher et al., "Sexual Behavior and Selected Health Measures: Men and Women 15–44 Years of Age, United States, 2002," in Centers for Disease Control and Prevention, *Advance Data*, No. 362 (Atlanta, September 15, 2005), 4 (table A).

42. *Lawrence v. Texas*, 537 U.S. 1044 (USSC, 2002) (granting review).

43. E-mail from Ruth Harlow to William N. Eskridge Jr., September 4, 2004.

44. Brief for Petitioners, *Lawrence v. Texas*, Docket No. 02-102 (USSC), 11 (first quotation in text); ibid., 30 (second quotation, quoting *Dickerson v. United States*, 530 U.S. 428, 443 [USSC, 2000]); ibid., 30–31 (third quotation, quoting *Planned Parenthood v. Casey*, 505 U.S. 833, 855 [USSC, 1992] [joint opinion]).

45. Brief *Amicus Curiae* by the Cato Institute, *Lawrence* (No. 02-102), 12–18; Brief of Professors of History, George Chauncey, Nancy Cott, et al., as *Amici Curiae*, ibid., 3–10; Brief *Amicus Curiae* of the American Civil Liberties Union and the ACLU of Texas, ibid., 11–26.

46. Brief for *Amici Curiae* for the American Psychological Association et al., *Lawrence* (No. 02-102), 11–23; Brief for the Alliance of Baptists et al. as *Amici Curiae*, ibid.; Garner telephone interview.

47. Brief of Petitioners, *Lawrence* (No. 02-102), 34–40 (Section 21.06 reflects antigay animus, requiring invalidation under *Romer*); ibid., 40-45 (Section 21.06 "brands" gay people as second-class citizens and imposes a broad array of disabilities on them); ibid., 45–50 (Section 21.06 encourages a culture of antigay violence). See also ibid., 44, noting that Section 21.06 was cited by the state as a reason to impose the death penalty in *Burdine v. Johnson*, 66 F.Supp.2d 854, 857 (U.S. District Court for the Southern District of Texas, 1999) (appeals denied).

48. Cato *Amicus* Brief, *Lawrence* (No. 02-102), 20–21 (quotation in text); Brief of the American Bar Association as *Amicus Curiae*, ibid., 12–14; Brief for Bruce Ackerman et al. as *Amici Curiae*, ibid., 14–17; see Christopher R. Leslie, "Creating Criminals: The Injuries Inflicted by 'Unenforced' Sodomy Laws," *Harvard Civil Rights–Civil Liberties Law Review* 35 (2000): 103–81.

49. Brief of NOW Legal Defense and Education Fund as *Amicus Curiae*, *Lawrence* (No. 02-102), 17–24; Koppelman, *Gay Rights Question*, 53–71; Edward Stein, "Evaluating the Sex Discrimination Argument for Lesbian and Gay Rights," *UCLA Law Review* 49 (2001): 471–518. See also Eskridge, *Gaylaw*, 218–31, arguing that the sex discrimination argument understates the role of sex-negativity in antigay discrimination but does capture the gender-based features of such discrimination, especially against lesbians.

50. ABA *Amicus* Brief, 7 (quotation in text); Cato *Amicus* Brief; *Amici Curiae* Brief of the Log Cabin Republicans and Liberty Education Forum, *Lawrence* (No. 02-102); Brief *Amici Curiae* Republican Unity Coalition and the Honorable Alan Simpson, ibid. Some of the amicus briefs supporting Harris County were grounded upon religious precepts but did not speak for religious denominations. For instance, Brief *Amicus Curiae* of the Family Research Council and Focus on the Family, ibid. (drafted by natural-law scholars Gerard Bradley of Notre Dame and Robert George of Princeton).

51. Brief *Amicus Curiae* of Mary Robinson et al., *Lawrence* (No. 02-102); *Knight v. Florida*, 528 U.S. 990, 997 (USSC, 1999) (Breyer, J., dissenting from denial of certiorari) (quotation in text); William N. Eskridge Jr., "*Lawrence v. Texas* and the Imperative of Comparative Constitutionalism," *International Journal of Constitutional Law* 2 (2004): 555–60. For examples where the Court has looked to international experience in constitutional cases, see, e.g., *Roper v. Simmons*, 543 U.S. 552, 575–78 (USSC, 2005) (Kennedy, J.) (death penalty for minors); *Washington v. Glucksberg*, 521 U.S. 702, 710, 718, 785–87 (USSC, 1997) (Rehnquist, C.J.) (constitutional right to die); *Poe v. Ullman*, 367 U.S. 497, 548 (USSC, 1961) (Harlan, J., dissenting) (marital privacy).

52. Respondent's Brief, *Lawrence* (No. 02-102), 8–26.

56. Ibid., 36–42; ibid., 39 (quotation in text); see *Griswold v. Connecticut*, 381 U.S. 479 (USSC, 1965) (constitutional privacy right prevents state from imposing anticontraceptive rules on married couples); *Buchanan v. Batchelor*, 308 F.Supp. 729 (U.S. District Court for the Northern District of Texas, 1970), reversed on other grounds, 401 U.S. 989 (USSC, 1971) (extending *Griswold* to rule that the Texas sodomy law could not constitutionally cover married couples); *Eisenstadt v. Baird*, 405 U.S. 438 (USSC, 1972) (invalidating on equal protection grounds a state bar to contraceptive use by unmarried persons).

54. Transcript of Oral Argument, *Lawrence* (No. 02-102, March 26, 2003), 3–5; interview with Paul Smith, New York City (Midtown), June 23, 2006.

55. *Lawrence* Argument, 20–21 (the kindergarten colloquy); ibid., 22–24 (Smith's arguments for overruling *Bowers*).

56. Ibid., 27–29 (record did not say defendants were homosexuals); ibid., 32–34 (Breyer: Why not overrule *Bowers*?).

57. Ibid., 37–38 (Breyer-Rosenthal colloquy).

58. The discussion of the justices' reactions in *Lawrence* is drawn from conversations with Court personnel. Cato the Elder's great line was *Carthago delenda est* (Carthage must be destroyed). Cato the Younger was the Roman libertarian after whom the Cato Institute was named.

59. The morning of June 26, 2003, Justice Kennedy read almost all of his majority opinion. The quotations are from his written opinion, *Lawrence v. Texas*, 539 U.S. 558, 562 (USSC, 2003).

60. Ibid., 566–67 (quotation in text); ibid., 567–73 (historical account, following Cato *Amicus* Brief, 9–17).

61. Ibid., 575 (first quotation in text); ibid., 578 (second quotation).

62. Ibid., 582 (O'Connor, J., concurring in the judgment) (first quotation in text); ibid., 584 (second quotation).

63. Audiotape of the Rally at Houston City Hall, June 30, 2003 (from Mitchell Katine).

64. Richard Connelly, "Back Door to History: Thank J.R. Quinn for the Gay Celebrations" (July 2003); "[Presidential] Press Briefing by Ari Fleischer," www.whitehouse.gov/news/releases/2003/06/20030626-5.html (viewed July 2006).

65. *Lawrence*, 539 U.S., 586–92 (Scalia, J., dissenting) (lambasting the Court for abandoning stare decisis); ibid., 592–98 (lambasting the Court for misunderstanding the nation's traditions); ibid., 598 (lambasting the Court for reliance on "foreign" views); ibid., 599–602 (lambasting Justice O'Connor); ibid., 602 (lambasting the Court for taking sides in "the culture war"); [Pat Robertson], "Operation Supreme Court Freedom," www.patrobertson.com/Press Releases/supremecourt.asp (viewed June 2006). For a temperate originalist critique of *Lawrence*, see Steven G. Calabresi, "*Lawrence*, the Fourteenth Amendment, and the Supreme Court's

Reliance on Foreign Constitutional Law: An Originalist Reappraisal," *Ohio State Law Journal* 65 (2004): 1097–1131.

66. *Corfield v. Coryell*, 6 F.Cas. 546, 552 (Circuit Court for the Eastern District of Pennsylvania, 1823) (No. 3230) (quotation in text). On *Lawrence* and original meaning, compare Calabresi, "*Lawrence*, an Originalist Reappraisal," 1109–15, with William N. Eskridge Jr., "*Hardwick* and Historiography," *University of Illinois Law Review*, 1999, 631–86.

67. Eskridge, "*Lawrence*'s Jurisprudence of Tolerance," 1058–64; Lawrence H. Tribe, "*Lawrence v. Texas*: The 'Fundamental Right' That Dare Not Speak Its Name," *Harvard Law Review* 117 (2004): 1918–36.

68. *Lawrence*, 539 U.S., 590, 599 (Scalia, J., dissenting) (end of morals legislation); ibid., 602–4 (adoption of "homosexual agenda"); "TFP Decries Supreme Court's Decision as America's 'Moral 9/11,'" www.sodomylaws.org/lawrence/lwnews089.htm (viewed April 2005).

Chapter Eleven: **American Public Law After *Lawrence***

1. Telephone interview with Steven Lofton, May 18, 2005; "The Lofton-Croteau Family," www.lethimstay.com/loftons.html (viewed June 2006).

2. 1977 Florida Laws chap. 77–140, codified at Fla. Stat. § 63.042(3).

3. *Lawrence v. Texas*, 539 U.S. 558, 578 (USSC, 2003) (majority opinion, holding that Texas advanced "no legitimate state interest" to support Section 21.06); ibid., 599 (Scalia, J., dissenting and observing that the Court's holding "decrees the end of all morals legislation"). In *Romer v. Evans*, 517 U.S. 620 (USSC, 1996), Justice Scalia assailed the majority opinion as deeply inconsistent with *Bowers*, a prophecy that *Lawrence* confirmed. 539 U.S., 574–75 (majority opinion), 588 (dissenting opinion).

4. Compare the broad readings of *Lawrence* in Randy E. Barnett, "Justice Kennedy's Libertarian Revolution: *Lawrence v. Texas*," in *Cato Supreme Court Review 2002–2003*, 21–41, and Laurence H. Tribe, "*Lawrence v. Texas*: The 'Fundamental Right' That Dare Not Speak Its Name," *Harvard Law Review* 117 (2004): 1898 (quotation in text), with more cautious readings by lesbian and gay scholars such as Dale Carpenter, "Is *Lawrence* Libertarian?" *Minnesota Law Review* 88 (2004): 1140–70 (no), and Nan D. Hunter, "Living with *Lawrence*," ibid., 1103–39 (reading *Lawrence* as an important but limited advance for lesbian and gay equality). Indeed, many lesbian and gay scholars find much to criticize and fear in *Lawrence*. For instance, Katharine M. Franke, "The Domesticated Liberty of *Lawrence v. Texas*," *Columbia Law Review* 104 (2004): 1399–1426; Marc Spindelman, "Surviving *Lawrence v. Texas*," *Michigan Law Review* 102 (2004): 1615–67.

5. William N. Eskridge Jr., "*Lawrence*'s Jurisprudence of Tolerance: Judicial Review to Lower the Stakes of Identity Politics," *Minnesota Law Review* 88 (2004): 1021–1102. The cautious approach I take to *Lawrence* is helpfully informed by an interview with Paul Smith, New York City (Midtown), June 23, 2006; Pamela S. Karlan, "Foreword: Loving *Lawrence*," *Michigan Law Review* 102 (2004): 1447–63; Andrew Koppelman, "*Lawrence*'s Penumbra," *Minnesota Law Review* 88 (2004): 1171–83; David D. Meyer, "Domesticating *Lawrence*," *University of Chicago Law Forum* 2004: 453–94; Miranda Oshige McGowan, "From Outlaws to Ingroup: *Romer*, *Lawrence*, and the Inevitable Normativity of Group Recognition," *Minnesota Law Review* 88 (2004): 1312–45.

6. The questions in the text are rhetorical, as Lofton and Croteau moved from Florida to Oregon in 1998, soon after their lawsuit was filed. Lofton telephone interview.

7. Compare *Griswold v. Connecticut*, 381 U.S. 479, 486 (USSC, 1965), with *Lawrence*, 539 U.S., 578. On the distinction between tolerance and acceptance, see Michael J. Sandel, "Moral Argument and Liberal Toleration: Abortion and Homosexuality," *California Law Review* 77 (1989): 533–38.

8. *Roe v. Wade*, 410 U.S. 113 (USSC, 1973); *Brown v. Board of Education*, 347 U.S. 483 (USSC, 1954).

9. *Maher v. Roe*, 432 U.S. 464 (USSC, 1977); ibid., 473–74 (first quotation in text); ibid., 475 (second quotation); ibid., 479–80 (third quotation); see ibid., 481–82 (Burger, C.J., concurring) (similar); *Harris v. McRae*, 448 U.S. 297 (USSC, 1980) (applying *Maher* to allow the federal government to deny funding for abortions).

10. *Planned Parenthood v. Casey*, 505 U.S. 833 (USSC, 1992) (Joint Opinion). Voting with the joint opinion to uphold all but the spousal notification requirement of Pennsylvania's abortion law were Chief Justice Rehnquist and Justices White, Scalia, and Thomas (all critics of *Roe*). Voting with the joint opinion to strike down the spousal notification requirement were Justices Blackmun and Stevens (*Roe* defenders).

11. *Naim v. Naim*, 350 U.S. 891 (USSC, 1955), vacating and remanding 87 S.E.2d 749 (Virginia Supreme Court, 1955). On remand, the Virginia Supreme Court reaffirmed its prior disposition, 90 S.E.2d 849 (1956), appeal dismissed, 350 U.S. 895 (USSC, 1956). *Naim* was abrogated in *Loving v. Virginia*, 388 U.S. 1 (USSC, 1967).

12. *The Federalist* No. 78 (Hamilton) (quotation in text); Alexander M. Bickel, *The Least Dangerous Branch: The Supreme Court at the Bar of Politics* (New Haven, CT: Yale University Press, 1962).

13. *United States v. Carolene Products Co.*, 304 U.S. 144, 152 note 4 (USSC, 1938); see David M. Bixby, "The Roosevelt Court, Democratic Ideology, and Minority Rights: Another Look at *United States v. Classic*," *Yale Law Journal* 90 (1981): 741–815; John Hart Ely, *Democracy and Distrust* (Cambridge, MA: Harvard University Press, 1980) (posing a "representation-reinforcing" theory of judicial review, drawn from *Carolene Products*).

14. *Railway Express Agency, Inc. v. New York*, 336 U.S. 106, 112 (USSC, 1949) (Jackson, J., concurring) (quotation in text).

15. *Bowers v. Hardwick*, 478 U.S. 186, 214–20 (USSC, 1986) (Stevens, J., dissenting).

16. See generally William N. Eskridge Jr., "Pluralism and Distrust: How Courts Can Support Democracy by Lowering the Stakes of Politics," *Yale Law Journal* 114 (2005): 1279–1328; McGowan, "From Outlaws to Ingroup."

17. In the classic game of "chicken," two guys drive hot rods on a collision course toward one another. The first to swerve is the "loser." If both swerve, they are both "losers." If neither swerves, they are both "totaled." From a social point of view, this is a very bad game.

18. Adam Przeworski, *Democracy and the Market: Political and Economic Reforms in Eastern Europe and Latin America* (Oxford: Oxford University Press, 1991), 26–37 (democracy is a self-enforcing equilibrium only so long as all groups see themselves better off under democracy than they would be under a state of nature). On the role of the Religion Clauses to prevent destructive group conflict, see *Zelman v. Simmons-Harris*, 536 U.S. 639, 718 (USSC, 2002) (Breyer, J., concurring); Noah Feldman, "The Intellectual Origins of the Establishment Clause," *NYU Law Review* 77 (2002): 346–428.

19. *Hurley v. Gay, Lesbian, Bisexual Irish of Boston*, 515 U.S. 557 (USSC, 1995); *Boy Scouts of America v. Dale*, 530 U.S. 640 (USSC, 2000). But see ibid., 665–78 (Stevens, J., dissenting), which

argues that the Boy Scouts' message was too unclear to merit the First Amendment protection accorded by the *Dale* majority.

20. William N. Eskridge Jr., "Some Effects of Identity-Based Social Movements on Constitutional Law in the Twentieth Century," *Michigan Law Review* 100 (2002): 2062–2194.

21. *Lawrence*, 539 U.S., 589–90, 599 (Scalia, J., dissenting) (several overlapping lists of morals-based laws nullified by *Lawrence*). Scalia's list is derived from Lord Patrick Devlin, *The Enforcement of Morals* (Oxford: Oxford University Press, 1965), which criticized the Wolfenden Report's proposal to deregulate consensual sodomy.

22. See *Limon v. Kansas*, 539 U.S. 955 (USSC, 2003), on remand 83 P.3d 229 (Kansas Court of Appeals, 2004), reversed, 122 P.3d 22 (Kansas Supreme Court, 2005).

23. *Lawrence*, 539 U.S., 564 (emphasizing that the only issue presented was the ability of the state to criminalize "private and consensual" activities between adults in the home); ibid., 578 (litany of variations the Court was *not* resolving, including sexual activities involving minors, in public, or for compensation). On the rise and dilution of the harm principle in criminal law, see Bernard E. Harcourt, "The Collapse of the Harm Principle," *Journal of Criminal Law and Criminology* 90 (1999): 109–94; Dan M. Kahan, "The Secret Ambition of Deterrence," *Harvard Law Review* 113 (1999): 413–500.

24. *United States v. Orellana*, 62 M.J. 595 (Court of Military Justice, 2004) (upholding adultery prosecution after *Lawrence*). On the harms of polygamy, compare Maura I. Strassberg, "Distinctions of Form or Substance: Monogamy, Polygamy, and Same-Sex Marriage," *North Carolina Law Review* 75 (1997): 1501–1624, with David L. Chambers, "Polygamy and Same-Sex Marriage," *Hofstra Law Review* 26 (1997): 53–83.

25. For an outdated but useful introduction to state regulation of obscene materials and prostitution, see Richard A. Posner and Katharine B. Silbaugh, *A Guide to America's Sex Laws* (Chicago: *University of Chicago Press*, 1996), 155–206.

26. *Lawrence*, 539 U.S., 578 (contrasting sodomy between consenting adults in the home with other conduct having third-party effects—rape, sex with minors [who cannot consent], public sexual conduct [that would harm captive audiences]); *New York v. Ferber*, 458 U.S. 747 (USSC, 1982) (liberal harm-based justifications for regulating child pornography); *Regina v. Butler*, [1992] 1 S.C.R. 452 (Supreme Court of Canada, 1992) (feminist harm-based justifications for regulating pornography generally); *Stanley v. Georgia*, 394 U.S. 556, 563–64 (USSC, 1969) (protecting "mere private possession" of pornography).

27. On the modernization of justification, see Reva B. Siegel, "'The Rule of Love': Wife Beating as Prerogative and Privacy," *Yale Law Journal* 105 (1996): 2117–2207. See also William N. Eskridge Jr., "No Promo Homo: The Sedimentation of Antigay Discourse and the Channeling Effect of Judicial Review," *NYU Law Review* 75 (2000): 1327–1411.

28. On bestiality laws, see Posner and Silbaugh, *Sex Laws*, 207–12. On the tentative link between sexual abuse of animals and of humans, see William M. Fleming et al., "Characteristics of Juvenile Offenders Admitting to Sexual Activity with Nonhuman Animals," *Society and Animals* 10 (2002): 36–37; Robert K. Ressler et al., "Murderers Who Rape and Mutilate," *Journal of Interpersonal Violence* 1 (1986): 277–78.

29. For a state-by-state analysis of age-of-consent laws, see William N. Eskridge Jr. and Nan D. Hunter, *Sexuality, Gender, and the Law*, 2d ed. (New York: Foundation Press, 2003), 142–46.

30. *State v. Freeman*, 801 N.E.2d 906, 909 (Ohio Court of Appeals, 2003) (quotation in text).

31. *Lawrence*, 539 U.S., 567 (quotations in text); ibid., 575–76 (antigay civil discriminations justified by the Homosexual Conduct Law); ibid., 581–82 (O'Connor, J., concurring in the judgment) (similar).

32. Ibid., 567–73 (Kennedy, J., for the Court). For a counterhistory, see ibid., 595–98 (Scalia, J., dissenting).

33. Ibid., 571 (Kennedy, J., for the Court) (quotation in text); ibid., 581–82 (O'Connor, J., concurring in the judgment). Justice O'Connor also took the position that "[m]oral disapproval of a group cannot be a legitimate governmental interest under the Equal Protection Clause." Ibid., 583.

34. Eskridge, "Jurisprudence of Tolerance," 1088–89.

35. Geoffrey Miller, "Law, Self-Pollution, and the Management of Sexual Anxiety," *Michigan Journal of Gender and the Law* 7 (2001): 261–89.

36. *Martin v. Ziherl*, 607 S.E.2d 367 (Virginia Supreme Court, 2005). Accord, *In re J.M.*, 575 S.E.2d 441 (Georgia Supreme Court, 2003) (pre-*Lawrence* opinion).

37. *Lawrence*, 539 U.S., 580 (O'Connor, J., concurring in the judgment) (Equal Protection Clause); see *Casey*, 505 U.S., 851–53 (joint opinion, including O'Connor) (similar heightened rational basis analysis for a woman's liberty interest in choosing abortion). Accord, Suzanne B. Goldberg, "Equality Without Tiers," *Southern California Law Review* 77 (2004): 481–582.

38. Posner and Silbaugh, *Sex Laws*, 129–42; *Israel v. Allen*, 577 P.2d 762 (Colorado Supreme Court, 1978) (invalidating incest law as applied to marriage between siblings by adoption).

39. On the survival of general incest laws after *Lawrence*, see *Alaska Civil Liberties Union v. State*, 122 P.3d 781 (Alaska Supreme Court, 2005); *State v. Lowe*, 2005 WL 1983964 (Ohio Court of Appeals, 2005); Brett H. McDonnell, "Is Incest Next?" *Cardozo Women's Law Journal* 10 (2003): 337–61 (arguing that adult incest laws are protected by the lack of social movement concern about them). Compare Christine McNiece Metteer, "Some 'Incest' Is Harmless Incest: Determining the Fundamental Right to Marry of Adults Related by Affinity Without Resorting to State Incest Statutes," *Kansas Journal of Law and Public Policy* 10 (2000): 262–81 (arguing that some adult incest is protected activity).

40. See Lawrence O. Gostin and James G. Hodge Jr., "Piercing the Veil of Secrecy in HIV/AIDS and Other Sexually Transmitted Diseases: Theories of Privacy and Disclosure in Partner Notification," *Duke Journal of Gender Law and Policy* 5 (1998): 9–88; Michelle Oberman, "Sex, Lies, and the Duty to Disclose," *Arizona Law Review* 47 (2005): 871–931.

41. See Marybeth Herald, "A Bedroom of One's Own: Morality and Sexual Privacy after *Lawrence v. Texas*," *Yale Journal of Law and Feminism* 16 (2004): 1–40; Danielle J. Lindemann, "Pathology Full Circle: A History of Anti-Vibrator Legislation in the United States," *Columbia Journal of Gender and Law* 15 (2006): 326–46.

42. See William N. Eskridge Jr., *Gaylaw: Challenging the Apartheid of the Closet* (Cambridge, MA: Harvard University Press, 1999), 243–63; Eskridge and Hunter, *Sexuality, Gender, and the Law*, 1332–48.

43. See Ian Ayres and Katharine K. Baker, "A Separate Crime of Reckless Sex," *University of Chicago Law Review* 72 (2005): 599–666; Lior Jacob Strahilevitz, "Consent, Aesthetics, and the Boundaries of Sexual Privacy After *Lawrence v. Texas*," *DePaul Law Review* 54 (2005): 671–700.

44. See Eskridge and Hunter, *Sexuality, Gender, and the Law*, 122–42 (sex work), 474–500 (child porn and cyberporn); Edward Stein, "Queers Anonymous: Lesbians, Gay Men, Free Speech, and Cyberspace," *Harvard Civil Rights–Civil Liberties Law Review* 38 (2003): 159–213.

45. See Eskridge and Hunter, *Sexuality, Gender, and the Law*, 142–64; Elizabeth Garfinkle, "Coming of Age in America: The Misapplication of Sex-Offender Registration and Community-Notification Laws to Juveniles," *California Law Review* 91 (2003): 163–206.

46. Eskridge and Hunter, *Sexuality, Gender, and the Law*, 474–500.

47. Cf. *Lawrence*, 539 U.S., 571 (private religious morality cannot be the basis for state criminal rules binding upon everyone).

48. Kansas Statutes § 21-3522 (2004 Supp.).

49. *Limon v. State*, 83 P.3d 229, 235–37 (Kansas Court of Appeals, 2004) (Green, J.) (various state interests, including public health); ibid., 242 (Malone, J., concurring for the reason quoted in text), reversed, 122 P.3d 22, 32–34 (Kansas Supreme Court, 2005).

50. *Limon*, 122 P.3d, 36–37 (Kansas Supreme Court), following 83 P.3d, 245–49 (Pierron, P.J., dissenting in the Kansas Court of Appeals).

51. Compare *Limon*, 83 P.3d, 235–37 (Green, J., Kansas Court of Appeals) (accepting the state's no promo homo justification), with William N. Eskridge Jr., "No Promo Homo: The Sedimentation of Antigay Discourse and the Channeling Effect of Judicial Review," *NYU Law Review* 75 (2000): 1366–70 (skeptical).

52. *Lawrence*, 539 U.S., 579–85 (O'Connor, concurring in the judgment). Because O'Connor was rigorously interpreting and applying *Romer* to the Homosexual Conduct Law, it is likely that the other five justices (in the majority of both *Lawrence* and *Romer*) would have agreed with her analysis. See ibid., 574–75 (majority opinion, agreeing that the equal protection claim is a "tenable argument," but insisting on the broader analysis so that all consensual sodomy laws are rendered invalid).

53. 1972 Ohio Laws H.B. 511, Revised Code § 2907.07(B), narrowed by *State v. Phipps*, 389 N.E.2d 1128 (Ohio Supreme Court, 1979), and invalidated on First Amendment grounds in *State v. Thompson*, 767 N.E.2d 251 (Ohio Supreme Court, 2002).

54. Compare *Sawatzsky v. Oklahoma City*, 906 P.2d 785 (Oklahoma Court of Criminal Appeals, 1995), upholding law criminalizing offers to engage in lewd (i.e., sodomitic) activities, with *Howard v. State*, 527 S.E.2d 195 (Georgia Supreme Court, 2000), construing such a law to require the object of the solicitation be sodomy that is *not* constitutionally protected.

55. See *Howard*, 527 S.E.2d, 197–200 (Sears, J., dissenting, objecting to the Court's limitation of sodomy-solicitation law to unprotected conduct, but without supplying specific guidance for what is unprotected); Cristina Breen, "Sodomy Arrest Guidelines Revised," *Charlotte Observer*, July 6, 2003 (Charlotte-Mecklenburg orders police to arrest people for sexual solicitation only if for sodomy in a public place).

56. For examples of homo-diversity, see Bruce Bawer, ed., *Beyond Queer: Challenging Gay Left Orthodoxy* (New York: Free Press, 1996) (opposing both antigay state discriminations *and* sexual orientation antidiscrimination laws); Sheila Jeffreys, *The Lesbian Heresy: A Feminist Perspective on the Lesbian Sexual Revolution* (North Melbourne, Australia: Spinifex Press, 1993) (lesbians who take pride in their "outlaw" status); Dennis Cooper, "Queercore," in Donald Morton, ed., *The Material Queer: A LesBiGay Cultural Studies Reader* (Boulder, CO: Westview Press, 1996), 292 ("punky, anti-assimilationist, transgressive movement on the fringe of lesbian and gay culture"); Diane H. Mazur, "The Unknown Soldier: A Critique of 'Gays in the Military' Scholarship and Litigation," *University of California at Davis Law Review* 29 (1996): 223–81 (most lesbian and gay soldiers prefer the ill-policed closet to the unwanted attention created by activism around the military exclusion); Spindelman, "Surviving *Lawrence v. Texas*" (highly critical of Lambda's assimilative, straight-affirming arguments supporting *Lawrence*).

57. "Roger Croteau and Michel Horvat Discuss Adoption by Gay Couples," transcript, *National Public Radio*, January 25, 2005 (first quotation in text); Lofton telephone interview (second quotation).

58. Transcript of Oral Argument, *Lawrence v. Texas*, Docket No. 02-102 (USSC, March 26, 2003), 20–21.

59. Rhonda R. Rivera, "Our Straight-Laced Judges: The Legal Position of Homosexual Persons in the United States," *Hastings Law Journal* 30 (1979): 799 and 50 (1999): 1015, part VII, surveying California and other state court cases involving dismissals of lesbian or gay teachers.

60. *Opinion of the Justices*, 530 A.2d 21 (New Hampshire Supreme Court, 1987) (opining that a proposed exclusion of gay people from daycare businesses would be unconstitutional); *Ratchford v. Gay Lib*, 434 U.S. 1080, 1084 (USSC, 1978) (Rehnquist, J., dissenting from the denial of certiorari) (analogizing homosexuality to measles, as both are contagious conditions that can infect and harm vulnerable youth); Carole Jenny et al., "Are Children at Risk for Sexual Abuse by Homosexuals?" *Pediatrics* 94 (1994): 41–42 (not at all); ibid., 42 (seventy-four percent of adult male molesters of boys were involved in sexual relationships with the boys' mothers or other female relatives).

61. For decisions upholding dismissal of bisexual and gay school personnel for reasons of institutional function, see, e.g., *Rowland v. Mad River School District*, 730 F.2d 444 (U.S. Court of Appeals for the Sixth Circuit, 1985); *Gaylord v. Tacoma School District*, 559 P.2d 1340, 1346 (Washington Supreme Court, 1977).

62. See *Tanner v. Oregon Health Sciences University*, 971 P.2d 435 (Oregon Court of Appeals, 1998), holding that sexual orientation is a suspect classification; state laws discriminating on this basis presumptively violate Oregon's Privileges or Immunities Clause.

63. *Lofton v. Secretary of Department of Children & Family Services*, 358 F.3d 804 (U.S. Court of Appeals for the Eleventh Circuit), en banc rehearing denied, 377 F.3d 1275 (2004). Although Oregon would allow Lofton and Croteau to adopt Wayne and Ernie, they have not done so, because that could fuel anxieties in the older children. Lofton interview.

64. Ibid., 818–19 (panel opinion).

65. In 2000, Mississippi barred adoptions by "couples of the same gender." Miss. Code § 93-17-3(2) (2006). Between 1987 and 1999, New Hampshire followed Florida in barring gay people from adopting children, and added a further bar to foster parenting. 1987 New Hampshire Laws chap. 343, repealed by 1999 New Hampshire Laws chap. 18. In 1999, Arkansas adopted an administrative rule barring gay people from becoming foster parents. Arkansas Minimum Licensing Standards § 200.3.2, invalidated in *Department of Human Services v. Howard*, 367 Ark. 55 (Arkansas Supreme Court, 2006). Nebraska's Department of Social Services has a rule prohibiting adoption by persons "known by the agency to be homosexual or who are unmarried and living with another adult." Administrative Memorandum #1-95, www.hhs.state.ne.us/jus/memos/AM-1.pdf (viewed July 2006). See also Utah Code Ann. § 78-30-1 (2006) (no adoption "by a person who is cohabiting in a relationship that is not a legally valid and binding marriage under the laws of this state").

66. *Lofton*, 377 F.3d, 1290–1313 (Barkett, J., dissenting from denial of rehearing en banc); ibid., 1296–98 (arguing that the discriminatory classification is way over- as well as underinclusive). Voting with Barkett for rehearing en banc were Judges Anderson, Dubina, Marcus, Tjoflat, and Wilson.

67. Ibid., 1302 note 31 (first quotation in text), surveying the legislative history and quoting from the tape-recorded proceedings of the House Judiciary Committee on May 19, 1977; ibid., 1303 and note 36 (second quotation), quoting Senator Peterson as reported in "Gay Bills Pass Both Chambers," *Florida Times-Union*, June 1, 1977.

68. *Lofton*, 358 F.3d, 817 (panel opinion); *Lofton*, 377 F.3d, 1298–99 (Barkett, J., dissenting from the denial of rehearing en banc).

69. *Lofton v. Secretary*, 543 U.S. 1081 (USSC, 2005). In 2006, at least sixteen state legislatures considered bills to bar adoption by gay people. www.usatoday.com/news/nation/2006-02-20 -gay-adoption_x.htm (viewed June 2006).

70. *Bottoms v. Bottoms*, 457 S.E.2d 102, 108 (Virginia Supreme Court, 1995) (quotation in text), gently following the antilesbian child custody presumption of *Roe v. Roe*, 324 S.E.2d 691 (Virginia Supreme Court, 1985).

71. Because the "interest of parents in the care, custody, and control of their children" is "perhaps the oldest of the fundamental [due process] liberty interests recognized by this Court," *Troxel v. Granville*, 530 U.S. 57 (USSC, 2000) (O'Connor, J., plurality opinion), the Court ruled that states could not disrupt parental control of their children to assure grandparents mandatory visitation rights. This constitutional interest is strongly inconsistent with the approach taken in *Bottoms*, which treated the grandparent's interest as similar to that of the mother's.

72. Compare *Ex parte D.W.W.*, 717 So.2d 793, 794–97 (Alabama Supreme Court, 1998) (plurality opinion by Hooper, C.J., upholding custody with the straight father and reinstating conditions upon the lesbian mother's visitation), with ibid., 797–99 (Kennedy, J., dissenting on the ground that the trial judge's opinion was based upon "prejudice" and ignored the documented abuses of the father).

73. Lofton telephone interview; *State v. Li*, 110 P.3d 91 (Oregon Supreme Court, 2005).

74. *Goodridge v. Department of Public Health*, 798 A.2d 941 (Massachusetts Supreme Judicial Court, 2003), invalidating that state's ban of same-sex marriages. Supporting the constitutional case for same-sex marriage are Cheshire Calhoun, *Feminism, the Family, and the Politics of the Closet: Lesbian and Gay Displacement* (Oxford: Oxford University Press, 2000), 107–15; William N. Eskridge Jr., *The Case for Same-Sex Marriage* (New York: Free Press, 1996); Morris Kaplan, *Sexual Justice: Democratic Citizenship and the Politics of Desire* (New York: Routledge, 1997); Richard D. Mohr, *A More Perfect Union: Why Straight America Must Stand Up for Gay Rights* (Boston: Beacon Press, 1994), chap. 3; Carlos A. Ball, "Moral Foundations for a Discourse on Same-Sex Marriage: Looking Beyond Political Liberalism," *Georgetown Law Journal* 85 (1997): 1871–1943; Mary I. Coombs, "Sexual Dis-Orientation: Transgendered People and Same-Sex Marriage," *UCLA Women's Law Journal* 8 (1998): 219–66.

75. See William N. Eskridge Jr. and Darren Spedale, *Gay Marriage: For Better or for Worse? What We've Learned from the Evidence* (New York: Oxford University Press, 2006), chap. 6, arguing that same-sex marriage is "identity politics" on both sides, with many traditionalists fundamentally invested in denying this institution to homosexuals. According to the Pew Research Center, thirty-nine percent of Americans favor gay marriage, while fifty-one percent oppose it. http://people-press.org/reports/display.php3?ReportID=273 (viewed June 2006).

76. *Washington v. Glucksberg*, 521 U.S. 702 (USSC, 1997) (Rehnquist, C.J., for the Court). Five justices were open to a "constitutionally cognizable interest in controlling the circumstances of his or her imminent death," but felt that it was premature to decide one way or another in 1997. Ibid., 736–38 (O'Connor), 738–52 (Stevens), 752–89 (Souter), 789 (Ginsburg), 789–92 (Breyer).

77. 2000 Vermont Laws P.A. 91., responding to *Baker v. State*, 744 A.2d 864 (Vermont

Supreme Court, 1999); California Domestic Partner Rights and Responsibilities Act of 2003, 2003 Cal. Stats. chap. 421 (A.B. No. 205).

78. *Goodridge*, 798 N.E.2d, 948, quoting *Lawrence*, 539 U.S., 571; ibid., 970–74 (Greany, J., concurring) (emphasizing O'Connor's concurring opinion in *Lawrence*). For a hard-hitting critique, see ibid., 983–1005 (Cordy, J., dissenting).

79. For instance, Pam Belluck, "Proposal to Ban Same-Sex Marriage Renews Old Battles," *New York Times*, July 11, 2006, A12.

80. Oregon Family Fairness Act of 2007, Oregon House Bill 2007, Regular Session of General Assembly, codified at Oregon Revised Statutes §§ 107.615, 192.842, 205.320, 409.300, 432.005, 432.235, 432.405, 432.408. See also Eskridge, *Equality Practice*; Jonathan Rauch, *Gay Marriage: Why It Is Good for Gays, Good for Straights, and Good for America* (New York: Times Books, 2004).

81. For "the sky did not fall" evidence from Scandinavia, which has recognized same-sex unions since 1989, see Eskridge and Spedale, *Gay Marriage*, chap. 5.

Chapter Twelve: *Lawrence* and Popular Constitutionalism

1. For early soundings of the themes in text, see William N. Eskridge Jr., "Pluralism and Distrust: How Courts Can Support Democracy by Lowering the Stakes of Politics," *Yale Law Journal* 114 (2005): 1279–1328; Reva B. Siegel, "Constitutional Culture, Social Movement Conflict and Constitutional Change: The Case of the De Facto ERA," *California Law Review* 94 (2006): 1323–1419.

2. Important explications of formal constitutionalism include *The Federalist* No. 78 (Clinton Rossiter ed., 1961) (Alexander Hamilton); *Marbury v. Madison*, 5 U.S. 137 (USSC, 1803); Akhil Amar, *America's Constitution: A Biography* (Cambridge, MA: Belknap Press, 2006); Robert H. Bork, *The Tempting of America* (New York: Free Press, 1989); Antonin Scalia, "The Rule of Law as a Law of Rules," *University of Chicago Law Review*, 1992; James Bradley Thayer, "The Origin and Scope of the American Doctrine of Constitutional Law," *Harvard Law Review* 7 (1893): 143–45.

3. For defenses of strongly dynamic common-law theories of constitutional interpretation, see, e.g., John Yoo, *The Powers of War and Peace: The Constitution and Foreign Affairs After 9/11* (Chicago: University of Chicago Press, 2005) (presidential common law, with congressional acquiescence); David A. Strauss, "The Irrelevance of Constitutional Amendments," *Harvard Law Review* 114 (2001): 1457–77 (judge-made common law). The examples in text are Memorandum from Jay S. Bybee, Assistant Attorney General, to Alberto R. Gonzalez, Counsel to the President, Re: Standards of Conduct for Interrogation Under 18 U.S.C. §§ 2340–2340A, August 1, 2002 (the infamous "torture memorandum"); *Printz v. United States*, 521 U.S. 898 (USSC, 1997) (Justice Scalia's opinion striking down part of the Brady Act, not because it was inconsistent with a provision of the Constitution, but instead based upon "principles" of federalism).

4. Compare *Lawrence v. Texas*, 539 U.S. 558, 567–73 (USSC, 2003), closely following Brief *Amicus Curiae* by the Cato Institute, *Lawrence* (No. 02-102), 12–18, with ibid., 595–98 (Scalia, J., dissenting). See also Brief of Professors of History, George Chauncey, Nancy Cott, et al., as *Amici Curiae*, ibid., 3–10; Brief *Amicus Curiae* of the American Civil Liberties Union and the ACLU of Texas, ibid., 11–26.

5. *Loving v. Virginia*, 388 U.S. 1 (USSC 1967) (striking down miscegenation laws, contrary to the original meaning of the Fourteenth Amendment, but consistent with its anti–class legislation purpose and antidiscrimination principle supported by precedent); *Mclaughlin v. Florida*, 379 U.S. 184 (USSC, 1964) (similar decision striking down law criminalizing sexual cohabitation of different-race couples); *Brown v. Board of Education*, 347 U.S. 483 (USSC 1954) (striking down state racial segregation in public schools). Compare Earl Maltz, "Originalism and the Desegregation Decisions," *Constitutional Commentary* 13 (1996): 223–31 (reflecting the majority view that *Brown* was inconsistent with original meaning), with Bork, *Tempting of America*, 81–82 (defending *Brown* on the grounds that it "realistically" chose to abandon segregation, accepted by the Fourteenth Amendment's framers, once it became clear that it had created a permanent racial caste).

6. *Corfield v. Coryell*, 6 F.Cas. 546, 552 (Circuit Court for the Eastern District of Pennsylvania, 1823) (No. 3230) (quotation in text). On *Lawrence* and original meaning, compare Steven G. Calabresi, "*Lawrence*, the Fourteenth Amendment, and the Supreme Court's Reliance on Foreign Constitutional Law: An Originalist Reappraisal," *Ohio State Law Journal* 65 (2004): 1109–15, with William N. Eskridge Jr., "*Hardwick* and Historiography," *University of Illinois Law Review*, 1999, 631–86.

7. *Congressional Globe*, 39th Congress, 1st Session 1088–89 (1866); ibid., 2766 (Senator Howard) (quotation in text); *Lawrence*, 539 U.S. at 574–75 (majority opinion); ibid., 579–85 (O'Connor, J., concurring in the judgment).

8. *Lawrence*, 539 U.S. at 579–85 (O'Connor, J., concurring in the judgment).

9. *The Federalist* No. 78 (Hamilton); Alexander M. Bickel, *The Least Dangerous Branch: The Supreme Court at the Bar of Politics* (New Haven, CT: Yale University Press, 1962). See David A. Strauss, "Common Law Constitutional Interpretation," *University of Chicago Law Review* 63 (1996): 877–935; Cass R. Sunstein, "The Supreme Court, 1995 Term—Foreword: Leaving Things Undecided," *Harvard Law Review* 110 (1996): 4–101.

10. *Brown v. Board of Education*, 349 U.S. 294 (USSC, 1955) (*Brown II*); *Roe v. Wade*, 410 U.S. 113 (USSC, 1973). The examples in text are developed in Gerald Rosenberg, *The Hollow Hope: Can Courts Bring About Social Change?* (Chicago: University of Chicago Press, 1991). See also Robert Post and Reva B. Siegel, "Popular Constitutionalism, Departmentalism, and Judicial Supremacy," *California Law Review* 92 (2004): 1030–34, discussing "departmentalist" theories of autonomous constitutional interpretation by each branch.

11. Models of polycentric constitutionalism can be found in Keith E. Whittington, *Constitutional Construction: Divided Powers and Constitutional Meaning* (Princeton, NJ: Princeton University Press, 1999); William N. Eskridge Jr. and Philip P. Frickey, "The Supreme Court, 1993 Term–Foreword: Law as Equilibrium," *Harvard Law Review* 108 (1994): 26–108; Robert C. Post and Reva B. Siegel, "Legislative Constitutionalism and Section Five Power: Policentric Interpretation of the Family and Medical Leave Act," *Yale Law Journal* 112 (2003): 1943–2056; Edwin Meese, III, "The Law of the Constitution," *Tulane Law Review* 61 (1987): 979–90.

12. *Naim v. Naim*, 87 S.E.2d 749 (Virginia Supreme Court, 1955) (reaffirming the constitutionality of its antimiscegenation law after *Brown*), appeal dismissed, 350 U.S. 985 (U.S. Supreme Court, 1956); Bickel, *Least Dangerous Branch*, 174 (explaining the Court's *Naim* disposition); *Loving v. Virginia*, 388 U.S. 1 (USSC, 1967); Randall Kennedy, *Interracial Intimacies: Sex, Marriage, Identity, and Adoption* (New York: Pantheon, 2003), 244–80 (tracing state repeal of their antimiscegenation statutes between *Naim* and *Loving*).

13. See chapter 7 of this book for the story of the House veto of the D.C. sodomy repeal, and chapter 8 for the unfavorable political circumstances (including AIDS concerns) for sweeping invalidation in 1986. See William N. Eskridge Jr., *Gaylaw: Challenging the Apartheid of the*

Closet (Cambridge, MA: Harvard University Press, 1999), 328–37 (appendix A1), for citations to state court opinions upholding consensual sodomy laws against right-to-privacy challenges.

14. See chapter 9 of this book for Judge Bork's defeat and the shift in public attitudes toward gay people, as well as successful state court challenges. See chapter 10 for the lineup of amici curiae in *Lawrence.*

15. For works that develop a social movement–driven popular constitutionalism, see Jack M. Balkin and Reva B. Siegel, "Principles, Practices, and Social Movements," *University of Pennsylvania Law Review* 154 (2006): 927–59; William N. Eskridge Jr., "Channeling: Identity-Based Social Movements and Public Law," *University of Pennsylvania Law Review* 150 (2001): 419–525; William E. Forbath, "Caste, Class, and Equal Citizenship," *Michigan Law Review* 98 (1999): 1–90; Doni Gewirtzman, "Glory Days: Popular Constitutionalism, Nostalgia, and the True Nature of Constitutional Culture," *Georgetown Law Journal* 93 (2005): 897–938; Reva B. Siegel, "Constitutional Culture, Social Movement Conflict and Constitutional Change: The Case of the De Facto ERA," *California Law Review* 94 (2006): 1323–1419. For other takes on popular constitutionalism, see generally Bruce Ackerman, *We the People 2: Transformations* (New Haven, CT: Yale University Press, 1998); Larry Kramer, *The People Themselves: Popular Constitutionalism and Judicial Review* (Cambridge, MA: Harvard University Press, 2004); Barry Friedman, "Mediated Popular Constitutionalism," *Michigan Law Review* 101 (2003): 2596–2636.

16. William N. Eskridge Jr., "Some Effects of Identity-Based Social Movements on Constitutional Law in the Twentieth Century," *Michigan Law Review* 100 (2002): 2062–2407.

17. Anthony Comstock, *Traps for the Young,* ed. Robert Bremmer (Cambridge, MA: Harvard University Press, 1967 [reprint of 1883 edition]); chaps. 2–3 and 7. For secular justifications of communitarianism, see, e.g., Amy Gutmann and Dennis Thompson, *Democracy and Disagreement* (Cambridge, MA: Harvard University Press,1996); Philip Pettit, *Republicanism: A Theory of Freedom and Government* (Princeton, NJ: Princeton University Press, 1997); Michael Sandel, *Liberalism and the Limits of Justice* (Cambridge: Cambridge University Press, 1982).

18. Walt Whitman, *Democratic Vistas* (1870), in Whitman (LOA), 946–47 (quotation in text). Both liberal theory, e.g., John Rawls, *Political Liberalism* (New York: Oxford University Press, 1993), and communitarian theory, e.g., Frank I. Michelman, "The Supreme Court, 1985 Term—Foreword: Traces of Self-Government," *Harvard Law Review* 97 (1986): 9–77, focus on developing people's capacity for self-governance.

19. Interview with Michael Bowers, Atlanta (Buckhead), January 4, 2004. The communitarian argument in text is inspired by various intelligent conservative voices, including Congregation for the Doctrine of the Faith, Declaration *Persona humana* (Rome: Vatican, December 29, 1975); Maggie Gallagher, "Normal Marriage: Two Views," in Lynn D. Wardle et al., eds., *Marriage and Same-Sex Unions: A Debate* (Westport, CT: Praeger, 2003), 13–24; Robert George and Gerard Bradley, "Marriage and the Liberal Imagination," *Georgetown Law Journal* 84 (1995): 301–20.

20. On the nation's growing love affair with heterosexual oral sex, see chapters 2, 4, and 9–11; NORC (1994), 96–109.

21. *Hardwick v. Bowers,* 760 F.2d 1202, 1211–12 (U.S. Court of Appeals for the Eleventh Circuit, 1985), reversed, 478 U.S. 186 (USSC, 1986) (first quotation in text); *Lawrence v. Texas,* 539 U.S. 558, 566–67 (USSC, 2003) (second quotation); Michael Sandel, "Moral Argument and Liberal Toleration: Abortion and Homosexuality," *California Law Review* 77 (1989): 535–38;

Carlos Ball, *The Morality of Gay Rights: An Exploration in Political Philosophy* (New York: Routledge, 2003), 139–70.

22. For a thoughtful example of a traditionalist who appreciates the emergence of lesbian and gay families of choice, see David D. Meyer, "Domesticating *Lawrence*," *University of Chicago Law Forum* 2004: 453–94.

23. Compare Ball, *Morality of Gay Rights*, 139–70 (arguing that homosexual relationships can constitute basic human goods), with Robert George, *In Defense of Natural Law* (Princeton, NJ: Princeton University Press, 1999) (arguing that homosexual sodomy can never be a basic human good), with Andrew Koppelman, *The Gay Rights Question in Contemporary American Law* (Chicago: University of Chicago Press, 2002), 86–93 (responding to George).

24. The questions in text are inspired by V. F. Nourse, "Reconceptualizing Criminal Law Defenses," *University of Pennsylvania Law Review* 151 (2003): 1741–45.

25. Corruption of police is an old complaint against consensual sodomy laws, see John Addington Symonds, *A Problem in Modern Ethics* (London, 1896), and was a key reason the Joint Committee to Revise the Illinois Criminal Code voted to decriminalize consensual sodomy (chapter 4).

26. See, e.g., David France, *Our Fathers: The Secret Life of the Catholic Church in an Age of Scandal* (New York: Broadway Books, 2004), arguing that the Catholic Church's official homophobia diverted attention away from priests molesting girls and boys under the church's authority.

27. On the idea that the state and society "produce" sexuality even when they are trying to repress it, see Michel Foucault, introduction, vol. 1 of *The History of Sexuality*, trans. Robert Hurley (New York: Vintage 1978), 42–43, 105–6, and "Afterword: The Subject and the Power," in Hubert L. Dreyfus and Paul Rabinow, eds., *Beyond Structuralism and Hermeneutics* (Chicago: University of Chicago Press, 1983). See also Vikki Bell, *Interrogating Incest: Feminism, Foucault, and the Law* (New York: Routledge, 1993); Judith Butler, *Gender Trouble: Feminism and the Subversion of Identity* (New York: Routledge, 1990).

28. David Cole, "Playing by Pornography's Rules: The Regulation of Sexual Expression," *University of Pennsylvania Law Review* 143 (1994): 177 (quotation in text).

29. Interview with former Georgia attorney general Michael Bowers, Atlanta (Buckhead), January 4, 2004; AEI Polls (2006) (collecting polling data on homosexuality, 1977–2006).

30. Adam Przeworski, *Democracy and the Market: Political and Economic Reforms in Eastern Europe and Latin America* (Oxford: Oxford University Press, 1991), 26–37 (democracy is a self-enforcing equilibrium only so long as all groups see themselves better off under democracy than they would be under a state of nature); William N. Eskridge Jr., "Pluralism and Distrust: How Courts Can Support Democracy by Lowering the Stakes of Politics," *Yale Law Journal* 114 (2005): 1279–1328.

31. *Boy Scouts of America v. Dale*, 530 U.S. 640 (USSC, 2000). On the role of the Religion Clauses to prevent destructive group conflict, see *Zelman v. Simmons-Harris*, 536 U.S. 639, 718 (USSC, 2002) (Breyer, J., concurring); Noah Feldman, "The Intellectual Origins of the Establishment Clause," *NYU Law Review* 77 (2002): 346–428.

32. *Reed v. Reed*, 404 U.S. 71 (USSC, 1971); *Craig v. Boren*, 429 U.S. 190 (USSC, 1976). For an account of the Court's movement, see Ruth Bader Ginsburg, "Sexual Equality under the Fourteenth and Equal Rights Amendments," *Washington University Law Quarterly*, 1979, 161ff.

33. Chapter 8. See generally Mark Tushnet, *Taking the Constitution Away from the Courts* (Princeton, NJ: Princeton University Press, 1999); Jeremy Waldron, *Democracy and Disagreement* (Oxford: Oxford University Press, 1999); William N. Eskridge Jr. and John Ferejohn, "Super-Statutes," *Duke Law Journal*, 2001, 1215–76.

34. Chapter 9. The "linked fates" idea is taken from Lani Guinier and Gerald Torres, *The Miner's Canary: Enlisting Race, Resisting Power, Transforming Democracy* (Cambridge, MA: Harvard University Press, 2002).

35. Patrick Egan, Nathaniel Persily, and Kevin Wallsten, "Gay Rights," in Persily et al., eds., *Public Opinion and Constitutional Controversy* (New York: Oxford University Press, forthcoming 2008), figure 4, showing a significant drop in public support for decriminalization after *Lawrence*.

36. Cf. Louis Michael Seidman, "*Brown* and *Miranda*," *California Law Review* 80 (1992): 673ff., arguing that *Brown* ultimately undermined the civil rights social movement and equal education for blacks in practice.

37. See Egan et al., "Gay Rights," for an excellent analysis of shifts in public opinion as regards the morality of homosexuality, gay rights, etc.

38. Elisabeth Young-Bruehl, *The Anatomy of Prejudices* (Cambridge, MA: Harvard University Press, 1996); Bowers interview.

39. NORC (1994), 101–9 (oral sex widely practiced, anal sex not so much); S. A. Sanders and J. M. Reinisch, "Would You Say You 'Had Sex' If?" *Journal of the American Medical Association* 281 (1999): 275–77 (almost all sexually active college students have had oral sex but do not consider it intercourse); Tamar Lewin, "Teen-agers Alter Sexual Practices, Thinking Risks Will Be Avoided," *New York Times*, April 5, 1997; William Ian Miller, *The Anatomy of Disgust* (Cambridge, MA: Harvard University Press, 1997) (anal sex is much ickier).

40. The analysis in the text is taken from William N. Eskridge Jr., "No Promo Homo: The Sedimentation of Antigay Discourse and the Channeling Effect of Judicial Review," *NYU Law Review* 75 (2000): 1327–1411.

41. *Powell v. State*, 510 S.E.2d 18 (Georgia Supreme Court, 1998); *Loving v. Virginia*, 388 U.S. 1 (USSC, 1967). For an argument that *Loving* supports an incremental and state-by-state approach to same-sex marriage by gay activists, see William N. Eskridge Jr. and Darren R. Spedale, *Gay Marriage: For Better or for Worse? What We've Learned from the Evidence* (New York: Oxford University Press, 2006), 228–41.

42. For a map of the states based upon their receptiveness to same-sex marriage or civil unions, see Eskridge and Spedale, *Gay Marriage*, 241–49.

43. The argument in the text reflects the views in William N. Eskridge Jr., *Equality Practice: Civil Unions and the Future of Gay Rights* (New York: Routledge, 2002); Jonathan Rauch, *Gay Marriage: Why It Is Good for Gays, Good for Straights, and Good for America* (New York: Times Books, 2004).

44. Compare John Rawls, "The Idea of Public Reason Revisited," *University of Chicago Law Review* 64 (1997): 779–80, 788 note 60, suggesting a narrow view of the government's interest in family formation except those "affect[ing] the orderly reproduction of society," with Carlos A. Ball, "Communitarianism and Gay Rights," *Cornell Law Review* 85 (2000): 451–57, suggesting that liberalism needs to take greater interest in families, including lesbian and gay families. See also Bruce Bawer, *A Place at the Table* (New York: Free Press, 1995); Rauch, *Gay Marriage*; Kath Weston, *Families We Choose: Lesbians, Gays, Kinship* (New York: Columbia University Press, 1991); Chai Feldblum, "Sexual Orientation, Morality, and the Law: Devlin Revisited,"

University of Pittsburgh Law Review 57 (1996): 237–336; Stephen Macedo, "Homosexuality and the Conservative Mind," *Georgetown Law Journal* 84 (1995): 261–78.

45. Marc Stein, "*Boutilier* and the U.S. Supreme Court's Sexual Revolution," 33–34 (draft, 2002), to be published as a chapter in *The U.S. Supreme Court's Sexual Revolution*; telephone interview with Eugene Willard Enslin, December 17, 2006; Joshua Lynsen, "Body of Gay Rights 'Hero' Languished After Death," *Washington Blade*, December 8, 2006, 14 (Garner's death; quotation in text).

46. Telephone interview with Susan Browning Chriss (Michael Hardwick's sister), October 7, 2006; interview with Susan Browning Chriss and Kathleen Blalock Hardwick (Michael's mother), Archer, Florida (near Gainesville), March 19, 2005.

47. Dr. Ron Godwin, "AIDS: A Moral and Political Time Bomb," *MMR*, July 1983, 2 (quotation in text). The Trojan horse metaphor was suggested to me by Kenji Yoshino, who found it in Monique Wittig.

48. Chriss telephone interview; Chriss Archer, Florida interview.

49. Interview with Robert Hardwick Weston, New York City (Café Raffaella, West Village), January 22, 2004. The quotations in the text are Robert's.

50. Ibid. (quotation in text).

Index